Navy Medicine
in Vietnam

Navy Medicine in Vietnam

Oral Histories from Dien Bien Phu to the Fall of Saigon

JAN K. HERMAN

McFarland & Company, Inc., Publishers
Jefferson, North Carolina, and London

LIBRARY OF CONGRESS CATALOGUING-IN-PUBLICATION DATA

Herman, Jan K.
Navy medicine in Vietnam : oral histories from Dien Bien
Phu to the fall of Saigon / Jan K. Herman.
p.   cm.
Includes bibliographical references and index.

ISBN 978-0-7864-3999-7
illustrated case binding : 50# alkaline paper ∞

1. Vietnam War, 1964–1975 — Naval operations, American — Personal
narratives, American.   2. Medicine, Naval — United States—
Personal narratives.   I. Title.

[DNLM: 1. United States. Navy.   2. Naval Medicine — history — United
States — Personal Narratives.   3. Naval Medicine — history — Vietnam —
Personal Narratives.   4. Vietnam Conflict — United States — Personal Narratives.
5. Vietnam Conflict — Vietnam — Personal Narratives.   6. History, 20th
Century — United States — Personal Narratives.   7. History, 20th Century —
Vietnam — Personal Narratives.   WZ 112.5.M4 H551n 2008]
DS558.7.H47   2009   959.704'37 — dc22   2008032761

British Library cataloguing data are available

On the cover: An x-ray showing a live mortar round in the
chest wall of a South Vietnamese soldier (BUMED Archives);
sandbags, emergency tent and x-ray pole ©2008 Shutterstock

Manufactured in the United States of America

McFarland & Company, Inc., Publishers
Box 611, Jefferson, North Carolina 28640
www.mcfarlandpub.com

To the Navy medical personnel
of the Vietnam War ...
and their patients

TABLE OF CONTENTS

Preface   1

1 — Passage to Freedom   3
2 — An American War   25
3 — Hearts and Minds   45
4 — Medical Battalions in a Frontless War   68
5 — Intrepid Surgeons   101
6 — Corpsman Up!   108
7 — Medal of Honor   150
8 — Naval Support Activity Hospital Danang   155
9 — Ships of Mercy   178
10 — Holocaust on Yankee Station   200
11 — Hue   211
12 — Khe Sanh   230
13 — Prisoner of War   251
14 — Mending   269
15 — Full Circle   289

Epilogue: The Journey Back   317
Appendix 1: The Cast   329
Appendix 2: Medal of Honor Citations   336
Appendix 3: Small Arms   339
Glossary   341
Chapter Notes   345
Bibliography   349
Index   353

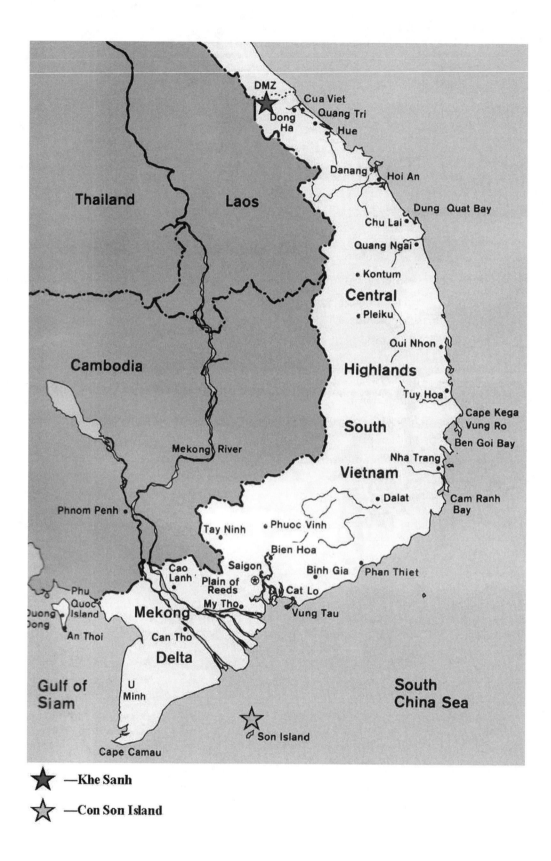

Thailand

Laos

DMZ
Cua Viet
Quang Tri
Dong Ha
Hue

Danang
Hoi An

Dung Quat Bay

Chu Lai

Quang Ngai

Kontum

Central

Pleiku

Qui Nhon

Highlands

Tuy Hoa

South

Cape Kega
Vung Ro
Ben Goi Bay

Nha Trang

Vietnam

Cambodia

Mekong River

Dalat

Cam Ranh
Bay

Phnom Penh

Tay Ninh

Phuoc Vinh

Bien Hoa

Cao Lanh

Saigon

Binh Gia
Phan Thiet

Plain of Reeds

Cat Lo

Phu Quoc Island

My Tho

Vung Tau

Duong Dong

Mekong

An Thoi

Can Tho

Delta

Gulf of
Siam

U Minh

South
China Sea

Cape Camau

Son Island

★ —Khe Sanh

☆ —Con Son Island

Preface

More than 30 years have passed since the end of the Vietnam War, a conflict that traumatized the United States as profoundly as the Civil War had done a century before. Despite the Gulf War of 1991 and the current wars in Afghanistan and Iraq, Vietnam is still very much with us. For some of the veterans who served in that prolonged combat and for those old enough to remember, Vietnam is the ghost that never leaves. Vietnam is also the touchstone by which we draw parallels to more recent conflicts. *Navy Medicine in Vietnam* is the story of Navy medicine's role during that war, an association that began a full decade before U.S. combat troops landed near Danang in 1965.

South Vietnam "was a place," recalls a former hospital corpsman, "where everything was trying to kill you—from the populace to the animals to the environment." With its hot, rainy climate and topography characterized by mountains, impenetrable jungles, swollen rivers, swamps, and rice paddies, American fighting men encountered flies, mosquitoes, leeches, worms, snakes, lizards, and, occasionally, a hostile tiger.

Vietnam was also a living textbook for endemic disease—tuberculosis, plague, malaria, smallpox, dengue, scrub typhus, trachoma, rabies, and infectious hepatitis. Stomach and intestinal maladies, such as amebiasis, dysentery, roundworm, and hookworm were common, as were fungal infections, including immersion foot and heat rash of the feet and groin.

Wounds were inflicted by the weapons of a determined enemy—automatic rifles, machine guns, rocket-propelled grenades, mines, mortars, and artillery. Low-tech but equally deadly booby traps also took a heavy toll on combat troops.

Even before Marines stepped ashore in 1965, Navy medicine had already established itself in South Vietnam two years earlier when Navy medical personnel converted an old Saigon apartment house into Station Hospital Saigon. Increased terror attacks by the Viet Cong guaranteed that the hospital would have a steady stream of casualties. And when the troops arrived, marking the war's escalation, accompanying them were physicians and corpsmen who soon were manning aid stations and mobile field hospitals—Charlie, Bravo, and Alpha medical companies. With helicopter medevac, these once mobile facilities then evolved into true fixed-in-place hospitals providing medical care in what soon became a "frontless" war. By 1968, when American involvement reached its peak, Naval Support Activity Hospital Danang (NSAH)—a 750-bed facility—was in full operation. Two hospital ships, USS *Repose* and USS *Sanctuary*, each with a capacity of 350 beds, cruised offshore, often a 30-minute helicopter flight from the battlefield.

Navy medicine's success is best illustrated by statistics compiled by the Marine Corps in that critical year of the war. During 1968, for every 100 Marines wounded, 44 were treated in the field and returned to duty, while 56 were admitted to a hospital. Of those admitted, only nine would remain in country and the rest would be evacuated. Approximately 7 percent would receive disability discharges and 5.5 percent would require long-term care. But, most notably, only 1.5 percent would die of their wounds.[1]

1

This last statistic is testimony to what had changed since the Korean War. The time from wounding to medical care had been drastically reduced. It was not uncommon for a casualty to be on the operating table within an hour after being injured. Indeed, helicopter evacuation was no longer a novelty. If Korea had represented the birth pangs of helicopter medevac, the Vietnam experience honed the system. Although helos had been used extensively in Korea, it was in Vietnam where the helicopter achieved its much deserved recognition. In a country of few roads, little infrastructure, and a varied and rugged topography, helicopters provided troop transport and resupply. The omnipresent UH-1 "Hueys" that airlifted Marines, soldiers, and South Vietnamese troops also doubled as ambulances. These choppers evacuated the wounded from where they had been injured to medical company hospitals, Naval Support Activity Hospital Danang, or to the hospital ships.

The practice of medicine also had changed. New drugs and antibiotics were available. Vascular surgery, only experimental during the Korean War, was now routinely saving limbs that would have been sacrificed just 15 years earlier. But, most importantly, the quality of medicine practiced at NSAH Danang and aboard *Repose* and *Sanctuary* was state-of-the-art with specialties such as neurosurgery, dermatology, urology, plastic surgery, ophthalmology, and ENT (ear, nose, and throat). "Every general surgeon, orthopedic surgeon, neurosurgeon, and ENT surgeon were all experienced in their given fields," recalls a former Navy nurse. Casualties who arrived at a treatment facility with multiple wounds might frequently have the attention of a general surgeon assisted by an operating room technician, an orthopedic surgeon, and a neurosurgeon — all working simultaneously.

The story of Navy medicine during the Vietnam War would be incomplete without discussing the other medical professional seen aboard every ship, in every medical facility, and serving with every Marine unit — the hospital corpsman. Throughout the war, some 5,000 hospital corpsmen and 300 dental technicians served in theater. As in previous conflicts, corpsmen did what their predecessors had done before them — stop the bleeding, clear the airway, protect the wound, and treat and prevent shock — with many performing these duties in the direct line of fire. No Navy personnel of any rating sacrificed more. The Vietnam Memorial in Washington, D.C., displays the names of 689 hospital corpsmen and two dental technicians who died in the war.

Whether hospital corpsman, physician, nurse, dentist, dental technician, or Medical Service Corps officer, each member of the Navy Medical Department saw the war from his or her own perspective. If the situation called for "winning hearts and minds" of Vietnamese civilians in a Mekong Delta hospital, saving the lives of injured sailors aboard a burning aircraft carrier, treating a critically wounded Marine for shock in the rubble-strewn streets of Hue, or rescuing a family of refugees on the high seas, Navy medical personnel were in Vietnam from the beginning of American involvement to the very end. *Navy Medicine in Vietnam* weaves their medical experiences into the fabric of the Vietnam War.

*   *   *

This book is based on documents in the Navy Bureau of Medicine Archives and interviews conducted by the author. All interview transcripts reside in the Bureau of Medicine and Surgery Oral History Collection.

1

PASSAGE TO FREEDOM

A full decade before the United States became embroiled in the Vietnam War, French colonial rule in Indochina came to a chaotic end. France hastily began withdrawing its forces in May 1954, following a climactic defeat by Ho Chi Minh's Viet Minh at Dien Bien Phu, a garrison in far northwestern Vietnam near the Laotian border. The pitiful and dispirited remnants of the French army that survived Dien Bien Phu suffered not only from wounds incurred during the 55-day siege, but they also had to cope with a variety of jungle diseases, malnutrition, and the cruelty of their communist captors. The Geneva Accords of 1954 that ended the fighting provided for the turnover and evacuation of French troops. Many French soldiers, temporarily marooned in Saigon, owed their rescue to the U.S. Navy.

The hospital ship Haven *(AH-12) had already seen action in World War II and four tours during the Korean War. Now the ship was again pressed into service. After docking at Saigon's Catinat Wharf, two French medical officers arrived to arrange for the boarding, embarkation, and medical care of 721 sick and wounded French military personnel. Many of these patients had come from France and also from colonial possessions in North Africa. Almost all suffered from tropical infectious diseases or wounds received during the recent fighting with the Viet Minh, or both. About 180 were ex-prisoners of war, some of whom survived the recent battle of Dien Bien Phu.*

Due to the oppressive climate, officials chose the early morning hour of 0300 to commence embarkation. It was 8 September 1954. The following passages are excerpts from an official report on Operation Repatriation sent back to the Bureau of Medicine and Surgery in Washington.

8 SEPTEMBER 1954

At 0200 reveille was held on all hospital corpsmen, medical, and hospital officers. Hot coffee and sandwiches were served to the embarkation party which not only refreshed, but also helped to awaken most of the sleepy sailors.

On the pier, in the early morning darkness, tables and chairs were set up for the purpose of checking each patient against a long, typewritten manifest of patients. A group of Legionnaires [French Foreign Legion], who were provided to assist in handling the tons of baggage, were huddled on the pier smoking cigarettes and awaiting their task. Aboard the ship, detail and litter teams were assigned, and the electric litter hoists were tested.

The wait was not long. The early morning stillness was suddenly interrupted by the drone of motors, and the dark streets became illuminated with the probing headlights of ambulances.

Without incident, the process of embarking 721 patients commenced at 0300. Of the total number, 247 were brought aboard in stretchers by means of electric litter hoists. There were 474 ambulatory patients brought aboard over the gangway. Accompanying the patients were nearly 3,000 pieces of baggage, varying in size from brief-cases to steamer trunks.

Once aboard, the patients were taken to their respective wards and made comfortable between freshly laundered sheets. Among the 721 patients was one woman, Mme. Renee Julien, a secretary in the French Colonial Army. The entire operation, from hoisting the first patient to lugging the last piece of baggage, was completed by 0900, 9 September 1954.

10 September

To the 721 French military patients aboard, the long voyage home began this morning at 1000 when the colors were shifted from the flagstaff to the after-mast, and the *Haven* navigated cautiously away from the pier. The ship moved so slowly that it hardly seemed to move at all. To those standing in the streets lining the harbor of Saigon, the ship, quietly sliding out of the port, must have appeared quite impressive, but certainly not earth-shattering. In actuality it meant that most of the patients were saying "fini" to their service in Indo-China, carrying away from them only vivid memories of the past hardships endured in prison camps, or suffering brought about by war wounds.

As the ship left port, traffic behind had picked up speed on the five-hour trek to the mouth of the winding Rivière de Saigon and the ship's activities once again returned to normal. Since almost all the patients speak no English, the big problem is the language barrier. Although three members of the crew speak fluent French, it is an impossibility for them to be everywhere at once. Consequently, information that is of interest to all French personnel is disseminated in French over the public announcement system.

It was decided to appoint a French patient from each ward to assist the Navy medical officers, nurses, and hospital corpsmen in his respective ward to maintain order and cleanliness. In this way, employing close coordination of patients with the French doctors, the many small problems, which go to keep a hospital clean and sanitary, could be accomplished with a minimum of misunderstanding involved.

12 September

After 48 hours at sea and 72 hours after embarkation, the general mess officers report that those ambulatory French military patients eating in the mess hall consume prodigious amounts of food, with emphasis on breads and sugar. A great many return to the serving line for second helpings, with copious amounts of food of starchy character taken. Those patients exhibiting malnourishment and emaciation are being given evening supplementary nourishment in the form of fruit juices and eggnog. The dietary scruples of Muhammadans against pork products has been considered and met by alternate menu selections.

13 September

Since the beginning of the voyage, a language barrier has been responsible for the limited amount of fraternization between patients and ship's company, but through various mixtures of German, French, Italian, Spanish, and English, this river of lingual helplessness is being spanned.

14 September

While there are many very ill among the French patients, only two have been considered to be in critical condition. These two patients have extensive intracranial wounds with profound neurological complications. The Navy medical officers attending the French patients are finding, to their astonishment, that those patients have not only one pathological condition but, in most cases, have three, four, or five infectious conditions concurrently. Most of the wounded or ill have malaria, pneumonia, amoebiasis, or some parasitic infestation superimposed upon the primary diagnosis. Extensive epidemiological laboratory analyses are being conducted on these cases.

15 SEPTEMBER 1954

At this point, the report details the circumstances of a 27-year-old Legionnaire corporal, Pierre MacIntosh. His chilling story of captivity under the communists seems to represent the experiences of his comrades-in-arms.

After spending a few years in France, [the Swiss national] satisfied his urge for adventure by joining the French [Foreign] Legion. In January 1952, he requested duty in Indo-China, where he has been until embarked aboard the *Haven* as a patient on September 9, 1954. Of the two and one-half years spent in Indo-China, all but the six months he was held as a prisoner of war were spent in combat.

The battalion to which he was attached was the first French unit taken at Dienbienphu. He, and those captured with him, spent thirty-eight days walking approximately 400 miles. MacIntosh walked the entire distance without shoes.

During the six months he was a prisoner of the communists, MacIntosh lost forty pounds. He was fed rice twice daily for six months, occasionally receiving a small piece of beef or pork. Vegetables, as the communists call them, were, as he said, "a little bit of grass." The prisoners received no soap or toothpaste while they were held. Tobacco was dispensed by leaf, and the prisoners used old newspapers or banana leaves as tobacco paper.

MacIntosh said there was no torture inflicted on the prisoners, except to those who tried to escape. However, they were subjected to vast amounts of propaganda in the form of lectures promising "peace" which, as he gestured, went in one ear and out the other. Russian-made movies spoken in French were also shown. He said the Americans were referred to as "Capitalists" and "Imperialists," while the French were called "Colonialists."

Life on the *Haven* is entirely different for MacIntosh. His eating is no longer a problem. He puts away three big meals a day, with supplementary nourishment between meals. Breakfast is his favorite meal. Suffering from malnutrition, MacIntosh has gained eight pounds since coming aboard five days ago. The only thing he really misses which the *Haven* cannot give him is his daily wine ration which is mandatory in the Legion.

His plans for the future are indefinite, but he is contemplating a career in the military life, hoping to be assigned someplace where there is "no rice."

17 SEPTEMBER 1954

One member of the Foreign Legion offered a possible explanation today for the enormous consumption of bread by the French patients. Approximately 400 loaves have become a daily necessity since the patients came aboard, compared with a pre-embarkation figure of 150 loaves for ship's company.

The Legionnaire pointed out that the butter ration in the Legion is two ounces once every three months, and small additional amounts on holidays. Butter is not rationed aboard the *Haven* and most of the patients are taking advantage of this abundance by consuming large amounts of the dairy product with it counterpart — bread.

The much-lamented lack of a twice-daily wine ration is evidently the commissary department's lone shortcoming in the eyes of the patients, while the unlimited flow of coffee is a tremendous hit. Approximately 120 pounds are consumed each day.

19 SEPTEMBER 1954

It isn't often that a plaster cast has to be reconstructed on account of a weight gain. One French patient, wearing a cast covering his chest and abdomen, has gained so much weight that his cast had to be split in such a way as to accommodate his increasing weight. Clinical records indicate that almost all French patients suffering from malnourishment have gained an impressive amount of weight, and continue to have hearty appetites.

Ward medical officers are still finding the language barrier to be a problem. One doctor, trying to question an Arab patient, needed three interpreters. The doctor would state his question to the French interpreter who relayed it to another French patient who spoke German. Using the German language, the question was then passed on to a German lad who repeated the question to the Arab patient in a language understood by the Arab. Receiving an answer, it was then passed back to the doctor after having been spoken in three entirely different languages.

In spite of fairly active seas, there has been no indication of seasickness among the French patients. The two patients on the critical list show slight improvement since they were embarked.

20 September 1954

The ship's store was authorized to accept French francs today and patients lined the counter from opening until closing time, buying a variety of American-made products.

In today's business, 499,000 francs or over $1,400 were spent by the French, with Argus C-3 cameras, Parker pens, and Pall Mall cigarettes leaders in sales. Although after-shave lotion is in demand, soap and toothpaste sales are slow, obviously due to health and comfort issues of these articles by the Chaplain's office.

24 September 1954

Approximately fifty patients of Islamic faith offered prayers on the flight deck this morning as the *Haven* came within eighty miles of their ancient shrine-city, Mecca. The ceremony reverencing the birthplace of one of the world's principal religions, Muhammadanism, involved a series of standing, bowing, and kneeling movements and lasted about fifteen minutes. Several members of the crew and other patients observed the rites.

26 September 1954

The USS *Haven* completed transit of the historical Red Sea early this morning and entered the channel of the highly strategic Suez Canal. Eighteen line handlers, employees of the Canal Company, were brought aboard with their boats as the ship stopped to receive her pilot. The *Haven*, edging down the Suez at a careful five knots, was through the first part of the canal before noon and anchored in Great Bitter Lake, awaiting permission to continue her transit of the 103-mile East-West connecting waterway.

27 September 1954

Nearing the northern entrance of the Suez Canal today, the *Haven* was welcomed by a fleet of enterprising Port Said merchants, hawking their manifold wares from a swarm of small, brightly-painted boats.

The salesmen, affected by a constant international movement through the canal, unquestionably accepted francs, dollars, piasters [Vietnamese monetary unit] and generally any form of legal currency in exchange for rugs, shoes, souvenir fezzes, or Coca-Cola and avocados.

While the flow of money and merchandise continued up and down the heaving lines of the Port Said gondoliers, 262,000 precious gallons of fuel streamed into the *Haven*'s thirsty reservoirs, readying the Navy Hospital Ship for another log of her current mercy cruise.

2 October 1954

The U.S. Navy hospital ship *Haven* completed part of her recently assigned mission today when the vessel docked at the North African port of Oran, Algeria and 420 of her 721 French patients were disembarked.

"Honneur Aux Combatants d'Indo-Chine," proclaimed a befitting banner paying homage to the Indo-China veterans and a French Army band and drum and bugle corps played the familiar "La Marseillaise," as French dignitaries paid official calls to the Commanding Officer of the *Haven*.

Drums were muffled and French troops and American sailors snapped to stiff attention as the flag-draped body of Maurice Lualhe, Foreign Legionnaire who died onboard the ship, was removed from the *Haven* and released to the French.

Less than an hour after the ship moored, disembarkation of ambulatory patients was initiated, removing one ward at a time. Litter patients were removed later and the entire operation was completed in approximately two hours. Each patient debarked was given a package of cigarettes and a small parcel of food by the French Red Cross.

At 1630 hours the *Haven*'s mooring lines were removed from the pier and the vessel departed the Algerian port en route to Marseille, France.

4 OCTOBER 1954

Completion of patient-debarkation at 1105 this morning at Marseille, France marked another "mission accomplished" by the US Navy hospital ship, *Haven*. A sea of anxious faces searched determinedly the groups of patients lining the rails of the ship as the *Haven* moved slowly toward the awaiting relatives and friends crowding the pier.

Suggesting a duplication of the Oran welcome for the Indo-China warriors, a drum and bugle corps and band played the Star-Spangled Banner, preceding a call from French civilian and military officials.

As the final patient was debarked, ward corpsmen started a cleanup drive and the relieved crew looked forward to liberty in Marseille and the trip home to the United States.

"Who Could Have Imagined?"

Bostonian Anna Corcoran joined the Navy in 1951 and served in several domestic and overseas assignments, including the naval hospitals in Guam and Yokosuka, Japan. When she was due to rotate home from Yokosuka, she was offered a roundabout way of getting back to Boston.

"There were about six of us. The chief nurse called us in and said, 'You will be having your orders back to the States but would you like to be assigned to the hospital ship Haven?'

"At that time they had reassigned a lot of their nurses either to Yokosuka or somewhere in the Pacific. They were short of nurses and asked us if we'd go aboard to supplement their number. So four of us said yes. They told us that we would be evacuating people who had just been released from prison, and we would be taking the Foreign Legion back to Oran, Algeria, and the French soldiers into Marseille."

Saigon was a beautiful city. It was so pretty and the buildings were so white. There were nice roads and streets. We didn't see a lot of destruction or anything like you'd see later. There was a cocktail party for us the first night after we arrived.

We had heard what happened to the French at Dien Bien Phu. One of our doctors at Yokosuka had been sent up to evacuate a lot of the Christians from the north down to the south part of Vietnam. His name was Dr. Tom Dooley.

I remember loading the patients in the middle of the night. And there were two rumors as to why we were doing that. One was that they didn't want the Viet Minh to know how many we were taking, and the other was that it was cooler in the middle of the night. We loaded over 700 patients starting somewhere about 3 or 4 o'clock in the morning. We had them all aboard by 10 o'clock. A lot of them walked aboard and some came aboard on stretchers or in wheelchairs. They were very thin and kind of grimy, and they looked malnourished.

I was assigned to the lowest deck, I think the E deck, where we had patients. There were two wards with 87 patients in each ward. We had triple-deck bunks. On that floor they all had to be able to walk upstairs to get their meals because there was no elevator that came all the way down and therefore no way to get food carts down.

None of us spoke French or Arabic, but we managed to communicate with the patients because we were with them all day. They would come up and try to tell you about themselves and their families. We had one man who was our interpreter. He had been a German SS trooper and afterward a prisoner in Canada. He spoke perfect English, perfect French, perfect German, and a little Arabic. When we had sick call, the doctor would stand on the second bunk to examine the guy in the third bunk, and the interpreter would squat on top of the third bedside table. Then the doctor would ask a question, the interpreter would ask the patient, and then the answer was relayed back to the doctor. It was certainly a very interesting and very different sick call than I'd ever done before or since.

Almost all the patients had worms. When I'd go down in the morning, they would bring their little boxes with stool samples for me to look at. We had to make sure the heads were on

USS *Haven* in the early 1950s (BUMED Archives).

the worms. We gave them medicine for that and had to check their stools all the time. Most of them had ascariasis, caused by a kind of worm that people got in those countries.

And after we had been under way for a while, we found that almost all of them had body lice. It was bad for one of my corpsmen who had long hair on his arms and he got some. We all felt so bad. But then when everybody found out that we had them in both wards, I went up to the wardroom for the movie one night and all the fellas said to me, "You can't sit here! You can't sit here! We don't want your lice." I hate to tell you how we got rid of them because we'd be arrested today. We lined the patients up in the heads and sprayed them with DDT. It was very effective but not good for them or us to inhale. But we did it. We didn't know any better.

When we first got under way, the patients enjoyed getting in the shower. We had to tie the showers off and only let them have a shower once or maybe twice a week because we were out of water. And the other thing they all did was eat bread. They ate so much that the bakery couldn't keep up with them.

A lot of our food, of course, was foreign to them. Because most of the North Africans were Muslim, there were restrictions on their diet as far as pork and things like that were concerned. The crew tried to accommodate them but at that point, most of them were so hungry they didn't adhere to the restrictions. They just ate whatever they could.

When we got to Oran, a band welcomed us. The Foreign Legion patients came off first. Most of them, at this point, were ambulatory. Some of their wounds had healed and they were in much better shape than when they had come aboard. Then we had a couple of hours' liberty in Oran.

When we left Oran later that afternoon and got under way, one of the soldiers jumped overboard. He had been drinking all afternoon in Oran and when he returned to the ship, he wrapped his wallet in plastic and decided to go back. They put the small boat in the water and the captain turned that ship around so quickly we almost crushed the sailor between the small boat and the ship.

There was also a ceremony when we arrived in Marseille and it was an emotional homecoming for them. There were a lot of people and we assumed that many of them were relatives because of the greeting they gave. One of the Legionnaires had died en route. They off-loaded the body in a casket with the French flag draped over it. That was very, very emotional to watch. Of course, at that time, we didn't know how many of our own would be going home that way from Vietnam. Who could have imagined back in 1954 that 10 years later we would be involved just like the French were and we'd suffer the same defeat they did.

* * *

The Geneva Accords of 1954 called for a cease-fire between French and Viet Minh forces, ending hostilities in Vietnam, Cambodia, and Laos. The provisions also allowed for the temporary division of Vietnam along the 17th Parallel, pending a nationwide election to be held in 1956. Meanwhile, French forces were to withdraw from the north and the Viet Minh from the south. Under the Geneva terms, the Vietnamese could decide where they wished to settle. Few in the south chose to go north, but with the collapse of French rule, hundreds of thousands of refugees streamed south to escape the communists. As with the humanitarian mission in evacuating the survivors of Dien Bien Phu, the U.S. Navy was also charged with conducting "Operation Passage to Freedom." By the time the mission was completed, Navy ships evacuated to South Vietnam more than 860,000 refugees, almost 500,000 of them Catholics.

Lt.(j.g.) Daniel M. Redmond, USNR, was attached to Amphibious Transport Division 13 (TRANSDIV 13) under the command of Capt. Walter C. Winn. As Winn's intelligence officer, Redmond had briefed his commander regularly about the progress of the war. Earlier that spring of 1954, as French forces battled the communist Viet Minh, it seemed quite possible that the United

States would intervene. But Dien Bien Phu halted any U.S. plans for saving the doomed French colony.

In the first days of August 1954, TRANSDIV 13 conducted landing exercises on Okinawa, when suddenly on 8 August the exercise was canceled and the division was ordered back to Japan. In new orders, TRANSDIV 13 was told to aid in the evacuation of refugees from northern Indochina. Capt. Winn would take command of Task Group 90.8 upon arrival at Haiphong.[1] This port city was located 60 miles east of Hanoi on the Cua Cam River in the Red River Delta. Lt.(j.g.) Redmond recounts what happened during the next several months.

By 15 August TRANSDIV 13 was at sea en route to Haiphong. Two days later in Indochina, the first Navy ship USS *Menard* (APA-201), carrying 1,924 refugees, embarked from the Haiphong area, just nine days after the initial American decision to assist had been conveyed to Vietnamese officials. By the time we arrived at Baie d'Along in the Gulf of Tonkin on 23 August, Winn had selected five officers and 10 enlisted men to be the nucleus of his staff for the embarkation phase of what was to be called "Passage to Freedom."

The next day we transferred to an APD, which was a small destroyer escort used to carry frogmen during amphibious operations. USS *Cavallaro* (APD-128), and at later stages two replacements, became the station ship and home of nearly all the staff of about 130 officers, sailors, and Marines. The French would only permit the officers of the Preventive Medicine and Sanitation Unit to live ashore at a hotel in Haiphong while we were there.

Transfer completed, *Cavallaro* raced up the reddish waters of the Cua Cam. Occasionally, on the river's low banks we saw small concrete blockhouses each flying the Tricolor against a luminous azure sky. It was very hot and humid. Everyone was edgy because we had been warned that a resumption of hostilities could occur at any moment. We arrived at Haiphong and moored to buoys a short distance upriver from the small French naval base.

Immediately, *Cavallaro* lowered a boat away with an armed crew to provide a 24-hour security patrol around the ship. Happily for the crews, who had to work in very tough conditions, Winn discontinued the patrol as soon as someone questioned how a Viet Minh sapper could swim in a current that often exceeded four knots.

Several hours after our arrival, Winn assumed command of CTF 90.8, and we began our embarkation duties. The Cua Cam was dredged to only 20 feet so shipping was limited to vessels of less than 10,000 tons displacement. Consequently, we used U.S. and French amphibious craft as lighters, loading them with refugees for the trip downriver to the Do San anchorage in Baie d'Along. There they would go alongside waiting APAs [Attack Transport], AKAs [Attack Cargo Ship], LSDs [Dock Landing Ship], APTs [Troop Barge]. Crews would move the refugees to the larger ships, often with great difficulty.

The trip south took about two and a half days of intense discomfort for crew and passengers. At first, Saigon was the drop-off point but overcrowding quickly shut it down. Cap St. Jacques on the South China Sea coast then became the landing site.

Movement from Haiphong had to be on an ebbing tide with enough time to ensure offloading in daylight at the anchorage. Night operations there were impossible because of heavy swells, frequent rain squalls, and the terror of the refugees. Although the Baie was only 10 miles away, the trip took about four hours. Conditions on the Cua Cam were hazardous to unsure piloting, and ships moved cautiously to avoid collision and running aground. Moreover, once an LST [Landing Ship Tank] left the river, it still had a lot of water to cover before it reached the anchorage.

Besides Vietnamese, we also had to remove large stocks of U.S. military equipment and ammunition delivered to the French in the later stages of the war. We used [transports] manned by American officers and Japanese crews and time-charted merchant ships of less than 10,000 tons. Pier availability and stevedoring problems in Haiphong really complicated this side of the

Refugees board an LST (Landing Ship Tank) for South Vietnam during Operation Passage to Freedom (BUMED Archives).

operation. Nevertheless, the Navy left nothing behind when it finally pulled out of the north in May 1955.

At Tourane [now Danang], located on the coast almost halfway to Saigon, CTF 90 established a logistics center. On the return trip to Haiphong a ship would put in to Tourane to refuel, reprovision, and receive needed repairs. When the northwest monsoon disrupted the anchorage, CTF 90 moved the center to the Baie d'Along.

For loading refugees, we employed a site called La Briqueterie about a mile upriver from Haiphong. Here a number of two-story and smaller stucco buildings barracked a Foreign Legion company that, surprisingly, included at least a squad of Vietnamese prostitutes. The Geneva Accords restricted the introduction of additional military forces so the French said we could have only 15 officers and men at the site at any one time, a constraint they later relaxed. They also refused to allow us ashore with weapons, but they did promise Legion protection wherever we loaded refugees at the main site, posts on the river, or at nearby Hongay, a coal producing center.

This turned out to be the case. But we always had one lasting complaint — our defenders often vanished down the road in their trucks a lot sooner than we wished. Once they left three enlisted men and me uneasily waiting for a boat in a lovely spot. Long after they were gone we had to listen to the threatening sounds of a very close but unseen firefight. We were very relieved to see our boat about an hour after the firing ended.

In the early days of the operation, the boarding area was very muddy from the intermittent heavy rains that drenched the delta day and night. Falling in torrents, the rain actually hurt when it hit you. And, strangely, often you saw the sun shining through it. Many times I stood in the rain eating C rations that must have been packed in the early 1940s. I stood in mud to my ankles, and rain and green dye from my cheap French Army raincoat ran into my shirt. I marveled at my new surprising life as a naval officer.

At first, the loading site — a cleared area about 100 yards wide and 50 deep in front of the buildings leading down to the river — proved too narrow for orderly operations. French tanks hemmed in the space on both sides. We had a long, frustrating talk with the senior military officer, a major general who flabbergasted us when he said he had to get clearance from Saigon to move his tanks back a short distance on each side. Capt. Winn finally persuaded him to widen the work area without consulting higher authority. Even widened, the site retained a crowded look because of large medical tents, parked vehicles, and numerous people.

Every morning military trucks jammed with refugees would arrive from Camp de la Pagode, the primary holding location just outside Haiphong. Shouting "Allez! Allez,!" the Legionnaires herded them forward, prodding them with rifles to move faster. The refugees were silent, not knowing what was in store, frightened by the soldiers and us. After all, the Viet Minh had said we would take them to sea and dump everyone overboard except the females we planned to sell to army brothels in the south. As for the soldiers, the refugees knew them all too well to trust them about anything.

The refugees were dressed in loose black cotton tops and trousers, most adults wearing yellow palm-leafed cones or thick, dark headbands. They were nearly all women, children, and old men, many barefooted and they shuffled between wooden control barriers in white clouds of DDT dust. The first time you got close to them you gagged, but somehow with time we came to tolerate their smell. Our corpsmen moved among them giving what help they could. It was not always accepted. Trying to help a woman in labor one wet day, two corpsmen were frantically waved away as she delivered the baby on the muddy ground, washed it in the river, and walked aboard a French LSM [Medium Landing Ship].

Once they were through delousing, a ship waited for them at water's edge, bow door open, ramp down. On the first day, Winn had made me embarkation officer, a role I played for much of our stay there. As the refugees passed me in single file, looking straight ahead, never smiling except for a rare child, a bosun clicked them off on his counter. We never got used to the misery we saw each day as thousands shuffled by holding their few belongings tightly or carrying them on balanceurs — the thin pole, bundle dangling from each end — seen everywhere in Southeast Asia.

They squatted on the well deck. Some tried to light cooking fires in braziers, but crewmen easily extinguished them. Occasionally, a fire would go undetected until the caramel smell of burning opium alerted sailors. Besides the real fire danger, drug use onboard violated naval regulations and panicked some ships to send messages like, "Pax smoking opium on board X What should we do?" CTF 90 quickly ordered the ship to confiscate the drugs until debarkation at which time they were to be returned. Opium and hashish use was uncontrolled in Indochina, so we did not destroy them on discovery.

It was very crowded on the well deck. We did not separate families or villagers. Once having only an LST available, we boarded about 3,000. Although such crowding made the trip to the Baie an arduous one, we did keep together a number of contiguous villages, as requested by their chiefs and Catholic priests.

The Red River Delta is beautiful. The Baie d'Along is spectacular with its turquoise waters specked with hundreds of limestone eruptions, some 500 feet tall. Unfortunately, the climate is tropical. Temperatures always seemed to be in the 90s or higher with 100 percent humidity. Even the river temperature was 96 degrees. The station ship berthing spaces below the water line were like steam baths, making uninterrupted sleep impossible. There was really not enough room to sleep on deck, and it rained during the night anyway. But still people tried it every night.

The French delivered water to the ship by barge three times a week. Our doctors added so much chlorine that it tasted like a swimming pool. Strict water rationing was the rule. Everyone seemed to suffer from skin rash, the worst case being the ship's baker who had to be evacuated because his whole body was covered with eruptions. And to make matters worse, the extra people onboard only intensified the "town-gown" friction between crew and staff.

Morale was terrible. Not only were living conditions bad, [but] we could not offset them with liberty. Even after the French allowed more of us on the beach, we could not solve the problem. CTF 90's liberal liberty policy stopped at the 17th parallel. There would be no liberty north of there. As a result, only 15 to 20 of us working got ashore every day — the embarkation party, the medical unit, and a few officers in Haiphong on official business. The rest were virtual prisoners aboard the station ship.

After senior petty officers began to show signs of stress, we had to do something. To everyone's relief, a clever staff officer came up with the "work party solution." If liberty parties were not allowed, we would put "work parties" ashore. The next morning an officer took 15 men ashore in their clothes — dungarees, blue shirt, and white hat. At the Navy base he briefed them on Haiphong's very real dangers, emphasized their obligation to make the plan work for all, and told them to meet him back on the base at 1500.

In all the work parties that followed, no one ever embarrassed us, and only one, a second class bosun, returned to the base and then went back into town. Two Marines and I found him that night just before curfew drunk and jolly at Le Sphinx, the French army brothel in Haiphong.

On 25 August, CTF 90 established Task Unit 90.8.6, the Preventive Medicine and Sanitation Unit at Haiphong. Headed by Cmdr. Julius Amberson, it consisted of three medical officers, one Medical Service Corps officer, and four corpsmen. Among the doctors was Lt.(j.g.) Thomas A. Dooley, who later became famous for his books and speeches about Passage to Freedom and his subsequent medical missions in Southeast Asia.

Under Winn's command, Cmdr. Amberson was to coordinate with French and Vietnamese officials all medical matters relating to the embarkation. In addition, his unit was to provide medical and sanitation assistance to evacuees.

Disease was widespread and shocking. Malaria, trachoma, smallpox, typhoid, worm infestation, fungi of all sorts, yaws, tuberculosis, dysentery, beriberi, rickets, conjunctivitis, pneumonia, measles, impetigo — we saw them all at Camp de la Pagode and the embarkation site. Refugees died at the camp, the site, and on the ships. Clearly, France had been indifferent or worse to the medical needs of the people it had exploited for a hundred years.

Dr. Amberson and his unit, assisted by Vietnamese medical teams, did all they could to deal with the enormous health problems they found in Pagode. The unit also took care of our medical needs which, fortunately, were not too demanding. And they treated other Americans in the area — MAAG [U.S. Military Assistance Advisory Group] personnel, diplomats from Hanoi, and the civilian pilots of Civil Air Transport [CAT] Co., an airline rumored to be partially funded by the CIA. The CAT pilots, a wild bunch of mercenaries, were famous with the French for their bravery in dropping supplies to the beleaguered garrison at Dien Bien Phu.

Besides the usual medical services, the unit set up a complete epidemiological laboratory that included bacteriology and parasitology. One afternoon I spent several hilarious hours with Dooley and a corpsman trying to capture a couple of monkeys in the garden of the Continental Hotel so they could get samples of simian body lice.

Adm. Querville, the senior naval officer in the north and very friendly toward us, gave Amberson the use of a small two-room building on the naval base for the medical unit's headquarters and laboratory. A refrigerator came with the building, and the doctors kept blood samples and an ample supply of Trente-Trois, the very good local beer. Dr. Amberson had issued an open invitation to stop by if you were on the base. It became the only place in northern Indochina you could get a cold beer. It goes without saying that wine and beer were the only liquids you could drink with impunity in Haiphong.

Dr. Amberson was an internationally known expert on tropical and arctic medicine. When he came to Haiphong he was 59, easily the oldest American in the north. At least six feet tall, he was overweight with a large belly. His face was fleshy and ruddy, his thinning white hair brushed straight back. Amberson's clothes somehow seemed more rumpled than ours, and he liked to wear a chapeau Breusse, a wide-brimmed hat with the right side fastened to the crown in the manner of an Australian soldier.

A fine officer, Dr. Amberson was a very friendly man, smiling often and usually in good spirits. He wore his fame modestly and everyone was quite fond of him. The night we received the ALNAV [message] announcing his selection for captain, two of us went over to Haiphong to tell him. Sure, it gave us a good excuse to get off the ship, but it also gave us the opportunity to deliver agreeable news to a good guy.

At the boarding site he was very helpful in keeping us informed as to what we were seeing among the refugees. Unlike most of us, he did not seem too surprised at the signs of French neglect. He used to say, "Give us enough bars of soap and clean water, by God, we could get rid of about half these diseases." Watching mothers give newborns their first bath in the filthy waters of the Cua Cam, he often wondered out loud at the slim prospects of the babies reaching their first birthdays. Shortly after his selection to captain, he received orders that took him out of Haiphong at the end of September.

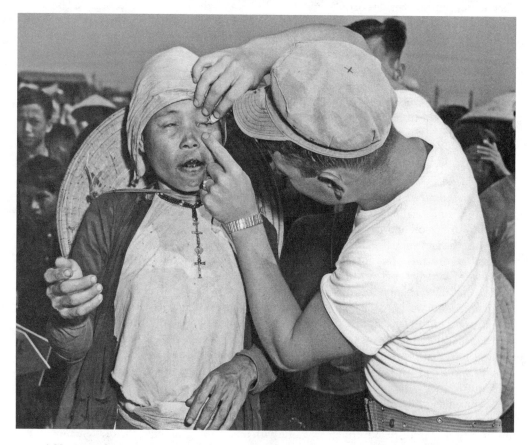

A Navy corpsman treats an eye infection at a Haiphong refugee camp (BUMED Archives).

As the weeks went by, the operation slowed and COMNAVFE [Commander Naval Forces Far East] started to return ships to normal training exercises. By the end of October, most of the Navy was gone. A small staff headed by a commander stayed aboard the station ship, and Dr. Dooley remained in Haiphong with five corpsmen. Refugees continued to depart on time-charted merchant ships. In May 1955, Passage to Freedom ended and the few remaining Americans departed the north.

By any standard, the operation was a success. During the nine months, we transported by sea 310,848 refugees (including 17,846 military), 68,757 tons of equipment and ammunition, and 8,135 vehicles. According to Bui Van Luong, the former General Director of the Refugee Commission, the French and Americans evacuated a total of 768,672 refugees, 555,037 by ship and 213,635 by French airlift. Others left the north on foot or by boat. In all, 928,152 went south, the vast majority of whom were Catholics.

In mid–October of 1954 the American ambassador in Saigon sent a message to CTF 90 that he in turn passed on to all the units involved in the evacuation. Former Ambassador [Donald R.] Heath summarized the operation as follows:

Upon occasion your depart from Saigon would like to reiterate my admiration for way in which you have carried out mission connection evac refugees from north X Conduct your officers and men both afloat and ashore deserves highest commendation X For their kindness and thoughtfulness towards refugees have left impression of individual Americans which will not soon be forgotten X Mission has been carried out in best tradition of naval service X

* * *

In a 1955 lecture presented at the U.S. Naval Medical School, Capt. Julius Amberson, Passage to Freedom's chief medical officer, reminisced about his role in this extraordinary mission.

Early in August 1954, the Commander of Naval Forces Far East received orders from Washington to mobilize a naval task force for the purpose of evacuating refugees from northern Vietnam to designated places of safety in southern Vietnam. The communists under the Viet Minh leader, Ho Chi Minh, had just broken the back of French resistance after seven years of war. Dien Bien Phu was their "Waterloo."

By the Geneva agreement there was a "provisional military line of demarcation" at the 17th parallel by which the commanders in chief of the Viet Minh forces on the north and Vietnam forces on the south were placed in charge of civil administration and relief on their respective sides of the line. Provision was also made for a small area around Haiphong for withdrawal of the French from the interior. All refugees were to congregate also at Haiphong for evacuation.

Naval Task Force 90, commanded by R.Adm. L[orenzo] S. Sabin, was dispatched to Vietnam to assist the French in the evacuation of both civilian and military personnel, as well as all military equipment which might be brought to the beaches and docks at Haiphong. Certainly the French forces deserve outstanding praise and credit for their efforts in this successful evacuation designated as the "Passage to Freedom."

The mission of the Medical Department was set forth succinctly in the medical annex of the operation order for this task force. In effect it said we would maintain sanitary conditions throughout each ship, prevent epidemics in our personnel, and provide humanitarian care and medical attention to the refugees as they came within the orbit of our operations, both ashore and afloat.

The task force began to assemble from various Pacific sectors in the vicinity of Haiphong about 15 August 1954. The admiral's flagship, USS *Estes* [AGC-12], arrived in Tonkin Bay on 18 August 1954. Many of these ships had too deep a draft to go up the Red River channel to Haiphong, but could be loaded from LSTs which were more suitable for embarking personnel from the beaches along the Red River.

The scene seemed peaceful with merchant ships plying toward the Red Delta. Sampans with butterfly sails were yawing and tacking about on an undestined course. We dropped our "hook" at 1700 hours. American Military Assistance Group officers from Haiphong came aboard for a conference on evacuation problems. We found it was necessary for us to establish good liaison with the French and Vietnamese in order to give medical assistance where and when indicated and to expedite the delousing of refugees at our embarkation points in the Red Delta.

On 19 August 1954 R.Adm. Sabin directed us to go ashore to establish the necessary medical sanitary facilities which would be needed for the refugees and, insofar as possible, to establish good liaison with the French and Vietnamese to expedite the mission. Our flagship lay about two miles offshore from the mouth of the Red River. We went ashore with a jeep and landed on the Do San Peninsula.

I was accompanied by Lt. Edward Gleason, MSC, USNR, a public health officer of the Navy. After disembarking on a hard seaplane ramp, we made our way toward Haiphong, a distance of 20 to 25 miles over a hard-surfaced tarmac road, passing many guarded roadblocks. French, African, and Vietnamese troops were manning these stations. The French Foreign Legion was very much in evidence. We passed over a broad plain being planted with rice. Many carabaos [water buffalo] were plowing the deep mud and water of rice paddies. These pastoral scenes were soon to stand out in sharp relief against conditions we were about to view in Haiphong and its environs.

As we entered Haiphong, we found every available vacant lot, parks, schools, and vacated buildings packed with refugees. We estimated there were about 200,000 at that time. They were living in the most squalid conditions— no sanitary conveniences. The human excreta combined with the presence of enormous numbers of flies were the making of epidemic diseases among these unfortunates. We visited other camps outside the city which had been set up from their meager belongings.

These camps were usually near a pool of rice paddy water. There were no sanitary arrangements. People were sitting under shelters, improvised from rice mats, cloth, or some type of plastic. Tents and shelter facilities were limited. Water was taken directly from the rice paddies and consumed raw. Wormy feces were common and carelessly scattered about. Flies were present in large numbers. The heat was intense. Strong odors permeated the air.

There were many pregnant women, as well as many small children and old people. The absence of young men was obvious. Family groups huddled together and seemed quite destitute.

Meetings were held with various French and Vietnamese officials, including Vietnamese Public Health people of Haiphong regarding assistance the Navy might render in expediting the welfare and evacuation of refugees from the city. Lt. David Davis, MC, USNR, and Lt.(j.g.) Thomas A. Dooley III, MC, USNR, served as French and English interpreters during these interchanges of view and expressions of international goodwill. We found the civilian Vietnamese to be very nationalistic and determined to run their own show. However, we indicated that wherever we might be of service in getting better camps set up, [ensuring a] good water supply and providing additional medical supplies, we would be glad to do so.

Our Military Assistance Group and a representative of the Foreign Aid Administration, Mr. Michael Adler, were primarily effective in bringing in tents and getting two new tent camps set up outside of Haiphong to be used as a staging area for about 12,000 to 14,000 refugees just prior to embarkation. After these were erected by Legionnaires and French Algerian troops, our Navy medical group took over sanitation of these camps and, under the direction of Lt. Gleason, we set up units for the filtration and purification of water.

At first the natives were slow to accept this clean, clear, chlorinated water but after some days took freely of it. There were saboteurs in these camps who slashed our large rubber water storage tanks, but this was stopped by erecting a barbed wire barrier around each tank and putting Senegalese guards from the Foreign Legion [on duty] to prevent such incidents.

As soon as the Military Assistance Group, Foreign Aid Administration, and French and Vietnamese Evacuation committees began moving the refugees from the staging area to our embarkation points along the Red River, we set up DDT dusting stations manned principally by U.S. Navy corpsmen and Beachmaster personnel, through which all refugees passed to have their bodies and personal effects disinsecticized [sic] before embarking on our ships. They passed through our lines at the rate of 1,000 per hour. Mechanical power dusters with 10 outlets were used. Several of these were in operation. The majority of the refugees were Catholic Tonkinese led by their priests. There were other groups as well, particularly Chinese families who had been in Indochina for generations.

In the staging areas and at our embarkation points, medical attention was provided mainly by the Vietnamese Public Health Services of Haiphong. We gave impetus to this service from the start, as none was provided the refugees during their great influx into Haiphong. The Vietnamese Public Health Service immunized all refugees against cholera and smallpox.

There was a lack of medical supplies among the Vietnamese, and these were provided from the American Foreign Aid Organization sources upon our recommendation and selection. It was evident that the peasants from the interior of the country had had little, if any, medical attention all their lives. One could surmise from the total number of medical practitioners in the country that 23 million people could not get adequate medical care from 500 doctors, the majority of whom were concentrated in the larger cities.

One was daily confronted with hordes of people with different eye diseases. Blindness was prevalent in the young, as well as the old. Pyogenic [pus-generating] infections of the scalp of young children were very common, as well as numerous other skin diseases. Dysentery and intestinal parasites were also very common, and one only had to walk through a campsite any morning to see the writhing worms in the fresh stools scattered about.

Malaria was prevalent in all groups, and some were too ill to accept passage at times. Whenever a person was found too ill to be sent to sea, usually the whole family would fall out of line and stay behind. The family ties were very strong, and they sensed that their best chance of survival rested in a family unit.

All were poorly clad, wearing only their cotton trousers, top shirts, and a peaked straw sun hat. Nearly all were barefoot and practically all children were half-dressed or naked.

Just before embarkation, each mother was given a blanket or a sheet for babies in arms. Funds for this were provided by the American Foreign Aid Organization and local Vietnamese social workers supervised by Mme. Vu Thi Ngai, who dispensed the cloth as indicated. Mme. Vu Thi Ngai also maintained her own private orphanage in Haiphong which enabled her to rescue many lost or abandoned babies and young children. She gathered about 400 to 500 around Haiphong. To all these children we gave medical attention. Her orphanage was eventually transferred to Saigon, but her efforts still required much outside support if these children were to survive.

All refugees were permitted to take as much personal baggage as they could carry on a split bamboo pole loaded at each end and mounted over their shoulders. Usually these personal effects consisted of a rice mat to sleep on, cooking utensils, and rice and fish. Rice constituted most of the weight. However, rice and fish were provided onboard ship for each contingent during their passage south. Each ship provided medical care to everyone during their sea journey, which for many was the first in their lives. Motion sickness was common. Their wounds were dressed by our corpsmen and more serious cases like fractures, obstetrics, and fevers were handled by a Navy doctor.

The disposal of the dead at sea posed some questions as to the nationality of the individual [and] his religion; the desires of the immediate family had to be taken into consideration. It so happened that almost everyone who died en route was Christian and burial at sea was permitted. It was estimated at the start of operations that we might have an average of four births and two deaths on each sea trip. These estimates proved to be fairly accurate. Burial paper was provided by the Navy in which the remains were wrapped and the usual Christian burial rites were performed before being committed to the sea.

I shall now refer to some phases of our work in connection with the evacuation. We anticipated the need for laboratory controls in our preventive medicine activities associated with our ships and their personnel. This laboratory had to be shore-based in order to serve our ships, which plied back and forth between Haiphong and Saigon and points between. We asked the French Naval Commandant, R.Adm. Jean Querville, for space in one of his buildings on the French naval base along the Red River at Haiphong. He quickly and graciously provided running water, electrical service, and an electric refrigerator. We were in business.

Lt. Richard Kaufman, MSC, and five corpsmen set up and manned departments in bacteriology, entomology, parasitology, and general zoology. This enabled us to collect and process important medical material, make water analyses for all our ships, identify insects of medical importance in the region, and ascertain the kinds of human parasites in this population.

We had two combat cameramen attached to our shore unit for the purpose of making a record of the refugee movement. All scenes shot followed a prepared script to assure complete coverage of every aspect of the refugees' lives from the time they were seen approaching Haiphong, arrival in villages and camps, medical care, food and shelter, DDT work and embarkation, and also their sea trip and life en route to destination in southern Indochina.

The lives of the refugees were not without hazard and discomfort even in our improved camps. Typhoons blew down tents; rain and high tides flooded them out on numerous occasions. Tents were struck by lightning, killing or injuring the occupants. We made many medical inspection tours among the people in our camps to administer to their needs in addition to the Vietnamese first aid arrangements which were set in motion by us.

We combated much of the adverse communist propaganda that was prevalent about Americans. Many erroneous ideas were sown: that our DDT was a slow poison;[2] that we were going to charge $60 a head for Passage to Freedom; that we might drown them at sea by opening up our LST bows; or that we might take them away from Indochina forever. Reports of communist atrocities on refugees were coming in, and we saw some evidence of beatings and bayonet wounds. Also, mothers reported the communists would wrench babies from their arms and run away with them in order to break up families and impede the exit of these people from communist-won areas. All these hazards and diversions thrown in their path were contrary to the Geneva Accords signed by both the communists and the French, which agreed to let each person have a free choice as to the side on which he wished to live and be allowed to go unmolested to that area.

By 21 September 1954, after a month's movement of refugees, the 100,000th refugee passed through our embarkation point. He was an itinerant tobacco salesman with a wife and four children. They were photographed, picked up by one of our helicopters, flown to our flagship, and taken to Saigon that way instead of the usual sea trip on one of the regular transports. This family was feted in Saigon upon arrival and given presents and made to feel that there was a bright future for themselves and all their people who had been rudely uprooted from their ancestral abodes.

By the end of September 1954, fewer refugees were coming in as the Viet Minh, or communists, were controlling their movements. All their sampans were confiscated and other means of transportation were taken away. However, the refugees continued to come through, and during late October and November 1954 thousands of people escaped from Bin Chi, Phat Dien, and Tani Binh areas of Tonkin.

Many managed to reach the three-mile continental limit on rafts and small junks where R.Adm. Querville's small naval craft picked them up and brought them up the Red River at night to our embarkation site. The health of these people was poor, as they had endured many months of hard labor under the communists rebuilding their railroad. In addition, they had to find their own food where they could, as none was supplied by the masters of northern Indochina. Many were found beaten and fractures were common.

By the end of January 1955, about 200,000 refugees had been moved by the U.S. Navy. The refugees were still being moved by sea at the rate of 6,000 per week and by French air at the rate of 500 per day. Haiphong was by this time a dying city. Nearly all business had ceased and moved out. Of the 100,000 French forces there in August 1954, less than 15,000 now remained. All Vietnamese Public Health people had gone south to Saigon.

By the middle of March 1955, we were able to strike our temporary camps for refugees and house them in the huge abandoned military barracks in the city of Haiphong. Our water purification units were re-crated and put aboard our transports for safekeeping. The water supply in Haiphong would suffice for the refugees. We continued to delouse the refugees before embarkation on our ships. Also, we sprayed for fly and mosquito control in the areas where refugees were housed in Haiphong as the insect problem was immense and almost overwhelming.

By this time about 750,000 refugees had been taken out — 250,000 of them in American bottoms. Adm. Sabin's task force expeditiously and with tender care moved these people to safety. The force medical officer, Capt. James Grindell, MC, coordinated the medical activities between the ships of the task force, and maintained continuous medical service for the refugees from the embarkation point to the debarkation points in southern Indochina. He also instituted preventive medicine measures for the maintenance of health of all our naval personnel manning Task Force 90. Weekly suppressive doses of chloroquine against malaria were taken by everyone, immunization boosters were given, rat and insect control measures were stepped up, and each ship was cleaned after each load of refugees debarked. Cmdr. Sidney Britten, MC, relieved me, and later he was relieved by Lt.(j.g.) Dooley, who remained in charge of medical activities in Haiphong until the communists moved in on 19 May 1955.

The French pulled out their last forces of 12,000 on 7 May. Their remnant forces were on the Do San Peninsula, the last bit of land at the end of the Red Delta. Subsequent movement would be removal to sea by their Navy.

Epidemics and famine were beginning to occur in Annam and Tonkin. All health and immunization programs had begun to break down in communist areas. The [Four] Horsemen of the Apocalypse have taken over where once peace, plenty, and happiness reigned. The U.S. Navy, however, wrote a new chapter in its long and glorious history in defending the weak, rescuing them from slavery and death.

Smoothing the Passage South

Dennis Shepard joined the Navy in 1951 and trained as a hospital corpsman at Naval Hospital San Diego. After additional training as an operating room technician, he went overseas and worked at medical treatment facilities in Korea and Japan. His qualifications were ready-made for his next assignment in Indochina — Operation Passage to Freedom. "I spoke Japanese, English, Spanish, and studied Latin. And I was able to learn languages quickly. I learned Japanese in five months and Lao in five months. I also had a medical-surgical background; I was a surgical technician who was also an expert marksman."

I got to Haiphong in August of 1954. First of all, it was really humid and I'd never been in a humid area before. The guys from Florida and New Orleans knew what humidity was; I didn't. And then, of course, we had some real rain that would last two or three days, then everything would be fine for a week. I was used to rain, being from Oregon, and that's the reason I don't live in Oregon anymore. But it wasn't like Vietnam. The stuff came down in buckets.

Of course, there was a tremendous French influence. You'd swear you were in an old, slightly decrepit part of Paris. It was really beautiful. The hotel was a gorgeous old structure with mosquito nets over each bed. There were fans in the ceiling and little geckos running around the walls eating the bugs. It was a very "romantic" place in appearance. The food was pretty good, if you like Vietnamese food. They put nuoc mam on everything. It's a fermented fish sauce. You could smell it a block away.

We were assigned to what they called "Beachmasters." That was a Marine Corps unit that goes in first before anybody else does and secures the beach. Everything in the Marine Corps is based on amphibious warfare. The "beach" we secured was the Majestic Hotel in Haiphong. We were brought in by ship to Haiphong and off-loaded from the ship with our personal equipment.

Our mission was to process 600,000 refugees. That's all we knew. We didn't really know what the word "process" meant. But then they started off-loading three or four jeeps with funny looking trailers. The funny looking trailer was a diesel tank with a fog generator. Think of a trailer about five feet wide and about six feet long with a big diesel tank on the front of it. On the back end, it had a generator that would create a fog. There was a nozzle. What you did was get in the jeep and drive to a location, then start up the fog generator on the back. Then you'd turn on the spigot which allowed the diesel fuel to enter the generator. The fuel would be turned into a fine droplet. Added to this diesel was DDT. We'd drive along the road with this thing spraying off the right side of the vehicle in the swampy areas beside the roads. They had irrigation ditches alongside the roads, and mosquito larvae would hatch in these ditches. We applied a layer of oil containing DDT in the ditches and eradicated the mosquitoes in a 10-mile radius around the city. People there were dying from malaria spread by these mosquitoes.

We all got malaria. I had it and also had hepatitis and mononucleosis. Half the time we were white and half the time we were yellow, depending upon what our livers were doing. Between the hepatitis and malaria, our livers were just swelling up and going down, swelling up and going down.

The Vietnamese people are small, but tough. They could carry a heavier load farther than we could. They used what the Marines called an "idiot stick." It's really called a balance pole. It was about six feet long and has a notch at each end. It's somewhat flexible like a ski. They hung a bag of rice at each end and balanced the stick on one shoulder. So one bag of rice might hang three feet in front of you and the other bag of rice about three feet behind you. They could carry huge loads for long distances using this balance pole. You talk about inventions that changed the world. That's got to be one of them. The problem carrying some things is that they are bulky and you can't get leverage on them. This device got the load away from your body so you could walk and carry at the same time.

When we were loading these Vietnamese aboard our ship to take them south to Saigon, they were allowed to bring personal items. Well, the most valued personal item was a sewing machine. So here you have a guy who weighed maybe 120 pounds and he's carrying a 50-pound bag of rice on the front end and a 50-pound sewing machine on the back end. He weighs 120 and he could carry this 100-pound load all day! He could carry it 15 or 20 miles. I had never seen anything like it in my life. These are strong, tough, wiry people with tremendous endurance.

That helps explain what happened on the Ho Chi Minh Trail years later. Those people were totally underestimated. When we were there, the Viet Cong as such did not exist. Ho Chi Minh was not obvious to us at that time. During our time in Vietnam the Cao Dai, a religious sect, was dedicated to driving out the French. We had to help evacuate some senior French Navy brass. One method of torture was to pound chop sticks into their ears. The inner ear would then get infected and they'd get meningitis—a terrible way to die.

When I went there, my commanding officer was Cmdr. [Julius] Amberson. He had been a mining engineer—a sweetheart of a guy. He was getting ready to be relieved and be shipped back to the States, and be let out of the military. He was a short-timer and was my commander for about six weeks. Then we got a new commanding officer, Tom Dooley. He was right out of internship at Camp Pendleton. When I was going through my operating technician school, Dooley was doing his internship. He said that he wanted to be an orthopedic surgeon, but at that time the Navy wasn't sending these guys to training, but sending them overseas as general medical officers, which is what he was at the time.

As far as enlisted personnel, there was a guy named Maugher and me. It's pretty hazy as to who else was there. A lot of these guys were not corpsmen. They were aviation boatswain's mates, mechanics, truck drivers. There were very few corpsmen. Maugher and I were the only two I can think of at that time.

We worked out of the Majestic Hotel. Then we had a little bivouac area where they kept the supplies such as the jeeps and diesel generators. We would be transported down to the docks where the LCVPs [Landing Craft Vehicle and Personnel] would be bringing in people from outlying areas along the river. They would stage these people there and then we would take them and run them past a little machine with a canister about the size of a half-gallon milk carton. It was filled with DDT powder. It looked like you were going to spray paint something. People would walk past us with their balance pole, and they would be carrying food and all their personal belongings like typewriters and sewing machines, and we would spray these people in the crotch. Most of them wore shorts. The women wore bouffant pantaloons. You could grab the top of the pants and spray downward into the crotch or you could grab the bottom of the pants and spray upward into the crotch. It was for lice.

This procedure was done just prior to them being loaded aboard LCVPs to go out to the USS *Montague*. I believe that was the main ship for transporting these people south. The other thing we were doing while we were spraying them was looking at all these people to see if they had any overt evidence of communicable disease. Did they have a rash or an eruption of the skin? Did they have pus coming from their eyes. We were looking for trachoma. Then the doctor would roll up the eyelid and look for the scarring and so forth. A lot of the trachoma was in 5- and 6-year-old kids. They came through there with flies on their eyes and pus coming down. They were in the acute phase.

The adults with trachoma were treated with tetracycline drops; the kids got an ointment. Sometimes they would pull someone aside and tell them they couldn't go because they had a communicable disease of some kind. I didn't know what some of these diseases were but the doctors were always on the lookout for something that might be communicated to the rest of the people.

One of the diseases we saw was leprosy. We were all afraid of catching it. It turns out that it's pretty hard to catch. At the time, we isolated them. One of the problems we had was that people with psoriasis looked like they had leprosy. When you're in the tropics, the humidity and heat make any disease look ten times worse. You could have some kind of minor little skin problem here and you get into the tropics and pretty soon it looks like some horrible contagious disease. The Americans were learning about diseases every day as to what was a serious versus what was just a common, ordinary problem, but looked a lot worse.

Most were families. But you also had men and women who didn't have children. And if there were men and women couples, you didn't know if they were married or not. I don't know of any sick person who was allowed to go south.

We knew about the partition at the 17th Parallel, and we knew that the people in the north would become communist and that the people in the south would stay "free." We knew our job was to help as many people to go south as we could and provide the medical support necessary to make their passage relatively safe.

* * *

Dr. Thomas Dooley was not new to Navy medicine when he went to Indochina in 1954. He had served briefly as a hospital corpsman during World War II before earning his medical degree

*at St. Louis University School of Medicine. He then joined the Navy Medical Corps. After complet-
ing a one-year rotating internship at Naval Hospital Camp Pendleton, California, Dooley served
briefly at Naval Hospital Yokosuka, Japan. A month after arriving in Japan, he volunteered for
duty aboard USS* Montague *(AKA-98), the ship involved in Passage to Freedom.*

In the summer of 1954, Dooley was reassigned for temporary additional duty from Montague
*to Commander Task Force 90 to serve as a French interpreter and medical officer for a Navy pre-
ventive medicine unit in Haiphong. During that assignment, Lt.(j.g.) Dooley stayed in touch with
one of his mentors, Dr. Melvin A. Casberg, former dean of St. Louis University School of Medicine.
Casberg had pulled strings to ensure Dooley's attendance at the school. In the following letter, the
ambitious young physician reported his personal view of Passage to Freedom.*

Lt. Thomas Dooley and interpreter explain to refugees how to use water purification tanks (BUMED
Archives).

USS *Montague*
Haiphong, Indo China
21 August 1954

Dear Doctor Casberg,

I have been sent out on TAD [Temporary Additional Duty] to this ship which is participating in Admiral Sabin's "Passage to Freedom." That is the evacuation of the Tonkin Delta area to Saigon. I can't give you the high level figures, but the numbers are around a half a million. CTF 90 is doing the job, and this AKA 98 is part of the force. There are a great deal of interesting facets and I'd like to pass them on to you. It is absolutely fantastic to me to think that there are some doctors who think that one never gets any experiences greater than the treatment for ring worm by being a Navy MD. Let them hear the below.

We were in Subic Bay when the word came that we were to take part in the evacuation. We had to leave in two days, and there was no Op. Order out yet. So we had to whip up imagination to the state of vision to figure out what would be needed. By the time we arrived here in Haiphong four and a half days later we were ready. It was then that the Op. Order arrived and we found that we had anticipated every point on the order, and had a few ideas which CTF 90 received most willingly.

Two thousand pounds of DDT were acquired through channels and by cumshawing[3] from the Epidemiology section at Clark Field in the Philippines. Also four dusters, but through Boatswain ingenuity, a large compressed-air-Venturi-wind tunnel-hopper machine was made with several hoses. This we hang over the side of the ship and blow the powder down their shirts and pants. Living spaces in our holds were made, with Lister Bags for drinking water, and half oil drums for wash water; and with portable honey buckets. On the deck six ten-seater latrines were made out of oil drums split lengthwise and welded together, with a hose in the forward end and a pipe going overboard on the after end. A continuous stream of saltwater. The tops were constructed Chinese fashion, with long boards to sit on their feet. You remember the Japanese Benjo [toilet], this is its sister equivalent.

I lectured to all the crew twice daily for four days on the diseases that would be brought aboard by these poor miserable refugees, and I didn't spare the punches. I believe my 300 men know all the layman can ever hope to know about Dysentery, Typhoid, Typhus, Intestinal Parasites, Malaria and Tb [sic]. And especially, they realize its infectiousness. They were inoculated (another thing I had to beg off of the sick bay at Subic as there was none left in the warehouse — serums) and anti-malarial treatment was started. We set the machine shop to work making screens for EVERY porthole on the ship.

All the plans for the messing had to be made, six tons of rice were acquired plus sardines, olive oil, corn beef, etc. The medical officer was involved in this because I have been in this part of the world and know what and how they eat. Pie tins and chopsticks were bought and made. Sawdust for the honey buckets was acquired. And the carpenters made ladders and ladders for the whole ship. Four levels to each cargo hold, and five holds. That takes a lot of ladders. The captain had conferences late at night to get the triage set up.

When we first arrived at this bay just outside of the seaport of Haiphong, we were scheduled to be the first to load. But it was changed, and three other ships were loaded. I went over to observe the first, the *Menard*, and the Captain of the ship was having a very difficult time with the French captain of the LSM [Landing Ship, Medium] that brought the refugees down the river. He could not get it across about how he wanted the LSM tied alongside, Chinese fashion etc. So I went on the Bridge, saluted per good line officer fashion, and introduced myself.

He bellowed, "What the devil do you want?"

I meekly explained that I spoke French as well as I did English and perhaps I could help him. With that he said, "Speak then man, speak...."

I took the loudspeaker and in my best sotto voce asked the skipper of the French ship to back away, turn around etc....

He replied with a broad smile and gentle "merci bien" and backed away.

From that time on I never left the Captain's side. I helped him handle the whole thing, speaking French to the French officers helping the unloading of the 1000 refugees from the LSM up to the AKA [Attack Cargo Ship]. I know enough Vietnamese to tell the people to walk up, faster, down, careful etc. ... so I was able to earn my pay there too.

Evidently the word got to the captains of the other vessels because each morning a dispatch comes to our ship requesting that I go over. This is good because not only is the collateral duty of an interpreter good training, but I was able to spy on the things they had set up on their ship, and what went well and poorly. I would return to my ship in the late afternoon and get the changes made accordingly. I helped in the loading of five ships before ours.

Yesterday we loaded, and we did it in record time, with little or no trouble. We had to stop only long enough to have a baby on the deck of the LSM. But a Stokes [litter] was lowered over the side and the mother and child brought to sick bay. The delivery was fast because it was her 9th child and there wasn't too much resistance from the pelvic floor, nor was an episiotomy needed. I should say not!

We are en route to Saigon now, a total of a 2-day trip. We have 2217 aboard, and all is going well. The stench is pretty terrible, and it seems these poor people devour tons of rice a day. Medically there are a great assortment of things to be seen. Some I treat, many I do not because the mission is the transportation.

There are a lot of staph infections of the scalp.... There are two full-blown cases of roseola. All the aged have the varieties of arthritis, and several good illustrations of that Marie-Strumpell spine.[4] Trachoma and other eye maladies are numerous. They seem to be completely free of fungus. Their feet, in spite [of] or perhaps because of standing for all their life in rice paddies, are in excellent condition. One very severe old asthmatic I am just keeping alive on epinephrine q4h until he debarks. All their teeth are coated with this betel nut [red] lacquer. All these you have seen in India I know, but you don't find them in every clinic in the states. Many of the unexplained fevers I suppose fall into the Typhoid and perhaps the Typhus group. One looks like it is rickettsial for sure. There are no lice left on them because they were thoroughly dusted, nearly bombed, when they came aboard....

I feel even more strongly about the Navy as a career than I did before. I believe they will allow me to continue my TAD after it runs out next month. I am sure they will. This medical corps is still tops in my mind....

Thanks again for making this all possible for me. I'll let you hear from time to time what becomes of this JG and I assure you someday about 22 years from now I'll invite you to my dinner when I am made the surgeon general....

Very sincerely,
Tom Dooley

2

AN AMERICAN WAR

Many provisions of the Geneva Accords ended French colonial rule in Indochina, not the least of which was the temporary division of Vietnam. In the meantime, before future elections were to decide the permanent status of that nation, Ho Chi Minh and his Vietminh ruled in the north; Ngo Dinh Diem and his family controlled the government in Saigon. Even though U.S. officials soon became conscious of his shortcomings as a leader, Diem seemed the best hope to hold the line against communism in Southeast Asia.

Yet little basis for optimism existed. Diem surrounded himself with friends and relatives, installing many of them in key government positions. He deposed Emperor Bao Dai, rigged a national referendum, and appointed himself the first president of the Republic of Vietnam. Most importantly, he failed to hold the elections as called for in the Geneva Accords.

But as the new bulwark against communism, the Diem regime received direct financial and later military aid from the United States. In 1955 Senator Hubert Humphrey characterized the strongman as "the leader of his people. He deserves and must have the wholehearted support of the American government and our foreign policy." At that time, such support was non-partisan.

Then other complications soon arose. Communist guerrillas, supported by the North, began a systematic policy of harassment, assassination, and sabotage. Diem responded by beefing up his army and putting social and political reforms on hold. Presidents Eisenhower, Kennedy, and eventually Johnson responded to the communist threat by sending military advisors.

Besides the communist challenge, other tensions confronted the new nation. Pressures came from the political and religious opposition that would culminate in the tumultuous overthrow of the regime and Diem's own violent death. This was the backdrop as Navy medical personnel began arriving in Vietnam to support U.S. military and civilian personnel.

First Navy Nurses in Saigon

Florence Alwyn had a full Navy career even before Vietnam. She had served at several naval hospitals during World War II before being discharged in 1946. Having retained her reserve commission, she was called back to active service in 1950 with the outbreak of the Korean War, and was stationed in Japan at U.S. Naval Hospital Yokosuka. Following several other stateside assignments, the veteran nurse received orders to Saigon. Sharing her colleagues' impressions, Vietnam seemed an unknown and distant place.

I was assistant chief nurse at Oak Knoll [Naval Hospital Oakland] then. The Chief Nurse called and told me I had orders to Saigon. My response was, "Where?" At that time, it was very early in U.S. involvement in Vietnam. My colleagues there at Oak Knoll didn't know any more about Vietnam than I did.

[Penny] Chloe Kaufman and I were the first Navy nurses to go. We were going to a dispensary [in Saigon], which was run by the State Department at that point. There was one State Department nurse and a couple of Army nurses, but they were switching over to become a Naval Support Activity. Some Navy corpsmen were there and some Army medics were still there. It was kind of a transition period.

We flew out of Travis [AFB, California] in February or March of 1963, and landed in Hawaii in the middle of the night so we couldn't even get anything to eat at the airport. Then we flew to Tan Son Nhut in Saigon.

When we arrived, it was hot, hot, hot. It was always 93 degrees in Saigon no matter what. As I recall, we had to hitch a ride into Saigon due to some confusion. That's what I remember most — the oppressive heat. And talk about humidity! That's the way it was the whole time. In some ways it was very exotic although I think I was somewhat prepared having already done a tour in the Far East in Japan. Yet it was quite different in a lot of ways.

We went to the Majestic Hotel right on the river and stayed there overnight. Then we went to our quarters at the Ham Nghi in Saigon. At that time, everything was hotels. It had been a hotel on the main circle in Saigon. We were relieving two Army nurses, but we never saw them; they left the very next day after we arrived. We were billeted on the eighth floor. On the floor below us were billeted a lot of the Army officers. An Army WAC major who lived there ran Army transportation. She was there for several weeks after we got there. She was interesting in that she had been brought up in North Vietnam and spoke some Vietnamese. Her father had been a diplomat.

We reported for duty at the dispensary, which was right downtown. Our senior medical officer was already there. His name was Capt. Lou Gens. Not too long after we got there, we started looking around to negotiate for a place to start a hospital.

At that point it was just an ordinary dispensary or clinic setup with several rooms. Of course, we didn't have any big cases. If anything was really wrong with any of our personnel, they were airevaced out. Most of the dependents were gone by that time, except some from the State Department. And, of course, there were quite a few embassy personnel.

By this time, the military was starting to build up and we knew we would have to have an inpatient facility because more and more of the Army and some of the Navy were arriving in greater numbers. We knew we needed something bigger and that's what Capt. Gens said. He and I subsequently spent quite a bit of time talking to people and trying to find a suitable place to set up a hospital. We eventually settled on what had been a hotel. In that part of the world, when it came time to negotiate, it was usually the women we dealt with.

We thought we had one place but that fell through. You had to take your time negotiating with the Vietnamese. Nothing happened overnight. We eventually settled on what became the Station Hospital.

Henry Cabot Lodge was ambassador at that time. His wife was quite a character and very nice. She'd come over now and then and say that she wanted to do some painting. We thought she wanted to put a painting of hers in there. But, no. She wanted to help us paint the walls, etc. The ambassador visited patients every so often.

The other six Navy nurses arrived as soon as we moved into the building. That was about halfway through my one-year tour. Jan Barcott, Bobbi Hovis, and Tweedie [Owedia] Searcy were with that group. Bobbi and Tweedie ended up billeted with us, and the others were billeted at another hotel.

Once we got the hospital set up, we began seeing patients. Some came from the field. There were a lot of Army personnel right there in Saigon at the headquarters. Because some of the dependents were still there, we did a lot of outpatient treatment for them as well as embassy personnel. But the patients were mostly military.

We had three or four Thai nurses on the staff. We couldn't use Vietnamese nurses because they weren't sufficiently trained. The Thais had been trained in Bangkok by the Seventh-day Adventist nursing school there.

This apartment house became Station Hospital Saigon (BUMED Archives).

The only casualties we saw early on were when the Capital Kinh Do Theater was blown up [16 February 1964].[1] That happened after we were all there. Previous to that, we'd get an occasional casualty from upcountry but if they were serious, we treated them and they were airevaced out.

At that time, the Buddhists were protesting by burning themselves to death. I remember one time telling the cab driver to get away from one place because we were heading into a group of protesters, and I wanted no part of getting in the middle of it. We had a big balcony at the Ham Nghi. The protesters would be on loudspeakers almost incessantly. There was always a lot of activity at the circle nearby, and we got to see a lot of demonstrations. Physically, it reminded me of Columbus Circle in New York City.

Oh, we knew the coup was coming. It was just a matter of when. That particular day [1 November 1963], I had been at the military attaché's house for lunch. I became fairly good friends with him and his wife because they had a child who was allergic to stinging insects. So we had to give him allergy shots. He was a funny kid who would only take the shots from me. The attaché got a phone call while we were at lunch, then came back and said, "The coup has started." He and I got in the car posthaste. He dropped me off at the hospital, and he went back to the embassy. He didn't seem at all surprised by the coup.

We couldn't leave the hospital for quite a while, but they finally allowed us to go home. Toward evening, a lot of the Army officers who lived at the Ham Nghi were forbidden to go to the Rex Hotel where their mess was. We had our own mess, so to speak, in that we had a cook and a maid. So we doled out what little food we had to help feed them.

Fortunately, the rebels weren't very good shots. Actually, the main fire occurred when they shot up the presidential palace. We could hear the shooting and once in a while a volley came a bit close. Mostly we could see and hear it but it was some distance away. When things calmed down the next day, we all went over to see the palace and the barracks that had been shelled so heavily, and I remember the wreckage.

When things quieted down the following day, we went back to the hospital and began taking care of patients again. We had an occasional Vietnamese patient, but I don't recall anyone who had been injured as a direct result of the fighting.

By this time, the Army had set up a hospital up in Nha Trang. Capt. Gens and I went up there on a visit one time to see the Army hospital. The fighting was starting to pick up, but we didn't get many casualties. The Army was getting most of them.

A typical day for us was very much like any other small hospital routine. We'd go in, care for the patients, make rounds. We did some surgery, but the procedures were relatively minor. We worked a five-day week, but I went in on a Saturday morning for half a day.

I left Saigon at the end of February of 1964. I was scheduled for a flight on a particular day, so I never met my relief. She must have arrived within days of when I left. I was very anxious to go home because Saigon was so confining. There were long periods when it was very quiet. When it was, we could go over to the old French Circle Sportif and eat, swim, and play tennis. Much of it was pleasant, and it certainly wasn't as hectic as when I was in Japan. Saigon had once been called the "Paris of the Orient," but one got the feeling that it was kind of an old has-been.

When you got home in those days, you just didn't run around saying that you'd been in Vietnam. There weren't any protests then and things hadn't turned ugly. Nobody seemed to know anything about it.

Station Hospital Saigon

Brooklyn-born Rosario Fisichella had just trained to be an obstetrician-gynecologist when he was called up during World War II. After serving in Europe and earning three Battle Stars, he left the Army to practice medicine. In 1956, he was offered a commission in the Navy as a commander with 10 years' seniority. "It was like the Mafia: It was an offer I couldn't refuse," he recalls. He served at U.S. Naval Hospital Yokosuka, Japan, and then became commanding officer of the 3rd Medical Battalion headquartered in Okinawa.

After another assignment as Force Troops Medical Officer at Twentynine Palms, California, now–Capt. Fisichella received orders to Vietnam. It was a shocking and unwelcome assignment for a man who had just gotten married. "So, what was my job over there? It was to establish a hospital in Saigon."

On the airplane going over, I met a wonderful lady who listened to me bitching to her the whole time because I had to leave my wife. She never said a word. When we arrived there was a huge crowd of people awaiting the plane. I soon learned that they were there to meet this woman, who turned out to be Gen. [William] Westmoreland's wife [Katherine]. It seems that I was bitching the whole time to the wrong woman. Well, we got to be really great friends. She was a delightful woman. Things were a real mess when we got there. They had just blown up a theater and there was mass confusion.

The hospital was on the main street, Tran Hung Dao, one of downtown Saigon's busiest thoroughfares. It was a five-story concrete building which at that time served as the only Navy hospital receiving American combat casualties directly from the field in Vietnam. The 100-bed hospital was established in October 1963 to meet the need for an inpatient facility in the southern portion of South Vietnam. The need was precipitated not only by an increase in the number of casualties in the Mekong River Delta area, but also by the distance involved in flying patients from there to the only existing American hospital at the time. This was the 100-bed Army field hospital in Nha Trang, 200 miles north of Saigon. In addition, increased terrorist activity in Saigon itself supported the need for a hospital in or near the capital city.

The building chosen was an old apartment house, and its age and layout of rooms and passageways created problems, which constantly tested the ingenuity of the Navy's Public Works Department during the conversion. It had one elevator, which was the French type, and it constantly broke down. No matter how we used it, it broke down, especially when we tried to transport a patient. Its unreliable performance complicated the transfer and feeding of patients. Food for patients was accomplished by transporting food in containers from a nearby hotel serving as an enlisted quarters. The hospital didn't have a kitchen. Right behind the main hospital building and attached to it by a series of stairways was another five-story structure. This annex provided an excellent isolation facility. A one-story stucco building was quickly constructed in the courtyard to house a central supply, emergency room, and operating room. We were operating outside for a while on improvised stretchers.

At that particular time, believe it or not, no American flags were flown in Saigon. And we were not permitted to fly helicopters over the city. It was a weird situation. It soon changed. We couldn't use our own sentries. We were not at war. We were just support people. Every man who was sent to Vietnam at that time was supposed to be kind of an ambassador. And they [the Navy] picked the special people to go to Vietnam, especially the officers. In four months, most of the officers ended up with ulcers because they were hobbled. They couldn't do what they were supposed to do in war.

The entire complex was surrounded by a concrete wall and topped by wire grenade screens. Everything had wire grenade screens because it was easy to throw grenades over the wall. These protective screens were common throughout the city. Terrorist activity was a constant threat making security a full-time job. In addition to the protective screen, U.S. military police armed with shotguns, and Vietnamese soldiers and police patrolled the compound 24 hours a day. The hospital vehicles, including four ambulances, were parked within this compound.

Some hospital equipment was already in Vietnam, but much had to be ordered from the States. Supply lines were long, creating some problems. Equipment improvisation and friendly borrowing, however, lessened the effect of a difficult supply service.

Directly across the street, two stories of a hotel building were taken over to serve as an outpatient clinic. The x-ray, pharmacy, laboratory, and administrative services were located there.

The senior medical officer was assisted by nine medical officers, including two general surgeons, an internist, a psychiatrist, four or five general practitioners, seven Navy nurses, and eight Thai nurses. We used Thai nurses because the Vietnamese nurses weren't trained well enough. We had two Medical Service Corps officers, 76 trained hospital corpsmen, and 40 Vietnamese employees, who were clerical assistants, drivers, and janitors.

Patients seen at the hospital were not limited to combat casualties. I think that was one of the reasons they sent me there. We also cared for personnel attached to the U.S. Embassy, United States Operations Mission, and the United States Information Service [USIS]. They had dependents there.

We treated dependents of American personnel until they were evacuated in February of 1965. The evacuation of dependents was regretted for many reasons, not the least among these being the loss to the hospital of a fine group of American Red Cross volunteers who contributed greatly to the welfare and morale of the patients. While in Vietnam, these ladies, including Mrs. [Katherine] Westmoreland, established a trained Vietnamese Red Cross volunteer service. We had Vietnamese patients admitted for emergency care and then we transferred them to local hospitals.

Then we established a helo pad on a soccer field about a five-minute ambulance ride from the hospital. Helicopter pilots carrying the wounded or sick were able to communicate by radio with the hospital, and ambulances and attendants waited at the helo pad ready to transfer patients with minimal delay. At other times, patients arrived on fixed wing aircraft from Ton Son Nhut Airport and were transferred by helicopter to us. That rapid transport saved a lot of lives at that time.

Terrorist bombs resulted in mass casualties more than actual combat for a while. On Christmas eve of 1964, a 200-pound bomb exploded beneath the Brink Hotel, which was the senior officers' BOQ [Bachelor Officers' Quarters] in downtown Saigon. We had 84 admissions. Four Navy nurses who were residents in the hotel were wounded. As in all these emergencies, a routine was followed which proved most adequate in handling mass casualties. All personnel were assigned to prearranged stations in the courtyard, emergency room, operating room, blood bank, and each deck of the hospital. A space on each deck of the hospital, except the first, was set up as a battle dressing station with a doctor and four corpsmen. This is where we dressed minor wounds and performed minor debridements.

Triage was rendered in the courtyard and adjacent emergency room, and we sent patients to the appropriate section for treatment. Patients were treated for shock and prepared for major surgery either in the emergency room or first deck of the hospital. Serious cases were always left on the first deck due to the unreliable elevator. As in all other emergency situations, a host of civilian and military volunteers quickly augmented the small hospital staff. The Military Assistance Command Surgeon and his staff of Army doctors, the director of public health, and the United States Operations Mission and his staff of civilian physicians offered immediate aid. Navy dentists also were on hand to help treat the casualties. The small Air Force hospital at Ton Son Nhut and the Army hospital at Nha Trang called — as soon as they received word of the bombing — that they were standing by to help in any way possible.

Now this is important. We obtained all blood by employing the walking blood bank system. We had no way of keeping the blood so when we sent out the call, people would come. This system was most effective and there was never a shortage of blood at the hospital.

While this was going on, the local Navy commander instituted heavy security measures to protect us from bombing since the accumulation of so many Americans at one time in one place could make a prime Viet Cong target.

In order to keep hospital beds open in anticipation of further casualties, we instituted a rapid evacuation system. Patients able to travel were transferred to the Army hospital in Nha Trang. This has been a common reciprocal system. The hospital employed a 30-day holding policy, and two air evacuation flights per week were used to transfer patients to the hospital at Clark Air Force Base in the Philippines. We attempted to keep the hospital at no more than 50 percent occupancy in anticipation of possible mass casualties.

Diseases accounted for a good deal of the hospital's day-to-day work. Malaria was endemic and everyone was required to take Chloraquine-Primaquine prophylaxis. Infectious hepatitis was not uncommon, and all personnel received immune globulin prior to or upon reporting in Vietnam. By far the most prevalent and annoying disease was amebiasis [amebic dysentery]. This disease responded well to a combination of Diodoquin and Oxytetracycline.

When the bomb went off at the Brink Hotel on Christmas Eve, I was thrown 20 feet across the room. I had planned on going to the Brink for dinner. Immediately, we got the word that the hotel had been bombed and we had to get to our hospital any way we could.

That night — with all the confusion and all the sirens going off — in comes Bob Hope and his troupe. They brought him to me immediately because the hospital had to be the safest place in the world because everyone was trying to protect us. And everybody, including Bob Hope and Jerry Colonna, got down to work helping with the wounded. I was loaded with wounded. And not only that, but we had to undress a lot of them because we figured some of them were Viet Cong who were trying to get into the hospital to blow it up.

Bob Hope and his group were wonderful. I have a picture of him where I'm ordering them out of the hospital because we thought there was a bomb in the next room. And he had blood on his sleeve. And one time he mentioned that it was the only time he was a little worried about his time out there because of the intensity of the situation. This picture is kind of cute because it appeared in the United States as "Captain Fisichella and Friend."

We evacuated as many of our patients as we could to Gen. Westmoreland's quarters that night. Bob Hope put on an impromptu show there for those wounded the next night. I thought that was a marvelous thing.

There was another sad outcome of that bombing. As the casualties came in and we were all exhausted, the chief nurse had a heart attack. There was also a dentist who was scheduled to go home in a few days. He was one of these straight arrows who never went out. He didn't show up and, as I was hoping he had escaped, they brought his body in. At that point, I just lost all my energy.

The hardest thing in the world would be to have a hospital blown up. Everybody loses morale like you wouldn't believe. Even so, we had to evacuate as many as we could fast because we didn't know how many we were going to get in. We would try to get them to Nha Trang and then to fixed wing aircraft to get them out.

I left Vietnam in March of 1965. I remember Gen. Westmoreland telling me not to leave until he got back from a mission he was on. When he got back he said, "This is what I want to tell you. We just got the word that we can now bomb the hell out of North Vietnam." And he wanted to tell me that personally before I left.

I remember that in my situation there, I was privy to a lot of things. It was a highly political situation. We were professionals doing a professional job and everybody had a specific job to do. We were all expected to be ambassadors. At the time I was there, it wasn't an American war. We were advisors. It became an American war after that. For me, it was the pride I had in the men and women I served with who were so brave. I'm glad I played a little part in it.

Coup in Saigon

Lt. Cmdr. Bobbi Hovis was in Saigon as the first Navy nurse to volunteer for duty in Vietnam. Along with her commanding officer and fellow nurses, she had recently helped set up the Station Hospital. As she settled into the daily routine of providing medical care to U.S. military advisors, the environment in South Vietnam's capital was increasingly unstable.

It was November 1st, 1963, and the pot had been stirring. The feelings against the Diem government were running higher and higher by the day. There were the pro–Diem faction and the anti–Diem faction. It was the Catholics versus the Buddhists. Diem and his family were Catholic and the [Buddhist] monks were stirring up trouble. You could just sense the tension in Saigon as it was building. You knew something was about to happen.

My senior corpsman, whose name was Paul ["Burnie"] Burns, went to lunch that day [1 November]. Most of my corpsmen lived in Cholon, which was the Chinese sister city to Vietnamese Saigon. There were a lot of small BEQs [Bachelor Enlisted Quarters] there where our enlisted people lived and they had to go back to their quarters to eat. We had no kitchens at all in the hospital.

Burnie came back and said, "There's all kinds of barbed wire strung across the street. There are gun emplacements set up with .50 caliber machine guns and they're all pointed right up the street at us."

I walked out in the middle of the street and couldn't believe what I saw. I was looking right into the barrels of two .50 caliber machine guns set up in sandbag emplacements. "Oh, my

Lt. Cmdr. Bobbi Hovis beside an Army ambulance at Station Hospital Saigon (courtesy Bobbi Hovis).

goodness," I thought. "What is happening here?" Well, it wasn't very long before the shooting started.

Fortunately, at that time, we had a minimum number of patients in my ICU and it was quiet. I went up to the fifth floor in the hospital on the front side so I could see better what was going on. I knew that if somebody needed something, Burnie would come up and get me.

Bullets were flying in every direction. Three T-28 aircraft being flown by anti–Diem rebels were dive-bombing Diem's palace. They were very close. As they released the bombs, anti-aircraft fire was being returned from the palace roof. An earlier coup [27 February 1962] attempt — in which the palace had been bombed — had prompted the installation of those anti-aircraft guns. The next thing I knew, I saw an airplane hit. It went into a dive and disappeared behind some trees.

Meanwhile, the pro–Diem Chief of Naval Operations had been shot at the Naval Station right there on the Saigon River. The fuel farm, also right there on the river at the Vietnamese naval base, blew up and was in flames. Bullets were flying in all directions, and civilians were trying to take cover in the streets. I saw one man shot. A bullet went through the back window of his car, through his chest, and out the windshield. Two men ran out from a store and dragged him out of the car. I don't know if this man lived or died.

The Civilian National Police were deserting like mad. They were taking off their uniforms, throwing them down, and running off.

A chief and I were standing on a fifth-floor balcony watching the bombing runs on the palace when suddenly a bullet hit right in front of us on the balcony wall, powdering the stucco. The bullet then ricocheted up from the balcony where it first hit, bounced off the overhead, and fell to the deck. Three inches higher and I would have been hit in my lower chest or abdomen. We both jumped back into the room and took cover under a table. I still have that .30 caliber bullet. When we didn't hear any more bullets hit, we ventured back out to watch what was going on.

The fighting went on for hours. About 1700 there was a lull and we were transported back from the hospital to our quarters, probably about three miles away. We were not receiving casualties at that time.

We barely got back to the quarters when the firing really began in earnest. The quarters were in downtown Saigon and very, very close to Diem's palace. Rebels had set up a 105mm howitzer out near the Gia Dinh Bridge on the road to Tan Son Nhut Airport, and they were firing that howitzer right into the palace. Many of the shells were going astray and hitting all around our BOQ and the roofs right near us. These shells were showering us with shards of red roof tile or glass from the next-door building; it was that close. This went on for 18 hours. It got so hot and heavy that I said to the girls, "In case we have to evacuate these quarters, we'd better have a little overnight kit packed, another uniform, and some toilet articles." So we each packed a bag. No sooner had we done so when the firing became even heavier and we took cover.

We lived on the top deck and so I suggested that we go down to the fourth deck and sit in the stairwell, which was in dead center of the building. Even though a 105mm howitzer shell would have gone right through that lightly built stucco, it seemed the safest area in the building.

Then some of the male officers who lived there joined us and we just sat there in the stairwell. I had my little Zenith Transoceanic radio with me. All we kept hearing on Armed Forces Radio Saigon was normal music while we were in the midst of all this. However, the BBC was relaying what was going on through Manila. That's how we learned of the *coup d'état* that was going on in Saigon. The one thing we did know was that we were under attack, even though we didn't know who was fighting whom.

It was about then that I decided to keep a journal. I went back up to my room to get a writing pad and a pen. As the coup proceeded and shells were hitting all around, I wrote minute-for-minute.

Eventually, the heavy firing died down and we heard the clank, clank, clank of tank treads. I then went back out onto the seventh floor balcony. I crawled on my stomach so as not to present a target. And I could just peer over the railing and look down. There on the street below I counted 27 tanks mustering right below our quarters. Several hundred fully armed troops accompanied the tanks. We didn't know who these troops were or what faction they belonged to. We certainly didn't know whether they were hostile to Americans.

Then everything appeared to come to a halt as they set up the command post below us. I could look right down and hear and see what they were doing. It appeared that they were mustering the troops and the tanks for the final assault on the Diem palace.

Suddenly the tanks began to fire right down the middle of the street. When those cannons fired within the confines of the city, you can't imagine the sound that reverberated off asphalt and brick streets and cement and stucco buildings. It was absolutely deafening. Between the thick cordite[2] and smoke and the deafening blasts and concussion, we all had headaches.

By then we were really fatigued; we hadn't had much to eat and were quite hungry. By now it was November 2nd. About 0400, the tanks and troops started to move out toward the palace. Just at sunrise white flags appeared over the palace even though we couldn't see them. We heard, on the radio, that the Diem government had surrendered.

I have a remarkable picture of an L-19 and a DC-3 that flew over town dropping thousands and thousands of colored leaflets. These leaflets were to inform the civilian population what was going on, explain there had been a coup, and that the Diem government no longer existed.

There was jubilation in the streets. The people were destroying anything that had to do with Diem. Then they really went crazy. The pro–Diem newspaper office was just within shouting distance of our quarters. The mob went in, got huge rolls of newsprint, set them on fire, and rolled them out in the streets. The fire became very severe, and it suddenly seemed ironic that we had lived through this coup only to have our building burn down around us. Then they set fire to a Diem-owned theater, and the pro–Diem police station across the street from us was grenaded.

The Diem brothers had made their way through a tunnel out to Cholon where they took refuge at a Catholic friend's house. But they were hunted down and put into an armored personnel carrier where they were shot and killed.

The fires eventually died down and people started to disperse. They seemed so jubilant as they rode on tanks and APCs [Armored Personnel Carriers]. There was a nice relationship between the soldiers and the civilians, and celebrations broke out throughout Saigon. Jukeboxes were turned on and people began to dance. Dancing hadn't been allowed under the Diems even though American GIs had taught the young Vietnamese to jitterbug and do the twist.

Finally, about 1000 or 1100 in the morning, we went out and walked to the palace. Just walking the five or so blocks, we really saw the destruction. I remember a black Volkswagen that had been parked on the street. It had been hit with so many bullets that it looked like a black piece of lacework. The heavy shelling had knocked down trees and power lines, and the destruction at the Diem palace was incredible.

The palace guards, the elite of the South Vietnamese Army, had been killed or wounded in the coup. What had been their barracks were just holes in building walls—105mm howitzer-sized holes. There were burned-out tanks with bodies still in them, and bloody boots were lying around within the palace grounds. The rebels were looting anything valuable.

Life never returned to normal while I was in Vietnam. An undercurrent of unrest was always present from one faction or another. Dissident generals continued to work behind the scenes, planning to stage another coup to overthrow the newly installed Minh government [headed by Gen. Duong Van Minh].

* * *

Prior to the autumn of 1963, the American presence in Vietnam — and particularly Saigon — was purposely kept low-key. Rather than constructing new, ostentatious facilities, U.S. personnel were billeted in converted apartments and hotels. Station Hospital Saigon occupied a rented apartment house, and some of its staff nurses lived in the Ham Nghi BOQ near Saigon's Central Market. Others occupied quarters in the Brink BOQ, a former hotel named for Brigadier General Francis Brink, head of the U.S. Military Mission in the former French Indochina, who died in 1952.

Despite the American low profile, Viet Cong terrorists were already very active, exploding bombs not only in the Central Market, but in bars and theaters frequented by American service personnel. On Christmas Eve 1964, a Viet Cong agent parked a bomb-laden car in the underground garage of the Brink BOQ. It detonated less than an hour later with devastating results.

Purple Heart Nurse

New Englander A. Darby Reynolds graduated from nursing school in 1961 and immediately joined the Navy. Her first assignment was working the surgical ward at Naval Hospital Pensacola, Florida. Receiving orders to Fort Sam Houston, Texas, for a mass casualty course, she arrived the same month President Kennedy was assassinated. "We had to wear [black] armbands while we were there. I came home for Christmas leave and got a special delivery letter saying, 'Congratulations, you have orders to Saigon.' I had no idea where Saigon was."

I remember the heat and the smell of Saigon when I stepped off the plane. The smell was just something that was indescribable. They rushed us right into a building so we could be debriefed. Cmdr. Ann Richman was the chief nurse in Saigon at the time. She had come out to meet me. I was a lieutenant j.g. We went through three or four days of orientation. We learned all the things we were not supposed to do in Saigon. We were never to go out alone. We were always to go in pairs. We were not to get into those *cycloes* [bicycle taxis] — you rode in front and the driver was behind you. They could throw a grenade if they wanted to get you. Be careful going into taxicabs. We were not to go out after dark. But the big thing was going in pairs. We heard that they had a price on the heads of the medical personnel. A nurse was worth $25 and a physician $50. So they always told us to be very careful because if they got one of us and took us across the river, that might be it.

My duty station was the Station Hospital Saigon. The hospital itself was unique. It was an old apartment building with five floors. The ICU was on the first and we had one elevator which did not work half the time. There was a water purification tower on top. We had a little annex attached to the hospital where we kept some of the other medical patients. And there was a little area in back of the hospital where they had built the operating room. It was really just one big room divided in sections for surgeries and recovery. There were two or three tables set up there.

When I first arrived, we had a lot of medical and surgical patients and those from terrorist bombings. There were a lot of shrapnel, punji stick[3] wounds, and other horrific injuries. We had a few burn patients from plane crashes. People came in from the field with these injuries. They were all American personnel. We could do just about anything. We did a lot of orthopedic surgeries and some amputations. We did whatever had to be done and then we medevaced them out.

I was the youngest member of the staff at the time, a jaygee [j.g.]. I remember when I checked in, everybody was so surprised I was there because I was so junior. We did everything, but I actually worked surgical, ICU, medical wards, and took operating room call. There were seven of us at the time — the chief nurse and nurse anesthetist plus four Thai nurses. With rotating shifts and days off, we usually had only three or four on duty at one time. The rest of us all rotated on nights for OR call. And that usually kept us quite busy because you never knew what was coming in. We started off working five days, and then as things progressed we worked six. I think for the most part we worked the six-day schedule during the time I was there. Later, as more casualties began coming in, they began working seven days. When I first arrived, the hospital had just been opened. The only other military hospital was one in Nha Trang, which was an Army hospital about 250 miles north. Between the two, depending on where the fighting was going on, we kept quite busy.

We'd get a call at night. A terrorist bomb had gone off in or outside the city. We would get so many casualties that everybody would be at work. You could be there for maybe 24 hours trying to get everyone settled and get them through surgery. As time went on, those times became more frequent. After the dependents left, the fighting really increased. And it seemed that every other day we were sending medevacs out because the hospital was so small. We just couldn't handle them.

Terrorist attacks were something you got used to after being in Saigon for a while. It was nothing to walk down the street and have a bomb go off in a movie theater or a restaurant. Saigon had a club called the Circle Sportif. It was like a country club with a swimming pool and tennis courts. I know I was there a couple of times when a bomb went off outside the perimeter. I remember walking by a couple of restaurants and had gotten just far enough away when a bomb went off. After a while, we almost got used to it. Fortunately, there weren't that many people who were injured when they did go off, at least when I was there. As the fighting increased, there were more and more casualties. Usually after a bomb attack, we had five or ten people injured so we were able to take care of them.

Our living arrangements in the Brink Hotel were actually quite good. It was seven stories and we had a suite on the first floor, which was really the second because the cars would park under the first floor. So technically we were on the second floor. Four of us shared a suite of rooms. We all had our individual bedrooms, which were air conditioned. We each had a balcony. And there were two large sitting rooms, two bathrooms, and a kitchen. When we went out the door of our suite, the elevator was right there. It would take you up to the top of the building, which was where the restaurant, the mess, and the officers' club was. Movies and entertainment were up there. Half of the top floor was open and you could watch the activity from the countryside. Sometimes you could hear bombs going off or see flares going up.

The hotel was a compound with a fence around it. In the beginning, things were pretty open. You could come and go as you wanted. But as the terrorist activity increased, MPs were on duty where you entered the compound. It really wasn't very secure because most anybody could get through. In fact, that's what happened when the bombing took place. Somebody drove through and the car wasn't really checked that closely.

The physicians and nurses lived separately. None of us all lived together in the same building. There were four of us in our suite at the Brink, and then later, another nurse joined the staff; she was billeted on an upper floor. Three other more senior nurses lived about four miles away from us. That's where Lt. Cmdr. Bobbi Hovis, Cmdr. Tweedie Searcy, and Cmdr. Ann Richman lived. We were separated in case anything should happen. That's also what they did with the physicians. None of them were all in the same building.

The Brink was about six miles or so from the hospital. Each day, we'd have breakfast at the top of the BOQ. Then we would come down and the car would come and take us to the hospital.

At the hospital we would get the report on the status of the patients from the night before. Then we did the bed baths, the medications, etc., and got patients ready for surgery. That was pretty much the routine. One memory that does stick in my mind is meals for the patients. There was no kitchen at the hospital so the food was prepared at the BEQ [Bachelor Enlisted Quarters] down the street. The food was then put on a cart and a man wheeled it up the street and into the hospital. For breakfast we had dehydrated eggs and milk. We prepared the trays and then delivered them to the patients. With the five floors—and since the elevator usually didn't work—we were always running up and down the stairs with food trays. It was a lot of extra work. Because of that elevator, we always had to keep the sicker patients on the first floor since there was no way to transport them.

We worked until about 3 or 3:30 when the other shift would come on. Then the car picked us up and took us back to the BOQ. Depending on what you wanted to do, you were free until the next morning. Many times we'd go out shopping because we were free to do that. Often supplies in the hospital were low so we would just walk along the sidewalk and find a lot of supplies and instruments we might need that never made it to the hospital.

There was a big black market for many items we desperately needed. I remember one time we had a very sick patient—an orthopedic patient—and didn't have the instruments for the surgery. We had to wait until a plane could bring the instruments down from the Army hospital in Nha Trang so we could operate. Once we finished, we had to send the instruments back.

I had few close calls in Saigon. One time I had gone shopping and caught a cab. At the beginning, you weren't supposed to go by yourself but I did. The cab was heading across the river. We all knew a little Vietnamese at that time. I knew how to tell him to stop and let me off. But we also had a price on our heads. This cab driver began driving across the river and didn't stop. Many of us carried a little knife or something. I had to pull my knife, tap him on the shoulder, and tell him to stop so I could get out.

There were other times when just getting back from the hospital was an effort because demonstrations were going on. One time they were burning cars going to the hospital. The city was in an uproar. Military police were riding in the car ahead of us, but we got caught in the demonstration and the bullets were flying all over. We had to duck down in the car or risk being hit. If we hadn't had the military police as escorts, we never would have gotten out of it.

If you wanted to stay in your room and do nothing you could do that. But if you wanted to get out and see a little bit of the city, which was called the "Paris of the Orient," or if you wanted to go to church on Sunday, or just meet other people, you had to go alone. You couldn't always rely on one of the other nurses being free to go with you.

Then we became the target of a terrorist bomb. It was Christmas Eve [1964]. I remember that very well because Christmas is always special to people. I also remember that I had the operating room call. I guess I was the unlucky one because I remember the doctor saying, "Okay, Reynolds has got the call again."

We had a pool going to see what time we were all going to be called back. I was in my quarters looking out, as we had a maid and we had given her her Christmas gift. They were checking everything very closely because Bob Hope was in town and was going to have a big show. He was staying across the street from us in another BOQ, and they wouldn't let the maid go out of the gate with her Christmas present. I was looking out of my room through the French glass doors and had my face pressed up against the glass. Ruth Mason had gone downstairs and was just returning when, all of a sudden, the bomb went off. The door blew in and the glass shattered and fell right down on top of me. I thought, "Oh, boy. Hospital OR call. Here we go!"

I was wearing sneakers and had remembered from one of my previous times in the operating room how uncomfortable I was standing for so many hours in sneakers. This time I wanted my nurse's shoes. So in a state of shock, I went back to my room to get those. I remember a couple of fellas coming in and saying, "You've got to get out of here. The building's on fire." By the time we got out the door and downstairs, you could see the flames and smoke. Out in the little courtyard, I saw all the damage and the victims starting to come out.

At that point, the nurses all checked on each other to make sure we were okay. Then we began checking all the casualties as they were coming out. When the ambulances began arriving, I got into the first one and took some patients to the hospital. I didn't realize at the time that I was bleeding. When we got to the hospital, one of the corpsmen said, "Oh, you need to be sutured so I'm putting a [suture] set aside for you." He knew that before long we would be short on supplies.

Then we just went to work taking care of patients and getting them settled. I waited until everybody was taken care of and then they sutured my leg. I remember one man in the next suite of rooms at the Brink. He was buried for several hours. They found him around midnight and brought him into the OR to try to save him, but he died on the table right across from me while they were working on my leg. That was something I'll always remember. Two men were killed in the suite next to ours.

Four of us nurses had been injured. Fran Crumpton had ear problems. The rest of us had lacerations and concussions. I also had a cervical injury. Later on, when I was stationed at Oakland, a physician told me my problem was probably from the bombing. Eventually, I also had to have a cervical fusion.

Later that night, Fran and I went back to the Brink. It was difficult getting through the city because everything was in an uproar. There were no lights. I finally got to my room. One memory really sticks in my mind. When I got there, my radio was still playing Christmas carols.

The Brink bombing resulted in more than 100 Australian, South Vietnamese, and American casualties, including two deaths among the latter. The four Navy nurses who had been injured — Lt.(j.g.) Ann Darby Reynolds, Lt. Frances L. Crumpton, Lt. Ruth A. Mason, and Lt. Barbara A. Wooster — were awarded the Purple Heart, the only Navy nurses during the Vietnam War to receive that decoration.

Lt. A. Darby Reynolds receives a Purple Heart for her injuries in the Brink Barracks bombing (courtesy A. Darby Reynolds).

In February 1965, a Viet Cong mortar attack on the U.S. base at Pleiku, in which eight Americans were killed and more than 100 wounded, prompted retaliatory air strikes against North Vietnam.

"I Knew I Was in a War"

Early in the summer of 1964, an incident in the Gulf of Tonkin had already turned the festering conflict in Southeast Asia into a full-blown war. On 2 August, USS Maddox (DD-73) was on what was termed a "routine patrol" in international waters when three North Vietnamese torpedo boats commenced a high speed torpedo run on the destroyer. What happened that day and shortly thereafter resulted in the Gulf of Tonkin Resolution. This resolution, which Congress passed on 7 August, gave the president the power "to take all necessary measures to repel any armed attack against the forces of the United States and to prevent further aggression." Escalation of the war in Vietnam was now assured.

Lt. Samuel Halpern, MC, USNR, had been raised on a farm in Kentucky's bluegrass region before attending medical school at the University of Louisville. He joined the Navy in 1963, the year the Diem regime was overthrown. "When I went into the Navy, suddenly I was an officer and a gentleman by an act of Congress. People saluted me. And they stuck my pockets full of money. I just couldn't believe it. When you've been a sharecropper for the first 14 years of your life, security means something."

USS *Maddox* (DD-731) (Naval Historical Center).

Soon placed in harm's way as medical officer of Destroyer Division 192, that sense of security quickly evaporated.

There were four ships in my division, the *Berkeley* [DDG-15], the *Maddox* [DD-731], the *Picking* [DD-685], and the *Herbert J. Thomas* [DD-833], which kept breaking down and didn't go to WESTPAC [Western Pacific] with us. We were in port and I was told that the commodore

[John J. Herrick] wanted me to board the *Maddox* immediately. Nobody told me what I was going to do or where we were going, but I was told to get the medical department in tiptop shape.

I didn't know anything at all when I went aboard the *Maddox*. I didn't even know how to salute. When I walked aboard, I saluted everything in sight until finally I began to catch on as to what I was supposed to do. But I had luck. On destroyers, you have what they call "independent duty corpsmen." These are guys who have been in the Navy for a long time, are highly trained, and are very good at their trade. They are easily as good as physician assistants and they also know the Navy. These guys would tell me what to do.

Maddox was a pretty scarred up old veteran, a 2,250-ton destroyer that had seen a lot of action during the Second World War. You could see the places where the kamikazes had hit the ship and where that damage had been repaired. Besides the punishment she had undergone then, *Maddox* had also fired a lot of shells in Korea.

As I went over the brow [gangplank], slightly to the right, I saw a twin 5-inch 38 mount. You could go up the deck on either side or through the passageways from there. Aft were racks with depth charges, spaces with ammunition, and the loading gear for the 5-inch 38s. Along both sides of the ship were 3-inch guns and torpedo tubes. As I went all the way forward, I came upon Mount 51, and behind and above it was Mount 52. Both were twin 5-inch 38s.

The bridge was behind and above the second turret. The wardroom was forward and officers' country was amidships. All the way forward was chiefs' country. Crew's quarters were aft. CIC [Combat Information Center] was in the middle of the ship.

The sick bay was about 5 feet by 4 feet. It had a cabinet containing all the pharmaceuticals—antibiotics, morphine, compazine, and anything else I might need. The nice thing about going to sea on a man-of-war was that everybody was young. If they weren't in good shape they wouldn't be there.

During combat, the wardroom table would become my operating theater, and there were surgical lights above the table. We had all sorts of supplies stuffed beneath the divan in the wardroom with lots of IV fluids, injectable anesthetics, and ether. I know what you're thinking. Ether is explosive! I know it is but we needed some way of putting patients to sleep. If you were hit aboard a man-of-war, you generally weren't going to have just one casualty. We had about 260 people aboard the *Maddox* packed in an area some 300 feet long and about 30 feet in the beam. If there was going to be combat, there would be a land office business. We were going to take care of people in the triage method. We would stanch the hemorrhage and keep the men alive as best we could until we could off-load them. And, of course, the crew hoped the doctor and the corpsman were not dead. Both of us would be in that wardroom so if we got wiped out, the crewmen would be on their own.

From the start, nobody told me a damn thing. They kept me in the total dark. I didn't know what was happening. I knew we were heading toward Taiwan. We pulled into Keelung [Taiwan], where they brought some Marines aboard. They were led by a captain who was in charge of an eavesdropping device, which was set up on the deck of the *Maddox*. There was a circle drawn around it and also the Marine guards. There was no question that if you got inside that circle, they would shoot you. These were mean-looking and very scary people.

We then took off. I wasn't totally stupid as to what was going on. I knew Vietnam was in the direction we were going.

The first time I knew we were at war was one morning when I woke up just at the crack of dawn and went out on deck. I liked doing that because the South China Sea is beautiful in August. It's still cool at that hour. The waters are in the doldrums, so it's flat and you have magnificent sunrises and sunsets. I could see some specks off in the distance, and they were moving faster than anything I'd ever seen on water. There were three boats and I didn't know what the hell they were. I found out later they were PT boats. But I figured that nothing could move that fast unless it was a PT boat. And they were really hauling. I figured there had been some action. I found out later that they had just raided North Vietnamese facilities.[4]

When we joined Task Force 77 — the *Ticonderoga* [CV-14] and a lot of other ships—I learned we were a DeSoto or intelligence patrol. But I didn't know what we were trying to become intelligent about.

After resupplying and refueling, we headed into the Gulf of Tonkin. We slowed down to a very slow 5 knots. At 5 knots you can go a hell of a long way on a tin can because you're hardly burning any fuel. It was hot. It was so hot! Unbelievable. We were surrounded by junks. Everywhere you looked there were junks, supposedly fishing vessels with nets out. We tried to avoid them but we had guns at the ready. I think we were at Condition 3, one condition before general quarters [GQ], and I believe half the guns were manned at the time. A tin can of that age had four boilers, and we had one and two boilers on the line and were just kind of lazing along. Nothing really was happening.

The day of the first attack [2 August 1964], I was lying in my bunk when we went to general quarters. I wondered why but I knew something was happening even before we went to general quarters. If you have been aboard a destroyer for some time, you could listen and tell the speed of the ship, where the seas were coming from, how many boilers were on line — the whole thing. And I was pretty good at deciphering what was going on down in the fire rooms.

We began picking up speed. The captain, Herb Osier, came on the 1MC [intercom] and said we were being approached by North Vietnamese PT boats and we had information that they intended to engage us. If they closed to 10,000 yards, we were going to fire warning shots. If they got closer than that, there would probably be an engagement, or something to that effect.

I went to my GQ station in the wardroom, and Chief Aguilar and I set up the hospital as best we could. We got out some mattresses and threw them on the floor for casualties. We secured all the supplies and equipment in case we took a hit. The *Maddox* had the watertight integrity of a sieve. She was just an old rust bucket. Nevertheless, we were ready.

When we let go with the 5-inch 38 warning shots, I thought that was it. We were really speeding up and I could tell we were bringing other boilers on line. The generators were whining like mad and we were doing somewhere between 25 and 28 knots. We could probably do about 31 knots in absolutely calm seas before we shook apart with all four boilers on line.

All of a sudden I heard, "Torpedo in the water! Torpedo in the water!" The 1MC was wide open. I thought, "This ain't real!" I didn't know anything about combat at sea. Aguilar kept yelling for me to get up and grab the big I-beams in the overhead and get off the deck. I didn't understand why he wanted me to do that. He looked like an idiot grabbing those beams and lifting himself up on his tiptoes. I found out later why he did this. If you're standing and the ship takes an explosion under you, it will break both your legs as the ship suddenly lifts up. I finally did what he said.

Our 5-inch mounts were just wide open — Boom! Boom! Boom! Boom! Boom! We were firing everything we could. And then I heard Crack! Crack! Crack! That was the sound of the 3-inch mounts. Our 5-inch guns had a range of about 10,000 yards. The 3-inch guns had a range of about 6,000 yards. That meant that if we were opening with the 3-inch mounts, our attackers had to be within 6,000 yards of us and were going to be on us real quick. We were throwing everything in the world at them. Some of the shells were even star shells. The only use these have is to light up the night. You're not going to hurt anything with a star shell unless the shell actually hits the target.

And then I heard "Torpedo in the water! Torpedo in the water!" again followed by "Torpedo is past us!" They were maneuvering the ship and the torpedoes were missing us.

I don't know how long the fight went on — not very long — and then it broke off. The planes from the *Ticonderoga* then came in and hit the three PT boats. At the time I was told we had sunk one, one was dead in the water, and the other limped off.

We had taken hits with some .50 caliber machine gun fire. One of them hit the after mount. Chief Keith Bain, the after mount director, was in there, and a bullet bounced all around him in that confined little space but missed him. Anyway, we got out without any casualties but for some ruptured eardrums from the concussion of our own guns. The men who were on the main deck didn't put cotton — or whatever we used back then — into their ears in time. If you are on deck and someone fires a 3-inch shell, it is absolutely painful. Your eardrums are splitting because it's a high-pitched crack. If a 5-inch shell is a muffled baritone, a 3-inch shell is a tenor. Everybody I examined that day who had a headache or an earache had blood behind the eardrum — in both ears. By then I knew I was in a war. Someone was trying to kill me and I knew that we had killed somebody.

We left the Gulf of Tonkin and rendezvoused with Task Force 77. Then we were ordered back into the gulf, this time accompanied by the USS *Turner Joy* [DD-951].

I prepared for major casualties. I had all I could use to stop severe bleeding and to insert endotracheal tubes to stop pain. I also had IV fluids, which I hung so that if it sloshed around, it wouldn't be smashed. There's a real problem. That destroyer rolled 10 degrees from the vertical in port. And when you're at sea bogeying along, you're not only going to roll but pitch and yaw. If you're going to use an anesthetic, you can't use a spinal because it will creep and the guy will stop breathing. If it's a severe injury, you're going to have to use ether. Then if anybody sets off a spark, you're going to blow hell out of the ship and kill everybody — yourself and the patient, too. We also had xylocaine, but the best anesthetic was going to be morphine. You hit a guy with 10mg of morphine IV, give him another 10mg IM [intramuscular], and he's going to calm down.

So we set up to triage as best we could. Aguilar and I had rehearsed this many times and we knew what we were doing. And then we just waited.

The worst part of combat was to be idle. During the attack, idleness is the worst thing that can possibly happen to you. You want to be doing something. You want to be watching the dial in the engine room. The best thing to be doing is firing a gun. You're going to slam those shells in, just shoot hell out of them, and this gives you a feeling of comfort. But when you've got nothing to do, that's like an execution. You keep waiting to die. Everything is out of your hands and somebody else is fighting your battle for you.

The night attack occurred on the 4th of August. I had gone to CIC [Combat Information Center] earlier in the day and saw things on the radarscope indicating that we were surrounded. Whether it was weather or not I couldn't tell. I was not a CIC officer. I wouldn't have known a hard target from a soft target. But there were things everywhere and they seemed to be surrounding us. I thought this didn't look too good, especially with the *Turner Joy* right behind us. We were scared to death of the *Turner Joy*. We didn't know how much combat experience the ship had. A misplaced 5-inch shell was not going to do an old tin can like ours very much good if it hit us amidships. In battle, you've got to know where each ship is. If you don't, you are going to sink each other.

The *Turner Joy* was right in our wake. Time went on and then we started picking up speed and zigzagging. It wasn't very long after that that we went to general quarters and the captain said we were being attacked. I heard a 5-inch mount go off. I thought, "Okay, this is it." Then, all of a sudden, I heard, "Torpedo in the water! Torpedo in the water!" And that began the wildest damn time you have ever seen in your life.

We were zigzagging. We were firing. I could hear talking on the bridge because the 1MC was open down in the wardroom. I heard the commodore say, "Shoot 'em! Shoot the sons of bitches!"

I talked to Bain later and he said that he would see a target and then it would disappear. He'd be fixed on it and ready to shoot and then it would vanish.

Meanwhile, we were being thrown all over the place in rough waters on the blackest of damn nights I'd ever seen. The *Turner Joy* was opening up and it was scary. I kept hoping some-body was not making a mistake. Anyway, we kept getting torpedo sightings. The sonar man was listening for high-pitched screws and doing the best job he could. I'll guarantee it because his ass was on the line. He's not going to be court-martialed; he's going to be dead if he's wrong. He kept hearing those sounds and had an option. He could either call them what he thought — a torpedo— or he could take a chance that it wasn't a torpedo and he was wrong. I would have done the same thing the kid did, namely, tell the bridge there was a torpedo in the water.

So we were zigzagging all over hell and every now and then we would open up with a one- or two-shot volley. I could also hear the thud of the *Turner Joy* out there. This went on for a while — the zigzagging and "Torpedo in the water! Torpedo's missed us!"

We had set "Zebra" throughout the ship which meant we were locked down. We had all the boilers on the line in the fire rooms and it got up to 140 degrees. Then the [heat] casualties started coming into the wardroom, and I did exactly what I was supposed to do. I jammed IV fluids into them, wet them down, and got them back into the fire rooms as quickly as I could. Of course, they came back after about 10 minutes. The second time they would be sicker, and I'd do the same procedure again and send them back. I hated to do it. The only time I decided not to send them back was when I thought they wouldn't survive the next time down in the fire rooms. If I thought they'd die, I'd keep them.

People were lying all over the wardroom floor, and I was stepping over them. Some had collapsed veins yet I tried to jam 18-gauge needles into a collapsed veins. It was amazing! It really helps to have something to do in combat, and I was so damned busy. I'd hear the shout-ing, "Torpedo in the water!" But I didn't give a damn. I had something to do. There wasn't any-thing I could do about the torpedo, but I could do something about the guys lying on the floor. And that's what I did. Those kids didn't realize that they did more for me than I did for them.

Eventually, the skipper came on the 1MC and said he thought the sound the sonar man was picking up was the sound of our rudder as we moved through the water, and we were break-ing off action. We slowed to about 20 knots, and the *Turner Joy* did likewise. Of course, every-one was waiting to see what would happen.

Finally, I got all the guys cleared out of the wardroom, and when we secured from GQ, I could not believe what I saw. All the officers came into the wardroom laughing hysterically. It was absolute pandemonium. It was one of the wildest scenes I had ever experienced. They didn't know what the hell happened but they had survived. The skipper, Commodore Herrick, and some of the old chiefs had seen combat during the Second World War, but the rest of us had never heard a shot fired in anger. Everybody was laughing. I didn't realize I was laughing but suddenly I discovered that I was laughing, too.

That ended the action. Jim Stockdale was our CAP [Combat Air Patrol] that night flying a lone F-8. He was it.[5] He was up there and kept looking for targets but couldn't find any. That's what he told me later when we discussed the whole situation. There wasn't anything there he could see and maintains to this day that he never saw anything. The commodore later told me that perhaps three of these torpedoes were real. I don't know what Osier thought.

Anyway, we left the Gulf of Tonkin and rendezvoused with Task Force 77. The next day the captain, the commodore, the XO, and Mr. Bueler got in the motor whaleboat and went over to the carrier. When they came back they were very somber. Something really big was happen-ing. And they were wearing sidearms. It wasn't more than a few hours later that every officer was wearing a sidearm and everyone was really grim. So I asked for a sidearm and was refused. They said I was a noncombatant. I kept wondering whether they realized my situation. Maybe I was a noncombatant to them but not to the Vietnamese.

We went back into the gulf — the *Turner Joy* and us. We began lolling around there and not going very fast. I kept waiting for something to happen. It was very tense. A Navy lieuten-ant kept running up to the bridge and monitoring everything the Vietnamese said. We had broken their code. Late one night I was sleeping and the staff ops [operations] officer came in, shook me, and said, "Doc, put your clothes on. The commodore wants to see you in his cabin." It was about 2 o'clock in the morning.

When I entered, the commodore looked awful. Herrick was worried that this thing was going to spread into a giant Asian war. He smelled a rat as to what was going on. How much of the rat I never realized until I'd had time to reflect on what was going on. Herrick had a headache and I gave him something for it. He said, "Doc, I want you to get out all the morphine and distribute a syrette to every man. We're gonna get hit tomorrow." That kind of got my attention.

An officer of USS *Maddox* kneels beside a North Vietnamese bullet protruding from the ship's superstructure. This projectile was a consequence of the first attack on the destroyer (Naval Historical Center).

Aguilar got out the morphine and we distributed a syrette to everybody. By this time I was a fatalist. I wanted a weapon. I felt that I had a right to defend myself. I did not want to become a prisoner of war. My family was slaughtered in Europe during the Second World War. We lost many in the concentration camps, and I just wasn't able to cope with the idea of dying that way. If I went in the water, I wasn't going to leave the gulf alive. I knew that because I wasn't going to rot in prison camp. But I never got the sidearm, and I was a farm boy and a better shot than 90 percent of the guys out there. Anyway, we were sitting there waiting for the attack that was supposed to come. And waiting and waiting and waiting. Then the staff ops officer came to me and said, "Relax, Doc. The attack's been called off." So I guess what happened was the Navy lieutenant operating the eavesdropping gear heard the enemy wasn't going to attack.

No more attacks occurred after that and we left the Gulf of Tonkin and rejoined Task Force 77. We then went back to Subic.

As you know, after that second attack, President Johnson addressed Congress and asked for the Tonkin Gulf Resolution. Twenty years later I learned that the bullet that had hit the after mount director in the first attack was presented to Congress as having hit the ship during the night attack.[6] That would have been a profound lie. We told the truth. Anything that happened afterward was done by the [Johnson] administration or the military. But I can tell you this: Anything that went off that ship that night and the next day was gospel. Nobody lied about anything. Whether or not there were ships out there that fired torpedoes at us, I don't know. But I know that what was reported to the administration was the truth. And how they dressed it up I don't know, but I can tell you that that bullet did not come from the night attack. Nothing hit us during that night attack — nothing at all.

3

HEARTS AND MINDS

So we must be ready to fight in Viet-Nam, but the ultimate victory will depend upon the hearts and minds of the people that actually live out there.

— Lyndon B. Johnson[1]

Although the phrase "winning hearts and minds" has become a cliché since President Lyndon Johnson first made it popular more than 40 years ago, the concept certainly made sense in the context of the Vietnam War. If the communist insurgency was to be kept at bay and finally defeated, winning the hearts and minds of the South Vietnamese people increasingly became the goal of U.S. aid. Encouraging them to resist the ideology of the communists was seen as making it more difficult for the Viet Cong to operate and sustain offensive guerrilla operations. Because medical care of any kind was a luxury that few Vietnamese in the impoverished countryside could afford, medical aid programs became a high priority.

The Department of State and the U.S. Agency for International Development (USAID) created a team concept that translated into Military Provincial Health Assistance Program teams or MILPHAP. The Department of Defense was to provide military personnel to staff these teams. In the spring of 1969, the Navy fielded seven MILPHAP teams which operated in Quang Tri/Quang Tri Province, Hoi An/Quang Nam Province, Tam Ky/Quang Tin Province, Bro Loc/ Lam Dong Province, Chau Doc/An Giang Province and Cao Lanh/Kien Phong Province, Soc Trang/Ba Xuyen Province, and Rach Gia/Kien Giang Province. Each team consisted of three general practitioners, one Medical Service Corps officer, and 12 enlisted personnel. The American military medical personnel, many on loan to MILPHAP, were to practice medicine in South Vietnamese civilian hospitals alongside their Vietnamese counterparts.

The experiences of these teams were as diverse as the geographical locations in which they operated. Even though all teams served in what was certainly a bona fide war zone, some teams encountered frequent rocket and mortar attacks on their facilities while others practiced their healing art in relative calm. What most MILPHAP personnel had in common was the lack of communication and frequent misunderstandings between American and Vietnamese colleagues. Few American medical personnel spoke Vietnamese. Their hasty preparatory State Department training for the MILPHAP mission did not include extensive Vietnamese language instruction.

One surgeon, Dr. William Gondring, summed up what became an all too familiar theme in Vietnam. "We Americans came and took over the surgical care in that hospital. But we didn't take it over to integrate, to teach, to communicate, to learn from, to have a dialogue with. We took it over to provide an American military system."

The Navy and the other services also began what were called "civic action" or "people-to-people" programs whose primary aim was to enable the Vietnamese to help themselves. Special Navy Construction Battalion (Seabee) teams taught villagers to build bridges, dig wells, and construct buildings. These programs also embraced English and technical training classes and on-the-job instruction, and they provided medical and dental assistance.

The Medical Civil Action Program (MEDCAP) was, in fact, one of the first civic action programs to be implemented. MEDCAP was intended to provide emergency care for civilian casualties and refugees in combat areas, offer sick call and limited dispensary care in populated areas not yet secure, and give professional medical assistance in secure areas and local hospitals. As a 1967 Marine Corps handbook pointed out, civic action was "applying the Golden Rule in the cause of freedom."

Hemostats and Barbed Wire

Even as Americans mourned the sudden and violent death of their young president, John F. Kennedy, in the late fall of 1963, medical personnel prepared to bring modern medicine to South Vietnam's hinterlands. Two of those personnel were Navy nurses, Lt. Cmdr. Ruth Pojeky and Lt. Cmdr. Bernadette McKay. Following their return from Vietnam, both nurses were debriefed by Quintin M. Sanger, an employee of the Bureau of Medicine and Surgery. Lt. Cmdr. McKay recalled how their adventure began.

"In November 1963 we received official notification that 'you have been selected as a nurse member of this team.' We wondered what we had been selected for, what it would be like on a team, who else had been selected. We discovered we were joining a Navy Surgical Team with Lt. Cmdr. James Beeby, MC; Lt. William Gondring, MC, USNR; Capt. Lawrence O. Bearson, NC, USAF; and HM2 William G. Sweeney. The group was to be loaned to the U.S. Agency for International Development [USAID] to work in a South Vietnamese civilian hospital for one year. It was composed of two surgeons, two operating room nurses, a male nurse anesthetist, and a hospital corpsman who was a combined x-ray/laboratory technician. The team, one of eight [actually seven] in the country, was then assigned to a provincial hospital in Rach Gia. The Naval Surgical Teams were to acquaint the Vietnamese [hospital staff] with some of the techniques and equipment needed to provide better patient care for the people of their country. The State Department told us that our mission was 'Teach ourselves out of a job.'"

One night in late 1964 about 2300, the phone rang. Maj. Wilson told Dr. Beeby we probably would hear mortar fire at fairly close range. Intelligence predicted that the Viet Cong were going to shell the nearby provincial headquarters. Most of us were asleep and Dr. Beeby elected not to inform us. Some of us had heard the phone but when no summons came, we turned over to continue our night's sleep. In about three minutes the room was lit up suddenly and vividly. This was followed by a loud explosion that seemed quite close. We went downstairs to determine what was going on and were surprised by four more quick explosions. They seemed to be coming from the canal directly in front of our "Hilton," the name we had given our house.

Maj. Wilson called about then and inquired, "Where are those damn mortars landing?" Dr. Beeby replied, "Right in our front yard!"

We were advised to remain in the house until MACV [Military Assistance Command, Vietnam] could ascertain from whence they came. We waited about 10 minutes for another call, but when there wasn't any, we all decided to go back to bed. As we were about to go to sleep, Dr. Beeby called us. "Let's move out."

We looked at each other, and in a split second both of us mentally packed our treasured loot and accepted the inevitable. "Move out where?" we asked.

"The emergency room! It's loaded with patients!"

And so it was. When we arrived, there were some 25 patients, mostly civilians. A group from MACV came by shortly to inform us they believed that the VC [Viet Cong] mortar attack had simply been "a little off target." Of the approximately 25 rounds, some had landed in a populated part of the city, others near our house, and one landed on the headquarters but did lit-

Rach Gia Hospital (courtesy William Gondring).

tle damage. In about three hours the victims of the mortar attack had received their indicated treatments; some cases went to surgery but most were treated in the emergency room. We were all safely tucked into bed again by 0300 — but not without saying a small prayer of thanks. That had been just a little too close for comfort, but all agreed a "miss was as good as a mile."

Rach Gia [pronounced "Rock Ja"] was in the Kian Giang Province in the Mekong Delta. The majority of the natives earned their living as fishermen and rice growers although the city had a few skilled workers. There was a six-month hot-wet season from April onward, and a hot-dry season the rest of the year. Life centered in the city markets. Here the team made friends at convenient opportunities. We were often greeted by "Hello!" and "Okay!" when we appeared in our green jeep.

Our house, which we affectionately named the "Rach Gia Hilton," consisted of two connected Vietnamese houses facing the Gulf of Thailand. The tile roof filtered out insects but did not keep out the monsoon rains. One storm caused an 18-inch flood on the first floor. The shower room was of Paul Bunyan size, but the kitchen sink belonged in a bathroom. There was one large room which served varied purposes, including entertainment of local American personnel. The "communication center" consisted of three green telephones used to keep in touch with the hospital and the U.S. MACV. Mosquito netting protected the sleeping quarters upstairs, but the bulkheads grew moss from soaking in rain.

These deficiencies were gradually repaired with the help of Maj. R. D. Wilson, USA, a MACV advisor, who supplied many hard-to-get items as if by magic. The overhead French-style fans were replaced by air conditioners, a normal kitchen sink was acquired, and a plastic "raincoat" was obtained to protect the refrigerator transformer against water damage. Our "Hilton-style" establishment offered Vietnamese management and hospitality with a blend of Western comfort, excellent dining facilities, and music on request to Americans serving in the Delta. The finishing touches were six to eight feet of barbed wire completely surrounding the house and three National Police guards on duty 24 hours a day.

Dr. Nguyen Phouc An, the hospital director, sent us two of his personal servants. Although a married couple, they soon became "Betty Crocker"—the cook and "Mr. Westinghouse"—the laundry man. They enjoyed calling each other by their new American names. The No. 1 house-boy was called B. Lewis, a corruption of John L. Lewis, because he was the labor boss.

Betty Crocker insisted on us eating all that she thought was good for us. After a time, in one way or another, the domestics were running us rather than vice versa. Compliance made everything so much easier. Yet the different cultures never completely meshed. We introduced green-colored items for a housewarming on Saint Patrick's Day. This was a mystery to the cook, and we soon found ourselves receiving varicolored drinks of all kinds, as if Betty Crocker thought Americans regularly ate and drank in Technicolor.

The Rach Gia Hospital [officially called Rach Gia-Phu Dinh Hospital] was a 450- to 500-bed institution. It was one of the few Vietnamese hospitals with a dental clinic. The team worked in the surgery department and also—especially during a large influx of patients—in the emergency room. The team trained Vietnamese staff members in techniques, such as anesthesia, and in the use of modern equipment, such as hemostats to stop hemorrhage. At first a surgical case had a team of five Americans and one Vietnamese, but as training progressed, there might be five Vietnamese and one or no Americans.

The Vietnamese were quick learners despite the language difficulties. They were amazingly dexterous at duplicating any manual skill. Their alert and willing manner never seemed to disappear. A large portion of the team's time was spent in teaching principles and practices and the use of varied types of equipment. In six months, three Vietnamese nurses mastered surgical aseptic techniques so thoroughly that they could skillfully assist at any surgical procedure anywhere. The use of pantomime and demonstration solved many sticky situations—with the help of a sense of humor on both sides.

General principles seemed far more difficult for the Vietnamese to grasp, perhaps because they were not tangible as were "how-to-do" functions. A period of one hour every two weeks was used to show technical American films to demonstrate a specific technique before it was introduced on the wards.

The team members' relations with their Vietnamese co-workers—doctors, nurses, and technicians—were cordial and mutually fruitful. The director and staff of the provincial hospital at Rach Gia readily accepted us and made us a part of their team effort. They taught us by their example and willingness to give of themselves. And through mutual respect, it was possible for us to gain the love and admiration of the people of Kien Gaing Province. The Vietnamese learned from Americans modern skills and techniques, and Americans gained a deep respect and admiration for the abilities of the Vietnamese people.

Our Navy Surgical Team soon learned what "mass casualty" and "this is no drill" meant at the hospital. In our first week a two-and-a-half-ton truck full of Regional Force and Popular Force soldiers rolled over.[2] The team was still unpacking its surgical gear when 25 casualties arrived in the emergency room. We worked together as a team — with some mistakes and duplication of effort—but managed very well our "baptism of fire." Gradually we developed a disaster plan which worked quite effectively. With a little trial and error, we could cover almost all contingencies.

From 500 to 600 patients were seen every month in the emergency room. This room was also an admission room, minor surgery clinic, cast room, blood drawings room, and triage center during mass casualties. Two tables were normally used for changing dressings, examining patients, and applying casts. The number was increased to five during emergencies. Duty in the ER was a combination of battle aid station, pediatrics clinic, and typical hospital emergency room in a large city. In several mass casualty situations, 35 to 140 patients were examined and treated in this area.

Mortar and bullet wounds, burns from bomb blasts, lacerations, and abscesses were the most frequent type of injury seen. When many patients were waiting to be treated, the entire crews of the operating room and emergency room plus the administrative personnel centered their initial activities there. Patients were bathed, their x-rays evaluated, and their further disposition made — all in this one room.

Our supplies were often short, our means of replenishing them often nonexistent, and our one autoclave was especially overworked. The first Vietnamese words the Navy Surgical Team learned were "*Kong Co*" and "*Het Roi*"— meaning "have not got" and "all gone." The team's supply officer performed a minor miracle to preclude the constant use of these words.

Support of any advisory or surgical team in Vietnam was a thankless, frustrating assignment. Supplies and every last bit of equipment had to be flown from a central warehouse in Saigon. Cargo planes, which were expected to bring the ordered supplies, were often diverted elsewhere to satisfy direct military needs. Those that did make the trip often faced VC attacks at the Rach Gia airfield, and some had to abort. When they did arrive, vigorous efforts by many staff members and laborers had to be made to unload, transport, and unpack the material in the shortest possible time. Opening a package that contained a critically needed item was very much like Christmas morning with delighted oohs and aahs from both Vietnamese and Americans. When supplies did not arrive in time, the team showed its traditional Navy talent for improvisation.

Past and present merged on the wards. The patients, commonly two to a bed in Vietnam except at Rach Gia, slept on wooden slats covered with a straw mat, but they could be receiving an intravenous through an intracath. All beds were covered with mosquito netting at night. Their frames served as a more than adequate intravenous pole by the simple addition of a bent nail to hold the IV bottle. Old alcohol burners and pots for boiling syringes were discarded in favor of a syringe exchange system initiated by central supply. Dressing carts were introduced, along with individual suture removal and dressing sets, to improve the old method of changing dressings.

When a patient was admitted to most Vietnamese hospitals, his family assumed responsibility for his meals while he was under treatment or recovering from surgery. A member of one's family prepared the food and served it to the son, daughter, wife, or husband on the ward. However, at Rach Gia, the hospital provided food service to most patients with the help of the Catholic Sisters.

The laundry service was an intriguing operation. The hospital had no washing machines or dryers. The clothes were gathered and washed by many hands and hung outside on bushes and shrubbery to dry during both the dry and wet seasons. Often the pajamas and linen attracted insects from the shrubbery. So the possibility of "ants in the pants" might often give unrest to the patient and disturb the quiet healing atmosphere expected in a hospital. However, this did not seem to bother the Vietnamese.

The most memorable experience of the year [1964] we were at Rach Gia occurred during a 36-hour period when 160 patients were admitted and 27 major surgical procedures were performed. At 1000 an American helicopter gunner walked in with a through-and-through gunshot wound of the face. He had been aboard a cover chopper for a dust-off evacuation chopper. He had gone in to pick up three casualties about 20 kilometers [about 12 miles] from the hospital. The soldier had a minor wound, but a spectacular message. "You may be a little busy because there was one hell of a firefight going on down there, Doc."

The wounded began arriving at 1130 in trucks, ambulances, and choppers in groups of 3 to 10 until 1500 the next afternoon. Luckily we had two extra surgeons on hand and split up two operative teams: two surgeons, two Vietnamese nurses, and one American anesthetist and one Vietnamese anesthetist on each of the two teams. Dr. Beeby, as the triage officer, sorted out the casualties, determining which had priority and what treatment or surgery was required. Dr. Gondring did minor procedures in the emergency room. Lt. Cmdr. Pojeky worked with two

Vietnamese nurses in the operating room replacing gear that was being used in both the operating and emergency rooms; I circulated between the two operating rooms and the recovery room. HM2 Sweeney and Mr. Troy worked as an x-ray team. The whole group worked extremely well with little duplication of effort. One member said, "Everyone had his job, did his job, and stayed at the job until every patient had been seen and treated." The next day they were not too energetic, but they felt pride in the job they had done under less than optimum circumstances.

Meanwhile, the daily surgical cases included the unusual. To list the surgical procedures performed during the year would be to write a text on what had happened that just couldn't be done. The surgeons operated on patients with types of surgical pathology that seemed unbelievable to us. They removed bladder stones the size of "boulders," took out a spleen that weighed one-tenth as much as the child who walked around with it, removed parotid tumors that had been present 2 to 17 years. Almost any piece of intestine that was removed contained some species of worm parasites. Often the surgeon had difficulty in finding an area free of worms so he could apply a Payr clamp to resect the bowel. Thyroid glands that weighed pounds rather than ounces were more usual than unusual. More than 100 surgical procedures were performed a month, and team members acquired unique slide collections of their most memorable pathologies. The specimens were sent to the Pasteur Institute in Saigon for pathological examination, and a report was sent back to the hospital for filing.

The team was not unaware of, nor indifferent to, the political situation in Vietnam. On some occasions members of the Viet Cong came to the hospital for treatment. They were not turned away but were treated as anyone else in need of attention. In fact, we knew we had really arrived when a VC hospital in another province referred a patient to Rach Gia. Impartial medical attention was also given to both Christian and Buddhist patients who applied for treatment. It would appear that this policy was especially notable because Buddhist Vietnamese have often charged they have been discriminated against in the troubled politics of the country.

Probably our most effective role was in helping the South Vietnamese people. Our presence and capabilities quickly spread by word of mouth throughout the countryside. According to the American advisors in the surrounding hamlets, the Navy Surgical Team was their ace in the hole. One district chief explained that the most frequent request made of him was for transportation to come to Rach Gia to see the American doctors. This aided the larger war effort in two ways. First, assurances of medical care by Americans improved relations between our advisors and their sometimes reluctant South Vietnamese counterparts. Second, the South Vietnamese government representative and his American advisor could assure an individual that he could get the needed medical care for himself or his family — a certainty he could not receive from the Viet Cong. At times this factor persuaded the men to support the Saigon government rather than communist rebels.

"Egotism of Our Superiority"

Missouri-born William Gondring knew he wanted to be a surgeon by the time he was in ninth grade. While attending Washington University Medical School in St. Louis, he signed up for the Navy's Ensign 1995 program, which allowed him to obtain invaluable clinical experience serving aboard the carrier USS Kearsarge *(CVA-33) for three months during the summer between his sophomore and junior years. After an internship in general surgery at the University of Oklahoma, a residency at Barnes Hospital at Washington University, and additional surgical training, he began active duty in 1964 assigned to the guided missile cruiser USS* Galveston *(CLG-3).*

After a six-month tour in which the ship carried out local operations off the Pacific Coast, the young surgeon yearned for an overseas assignment. He didn't have long to wait. He and his wife, who was a civilian nurse, were selected to go to Vietnam with Advisory Team 54. Related 40 years after his experience in Vietnam, Dr. Gondring's evaluation of the team's effectiveness differs from the previous, more contemporary account of Bernadette McKay and Ruth Pojeky shortly after they returned home. The outcome of the struggle in Southeast Asia still looked very bright in 1964.

Our assignment was a provincial hospital at Ban Me Thuot in the Central Highlands to provide care to the Vietnamese, the Vietnamese military, and anybody else who showed up. We were transferred from the Department of Defense to the Department of State and then were paid by and became completely under the control of the State Department. We went to Washington for about eight weeks and took a course on Vietnam at the Foreign Service Institute. There we met the rest of our team — Ruth Pojeky, Bernadette McKay, Jim Beeby, Larry Bearson, and Bill Sweeney. All had been transferred from the Navy to the State Department and were in Washington for the State Department orientation.

My observation was how little our instructors knew and how little intelligence they had about the diseases we would expect to see. We really had minimal preparation.

My wife and I were going to take a holiday in Tokyo and Hong Kong on the way over but they canceled our leave. They canceled everything. So we went to New York instead and were interviewed for the news show *Monitor*. They asked us whether we'd heard that President Johnson had just announced that no more dependents were going to Saigon or Vietnam. It was right about the time the war escalated [1965] and all dependents were to leave Saigon. So we had to make arrangements for my wife to go somewhere else. The situation really had changed all of a sudden. She went to Oklahoma City for a BSN [Bachelor of Science in Nursing] program and worked. I flew from Washington to Saigon.

In Saigon, we found that our assignment had been changed from Ban Me Thuot to a place in the Mekong Delta called Rach Gia. We stayed in Saigon for a while at a small villa, and had more orientation as to what was going on — but no medical orientation. This was a team put together to provide health care — but without all the other instructions and meaningful knowledge we needed. How do you take care of typhoid perforations? How do you treat cholera? How do you take a land mine casing out of a guy who is eviscerated [disemboweled]? How are you going to handle patients when you run out of chromic [catgut]?[3] Or how are you going to handle patients when you run out of antibiotics? How do you operate at night when the power source goes off?

We flew from Saigon to Rach Gia. When the plane landed, AID vehicles— old jeeps— transported us. That very day, a truck drove over a land mine. We went to a soccer field where about 20 or 30 injured Vietnamese soldiers were brought. We had no instruments. In fact, we found that all our instruments were packed in cosmoline[4] and sealed in aluminum canisters. We first had to clean the cosmoline off the instruments and then manage the injured.

One of my patients was a young lieutenant with a penetrating wound of the chest that had developed into a tension pneumothorax. I took a 15-gauge needle, poured merthiolate over it, poured merthiolate over his chest, and cut a finger off a glove. I looped the glove finger so it became a flutter valve with a ligature around the hub of the needle, and then stuck it in his chest. The valve I made would expand when the patient exhaled and then collapse when he inhaled. After I finished, he was put in a helicopter. The only trouble was the chopper flew too high, there was nobody monitoring him, and he died. I'm not sure he had oxygen.

The hospital at Rach Gia was called Rach Gia-Phu Dinh Hospital. The Agency for International Development [AID] had built two operating rooms right in the center of the courtyard, but they had never been used. The Vietnamese nurse put together all our surgical packs, which contained standard Navy instruments that came out of a regular surgical instrument set. The packs had scalpels, retractors, and hemostats.

We used an ether-air anesthesia machine, which was safe and required little maintenance and no oxygen. The ether was evacuated via tube out of the room because we used an electric cautery for hemostasis.

For antibiotics, we had penicillin and chloromycetin. Chloromycetin is no longer sold in the U.S. because it causes myeloid depression in 3 to 5 percent of patients. We used a lot of chloromycetin. We also used biologicals for treatment of tetanus and rabies that were made in Paris by the Pasteur Institute.

I ended up doing half the general surgery—the simple cases like abdominal exploration. The general surgeon, Dr. Beeby, did the more complicated cases. We got so we could do an amputation in 14 or 15 minutes. Once we determined that the patient had two kidneys and that one of them functioned, we could resect a kidney in 15 minutes.

Three-quarters to seven-eighths of our patients were Vietnamese but, being in the Mekong Delta, we also supported the junk force fleet. The junk force was made up of young Navy lieutenants with language skills and senior enlisted who went to sea on maritime patrols aboard Vietnamese junks. We also saw the first Swift Boat casualty. This is reported in a book about the "Brown Water Navy," small, fast Navy combat craft that plied the Mekong Delta's muddy rivers and channels. It mentions the Swift Boat episode which occurred on an evening when the skipper of the boat saw a Viet Cong flag and thought it was an arms cache. When he went to investigate, the boat was ambushed and the VC destroyed his boat. We got the radio request and sent out a Boston Whaler[5] and a helicopter. But due to mistakes and misjudgment, the helicopter brought back the patients who were least seriously injured and the Boston Whaler brought back the most seriously wounded. On the way back, one man expired.

We took everybody to the operating room, and I worked on a broken tibia which had an open fracture. One or two guys died and we temporarily lost their bodies in the middle of the night. It was a lack of communication between two cultures. The Vietnamese had taken the bodies to their morgue and we didn't locate them until the next morning.

Sometimes night would be interrupted by star shells[6] or the VC would attack Rach Gia with mortars. On one occasion an assault occurred on one of the roads leading into the community and we began getting casualties. We finished with them, went back to the house, and then suddenly the mortars started falling within 20 yards of our home. You don't hear mortars until they hit.

The next day we found that the mortar plate[7] our attackers used had been placed in a rice paddy. Because the paddy was wet, when the mortar went off, it skidded and changed direction. And so it missed us. Once the attacks were over, we went about our jobs. We had a defensive bunker we'd get into in

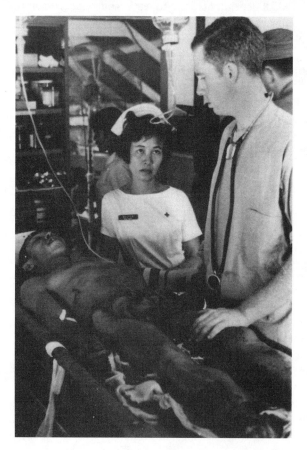

Navy doctor Lt. Raymond Osborn confers with a Vietnamese nurse at Hoa Kanh Children's Hospital. Their patient, injured in a truck accident, will lose his leg (BUMED Archives).

case the situation was really nasty. But the bunker had water in it — and snakes and lizards were always in there.

Vietnamese guards provided our security. They always kept their M1 carbines wrapped in a carbine cloth because they didn't want dust or moisture to get in. And the barrels were stuffed with cotton because they didn't want the barrels to get rusty or dirty. Let's say the security was less than optimal. In my hip pocket I carried a .38 pistol that my father had sent me, and I operated on prisoners of war with a .22 Browning in my surgeon's scrubs just for self-protection. Our episodes with combat were all defensive. The army gave all of us M1 carbines but none of us ever fired a weapon in anger.

On the walls of the building around Rach Gia were signs that said, "Have you done your good deed for the day — killed another American?" There were also other signs offering 20,000 piasters to kill an American. That was about $200.

I learned from many of the prisoners we operated on that, by and large, they were not communists. They had been fighting against the Vietnamese central government for years. But they had no real knowledge about what the world situation was and knew nothing about Marxist-Leninism. It was more individual civil disobedience.

A Special Forces team at Ha Tien was about 30 kilometers [almost 19 miles] down the road from us. They had killed a 12 year old a couple of weeks before who had thrown a hand grenade at them. So we were aware that children could become aggressive. One day, while we were walking down a nearby road, three people suddenly jumped out. The roads were sloped with water on either side. One youth had something that looked like a hand grenade and threw it. I jumped but made up my mind that I would never shoot a 12 year old. What I thought was a hand grenade was a firecracker. The group had done this deliberately to have one of us provoke an incident in which we would shoot somebody. Then they would claim we had no caring for people. I knew then that I couldn't shoot anybody anyway. My job was not to kill but to take care of people and put them back together again.

I always looked at cases by type and episodes. We could handle 15 napalm burn care cases an hour. We had Regional/Popular Forces and ARVN [Army of the Republic of Vietnam] forces and the differences between the two were determined by their levels of experience. There was ARVN–controlled territory, VC–controlled territory, and the intermediate area. The intermediate area was the area where the CIA worked.

The Regional/Popular Forces, which were poorly trained, poorly led, and poorly equipped, always moved with their women and children, cats and dogs. A French-built fort was often situated around a canal or river. The VC would attack these forts at night, usually by setting up an ambush. The Americans finally learned that if they tried to reinforce these forts at night, they would also be ambushed. So they would never reinforce those people at night. On this occasion, the little outpost was completely overrun and all the people were killed. The women and children were crucified to the front gate.

For U.S. forces to make an air strike, the rules of engagement had to be followed. The coordinates had to be okayed through the Vietnamese command. And by the time all that was done, the VC knew what was going on and were no longer around. So this time the whole area was napalmed and the people we got were the women, children, and old men who were still left.

Nevertheless, we took care of the whole group. Every patient was treated the same. They were placed on a gurney, they received IV fluids, and their wounds were debrided. They received penicillin, chloromycetin, tetanus, then morphine. Afterwards we applied a yellow sulfa preparation. We had no dressings so we cut up parachute silk. The patients were then put on the ward.

The hospital could treat more patients by pushing the beds together. You could have three children in the same bed with two in traction. When we had so many patients on the ward that it overflowed, we rolled the beds together. Some patients were actually placed on cracks between the beds. Instead of having one patient to a bed, we had private and semi-private beds. With this system, we could really expand the hospital in a hurry.

The beds had a rice mat with no mattress, a mosquito net over the top, and few covers because it was always warm. The care and the nursing would be provided by the hospital, but the patient's family slept beneath the beds with their own cooking instruments, and they were responsible for feeding their family member.

We went to the market place and had carpenters or seamstresses make our traction materials. They would cut old bicycle tires so that we could run the rubber up and down the sides with an Ace bandage. A piece of wood was at the end and a parachute line out the end for holding the weights. The weights were bags filled with sand. A traction system requires pulleys. Back in the U.S. we used metal pulleys. At Rach Gia, carpenters hand-carved the pulleys. We had a lot of fractures so we did a lot of traction. And those patients were always put in a traction system made of materials that were obtained close by.

The supply system worked poorly. We frequently ran out of antibiotics and suture material. Even though we knew supplies were coming into Saigon, they frequently would be stolen. We also realized that some of what had been stolen was being used by the other side.

At that time we had glass bottles for IV fluids. We needed antibiotics and suture material even though everything else was reused. We had no disposables. Everything had to be washed, cleaned, and dried. Surgical scrubs were hung up on the clothesline, but there was a problem with doing that. Fire ants got into them. So when you put on a surgical scrub, it was almost unbearable trying to get rid of those little things that were biting you.

We also had a problem with our generators. We had power at night but if it was interrupted, we needed the generator. But that meant the generator had to be kept in good condition and the battery that turned over the diesel engine to run the generator needed to be maintained. Invariably, that battery was not taken care of. You might try to do a case at night but knew the diesel wouldn't start. So you were forced to use the battery in the jeep to turn over the diesel to get the generator to work.

Everywhere you turned problems arose that you would never have dreamt about until you'd been through this sort of situation. You had to have the flexibility and agility of mind to adapt. And, by the way, everyone on the team had that adaptability.

We had a self-selection system for treating patients. The patient transportation system was not available at night because of fear of ambush and the fear of sending ambulances out after dark. Patients often had lost a great amount of blood before they got to us. They only brought us the patients who survived.

At first we really didn't have a referral system. When we got there, the 3rd Field Hospital was not available. The Saigon Naval Station Hospital had closed. From the standpoint of American care, it was quite clear that we would give patients primary care and then transfer them out for more definitive treatment.

We pretty much did as much as we could within the limits of our blood supply. Due to the blood shortage anyone who required massive reconstruction we transferred out. Blood was always the limiting factor. The ARVN and Regional/Popular Forces donated it. On one occasion, after a major military operation, we needed a lot of blood so we got it from them. They knew we didn't use it all so they wanted their blood back. They had a mini-riot. They didn't know you could keep blood and use it for somebody else.

And I think the situation got worse while we were there. A guy named "Killer" Houng, ran an assassination squad. He was controlled by the CIA and received American support. They were ARVN and they had an independent operation — ARVN troops that were supported by the CIA. On one occasion, Houng was wounded and they brought him to the ER along with his men who had come along to protect him. They all had carbines and crowded up close to Houng to protect him with their bodies. As I debrided his wounds, they had their guns right underneath my chin. I was afraid an accident would happen in the ER simply because these guys carried their weapons so carelessly. I requested them all to leave. They departed and then deployed around the hospital. Killer Houng finally got well and left.

My next encounter with Killer Houng concerned an incident with his wife. She was downtown watching some men play cards. When Killer Houng observed this, he took her hand, put it on the table, and cut her little finger off. Afterward, he instructed her never again to watch other men play cards. I took care of the amputated finger when they brought her to the hospital.

The next episode with Killer Houng was the last. He was brought to the hospital, only this time he had been shot in the head and died. He killed on both sides in addition to doing away with anybody he had a grudge against. His family and his relatives carried sidearms, but they also had heavy weapons located in their home under lock and key in a glass cabinet.

After he died, they went back home and, in their excitement, one family member thrust his hands through the glass and cut all the tendons in both hands. I took care of the remnants of the lacerations of the tendons of the wrist and medial nerves.

I kept track of these events as they occurred because I was participating in them. I was taking part in their lives but always indirectly and on the outskirts. You never knew who you were taking care of. The victims were put on a general surgical ward. Then the Vietnamese intelligence would go in there and, pretending to be sick, lie there beside them to see if they could develop a bond or a friendship to get intelligence. After a while, I had skill enough to speak to the prisoners of war after they had been wounded and before we operated on them. My technique was always to be friendly to people and never to try to hurt them ... and gain their confidence. I would ask them philosophical questions. Did they understand Marxism-Leninism? What was their philosophy? What was their reason for participating in the war? Who were they fighting?

I found that in our area these people had been fighting for years. As near as I could tell, they had been fighting the central government regardless of who was the central government. They weren't fighting for the hearts and minds or for the freedoms that we fight for. They just fought and accepted their destiny.

Many of our problems were due to communication or the lack of it. With the lack of communication, the system broke down. Our Navy Surgical Teams didn't have a Vietnamese surgeon who would operate with us. We Americans came and took over the surgical care in that hospital. But we didn't take it over to integrate, to teach, to communicate, to learn from, to have a dialogue with. We took it over to provide an American military system. We did not work within the Vietnamese system and their style of medical treatment. We used our own instrument system; we didn't adopt their instrument system. We didn't explain our instruments and our techniques to them. We didn't have a dialogue about their instruments and their techniques. And we really never knew what their referral system was.

Our senior leadership, including myself, never knew that we should have integrated ourselves into their system so that we could have had a dialogue. Ultimately, the way you bond with people is through similar circumstances. We never bonded. We could have been more successful — on levels other than operating, amputating, and removing kidneys — if we had had an opportunity to bond over common experiences and learn about their life and then integrate and teach.

So we segregated our American culture from the Vietnamese. And ours was less segregated than most because we lived in a Vietnamese house and had a Vietnamese cook. Americans had air conditioning. The Vietnamese didn't have air conditioning. We had transported our way of life, our society, and our health care into Vietnam. The "hearts and minds" campaign was designed to fail simply because of our arrogance and ego. I always felt that *I* wasn't arrogant because I went to Vietnam. But in reality I *was* arrogant and had an ego or else I would have insisted on having the Vietnamese physicians scrub with me and make decisions on health care, ER coverage, rounds, and medications. Never once did I ever go into a Vietnamese doctor's home. Never once did I ever integrate myself into the community like I did in 2003 when I operated with a former North Vietnamese Army surgeon in Vietnam.

My message is that we have the egotism of our superiority. We felt we could help the Vietnamese. We could give them health care. We could take care of diseases. We could give them democracy. But that's not the way it worked. We never understood how unsuccessful we were because of a lack of cultural understanding and training.

Buzzing the Doctors' House

Almost four years after Americans came to Rach Gia hospital to help provide medical care to the town, a Navy presence was still there. For new arrivals such as Navy nurse Winifred Copeland, the Mekong Delta, if not an exotic place to practice medicine, was still very much a war zone. In a letter to Navy Nurse Corps Director, Veronica Bulshefski, dated 30 March 1967, the young nurse described her introduction to Vietnam duty.

Dear Captain Bulshefski,

Our team arrived in Saigon on the 9th of February after some 26 hours en route via Northwest Airlines. We were taken to Koepler Army Compound in Saigon for the in-processing and the beginning of many briefings. Since there are no facilities at Koepler for women, Miss Wilson and I stayed at the USAID guest house and commuted by taxi. The army briefings, though interesting and well organized, were more geared to the jungle fighting soldier.

Saigon was interesting but hectic. We arrived at the beginning of TET or Vietnamese New Year, which resembles a combination of Christmas, New Years, Thanksgiving and Fourth of July. One notes the elements of the Fourth of July very readily with the firecrackers going off day and night. Apparently the Vietnamese sleep very little during this holiday. The crowds, heat and dirt of the city made the delta sound appealing. We were not too sorry to leave Saigon after a week.

From Saigon to Rach Gia was an hour and a half by Beechcraft. The pilot pointed out the interesting landmarks en route including the mountains along the Cambodian border. The rivers cross the delta in a very picturesque fashion and the whole area is deceptively peaceful from the air. Travel here is primarily done by air because the VC have mined many of the roads and blown up the bridges. The pilots maintain as high an altitude consistent with safety for as long as possible because of the instances of rifle fire from the ground. Also the pilots won't land here at Rach Gia until they can recognize "friendly" transportation on the ground. Since communications of all kinds are difficult here, the pilot signals his wish to land by buzzing the town — notably the doctors' house and the hospital. Such buzzing will bring 2 or more men to the air strip, in a Jeep and with weapons.

Our hospital is considered to be one of the best in Vietnam. It is very old and unscreened so that the insect and rodent population on every ward is unbelievable. The wards are crowded with patients and family who set up camp during the illness.

The patient furnishings on the wards consist of an iron bed with wooden slats, covered with a straw mat. The only mattresses that I have seen are in the recovery room and the post-operative ward. As soon as a patient feels well enough he "escapes"— or leaves unannounced. This is often done just before scheduled surgery, but may occur at any time. It is most disconcerting to our medical officer to find that his patient in traction has "escaped," traction and all. Apparently we have rather stiff competition from the local practitioner of "Chinese Medicine." This is the local witch doctor who gives us many "headaches" by attempting to treat diphtheria, for example, by kneading the skin on the neck of an infant. We get the child just in time for a tracheostomy[8] but too late for much in the way of therapy.

We have not had an American hospital administrator here since last October. I have been attending to the administrative matters with the very capable assistance of Miss Wilson. I have always felt that hospital administration would be a challenge but what a place to begin! We are currently preparing all reports, answering communications from Public Health on the number of cases of cholera, diphtheria, etc., and reporting on immunization programs in our province. Our hospital administrator is due to arrive on April 15 and we shall welcome him.

Our nursing time is divided among the operating room, emergency room and recovery room. The number of surgical cases is going up because of war casualties and we have asked for more surgical beds and an additional operating room. The VC continue their harassment by mining roads and blowing up local buses en route to neighboring towns.

The role of nurse advisor is challenging, though not without its problems. The cultural setting is so different and nursing standards as we know them do not exist. Last Monday, I was privileged to attend the opening of a workshop for Vietnamese chief nurses. The workshop lasts two weeks and is an attempt to teach the chief nurse what his job is. Almost all chief nurses here are men. I hope to work closely with Mr. Cao when he returns from the workshop in the organization and administration of the nursing service here. We will have to begin from the very beginning! Mr. Hasaka is giving anesthesia and instructing two Vietnamese in anesthesia. He is also helping with administrative duties.

Our house is located 5 blocks from the hospital and we have a car (International Scout) to drive to work. Miss Wilson and I are sharing the house with 2 USAID nurses. There is plenty of room and by VN standards the house is a good one. We are having problems with the electricity and water — in that they are both off sometimes for 12 or 24 hours at a time. The local "power and light company" turns the generators down too low and blows the fuses. We have obtained a good supply of candles, flashlights and one battle lantern. Now if we could just find a way to keep the food from spoiling. We have two very willing maids who speak only Vietnamese. Most of our food is obtained from the local economy since the nearest commissary is in Saigon. We can get some canned goods through supply channels but it is difficult.

We have made several interesting rural health visits. One was down river to a navy junk base. The medical officer, Miss Wilson and I held sick call and were almost overrun by the villagers. We saw 200 patients and it was a very long hot day. The afternoon temperature has been between 115 and 120. We are told that this is a prelude to the monsoon.

Sincerely,
Winifred Copeland

Seven months after arriving in Vietnam, Copeland's team was withdrawn from Rach Gia. "We were very much surrounded by the Viet Cong down there, and there was a lot of harassment at night. It wasn't a very safe place for a group of medics to be because we had no defense. In fact, there was a problem keeping track of us administratively. Most people were surprised to learn that we were even there, way down in the Delta."

When Not to Wear a Flak Jacket

Dr. Stanley Bloustine well remembers his orientation into Navy life in 1967. "We had to show up about three or four days early and they told us how to wear the uniform, how to salute, a little bit about the rank structure, but it was very informal." After serving his general surgery residency at Naval Hospital Chelsea, Massachusetts, the neophyte surgeon heard about the MILPHAP program. He applied and was accepted. In November 1967 he went to the National Naval Medical Center in Bethesda, Maryland, for two weeks of training. He then packed his bags and flew to Vietnam as a member of Field Advisory Team 2. His assignment was a Vietnamese hospital at Hoi An, the capital of Quang Nam Province, about 25 miles south of Danang.

I stayed overnight in Saigon at some officers' club. At that time, the airline that flew us around was Air America, which was run by the CIA. The next day I flew up to Danang. I spent a day there in-processing, and then the Medical Service Corps officer with my team met me at Danang airbase and drove me in a jeep to Hoi An.

I didn't feel any sense of dread. I was just trying to understand what was going on and trying to adapt and figure out what I was going to do.

Hoi An was a nice little town. The American contingent was in two sections — a little Army post and the State Department compound. Initially, they had room for me in the latter. I had a private room with air conditioning. We joined the mess there with a monthly fee, had Vietnamese cooks, and ate very well. I was not a State Department employee but was still in the Navy and wore my Navy uniform which looked like utilities.[9]

We didn't have a bad time while we were there but had to play by the rules. The rule was that you didn't go out at night outside your town. The Vietnamese army guarded the main roads into town and they put up barbed wire. You would have been stupid to be on the roads at night. And you would be stupid to be on the roads before an American or Vietnamese unit swept the road for mines every morning. But once that was done, it was pretty safe. I never felt like I was in imminent danger. There was always that possibility of risk being in a war zone. Some of it was probably fatalism. You had to feel that way or you'd be paralyzed and never do anything. We took reasonable precautions and went about our business.

When we took the jeep to Danang or a village somewhere, we didn't go until the road had been swept, and then you took your weapon and helmet with you. Back then you didn't wear your flak jacket; you sat on your flak jacket. The likelihood of running over a mine was greater than getting shot by a sniper. You figured that if you were going to get hit by a mine, the fragments were going to come up through the jeep. So if you had another layer — your flak vest — there was a greater chance of having lesser injuries.

When I made trips by jeep from Hoi An, I was armed with a standard M16A1 and a .45 pistol even though I never had any training with these weapons until I got to Vietnam. In fact, I never fired either one of them in my life. One day they took us to a firing range near the beach. We were very near the South China Sea. A soldier or a Marine — I can't remember which — showed us how to fire the weapons and clear them if they jammed. That was our only training. We got to fire a couple of clips and that was it. Thank God, I never had to fire my weapon in anger.

The hospital we were assigned to was a Third World hospital staffed by Vietnamese army doctors. They took care of South Vietnamese soldiers in a separate ward, and we took care of the civilians and the North Vietnamese and Viet Cong prisoners of war who had been wounded. The Vietnamese doctors, because they were paid so little, worked in the Vietnamese army hospital in the morning and then had their own private practices in the afternoon. Even though the Vietnamese ran the hospital, we had very little contact with them, which was one of the problems I had to deal with.

We saw some serious cases but not really the worst ones. If those serious cases were South Vietnamese soldiers, they were helicoptered out to the hospitals in Danang. If the critically injured were Vietnamese civilians, they weren't going to make it to our hospital. They would either die on the spot or an American unit nearby might helicopter them to a hospital in Danang. We got the lesser injuries.

A young man and a young woman did our translating for us. Even though I had an interpreter assigned to me, the language problem always contributed to misunderstandings between us and the Vietnamese. I'm not very good at languages. A young man from the State Department was with me, and I paid a Vietnamese to come and give us language lessons. I picked some up so I could survive but it was not much more than "hello," "goodbye," and "where's the bathroom." At least I tried. Unfortunately, a lot of people never tried.

The hospital had an OR and we were able to do certain types of surgery. Because I was the only surgeon, even though I had just over a year of training plus an internship, I did the C-sections and helped the midwives with difficult deliveries.

Every province was quite different. It depended on who was there. An Army MILPHAP was in one of the provinces in the south of I Corps. Their team leader was a fully trained general surgeon who had come out of retirement and was in his mid– or late 50s. He had gray hair and was very experienced. The Vietnamese have a lot of respect for the elderly. So this guy was able to get their attention much better than a young nobody like I was. They listened to him. He did a lot more cases and seemed to have a better relationship with his Vietnamese counterparts than I ever did. So the situation was very different from province to province.

The Vietnamese doctors were very proud. They had been trained in the French and American literature. But the main point was they felt fully trained and that we had nothing to teach them. They felt they were just as good as we were. They knew everything plus it was their country and thought there was no value in cooperating with us. Not too long before I left, I finally got the big shots to get together and confer so we could somehow collaborate. But it was a struggle the whole time I was there.

Occasionally our people would go out on MEDCAPs [Medical Civil Action Program]. They were purely American run and that was one of the problems I was trying to address. The Americans looked down on the Vietnamese. I had so much trouble trying to convince them that the Vietnamese people were not stupid. I'd tell them, "Listen, they know we Americans know how to do things. They also know that we've got lots of medicines and fancy stuff and we know how to deliver care." The Americans would go out on these MEDCAPs only with their own people and give out a bunch of pills and candy to the children. Maybe they'd find a couple of kids with something that might require an operation. So they'd take the kids back, do what had to be done, and send them home. They thought they were doing a wonderful job but they never included the Vietnamese health care system. I'd try to tell them our job was to convince people that the Vietnamese government could take care of them, not that we could take care of them. But I was never successful. Resistance came mainly from our own people. The other side was not the Vietnamese army doctors; it was the Vietnamese civilian health care system — the nurses and other medical staff. They had a whole infrastructure of their own we tended not to use.

Even though I didn't go out on MEDCAPs, I visited villages. I had a jeep most of the time or I'd ride on Army helicopters or Air America helicopters. We visited outlying American units

A Navy physician examines South Vietnamese villagers during a MEDCAP (Medical Civil Action Program) operation (courtesy Bob Ingraham).

During a visit to their village, a Navy dentist teaches Vietnamese children the proper way to brush (BUMED Archives).

and talked to them about public health or visited Vietnamese village chiefs. We went out as much as we could. I didn't want to stay in Hoi An all the time.

We did our best to support the Vietnamese. The Marines had a field hospital up in Danang and, as there was less need for this hospital, they closed it. The Marines had truckloads and warehouses full of IVs, surgical supplies, etc. I knew they weren't going to drag it all back to the States so I talked with people through the Marine chain. They supported me and brought these supplies to us. In fact, they delivered truckloads of stuff to us but it was stolen. I'm sure some of it went to the Viet Cong or the black market. We used to say that we were trying to win hearts and minds. And the Army and Marines were saying, 'You drag them by the balls and their hearts and minds will follow.' Those two philosophies were always at odds with each other. Unfortunately, neither worked very well.

"Charlie Said, 'Hello'"

James Soliday grew up in Punxsutawney, Pennsylvania, where the groundhog seeks its shadow every February 2nd. He joined the Navy in 1963 and, after boot camp and corps school at Great Lakes Recruit Training Command in Illinois was sent to Naval Hospital, Portsmouth, New Hampshire. His next assignment took him to Camp Lejeune, North Carolina, where he attended the Field Medical Service School. Following graduation, the young hospital corpsman went with his new unit, the 1st Battalion, 8th Marines, 2nd Marine Division to the Dominican Republic when the U.S. intervened in what was a short but chaotic civil war. "That was in May, 1965, after just learning to wear a green uniform and carry a Unit One [medical bag]. It was an experience."

After dodging bullets in Santo Domingo for several months, Soliday reenlisted then volunteered for duty in Vietnam. His new orders were to the Navy MILPHAP Team Five. It was February 1967.

The team leadership consisted of three physicians and a Medical Service Corps officer, then Lt.(j.g.) Richard Gutshall, who had gone ahead of us to Vietnam to make way for the team. The rest of us went to Bethesda [National Naval Medical Center] for a three- or four-week indoctrination provided by previous MILPHAP team members. They gave us a good brief on how we would fit in, what we would be doing, for whom we would be working. We had three weeks of language training. They had actual Vietnamese instructors, and we spent many hours a day learning basic Vietnamese.

There were, however, a couple of glitches. We were the second Navy Team Five that went into Chau Doc Province. The Navy was not the only service that had these medical teams. The Army and Air Force also had MILPHAP teams. The first teams that went over in 1966 and 1967 worked strictly for the USAID Program. They had no military connotation whatsoever. In fact, the team members wore civilian clothes. When it came time for our team to go, the Department of Defense decided that we would go as a military team and coordinate our efforts with USAID. But it was decided that we would stay with the MACV [Military Advisory Command, Vietnam] advisory groups. In our case this was the MACV Advisory Group 64 and Special Forces Group 5.

The other thing that was comical—and even embarrassing to us—was the Vietnamese we had learned. We found out after we got there that we had learned the North Vietnamese dialect. The instructors had been from the north. The people we encountered could understand us, but by the way we were pronouncing words, they knew that we had learned our language from northerners. "Who are you people?" they probably thought. Eventually we learned their dialect.

The area we were in—Chau Doc Province near the Cambodian border—was predominantly Chinese with very few Vietnamese. That was because the area was interlaced with waterways, and the Chinese congregated in those areas and used their sampans. They were even more aware of us pronouncing words in the northern dialect.

Of course, we were never relieved of our military duties. If we were caught in a situation where living with the Special Forces and the ARVN would bring us under attack—and our military duties were required, we provided our expertise. But our primary duty was to work with and develop the civilian hospitals, first aid stations, and midwife groups throughout our area of assignment. In our case, it covered about 100 square kilometers [39 square miles] and about three of what we would call "counties." Under us was one major hospital in Chau Doc. Since Chau Doc was a province, it had a province medical chief, who would be like a state health director. Four or five small towns within our area of responsibility had smaller medical activities and had sub-medical chiefs.

Eleven other MILPHAP teams stretched from the DMZ to the bottom of Vietnam, but my group, Team Five, was broken off into two groups. Initially, Team Five had three physicians. One had a general surgical background, the other two were general medical officers. We also had a Medical Service Corps [MSC] officer and a leading chief petty officer, plus 10 corpsmen and one dental technician, all with FMF [Fleet Marine Force] backgrounds. Also within the team were some specialties consisting of one lab tech, an OR tech, a preventive medicine tech, and the dental tech who had an operative background and had worked in operating rooms with dental surgeons. And, like myself, there were three general FMF corpsmen as part of the team.

Because the Mekong River split the two provinces we were responsible for, our team was split into two groups. One physician and two corpsmen went downriver from us. Two physicians, the MSC officer, the chief, the remaining corpsmen and dental tech were in the Chau Doc team. Within this team, we split out. The two physicians, the MSC officer, the chief, the OR tech, the lab tech, the dental tech, and at least one general corpsman stayed in Chau Doc. Two small towns had rather large ambulatory care type of facilities. These towns also had splinter groups of the Army advisory teams to which they assigned each of us team members. That's how I ended up in the village of Tan Chau.

This was very rural and the major problem was the poor roads. In summer it was dry enough for us to travel the riverbeds by jeep; during the monsoons we traveled by boat. Those same roads during the dry season became rivers during the monsoons. The houses during the dry season were up high on stilts; during the wet season, the water was right to the floor. I seldom traveled to our team site at Chau Doc. If I did, for safety, it was by boat. Our location, where the Mekong River comes through the Cambodian border, was a main supply line for the Viet Cong and the North Vietnamese, and these rural areas away from the towns were well traveled by both. Consequently, we did very little traveling by road. Our main transportation by water was a little 17- or 18-foot Boston Whaler type boat with a 75 hp Evinrude. It belonged to the Special Forces we were attached to.

Technically, we weren't supposed to be armed because medical personnel weren't required to carry anything other than a .45 sidearm but, as MILPHAP team members, we were issued M1 carbines.

I had no special status being a corpsman. The collar device we wore at that time was a shield with a caduceus on it, the symbol of the medical profession. Unless you were right on top of a guy, you couldn't tell he was a medic. If the Viet Cong saw a guy carrying a Unit One and a .45, they knew he was a corpsman. The radio antenna and the people with the .45s were the first ones they looked for. I didn't carry a pistol but did carry a carbine.

Even though security was really tight, I don't think it deterred our work. Because once we got wherever we were going and began working with the midwives or the first aid stations, it was just everyday business. It was the traveling part when we got super cautious.

When I was in Tan Chau, I had the medical advisory responsibility for the Tan Chau medical district. I had a civilian counterpart, the associate health director, who ran the local clinic. He also had the responsibility for about six or eight first aid stations and a couple of midwife stations scattered up and down the river. We made frequent visits to them by boat. I traveled with my counterpart, often one of his assistants—an interpreter—who was usually an ARVN soldier who was assigned to me, and frequently with one member of the Army MACV [Military Assistance Command, Vietnam] team. It was safe travel and we had no problems.

As I previously stated, the team split into two groups. The group that remained at Chau Doc was further broken down. One member of the team was sent to Tan Chau, another to the little village of Tinh-Bien, and still another to the village of Triton. I originally stayed in Chau Doc with the main team and worked in setting up the supply system with my counterparts in the Vietnamese civilian hospital. They had received about four huge Connex boxes[10] from the USAID program filled with hospital supplies that were sitting in the backyard of the hospital, rusting. A whole hospital unit was contained in those boxes. You name it, it was in there. Everything from the OR to the lab, to x-ray, ward furniture, pills—everything. The outside of the boxes had begun to deteriorate but fortunately everything inside was in great shape. My main function was to teach my counterpart in the supply system that those were good supplies, that we needed to get them out, get them in place, and account for them. We needed to set up a stock system for those supplies—everything we do in the military system. We didn't have a problem. They were very receptive people to work with. As luck would have it, they were also reserves in the Vietnamese Army.

A typical day for our MILPHAP team varied depending where you were. In Chau Doc, you got up around 5:30, 5:45. You cleaned up and went to breakfast. Both locations had a mess hall of sorts manned by Vietnamese. All our cooking was done by Vietnamese men or women. Usually they were pretty good meals. We drew rations in kind—money. So they collected from us and then they would go to the commissary at Can Tho and buy pretty good products for preparing meals. So we would have a meal and count the bugs in the bread. They made loaves of French bread—bear in mind the French background in Vietnam. The majority of the Vietnamese who cooked did so in the French culinary tradition. All the flour had bugs in it and they didn't bother to take them out. It was protein. The big joke of the day at both breakfast or the evening meal was to put your bread up to the light and see who had the most bugs.

As a team, we were also part of the military group that lived in that barracks. Usually we had a group meeting with the Army around 7:00 or 7:15 just to get a brief for the day on any incidents in the area or scuttlebutt about movements. We didn't want any surprises.

By 7:30 or 7:45 we were in our three vehicles, which were jeeps and an old French personnel carrier, headed for the civilian hospital. After arriving at the hospital, each of us had his own area we were responsible for. The doctors would make rounds on the wards, check the surgical schedule for the day, and I'd take off for supply to see what was coming in or what we needed to order. If there wasn't much going on in supply, I'd make rounds with the doctor or go see if I could help out in sick call. It was a normal, routine medical day once we got to the hospital. It was like being in any Navy facility here.

But there were challenges. When we first got to Chau Doc, even though a team had been ahead of us, the very first ward we walked on had no beds, just bamboo mats on the floor. The shutters were all closed; it was very dark. The whole family was there. The Vietnamese tradition is that if you are admitted to the hospital, the whole family comes. If they owned cows and chickens, they also came so they wouldn't get stolen — although they were outside the hospital building in the yard. Inside was the whole family group with the cooking pot and whatever else because they took care of that person. Anyway, we got that straightened out.

But that hospital needed some corrections. Before we arrived on the scene, they were using the same medicine cup to give patients cough syrup. They had been using the same needle to give shots — over and over again.

This had us puzzled. A MILPHAP team had been here before us, and we couldn't understand why these unsanitary practices were still going on. We figured they were resorting to such procedures because they had been unable to get supplies on a regular basis.

Anyway, we broke open the Connex boxes and inside were beds to equip entire wards. We finally convinced them through the head doctor of the hospital to give us one ward to set up to show them correct methods. We screened the windows, opened the shutters, put up the beds, put on mattresses, got medicine carts out, and got sterile techniques going. We trained the two nurses that you don't use the same needles, don't use the same medicine cup.

We got that working pretty well. The hardest part was getting the families out of there. By tradition, they still felt it was their responsibility to be with the ill family member 24 hours a day and to prepare their food, take care of the bed, and get their drinks, etc. I don't think we ever really changed that. But at least we finally got them to leave their cows and chickens at home.

The OR in that hospital was antiquated. The physicians in surgery were lucky in that the head Vietnamese OR nurse trained on the SS *Hope*.[11] Somehow she had managed to get out of Vietnam and get assigned to the *Hope*. She had spent a year on the hospital ship and learned English very well. She was just a super OR nurse. The problem was that she was having trouble like we were in getting members of the Vietnamese medical community to understand sterile technique such as reuse of instruments and gloving, etc. As our physicians got more and more involved with surgery, their physicians got less and less involved.

We had an OR tech on the team, but the rest of us filled in whenever we had to. When it got really busy, all of us would take a turn scrubbing and doing what we had to. The uniqueness of the team was that we did everything, whether it was lab, x-ray, OR, sick call, supply, ward rounds, standing watch on the "preemies," etc. We had nobody backing us up. We didn't have another medical team somewhere to come in and replace us when we got tired. We were it. So it behooved us to train the Vietnamese as quickly as we could, but it took nearly the entire year we were there to get that done.

One of the other matters we got deeply involved — for our own sanity and well-being —

was with the orphanages. Chau Doc had two very large Catholic orphanages. They were run-down and unkempt with no running water and no bathroom facilities. The kitchen area was just a rat pit. It was because nobody cared for these kids. Most of them were Eurasian and they were considered outcasts. Early on in our tour, we traveled by one of those orphanages every day. As a team, we decided to do something. We spent every off-duty minute of time at the orphanage. We eventually convinced the USAID program to build them a new one.

From June of 1967 when we arrived in the country until October, the situation was very serene. We did our day-to-day work, taking care of hospitals and working with our people. There was little combat action in our immediate area. Occasionally we treated wounded civilians from the outlands where they had stepped on a mine or got hit by a stray shell. All of us had kind of a complacent attitude. And then on Columbus Day [1967] at 3 o'clock in the morning, "Char-lie" [the VC] said, "Hello."

The Special Forces compound, on which we were berthed, was an old French hotel. It sat right along the Bassac river. Charlie set up across the river and gave us reveille. Rockets, every-thing, you name it. Several Army guys were killed. I was the only one of my team who was injured. Charlie, knowing where the communications center was in the building, threw a rocket through the window and knocked out the two communicators and our communications. They also zeroed in on the fuel tanks. At that time, the compound was rather open. A barbed wire fence was strung around the compound, but we had very few sandbags and only a couple of bunkers that you could get into. After that attack, we got massive sandbag walls. But that night was hell. The attack lasted about two and a half hours with constant small arms, mortar, and rocket fire.

We couldn't set up any kind of defense line because we were pinned down and able only to return minimum fire and some mortars. We had no idea where they were across the river. It was just a matter of keeping our behinds down. What ultimately saved us was an aircraft called "Puff."[12] It took him awhile to get wherever he was to Chau Doc, but sometime around 5:00 or 5:15, Puff flew over. Shortly thereafter, all the incoming stopped. That was it. There were some serious wounds and deaths and a need for body bags.

I was with Col. Smith, CO of the compound, trying to make rounds when I got hit. I had a hard time keeping up with him because he was a big tall dude who could move fast. We came around a corner when a mortar shell went off, and it flipped me back against a wall. I didn't realize I was hit in the knee until the next morning. We were busy because the wounded were all over the place.

We finally got a couple of choppers in to get the medevacs out. As we sat there right after sunup trying to recap everything that had happened, one guy said, "What happened to your pants?" There was a little bit of blood dripping. It wasn't anything major, and it didn't require a medevac. We dug the fragment out, cleaned it up, and it healed up in about three weeks. It took that much time to clean up the compound, patch the windows, build the walls back up again, and replace all the tires that were shot out and fences that were torn up.

The Special Forces "snoopers," which were Vietnamese undercover, said it was a VC unit, a full company with some NVA [North Vietnamese Army] with them, but that was never confirmed. The snoopers found where they had been and they found blood, but never as much as a body.

After that, everybody became very guarded, suddenly realizing that life was fragile. This playpen we were in was not so serene. There were people around us who would do us harm. The complacency changed. The distance from the military compound where we stayed to the civil-ian hospital was about five kilometers [three miles] through back roads and streets of the town. We used to think nothing about getting into a vehicle and not paying attention to what was going on. But now we looked around to see what might be there. However, it didn't reach the point where we became paranoid or forgot we were there to work with the civilian community.

Our relations with the community were very good. The MILPHAP team's most dangerous time was when we were intermingled with the U.S. military. To our way of thinking, our safest time was when we were at the civilian hospital because we didn't know who we were taking care of. The patients didn't wear uniforms. We didn't know who might be Charlie. We took care of everybody. And we learned through our interpreters that we were the good guys. The Viet Cong didn't see us as a threat. We were a plus. They didn't mess with the MILPHAP teams. Sometimes when attacks were going on around us in the town we were ideal sitting ducks in that hospital. They never messed with the team as long as we were taking care of the people. If we were on a convoy or if we were back at the military compound and they happened to attack it, then we were vulnerable.

The teams before us wore civvies; we had to be in uniform while working. We were the medics. We took care of the Viet Cong as well as the good guys. Unless one of our interpreters, one of the police, or one of the Vietnamese soldiers pointed somebody out, we didn't know the difference. And it really wasn't our job to determine who was who. It was kind of an unwritten law, according to our interpreters, that the MILPHAP teams did not get messed with. Every opportunity was there because we were unguarded, except for the little weapons we carried. We were in an ideal situation for any kind of terrorism — hand grenades, shootings, you name it. The night of the attack, we just happened to be on the compound the night when Charlie decided the Special Forces needed a lesson.

In December 1967, I went out to relieve the corpsman at Tan Chau when he became ill, developing some problems with blood clots in his leg. I can't recall the diagnosis but it had something to with the tropics and humidity. Anyhow, they medevaced him out, and I replaced him at the Tan Chau compound, which had a small MACV team of five Army guys and myself. I was the only American medical person in the area to support the U.S. forces and the civilians.

Tan Chau had a small ambulatory care clinic where my work was less involved. I had ample time for teaching and implementing medical/supply systems. I took care of sick call with the military and worked with the civilians. I also completed training two Vietnamese nurses so they could help with sick call on the military compound. That freed me up so I could go back to doing the job I was supposed to do. That took a couple of months but it was worthwhile.

Caught Between the Villagers and the VC

Cmdr. James Ryscamp was head of Surgical Team Alpha stationed aboard the amphibious assault vessels USS Okinawa *(LPH-3) and USS* Iwo Jima *(LPH-2). The four ships in the group included the World War II–era aircraft carrier USS* Princeton, *which had just been recently redesignated amphibious assault carrier (LPH-5). "We had a 300-bed hospital on the helicopter carrier, and I had 11 doctors and 30 corpsmen with my surgical team."*

Cruising off the northern coast of South Vietnam, these ships were home to a battalion of Marines who conducted periodic amphibious landings in support of operations in I Corps and II Corps.

"When they conducted an amphibious assault, they put all the Marines on the hangar bay to pick up their ammunition and weapons. Then they went up on the flight deck and boarded helicopters — four or five per helicopter and fully combat-laden. Then that helicopter lifted off from the flight deck and cruised around in the sky overhead until all the helicopters were loaded and airborne. In the meantime, the task group loaded their Marines aboard landing craft. It was all timed so that those landing craft hit the beach at the same time the helicopters landed in zones inland from the beach. With Marines on the beach and Marines in the landing zones, they'd squeeze together. And everything in that circle was dead meat."

Dr. Ryscamp and his medical personnel had treated all the casualties. If there was a lull in the

*action, he occasionally requested the commodore's permission to go ashore and conduct a MED-
CAP (Medical Civil Action Program). He and his hand-picked team were then helicoptered ashore
to bring modern American medicine to yet another Vietnamese village.*

We had a Marine sergeant who acted as an interpreter and could speak Vietnamese, but
we found that sometimes they didn't want us there. One time we were heading for a village to
do a MEDCAP and some villagers met us before we got there and told us to go back. We asked
why. They took us a bit further and showed us a pregnant girl hanging in a tree from all four
limbs. The Viet Cong had slashed her belly and her baby was dangling from her abdomen by
the umbilical cord. They said, "Don't come. If you do, this is what will happen to us."

The villagers were stuck. We'd come through and treat them nicely, and then the VC would
return and kick their butts because the villagers had been friendly to us. They were caught in
the middle and just couldn't win.

When we were able to enter a village, we saw a lot of skin diseases. Most of the people just
needed to be cleansed. We gave them soap but they wouldn't wash themselves; instead they
washed their hooches [thatched huts] with it. They didn't understand what soap was for.

Occasionally, we encountered some interesting cases. On one MEDCAP, we found a girl
who had been shot from the side and the bullet had gone through her eye, the root of her nose,
and out the other eye. Both eyeballs were destroyed and she was totally blind. Her only medical care had been a German MEDCAP team that came through about every six weeks. The German medical personnel just wrapped a piece of material around her head and over her eyes.
When I saw this, I suggested we take her back to the ship and clean up her infection and debride
all the dead tissue. She couldn't go on living with draining pus out of her eye sockets.

We had to get permission from her mother to take her to the ship. She was 19 or 20. The
mother consented only if her 12-year-old sister could go along with her. The ship's company
called the sister "Baby san." We took her older sister to the operating room several times and
debrided everything. Then I removed all the epithelium from the inside of her eyelids because
if you bury epithelial tissue, a cyst will form and become infected again. So I had to remove all
the skin lining inside the eyelid. Then I sewed her eyelids shut permanently so that she wouldn't
have to live with pus draining continually.

We cleared up the infection and, before we took her back to her village, I gave her a little
transistor radio I bought in the ship's store. She would sit on her bed holding that little radio
to her ear. I don't know whether you've ever heard Vietnamese music. It's a real monotonous
sounding music that Americans couldn't listen to. But she enjoyed it.

Then we brought her back to her mother who had a house that was maybe six feet square
and raised about three feet off the ground. The flies were just everywhere because the people
nailed fish to boards outside their hooches to dry them.

I went back to see the girl about a month afterward and found that she no longer had her
radio. Our Marine interpreter asked her where it was. She had sold it for rice. It had been such
a pleasure to her because she was blind. Yet she couldn't keep it because it was more important
to eat than to have pleasure.

We treated another girl whose name was An Hoa. I'll never forget her. She was a sweet girl
but very shy at first. She had had her leg blown off just below the knee and it had healed by scar
contracture. My orthopedic surgeon, Lt. Eric Widdel, and I knew that her little village was all
sand. Can you imagine walking on the beach with crutches and every time you put the crutch
down, it would dig into the sand? Well, that girl struggled with those crutches. We brought her
back to the ship and made a device to help her. Down in the hangar bay's machine shop we
found everything you could imagine. They had leather and every other kind of material. We
used a crutch for the main strength of the apparatus. Then we made a plaster mold of her stump
and a leather harness to that shape so that she could strap it onto her leg and around her waist.

We then attached a boot to the bottom of the crutch. It was a real crude thing but An Hoa could strap it on and walk without using crutches.

I wish I could have taken those girls back home with me. I don't know what happened to them. They probably ended up in prostitution in order to eat.

We conducted four or five MEDCAPs while I was in Vietnam, but I don't know if we were very successful.

4

MEDICAL BATTALIONS IN A FRONTLESS WAR

On 8 March 1965, the first U.S. combat troops arrived in Vietnam to defend the Danang airfield. These forces were the Marines of the 9th Marine Expeditionary Brigade. Marines were soon deployed to Chu Lai, located about 50 miles south of Danang, to protect the airstrip. They were also sent to Phu Bai, about 40 miles north near the city of Hue, to defend its airfield.

It was not long before the Marines shifted from defense to offense, actively patrolling the countryside and searching for the enemy. With a force of 3,500 troops now on the ground and escalation of the war seeming to be a foregone conclusion, medical assistance became a high priority. The 3rd Medical Battalion would provide that support.

In 1965, the 3rd Marine Division consisted of three infantry regiments, an artillery regiment, support forces, and its own medical support organization — the 3rd Medical Battalion. Each of the infantry regiments had a collecting and clearing company plus one at the Division headquarters. The collecting and clearing company was intended to be mobile so it could move within its respective infantry regiment. Because the war in Vietnam was essentially a "frontless" conflict with little movement, the collecting and clearing companies remained stationary. These companies traditionally were not designed as definitive treatment facilities, but as then 3rd Medical Battalion commanding officer Cmdr. Almon Wilson pointed out, these were the only companies currently available to assign to Danang, Chu Lai, and Phu Bai where airfields needed protection.

Despite their limitations at the outset, within a few short months these collecting and clearing companies had, by necessity, become actual hospitals. Charlie Company organized at Danang, Bravo at Chu Lai, and Alpha at Phu Bai. During the early summer of 1965, equipment and supplies for Delta Company remained in storage in Danang.

* * *

Almon C. Wilson was a Navy man through and through. In 1944, a year after having enlisted as an apprentice seaman, Wilson was commissioned an ensign. In January 1945, he joined the crew of USS Liddle *(APD-60) and saw action in the Pacific. His service as a line officer and his thorough understanding of the ways of the operational Navy put him in good stead as he made the transition to the Medical Corps in 1952. After several assignments in Navy medical facilities, Wilson (now with a medical degree) received orders for his most challenging job yet: commanding officer of the 3rd Medical Battalion in Danang, South Vietnam. The creation of C Medical Company, "Charlie Med," was Cmdr. Wilson's task from the very beginning.*

We flew to Vietnam in a C-130 that was loaded with supplies and equipment. We sat along the side of this airplane with our knees tucked up under our chin and our legs straddling cargo chains that were tied so tight that you could almost hear them sing if you touched them.

In the middle of July [1965] in Vietnam — at least in the northern part — it was hot, it was humid, and it was dusty. The dust was a fine red powder, and it stuck to any wet surface. If you perspired a little bit, you turned dusty red very quickly. We landed on the Danang airstrip, and as we flew in there and looked out the window to see what the terrain looked like, it was absolutely gorgeous. Danang sits on Tourane Bay, surrounded by these lush fields and tree-covered mountains in the background. We saw China Beach — the beautiful white beach — and the blue water and the sunshine. Then looking at the airstrip, one saw all the scars of ammunition dumps, refuse dumps, motor pool parks, and the helicopter landing pads that kind of destroyed the landscape.

When we arrived in Danang, we were met by a man who I came to know much better. He was a black Marine private, and he was one of the most lighthearted and happy persons I have ever met in my whole life. He always had a broad smile on his face. He was a very willing, hard-working kind of fellow. He just happened to be there when we landed, and he drove us out to the camp. It might be interesting to note that the transient barracks at the time consisted of one GP [general purpose] tent on the edge of the airstrip. It was so filthy dirty and dusty that I don't see how anybody could live in it.

At any rate, this happy young private drove us in a "Mighty Mite," which is sort of a diminutive jeep, out to the foot of Hill 268 — recently a rice paddy. There I cast my eye on what was to be my home for the next year. It was a group of tents, most of which were on the ground in the former rice paddy. A few of them had been framed out. The headquarters tent and two operating rooms had been framed out. The operating rooms had been lined with plywood and had air conditioners in them. That was all. These were small operating rooms. They were based on a GPM tent, a general purpose medium tent, which is 16 by 32 feet. That is a poor dimension for an operating room. Operating rooms are much handier if they are about 20 feet square. At any rate, while there was a lot of square footage in them, they weren't as useful as the versions later developed.

Throughout the first three or four months in Danang, we were constantly beset by shelter problems. The tents we had were old, worn out, and decaying in the heat and the rain. It was a constant problem to get materials to improve the facilities. The technique that we employed was to take a tent that was pitched on the ground and frame it out with 2 by 4s and build a plywood deck, then put the tent back over it. When we had the screen, we put screens on the outside of them and eventually replaced the tents with corrugated tin roofs. The problem was always the availability of lumber and screen and tin roofing. We went through all sorts of gyrations to get these materials.

The staff at Danang at the time consisted of about nine medical officers. Everybody slept in tents. Most everybody slept on a cot that was sitting on the ground. There was, of course, no air conditioning. It was hot and dusty. We ate out of mess kits. We did our own laundry. The shower consisted of a 55-gallon drum with a small pipe with a valve on it in the bottom. Water ran into a large fruit juice can with holes punched in the bottom to give the effect of spray. To make this thing work, you took a five-gallon water can and carried it up the steps that were attached to the support for this barrel. You dumped the water in and went down and took a shower. We did not have hot water for nearly a year.

Food was remarkably good, considering the difficulties that the cooks faced. We had a lot of B rations— the canned rations, as opposed to C rations— the dry ones that nobody liked. Eventually we had a lot of A rations, which are fresh-frozen foods.

During those early days of our time in Vietnam, supplies were very, very low. For example, after having been in Vietnam about a month or a little bit longer, I went back up to Okinawa to see if I couldn't do something about our supply plight. We were having terrible difficulties getting enough supplies. When I left, there was something in the order of a day and a half of fuel for the aircraft and the motor transports. This was for the entire division. I had two days of food and two days of ammunition. They got to the point eventually where they were flying 105mm ammunition from Okinawa down to Vietnam to keep the artillery supplied, which is, of course, a very, very wasteful use of aircraft. But the situation was that tenuous.

Fortunately, we didn't have a lot of casualties at the outset. The war was just starting. We would get an occasional group in that had been hit by some mortar fire or had been involved in an accident. You have to remember that when you go to war, you take all the non-hostile kinds of injuries and illnesses with you. You also pick up the illnesses which are inherent in being in the field—dysentery and diarrhea in particular. But the hernias, hemorrhoids, common colds, pneumonias, sprained ankles, automobile accident injuries—and particularly jeep accidents were all there. History from earlier conflicts repeated itself. In the postwar analysis, we learned that over half the admissions to hospitals had nothing to do with combat injuries. These admissions were from illnesses and injuries relating to non-hostile acts.

We were going through the typical learning curve of young surgeons in a war. It has to be said that when each war comes along a new population of surgeons has to learn war surgery. Fortunately or unfortunately—however you wish to put it—in the civilian sector few injuries are true counterparts of combat injuries. That may sound funny but it's true. True combat injuries, by and large, are due to high-velocity missiles.

Most of the surgeons were lieutenant commanders. I was a commander at the time. As it turned out, I did very little surgery personally. I was much too busy with the logistics of keeping the commands running and various hospitals running. We had surgeons to do the job and do it well.

The morale was tremendous. I can never recall ever having to call a surgeon or any of the

Corpsmen hustle to retrieve incoming wounded (BUMED Archives).

other physicians, or a corpsman, or a Marine to go to work. By the time the second helicopter had landed, even in the dead of night, the entire camp would be on its feet and everybody at his duty station. The Marines would be out on the airstrip waiting to unload the helicopters to act as stretcher-bearers, or they would load the medevac birds if we were shipping patients out.

When the patient entered the system at the helicopter pad, he went one of two directions. He went immediately to the place where we did the acute care, the so-called "shock and resuscitation tent," or he went to a holding area for the less severely wounded. In these locations patients were examined, evaluated, and moved to the proper area for either minor surgery or put in the priority system for major surgery. In these holding areas they had their x-rays and laboratory studies completed and had intravenous fluids started. Once the patients entered the system at these two portals, the flow pattern was such that they would never have to backtrack. It was forward progress all the way.

We had 75 beds, but didn't have enough people to run 75 beds. So when we got individuals who were badly hurt and couldn't go back to duty, we would keep them long enough to make sure they were stable. We would then evacuate them to Clark Air Base Hospital [Philippines], which was 800 miles away.

As the situation progressed and we got busier, we very frequently had to move patients immediately after they were operated on. We had insufficient beds to keep them, and we didn't know what the next hour was going to bring. We didn't know how many more casualties we were to get. So one of our experiences was standing on the airstrip during the monsoon season, watching incoming patients being off-loaded from helicopters, and then those same helicopters being used to move patients down to the airstrip for evacuation.

We got to know a lot about helicopters in the sense that we could identify them from afar, and on occasion we could identify the nature of the problem. It's a fact of life that the fastest way a helicopter can travel is to tip up on its nose and fly down at treetop level where the air is densest. When we heard helicopters coming in making the very characteristic noise of a high-powered, full-throttle approach at low level — and it's a very distinctive sound — we knew full well that there was somebody very critically injured aboard.

When helicopters landed, they were on the ground in less than 20 seconds. We had people always available to take patients from the helicopters. Standard procedure was for somebody to take the stretcher under an arm and rush out to the helicopter with another stretcher-bearer. They would get the patient out of the helicopter, put the fresh stretcher in, and move the patient into the shock and resuscitation area. The helicopter could then leave, and this was a matter of 20 seconds if just one patient was involved.

We did not have radio communication with the helicopters at our station at the time. So the only notification we had usually was the helicopter landing. On quite a number of occasions, we would get casualties and the division would not know that there had been an action in the field.

Typically, a Marine was wounded, say, one or two or three hours before we received him. Upon entering the hospital system, that wounded Marine was resuscitated, underwent a three- or four-hour operation, came out from under anesthesia, and within an hour or two could be in an airplane headed for Clark Air Base.

This was possible for several reasons. First, the Marines were tough. They were young and healthy — pretty rugged kids. Second, we were able to resuscitate them adequately. We had enough fluids and blood so we could restore their vital systems promptly. Third, as long as they came out from anesthesia without any difficulties with their breathing and their blood pressures steady and stable, it was a golden time to send them. This was true because they would travel before they had time to develop any complications like pneumonia or atelectasis [collapsed lung].

Our batting average for keeping patients alive was very good. Our analysis showed that if a patient got to us alive, he had a 98 percent chance of living—at least to get out of our shop. Now, having said that, we understood full well that we were shipping some desperately injured people. We knew that what we did was only the first stopgap measure. Even though it was looked upon as being definitive in the sense that the patients were operated on and the holes in their intestines were patched up, it was only part of the solution. Problems of infection and other complications can always happen with patients. To the extent that that's true, we shipped a lot of potential problems, as well as some early successes.

What the surgeons and anesthesiologists had to learn very quickly is the concept of sorting and the difference between triage and sorting. "Triage" is a term that was brought into play when the world at large began to talk about nuclear casualties, which were estimated to be in the tens of thousands. In that case patients are going to die, and there is nothing in the world you can do about it. A triage has three categories: those expected to die, the seriously wounded, and the lightly wounded.

In the methodology that supports triage, the lightly wounded and the intermediately wounded are the ones who are treated because they are the greatest source of people who can continue to live and to help with the problem. Those who are over-radiated and cannot be expected to live will not have resources expended in their care. This is something very foreign to our nature, but this is the way the thinking is run in relation to triage.

In Vietnam, we did not use triage; we "sorted" patients. We sorted them out and took the most seriously wounded first. By this technique we applied the immediate emergency resuscitative and therapeutic measures earliest on the most severely wounded. It's of interest that an analysis of our first experience in the field of this shock and resuscitation team revealed that the team probably saved at least seven people from certain death by their prompt resuscitation efforts.

One of these was a colonel and operations officer for the 1st Marine Air Wing. He was hit in the left leg by a .50 caliber bullet and brought to us. The bullet blew out four inches on his left leg, left shin, and left both arteries open. The fellows [corpsmen] in the field put a tourniquet on him, gave him some blood and fluids, tied off his open arteries, and sent him on to the Danang hospital where he was resuscitated. He underwent amputation and even agreed to have it photographed.

In early December [1965], the Marines tangled with the VC in this operation called Harvest Moon.[1] We took a lot of casualties. We had so many casualties that on one occasion the field unit from the 3rd Medical Battalion, the shock and resuscitation team, saw 94 wounded in 24 hours. Seventy of those casualties were flown into Danang. Since we were unable to get to all of them with the necessary dispatch, some were sent immediately to Clark Air Base.

Harvest Moon had much to teach us. First of all, we had only two operating rooms. It's a fact that the average operation in a war zone such as that requires between three and four hours. You cannot count on doing more than six cases in one operating room in a 24-hour period. When you consider operating time, cleanup time, and preparation time for the ORs, you are lucky to get six patients through there. Some people even use five per operating room per day for planning.

It was obvious from our Harvest Moon experience that we did not have enough ORs to keep up with the heavy casualty load. I made this clear to General [Lewis] Walt. Almost immediately, three Quonset huts were made available to us in Danang, and several were made available to the other units—a couple down at Chu Lai and a couple up at Phu Bai. Phu Bai was a smaller unit, which used one of the Quonsets to incorporate two operating rooms, expanding them to three. The other Quonset hut was used for an intensive care ward. In Chu Lai they did essentially the same thing. In Danang we got three Quonsets; two of them were made into ORs, giving us a total of four, and the other one was made into an intensive care ward. The addition of those Quonset huts, which were air conditioned and plumbed, was an immense improvement in our capability. These improvements were stimulated by the Harvest Moon operation in which we were essentially overrun with casualties.

This was my first command, and I had much to learn. I had been around the Navy and had witnessed a lot. But once you're on the spot, you're the guy with the responsibility, particularly in a very unstable situation like this. It gives you time to think about the situation very critically, for example, ordinary circumstances. Do you let people go around armed? These are medical people. Should they be armed or should they not be armed? If they have guns are they well enough trained so that they are not going to shoot themselves in the foot or shoot each other? If they do not have weapons what do you do about the sniper problem? We had snipers around the camp all the time. During the first few weeks, we had to shut the lights out in the evenings because snipers out in the rice paddy would shoot at us in the glow of our own lights.

The Geneva Convention is quite clear in stating that medical personnel should not be armed, but it also says the enemy shouldn't shoot you. The upshot of the whole ordeal was that we did not require that medical personnel be armed in the camp, except under special circumstances. We did require that they be armed when they left the compound. I personally had a .38 revolver and I lived with it. I kept it under my pillow at night, and I wore it in my hip pocket all day because I was in and out of the camp all the time.

I used to do a lot of flying early on in the game because for a time Chu Lai had all the business. For some reason or other, the Chu Lai sector had more casualties in the first four months of my presence in Vietnam than anywhere else. Chu Lai would call in and say they had "x" number of casualties. We had only one anesthesia person in that camp, and the wounded always called for blood. The telephone connections were so bad that I sometimes could not get any more information than just the fact that Chu Lai had casualties and needed help. So sometimes in the middle of the night, I would get an anesthesiologist, pick up a load of blood, and get in the helicopter and fly down to Chu Lai to see what their situation was.

The standard doctrine at the time was for two helicopters to go. One was a gunship and the other one was the cargo bird, carrying the supplies and the people. The doctrine was that if your helicopter was shot down, the gunship would land right next to you. You just got out of one chopper and into the other — and don't bother with anything. Fortunately, we did not have any trouble, but it wasn't all that much fun flying at night over VC territory in a helicopter. It was never my idea of a Sunday afternoon excursion.

I got to Vietnam in the summer of 1965 and left in the spring of 1966. I like to draw the parallel between being broke and having a dime, and then between having a dime and having a lot more money. When you're broke, you're broke and that's a fact. That's not measurable; that's infinite. When you have a dime, you're not broke and you can measure your wealth. When we went out there, we were broke. By the springtime, we probably had a quarter. We were not broke. We weren't all that well off, but we were one hell of a lot better than we were when we started. The situation got continually better.

Supply and Demand

Shortly after the 3rd Marine Division landed in South Vietnam, the 1st Marine Division arrived to join combat operations in the I Corps area of northern South Vietnam. Providing medical support was the job of the 1st Medical Battalion. As with the 3rd Medical Battalion, the new unit had to begin from scratch, and getting a medical unit up and running was more than a challenge for its personnel.

George Harris had wanted to be a physician before he joined the Navy at age 18 in 1951. Following boot camp and hospital corps school, he went off to Korea. When his first hitch was up in 1955, he reenlisted. The upwardly mobile corpsman was soon a hospital corpsman first class. He recounts, "[I] was determined to make chief, warrant, or MSC [Medical Service Corps officer] by the end of my enlistment or I was getting out of the Navy." Four years later, Harris was selected for the Medical Service Corps and commissioned an ensign. After several assignments, he received orders to the 1st Medical Battalion, 1st Marine Division, which prepared to deploy to Vietnam in January 1966. As commanding officer of B Medical Company of the Battalion, Harris found that preparing his unit to go to war was not a simple proposition. Half his company had already left for Vietnam, and, without his knowledge, they had helped themselves to most of the unit's gear and supplies.

I had just half a company — one clearing platoon in the headquarters and that was it. It had a 30-bed capability. The other 30 beds were gone. As a whole company, they were 60-bed units. I was attached to the 5th Marine Regiment out of the 1st Medical Battalion. When I started going through all our gear, I found that we hardly had anything. The other half of the company had taken almost everything with them.

That was almost the end of my career because I had signed for everything without looking in a single box. We were supposed to have 50 Coleman lanterns. There were no Coleman lanterns, just the empty boxes.

The CO of the 5th Marines was a very understanding guy, Col. [Charles F.] Widdecke. Later on, he became a general. He always looked over all the requisitions and, not surprisingly, he noted that we were ordering all these lantern parts. I had a lantern factory set up and we were ordering all the parts for Coleman lanterns, building them, and putting them in boxes.

After a meeting one day, he said, "Harris, you got a lantern factory going on over there in your warehouse?"

"Oh, no, Colonel, I'm just getting spare parts."

When you're getting ready to deploy, you're expected to have your basic outfit plus 30 days of operating stocks. Well, what's 30 days of operating stocks for a medical unit in a combat zone? I didn't know. And there weren't any books written to tell you what it was supposed to be. All kinds of guides tell you that you should have 30 days POL [petroleum, oil, and lubricants]. There are requirements for those and you can calculate that. I've got this many 6 by 6 trucks. I've got this many jeeps. I've got this many diesel engines on generators, and they burn this much fuel per hour. And I'm going to run them "x" number of hours a day. Therefore, I've got to have this much fuel. And if I need that much fuel, then I have to have.... If you've got this many gallons of fuel, you require this many gallons of oil, and this many pounds of lubricants. So you can figure out how many spark plugs you need and spare tires. There are requirements for all that — but nothing for medical supplies.

I had a first class OR tech named Sugden. He checked into my company and I asked him, "What do you do, Sugden?"

"Well, I'm an OR tech, sir."

"Well, not now. You're a medical supply guy for this company."

"But, sir, I don't know anything about medical supply."

"I don't care. I want you to run medical supply. You're an OR tech. We do surgery here. You can at least tell me whether or not we're ready to do that because you know what we need in the way of surgical equipment."

We had lists of the basic required equipment. One was the AMAL [Authorized Medical Allowance List].

"I'll tell you what I want you to do. Every time you order something for the clinic, you order one to put into operating stock that we're going to take with us. If you order a case of bandages, you order two cases, and put one in the box we're going to take with us." And that's what we did for several months before we went to Vietnam.

This was August and we knew we were going to go sometime after the first of the year in

1966. The Marine Corps came out with these 27-cubic-foot wooden boxes— 3 by 3 by 3. It was a great idea for packing stuff because they had inserts in them. They also had a locator system that told you where items were contained. If you had a 5-inch curved Kelly hemostat in one of those boxes, and it was in insert number 4, you could look it up and find that it was in insert number 4 in this box, in this row of the warehouse. So that's how we packed up all the extra stuff that we brought along.

No one in the medical battalion — either the 3rd Medical Battalion when I was there or in the 1st Medical Battalion —followed the Marine Corps procedure for warehousing. Everyone said, "We're different. We pack our stuff differently." But you never could find anything. For years— and perhaps today — medical units had a bastardized system of warehousing AMALs. This system did not match up with anything the Marine Corps was using. I found — by using the Marine Corps Field Warehousing System — we could easily track gear and could locate boxes that had dated items. We could also find boxes that were awaiting items that had been on order.

I sat down and read this manual about field warehousing and said, "Hey, this thing makes sense." So we went back and redid all our stuff. Col. Widdecke had told everybody in the regiment and all the units that were attached, "You're going to pack up all your loose ends in these 27-cubic-foot boxes."

I went to Medical Battalion and asked for 50 27-cubic-foot boxes. Nobody had them yet; they had to make them. So I asked for the material to build the boxes, but they told me I couldn't have it. I went back to the colonel and told him my unit would not give me the boxes. He said, "How many boxes do you need?"

I said, "50."

The next day a low-boy [truck] drove up with 50 27-cubic-foot boxes. That's the kind of guy Widdecke was.

The end result for us in B Med., 1st Medical Battalion tells the story. When we landed in Okinawa to let our logistics tail catch up, we had everything warehoused in two days using only a hand-operated pallet jack. Col. Widdecke had people come to our warehouse to see "how it was done." When we finally arrived in Vietnam, we got there with everything we started with — in operating condition — with the exception of one mechanic's tool kit, which was stolen on the USS *Talladega* — probably by a sailor! I don't think any other unit in the 1st Medical Battalion could make that claim.

We landed in Chu Lai and off-loaded our stuff out in the Sam Hai River aboard mike boats.[2] The Seabees had what they called a "sand ramp" on the river, and that's where our gear came ashore.

When the 3rd Medical Battalion had arrived in Vietnam, it was split into companies. One company went to Chu Lai, one company went up to Phu Bai, and the balance of it went to Danang. When we arrived, we absorbed the unit that was in Chu Lai. And 3rd Med took a company of our Battalion, which went up to Danang.

Even before we got to Vietnam, we had an interesting communication from the Army on Okinawa. Sugden came into the office one day and said, "Boss, I got a call from the Army supply people. They say they've got a bunch of Navy medical gear in a warehouse and they need room in the warehouse. They're just gonna set it all out on the warehouse loading dock in the weather."

So I sent him down there to see what it was. He went and then called me. "Boss, there's a surgical team block and a surgical team resupply block here."

I said, "Good. Load it up. We're gonna repaint it, re-mark it, and make it part of B Med."

And that's exactly what we did. I don't how it ended up there, but it wound up in my hands. It had Navy markings on the boxes, so we repainted it number 23 Marine Corps green, put 1st Medical Battalion markings on it, and took it to Vietnam. We had enough equipment to fill this room from floor to ceiling with instruments, dressings, oxygen, anesthesia machines,

OR tables. When we arrived in Vietnam, we not only had this surgical team block and resupply block that we had purloined from the Army warehouse, but also all the vehicle spare parts we were entitled to along with 30 days of "operating stock" for our company.[3]

When we first got to Chu Lai, everything was still in tents. All the wards were in tents. The Seabees then came to build a hospital. At that time, they built Southeast Asia huts out of Philippine mahogany—luan. They had corrugated tin roofs, the sides were open with screens on them. So that's what this whole camp was. We had four ORs in Quonsets with concrete floors. By the time they got everything done, it was about July of 1966.

All the 1st Medical Battalion's companies were in the same place. We stayed together until the end of 1966 when the Division started moving north; 3rd Medical Battalion moved north around Dong Ha, and we moved into Danang.

Once we got set up, we saw pretty much of everything. Almost every day somebody got banged up or was injured from enemy action. We saw the whole gamut—from rashes and gunshot wounds to shrapnel wounds and burns.

If a major operation was under way, we would deploy what we called a "shock surgical team." It consisted of an MSC, a couple of docs, and a handful of corpsmen. They would set up in whatever logistics support area we had for whatever operation was going on. They would become like a large battalion aid station and would treat patients before sending them to us.

In fact, the battalion aid stations concept as such wasn't really used in Vietnam at all. The whole theory of medical support was the capability to echelon. It was also the same for the concept of what had been called "collecting and clearing companies." The collecting and clearing companies became the medical companies, and then switched back to being collecting and clearing companies. No one understood what collecting and clearing companies meant. That's why we changed the term to "medical companies."

The medical company consisted of two platoons that were identical—two x-ray machines, two operating rooms, two medical supply sections, and a headquarters platoon. The headquarters platoon was basically an administration group and wasn't a very big outfit. It had the CO and the first sergeant.

Each platoon was a 30-bed unit identical to its sister platoon. If combat was going on, you could close down the 30-bed unit, move it, and set up operation at the new location. Then you could clear patients out of the other 30-bed unit and move that platoon forward in a leapfrog manner. That was the theory. It may have been used in World War II, but I don't know whether this system was ever employed in Vietnam.

It probably remained theoretical because Vietnam was a pretty static war with no fronts. Everybody set up cantonments and then went out, operated, and then came back. You might have a whole battalion out at one time so there wasn't any way to make use of the echelon kind of arrangement.

Not many casualties in Vietnam moved very far by ground. You might move a casualty a mile or less by ground, but most of the time the Marines operated in terrain not friendly to motor transport—out in the jungle someplace. So casualties moved by air as much as they could.

Helicopters played the biggest role. We started with helicopters in Korea, and by the time we got to Vietnam, a guy would get hit and 20 minutes later he'd be at the medical battalion. But we never had any dedicated helicopters, that is, helos used only for medical evacuation. They were available on a catch-as-catch-can basis unlike the Army which had whole companies of helicopter ambulances. The Marine theory was that an airplane is an airplane is an airplane, and a helicopter is a helicopter is a helicopter. The belief was that they couldn't afford to sideline a helicopter to move casualties so we didn't have dedicated "dust-off" helicopters, or "slicks," as we called them.

If we had to move a casualty out to the *Sanctuary* or the *Repose*, we would call MAG-36

Under fire from the enemy, Marines rush one of their wounded comrades through a rice paddy to a waiting helicopter (BUMED Archives).

[Marine Aircraft Group] and MAG-36 would send a helo. Marine Air Group-36 was cheek-by-jowl with us. They would fly a helicopter over and land on our pad. Then we'd load the casualty and they'd take him out to the hospital ship. The biggest problem was urgency. It was very difficult getting the Marine helicopter drivers and the dispatchers over at MAG to understand that the medical battalion could have an urgent requirement just like they could have one out on the battlefield. If we got a head injury, our surgeons might make a small hole to relieve pressure, but we didn't really mess with heads because we didn't have the capability to do neuro-surgery. We wanted to get him out to a hospital ship where he could be seen by a neurosurgeon. Head patients went to the hospital ship or, if they were stable enough, they went to Clark.

Yet it just never made sense to the MAG dispatchers—or so it seemed while I was there. We might say, "We've got an urgent request to move a guy from here to the hospital ship."

And they might respond, "Well, we'll get you a bird as quickly as we can."

"You don't understand. This guy's life is in the balance here."

The worst part about not having dedicated helicopters was making somebody understand that you could have a requirement that was just as urgent as when they had someone out in a rifle company calling in for a medevac.

We always had problems with communications. Telephone communications were terrible. We had field telephones so we'd have to go through a switchboard and get bounced down the line. Our call would go first to FLSG [Force Logistic Support Group]. Then from FLSG it would go to Division. From Division the call might go someplace else. Of course, every time the call would get passed along to another switchboard, the chances of dropping that call multiplied exponentially. And they all had call names. "This is Whiskey 2. Give me Foxtrot 1."

I had a kid named Green who did most of my medevac setups. You would have to give him the next day off because he couldn't talk from shouting on the phone at the top of his voice. He probably could have stood outside with a megaphone.

And we also had lousy radio communications. We had a big radio unit but it was seldom used. We did all our business by land line. We talked to the *Repose* by radio, but as far as talking with the medevac people, it was all done by land line.

Supply was also a problem for a long time until "Red Ball" was instigated. A red ball painted on boxes meant urgent movement. The supply point was Okinawa. The supply officer would get on the telephone—which often was very hard to do—or get on the radio to Okinawa to get medical supplies. He would get the supplies "red-balled" to his unit so we could get supplied.

Fresh blood was always a problem. You would get blood and it might be good for a week. This was before we had frozen blood. FLSG Bravo was a huge organization, maybe a thousand people. They became our walking blood bank. We had people typed and cross-matched ahead of time.

Warm running water was also an issue so you could scrub. We finally got it but it took awhile. For a long time the only water we had was what was available in water buffaloes.[4] Then the Seabees finally came in and drilled a well and put up a water tower so we could have water under pressure. When we installed water heaters, we finally got warm water for the surgeons to wash their hands.

Medical oxygen was a problem. A big airfield nearby was our supply for oxygen. And the quality of that oxygen was debated for a long time.

"Well, it's not medical oxygen," someone would argue.

"What do you mean, it's not medical oxygen? The aviators are breathing the stuff. It's good enough for them; it ought to be good enough for us."

X-ray machines were always a problem in that they were not very powerful units. And we were still using a wet process for film. You had to go through all the hand-processing, and it was always a nightmare as was getting good resolution on the films and getting them in a timely way. You might have 60 casualties stacked up. Maybe 20, or a third of them, had to go in for major surgery. We had four operating rooms, and if they were all up and running, you might be handling four patients. Each patient might take an hour. Then the docs would have to change gowns and scrub up again while the crew sloshed out the OR and set up for another patient.

And more patients were stacked up. The first few were always a problem because X-ray was a bottleneck. To go from the admissions-sorting area to the operating room, you had to go through X-ray. Not everybody went through X-ray—but most did. Anybody with major holes who was going into the OR needed at least one or two pictures so X-ray was always a slow point.

Many of the casualties went into our debridement area. Cmdr. Ray Ashworth, our triage officer, was a hand surgeon and this was his second tour in Vietnam. He had been in Vietnam when Tom Dooley [played a significant role in Operation Passage to Freedom, 1954–1955; see Chapter 1] was there. He had gotten out of the Navy but then volunteered to come back in. Ray triaged the patients, then Ken Ponder who was a dentist, a couple of operating technicians—first classes—and I did all the debridements. Ray would circulate and if we ran into a problem with a bleeder[5] that we couldn't control, he would put a pair of gloves on and fix it.

I had a really good crew of guys who worked for me in Patient Affairs. We'd get that operation up and going for admitting new patients and then I had nothing to do. And always being a frustrated physician, I'd go over to the debridement area and help out. The first few times, Ashworth watched me. You debrided the wound, packed it with iodoform gauze, or put a Penrose drain in it. Maybe you would put one stitch through the drain to hold it in place and leave the wound open. Then you covered it with gauze pads and wrapped it up.

These were all minor wounds. You might get a guy in with 20 little pieces of shrapnel, anything from the size of a match head up to something less than a quarter of an inch, but usually not very deep. It was kind of neat, I thought. I'd been a corpsman and knew how to do this stuff.

It's difficult to remember the names of all the operations we supported, but it seems like all during the summer and fall we were busy. Whenever the Marines had an operation, we were busy. You'd know something was coming up because you'd send one of the shock surgical teams out to where the action would be. And we'd get ready for casualties. The most demanding operation was "Operation Hastings/Deckhouse II" in the summer of 1966 [7 July–3 August]. Some 448 Marines were wounded and another 126 killed. Many small unit operations resulted in casualties, but Hastings was by far the worst. "Operation Colorado/Lien Ket 52" [6–21 August 1966] was another busy time.

A patient would arrive with a field medical tag on him. So that provided the basic information. You had the guy's name and his unit. Sometimes a patient arrived without a tag. I remember one time a truck-load of guys—maybe a dozen—came in. They had been riding a truck when someone set off a command detonated mine which blew up the truck. A number of them were killed and a lot were wounded. Another truck came along right behind them and picked them all up, threw them on the truck, and brought them in to us. So then we had to rely on dog tags. Hopefully, they had their dog tags on.

When a patient arrived, we'd open up a medical record on him just like you'd do today, except we had a different starting mechanism — the field medical tag. And when he left, that record went with him when he was evaced out.

We didn't keep guys very long. I think we might have had a 15-day evac policy. If you couldn't get a guy back to duty in 15 days, he went out — either to the hospital ship, Danang, the Philippines, Okinawa, or Japan.

You'd go for days with hardly anybody. And then it would just become complete chaos. We had a few casualties all the time, but then there would be periods where we would get anywhere from 25 to perhaps 65 casualties in a few hours. During the busy times everyone turned to in order to get the job done. Long hours were the order of the day, particularly for the folks in surgery. This made triage very important since the effort was aimed at screening out those who did not have to go to the operating room to be cared for. This triage resulted in leaving folks to the ministrations of those of us who did the minor debridements. Things get done in wartime that you would never see in our brick-and-mortar hospitals because of "credentialing." "Credentials" in Vietnam consisted of a willingness to work and the ability to learn along with the oversight of more talented folks.

In addition, the dead would be brought in, and someone actually had to pronounce them dead. Then the dead had to be identified. If they didn't have any tag on them, hopefully some-body from their battalion or their company would come back and be able to help identify them.

When I was in Vietnam, there was only one hospital ship — the *Repose*. The *Repose* moved back and forth between Danang and Chu Lai and the Philippines. The ship came near us about three days a week. The rest of the time you couldn't rely on it. If you got bogged down, that was it. If we got a lot of casualties and it looked like we would really be hard pressed, we emp-tied out the wards as much as we could. Then we would call the Air Force to set up a medevac for maybe 25 or 30 patients. Then they would be transported to a fixed wing air group and flown to Clark to make room for new guys. We'd be doing that while fresh casualties were already arriving.

We were also involved with the Medical Civil Action Program [MEDCAP]. One time we visited a little town not too far from us as part of MEDCAP, and I administered a plague vac-cine because there was a plague outbreak. But it was funny because people would get a shot, leave, and you'd see them getting back in line. They figured if one is good, two would be bet-ter.

A young Vietnamese nurse worked in this village. We would coordinate with her. If the Viet Cong were in the area, she would tell us, "Don't come today." So we wouldn't go. We did checkups and other care. We saw people who had walked for two days because they knew we were going to be there.

Punji Sticks and Bear Traps

Ohio native William Mahaffey received his medical degree from Ohio State University Col-lege of Medicine and then trained as an anesthesiologist before joining the Navy. "In those days, any able-bodied young physician — who had two arms, two legs, and who was not already a vet-eran — could expect to be drafted at an inconvenient time in their medical career if they didn't han-dle things right." He signed up for the Berry Plan,[6] which enabled him to complete his anesthesia training before reporting for active duty. Dr. Mahaffey had chosen the Navy because his uncles had been sailors, and he had always been interested in all things "Navy"— naval history, ships, and submarines.

First assigned to Naval Hospital Portsmouth, Virginia, Dr. Mahaffey soon learned that he was heading for a place called Vietnam via Camp Pendleton and Okinawa. It was October 1965, and very little was known about that beleaguered little nation in Southeast Asia.

I arrived at Camp Pendleton on the Marine Corps birthday [10 November], and was there for two or three weeks. We learned more about medical treatment in Korea than the realities of combat medicine in Vietnam. They taught us cold weather medicine because there wasn't enough experience coming out of Vietnam at that time.

We first flew to Okinawa on a chartered commercial plane. After two or three days there, we caught a Marine Corps aircraft to Vietnam with a group of Marines, physicians, dentists, and chaplains. The Marines were told not to puke — but, if they had to, they were to do it in their helmets and not on the deck.

We landed late on a very rainy and muddy day at Danang on the 23rd of December. I remember standing under the wing of a C-130 aircraft waiting for someone to tell us where to go. A couple of blindfolded Vietnamese prisoners were sitting there. In Field Medical Service School we were told not to call them "gooks," but they were certainly called "gooks" by the Marines who introduced us to the area.

Eventually, after waiting until 7 or 8 o'clock in the evening, a dental tech drove up in a

Aerial view of Charlie Med in October 1966 (courtesy William Mahaffey).

jeep. It was still raining. Mud was everywhere. He offered us a cold soda to drink and drove us back to the 3rd Marine Division headquarters in Danang where I met the Division surgeon. His name was Hap [Homer] Arnold. He told me they were busy down there, "there" being a couple of miles back up the road in the mud. He said, "Lt. Mahaffey. You're going to be busy tonight." Then he sent me on my way in the rain.

Another jeep took me to Charlie Med — C Company, 3rd Med Battalion. Lt. Bill Self [MSC, USN] took my foot locker and my briefcase and sent me right to the OR. Literally minutes after I got to Charlie Med, I was in the operating room dumbfounded, facing my first anesthetic in a combat zone.

In a regular hospital, I was used to ordering pre-op medications, usually a narcotic and some atropine. So I walked into that operating room trying to sound experienced and calm. The corpsman told me that my first patient was on his way up. So I said, "Give him some Demerol and atropine," just as I would have ordered in a hospital. I'm sure they didn't even pay any attention to this request down in the triage area. They probably laughed at it. They didn't know who this neophyte was. I'm sure that patient never got any pre-op medications, and I never again ordered any in the future. It certainly wasn't a combat zone routine.

Charlie Med sat on what was just a flat, sandy area bordering on rice paddies between us and the ocean. A helicopter pad was located in the center of Charlie Med. When we had an overflow of casualties, we let them lie in the shade of a big mango tree in the middle of our compound.

When I first got there, I was put in what looked like an oversized pup tent, which belonged to one of the surgeons who was on emergency leave. It was damp and cold. But then I moved into the new hardbacks that were being built. These were wooden framed structures built by Seabees that had screening around the outside for ventilation, and they also had corrugated metal roofs. The hardback that I was in had two dentists, two general medical officers, and another anesthesiologist.

The enlisted eventually had about the same housing facilities, but I think they were more densely packed. They were on the other side of the compound up on the hill. They had an outdoor movie theater and we had an indoor movie theater.

Creature comforts are essential in any situation though they vary in significance according to the circumstances. The creature comforts we enjoyed at a medical battalion were vastly more pleasurable than those enjoyed by Marines in the field. We never forgot that. But they were far fewer than those enjoyed at NSA [Naval Support Activity] Hospital near Danang or on USS *Repose* [AH-16] out in Danang Harbor where air-conditioned living quarters, flush toilets, hot showers, and chilled drinking water were standard comforts. I wonder if they served Spam on *Repose*.

One important creature comfort at Charlie Med was the shower. When I arrived, the officers' shower was an unenclosed stall made of 2 by 4s. The users' privacy and modesty had not been considered. A crude ladder leaned against the side of the structure. At the top was a 55-gallon barrel fitted with a kerosene-fired immersion burner borrowed from the galley. Lighting the burner was tricky so its use was limited to cool weather. Normally, each of us kept a 5-gallon can of water in the sun all day. We would then climb the ladder, dump the can of warmed water into the barrel, then return quickly to the stall to enjoy a brief 5-gallon shower as water was allowed to flow through a tin can with holes punched in the bottom.

On my second day in country, I discovered how the shower was used. Naively and without asking permission, I picked up a 5-gallon can of water a senior dental officer had been warming all day. Perhaps I was thinking that such cans of water were distributed for our convenience. I used it for my first shower in Vietnam. When I finished, the dentist asked me, "Did you enjoy your shower?"

Early in the game, hyper-chlorinated drinking water was towed in to Charlie Med in two-wheeled "water buffaloes." Containers were then filled for various purposes from those centrally placed water buffaloes. By late summer when running water was being piped in from a central source, a common shower tent had been built, complete with waist-high outer walls, multiple showerheads, soap dishes, and lights. Water for the showers was stored in a cumshawed wing tank from a former jet fighter. The sun would warm the stored water considerably during bright days and a warm shower in the evening. Though the temperature of the water could not be regulated, a shower became a real luxury that we soon took for granted.

Our galley or dining facility was run by the Marines. It served us well though we never had a relish plate. And they never offered "chilled this" or "fricasseed that." Everything was thoroughly fried or roasted or boiled or mashed, though occasionally we had steaks to broil. Each of us had his own mess tray and utensils suspended from a piece of wire. As we approached the mess hall, we first encountered a large garbage can of water heated to boiling by an immersion burner. We would hang onto the piece of wire and dip our mess gear into this cauldron, ostensibly to sterilize it.

Breakfast invariably offered canned orange juice, toast or dense sticky buns, eggs— sunny side up or down, but never scrambled — and bacon or fried Spam. Huge pancakes and sausage links occasionally provided variety.

Large portions of that day's menu selections were served — not presented —cafeteria-style absolutely devoid of decorations, such as parsley, herbs and the like, and eaten at tables in a screened "dining room." Lettuce and fresh salads were unknown. The reconstituted milk and the hyper-chlorinated water were unappetizing so we usually drank bug juice (Marine Corps "Kool-Aid") or coffee. Baked Marine desserts were plentiful at mealtime and for snacking day and night, but they were certainly not delicate. The Marines' favorite seemed to be an inch-thick dense spice cake made from a mix and topped by a very thick layer of generic khaki frosting. Also available any time of day or night were makings for cold Spam sandwiches. Occasionally, very soft tan — almost khaki — Marine ice cream showed up, but it was normally diverted to the patients' trays. After a meal, we each scrubbed our mess gear in a hot soapy cauldron, then dipped them again into plain hot water. Some fresh bananas, melons, mangos, and pineapple, which could be consumed safely, were eventually procured from the local economy. When a visit to the mess hall just didn't sound very appealing during quiet periods, we snacked in our hooches on the surprisingly good items found in commandeered C-rations, or on items from the PX, or on precious goodies received from home.

Early in 1966, the occupants of each hooch in the compound were given the option of hiring a "House Mouse," or Vietnamese woman who would do laundry and tidy up our living spaces in the hooch. No matter how well they scrubbed our uniforms and skivvies, drying laundry in Vietnam's humidity was a slow process especially during the rainy season. Our House Mouse was named Mỹ. The Vietnamese language is tonal and the real meaning of a word depends on the proper rising and falling pitch of the voice. We apparently never mastered the pronunciation of Mỹ's name since she would usually giggle when called. We lost Mỹ's services when it was discovered that she had a positive tuberculosis skin test.

We occasionally had an all-hands party in the OR. The fanciest party was when drinking containers had been fashioned from small hollowed-out local pineapples. To the juice made from the pulp was added 7-Up, ice, and just a little "gilley" — or medical-grade ethyl alcohol. Each Quonset housed two ORs. During that party in one OR, an emergency appendectomy was performed in the other OR in the same Quonset. The party continued.

Beer and distilled spirits, as well as a variety of soft drinks, were always available on the honor system in the clubs. A cold beer or a gin and tonic sometimes settled well, especially after supper while waiting for a movie to start. But without any specific orders, we had a very responsible attitude toward alcohol in a compound where casualties could swamp us at any minute. Our commanding officer dealt sternly with the rare abuser. One such senior officer was "restricted to quarters," meaning that except for work and meals, he remained in his hooch for a considerable period.

The Marine Corps's attitude is to take care of their people. We realized how high on the hog we lived. There were a few guys who bellyached about this and that. But we knew that we were living pretty damn well compared to the Marines in the field who were just trying to survive each day at a time.

A constant source of electricity was essential to our work. Near the helicopter pad, two of our four noisy diesel generators were always running. Only rarely did we lose all power. At those times I think that the dead silence was more noticeable than the absence of lights.

Was money a creature comfort? It was! It now seems unbelievable that in those days — long before the convenience of direct deposit of military paychecks — paper paychecks of the "Do not Fold, Staple, or Mutilate" type were issued to us twice a month. We could, of course, direct an allotment to a spouse or some financial institution. Our paychecks could either be cashed at the BX [Base Exchange] or they could be mailed back home to a bank. I wonder how many paychecks were never cashed. To avoid a black market situation, we could not spend greenbacks in Vietnam, only ornate MPCs, or Military Payment Certificates issued in various dollar and fractional denominations. For any dealings with the local economy, such as buying souvenirs, paying a House Mouse, or, I suppose, even settling up with a prostitute, some MPCs had to be converted into Vietnamese Dong currency. The rate was a thousand or so Dong to the dollar.

At that time, Charlie Med was entirely canvas except for a few hardback tents that were just beginning to be built. Our operating rooms were two plywood boxes side by side inside of a canvas tent. The tents were surrounded by sandbags. We were told later that these were to protect the rest of the compound in case something imbedded in an injured patient would explode in the operating room. Between the two operating rooms was a larger tent enclosing a plywood box. This larger tent served as a recovery room and sort of an ICU [intensive care unit]. A couple of open-air wards were hardbacked.

A little electric autoclave was located in the operating room. It was probably as big as a toaster oven, and used for quick sterilizing of a small number of instruments. The big autoclaves were gasoline-powered and were in another tent slightly down the road from the operating rooms. We facetiously called this other tent "Central Supply." These autoclaves used gasoline to create steam to autoclave our packs, instruments, and also our irrigating fluids.

The corpsmen showed a duplicity of attitude toward these autoclaves. They were a little frightened of them because of the roaring noise they made. I think they suspected they were capable of blowing up. On cool winter nights, they also put out some heat so that was a good place for corpsmen to lie down and catch some Zs.

Our x-ray equipment was primitive. It was a field model x-ray, the kind that folds up into a case. But it served its purpose.

We always had plenty of IV fluids. This was back in the days when IV fluids came in glass bottles. Nowadays, they come in plastic bags. We did not have irrigating fluids. Of course, in an operating room you have to have abundant supplies of saline for irrigating wounds. Without any special recipe to make the right concentration, the corpsmen would take hyper-chlorinated Marine Corps potable water, fill empty 1-liter IV bottles, and add a few salt tablets. Then they just taped the stoppers back on and autoclaved the bottles.

Back in my university hospital setting, I had everything I could possibly want just by reaching in the cabinet behind me. But at Charlie Med we had a primitive field anesthesia machine, which had a tank of nitrous oxide on it attached by a hose to a larger tank of aviation quality oxygen. We had plenty of pentothal, which is no longer part of the anesthesiologist's armamentarium. We also had spinal sets because at that time spinals were much more common than epidurals. But beyond that, we learned that we could and had to do with just the very basics.

We got a respirator halfway through my tour. Today's anesthesiologists think they can't do an anesthetic without a respirator. Back then we had one respirator we had to spread out evenly for four operating rooms and possible use in ICU.

Sometimes we had fears about our blood supply. It was primarily drawn from dependents and active-duty people in the Philippines, Guam, and Okinawa. The blood was about a week old by the time we got it. But we never ran out. One standard procedure when administering this blood in large amounts was to warm the blood to body temperature as it was being transfused. But we didn't have that luxury at Charlie Med where we were using large amounts of cold blood. Sometimes we'd run some IV tubing through a basin of warm water, hoping that would warm the blood to some degree. Our patients often were somewhat hypothermic by the time they got to ICU, partially because of the cold blood we administered and partially because we had effective air conditioning in those operating rooms.

We used blood by the gallons, sometimes more than 50 units of blood on any one patient. We had a chalkboard in the operating room so every time we administered more than 50 units of blood to a patient, we put that patient's name on the chalkboard. The number was not all that great but the last time I looked at that chalk board, we had 8 or 10 names on it.

We had no modern facilities to help warm the patient and no warming blankets and pads with warm water flowing through them. All we could do in the ICU afterwards was to allow the patient to begin shivering which, of course, generates heat, cover him with blankets, and put some incandescent lights over his body to try to warm him up as he awoke from his anesthetic.

We always had the essentials for an anesthesiologist such as oxygen, which is vital. The Air Force gave us all the aviation quality oxygen we needed. But medical supplies in general were very high priority items. The items I thought were essential — which I was used to when I was a pampered resident — were not available.

The bulk of our patient load at Charlie Med consisted of combat casualties requiring surgery, but we had many patients in other categories to keep our medical personnel busy. Malaria patients among the Marines were surprisingly numerous. We also had surprising numbers of Marines with disabling diarrhea. They required admission to our medical wards so that their severe dehydration could be corrected. During the cooler wet winter nights of the monsoon season, a number of Marines arrived at Charlie Med with pneumonia.

Sexually transmitted diseases, primarily gonorrhea and some syphilis, are common in any combat zone, though they were often treated at the Battalion Aid Station level. But in Vietnam, we were seeing a new problem. Gonorrhea normally responds promptly to penicillin and is usually not a therapeutic challenge, but in Southeast Asia our physicians were beginning to see a form of gonorrhea which did not respond to penicillin. It was labeled PPNG or penicillinase-producing *Neisseria gonorrhœae*. This new strain of the gonorrhea bacterium produced penicillinase, which destroyed penicillin in the body at the site of the infection. These numerous PPNG patients were retained on the wards long enough to do antibiotic sensitivity testing so that the right antibiotic could be started.

Our psychiatrist was kept busy seeing and treating many combat fatigue[7] victims and others who temporarily went off the deep end while facing the realities of war. His office and hooch were away from the other clinical areas of Charlie Med. Near his office were two wards housing his patients.

From any large population of young adults such as the 3rd Marine Division, a goodly number of appendicitis cases can be expected, unrelated to war. During a period of heavy casualties, it was not uncommon to hear that the next patient coming to the OR would be an "appy," or appendicitis patient. If the seriously wounded casualties were particularly numerous, however, an appendicitis patient could safely be put on hold for some time with intravenous antibiotics and other conservative measures.

Injuries ran the scale from small and almost insignificant to some of the most incredibly horrendous wounds imaginable. One of the smallest wounds that I recall in the OR was an Air Force man who caught his wedding ring on something as he jumped to the ground from a parked aircraft. This injury stripped or avulsed all of the skin from his ring finger. It seemed so insignificant compared to other injuries we took care of, but the services of a skilled surgeon would be required to preserve that finger's function.

Another frequent but relatively minor injury was that resulting from a Marine stepping on a concealed punji stick in the jungle. A punji stick is a pencil-sized piece of steel with a very sharp barb on one end. Like a barbed fishhook, it cannot easily be removed from even soft tissue. Several of these punji sticks would be imbedded vertically in a slab of concrete or mounted on a piece of wood so that they could be concealed in the underbrush where Marines on patrol might walk or run. It was rumored that punji sticks were coated with feces. When a running Marine stepped forcefully on the punji stick, the sharp barbed tip immediately pierced his boot and foot. While pain was severe, the injury was not all that serious. However, it disabled the Marine by having a heavy slab of concrete or wood painfully and firmly attached to his foot. He then had to be removed to a location where the barb could be cut off and the punji stick removed. In the field it also effectively incapacitated one or two uninjured Marines or corpsmen when they had to carry the injured man.

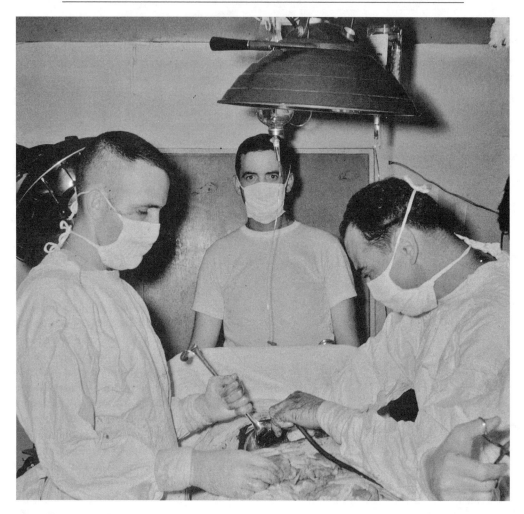

Lt. William Mahaffey, anesthesiologist (center), is a member of the operating team at Charlie Med (courtesy William Mahaffey).

On display in Charlie Med's triage building was a huge trap, nicknamed a "bear trap," operating like a huge rat trap. Early in Charlie Med's presence in Vietnam, a Marine was brought in with his leg in this bear trap.

A number of Marines had belly wounds resulting from a piece of flak ripping an opening in the abdominal wall. Usually a sizable loop of small or large intestine would be protruding through the wound when the man arrived at Charlie Med. Though this injury would require a general anesthetic, only a fairly brief surgical procedure would be needed to check the gut for perforations and then close the wound. This Marine would be up and around in no time. After USS *Repose* arrived, casualties such as these would recuperate on the hospital ship and — unfortunately — return to battle unless this injury had earned him his second Purple Heart in Vietnam.

Some people assumed that all we did at Charlie Med was stabilization. No way. We did definitive surgery. We treated a lot of chest injuries. The head injuries we saw were either minor — some of which could be treated by the oral surgeons— or they were instantly fatal. We actually had a portable open heart machine which we never used. Eventually, a vascular surgeon, Jim Chandler, joined the staff. We occasionally had vascular injuries, especially the femoral artery in the legs because of the land mine explosions. They usually affected the lower extremities, but vascular injuries, per se, were not all that numerous.

In fact, at least half our procedures concerned injuries to the lower legs, especially the posterior aspect of the lower legs due to land mines. When a Marine would turn to run away from a land mine that was about to explode, the flak from the land mine would just destroy the back of his buttocks, thighs, and legs. Many of these mines were the so-called "Bouncing Bettys." I've never seen one and I've never heard one, but I've certainly seen their results.

Our big thing was orthopedics and general surgery to handle this massive soft tissue trauma from the Bouncing Bettys. Most of what we saw were massive soft tissue injury and utterly destroyed femurs, tibias, fibulas, and ankles—wounds that I had never seen in a civilian setting.

There was nothing like a typical day at Charlie Med. We could go two or three days on end without a single patient. Our day's work was never scheduled. Our work started when the helicopters arrived. I'm not an aviator but I could tell the difference between a Huey and a CH-46 [Sea Knight helicopter]. If we heard that "whop, whop, whop" of a Huey coming in at night, it wasn't a general making a presentation someplace. It meant casualties coming in. We had an order: first call, second call, third call, whatever. If the guy who was on first call was in bed, he got up when he heard the helicopter coming in. We anesthesiologists wanted to be there for the initial phases of resuscitation. We felt we were pretty good at restoring body fluid and maintaining airways and conditions like that so we didn't wait to be called.

We rarely had advanced word that patients were coming in. It could either be a Huey with just two or three casualties or maybe just one severely injured patient. Sometimes the big '46s would come in with 40 or 50 less severely injured casualties and, of course, a lot of dead bodies.

At first I don't think I even realized what I was actually experiencing. I had seen a lot of death, of course, but I'd never seen death in that number. Maybe two or three months into my tour, all of a sudden it hit me that these were young Americans piled up like logs—dead. I especially remember when I'd see a left hand sticking out of the pile with a wedding ring on it. I knew the guy was dead, but his family at home didn't know yet.

In the operating room we never actually counted patients and never counted cases. Even though we counted the number of units of blood we used, we never kept anesthesia records. So I can't guess how many casualties passed through that place. Nor can I even guess how many dead bodies our graves registration guys handled, but we had hundreds and thousands.

A few of the patients we treated stand out. I remember one who had a simple injury, usually taken care of by a spinal anesthetic — no challenge at all medically — but it was the day that Hollywood comedienne Martha Raye was visiting our place. Martha Raye was a nurse in the Army reserve. So she came into the operating room with a mask on. I stood up from my anesthesiologist's stool, and she sat down and took the patient's blood pressure and chatted with him. He was just overjoyed that Martha Raye would talk to him while he was having his leg operated on.

I remember some patients from the personal side, but I also recall a few from the medical side. One of those was a Marine who had tried to launch a flare when it became lodged between his flak jacket and his chest wall. I still have photographs from my position in the operating room removing this unignited flare from his chest cavity. It was the only case we did without prepping and putting on anything more than just gloves. It was just a matter of seconds before we anesthetized the patient, opened him, took the flare out, and gave it to another Marine who took it out of the operating room.

I also recall a patient who came in with his mandible pretty much destroyed. He learned by experience that the only way he could breathe was to get up on his hands and knees. Gravity then allowed his jaw to fall away from his pharynx so he could breathe. If we tried to put him on his back to induce anesthesia, of course he couldn't breathe. With him standing on his knees and face down, I got on my knees and looked up to intubate him.

I also remember a lot of the corpsmen. One was nicknamed was Andy. I don't know what his first name was, but they called him Andy Anderson. By the time surgery was over, he had lost one leg below the knee, one leg above the knee, and one arm above the elbow.

Another corpsman, Aldon Asherman had worked with us at Charlie Med before going out in the field. Very few patients died after arriving at our place. Asherman arrived technically alive, and we sort of sensed that he knew where he was, but he died while we were taking care of him. Later, when I was stationed at BUMED [Bureau of Medicine and Surgery in Washington, DC], I would eat my lunch at the Vietnam Wall and knew where to find his name. Of course, I knew many other names on the Wall but Doc Asherman was one of those names I always searched for.

The team at Charlie Med was just remarkable. The lab techs never had to be told how much blood to set up. The x-ray techs never had to be told what to x-ray. And by the time we got the patient into the operating room, the OR was set up for whatever procedure was necessary. Of course, I wanted to return home and when it was my turn, I really wanted to go. But I think I shed a tear when I had to leave that team because it was the finest team I ever worked with.

I saw the movie *M*A*S*H* [released in 1970] for the first time within months after I returned to the States. It upset me because we were a very serious organization. We had fun when we had no work, but when we did have work to do we were serious. We had none of this tomfoolery.

The silence in our situation when casualties came in was overwhelming. Everybody knew their job. We did not scream for this or that or say do this or do that. The surgical teams did their jobs mostly in silence. We had none of this chaos you see on *ER* and other shows like *M*A*S*H*. Teamwork transcended the officer-enlisted boundary. We respected one another.

"Good Morning, Vietnam"

James Finnegan is a product of Pennsylvania — born, bred, and educated. He graduated from Hahnemann Medical School in Philadelphia, spent a year at Hahnemann Hospital for his internship, and then attended the University of Pennsylvania to train as a surgeon.

After completing his second year of medical school, he considered service in Vietnam. "My father came from a long line of warriors but was kept out of World War II because he was a steelworker. He spent his life regretting it. He actually tried all kinds of subterfuges to get in the service, but they blocked him at every point and sent him back to the mill to make guns or howitzers. All through my childhood he would say, 'You're going to serve in the military no matter what else you do.' I wanted to go to war perhaps subconsciously to please my father."

Finnegan was already studying under the Berry Plan with the Navy, and after relinquishing his deferment, found himself at Camp Lejeune, North Carolina, assigned to the Marines.

It was an amazing experience for me because I literally went from home to the Marine Corps. There was absolutely nothing to suggest the existence or presence of the United States Navy. I was in Lejeune in fatigues and combat boots, running the obstacle course and sitting through their classes— the usual stuff that you do for six weeks with the Marines. It was bearable. We obviously, we didn't do what the typical Marine grunt would do, but, nevertheless, they made it pretty serious and scary in the sense that this is what you're going to do.

My orders were to go from Travis [Air Force Base, California] to Okinawa to Vietnam. It was September 1967. My dad came down to Philly from Pittsburgh to see me off, and took me out to the Philadelphia International Airport. My dad was a regular lower middle class guy. He pumped gas, sold storm doors. He never got beyond that level in his lifetime, but he thought like a big shot. He always did. I had a TWA coach ticket to San Francisco. When we arrived at the airport he went up to the TWA counter and said, "I'd like to speak to the manager." I was off to the side as this guy comes out, and my dad said to him, "This is my son, Dr. Finnegan. He's a surgeon from the University of Pennsylvania and he's leaving for Vietnam to operate on the Marines. I want him to fly first class." I wish I had that much chutzpa. My dad did it all the time. Needless to say, that's how I went, first class.

I went through Okinawa and landed in Danang. I got there late in the evening. It was just dusk. The building at the Danang airport was basically a big tin hut. I was standing on Vietnamese soil, and had no clue what I was supposed to do or where I was supposed to go. I was assigned to Headquarters 3rd Medical Battalion, 3rd Division. I went up to a counter to talk to an Air Force airman and said, "I just got here and my orders are..."

"Oh, you have to go to Phu Bai. And there's nothing going out to Phu Bai until tomorrow morning."

I was very naive so I said, "What am I supposed to do until then?"

He said, "Doc, if I were you, I'd find myself a patch of ground out there and get some sleep."

There was a dirt road, no lights, and a big cyclone fence. And by now it was dark. So I went out looking around and found a patch of grass. I put my satchel down, stretched out on the grass, put my head on it, and fell asleep.

At pre-dawn, with just the barest streak of light coming over the horizon, a noise literally blew me awake. I was scared and bolted up in the grass. It was still kind of dark. I had fallen asleep under the back end of an F-4! This guy had just started up the plane. I don't know where he was going, but these engines came on behind that cyclone fence. I don't know how far it was from me, maybe 20 yards or so. I thought I was going to lose it all right then and there. That was my welcome — my "Good Morning, Vietnam."[8]

Later in the day I got a ride up to Phu Bai, my first official stop. I got a bunk in what we used to call "Southeast Asian" huts — plywood with a tin roof. A triage area with a big mud yard was in front of this hut. The airstrip was out there. I still remember the awkwardness. What I didn't realize was that the battalion was in the process of moving north to Dong Ha, which became the headquarters of the 3rd Marine Division, and the 3rd Medical Battalion was also moving to Phu Bai. I think I arrived as that [deployment] was beginning.

Phu Bai was kind of a quiet blip in my experience. There were casualties but never big time — and not much incoming [fire]. Sometimes you'd hear something off in the distance. Then we got word that we were all shipping up to Dong Ha. They had built that combat base, which was actually quite large. The headquarters of the 3rd Marine Division was about half a mile down the road from us.

We took casualties at Delta Med at a much more frequent rate because now we were servicing the whole 3rd Marine Division along that stretch of the DMZ [Demilitarized Zone]. A lot of action occurred at that point — patrols, clashes, battles, and everything else. Then the NVA [North Vietnamese Army] began shelling Dong Ha. This was dramatically more than at Phu Bai.

Dong Ha had a huge triage area, maybe 2,000 feet, where you could put a whole row of litters. We could take a dozen litter casualties at the same time. Remember with [Dr. John] Parrish's book, *12, 20, and 5: A Doctor's Year in Vietnam* [published in 1972], when the chopper pilots called in? That was the code. That meant walking wounded, litter wounded, and dead. That's what the numbers were. When you heard the numbers, you knew what to expect in terms of getting everything set up.

We could take a pretty large load of casualties at one time, and we did so with some frequency. But we were also within range of the NVA gunners just on the other side of the DMZ, and they used to shell the medical area. The bunkers were located out in the front of Triage. A big steel revetment about 10 feet high and maybe 40 or 50 feet long had been built. As I recall, it wasn't exactly facing north. Nevertheless, when we'd take incoming, we'd all run out and jump in these bunkers—always with a lot of swearing. Why the hell are they firing at the hospital?

Well, we discovered that we had a big white flag with a red cross sticking up on top of the hospital. Somebody pointed out that enemy artillery observers absolutely loved that flag. It gave them a perfect target to sight on and measure their distances. We took the flag down.

I was at Dong Ha from October 1967 through January 1968. We surgeons would alternate call. You would go Triage, first call, second call, third call. One surgeon was designated "triage surgeon." That meant whenever the call came.... Actually, you didn't need much of a call because you could hear the sound of the helicopters coming in from miles out. It could be anything— Hueys and the larger helicopters—the Jolly Green Giants also. It was almost all helicopters at that point. Over that four-month period, we had a steady flow of casualties. If a battle was going on or a recon patrol got into trouble, that would generate a large number of casualties.

When I got to Dong Ha, only a handful of surgeons for the whole 3rd Marine Division were on staff. We didn't have that many people. After operating a little bit, they kind of checked me out and I was pretty much on my own after that.

Although I had been trained as a civilian surgeon, for the most part, the application of basic surgical principles is still your first line of care. It's not as though we invented anything brand-new or that we had never heard of it before. Stop the bleeding, get rid of the bad parts, put the other stuff back together. It's basic surgical principles, but applied a little more rapidly than you would at 34th and Spruce in Philadelphia. But, nevertheless, it was basic surgery. Combat casualties reflect the two big differences between practicing surgery in Philadelphia and practicing surgery in Vietnam.

Many surgeons who have only civilian experience don't have a working knowledge of ballistics—muzzle velocity, missile size, and kinetic damage to tissue. I used to give a lecture on it. If you take the human hand holding a knife and stabbing someone, that hand is moving on an average of eight feet per second as it approaches the body. That's very slow. What that means is that the only injury will be the track of the knife blade. There's no kinetic energy associated with that. Now if that knife blade happens to be tracking into your left ventricle, you're going to die. If the blade just goes through the ribs into the lung, you're going to have a hole in your chest and a lung injury. But you're going to be fine because nothing else happens except that track.

If you take a police .38 special revolver that's clean and well cared for, the muzzle velocity is 938 feet per second. That velocity imparts a reasonable amount of kinetic energy, which means the amount of destructive force that passes through tissue as the missile goes through the body. So that bullet, for example, as it goes through your belly, is not just going to make a hole. Everything a couple of inches around it is going to be damaged severely by the kinetic energy of that missile and the energy it imparts.

If you move to the M16 or the AK-47, you're talking about a muzzle velocity of 3,250 feet per second. It's nothing more than a variation of $E = MC^2$, only E is KE—kinetic energy. Translation: destructive force to tissue equals mass or bullet times velocity squared—3,250 feet per second squared to make up that kinetic energy. For example, if an AK-47 round goes through your chest and just slides beside your heart without hitting it, it will blow off the side of your heart even though it didn't hit the heart.

The first difference you see in casualties in a combat zone—that you're not accustomed to seeing in the civilian world—is the amount of tissue damage from these missiles because of the tremendous velocity they carry.

The second difference in a combat zone is the use of the helicopter. Because it was a helicopter war, almost the instant a casualty occurred, [someone called] "Chopper!" I still think that the great unsung heroes of the war are the chopper pilots. I don't know why they all don't have the Medal of Honor. Every time casualties go down — under any circumstances — the first step is to call for a chopper. And how many times did these guys have to fly into hot fire zones! They had to slow down to land — becoming total targets. They'd go in under fire and pick up casualties. I have to imagine that the amount of injury and destruction to them was considerable. My point is that when they succeeded, they delivered to us 18-, 19-, 20-year-old Marines, the healthiest people on the planet Earth. They had massive injuries that — under any other circumstances — would kill anybody else, or certainly — within a short period of time — would kill anybody.

By chopper, they would arrive at Delta Med in Dong Ha in seven minutes! They were barely alive, but still alive. The new experience was actually seeing these people sooner. Under other circumstances, they would just be dead as in World War I when they would wait for an ambulance to be driven 20 miles to the rear, or during World War II, which was pretty much the same situation. In Korea, helicopters were used. I don't know the percentage of casualties they actually evacuated, but it was pretty small. The movie or TV series *M*A*S*H* would make you think they all came that way but that's not true. They had these tiny helicopters that could just take a couple of people.

It really wasn't until Vietnam that we had the experience of having huge fleets of helicopters on the ready in the fire zones. They would take out massively wounded kids and plop them on our triage tables alive or barely alive, sometimes within minutes.

We had a resuscitation system that was honed to the point where I don't think any civilian organization, at least at that time, could begin to match. It was basic — but extremely effective. For example, sometimes we had a kid come in all shot up and nearly bled out with no vital signs and zero blood pressure. The first job was to resuscitate him.

If I were the triage surgeon and we got in a big batch of casualties, the first step we'd take was to sort them. We had 12 litters and we'd want the worst casualty in litter number 1, the second worst on 2, etc. Let's say the 12th was a guy who maybe had been shot in the belly, but his vital signs were stable and he was fine. He would have to be explored but he was stable and could wait. This other guy who had no vital signs was bleeding like a stuck pig, and we either resuscitated him or he'd die.

We could do all this in a second. It got to the point where you could look at each casualty and put him there and him down there. That's how fast it went. The first team went to the first litter. This is where the criticality was at its height. The chaplain, the orthopedic surgeon, and the corpsmen began cutting off every stitch of clothing. In seconds, the patient was completely naked. In a few seconds more, both groins were opened with a scalpel and both saphenous veins were cannulated with IV tubing. Forget needles. We put the tubing right into the veins. Two pumps — boom!

Within minutes of that kid coming through the door, we were literally pumping stuff into him to restore his blood volume. We never cross-matched a unit of blood the whole time I was there. We used type-specific blood. That would horrify people nowadays. A trial lawyer would have a field day if you ever even mentioned that today. We never cross-matched anybody because we knew what the blood type was based on his dog tag. If he were type A: "Bring me 20 units of Type A." In a matter of minutes, this kid was getting blood and fluids through two huge bore IV cannulas. He had already been intubated instantly by one of our anesthesia people. If there was no heartbeat, the chest was opened very quickly. So the resuscitative effort was slick, quick, skilled, and effective.

I've been asked, "Did anybody ever fall between the cracks?" And I can honestly say, "No." I never knew of anybody dying because we couldn't get to him once that casualty got to us. You would think that with volume casualties that a [low mortality situation] wasn't possible. But I never saw that happen. We took care of everybody.

Tiger in the Night

As a medical battalion physician with the 3rd Medical Battalion in Vietnam, G. Gustave "Gus" Hodge had seen just about every type of wound the North Vietnamese and Viet Cong could inflict. That was before he saw what a hungry four-legged enemy could do.

On the 11th of February 1967, I came in from the field and joined Delta Company, 3rd Medical Battalion, which was at Dong Ha. We had five GMOs [general medical officers], an orthopedic surgeon, a general surgeon, and a couple of anesthesiologists.

At Dong Ha, we were seeing between 1,500 and 1,800 battle casualties a month. A number of casualties were brought in post-concussion from mortar or rocket attack. One fellow came in pretty shaken up. I examined him with my otoscope and ophthalmoscope. When I looked in his left eye, I noticed that it was all black and thought maybe he had blood in that eye. I asked him to move his eyes left and right and his left eye didn't move as well. Then he started chuckling. I asked him what was going on.

He said, "That's my artificial eye." I asked him what his MOS [Military Occupation Specialty] was. He replied that he was a machine gunner. I asked him how he did that with one eye. He said, "My ammo bearer gives me the range and he's also my spotter so if I'm shooting over or under, we correct. It's even better than that Doc. On Okinawa, I was an ammo truck driver."

I asked him how he passed the physical.

He said, "I'd be looking out of my right eye. And they'd tell me to cover my eye with my hand. I'd put my left hand to my left eye. Then they'd say, 'Other eye.' And I'd put my left hand to my left eye. Then I'd put my right hand to the left eye. And it worked three times."

Another fellow was disarming a shoulder-fired rocket launcher. He was disarming the wires that were attached to the rocket launcher, and it went off while he had his hand up. I asked him if he were right- or left-handed.

He said, "My friends call me 'Lefty,' but I used to be right-handed."

He lost his right arm to about mid-forearm. There was nothing left to reconstruct.

The humor that came through in the triage area was amazing. How resilient these folks were. One day they brought in a wounded Marine who was point for his company.[9] As we were about to medevac him, he resisted evacuation. "Doc," he said, "I can smell 'em. If I'm not there, someone's gonna get hurt." He said that his ability to smell the enemy got him out of a couple of bad scrapes.

Another incident created a lot of interest. A Marine was brought to our triage area with an unusual wound in his right arm. I asked him what had happened and he said that he really wasn't sure. Something had picked him up and shook him like a rag doll. I examined the wound and found an avulsion [torn-away tissue] of the anterior right arm with significant damage to the biceps and some individual punctures.

He thought that he had been bitten by a tiger. Everybody ridiculed this notion, but after looking at the wounds, we felt that this was most likely the case. He said that he and his comrades had taken off from Route 9 and gone into the bush. They climbed up a hill and began digging in for the night. He was in a shallow foxhole with his arms out of the foxhole and his rifle across the edge. Just about the time he began to doze off, the tiger grabbed him by the arm. The Marine began beating the animal with his fists and didn't know whether he hit it in the nose or the eye, but it let go and headed down the hill. He grabbed his rifle and fired a couple of rounds at the retreating mass, but didn't think he hit anything. Suddenly he realized that he had just shot his rifle so he couldn't have lost his arm. He told us that at first it didn't hurt but for a burning sensation.

We cleaned up the wounds. According to my notes, he went out to the *Sanctuary* for further treatment on April 17, 1967.

"Tiger Dave"

Cpl. David Schwirian of Lima Company 3/3 was the tiger's victim. He had been ordered to set up an after-dark ambush along Highway 9. This road was west of Ca Lu and just south of the DMZ, not far from the Laotian border. The young Marine never suspected that a four-legged enemy lurked nearby.

I set up in the middle and had a machine gunner on one side and a rocket man on the other with an automatic weapon. The radioman was to my right and my corpsman was behind us. We were on a turn so that we could fire in either direction down the road in case something came up from either direction.

We were making radio checks every half hour by clicking the mike key on the radio. We wouldn't talk but just key the mike. The code was either one or two clicks. This was about 11 or 11:30 at night and you couldn't see a hand in front of your face. There was supposed to be a click but I didn't hear it. I was reaching over to see whether my radioman was awake or if he made that connection. When I reached over, the tiger grabbed my right arm from behind. I didn't know it was there until it grabbed me and, at that time, I didn't know what it was.

I thought I had punched him in the nose but I'm not sure that happened. On these patrols I kept a Ka-Bar knife[10] in between my legs because I always sat up. Well, that Ka-Bar was missing; we don't know what happened to it. I don't know whether I stuck it in the tiger or it just got lost in the shuffle. I heard nothing until the tiger ran away. It sounded like a freight train. The whole thing took milliseconds. It was very quick.

I don't remember what happened right after that because I went into shock — but I had no pain. I had no feeling in that arm whatsoever. The tiger had severed the nerve because he had taken so much muscle out. And because it was so dark, there was no way to see what the damage was. The corpsman had one of those BIC lighters and was able to assess what had happened. He said I was in bad condition and he needed to get me out of there.

The corpsman was trying to patch me up and call out on the radio without any lights. Because it was so dark the first time he tried, he wrapped the microphone from the radio up in the bandages and had to take it all apart and re-do it. He was trying to get permission to break the ambush, but back at headquarters, they were having a hard time trying to comprehend what was going on. So it took them 30 minutes or so to decide to let us break the ambush and leave.

The corpsman and I decided that I would walk back with him as far as I could until I couldn't walk anymore. Then he would give me morphine. Up until that point, I had no feeling in the arm and it wasn't hurting.

About two-thirds of the way back I got to the point where I had probably lost so much blood I couldn't go any further. So they took some rifles and ponchos, made a stretcher, and carried me the rest of the way.

We came to a bridge we had to cross and had to do it single file and I have no idea how we did it with no lights. We were trying to move as quickly as possible to get back inside the perimeter before we got caught by the enemy. That was a big concern and that's why we wanted to break the ambush as soon as possible. When that tiger got me, I must have made enough noise to wake up Laos.

They carried me back to the company at Ca Lu because restrictions kept them from flying the choppers. When daylight came, they put me in a jeep and a squad riding in a dump truck escorted us back to Delta Med.

At the same time, they sent another squad back to the ambush site during the daylight and found the tiger tracks which confirmed that it was a tiger.

I remember a corpsman pouring some saline solution on my arm and I went ballistic. I think he had given me a shot underneath my arm. When he put the saline on the wound to clean it, I went out. I was out until they were wheeling me down the ramp from the chopper into the USS *Sanctuary*, and down a hallway right into the operating room. I didn't know how serious my wounds were, but later they told me I was within millimeters of losing my arm. The tiger had taken my bicep and just removed everything on the front side of the arm down to the bone.

The surgeon put everything back together but left the wound open for two or three weeks while I was on the ship so it could be cleaned out to prevent any infection. They also gave me the 14-day series of rabies shots. After that, they did a skin graft, taking the skin off the front of my legs. There's no muscle in there. The skin graft just covered up the area.

I spent about 30 days or so on the *Sanctuary* and then they shipped me back to the Philadelphia Naval Hospital. Dr. Smith did a tendon transplant so I could use my hand. He used tendons that went to my shoulder, and my shoulder muscles help to move my hand. Then I was discharged.

I have a lot of problems but the arm is usable. I can't lift anything; I've got no strength because I have no muscles.

HM2 Paul Churchill was on duty at Delta Med the night they brought in Cpl. Schwirian.

That night, we heard that a medevac helicopter was coming in so we got up and ran down to the pad. Dave [Schwirian] was on that helicopter, and when it landed we grabbed a stretcher and took him in.

Truthfully, I don't remember the other wounds; I remember the arm. He was on the stretcher and his arm was beside him. It was almost as though a surgeon had removed his biceps. The humerus was lying there perfectly clean and just white as snow. It wasn't even bleeding. Doc [Dan] Fuss did a great job out there in the field. It was unbelievable.

We had to apply saline to hydrate it because it was already drying and the surface was beginning to scab over. We then wrapped it and got him ready to move on to the next stop which was the hospital ship. We basically cleaned and wrapped it. At that time, we routinely applied Furacin [ointment used on skin grafts]. I had been using a Furadantin impregnated gauze on burn victims in the field. I'm not sure that's what we used, but we covered the wound with something to protect and keep it hydrated until we could medevac him to where they could do some real surgery.

There were other tiger incidents. Even before that attack, I was on a patrol probably 8 or 10 clicks north of the base camp with about 8 or 9 others. I was walking in a line with a Montagnard PF [Popular Forces] behind me who was carrying a grease gun [.45 submachine gun]. All of a sudden, he opened up and nobody saw what he was shooting at. We motioned to him to ask what he was shooting at. He took his hand and made like a big mouth closing and he growled. He then pointed at my pants. I looked down and there was blood on my pants leg. Apparently, the tiger had been close enough that when he shot it, the blood spattered on my pants. I never even saw the tiger. We were in elephant grass about nine feet tall. But somehow he saw the tiger and shot it. Even though it left a blood trail, we never saw the tiger. The PF wanted to go after the tiger, but we all thought it was better not to—especially since he had fired that grease gun and gave away our position. So we decided to get out of there. About four months after that, Dave was bitten. You got to where you were watching behind you as much as in front of you when you were on patrol.

Doctor to the Rescue

It was late afternoon on 4 September 1968. A Company, 1st Battalion of the 61st Infantry Regiment (Mechanized) had been engaged in a "search and clear operation" beside the destroyed vil-

lage of Lang Dong Bao Thuong. The village was located in the vicinity of Hill 162 in Quang Tri Province. Without warning, a numerically superior force of the North Vietnamese Army ambushed the company. Using automatic weapons, rocket-propelled grenades, mortars, and artillery, the enemy tore the hapless troops to pieces, inflicting many casualties. Within minutes all the company's officers and NCOs (noncommissioned officers) were either killed or wounded. The survivors huddled in or behind their armored personnel carriers (APCs), several of which had been disabled by incoming fire. Some had become mired in the mud and were immovable. A few soldiers returned a desultory fire against their attackers. The others were too demoralized to respond.

As North Vietnamese soldiers were closing in for the kill, an Army helicopter landed at the Quang Tri Marine Corps hospital complex with news of the embattled company. Lt. Edward Feldman, a 3rd Medical Battalion physician, who had recently lived through the 77-day siege of Khe Sanh, was in the facility's Triage preparing it for the possible arrival of casualties.

It was about 5:30. Suddenly a chopper came into the landing pad, and a crewman said they needed a doctor out at the aircraft. I wasn't sure whether they had a casualty they didn't know how to move or whether there was a casualty who needed immediate care. I followed him out to the Huey, climbed aboard, and they immediately took off. The door gunner gave me a headset and I began talking to the pilot or co-pilot. They told me there were troops engaged who had been attacked and who couldn't get their casualties out. It was an Army armored unit and would I come with them. I said I would.

We flew for 15 or 20 minutes at a low altitude in very bad weather, being buffeted and with rain coming into the chopper. When we landed, we immediately began taking incoming rounds on the left side of the aircraft. You could just hear them hitting. I jumped out onto the ground. It was dark, overcast, and rainy. I saw the enemy off to the left beyond the armored personnel carriers. I also saw movement of troops but couldn't tell if they were friendly or enemy.

A person — whom I would characterize as a senior NCO or field grade officer — briefed me as to what was happening. I found a casualty with a head wound in one of the first vehicles. He was either dead or close to it. With that head wound, he was not someone whom I could have salvaged or would have evacuated at that point. I took his helmet, flak jacket, his M16, and a pouch like a bandolier. The guy who was briefing me got pissed off because I wouldn't evacuate the man. I said, "He's not going out. Let me see some other wounded." I certainly was not going to allow him to be evacuated on the chopper that had just brought me in. It would be needed for the wounded who had a chance. I added very firmly, "That's not how it's going to happen."

We went to the next trac [APC — Armored Personnel Carrier] and found some more wounded men. I had no medical supplies with me. I found some gear, mainly dressings in the APCs and had one of the NCOs bring me whatever medical equipment he could find. We ended up just using some of the dressings he had found. I don't recall having anything else besides some morphine.

We continued to take a lot of incoming — RPGs [rocket-propelled grenades] and automatic weapons fire. I remember getting to one trac and observed maybe two or three soldiers on top who were not firing their weapons. I could see the enemy just a little bit above us, off to the left and not far away. I could also see the greenish yellow tracer rounds coming at us and at the other vehicles. I knew the enemy was out there and we needed to return fire. I said, "You need to fire your weapons." And I began to fire my newly acquired and mud-encrusted M16 in that direction.

When the soldiers finally began firing their .50 caliber and M60s, I then went from trac to trac looking after casualties. These soldiers were either dead or dying, and I had to evaluate them based on their appearance or the condition of their wounds. If I knew they were dying or almost gone, I gave them morphine. Although I found some casualty tags and signed my name on them with a pencil or pen, I knew something else. When casualties were received at an aid station, it was customary for them to be freshly evaluated and the only information that anyone seemed to see or was interested in at that point was the time they had gotten their last morphine. We paid attention to the tag, but we mainly just looked at their pupils and their vital signs, checked out their wounds, and then treated them accordingly. No one paid much attention to the description of their wound on the casualty tag. What you saw was what you got.

The enemy was getting closer, and down at the last trac I saw movement that wasn't friendly. We began firing at them.

After a while, it became very evident that no one was changing any of the dynamics of our predicament. We were taking fire and just halfheartedly responding. We were dispersed, couldn't really concentrate our forces, and were clearly not in control of the situation. By now the helicopter that had brought me was gone, and I don't know who had been evacuated. It became clear to me that we had to get to higher ground on an adjacent hill.

The armored personnel carriers [M113s][11] were armed with two or three M60 machine guns and a .50 caliber in the turret. I wasn't seeing a lot of people around. Sometimes the soldiers were out and around the vehicles sometimes on them sometimes in them. To rouse those inside, I knocked on the rear hatches with the butt of my M16. Actually by that time I had two M16s. I said, "We need to move these vehicles."

And so we began to move the tracs up that hill. I walked at first, then rode on one of them. Even though it was dark and raining, we moved under constant mortar, RPG, artillery, and machine gun fire.

When we got up the hill, the troops lined up the vehicles, pointing them in the direction from which we had come. This hill has since been called Hill 162 although I didn't know that at the time, not having a map. We faced the APCs outward with armed soldiers in and between them, and put out some concertina wire. I was told that we had Claymore mines[12] so the soldiers put them out also.

Because we had taken some more casualties during the course of this movement, we collected them in the center of the remaining eight vehicles in a kind of convex formation. There were no medics but several guys began helping me. I remember one casualty in particular, Lt. [Philip] Hesli. One of his eyes was gone and the other was closed. He had also been wounded in the thigh, groin, or leg because I recall cutting off his pants leg. He was stable but really needed to be evacuated.

I asked the radioman to call back to base and get me on the line and I would talk. I told them we needed a big chopper. We also had to clear a landing zone. I didn't know how to clear a landing zone so I said, "Clear a landing zone!" And they did it. As we got the casualties ready for evacuation, we were still getting some rifle and automatic weapons fire but no more RPG or mortar fire.

By this time another unit had joined us on the hill, but I had made no contact with its commander. I was just taking care of casualties because no one else was there. The main goal was to get the casualties out. I didn't know it at the time but I know from the log what time it was. It was 10:45 when a [CH-47] Chinook came to pick up our five dead and some of the most serious casualties.

As it came in, we began getting a lot of machine gun fire in the landing zone. I didn't know whether they were firing at the chopper on the ground, at the casualties and those of us loading them, or all of the above. Nevertheless, we got all the casualties aboard that we could manage — aboard, and also some of the dead. And then the chopper took off under heavy fire, after which everything kind of slowed down. Throughout the night I remained awake, sometimes taking shelter inside and sometimes alongside one of the tracs, always letting the men know where I was.

The next day we got just the occasional incoming round but nothing of any consequence.

The men then tried to get some of the mired vehicles out of there by towing them with chains. Several were very badly damaged.

Eventually, we moved out and went back to an area called C-2 or C-3, where I met the battalion commander, Lt. Col. [Bernard] Wheeler. He was very laudatory as to what I had done. No one back at my unit knew where I was. When I told Lt. Col. Wheeler that I had to get back to Quang Tri quickly, they got me a chopper and took me. This was on September 6th.

When I arrived at headquarters, I was treated like an MIA. It looked like someone had taken ice tongs, put them in my ears, dropped me into a mud bath, and pulled me out a day later. When I learned that I had been considered MIA, I immediately became concerned that my family would freak out. I went to 3rd Marine Division headquarters, not trusting anyone with the kind of paperwork that would be required.

One big event happened at headquarters. Here I was, an absolute filth box — unkempt, unshaven, in a mud-encrusted uniform, and still carrying the M16. And who do I run into but General [Ray] Davis [Commanding General, 3rd Marine Division]!

This was Division headquarters. It didn't matter where Division headquarters was. It was always squared away. It was always policed. And all the people, both officer and enlisted, were always wearing starched utilities. I saw the general and saluted him. I had met him two months before and had dinner with him twice after he had given me the Silver Star and once after that. He looked at me and said, "Doctor, if you're going to get yourself into trouble, you should at least have the good sense to do so with the Marines."

"The Price of Doing Business"

Not all casualties can be repaired with scalpels and sutures. As in all wars, the stress of combat — with all its horrific by-products — takes a toll on the human psyche. In Vietnam, men broke down, became contentious, or grew increasingly depressed. Units sometimes spent weeks in the bush living, fighting, and enduring an inhospitable environment. These surroundings took the form of heat, humidity, insects, snakes, leeches, booby traps, and an invisible but deadly enemy. For the men defending isolated hilltops or the combat base at Khe Sanh, NVA shelling deprived men of sleep, leaving them exhausted, disoriented, and unable to function. The bloody month-long combat in the streets and buildings of Hue added to the rolls of the mentally wounded.

Everyday confrontation with fear, violence, trauma, the loss of friends, and their own mortality sometimes left even the best fighters worn out and burned out. Given such unsettling conditions, all men were susceptible to these symptoms, but those with previously undetected mental illness could also become threats to themselves and their comrades.

Attending to this kind of disturbed and disabling mental casualty was the job of Navy psychologists and psychiatrists. Never in adequate supply, these mental health specialists practiced their healing art in medical battalions and aboard the two hospital ships. Their approach to dealing with psychiatric casualties was to treat them as close as possible to the scene of action and then quickly return them to their outfits. As 3rd Medical Battalion commanding officer Cmdr. Almon Wilson noted, "Confidence building was [the psychiatrist's] biggest contribution. He might say to a patient, 'There's nothing wrong with being afraid once in a while. There's nothing wrong with saying this is a dirty, filthy, rotten place, and that you'd rather be home. It's perfectly normal to feel as you feel. If your buddies don't feel like you do, they're just not telling you.'"

It was early March 1968 when Lt. Stephen Edmondson arrived in Vietnam. A graduate of the Medical College of Georgia, and with residencies at the Psychiatric Institute of the University of Maryland and Emory University, Edmondson reported for active duty in August 1967. He was assigned to the 3rd Medical Battalion at Phu Bai in late February 1968. The Tet Offensive had been raging for a month.

Most of the patients we received were referrals from general medical officers. They were extreme stress cases relating to combat in the bush where the Marines were doing the fighting.

We kept anyone in really bad shape — who couldn't be sent right back to his unit — in our little 10- or 12-bed unit. We used the sole bottle of Thorazine [anti-psychotic drug with sedative qualities] on these patients. When I got to Phu Bai I discovered we had almost no psychotropic medication available — just this one big bottle of 75mg Thorazine. If the patients were really bummed out, were psychotic, disorganized, or extremely fatigued and not able to function, we gave them enough Thorazine to make them sleep for two or three days. I instructed the corpsmen to wake them from time to time, help them to the latrine, get some fluids into them, see that they had something to eat, and then just let them go back to sleep. Usually after a day or two of rest, most of these fellows improved drastically and were able to go back to their units. Others, aided by the medication, food, and support in a safe quiet place got turned around pretty quickly. In fact, our evacuation rate dropped like a rock.

I had a standard procedure with a new patient. In the patient's presence, I read the referring information written up by the general medical officer. Then I established a talking rapport with the patient by reviewing some of the points made in that referral. I would then ask for the patient's opinion based on what had been said. I would simply keep him talking — as I would anyone back home — but with a focus, of course, on the particular complaints that he was supposed to have had.

Most of these fellows would give me a pretty accurate account that agreed with the referral information. Sometimes the patient introduced new material that was a lot more detailed than what the referral had provided. I found that only a few patients were trying to pull a con operation.

After discussing all this with the patient, I told him what I thought and whether or not he needed to get himself ready to go back to his unit. Somewhere in the course of the interview, I would say, "Now listen. After we talk, if I don't see any problem severe enough for you to stay here for a while or be evacuated, you're going to have to go back to your unit."

This was particularly tough with some of the young men coming out of Khe Sanh. But most of them accepted it quite well, and most of them went back. We never thought about returning anyone to their unit while they were on medication.

As soon as these young fellows were able to get on their feet and do something, we assigned them a number of chores around the medical battalion to keep them in harness and to help them rebuild their function. It also enabled us observe how well they were functioning.

As I said, most of them were able to return to their units after a few days. Those we had to evacuate were clearly dangerous. We pretty quickly shipped to Danang those who might have been trying to kill others [their own troops] or themselves.

We had very few really dangerous cases but I recall one in particular. In the interest of trying to help the young man with his very strong motivation to be a successful Marine, I made a big mistake. He was a young fellow, fairly slim, seemingly mature, and from a New England family with a very strong military focus. He wanted to prove to them that he could be a good Marine.

His unit had seen a lot of heavy combat, and he had gotten to the point where he was not functioning properly. He wasn't making good decisions or carrying out orders very well — not because he wasn't trying — but because he had deteriorated that much. We kept him for a while and I talked to him. He was so focused on wanting to return to his unit and prove himself that he seemed to get a lot better, and he functioned okay with the little assignments we gave him.

He stayed with us for about two weeks and then we sent him back. A few weeks later, something really dramatic and terrible happened. In the middle of the night, he went into what looked like a fugue state. This is a disassociated state in which he thought something was happening that wasn't really happening at all. He grabbed a machine gun and began to fire in every direction — over the camp and out into the wilds. It took his sergeant and others several hours to distract him enough so someone could disarm him. Nobody was hurt, but they certainly could have been. Frankly, I hadn't anticipated this happening, and I doubt most people would have.

I had another interesting case while I was in Vietnam. The patient was with one of the units that was going through a lot of combat up near the DMZ. They had many wounded and killed.

Somewhere along the way, he lost his glasses and, being where they were, he couldn't get another pair. So his friends looked after him until things cleared up a bit. They literally told him what direction to shoot in. After a while, he had classic battle fatigue and so they sent him to see me. After I spoke with him, I learned that he, too, just wanted to serve. We had gotten him a new pair of glasses by this time, and he begged to go back to his unit.

I told him that it would never do and that he had been through this once already — and he had become a hazard to his unit. "This could happen again at any time if your glasses get broken or lost," I told him.

While he was with us, he demonstrated a remarkable artistic talent, drawing all the time. I asked the division office if they could use someone to illustrate their publications. I took him to the division office and they put him to work. He stayed and finished his tour helping with their publications. And he was very good.

As a psychiatrist, I certainly watched out for psychotic symptoms since the patients were inconsistent with functioning even back in a quiet situation. I saw occasional cases where we were sure the patient was a functioning psychotic — a person who might not have succeeded in a civilian situation but might actually take to the violence of war. Our goal was to make sure the patients were able to think straight, cooperate with other people, carry out orders, and tolerate that very high degree of stress that combat situations included.

We determined "psychosis" by looking for evidence of schizophrenia and any other kind of psychotic state. We also looked for depression that was so severe that the individual could not concentrate on his work. He might make a mistake and get himself or other people killed. He might become so depressed that he would try to kill himself — and the weapons were there to do that. Many opportunities occurred to get killed indirectly by putting oneself in the line of fire.

We found a number of men who had seen so much death and loss among their comrades or had been out in the field so long that they were totally "burned out." It was the kind of depression that was not going to improve very quickly. These patients included some pretty high ranking officers. One lieutenant colonel in charge of a battalion had been out in the field so long and had dealt with so much that he could no longer function. He had to be evacuated.

Anxiety was a condition most everybody experienced to one degree or another, but it was only a danger if it led to virtual paralysis in certain situations. One patient in this category was a young corpsman who had been at Khe Sanh. He had rushed out to get some casualties onto an aircraft that had just touched down on the runway. Aircraft that landed at Khe Sanh rarely stopped completely but kept rolling to keep the NVA from targeting them with mortars. The corpsman had just loaded a patient into the plane when a mortar landed about a foot and a half in front of him. But it failed to explode. He froze, expecting the shell to detonate at any moment. When his fellow corpsmen saw what had happened, they grabbed him and threw him aboard the very next plane that came in. The man went to Phu Bai — not only to get out of harm's way — but to be evaluated. He was badly shaken but was all right.

During my practice in Vietnam, I saw the acute version of what became known as PTSD [Post Traumatic Stress Disorder]. It was as common as dirt. But most of the troops had to carry on. If they could seal it over enough to go back to duty and continue functioning, they did so. If everyone who had experienced this typically acute disorder had been evacuated, we would not have had an army over there. It was part of the price of doing business in a war.

We were encouraged to continue to use the terms "combat fatigue" or "combat stress syndrome" to define this particular kind of condition. I usually called it an "acute situation reaction." Certainly that applied to that young corpsman at Khe Sanh who had the experience with the mortar. And adding to that was the fact that he had already seen numerous wounds and people dying.

Of course, many of these patients swallowed hard, shut it out, and went back to duty. The chronic symptoms would begin to emerge later on. While they were in combat, they never had a chance to work on it and work it through. But later they would have this horrible wringing-out condition hitting them over and over again for years and years. When I got back and had my practice in Atlanta, I saw a lot of these fellows because some of the other psychiatrists knew I had been in Vietnam and they referred them to me.

It was a very sad condition to see because a lot of them were truly disabled by it. But we didn't have the technical or the diagnostic concept of PTSD at that time.

5

INTREPID SURGEONS

The Vietnam War generated the kinds of injuries expected in a mid–20th century conflict fought with high velocity small arms, mortars, rockets, artillery, and the most insidious weapon of all — land mines. As the war ground on, medical personnel became proficient in treating hideous wounds inflicted by these instruments of war. Yet surgeons were also forced to confront the unimaginable — fighting men who had survived violent encounters with ordnance that had inexplicably failed to detonate. What to do with an unexploded mortar shell embedded in a soldier's chest wall or an armed rocket protruding from a patient's knee? These were situations that required caution, skill, and courage. Here are the stories of three heroic surgeons who went above and beyond their normal medical routine to save a life — and with their own hanging in the balance.

Dr. Dinsmore's Souvenir

One of the most curious photographs to come out of the Vietnam War is an x-ray showing a mortar shell lodged beside the victim's chest wall. The patient, a South Vietnamese soldier, had been riding in an armored personnel carrier near Danang in the late afternoon of 1 October 1966 when he spotted a Viet Cong mortar squad. It was already too late. A 60mm mortar round[1] struck the open hatch, deflected off his steel helmet, and penetrated soft tissue between his collarbone and shoulder. The round then plunged beneath his skin before coming to rest below the left armpit. Within minutes, his comrades rushed him — still conscious and very terrified — to the nearby U.S. Naval Support Activity hospital at Danang. Capt. Harry Dinsmore describes the traumatic experience in the OR.

I was eating my evening meal in the officers' mess hall at about 5:30 P.M. on the evening of 1 October 1966. The mess hall was located a few hundred yards from the Mass Casualty Center [MCC], where many of our casualties arrived by helicopter. I was just finishing when the officer of the day walked in with an x-ray in his hand. I vividly recall thinking my colleagues were playing a trick on me as we sometimes did to each other to break the boredom. I was assured it was no trick, and the patient was at that moment in the MCC. I and several other physicians hurried down there to take a look.

An ARVN [Army of the Republic of Vietnam] soldier, Nguyen Van Luong, age 22, was conscious and had no wounds other than the entrance wound in the anterior aspect of his left shoulder — and the obvious 60mm mortar round beneath the skin of his left anterior chest wall. His heavy denim army shirt was pulled into the wound, and, as it later turned out, the cloth was badly entangled in the mortar round's tail fins. Most of the shirt had been cut away by the time he arrived. It was immediately obvious what had to be done.

I was chief of surgery and the senior surgical officer present. However, I did not have the first surgical call. Although three to four other general surgeons were on my staff, with the gravity of this situation, I felt that I could not ask or order anyone else to do the surgery.

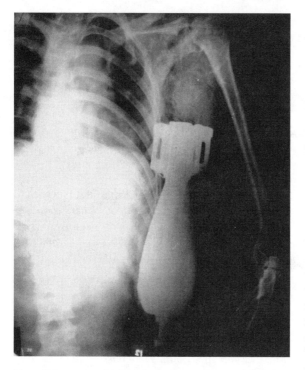

One of the most gripping photos to come out of the Vietnam War is this x-ray showing a live mortar round lodged in the chest wall of a South Vietnamese soldier (BUMED Archives).

We called the Navy Ordnance Depot and told them our problem. They agreed to send a demolition expert to the hospital. He arrived about 20 minutes later. When shown the patient, Engineman First Class John Lyons just shook his head in disbelief. The round, he stated, contained between one and two pounds of TNT. After measuring the firing pin on the x-ray, he pointed out that it was already partially depressed. The round could go off at any time — even without being handled!

In the meantime, several corpsmen and other staff members were starting to position sandbags around the operating table in the OR at one end of a Quonset hut. However, their activity was stopped for two reasons. One, the round was of such a size that it could not be held in place with an instrument during surgery; it had to be handheld. There was no way this could be done from behind sandbags. The second reason was the more determining one. Lyons told us that sandbags would do no good. If the round went off, the whole Quonset hut would be gone!

The patient was taken to the operating room by stretcher, and I never saw such careful, tiptoeing stretcher carriers. They placed him on the operating table, stretcher and all. He was sedated, given a general anesthetic by our anesthesiologist, Lt. Jerry Warren, intubated, and then attached to the Bird machine, an automatic respirator. Warren then left. I made the decision that no unnecessary personnel should be in the OR. Several corpsmen — OR techs — volunteered to assist me, and while I was in the locker room changing clothes, one of the other surgeons offered to do the surgery. He could see how scared I was. The OR techs set up the Mayo trays and then left. Only Lyons and I would stay. Lyons would take the round and disarm it after removal.

I chose not to do a skin prep. Lyons urged that I not move the round within the tissue — no twisting or lateral motion. He felt the round should not be moved at all until it was lifted straight from the chest wall. To accomplish that end, I planned to make an elliptical incision all the way around and away from the mortar shell. I proceeded with the surgery.

When the round had been completely encircled, I lifted it with the overlying soft tissues directly away from the chest wall, thinking every second that my world was going to end — the shell was just a foot from my face.

Then a major problem became evident. As the shell came away from the chest wall, I felt something restraining it. The patient's blood-soaked shirt, which was also firmly trapped within the entrance wound, was badly entangled in the mortar round's tail fins. With Mayo scissors, the heaviest we had, I spent another harrowing 10 minutes cutting through multiple folds of heavy, wet cloth to get it free. I handed the shell, with the surrounding tissues, to Lyons and then hurried over to open the door for him. He took the round to a nearby sand dune where he defused it and emptied the TNT. He later returned it to me as a keepsake.

The entire procedure had taken about a half hour. The OR techs then returned. After re-gloving, I completed the procedure by obtaining hemostasis, removing the remaining cloth fragments, and further debriding the wound, all accompanied by copious irrigation. This took an additional 30 minutes, but that part of it I barely remember. We applied sterile dressings; skin grafting was planned for later.

It was Saturday evening. I went back and wrote a letter to my wife after I stopped at the chapel for better than half an hour. And then I went to bed. I don't know what time it was — 6:30 or 7:00 Sunday morning — when someone was beating on my door. The messenger said, "Doctor, the OD [officer of the day] said you'd better come down here. There are press reporters all over this place." So we went down there and he was right. They were everywhere. I would try to answer as many questions as they asked. And they wanted all kinds of pictures. All the major networks had reporters on the scene — from ABC, CBS, and NBC.

The patient's postoperative course was uneventful, and he was very grateful. The wounds were closed with split-thickness grafts about a week later, which took well and healing progressed satisfactorily. He had some resultant weakness of the left shoulder because of the loss of a portion of greater pectoral muscle, but the functional result was good. The patient returned to full-duty status within two months.

Surgery Under Fire

Lt. Edward Feldman of the 3rd Medical Battalion was on temporary duty at Khe Sanh and under fire every day. At 5:30 on the morning of 21 January 1968, the North Vietnamese

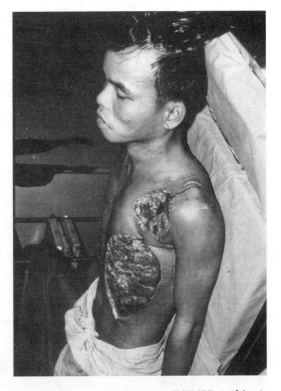

Nguyen Van Luong post-surgery (BUMED Archives).

Capt. Harry Dinsmore receives the Navy Cross and congratulations from Gen. William Westmoreland, commander, U.S. Military Assistance Command, Vietnam (COMUSMACV) (BUMED Archives).

launched a ferocious mortar and rocket attack. Lt. Feldman and many others at the besieged Marine base that morning, took whatever cover they could. Crouched in his two-man, above-ground bunker, he reacted with fear and dread. "I was trying to tie my boots and my hands were shaking. I was in no position to help anyone in this bunker by myself. Suddenly, a huge round landed just outside. If it had been in the passageway that led to the outside, I would have fallen into a hole the size of a Volkswagen." Minutes later, Feldman had enough casualties to keep him busy for a very long time. Thirty-six years after the Siege of Khe Sanh, he recalled one wounded Marine above all the others.

Fortunately, I had increased our defensive posture. I had two automatic weapons positions at either end of the triage bunker, our so-called "holding bunker," and they were manned by some additional Marine personnel to operate the weapons.

I waited a little while and then headed for the battalion aid station [BAS] but it was on fire, having taken a direct hit. The BAS was essentially gone. Instead, I went to an above-ground bunker, which was our holding bunker, and moved out the guys who had resided there in a two- or three-day hold situation. I sent them elsewhere. They weren't wounded but just had rashes and other minor ailments. We salvaged as much as we could from the battalion aid station tents and put all that gear into one corner. One person then started sorting gear so we could utilize the holding bunker efficiently.

Then casualties began streaming in. They brought one guy in on poncho liners with an abdominal wound. I cut off the battle dressing and saw a pipe about the diameter of a hand-held flashlight pointing upward from the upper left quadrant of his abdomen. We didn't know what it was. A first class corpsman named Richard Asquith said to me, "Hold everything! That's something else."

When we realized that the casualty could have unexploded ordnance in his belly, I backed away and had some of the men bring in sandbags from the side of the bunker. We then put the wounded Marine in one corner surrounded by sandbags. With his IV hanging down, I talked to him. I told him that part of his gas mask was in his wound and I had to take it out. I said to just lie still. Nobody was going to leave him. We were just improving our defensive position with the sandbags. He had no clue.

I gave him a syrette of morphine and then told Lt. Kim Johnson, "If anything bad happens, just get rid of these personal letters of mine."

"Oh, nothing is going to happen," he replied.

I got a corpsman to volunteer. We taped four flashlights together and then I sent for an EOD [explosive ordnance disposal], but with all the chaos we couldn't find anyone. The ammo dump had been hit, we were still getting incoming, and our ordnance was exploding all over the place. Huge fuel bladders filled with JP-4 [aircraft fuel] for our choppers were on fire. The whole place was on fire and shells were cooking off.

Anyway, they found a staff sergeant engineer named Ronald Sniekouski who said he'd help me. He told me what not to touch. I had a few instruments I had salvaged. One was a huge hemostat which was in my pocket.

With the instruments and my fingers, I got around the pipe-like object. A lot of tissue had adhered to it because the metal had been hot when it hit. I got my hands under it, lifted it up, then passed it over to the staff sergeant who carried it outside and deposited the ordnance in a safe area — a square about two or three feet high that had additional sandbags.

I'm not really sure, even now, what it was. Some said it was the warhead and fuse assembly from an 82mm mortar. I then evacuated the patient down to Charlie Med because at that time I was still attached to the battalion aid station for the 1st Battalion, 26th Marines. The patient then went into shock because I had missed his liver laceration. They took him into the OR, sutured the liver laceration, and evacuated him to what I believe was Phu Bai. I saw 60 more casualties that day.

Rocket Surgery

Navy surgeon Dr. David Taft had his own encounter with a life-threatening surgery. As he remembers, he was lying in his rack at Charlie Med reading a book that fateful afternoon in August 1967 when a corpsman disturbed his rest.

"Doctor, there's a young kid up in Triage, and he's got something sticking out of his knee." I asked how big it was.

And he said, "It's about three inches in diameter, and it's long."

I pulled on my boots, and the corpsman and I walked up to Triage to see what the object was. It was obvious to me what it was—a 2.75mm rocket, probably from a Huey helicopter. I had seen those pods with multiple holes on the sides of Hueys and this type of rocket fit in one of those holes.

The whole damn rocket had gone right through the kid's patella, and his leg was flexed at the knee. I leaned over and asked him, "Were you being supported by helicopters?"

He said, "Yeah."

"Were they firing rockets?" He nodded.

I turned and whispered to the corpsman to get everyone out of there, and then said, "I think this is a live rocket."

I had an EOD man standing by—a Marine. He motioned to me to come over to him. "Doctor, if I were you, I'd be most careful with that thing."

I asked him if I should take any special precautions. He suggested that I not be too rough with it.

He then said, "There's no reason for me to be in here too."

I told him I wouldn't let him stay anyway. "If you want to see surgery some time, I'd be happy to take you into the OR, but right now I don't want anybody else getting hurt."

Pretty soon the whole place was empty except for the patient and me. He said, "What's up?" and I told him that we would have to take him to the operating room to remove the rocket. I left him and went out to try to find some help but most everybody had disappeared. I asked a first class corpsman about anesthesia, and he said that nobody wanted anything to do with this situation.

I knew how to give a spinal so I requested that he get a tray ready for me. I then asked for a corpsman to help me, just to pass things. Was there anybody there who could do that?

A corpsman named [HM1 Daniel B.] Henry said he would help me. So he and I took the young patient back to the OR. I had already done the spinal and given him heavy sedation. By this time, we were wearing flak jackets. I told Henry "This is ridiculous. Are you going to put a flak jacket over my head, too? If this thing goes off, it will blow the hell out of both of us."

I examined the x-ray and it looked to me like the rocket had destroyed his knee. In fact, on the x-ray the knee looked like a handful of dice. The rocket was just jammed in there. Henry said that one of the orthopedic surgeons had suggested that I just cut the leg off because all the vessels and nerves were destroyed.

We applied some Zephiran [topical anesthetic] to the knee and I began working. Initially, I tried to rock the projectile but the rocket was stuck. The knee is an interesting structure. It's under tension. If you stick something in between the tibia and the end of the femur, it's stuck there! I could have cut into the joint and removed it, but by that time the foot was really looking bad. It had been a couple of hours since the knee had been so badly smashed. It was better surgery to just remove the leg.

The lad was already asleep so I proceeded, cutting through soft tissue about three inches above the knee. Of course, I knew what could happen but we had no other option. I remember thinking, "If I get out of this one, I'm sure going to be a good boy from now on." The part that made me nervous was putting the saw to the femur. I had originally asked for a Gigli saw—a flexible wire saw. It has a handle on either end and you pull it back and forth. When I got down to the bone I said, "I don't want to put a saw on that bone." So I made a tunnel behind the femur and threaded the flexible blade through. Then I told Henry to hold onto it as tight as he could, but it wasn't working very well. I pulled it out and went back to the old standard Civil War–era rigid saw. I knew somebody else would have to revise this amputation because, under the circumstances, I couldn't create good skin flaps. So I held the leg with one hand and sawed with the other. I finished cutting through the remaining soft tissue and clamped off bleeders.

Then I took the leg and carried it outside. I looked around and noticed that there wasn't a soul to be seen. Ordinarily the place was a beehive of activity. Way out in the field I spotted a Marine lieutenant, one of our security people. He said, "Hey, Dave, bring it over here. There's a big hole. Put it in the hole."

I very carefully carried the leg with the rocket sticking out of it and very gently placed it in the one-foot-deep hole. Someone had already placed C-4 [explosive] in the bottom. As I turned to head back to the operating room to dress the wound and clean things up, the lieutenant was waiting for me up ahead. "Dave," he said, "That really took balls."

I said, "I figured if the rocket hit the guy that hard and didn't go off, I probably wasn't going to set it off fooling around with it."

He said, "That's not necessarily the case. Generally, if they haven't gone far enough, they don't explode. It has to go beyond a certain distance for it to be armed."

"I'm glad I didn't know that," I answered.

He patted me on the back and said that when I finished up in the OR, he'd buy me a drink. I accepted his offer.

When I went back into the OR, Henry and the patient were talking.[2] While we were cleaning up the wound, suddenly we heard a huge explosion and debris began falling on the roof of our Quonset hut. The patient looked up and said, "Are we getting hit?"

I said, "No. There's a gravel pit across the way and they always set off a charge about this time in the afternoon. That's what it was. Go back to sleep."

Even now, it's not clear in my mind whether they set off the explosion that destroyed the rocket or if it went off spontaneously.

That afternoon and evening I went back to see the patient to make sure he was okay. He asked me what I had done with him, and I had to tell him that it required an amputation.

I said, "Son, your leg was amputated above the knee. But it should not be a problem. They will fix you up with a prosthesis and everything will be okay."

"Sir, I've got a basketball scholarship waiting for me."

"Well, I don't think you'll play basketball for a while."

I asked him where the scholarship was from, and he told me it was one of the

Lt. Cmdr. David Taft of the 1st Medical Battalion received the Navy Cross for his dramatic surgery (BUMED Archives).

upstate New York universities. I asked him for the address. I wrote a letter explaining what happened, and they gave him the scholarship anyway!

The patient's name was Ray Hutton. He went home and I saw him again at Walter Reed [Army Medical Center] when I got back. The ward reminded me of Walt Whitman and the Civil War hospitals he worked in as a nurse. It had 15 or 20 beds per side and patients with all kinds of amputations— arms, legs, or both. And there was Ray Hutton. I went over and gave him a big hug and asked how he was doing. We had a good talk and down through the years I got letters from him. I was at Camp Pendleton in the 1990s when my wife gave me a letter and said, "Ray Hutton has written you a letter."

I looked at the envelope and realized it wasn't from Ray; it wasn't his writing. The letter was from his son and I didn't want to open it. It seems that his father had suffered a coronary and died. Ray's son wrote: "You gave him a lot of great years and we'll never forget what you did."

For his heroic surgery, Capt. Harry Dinsmore was awarded the Navy Cross. Lt. Edward Feldman received the Silver Star for his surgery. Lt. Cmdr. David Taft was also awarded the Navy Cross, as were two other Navy physicians, Lt. James Back and Lt. Cmdr. David Lewis, for removing live ordnance from their patients.

6

CORPSMAN UP!

A Vietnam-era corpsman was very special to the Marines he served. The corpsman was the man the Marines protected because they knew his job was to take care of them. "Doc" had the skills to save their lives if they were hit.

But that respect had to be earned. The corpsman had to be tough physically and psychologically to stay with the troops during the mission. It was not enough merely to reach the objective. Once at his destination the corpsman's job really began. He had to carry a heavier load, handle stress, and monitor the daily condition of his men. And when the call "Corpsman up!" rang out, he had to remain cool under fire and override the adrenalin pump to get to his man and treat him.

If experience is the best judge of performance, retired Marine Richard Zink speaks with authority. He owes his life to a Navy corpsman. In January 1967, Zink and his company were patrolling a rice paddy not far from Khe Sanh when a reinforced regiment of NVA regulars overwhelmed them. Zink was hit in the hip and knee by AK-47 fire, and most of his buddies were killed or wounded. The fighting was so furious that two F-4 Phantoms providing close air support were blown from the sky above Zink.

"We lost our entire company in less than 15 minutes. There were no trees or cover. The corpsmen had to run about 125 meters to get to us, and every time they tried, they got knocked down. Six of them lost their lives. That night when the sun went down, those who could manage crawled the whole distance. Five hours had gone by since I had been wounded. The corpsman who got to me used up his battle dressings and then what was left of my skivvy shirt. When that was gone, he used his own shirt to stop the bleeding. Those guys who got to us had to carry out the dead and wounded; there were no Marines left to do the job.

"They were all magnificent. When it hit the fan, they were there. No one could have put anything better on this earth than Navy corpsmen. I've always felt — and I've told my men time and again — that when you lose your corpsman, you've lost everything."[1]

The hospital corpsmen Zink praised not only served with Marine units but everywhere else the Navy operated in Vietnam. And, as a group, they made quite an impression on those they tended. Cmdr. Almon Wilson, commanding officer of Charlie Med in 1964, never forgot his association with them.

"First of all, the corpsmen were an absolutely superb lot of people. They were of all varieties — all the way from hospitalman apprentice up to master chief hospital corpsman. What bound them together was their commitment to taking care of patients. Never once did I have to call a corpsman to duty. They were always ready and available and responded quickly. The corpsmen worked long hard hours on their feet, sometimes doing tedious tasks, sometimes just doing ordinary hard work. The scrub corpsmen were on their feet 12 to 16 to 20 hours at a time. They were a superb group, and they worked above their heads most of the time."[2]

Hospital corpsmen were not strangers to Vietnam when the U.S. increased its troop commitment in 1965. They had been in Vietnam as far back as 1954 during "Operation Passage to Freedom." Five years later, several corpsmen were assigned to the dispensary at the U.S. Embassy in Saigon.

As the conflict escalated, corpsmen supported both Navy and Marine Corps units. They manned medical departments aboard aircraft carriers, cruisers, destroyers, oilers, amphibious vessels, the battleship New Jersey, and also with the riverine force—the so-called "Brown Water Navy"—in the Mekong Delta. In addition, they served in large numbers aboard hospital ships Repose and Sanctuary.

Ashore, they were assigned to Station Hospital Saigon beginning in 1963, and later sent to the Naval Support Activity Hospital Danang. Corpsmen provided medical support to the Marines as members of air wings, reconnaissance teams, artillery fire bases, and with the 1st and 3rd Medical battalions of the 1st and 3rd Marine divisions. They also accompanied Navy SEAL teams on their secret missions.

It might be argued that corpsmen made their greatest contributions in sup-

Equipped for a mission: HM1 Craig Jimerfield served as a medical advisor for Amphibious Task Force 211 in Dong Tam (BUMED Archives).

porting individual Marine rifle companies not only by providing rudimentary medical care but by being "first responders" to disease and traumatic injury. Throughout U.S. involvement in Vietnam, approximately 5,000 hospital corpsmen and 300 dental technicians served in theater. The statistics testify to their familiarity with combat. More than 4,500 were awarded the Purple Heart, 290 received the Bronze Star, 127 were given the Silver Star, 29 were bestowed the Navy Cross, and 4 earned the Medal of Honor (2 posthumously). The Vietnam Wall in Washington, DC, memorializes the names of 689 hospital corpsmen and 2 dental technicians who died in that war.

One platoon commander, Marine Lt. Michael Holladay, truly appreciated what his corpsman had to face. "We spent so much time in the bush that our clothing stayed wet damn near all the time. Because we went through tiger grass, which had a razor edge on it, the crotch of our utilities[3] was cut out all the time. A lot of us also got to where we just didn't wear socks because it was a waste of time; they were always wet. As a result, we had a lot of foot problems and a good deal of jungle rot. Many of us also had groin infections and boils. The corpsman spent much of his time trying to deal with some of the health issues that came up with men who were constantly living in a muddy, wet environment."

Corpsmen were theoretically equipped to deal with these challenges but many accomplished their missions in the high-heat, high-humidity jungle by shedding much of their gear. HN William Barber recalls his experience:

"After a while I got rid of my flak jacket. I didn't even wear a helmet. It was just too hot. I never changed clothes when I was out in the field. When we were traveling on foot in 100-degree temperatures up and down mountains, we wanted to carry the least amount of equipment we could. I didn't need to carry ammo, grenades, or an M16 because during a firefight, all that equipment became available.[4] So that's why I only carried a .45 pistol. My original wardrobe consisted of a *green sweatshirt that — from wear and the wet — rotted off me, a pair of dungarees, carriage belt, boots, and a soft cover. I also carried a Unit 1, which to me was ceremonial.[5] I couldn't carry drugs/*

medicines in it for long durations due to the weather, and I was constantly out of powders or ointments."

Corpsmen often found that their biggest problem was trying to force their men to practice rudimentary sanitation and take care of themselves. Barber noted that his second most common concern was heat exhaustion. "A Marine would go all day loaded down with extra gear and not drink his water. When they were exhausted, the gunny sergeant would get up behind them and just keep kicking them to make them move. That was typical. 'You're a Marine. You can do it.' They were young like I was and just didn't know how to take care of themselves or, because of the Marine image, never com-

Unit 1 medical bag (collection of Mark Hacala).

plained. A guy would cut himself and just blow it off. 'I'm 18. I'm invincible.' The next thing you knew his finger had swollen up twice its size."

As with corpsmen in previous wars, "Doc" found himself playing other roles. He was also mother, father, and psychiatrist. Lt. Gen. Ernest Cheatham, former commanding officer of 2nd Battalion, 5th Marines, observed the special bond between corpsmen and the Marines they served so faithfully: "The doc — small 'd' — was always with us and was just another Marine. He was the one who carried the medical bag. There's always been a real fondness and a real close bond going both ways. A lot of corpsmen are very proud that they served with the Marines. And the Marines always tried to treat the corpsmen as best they could because they knew their lives depended on them."

The Training: Stay Alive and Keep Them Alive

Following boot camp and hospital corps school, some fledgling corpsmen received orders to naval hospitals, most likely to work with patients as ward corpsmen. Others were assigned to the fleet as ship's company aboard vessels with medical departments. Still other corpsmen learned, much to their shock and dismay, that the Navy provided medical support to the Marine Corps. They found themselves assigned to the Fleet Marine Force (FMF), facing additional training at Field Medical Service School (FMSS) at Camp Lejeune or Camp Pendleton. For young men who had once envisioned their military service in a stateside hospital or aboard a nice clean ship with a comfortable bunk and legendary Navy chow, the new reality meant preparing for duty as an infantryman. They were trading white uniforms for Marine green.

Field Medical Service School was designed for one purpose — to turn a sailor into a corpsman fit to support Marines in combat. During a vigorous and grueling few weeks, these men went through what might be described as a "mini Marine boot camp" of physical conditioning, rudimentary weapons training, and learning advanced life-saving techniques.

HN James Maddox, Golf Company, 2nd Battalion, 9th Marines

We went for an extra month of training at Camp Del Mar near the Marine Corps base at Camp Pendleton. It was a month of what they called "Field Medical School." We practiced taking care of fake plastic wounds. A lot of the training was just learning how to stop bleeding. The instructors emphasized how to apply a battle dressing and how to get it tight. If it was a sucking chest wound, you had to make sure to put the plastic — which was wrapped around the battle dressing — on the wound first. They taught us some very basic practical skills, such as "stay down and apply pressure to the wound." At a model Viet Cong village, we learned how and where booby traps had been set and what punji sticks were. We threw some live grenades from behind a barrier, pulling the pins and throwing them. We also fired .45 pistols.

It didn't seem really scary although our instructor was a young Marine who had just gotten back from Vietnam. He had some scars on his face where he had been hit by shrapnel. He was trying to tell us that it was worse than we knew, but how can you tell a bunch of young naive kids? His demeanor was more serious. I remember sitting up in the bleachers getting ready to graduate and one instructor said, "Look, some of you won't be coming back." I know that kind of put a lump in my throat. But it's just like anybody going out driving his car on the freeway and facing the odds of being killed in a wreck. You think, "Not me!"

HM1 William Gerrard, Mike Company, 3rd Battalion, 26th Marines

Field Medical Service School was both classroom and fieldwork. Some of the training was about guns. We got to go out and shoot the .45 caliber pistol on the range — two clips — 10 to 14 bullets. We listened to guys from the Korean War era and what they had done. They taught us a little bit about field sanitation and treating the wounded.

When I got to the 5th Division, I got to fire everything. I was a country boy and liked going in the woods so I volunteered to do that. I also got to shoot the .50 caliber machine gun, throw grenades, fire mortars, and use the M14 and the M60 machine gun. They'd give me one or two of those green ammo boxes filled with ammunition and tell me to go out and have fun. And I did. Sometimes I'd come back in and my ears would be ringing for the next three days.

HN William Barber, India Company, 3rd Battalion, 4th Marines

They taught us basic military subjects to buddy care and how to save lives in the field. The military subjects ranged from facts about the Marine Corps to navigation at night by reading a map and learning how to use a compass. But mainly the lectures focused on sanitation in the field — how to dig trenches for latrines. It was basic field medicine — what you needed to know to keep someone alive until he was transported to the next level of care.

HM3 Roger Ware,
Fox and Hotel Companies, 2nd Battalion, 5th Marines

We had a lot of infantry training with the Marines. The instructors showed us different combat tactics: ambushes, a wedge formation, how to support a fire team, how the Marines do their frontal assaults, defensive positions, and how to shoot the old M14 and the .45 pistol. We also learned how to get our 782 gear [equipment issued to a Marine that, among other necessities, included a poncho and shelter half] squared away. Sgt. Brand was one of our platoon sergeants and was a Vietnam vet. He said, "Guys, I'm telling you. A lot of you are going straight to the Fleet Marine Force in Vietnam, and you're gonna see a lot of combat so I'm trying to teach you to stay alive. So everything I'm teaching you now is gonna help you."

We walked down the road and Sgt. Brand would yell, "Sniper!" And then we'd have to jump in the bushes and trees and learn how to provide cover fire in different directions. I think he was just preparing us to stay alive and how to use the different terrain and equipment to do that. The whole purpose of a corpsman is to stay alive — not be a hero — and take care of Marines in combat. Your primary mission is to protect yourself, but, at the same time, do your job.

We had medical training, too, going through the different scenarios as far as compound fractures, sucking chest wounds, protruding abdomen, fractured jaw with an airway protection, and amputations. We were also taught how to do a trach, how to start IVs, how to apply different bandages, and how to use litters and ponchos to carry people. It was a given that we had had a lot of the first aid training in basic corps school, so the training we had at Camp Lejeune was primarily for combat wounds. It wasn't basic first aid but more for combat wounds. We also learned to take care of burns, give fluids, and treat heat casualties. We practiced getting in and out of helos — the old H-34 helos [Sikorsky H-34 Choctaw used for transport] — and how to load and unload casualties.

This was 1966 and Vietnam was going pretty heavy. They needed corpsmen in Vietnam very quickly to replace the ones who were being killed or wounded. So they got us through very quickly.

The Arrival: Welcome to Hell

Perhaps one of most sobering and indelible scenes in the 1986 Oliver Stone film, "Platoon," is the arrival in Vietnam of Pvt. Chris Taylor, played by Charlie Sheen. The young soldier, barely out of his teens, steps from the plane into an alien world. He immediately confronts the taunts of hardened veterans and a row of bodies on the tarmac ready for shipment home.

Bewilderment, fear, and disorientation were the most prevalent emotions felt by military personnel about to begin their one-year tours in South Vietnam. Almost without exception, each arrived as an individual, that is, a replacement, and not part of a military unit. In fact, assignment to a unit might take place right there at the airport or certainly within a day or two. Unit needs dictated those decisions. And once a new arrival was assigned his battalion and regiment, finding his unit's location and getting transport to that site were his responsibilities.

HM3 Dennis Noah, Hotel Company, 2nd Battalion, 5th Marines

After we landed at Danang, we were taken to a hut right at the end of the airstrip. F-4s were constantly taking off with their afterburners, which would rattle your teeth.

The next morning three or four of us were assigned to 2/5 [2nd Battalion, 5th Marines]. Then we boarded a C-130 and flew to An Hoa, which was located southwest of Danang. As we were landing and got real low, all of a sudden we started taking rounds in the belly. The crew chief looked at us and said, "We're taking rounds. Hold on."

The C-130 had no seats so we were sitting on the floor. As the pilot went for the ground, all of a sudden the plane dropped just like a fast elevator. "Clank! Boom! Bang!" and the plane was bouncing. I can still see the faces of some of the guys. A red-headed corpsman named Graham said, "We're screwed." We thought we had crashed. We didn't know what steel-matted runways were. We had no experience and nobody told us we were going to land on steel mat, which is noisy under the best of conditions.

The plane then stopped and the grizzly old Air Force crew chief looked over and started laughing at us. We had arrived in An Hoa.

HN William Barber, India Company, 3rd Battalion, 4th Marines

As we arrived in Danang, the plane actually came under fire. After we landed and got off, it seemed as though the system fell apart. I thought someone was going to pick us up and take us somewhere. But it was really more like, "What the hell was going on?" After a day or two, somehow I found out where to go to be assigned — a little shack. From inside, I heard names being called out. When you went in, you were told where you were going. "You're going here. You're going there."

At that time you were assigned according to the needs of the units. Finally, it was my turn and I was assigned to India Company, 3rd Battalion, 4th Marines, 3rd Marine Division. I was informed that my unit was somewhere in Dong Ha and that I should go find it. It was almost like you were on your own.

I took a truck convoy out of Danang to Dong Ha where I finally found India Company's rear in Dong Ha. I stayed at Dong Ha about a week to get acclimated. Third Battalion, 4th Marines had four companies — India, Mike, Lima, and Kilo. I met the other guys who, like myself, were just coming in. That's the first time I met [Donald] Ballard. He later got the Medal of Honor.

HM3 Raymond Felle, Kilo Company, 3rd Battalion, 9th Marines

I was so taken aback by the whole situation. I was scared and don't think I was recording information the first couple of days. I don't even remember landing at the airport. I remember sitting there and thinking, "God, I'm here! Am I going to be okay?"

I must have spent only a day in Danang and then went to Phu Bai via a C-130 transport. I don't remember that landing either.

I was told to report to the battalion aid station in Phu Bai. I then got on a plane and flew back to Dong Ha, and from there caught a helicopter or a truck to [Camp] Carroll. That's where I met up with 3/9.

HN James Maddox, Golf Company, 2nd Battalion, 9th Marines

When we arrived in Danang, I felt a blast of heat — I mean really hot! I recall waiting for my sea bag and looking over at some guys behind a fence who were waiting to get on a plane. They were all hootin' and hollerin.' Boy, they were really letting us have it with "here comes the new meat" kind of stuff. "We're going home and you're just arriving. Good luck!"

I got my bag and stumbled into a big hangar really confused. I didn't know where I was going or what was happening. I ran into a Marine who told me a story about getting a testicle shot off and that he was going back to his unit. He was probably just "playing with the new guy."

I then found myself out on the tarmac with a crowd. A C-130 transport plane had its big ramp down at the tail end. I got on it, packed in with others like sardines, and we flew up to Dong Ha.

I ended up in a tent area at Dong Ha where I had to wait until the next day to get to my unit. I slept in a tent on a cot that night, and that's when I first heard really loud artillery. It was so loud that the ground shook and it just blasted me right off my cot. One Marine was lying on another cot and, without even getting up, he said, "Outgoing." I didn't even know what this term meant at the time. That's how green I was.

HM1 Alan Kent, Delta Company, 1st Battalion, 5th Marines

Tet [February 1968] was going on but we didn't know what the hell that was all about. All we knew was that new troops were needed badly and we had to get going.

We landed in Danang at night and rockets were going off all over. Even though the airfield was getting hit, we got to the end of the runway and everybody bailed out onto the edges of the runway. We all lay pretty low until the rocket fire died down. Then they piled us in vehicles and took us to a staging area that night, not too far from the airport. It was my welcome to Vietnam without any prior introduction to combat. I had no gradual orientation. I was told, "Right now you're going into battle!"

HM3 Roger Pittman,
Golf, Hotel, and Fox Companies, 2nd Battalion, 4th Marines

I wound up in country about the 5th of October and then spent two or three days at Dong Ha trying to get to the 2nd Battalion, 4th Marines. At that time they were in the outer perimeter duty at Con Thien, which was under siege. That was my first experience with combat.

It was an absolute mind-bending experience. In fact, they just shoved me out of the helicopter onto an LZ [landing zone]. The last words I heard out of the chopper from the crew chief were, "Just keep low!"

I landed down on my feet and stayed low. As soon as the chopper left, I heard a voice coming out of the bushes saying, "Stay low and come over here."

They were getting incoming at that very moment, and I didn't even realize what it sounded like. The first round I heard came in and landed maybe 75 or 100 yards away. I saw the flash and it just didn't register what was going on. I looked down and noticed that everybody was in their hole and looking up at me as if to say, "You stupid fool!"

HM3 Richard Thacker, Golf Company, 2nd Battalion, 5th Marines

I think the movie "Platoon" wrapped it all up for me and a lot of other vets. When the door of the C-130 opened up, I remember the heat from the runway. The smells were entirely

A Navy corpsman treats a Marine for heat exhaustion during a jungle patrol (BUMED Archives).

alien to what I was used to. It was very, very hot and humid. An air strike was going on over a hill in the distance. We all felt a lot of anticipation. We didn't know where we were going.

We were sent to a little staging shed area. A corpsman from the Division Surgeon's office came by, picked up our records, and told us to wait there for our assignments. Three or four hours later he came back and said I'd be assigned to the 2nd Battalion, 5th Marine Regiment, which was in An Hoa, about 36 miles southwest of Danang. Since the roads were being ambushed really bad, they'd have to fly us out on a C-121, a little twin engine cargo plane full of 55-gallon drums of gasoline they were delivering. Five of us corpsmen were on that plane.

Playing God

Donald Ballard joined the Navy in 1965 to finish his education and begin a career. "I wanted to make a career in the Navy as a dentist." But as with so many of his contemporaries, fate had another plan for him. After a short stint as a ward corpsman, he was assigned to the Marines.

In November 1967, he received orders to Vietnam, and, as was customary, did not go to war with a unit but as an individual replacement. When he arrived, reality smacked him in the face.

The day after I arrived in Vietnam I was given my first assignment—inventorying some personal gear of a corpsman who had been killed. I was putting what the Marines call "782 gear" in one stack and the personal stuff and the sea bag in another. Then I was making a list of both sets of items and taking everything back to supply. Later the same day I found out that this was the corpsman I was replacing. So that was my second in country impression of Vietnam—and it was just the second day.

The third day a corpsman told me "You're going to be joining my unit so I'd like to get to know you and take you out there." We went to the battalion supply area where we drew supplies. That was his main purpose. He came back to get supplies and pick up the replacements. And I was a replacement.

In about an hour or two, we got on the helicopter and landed in an area that looked just like the place we had come from. It was all jungle and all hostile looking. The remainder of the day was spent introducing myself to Marines in Mike Company.

All we did that night was dig in. They wanted me to dig a foxhole. I later learned that wasn't going to work because when I'm doing my job, I'm not lying in my hole. So I only dug one foxhole the whole time I was in Vietnam. I told the Marines, "If you want me to come and treat you, you'd better dig a hole deep enough for both of us."

They gave me a .45 with no magazine or bullets. I asked, "Sergeant, what the hell am I supposed to do with this?"

He said, "Regulations say I have to give it to you."

I said, "Well, it's worthless. If they ever get this close, I'll have to hit them on the head with it!"

His memorable line was, "Doc, if you want a weapon, don't worry about it. There's plenty of 'em lying on the ground down there."

And he was right. Right after the first firefight, I saw all kinds of weapons. The helicopters wouldn't evacuate people with their weapons. If we had casualties we were medevacing, we had to hump the extra weapons out of there.

We operated out of Dong Ha, Cam Lo, and some of the base camps—J. J. Carroll, and "the Rockpile." The 4th Marines were the farthest north unit. We were probably in North Vietnam sometimes, but again, we didn't have a need to know. The lieutenant wouldn't say anything. There were no signs in the bush that said "You're now leaving Vietnam and going into Cambodia." There were no customs stations or welcome centers. It was just plain jungle. A lot of times we didn't see any signs of life — no villages or other signs of civilization. It was pretty desolate.

It was 10 days before I saw my first firefight with casualties. We were on the trail just walking through the jungle, not on any path. We never took anybody else's path because of booby traps. We were cutting through the jungle and getting slapped in the face with foliage. It was just a mess. I couldn't see 20 feet on either side of me because of the elephant grass and overgrowth. All of a sudden I heard the familiar small arms fire. The AK-47 has a distinct sound, as well as the M16. You could hear the two chattering back and forth. We hit the deck. I hadn't been lying there maybe 15 minutes before I heard the Marine Corps battle cry — "Corpsman up!"

So I had to get up out of my safe place — and I didn't even have a weapon — and go to whoever was hollering at me. And some Marines kept yelling, "Corpsman up!" They kept pointing farther forward where the first or second guy in the squad was located. The damn enemy knew where I was because they'd already shot the Marine. I was leaning over the guy trying to treat him. And that's how most corpsmen got killed. They were paying attention to their patients and not keeping track of the enemy.

I tried to treat him as best I could while I was lying flat on the ground. He had an abdominal wound and an extremity wound of the arm. The bullet must have gotten his stomach and arm at the same time. I was able to control the hemorrhage and treat him for shock. The rest of the Marines took off after the sniper. I learned later they kept on going until they killed the sniper. They never gave up and were relentless in getting their man. But I didn't have a need to know. My job was focused on the injured Marine.

The other corpsman was senior to me so he joined us. We called in a medevac helicopter and medevaced the guy out. I had to learn radio procedure in a relatively short time. You did the best you could in a very stressful environment.

I have concentrated most of my life trying to forget Vietnam because of the inner feelings I have — and there were no good feelings. It wasn't a party and we didn't have any good times. We might sit around and complain about the C-rations or about the "gooks" we'd just killed but I never had a day that didn't have some negativity about it.

If we weren't fighting, we were remembering the buddy we were talking to the day before but who was not here today. You remembered him because you treated him. As a corpsman you had to play God in a mass casualty situation. You worked on so many people, and often you had to choose who was gonna live and who was gonna die. And I didn't want anyone to die so when I made those unconscious decisions, I had to think back on my qualifications and whether or not I did the best I could. Today, when I think back, all I can do is remember the bad days and wonder if I did all I could have done to save the guys. I have a lot of guilt feelings. I have to work hard to put Vietnam behind me.

First Blood on Valentine's Ridge

Raymond Felle was born in California and raised in Oregon. He joined the Navy in 1966 with the troop buildup in Vietnam. Although he sought shipboard duty, it was during hospital corps school that he realized the Navy had other plans. Felle was assigned to Field Medical Service School at Camp Pendleton. As he now points out, during his entire stint in the Navy, he was never on a ship.

In October 1967, the 20-year-old corpsman received orders to Vietnam. Upon arrival, he was assigned to the 3rd Battalion, 9th Marines, and met up with his new outfit at Camp Carroll near Dong Ha. He would soon experience combat for the first time.

I remember the smell, the heat. I remember looking at the mountains around us and thinking, "Am I gonna make it here? Did I make the right decision?" My dad died while I was in boot camp and I was the only surviving son. So my mom didn't want me to go to Vietnam. She told me that being the only surviving son, I didn't have to go. But I told her it was my duty to go. Did I really make a wise decision coming to this country and being with the Marines? I was proud to be with them but I didn't know a hell of a lot about them. I didn't know how to survive. I was a Navy corpsman — not a Marine — at least not yet.

They gave me all my gear and my Unit 1 and, from that point forward, my comrades started looking at me as the person who would treat and take care of them. I was also issued a .45. Before I went into the service, I was familiar with shooting guns. I had spent many hours hunting so I knew how to shoot rifles and pistols. I just wasn't familiar with the automatic. This pistol was pretty beat up. It was probably from World War II. The barrel was loose and I couldn't hit something 15 feet away. It made a lot of noise but it just wasn't very accurate. It probably came from the previous corpsman — and the one before him and the one before him.

When I was in battle, I usually had an M16 to take with me. I'd get a rifle from the Marine I was treating. He'd either be wounded or killed and I'd just take his rifle. Since I wasn't responsible for it, I could put it down to use both hands. If I lost it, I could always get another one.

We got on a truck convoy on the 24th of December [1967] and headed out Route 9, which pretty much followed the McNamara Line[6] of combat bases. We finally ended up at the Rockpile, which was very impressive. It was a huge pile of rocks with clouds and fog layers hovering over the top. It was mystical. You knew the enemy was out there somewhere. I had an eerie feeling and certainly didn't feel secure. I pulled into the BAS [battalion aid station] and checked in with Jerry Behrens, my battalion surgeon. He took my name and asked me what I needed. I asked him where I was going but he wasn't sure. We had Christmas dinner at the Rockpile.

On 14 February, we went out on a two-day patrol. We left early in the morning and moved up about two miles west of Ca Lu toward Khe Sanh. Very early that morning, Capt. Alexander Ward, our commanding officer, cut his finger. It was probably about 2 o'clock in the afternoon when I saw him talking with someone. We had passed him by as we lined up our platoons to go up on what would later be called "Valentine's Ridge." I told him he needed to take care of the cut. He said, "I don't need to."

I said, "You've got to put a Band-Aid on it or you're going to get jungle rot and it will get infected." So he let me put a Band-Aid on his finger and that was the last time I ever saw Capt. Ward.

Someone then said they had seen some NVA moving out of a valley up onto Valentine's Ridge. It was about 3 o'clock in the afternoon. We were heading down into a valley and across a creek. We then started up the side of Valentine's Ridge on a well-made trail. Because the mountain was so steep, the trail zigzagged its way up the side of the mountain. We had gotten part way up the trail when our platoon commander, Lt. [Michael] Holladay, made the decision to get off the trail, cross a little gully, and head up the side.

About 15 of us then got off the trail. We were trying to hustle up the side of the hill, but it was so steep that rocks were rolling back down again. We had gotten pretty close to the top of the ridge when an NVA fired an RPG [rocket-propelled grenade] which hit a rock, blowing it apart and throwing shrapnel and rock fragments in all directions. It was a trap! With three platoons heading up the side of the hill, they opened up on the second platoon with .50 caliber machine guns. I and four other men to my side and front were wounded. One of the Marines in front of me had half his rear end blown off.

We returned fire. For me, it was my first contact and I was pretty scared. Someone began yelling "Corpsman up!" I wasn't very far from him.

There was tremendous confusion — mortar rounds, RPGs, and machine gun fire. My part was taking care of the wounded. Even though I had been wounded, I didn't even know it because I was so scared—and the adrenalin was running.

One of the guys had his M16 jam just when he had one of the NVA in sight. I also remember that someone threw a grenade toward the RPG nest, but it hit a tree and started rolling back towards us. Someone said, "Get down! It's rolling back toward us!" We hid behind a log so we were pretty well protected from the blast.

I then attempted to control the bleeding on a gunny sergeant. Because he was starting to feel pain, I gave him a shot of morphine. I remember losing contact with the command group until we were just our own little group of people and didn't know where everybody else was.

Then they started lobbing in mortars. We lost contact with the command group—Capt. Ward, our commanding officer, and Lt. [William R.] Reese, our executive officer. Early in the battle, a mortar had landed, critically wounding both of them. They died a short time after that. The battalion corpsman, HM2 [Larry J.] Goss, was also killed by that mortar round.

So the battle raged on and we took out the RPG nest. We couldn't contact the rest of the company so Lt. Holladay took what was left of our platoon, including the wounded, and we went over the top of the hill and waited for instructions from Ca Lu. Just before we did that, he called in jets which dropped napalm and 500-pounders on the enemy. They dropped those bombs so close to us that we were told to set off green smoke so they would know where we were. Those explosions literally lifted us off the ground when they hit. I could only imagine what they did to the NVA. I just remember the big shards from the bombs cutting off the tops of trees in that triple-canopy jungle. Pieces of those trees fell down all over the place.

We got off the hill that evening and waited on Route 9 for more reinforcements, which came up at 2 o'clock the next morning. Then we took our wounded and went back to Ca Lu. The rest of 3rd Platoon was still up on that hill, and India Company 3/9 went up to assist them and bring them down. The final tally included 10 Marines and 1 corpsman killed.

I was so scared I didn't even know I was injured. I had a perforated left eardrum, shrapnel in my neck, back, and the side of my arm where it wasn't protected by my flak jacket. And I had blood all over me from treating people.

I gave them morphine and was able to control the bleeding with large battle dressings and tried to give them moral support. That's all I could do in the field. I had serum albumin but it was kind of useless. It's hard to start an IV when you can't see the person's arm in the dark. Many times the people you were dealing with were dehydrated anyway. Serum albumin is a volume expander and when you inject it, it sucks fluid out of the surrounding tissue to expand the fluid volume. If the person is bleeding severely, he is already dehydrated so you're not going to do him a lot of good. In the field, I could do better by just controlling the bleeding rather than trying to start a useless IV.

At 2 o'clock in the morning they told us to start heading back down to Route 9. That was 1st Platoon and 2nd Platoon. We were meeting up with stragglers coming out of the jungle. It was dark and they couldn't see. We just coaxed them in by radio, telling them which way to go.

This was the first battle many of us had been in so we were pretty shook up. I was scared but did my job. I did what I had to do and earned the respect of my platoon. I was no longer "Squid." I was "Doc."

The Smell of Death

Following what became known as the "Battle of Valentine's Ridge," Raymond Felle and the survivors of the carnage set up camp within sight of the ridge they had just abandoned. Lt. Michael Holladay, Felle's platoon commander, picks up the story.

Holladay: The plan had been set for Pegasus, which was the operation to relieve the siege of Khe Sanh. Our battalion was told to hold fast. By now it was about 23 days after the fight on Valentine's Ridge. During that time our battalion had started raising so much hell because of what was happening on the ridge. The buzzards were really working the ridge line. We had a number of Marines and a corpsman who were MIA. The worst possible situation is to have MIAs. MIAs are a big deal. You just don't want to be in an organization that has MIAs. KIAs and WIAs are bad enough but if you can't find and identify your missing, you've got a problem. Marines do not leave their dead on the battlefield. They bring them out. But at the same time we were told we could not go back for them.

Felle: After we got off the mountain and were back in Ca Lu on the 15th [February 1968], we didn't know the condition of the rest of the company. It wasn't until the evening of the 15th that we discovered how many people had been killed or were missing. We wanted to go back and get our dead. We didn't want them to be MIA, and that's how they were classified. Even if you had seen them get killed, they were still classified as MIA. We were told not to write home to tell any family members that you saw them killed. You couldn't do that.

Then our minds began playing tricks on us. From Ca Lu, we were within view of Valentine's Ridge. At one point, we even thought we had seen an NVA tie one of the bodies up on a tree. But it wasn't so. We knew that the NVA were on that ridge, but we weren't allowed to sacrifice any more men to recover the Marines who had been killed.

Holladay: After we raised a lot of hell, they finally assented — but only after we sent in a recon team to see what was out there and locate the remains. The recon team went, located the remains, but refused to bring them in. So I volunteered our platoon.

We went with an old half-track that would provide us with a way to carry the remains back in. By that time it was well into the first part of March [1968] and it was getting hot. As we got up on the side of the ridge line, we found all the remains except one whom we could identify.

We found the remains very decomposed. There were some torsos that were intact but others had appendages that were separated. Several had the fingers eaten away. But as we were heading out, my last order was to get some kind of jawbone to identify the teeth, if at all possible.

We had no body bags. All we had were ponchos in which we wrapped the remains. Then we cut bamboo poles. It wouldn't take five minutes before the body acid would eat right through the ponchos. And we're not talking rubber gloves. We'd put the remains on the ponchos and then they would fall out on the ground. It just took all day long to recover those remains.

Felle: All I can remember are ponchos coming down off the mountain. At the base of the poncho that's fitted for the head that's where stuff would leak out as we carried them down off the hill towards Route 9. I don't remember much else, and I just don't know what I did with that information in my head. I do remember other Marines who were carrying them off the hill, saying that everyone was puking all over the place. The smell of death was just everywhere. And once you got that smell of death on you, you just couldn't get it off.

Holladay: We had decided to make the extract point the closest point to Route 9. We had to traverse about 400 meters back and forth. The difficulty was the heat. It was just so damn hot. The canopy was wet and the humidity was a thousand percent. Combine that with the smell of the dead, as Doc talks about, and I can smell it right now. It just never leaves you.

It took us most of the day to get the remains down to Route 9. We got them in the back of an old vehicle that was as big as your present-day Humvee. I had to have a resupply of ponchos brought out to us. By that time we had gotten orders to bring in every bit of material we could find — boots, belts, helmets, whatever.

Felle: We took all the bodies back to Ca Lu and put them on the landing pad. When they removed the bodies from the helicopter, they had to saturate the place where the bodies had been lying with kerosene and diesel fuel. They had to light it on fire because the smell was so bad. Jerry Behrens, the Battalion Surgeon, then had to identify the bodies.

Holladay: That was the end of our aspect of the mission. Besides everything else, we were dealing with the constant threat of disease. Every time you got a cut, it got infected. There just was no way to stay clean. One of the biggest jobs I had, and certainly Doc [Felle] had, too, from a medical standpoint, was to force the Marines to take care of themselves. We were given orders to ensure that we washed as carefully as we could — hands, arms, and fingernails. But you just couldn't get that smell off of you.

Saving Lt. Holladay

A month after the tragic firefight on Valentine's Ridge, HM3 Ray Felle found himself in another hot spot — again in the thick of the action. By that time, manning the so-called McNamara Line near the DMZ had settled into a deadly routine.

On March 27th [1968] we received information that an NVA tank had crossed the DMZ into South Vietnam so we set out on an operation to find it. We were near Camp Carroll and just starting to settle in for the evening. I began digging a fighting hole while my fighting hole buddy, Cpl. [Clifford] "Will" Williams, went up to the command group with Lt. Holladay, our platoon commander, to find out what we would be doing the next day. Cpl. Williams then came back from the meeting. He took off all his gear and piled it in front of the hole so he could help me dig. Just then we heard the "pop! pop! pop!" of mortars leaving the tubes. Knowing they were on their way, we yelled, "Incoming!"

My hole was only about half dug but both of us got in. Suddenly, Will got out to grab his flak jacket to cover the hole. I grabbed him, pulled him back in, and put my flak jacket over both our heads just as the first round landed about three feet in front of us. That round blew up all his gear and wounded the platoon commander who was running back to his hole.

About seven or eight more rounds fell. Then I heard, "Corpsman up!" I could see that someone was wounded. I ran to him and found that the injured Marine was our platoon commander, Lt. Holladay. I called back to Cpl. Williams and he immediately came up to help me.

The lieutenant was only a few feet from the mortar round when it went off, and I could see he had a neck wound, a face wound, and a large gash in his leg. Because he was spitting up foaming blood, I also thought he had a sucking chest wound. Just as I took off his flak jacket, we heard more mortar rounds come out of the tubes. The two of us lay on top of Lt. Holladay to protect him from being injured any further.

It was getting really dark and I could hardly see. I patched up what I could and we called for a helicopter which took about 20 minutes to arrive. The lieutenant was bleeding profusely and I wasn't able to control it. A mortar fragment had taken out two teeth and part of his jaw. It had gone through his mouth and then through his neck, partially severing his jugular vein. He had a six-inch gash in his leg, and the mortar round had also busted his pelvis and broken his arm. I didn't know about those injuries at the time. I was only interested in stopping the bleeding as best I could.

Just as the helicopter came in, the NVA mortared us again. We tried to lift Lt. Holladay up into the helicopter but the pilot got jumpy and lifted it about four feet off the ground. Cpl. Williams and I couldn't lift the lieutenant that high. After the pilot lowered his chopper a bit, we finally got him in and they took off.

And that was the last I heard about him until I began looking for Cpl. Williams's son a few years ago. That's when I found Lt. Holladay and learned that it took him a year to recover. He retired from the Marine Corps as a colonel. The Discovery Channel was looking for a corpsman who had found the person he had treated in the field and so I submitted my story to them. The Discovery Channel did a special on it in a program called "Real MASH." I hadn't seen him since the battlefield. After I put him on that helicopter, I never knew his fate. While he was in the hospital in Guam, he submitted medals for both Cpl. Williams and me. When I told him I had never received any medal, he resubmitted the paperwork. My bronze star was awarded in 2000 at a ceremony in Portland, Oregon.

I also found the son of my fighting hole buddy, Cpl. Williams, who was killed on the 30th of April [1968]. Col. Holladay and I then went to Michigan — to Will's gravesite — and had a ceremony in which we presented the Silver Star he was awarded for his action that day. Will had helped me take care of Col. Holladay and took command of the platoon after Holladay was wounded.

Acts of heroism in the field were rarely recorded, and many times the people who actually witnessed the events were killed themselves. Many more of those events either were written up and then were never submitted, as in my case — or the awards were never issued, which is sad.

"Corpsman! Come and Get Me!"

Roger Pittman grew up in rural Kansas and decided early on that farming was not for him. While attending college, he took an operating room technician course and subsequently learned about the Navy corpsmen program and how well trained they were. "I filed that away as an interesting possibility. Everything then seemed very hopeless. So looking at my chances, I considered the Marine Corps but knew that I didn't want to dig foxholes and be shot at. I wanted to have a regular bed and a comfortable life, and decide what I wanted to do with my life. Then I'd get out and go to school."

Pittman joined the Navy in May 1965. After boot camp at Great Lakes, he moved across the street to hospital corps school. He recalls sitting in the hospital dining room about halfway through the program and having a rude awakening. "This guy walks by on crutches. He's got his dress greens on. He's wearing a Purple Heart over his left breast pocket but he's got Navy insignias exactly like mine with a Navy caduceus [the medical profession symbol of two snakes entwined around a winged staff] on top. I asked, 'What is that?'

"Some senior petty officer at the dining room table said, 'That's a hospital corpsman. He's been wounded. He went with the Marines.'

"I said, 'What do you mean he went with the Marines?' So that was the first time I heard that corpsmen were actually attached to the Marine Corps. And it was a most disheartening fact. That was not part of my plan."

Pittman went to Vietnam in September 1967 and was assigned to Fox Company, 2nd Battalion, 4th Marines. Barely a month later he had his introduction to combat.

We moved down the hill from Con Thien for — what they told us — a few days of rest and relaxation at Dong Ha. On the way, we had to stop at a bridge called "the Washout." It was the road that left Route 9 at Cam Lo and went up to Con Thien. It was a little dirt road that had been paved by the Seabees. It was a good road but it was always mined.

The Washout was a bridge over a good-sized river that we had to guard for a few nights. During the second night by this bridge we had stayed alert until midnight. In fact, everybody in the platoon had to stay alert. Then 50 percent of the people could sleep. The corpsmen didn't have radio watch in that platoon so the other corpsman and I went to sleep. I wasn't fully asleep when I heard a flare go up in the air. It was a red flare. I remember the corpsman having told me that a red flare was a bad sign. A red flare was shot up only if a position was being overrun. And, in fact, that was just what was starting to happen.

We were overrun that night and I treated my first casualties. A lot of tear gas and smoke filled the area so we had to put on our gas masks. Those fogged up immediately because we were all hyperventilating and it was a hot, muggy night, as you might imagine.

During that night I somehow got separated from the platoon. A sergeant found me and said he had casualties up the hill. He gave me the general direction, but when I got up there, I found myself all alone with nobody in sight at all. The only light was made by occasional flares going off. I couldn't use the flare light because I was on top of the hill — and very visible and highly silhouetted.

So I stayed down and finally found a shallow trench. A Marine was in the trench with a head wound. He had some bleeding from his scalp and was in and out of consciousness; he was not coherent at all times. He would occasionally vomit. I kept looking at him to see if he was okay, but I knew I had to get him out of there. This was around midnight with not much of a chance of getting evacuated.

A second Marine finally came up. I was happy to see him. His name was Capt. Nigh and he had been shot through the thigh. He had an M16. I only had a .45 with seven rounds of ammo. That's all they could spare when I checked out the weapon. This is very important. The supplies and the support we had were horrendous. I had a poncho but no poncho liner. I had no air mattress. I didn't have jungle utilities.

I had a Unit 1, which was fairly well stocked but had no 782 gear. We had canteens but no canteen covers. I had an old torn-up flak jacket. I look back on it now and think about how we were told we were the greatest army in the world. But as far as I'm concerned, we were third rate. I had seen guerrilla units better equipped than we were. The battalion's combat effectiveness was at best borderline.

My .45 didn't work all the time, and I was given only one clip of .45 ammo. Later on, I had a misfire in the middle of a patrol at night with the gun in my holster. It misfired and almost blew my foot away so I never trusted it after that. When I fam fired [familiarization] the weapon after I first got it, it did not fire correctly. It would sometimes misfire and jam. But it was the best they had at the time. And, as I said, I only had seven rounds of ammunition. And this was a Marine unit that was involved at the time in the heaviest combat in Vietnam.

By now the M14s were gone and everyone was supposed to have an M16 — at least that was the theory. The battalion had just gotten their M16s shortly before I arrived. The platoon commanders and the company commanders didn't quite trust the M16 so we had at least one M14 in each squad.

The M16 was horrendous. It was the worst weapon I had ever seen in my life and I had grown up with a lot of firearms. Initially, the M16s just didn't work in those jungle conditions. I know the M16 was investigated, but from the platoon's standpoint down to the squad, the Marines in Fox Company, 2nd Battalion, 4th Marines had no confidence in this weapon.

Everybody had a cleaning rod already put together and ready.[7] The problem we were having in firefights was the ammunition. The shell casing would jam in the chamber, and the extractor mechanism would extract just the butt of the casing, leaving the body of the cartridge in the firing chamber. This was a really bad situation and caused a lot of Marine dead. Everybody knew that if you couldn't punch the round out of the chamber because it had jammed, you were really screwed. And this was not an uncommon occurrence. In fact, it was a very common occurrence — too common not to do something about it. They tried to correct it with a chrome sliding mechanism, which helped a little bit but it didn't correct the whole problem. That situation continued for several months.

Anyway, that night I knew our position had been overrun and the NVA were all over the area. Most of the fighting occurred in a ravine which was about 50 yards below me near the stream. That's where the battalion headquarters had been overrun. During the night, we heard a lot of screaming and yelling. Every once in awhile someone would say, "Corpsman! Corpsman! Come and get me!" Or they would cry for their mother. And I'd hear them.

So I started down into this ravine two or three times. Each time Capt. Nigh said, "If you go down there, Doc, you're dead! That could be the enemy. It could be a Marine, but you don't know. So don't go down there!"

That bugged the heck out of me — and still does. But he was right. I could not assume that whoever was calling for his mother or a corpsman was legitimate and not an NVA.

I stayed on top of the hill the rest of the night. The fellow with the head wound was okay. When the sun came up, I carried the wounded Marine down to the chopper that was coming into the LZ. I felt sad because they were loading bodies onto the chopper. Twenty-one individuals died that night. Four were corpsmen. I saw the bodies of three or four brand-new lieutenants — second lieutenants — who had come in that day. They didn't even last six hours before being killed when Golf Company's position was overrun. They were all in the same foxhole together and were told to stay there. The NVA came in behind the fighting positions dressed in Marine Corps 782 gear and carrying M16s and satchel charges. That's how they opened up a wide breach in our perimeter. The name of that battle was "The Washout." It took place on October 14th, 1967.

After my first night of treating combat casualties and several hours of adrenalin flowing through my veins—and tear gas still irritating my eyes, I felt exuberant but also sad. I didn't think I knew any of the people who were killed that night but it turns out that I did. I was glad it was over because it was worse than I thought it would ever be. The confusion and the total chaos were compounded by everything else—not knowing where the enemy was, not having an adequate weapon, and feeling fairly exposed.

They pulled us back to Dong Ha that day. We mounted a convoy, and as we were going back, we passed some civilians as we got closer to Cam Lo. Some of the kids were giving us the finger. I thought, "This is not gonna be a good deal. The civilians don't appreciate us being here." My dissatisfaction grew with being involved in a war that we shouldn't have been involved in at all. Maybe our intentions were right, but the way we fought it was wrong.

A Tough Call

Fox Company, 2nd Battalion, 4th Marines saw a lot more combat, but by this time HM2 Pittman had been transferred from 1st Platoon and promoted to senior corpsman of Fox Company. It was February 1968 and Tet was in high gear. One night while guarding a bridge along Route 9 near Camp Carroll, he faced a terrible dilemma.

During the night, one of the corpsmen from the platoon came to the company command post where I was sleeping and said, "We've got a really sick Marine. I don't know what's wrong with him. We need some help."

I then went down to the platoon position in the middle of the night and found this Marine whom I knew. He was just withering in pain and practically incoherent. I couldn't get any kind of history out of him. It didn't look like anything I had ever seen, such as malaria, diarrhea, or any other disease like that.

I decided that I had to give him something for pain so I gave him a shot of morphine. It may have helped a tiny bit but not a whole lot. The guy was still in a lot of pain. I knew this Marine and knew he wasn't faking it. It just didn't seem right.

I finally gave him another shot of morphine and he relaxed a bit. His abdomen was hard and he was vomiting by that time. With another corpsman, I made a decision to get the man out. I went to the command post and the radio operator put me in touch with the battalion surgeon, who was about a mile up the road with the battalion command post. I told him the patient was really sick and we needed to get him out right away. The battalion surgeon said that we couldn't get him out. Lt. Col. [William] Weise [commanding officer of 2/4] said that nobody was going to go down the road [Route 9] because the chance was just too great for an ambush. "There's no way!" he said. "Sit on him."

So I went back. The guy was just getting worse and worse. He was starting to run a fever so I returned to the company command post a second time and said, "This guy is in bad condition and my feeling is that he's gonna die."

Lt. Col. Weise came on the radio and said, "You've gotta sit on him."

I replied, "I'll sit on him but he's gonna die."

Weise then said, "Well, I don't want to risk coming down the road tonight to pick this guy up. We can't fly him out of where you are because the hills are too steep and there's no way to get a medevac into your position tonight."

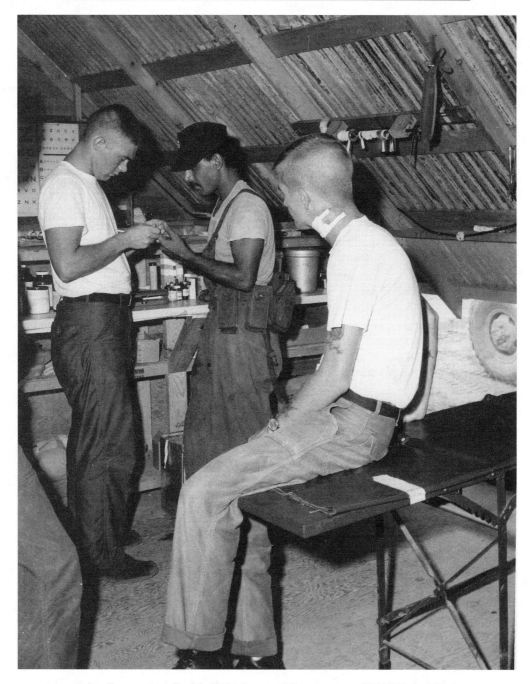

Sick call at most medical facilities began with a corpsman (BUMED Archives).

I said, "It's your call, sir. The man's gonna die."

And he replied, "You had better be right."

They soon sent a couple of tanks with some infantry on top of them, picked up the Marine, and took him back to the battalion command post, which was in a level, clear field. They medevaced him out that night.

I then went to sleep for a little bit. The battalion surgeon then asked me to come and talk

A Navy hospital corpsman comforts a wounded South Vietnamese soldier (BUMED Archives).

with him as soon as possible. He sent a patrol down to get me. The battalion surgeon said, "We're reassigning you to Echo Company, 2nd Platoon."

This was quite a demotion from being the company senior corpsman. He was doing this because I had insisted on getting the Marine out that night. The only question I asked the battalion surgeon was, "How's the Marine?"

He said, "Well, he had a ruptured appendix." I did what I had to do and learned a valuable lesson. You're gonna suffer the consequences if you make a decision that's not favorable to the process. I've carried that for my whole medical career. Occasionally you have to go against conventional wisdom and stand up for the patient.

Was it right to risk other people getting him out of there? That was not my decision. I just told it the way it was. We had a very good probability of a very bad outcome if we hadn't gotten him out that night. So even though my initial impression of Lt. Col. Weise wasn't positive, he taught me a valuable lesson. If you know right from wrong, you always have to go with right and do the right thing. Luckily, the rescue party wasn't ambushed.

"A Roll of the Dice"

For whatever reason he was reassigned, Roger Pittman was a platoon corpsman again going out on nighttime ambushes and patrols. On two or three of those patrols the Marines themselves were ambushed.

The battalion was eventually flown out of the hill country near Camp Carroll to the flat-lands — an area of rice paddies northeast of Dong Ha. From there Fox Company began manning a little outpost along the coast above the Cua Viet River in an area called "C-4," located between Cua Viet and the DMZ. Pittman recalls that most of that territory had been converted into a free-fire zone. The NVA were around and in much more strength than anybody expected. Moreover, Tet was still in full swing.

We slept at Mai Loc, a village along the Cua Viet River. When we woke up the next morning, we moved into the battalion perimeter and then immediately followed Fox Company out of the perimeter. Fox Company didn't quite get into the village but was shot up pretty badly trying to do so. I lost two friends—both corpsmen—that first morning. In fact, I greeted them and five minutes later they were both dead along with six Marines. It was just a horrendous firefight. We held a position just above them so I could see what was going on, but it was just a really bad situation.

Every day after that we were in a firefight. It was very stressful. Before this frequent combat, maybe we'd get into a firefight once, twice, or three times a month. And maybe you weren't directly involved but were a few hundred yards away. Maybe rounds were whistling over your head. But now the firefights in these small, abandoned villages were very intense, and I was always heavily involved. I had people shot and killed right next to me. So I went into a different survival mode at that time.

We had what they called "scoop meetings" the night before. The officers would tell us what we were going to do the next day — the general layout of the operation, platoon location, objectives, and expectations. Well, we knew what to expect. We knew what we were going to do. We were going to walk up to the village tree line, and the first Marines arriving were going to be shot and killed. Then the corpsmen were going to get up and treat the wounded. And if they made it, they made it. And if they didn't, they didn't.

This absolutely horrendous combat went on for six or seven days. It really got difficult to live. I knew I wasn't going to live. The people around me were not living so why should I expect to survive? It was not a matter of *if* but *when*.

I would get so nervous after one of these scoop meetings that I'd get diarrhea and cramping. The dysentery made it so much worse. I'd spend two or three hours having the worst diarrhea of my life along with stomach cramps, compounded by this nervous feeling and anxiety of knowing I wouldn't make it. Everybody with me had the same feeling even though nobody was talking about it. You could tell that everybody was depressed. We couldn't play around and we did not do a lot of talking.

But the situation changed for me. I began to personify death. I saw an image in the sky above me. Death was the Grim Reaper, a bony skeleton figure dressed in a black robe. I said, "No, I'm not gonna do this. You can go to hell! I'm not going to die! I'm not gonna allow you to take me today!"

And for some reason this new-found determination worked for me. And from that point, I was not even half as anxious as I was before. My goal was beating the Grim Reaper. It wasn't foolproof but it worked most of the time!

We'd be sitting in a rice paddy or in a village getting ready to jump off into an assault position moments away. We'd get the word: "Okay, guys, let's move out." And from that step on, you knew that you were subject to being killed. As soon as you moved out, you were in that assault mode and you knew that people were going to die. Was it going to be you or somebody next to you? You didn't know. It was a roll of the dice. And many times I saw several rolls of several dice and a lot of guys died.

The chaplain held memorial services at the battalion CP once a week, and we saw 10, 15, or 20 helmets on M16s with their bayonets stuck in the ground. Those of us who believed in

God and wanted to say a prayer for these guys would line up and the chaplain would lead us in prayer. We knew that next week, this service could be for one of us.

At that time I realized the war was fruitless. I was coming to an overall realization that we shouldn't be there, or at least that we should be fighting this war differently. We were still poorly supplied, maybe better than we were previous to Tet but not that much better. We would assault the same village two or three times in two or three weeks, take it, and then abandon it. Then we'd have to come back the next week and retake it. And people were dying as a result of that strategy. None of this made any sense. Not to me. I'm a farm kid and you survive on the farm by being practical and using common sense. But this was just not anything close to what I ever saw in my life. It was a waste of human beings. It was a waste of young men. And I must have become overtly disenchanted with the whole situation. I got to the point where I realized that I wasn't in Vietnam for my country. I was in this country for the guys who were around me. We were there for each other and that's the way it was. And we were going to try to help each other survive — whatever it took. It was an unspoken pact among all of us.

Dai Do

At the beginning of April 1968, the fighting suddenly died down and casualties dwindled notice-ably. Pittman and the Marines of Fox Company were uneasy. "I got this really bad feeling that this wasn't right. All our patrols and nighttime ambushes went out and then came back with no contact," he recalls. Two weeks later he learned he had been promoted to HM2 and was taken out of Hotel Company for a month, transferred to the battalion aid station, and assigned to doing sick call.

One day Chief Gorsage said, "You've got really bad jungle rot. You look like shit. You need to go to the ship, catch a movie tonight or tomorrow night, and pick up some rabies vaccine and medical supplies. Get yourself a shower and get cleaned up."

I was excited. I hadn't seen the rear for four or five months — not a shower, not any bathing at all to speak of except out in the rain. So I got up early in the morning before the sun came up and went out to the LZ. The landing zone supply radioman was on the LZ and we were just talking. All of a sudden, we heard gunfire off in the distance. I knew it was Hotel Company because it was their TAOR [tactical area of responsibility]. A chopper came as the firefight grew. I thought, "This is not good."

I got on the chopper and flew to the ship — the *Iwo Jima*. It was our rear because we were still a battalion landing team at that time. The Marines and corpsmen in the field never saw the rear. To see the ship was like hoping to go to heaven. It wasn't routine for someone in the field even to see the ship. It was kind of a sacred area to be enjoyed by rear echelon personnel.

So I turned in my list of medical supplies and went to the shower area. The ship's corpsmen lived in this area. I got a towel and had just walked into the shower with my clothes on because I was going to wash those, too. As I was doing that, one of the other corpsmen came in and said, "Hey! Pittman! Get your shit together! The Chief wants you back at the BAS ASAP!"

This was bad news. I wasn't gonna catch a movie. I wasn't going to be able to relax a little bit and have a decent meal. As I was putting my clothes back on, which were still wet, I heard the public address system announcement. "Medevacs inbound! Medevacs inbound!"

So I got my medical supplies and got on one of the choppers that had just delivered some of the casualties. Blood was still on the floor of the chopper. I just knew that this wasn't going to be good. As we were coming into the LZ, I could see what was going on. The landing zone was packed with casualties.

I jumped off the chopper. We had two docs in the battalion landing team. I went over to one and he said, "I need you to start CPR on these two guys right here."

I asked "Who's gonna help me?"

He said, "You've got to do it by yourself."

So I lined up these two guys who needed CPR and started giving them mouth-to-mouth and chest compressions. We flew to Dong Ha by chopper while I was working on both of them at the same time. We flew over Dai Do as the battle had just started.[8]

We worked all that day, maybe got an hour or two of sleep that night, and worked all the next day. On the third day of the battle, the Chief called me and another corpsman—a friend of mine, Jack Fillinger—to the bunker of the battalion aid station. The BAS was just a short distance from the landing zone where we were working on casualties. The Chief said, "You and Fillinger need to go up to the front. Pittman, you're going back to Fox Company and Jack, you're going back to Golf Company." That was 10 o'clock in the morning.

Jack and I got our gear and took an outboard motorboat up the river to Dai Do. It was maybe a mile or so. I joined Fox Company. We received incoming immediately. Jack and I got down in a trench together. This was really heavy artillery. I think it was 152mm NVA howitzers from the DMZ. Jack, who had already been wounded twice, said, "Rog, I think I'm gonna pass out. Take my pulse."

I reached over as we were lying in the trench and took his pulse. It was 140 something. Later on, in 1988, Jack and I got together and I said, "Jack, I don't know whether I took your pulse or mine."

So Jack went to Golf and I went to Fox. I was sitting next to the radio operator of Fox Company. I could hear gunfire off and on in the other part of the battle area. All of a sudden, Lt. Col. Weise's voice came up on the radio. "Golf Company is being overrun for the second time. We need help now! Break, Fox 6, Fox 6. This is Dixie Diner 6."

I'll never forget those words. "Dixie Diner 6" was Lt. Col. Weise's call sign. "Fox 6" was Capt. Butler's call sign. He was the CO of Fox Company. Weise said, "I want you to join up with Golf Company's right flank now. Move out now!"

We moved out single file through the village and went through the bottom part of Dai Do, which was an L-shaped village. We were the lower part of the "L" as we assaulted through Dai Do. It was fairly quiet with dead NVA all over the rice paddy. They were starting to bloat and stink. We got through most of Dai Do. I was on the right flank of the company. As I looked across the rice paddy on the far right flank, I saw probably a dozen or so NVA in front of me about 75 yards away running at right angles to my position. I had just passed a sniper team a few moments before. I yelled back to send word to the sniper team that we had NVA to our front. I then got distracted more to my left. As the firing picked up, I took shelter behind a house wall that had been bombed out. The wall was probably up to my chest in height.

I knew Marines were in front of me in the tree line. They were looking out across the rice paddy that we were going to have to cross in order to get to Golf Company's right flank. I was kneeling down behind the wall for protection because of all the small arms fire we were getting. Somebody suddenly yelled "Charge!"

I couldn't get around the wall in time to join the assault but I looked up over the edge of the wall slightly. All I could see were Marines going out into the rice paddy; they had gotten out of the tree line maybe 10 feet in front of me. They were going down like rag dolls, half spinning and falling in a way that was not natural. I realized that they had all been shot. Everybody in front of me had been killed. There was nobody except me.

I finished going around the wall after a few moments of hyperventilating. Nobody was there. Nobody was around me. I couldn't find anybody. I couldn't go out into the rice paddy and expose myself because I still heard heavy small arms fire. Going into that rice paddy would have meant meeting the same fate as the Marines. And nobody was even hollering for "Corpsman up!" As near as I could tell, I was one of six survivors in that assault group.

The village was infiltrated with NVA. They were all over the place. Pockets of NVA were just overrunning everybody. They were coming out of the rice paddy and shooting Marines who were still alive.

What I next remember is crawling on my stomach through Dai Do and running across some jungle boots sticking out of bushes. And for the first time I realized that maybe I was back with some Marines. And indeed I was. I linked up with them. A lot of casualties were now coming back through the village. I looked up and saw Lt. Col. Weise and all the radio operators maybe 30 feet in front of me.

I knew the CP [command post] was ahead of me. I got down into a big bomb crater and started treating casualties. The Marines around the bomb crater's rim were some guys I knew from Fox Company's mortar platoon. They were grabbing the wounded as they were stumbling by and bringing them down to me at the bottom of the crater. They were very badly wounded and I was patching them up. What saved them was the fact that they were walking. If they couldn't walk, they wouldn't be down in that crater. They were in shock. Another's arm was half off. The men had terribly horrendous wounds with advanced shock.

There was no way I could hold them in that position and do them any good. I would hold one badly wounded Marine until I got hold of another that wasn't as bad. And I would link those two guys up and point them to the rear — the south edge of Dai Do — and send them back by themselves. We couldn't spare anybody to take them back to the rear.

All of a sudden, the Marines on the lip of the crater got terribly nervous. We could hear the NVA assault coming our way. We knew that if we gave up this position, we were all dead. I was at the bottom of the crater trying to get to the lip to see what was going on. I looked up and saw Capt. [Manuel S.] Vargas coming along the edge of the crater. He had his right arm around Lt. Col. Weise, who was stumbling and not walking very well. In fact, I don't think he was walking at all. And Weise had his right arm around his radio operator, who was severely wounded with blood all over him. Weise looked like he was in shock.

We could see the NVA now coming from our front — the north side. We could smell 'em. We could feel 'em. They were trying to get around us on the left side. Lt. Col. Weise looked down at me directly and said, "Doc, let's get the hell out of here!" And those were the greatest words I had heard in a long time. I stumbled in behind him. We all grabbed somebody who was wounded and started stumbling through the village. It was every man for himself — and grab a friend. I saw men in rags, blood everywhere, smoke filling the air, splintered trees, explosions, and white, dirty faces. It was time to die but the Marines' faces said, "Not without a fight!"

It was an uncontrolled controlled fighting retreat. None of us were running. We wanted to but we couldn't because the NVA had come around us, and they were blocking our exit from the village to the south.

I didn't want to go through the village. I wound up with a corporal on the village's west side along an irrigation ditch. He and I crawled and ran our way through the bloody, watery ditch. He was in front of me as we ran down that ditch bent over as low as we could. And all of a sudden, he stopped and I almost ran into him. He looked off to the left and said, "Doc, look at that!"

About 100 or 150 yards through the clearing I could barely see little trees stirring at the bottom of the tree line. The trees appeared to be moving. I wanted to think I was hallucinating. I wanted to believe I was not seeing what I was seeing. And then I saw the whole tree line moving. Oh, man! And we had at least a quarter of a mile to go before we reached the river [Cua Viet River], which I thought we could swim and get the hell away from there.

The corporal lifted his M16 and said, "I'm gonna open up!"

I said, "No, you're not! We're gettin' the hell out of here! You open up on them and that's just gonna piss 'em off. What are you going to accomplish with your M16? Nothing. We're gettin' the hell out of here!"

So I started out crawling — moving a little slower this time. But we realized that we were not gonna make it before this movement out of the tree line was going to intercept us. I looked down through the ditch toward the river. I could see that the ditch formed a little "V" as it emptied into the Cua Viet River. I also saw a Navy gunboat come into the "V" and stop. That was not all good news. We looked like NVA with mud all over us. We couldn't be identified. So I kneeled down and waved my hand. I knew they were looking at me. I waved my hands to let them know we weren't NVA. That was a very good decision.

Then I saw their guns swing away from us toward the tree line, and they opened up with a breech-loaded 81mm mortar, a 20mm, and a couple of .50s that worked over the tree line. Once they opened up, we just ran like hell down that trench and got to the bottom south edge of Dai Do. We found other Marines at that site who had come down parallel to us through the village. We had wounded that we got out. We did a headcount and then set up for the night. Six of us were left out of my platoon, and only about 25 guys were left from Golf Company. The whole battalion at that time, which included cooks and clerks out of the rear, maybe amounted to only 250 guys left in the whole battalion.

The following night I was in charge of setting up the battalion aid station for counting the dead. I think 70 KIAs were logged in, counted, identified, tagged, body-bagged, and left on the LZ for first light to be evacuated. I know, for a fact, that these KIAs represented only a part of the casualties and KIAs of the battle. It was a really bad experience because I knew some of these guys, and so I purposely chose not to identify the KIAs from Fox Company that night. It was 2 or 3 o'clock in the morning when we finally got to Fox Company's KIAs. When they came up to be identified, I left. I just didn't want the memories.

Dai Do was the worst and longest experience of combat any of us had ever seen. Some historians have used the words "Tarawa," "Iwo Jima," or "Peleliu" for comparison. It was horrendous and unrelenting. And it was worse than we thought. When the numbers were counted on both sides in full detail, it turns out that we were up against a whole division of NVA with something like a 600- to 800–Viet Cong cadre attached. They were also supported by heavy artillery during daytime, which was a little unusual for that time of the war.

"No Medevacs on This Operation"

After the Battle of Dai Do, Roger Pittman went on a short R&R to Bangkok. When he returned, he was reinstated as the battalion's senior corpsman. At the time, 2/4's rear was in Dong Ha, but the battalion was operating in the Khe Sanh Valley area. It was late spring 1968 and the embattled base was still under heavy NVA bombardment.

I remember sitting on top of a hill on the west side of Khe Sanh inside the perimeter. I was watching counter-battery fire from 155s. The base was sandbagged and catching these big rounds coming into their position. The NVA shells were just impacting into these 155mm positions and I thought "Well, those guys [Marines] are toast!" The NVA had those 155s pinpointed. I think they were even shooting for each individual 155. You could see the 155 guys working the breeches of their guns as the shells were impacting around them. These Marines were some of the gutsiest guys I've ever seen in my life.

The officers called me up to the battalion command post one evening for a scoop meeting. We were going to air-assault into the Ho Chi Minh Trail area. It was inside the Laotian border south of Khe Sanh and just above the A Shau Valley. Casualties were expected to be heavy. We could anticipate heavy anti-aircraft fire on the choppers coming in. A Special Forces team was in the area that night and they had the radio open. You could hear them saying, "We have beaucoup NVA." They were describing tanks, elephants, engineering troops— probably in the several hundreds in their area alone. And this was the area where we were going to be flown into.

Everyone was just freaked out. Lt. Col. Ryan, who had been one of the battalion commanders in the 26th Marines, was an old salt. He came to Medical and asked me, "Doc, do you have any questions?"

I said, "No, sir."

He said, "I just want to tell you that there will be no medevacs on this operation. Whoever gets hurt, you will not medevac them. We will not give our position away by evacuating casualties. So suck it up and get it right!"

I said, "Yes, sir."

Then I thought, "This is a smart guy." That's exactly what the NVA used to determine our position. Not just our position but the center of our position. Because Marines always had the habit of putting the LZ in the middle of something. It usually wasn't off to the side. It had something to do with the CP [command post]. I thought maybe we could do some good on this operation. And we did.

We kicked their butts all the way down the Ho Chi Minh Trail. That road was literally strung with trucks and bicycles. One of our advance patrols found bicycles whose wheels were still spinning. We came upon base camps with triple-canopy jungle and cook fires still lit and smoking. They had recreation areas with volleyball nets. It was their rear and we were in it. We were kicking their butts and that felt good. Needless to say, the enemy had interfered with my recreation for a long time so it was about time we got even.

Downgraded to a Navy Cross

William Barber did what many young men did in the 1960s. He joined the Naval Reserve for two years of active duty so he could use the GI Bill to get an education. He then spent a year at the Naval Reserve Center in Austin, Texas, learning to be a corpsman. When he went on active duty, his detailer obtained a billet for him at the corps school in San Diego.

Following graduation, he attended Field Medical Service School at Camp Pendleton. Curiously, his first assignment was Naval Hospital Oakland — not the Fleet Marine Force — and then immediate deployment to Vietnam. At Oakland, he worked on a ward caring for paraplegics — mostly casualties from Vietnam.

Barber received his own orders to Vietnam in June 1968. "The reason I got orders so quickly was because they wanted to get a 12-month tour out of me before my two-year active duty obligation ended. This order was obvious from the day we graduated from corps school as reservists. Every one of us was sent to the West Coast so we could get some OJT [on-the-job training]. Then, with about a year left, they finally cut us orders to the FMF."

When he arrived in Vietnam, Barber was assigned to India Company, 3rd Battalion, 4th Marines.

My platoon had only 10 guys. It should have had 20 or 30. On the one hand I thought, "This is great; I have only 10 guys to take care of." On the other hand, I thought about staying alive. So I thought, "Oh my God, we're gonna get wiped." I was 18 going on 19 and wondered if I was going to see 20.

My company had four corpsmen and a senior corpsman. The senior corpsman was an E-4 or senior E-3, while the rest of us were E-1s, E-2s, and E-3s. [E indicates enlisted grades.]

At 19, all I was concerned about was not ending up like the paraplegics I had taken care of at Oakland. My main concern was coming back without any legs or arms. Getting killed was nothing. You're dead and that's that. I was afraid of stepping on a mine and losing an arm or both my legs. Losing a limb or limbs scared me more than getting killed.

But the longer I was there, I began to take on traits of the old-timers. If someone new came in, I didn't want to know him. Too many times I saw people I knew get killed. We were so young and immature. Probably the majority of us had never been away from home. We were more scared than anything else. But, as a corpsman, it was only through my actions that the Marines really and truly came to trust me when they needed medical attention.

I got their respect and admiration through hard work and time. When they went out on ambushes, I went because to win them over you had to do more than have knowledge of medicine. Of course, I took care of them, but I had to be one of the boys. Corpsmen fell into different categories. Some were only corpsmen, kept to themselves, did their jobs, and thus were friendless. Others were more outgoing and did well with the Marines. Finally, there were those — like myself — who were both corpsman and Marine.

In November of 1968 we were in a firefight and discovered an NVA underground complex up in the mountains. Our area of responsibility was I Corps — the northwest corner of South Vietnam close to the Laos border. On our east was Khe Sanh. To our west was Laos. To our north was the DMZ. Our rear was Camp Vandergrift, which was our forward position. From here we began our missions.

The whole complex was underground and connected by a tunnel system. The complex had a command post, a hospital, and sleeping quarters. Since we had all the air power, the Marines always traveled on the tops of mountains while the enemy always seemed to stay down in the valleys so they could hide. When the NVA got into the mountains, they didn't want to have a command post which could be seen so they did a lot of tunneling. In this case the compound had one big room that may have been a radio command post. Maps hung on the walls. The next room had a treatment table with drugs. And the room next door contained bunks where they slept. They also had a large number of exits going in all directions. This could have been a stopping-off place for the NVA on the way down the road or just a forward position to stay for R&R.

Anyway, we got a radio message at that time telling us that a general and some press were coming out to see us and inspect the complex we had discovered. My platoon was ordered to go and secure a landing zone several clicks [kilometers] away where the general and his party could land.

I should point out that after you had been in a firefight or a battle, you were not mentally or physically prepared to do this kind of duty. If you had been fighting, you were both mentally and physically exhausted; you were not mentally sharp. So when they told us — 3rd Platoon — to go and secure this landing zone, I guess we weren't in the best mental state at that time. Some of the guys weren't dressed. Some guys didn't even take their weapons. We weren't battle-ready, to say the least. The attitude was, "Why us? Get somebody else."

From the beginning, this simple tasking was doomed. When you approach a landing zone, you go around it and secure it. You don't go right down the middle and sit down. Instead of doing what we were trained to do, our guys started walking down the middle of the landing zone. When we got about three-quarters of the way across, all hell broke loose. We had walked into a horseshoe ambush. We were trapped in the middle of a landing zone and the NVA were blasting away.

I saw no way out and honestly thought I was going to die. In a circumstance like that, it's amazing to observe how people actually react to their situation. Some guys couldn't get close enough to the ground, but they still returned fire. Some guys were just sitting up and crying. Others were wandering around and calling for their mothers. And others, even though they knew they were surrounded, ran right toward the enemy guns that were shooting them. It is an eerie scene when you believe you are going to die. And yet, as individuals, we handle it differently.

Most people are creatures of habit. If they drink, they usually go to the same bar. Well, we had come onto the landing zone from a certain direction. We thought the best way to get out of there was to go back the way we came. We figured that it must be safe because we just came from there. But the NVA had moved two machine guns around to where we had come. We didn't know that but maybe that was a blessing.

So I lay on the ground scared, confused, and wondering. I could hear bullets whizzing and observed puffs of dirt being thrown from the ground as the bullets walked up to us. I finally realized that if I stayed where I was, I was going to die so I decided to get out of there. What makes a man or group of men react like I did at this time must be the basic instinct of survival. I wanted to live.

All at once we got up and started running down the trail back to where we had just come from. At that time I was about the fourth guy in line. Three Marines were in front of me. That was the first time I ever saw machine gun fire actually pick a guy up in the air and hold him there while the enemy continued shooting him. Finally, when they stopped, he fell to the ground right in front of me. It is a sight that has lingered with me. He was a human being and I knew him.

He was the first man killed. The second Marine was also shot. The third guy, if you can believe this, got hit and fell across the machine gun on the right knocking it over. As I came down the trail, the machine gun on the left suddenly jammed. I guess it wasn't my time to die.

I already had my .45 in one hand and a Ka-Bar [a seven-inch Marine fighting knife] in the other. When I got to the gun on the left, I shot the guy who was firing the machine gun. When the guy holding the ammunition belt came at me, I stabbed him. Then I turned around and took care of the two-man crew on the other machine gun.

After that, I called out to the others to come to the safety of the bush. People started coming. This is when you actually ask, "What does it mean to be a corpsman? Why am I here?" That's the only way I can explain what I'm about to tell you. I can only say that there were still Marines left on the LZ and unable to come to the safety of the bush.

I then went back onto the LZ. I don't know why. Maybe because Marines were still there and we lived by the code: We wouldn't leave anybody out there. Maybe the answer is simple. It was my job.

I crawled down the trail and got to the first Marine. He was dead. I dragged him back. Then I went out again and got the second man. He had been shot in the leg. I brought him back and stabilized him with a rifle as a splint. Then I went out and got the third guy and brought him back.

Then, being stupid, I went back a fourth time. As I was dragging the fourth guy back, the firing stopped. Off to my left, I saw an NVA with a rifle raised to stab me with his bayonet. On the ground, lying flat, and having my attention focused on a patient made me an easy mark. As I said before, "If it's not your time to go, it must not be." He tripped over something — a root, a tree stump, or his own feet; I don't know what it was. But he tripped across the trail in front of me. I shot him and he fell face down.

Then, all of a sudden, all hell broke loose again. As I lay there with my face in the dirt, I felt this cool stuff all over me. It was his blood. I don't know how long I lay there staring at my hand covered with his blood.

As my senses returned, I figured I had better get the hell out of there. I began crawling down the trail dragging the wounded Marine. But first I had to push the dead NVA out of the way with my left hand because he was lying across the trail immediately in front of me. I had just killed this guy and yet I stopped and turned his face toward me. His eyes were open, just staring. All of a sudden, I put my left hand on his cheeks. I don't know why I did that but I remember thinking, "This guy is so young, he's never gonna shave." He must have been no older than 10 or 12. We weren't fighting an old man's army. We were fighting young kids.

I pushed him out of the way and continued dragging the fourth guy over to the safety of the bush. It may have been 100 degrees that day, but as I came out of shock, I was shaking as if I had a good case of pneumonia.

I was nominated for the Medal of Honor and, as it went up the chain, it was approved at each level. When it got to a Navy admiral [Adm. John S. McCain, Jr.],[9] who, I understand, commanded all the forces in the Pacific, he thought it should be disapproved. So it went back down the same chain and was re-submitted recommending downgrade.

This sounds terrible to say, but a year later a guy called to inform me that I was going to get the Navy Cross. He stated that getting the Medal of Honor would have been a hard sell. When I asked why, he said, "America sees her heroes dead, mutilated, or at least wounded. The best thing you could have done that day was to have pulled out your John Wayne [fighting knife] and cut yourself."

I didn't have any medals at that time so I figured you couldn't go directly to the Medal of Honor right off the bat. And even though the Navy element in Vietnam suggested that I call/write my parents and get them involved politically, I didn't. I didn't even have the National Defense Medal. But at age 19, I guess I was at the apex of my career.

"Bait for the NVA"

Missouri native Dennis Noah joined the Navy in 1965, but he did not go on active duty until early the following year. After boot camp at Great Lakes, he remained there to attend hospital corps school. Noah then worked at the dispensary administering shots to thousands of recruits passing through that facility.

"One day the senior chief said, 'There's been a request to amend orders for two, three, or four of you, and you're going to go FMF.' The other guys didn't want to do that. My best buddy didn't want to but I said to him, 'Hey, man, let's go do this. It sounds pretty neat.'

"So we volunteered and went to Camp Pendleton — B School — or as I like to call it, the 'Reader's Digest' version of Marine Corps boot camp. They ran us around with packs and tried to make Marines out of us. That was in January of 1967."

After he arrived in Vietnam, Noah was assigned to 3rd Platoon, Hotel Company, 2nd Battalion, 5th Marines. "There was no orientation at all — zero. We got a B-1 bag — a Unit 1 bag. They gave us battle dressings and some morphine syrettes, some atropine syrettes, a bandage scissors, which I still have, suture scissors, a suture set, a cut-down set, amyl nitrate ampules, which I threw away, and some aspirin. Not much. When we went into the field for the first time, we learned pretty quickly. The very day I joined my unit, the unit was assigned in the morning and I was up in the weeds that afternoon.

"Militarily, they never kept the corpsmen up to date, but we didn't really care. We just followed the guy in front of us, and when they yelled, 'Corpsman up!' we went."

In November 1967, Noah and his platoon were on patrol walking across a small rice paddy, as they had done countless times before. But this time, it would be different.

Not too long before this we had looked across a big rice paddy and saw a bunch of guys about our size with flak jackets and gas masks. We thought they were Marines and so we waved at them and they waved back. They went on their way and we went on ours. As we walked across this small rice paddy toward a tree line, an NVA weapons platoon hit us. These were the guys we had been waving at.

About six Marines went down in the first volley. [Sgt. William] Stutes was killed with the first shot and Steve Irvin was also killed. Sgt. Wadley and I ran across the rice paddy. The ground was just exploding all around us and I couldn't hear. A huge bomb crater was right in front of the tree line so we hid behind it to help the guys — but they were already dead.

Then Wadley took a couple of rounds. Our platoon radioman, a guy named Crabtree, was shot in the leg and broke his femur, but he was still radioing back to the company. And that's when we had our mighty "Mattels," the M16s with the plastic stocks made by Mattel.[10] We had four men from what they called "shore party" who had M14s. The rest of the guys had M16s and every damn one of them jammed. So here we were pinned down with a couple of wounded guys behind a rice paddy about 50 feet from the enemy and the only firepower we had were four M14s. And those NVA were good. When they shot, they hit. By this time, the platoon had pulled back and left us out there because they didn't have any firepower.

Second Lt. [Allan] Herman kept running out and sticking his head up. He was one of the new second "louies" we had just gotten about a month before. I said to him, "Lieutenant, they're gonna pop you!" And there he was throwing hand grenades at them. "Lieutenant, you're just gonna piss 'em off! We're not gonna defeat those guys."

And sure enough, the NVA plugged the lieutenant right in the eye and killed him instantly. A lot of the dead had been shot in the eyeball. Stutes also got it that way and so did Irvin. As I said, those NVA were good.

Gibson kept running back and forth like a crazy man. I yelled, "Gib, quit running back and forth! They're gonna kill you!" He and Stutes had gone through boot camp together and were very close buddies. And now, of course, Stutes was dead. So here I was lying there with two wounded men. I found out later that we were the bait for the NVA to kill more Marines. Every time someone tried to come get us, the enemy would plug those Marines.

For about 12 hours we were ground zero for F-4s, A-4s, Hueys, mortars, and the artillery. All this stuff was coming in right on top of us—napalm and everything. The only cover that protected us was this huge bomb crater we were on the back side of. The bomb that had created it had kicked up dirt that was raised up so we were hidden. And every time we'd stick our heads up, they'd take a shot at us. At one point, Wadley leaned over and said, "Pull out your .45, Doc."

Even though I carried a .45, I couldn't hit the broad side of a barn with it. I didn't carry any ammo with it and I never cleaned it. So I pulled it out. I actually had a clip with six rounds in it but when I pulled the slide back, it jammed. Wadley then said, "They're gonna overrun us. Get ready!" Of course, they didn't overrun us, but when one of the NVA stuck his head up, I threw my .45 at him.

We spent the rest of the evening being bombed. Every time one of the F-4s or A-4s came in you'd hear "Click! Click! Click!" That was the NVA's signal to go into their holes. After the plane dropped whatever, they'd go "click! click!" I found out later that our guys hadn't dropped anything bigger than 250-pound bombs because they thought we might still be out there—and they didn't want to kill us. Each time one of those bombs went off, our bodies came off the ground about three or four inches. And the napalm was really something. When napalm exploded, all the air would go that way, then come back.

In that crater we had about half a dozen dead plus myself and Wadley. He got plugged twice and I, too, by this time had been hit by shrapnel in the shoulder and back. And then there was Crabtree, the radioman, who was behind us. They had tried to pull him out earlier but he had refused to go because he was trying to direct the air strikes from hitting us. So three of us were still alive. Lt. Herman was lying right next to me and he was dead. In that situation, I couldn't do much to provide medical attention. I couldn't move so I threw Crabtree a battle dressing. I yelled, "Crabtree, are you okay?"

"Yeah, I'm shot in the leg and it's broken."

I asked, "Is it spurting blood or anything like that?"

"No, nothing like that, just oozing." He put the battle dressing on. Then I put a couple of battle dressings, as best as I could, on Wadley. He was hit in the shoulder and chest.

Hours later, two or three guys came crawling up and asked, "You guys are still alive? Do you want to go back?" I thought that would be a good idea.

When they finally pulled us out, the NVA were still there. A CH-34 [Navy transport helicopter] then came in to pick up the wounded guys. I'll never forget this. He had to land in this really tight rice paddy and these '34s were really good-sized helicopters. His rotor blades were shattering the tree tops but he got it down. After we got everybody on, I grabbed the crew chief and said, "Tell the pilot to turn this thing around and go out the other way because you're gonna fly right over the top of these guys—and they apparently have a couple of heavy machine guns."

The crew chief said that he understood. And sure enough, the pilot took off and headed right across the NVA. We took fire and a few of the guys in the helicopter were wounded again.

Prepared for Gruesome Business

Roger Ware grew up in West Virginia. When he received a draft notice in 1965, he and a friend immediately contacted a Navy recruiter. "He came, got us, and signed us up that same evening."

After boot camp and hospital corps school in Great Lakes, he was assigned to Naval Hospital Jacksonville, Florida, and worked on the isolation ward taking care of patients with tuberculosis and other communicable diseases. Four months later, Ware received orders to report to the Fleet Marine Force and Field Medical Service School at Camp Lejeune.

After arriving in Vietnam, Ware found his company operating near Con Thien near the DMZ in what was called "Operation Prairie." It lasted 53 days, ending in early November 1966. Combat soon gave him perspective as to what was expected of a corpsman.

I wore a flak jacket and four canteens, two hooked on my flak jacket and another two onto my web belt. I also carried a Ka-Bar, a .45, and four clips for the pistol. Then I had to carry my Unit 1 and my pack with C-rations and extra gear.

Each person in our unit also had to carry either 100 or 200 rounds of machine gun ammo. If we had one M60 machine gun, each man carried a hundred-round belt. If we had two machine guns, each guy carried two 100-round belts. In addition, I carried smoke grenades for the medevacs, an E-tool [shovel], and a poncho.

When we had to pop smoke, it was usually yellow smoke. Red smoke meant enemy. We would let the incoming helo know what color smoke we were going to pop. I also carried fragmentation grenades and a cleaning kit for the .45 in my pack, C-rats, extra socks, a long-sleeved shirt, and an extra pair of trousers if we were going to be out in the field for five or six days. Some had three or four plastic bottles of insect repellent, which never worked but we carried it anyway. I once weighed my gear. I carried 82 pounds plus the helmet.

We were also issued what was called a "rubber lady"—an air mattress—but we never carried the mattresses in the field. We were also given a blanket, poncho, and shelter half with poles and rope. In addition, we had a nylon bag about the size of sea bag we called a "willy peter bag," in which we could pack all our gear to store in the rear.

We were supposed to have a nylon litter but we found them useless. You were better off just putting a guy on a poncho and dragging him out. Combat doesn't mean having just one guy shot every hour. You might get 20 every few minutes. I never used that nylon litter—not even one time.

I carried many different sizes of dressings in my Unit 1—large, medium, and small. I had scissors, tourniquets, and morphine syrettes. I think I had about 10 syrettes of morphine, maybe more. I geared up my Unit 1 to where I was going and how many days I was going to be out. If we were going on a major operation, I'd take extra supplies in my pack. I might take 20 syrettes of morphine. My initial outfit contained two cans of serum albumin. I'd have two large battle dressings, gauze for burns, [copper sulphate] powder for willy peter [white phosphorus] burns, and petroleum jelly gauze for burns. We had atropine syrettes in case they used nerve gas on us but I never used them. The Unit 1 bags also contained Ace wraps and Band-Aids. I had a penlight, tongue blades, oral airway, Q Tips, 4 by 4s, 2 by 2s, eye patches, wire splints, and slings. Then I had a medical book I wrote in using an ink pen. It was a coupon-type book that had medical tags with carbon copies. You could wire that to a person's collar. We had medicines for diarrhea and upset stomach and Tylenol for headaches, muscle relaxers, antihistamines, eye drops, and malaria pills plus Bacitracin ointment. I had some Tetracaine ointment for burns. We had Merthiolate, a few salt tablets, and calamine lotion, a couple of pairs of scissors and lots of moleskin [heavy cotton material] and tape for blisters.

I also had a surgical kit with suture needles, prep blades, scissors, forceps, tweezers, probe, and a knife handle. It was called a "minor surgical kit," and went inside one of the pouches of the Unit 1.

When we were on patrol, we carried our ponchos rolled up and tied below our packs. I usually carried extra supplies in my pack, such as three extra cans of serum albumin, three or four extra large dressings, two or three extra tourniquets, a handful of small dressings, and extra salt tabs because my job was to give them out. And I'd carry extra Tylenol, aspirin, sunburn ointment, malaria pills, and Merthiolate. I also carried an ammo bag to hold extra supplies. If a guy hit a mine and got a massive blast injury, he might have 20 wounds! I would use large dressings and a couple of tourniquets on his amputations plus five or six other dressings. Bang! You might use your whole load just on one man! And we saw a lot of mines and booby traps.

I carried extra supplies in ammo bags. Each Marine had halazone [water purification] tablets in his individual pouch on the web belt, and also two bottles of halazone tablets, 100 tablets per bottle. Each Marine also carried a little first aid in the back of his web belt, which contained a couple of medium dressings and a few small dressings and a tourniquet. The pouch was about four inches high and about four inches wide.

Many times I would be the only corpsman in my platoon. We normally had eight corpsmen to a line company. That's two corpsmen per platoon. But often we'd be down to three or four corpsmen per company—one for each platoon. Sometimes we had so many wounded Marines in a good battle or firefight that I didn't even get to them until the medevacs had arrived. Most of the time I didn't even have time to fill out the medical tags that were made of paper. These paper tags didn't do well in the humidity. After treating a casualty, the corpsman was expected to fill out the tag and make it readable—while working in a rice paddy and mud or while it was raining. Often I didn't even get a chance to do that because I'd be going from one guy to another. Was it more important to save a guy's life or do the paperwork documenting what I had done?

As soon as a man was hit, the question was asked, "Doc, what kind of medevac do you need? What priority?" "Emergency" meant as soon as you could get one. "Routine" meant some time today. "Priority" meant about two hours. And you wouldn't know when a helo was inbound. I may have had plenty of time to work on a guy or a bunch of wounded, but often we had so many wounded, I didn't get to all of them. Then all of a sudden a medevac was inbound.

The helo didn't always land exactly where we were. It might land in the middle of a rice paddy, and we had to drag those guys out to where the helo was—many times under fire.

Often we'd just carry our wounded in ponchos or grab their clothes and drag them out to the helo. I'd have three or four Marines help me, but I'd always go myself. As I stood right beside the helo, bullets would be coming in. If we were in a hot LZ—and almost every medevac was under fire—I was out there in that LZ getting shot at.

What was it like waiting for a helo? Suddenly the enemy heard the chopper coming in and knew it was going to come in into the wind. So if you were the enemy, you would want to take that chopper down because it was big and you could see it. For the enemy, that was quite an achievement to knock down a helo. It certainly was more important than shooting one person.

When that helo was inbound and I saw it, I began moving the casualty to where it landed. I didn't care whether or not it was under fire. I just wanted to get my casualty aboard and give him a chance to live.

I often saw guys wounded all over the place. If I were the only corpsman, I didn't have a chance to get to all of them. Most of the time they'd just throw the casualties on the helo without me even getting to them or treating them. I remember people with multiple amputations. I'd be trying to get an IV into them because they were in such shock. I'd hear that a medevac was on the way. But three hours might have gone by, and I was trying to keep the patient alive as best I could.

What made it even more difficult for me was that I knew these people. I'd spent a lot of time with them and they were my friends. Here I was a corpsman in Vietnam 18 or 19 years old and I had guys' lives in my hands that 30- and 40-year-old surgeons would be treating later. But as the corpsman, I was out there as the first care giver. That's something I never thought about until after it was over. More than once I wished I had better training or better supplies to take care of those men.

Even before I heard a Marine yelling, "Corpsman up!" I'd already be running. Imagine what it must have been like. You're on patrol and suddenly a mine goes off. Everybody stops in their tracks except one guy. One guy is moving. That's the corpsman. So if you were the enemy and you saw that one guy running, you knew he was the corpsman. I might have to run a quarter of a mile to get to somebody. I had just come through that rice paddy maybe waist-deep in water. Now I'd have run back through it to get to somebody. And I couldn't run that fast in the mud with all my gear on. I just hoped I'd get there in time to do some good.

When a man was badly wounded, I always tried to control my own stress and fear because until I got to him I wouldn't know what kind of injury he had. When I reached him, I'd think, "Oh my God, what's this guy got?" It was difficult to look at a friend of yours you had known for months and realize that he had his legs blown off or had massive blast injuries. I'd work as quickly as I could and do the best I could. Sometimes it seemed as though I just wasn't doing enough, particularly when the man had multiple amputations. As I applied tourniquets, I wondered what to do next. I went through checks in my mind. What to do next? The casualty would ask, "How bad am I, Doc?" Many times I lied to the casualty to give them hope to live.

If I had two casualties exactly the same, I might not have treated them exactly the same. It all depended where I was and what the conditions were. Was he lying in a rice paddy? Was I under fire or being mortared? The casualty would often be scared and excited, in shock, or disbelief. I'd talk to him, always trying to calm him down while trying to control my own stress.

Once I treated the casualties and got them medevaced, we moved out to finish our patrol. It was not unusual to walk 20 to 30 miles a day on patrol. One time our M-79 [grenade launcher] guy was killed and I ended up carrying his M-79 with about 30 rounds. That was the biggest mistake I ever made. We had a 12-mile speed hump and I was the last guy who came in. Occasionally I carried a shotgun or an M14 on ambushes. If we captured enemy weapons, I'd help carry these out. I never carried an M16. My standard weapon was a .45, which I carried in a shoulder holster. I never shot any NVA, but I did shoot at a couple of Viet Cong to protect my patient during "Operation Tuscaloosa" in January 1967.[11]

Grasshopper 16

The helicopter is one of the lasting symbols associated with the Vietnam War. By the time U.S. combat troops arrived in South Vietnam in 1965, this unique aircraft was hardly a novelty.

Unlike the Army, which had designated helicopter ambulances ("dust-offs,"), the Marines provided medevac on an as-needed basis. During the early phase of Marine operations in Vietnam,

Lt. Cmdr. George Harris, commanding officer of B Medical Company of the 1st Medical Battalion, recalls that his unit "never had any dedicated helicopters, that is, helos used only for medical evacuation. They were available on a catch-as-catch-can basis unlike the Army which had whole companies of helicopter ambulances. The Marine theory was that an airplane is an airplane is an airplane, and a helicopter is a helicopter is a helicopter. The belief was that they couldn't afford to sideline a helicopter to move casualties so we didn't have dedicated 'dust-off' helicopters, or 'slicks,' as we called them."

If a casualty required transportation to one of the hospital ships, a phone call to the local Marine Air Group would usually bring a helicopter to the hospital helo pad in short order, if one was available. As Harris and his colleagues learned, an "urgent" ambulance call might well go unheeded if all the group's helicopters were out on a mission.

By 1968, Marine helicopter squadrons located in the I Corps area in northern South Vietnam at Quang Tri, Phu Bai, and Danang were flying daily medevac missions on a rotating basis with designated air crew usually comprising the pilot, co-pilot, crew chief, hospital corpsman, and, if the CH-46 were the aircraft, two gunners for suppressing enemy ground fire.

Duty as a medevac corpsman was strictly voluntary and no specific training was required. HM3 Roger Ware, once back from the field and assigned to a battalion aid station, frequently volunteered for medevac flights. "If they needed a corpsman, I'd go."

Our call sign at the BAS [battalion aid station] was Grasshopper 16. They'd call in, "Grasshopper 16, this is Flight Line. Need a corpsman for a medevac. Do you have one available?" When the chopper landed at Medical, I'd go out and take off with it.

I remember quite a few medevac flights. I'd ride out in a helo somewhere in the field and wouldn't know where I was. I wouldn't be hooked into the flight helmet. I'd just be a body inside that helo. We'd land in an LZ, a field, or rice paddy. They'd then bring a guy up, throw him on the helo, and we'd take off.

Then I'd do my job. I might start an IV, do CPR, or maybe check him for more injuries. Maybe there were three, four, or five casualties had never been treated on the ground. So now I'd be treating them as the helo was flying back to 1st Medical Battalion. When the helos landed, I'd get out and see the bullet holes.

The biggest risk I always worried about was going on a night medevac mission. I couldn't see and had no idea where we were going. When a helo began going down into an LZ at night, we flew with no lights on, and just hoped to goodness there were no trees

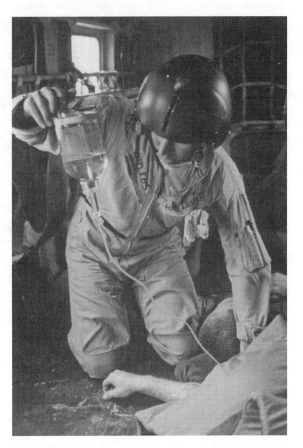

HM3 Ira Leavitt hydrates a casualty with intravenous dextrose during an evacuation flight to a hospital at Phu Bai (BUMED Archives).

below us. We were being talked down by the radioman on the ground. When I was inside those helos, all I had on was my flak jacket and my gear. The gunners had reinforced armor vests and some extra protection around the machine guns. But if I stood in those doorways, I had no extra protection. It was a hairy feeling being in a helo like that.

In my case, I controlled my fear. I actually was afraid until the helo landed. Then instinct took over and I did my job. When you were doing your job, you never worried about getting shot down. The fear went away. It was the same fear I felt in combat. When I was on patrol, I always worried about something happening that I could never take care of. When I saw some of those injuries, I would be in such shock myself. No matter how much I'd seen, it was never the same. But, as I said, instinct took over.

At night I had to feel for the injuries. I might have had a red flashlight but wouldn't want to use it at night because I didn't want the enemy to see where I was. My biggest fear at night was that one guy would trip a mine and maim everybody around him — and I might be one of them. I also wondered what would happen if I got hit. Who would take care of me?

First Patrol: Search and Destroy

James Maddox was 19 when he joined the Navy in 1966. Because of a special Naval Reserve program which featured delayed enlistment, he went through basic training but didn't report for active duty until almost a year later. In June 1967, he attended corps school in San Diego and shortly thereafter was assigned to the Marines. "When you don't know something, you use your imagination and kind of make a little movie. Well, my movie was, 'If I go with the Marines as a corpsman, I'd get to wear the Marine uniform and be an extra special guy.' We knew Marines really liked corpsmen — or most of them did. So I had kind of a pumped up feeling." When Maddox arrived at Dong Ha, that feeling was already turning to bewilderment.

I hadn't yet been assigned to a unit but was told to report to the rear area main tent for corpsmen going to the 3rd Marine Division. The next morning I recall someone telling me, "Try to become a driver or get with artillery." I asked a guy behind a desk if I could go with artillery. He gave me a cynical laugh. "Oh yeah, right, artillery." And then he assigned me to infantry — 2nd Battalion, 9th Marines. At the time, that unit was not far below the DMZ. It was south of Dong Ha out in a rural area in a big tent city.

A jeep dropped me off and I crossed an open area to get to the tents. I went by a group of a half dozen Marines and asked how to get to so and so. One Marine told me he was in the rear area because he had gotten a rat bite. Everyone began laughing. He held up a little metal can opener called a "P-38." It had a small sharp-hooked point used to puncture and open C-ration cans. A P-38 could also inflict a rat-tooth-looking wound. He said, "Here's how you get a rat bite. I'm back here to get two weeks of shots." I found out later that a fake rat bite was one way to get out of the field for two weeks.

Anyway, I was ordered to travel with a Marine who had already been out in the field for about six months. We were to catch a helicopter to a "grunt" company that was out in the field and about to start a search-and-destroy operation. I looked out the door of the helicopter and saw bomb craters everywhere. It looked like a moonscape down there. It had gone from green lush trees to barren, reddish brown dirt and bomb craters.

When we landed and I got to my unit, the situation started getting crazier and crazier. The corpsman I was relieving came running up to me. He was filthy, skinny, wide-eyed, and so happy that he gave me a hug like I was some beautiful blond babe who had just come into his life. And then he grabbed his gear, got on that helicopter that had just brought me there, and away he went.

While this was going on, jets were shrieking overhead and bombing a nearby hill that seemed only a few hundred yards away. The bombs were going off very loudly and I could see black smoke billowing up into the sky. The Marines were cheering like they were at a football game. Little did I know that that hill was where we were going the next day.

The chief hospital corpsman told me where to sleep and how to get my gear. I got my jungle utilities and helmet. Then they had me fire an M16 and the .45 I was issued. They didn't bother issuing me a Unit 1. Instead they gave me a big ammo bag about 16 or 18 inches deep. The chief then said, "This is what you're gonna need. Pack it with battle dressings." They gave me some M16 clip bandoliers, and I stuffed them with battle dressings. I got a little box of morphine syrettes, some plasma, and bottles of pills.

That night we used our shelter halves. It was like a poncho and I just grabbed some branches or sticks and made a little tent. Then you lay down on the ground in your clothes. Most guys slept fully dressed — boots and everything. It wasn't raining but it was sweltering hot and extremely humid. Anyway, we were going on a patrol the next morning — my first patrol.

We got up about 4 A.M. Everybody was very quiet putting on their gear. One guy said very solemnly, "Okay, Doc, you're going to march behind this guy." After eating our C-rations, we got in line and went marching off. It was still dark when we started out; it seemed like we walked for hours. It wasn't real jungle but more like a piedmont area with tall grass and scattered trees.

We stopped when we reached a river. Our unit then fired some mortars across the river and I saw them explode. I had never seen anything like that before. Someone said that they had seen some movement. The guys in the company were all agitated. I didn't know that when you saw movement, it meant that there was probably going to be a fight. I talked to the guy walking behind me — a young red-haired kid. He was nervously going on and on about trying to find a way to get out of the field.

That night my platoon was assigned to be point platoon in the company patrol that was to return to where they had seen movement earlier. This made the guys in my platoon terribly afraid. The platoon leader — a corporal — came back and said, "We have lead in the patrol." Everybody suddenly was really down with a terrible, sad feeling you could cut with a knife.

After another pre-dawn awakening, we marched out in file again. About 9 or 10 in the morning we came to a hill. A few guys yelled, "Fire in the hole!" I didn't know what this meant at the time, but I remember seeing them gathered around what turned out to be a bunker. I heard a loud explosion and saw black smoke.

We kept moving slowly up a hill. It wasn't jungle but hollow reed grass with trees here and there. Then we were ordered to halt. I got down on one knee and started daydreaming about being home because I was feeling so out of sorts. I don't think I had had a bowel movement in almost a week, and I was very fatigued.

Suddenly I heard several explosions behind me, loud and close. Everyone instantly lay down on the ground. And then all hell broke loose with a roar of gunfire that sounded like the inside of a fireworks factory going off. Then they started yelling, "Corpsman!" A guy lying ahead of me was screaming, "Doc, you've got to get up there. But stay down! Stay down!"

I crouched down with all my gear and began moving up towards the sound of where the shooting was getting heavier. Someone shouted for me to get down lower. I crawled into a huge bomb crater about the size of my house, probably 10 or 15 feet deep. Over the sound of all the explosions and guns going off, they were yelling, "There's a guy hit down on the side of the hill."

I crawled over the hill — the bomb crater — alone, nobody with me, and down through some little trees. I ended up crawling right through the middle of an NVA toilet. Everywhere were little cans with shit in them — piles of it everywhere. I had it all over my shirt front and between my fingers and it stunk badly. Here I am crawling through shit with all this gunfire going on, not knowing what to expect. Ironically, I have to work on an open wound with human feces smeared on me. Not exactly sterile procedure.

I finally got to a Marine crouched down and holding a battle dressing to the side of the wounded man. I said, "I'll take care of things." I looked at the wound and said, "Oh my God!" The guy — Murdock — had taken shrapnel through his flak jacket and shirt and was hit in the upper left part of the back near his chest area. It looked like you could easily stick two fingers in the hole. And what looked like raspberry Jell-O was clumping out of his wound. This was nothing like the fake wounds in Field Medical School. This was the real thing. He was bleeding like a sieve and was very pale. He barely whispered that he couldn't feel his legs.

My field medical training came in. I tried to move him so I could get that battle dressing around tight enough. The situation was getting crazier and crazier. The fire was intense and smoke and dirt filled the air everywhere. Since the Marine left me, a grenade had hit him and now he had crawled back up to me.

I looked at his wound and thought, "This is too much. I'm terribly frightened for myself, but I have to deal with these wounded guys." I yelled at him to take care of his arm wound himself. I knew I had to get Murdock up on his bad side to allow his good lung to help him breathe.

As I was doing that, someone came to help me. I think it was a Marine photographer who was traveling with us. He had no helmet or any other kind of protection. I tried to get some blood plasma into Murdock because he had lost a lot of blood, but I couldn't find his veins. They had all collapsed. I felt myself beginning to panic by now when, all of a sudden, the guy who was helping me was gone and I was alone again.

Suddenly I heard a thud. I looked over and saw a grenade that had landed near me. It had a black iron head and some kind of hollow wooden handle with whitish smoke coming out of it. I did what I was trained to do. I lay on top of my patient as the grenade went off.

I think it knocked me unconscious for a second or two and the concussion rolled me over. When I came to, I was terrified. I thought I was wounded because it felt like my legs were numb. It turned out I wasn't hit, but I started screaming for some help. Finally a young black Marine named [George] Gipson came sliding down on his rear with no helmet, yelling that he'd help me.

He then jumped over on the other side of the wounded Marine. I grabbed Murdock under the arm and told Gipson that we'd drag him up to the bomb crater. I said, "Let's go!" And then he lurched forward and screamed that he'd been hit.

This is where I'm confused in my mind. Maybe I started crawling away. Then I got hit in the hip with shrapnel. I don't remember the explosion, but it felt like someone had whacked me with the claw end of a hammer. Looking down, I saw that it had blown a large hole in my jungle utilities, and I had a big hole in me that started to bleed. I was screaming for God to help me. "God, don't let me die!"

I crawled up to a tree and got behind it. As my helmet went rolling off, I looked back at the man who had just come down to help me. He had his arms wrapped around his chest and was screaming for me or someone else to help him. I yelled back for him to crawl to me. He looked right at me with his eyes wide open and replied that he couldn't. I yelled, "You're a Marine! Crawl to me!"

He then said, "I can't move." I knew I had to get out of there. I felt like all hell was breaking loose. I began inching my way up the hill when I came upon a radioman who was lying on his back talking on the radio. He told me to get back to the bomb crater so I crawled up and into it. Another corpsman named Deweese came and put a battle dressing on me. It was mayhem everywhere.

Then they pulled Murdock — the guy I had originally treated — and Gipson up into the bomb crater. More guys crawled in and began returning fire. I continued treating Murdock, again trying to forget my own wound. I heard someone say that Gipson was dying so I shifted my attention to him. This other corpsman and I tried to revive him but he just didn't make it. I saw his pupils go all the way out to the hilt. And something else to remember: His pants had somehow come off, and sperm began pouring out of his penis and running down his leg. Certain sights you never forget. This was the first person I had seen die before me in such a violent way. I will never get that sight out of my mind.

The firefight continued and more people were shouting for help, more people were bleeding. We had to get the wounded to a place for the medevac helicopter. "Thank God, I was wounded," I thought, "because I also get to go on the helicopter." There must have been a dozen or more wounded and three killed. That was my introduction to Vietnam. It was July 20, 1968, and it's burned into my mind forever.

"A Hole in My Soul"

Maddox and his dead and injured comrades were brought to a hilltop to await evacuation even as the firefight went on around them. As he continued doing what he could for the wounded, a Huey gunship fired down into a nearby ravine and jets dropped napalm and bombs.

The ground shook tremendously and dirt clods rained down on us. The planes came roaring by extremely close and the napalm made a wall of flame. Some guys later said it took the oxygen out of the air and it was hard to breathe. I just remember it was all very close.

A big CH-46 [Sea Knight] helicopter came in and hovered, lowered the rear ramp, and we corpsmen and some of the Marines loaded the bodies on while it was hovering just above the ground. Being the corpsman, I was one of the last to get on. About 14 or 15 of us wounded crowded in there. All this time a machine gunner was firing away out the side of the '46. As he fired, hot shells flew down onto the floor near me and around us. I remember thinking, "Let's get outta here! Outta here!" I was really afraid bullets would come tearing through the skin of that chopper. Anyway, he kept up the fire, they closed up the back of the '46, and it banked on away.

A corpsman came over, looked at my wound, and then applied a battle dressing. My pants were kinda hanging off me because the shrapnel had also cut my belt in half. I had the battle dressing tied real tightly around my hip.

They flew us for what must have been about 15 minutes—I and all these freshly wounded and traumatized guys crowded in together. It was very surrealistic and relatively quiet after the shooting stopped. I can't recall what went on in that helicopter except I still was more or less dealing with Murdock. I had him rolled over on his bad side because I was pretty sure that a lung had collapsed. He was losing a lot of blood, and I was just trying to keep him awake. I had one hand on his pulse.[12]

We landed at the medical facility at Dong Ha, which, at that time, was called "Delta Med." They opened the hatch and some corpsmen were there to greet us. They immediately began carrying off the worst of the wounded. I got off on my own but was pretty woozy and confused. A chaplain handed me a cold Coca-Cola.

It was already about 115 degrees out by noon and everybody was heading into a Quonset, which was the medical facility at Dong Ha. It was a large place and full of wounded. I was staggering about holding my pants up. I was missing my helmet and was wearing a battle dressing with blood running down my leg. I began screaming that all this was insanity. A corpsman ran over, grabbed me by the shoulders, shook me, and told me to shut up. One guy yelled. "We've all been through it. Get your act together." I kind of stuffed everything right then, realizing that you couldn't have someone losing it in the middle of these casualties.

So I calmed down and they led me into a little side room off the main area. Sawhorses with stretchers were lined up in a row. It reminded me of babies at the hospital all lying next to each other in little cribs. Corpsmen and doctors were hard at work removing shrapnel and bullets. As they led me in, they brought a South Vietnamese soldier by on a stretcher. I looked down and both his legs, just above the ankles, looked like someone had taken a big axe and cut both of them nearly off; they were just hanging by threads.

They lay me down on my stomach and examined my wound. A corpsman gave me some lidocaine [local anesthetic] shots in the side. Another guy was standing over me with a clipboard getting the details. Since I was lying on my stomach I looked over next to me. Curley, a man from my platoon, was having some shrapnel removed from his arm. I remember those forceps being way up inside his biceps and he was screaming to beat the devil. So it wasn't like this was a nice, quiet, clean place with pretty nurses.

They were just running us through like cattle. I'm not saying they were being mean, but they had a lot of customers. Everything was just matter of fact with no time for warm fuzzies. It was just business as usual. They had stitched me up with wire sutures because my wound was pretty wide but not very deep. The shrapnel had just taken a chunk of meat out in back of my right iliac. If it had penetrated any further, it might have gone through my gut. If it had been a little more this way, it could have severed my spine. But the way it hit, it just took a chunk of meat out of the back of my hip, just missing the big pelvic bone. My web belt, the one that held up my pants, had been blown in half; I still have it. I always felt that belt helped deflect the shrapnel and prevented it from penetrating as deep as it might have.

I was moved to a tented area near Dong Ha that housed a bunch of us "walking wounded." Then they loaded us in the back of a "6 by" truck and took us back to that main area in Quang Tri where I had first checked in. It was a Marine Corps rear area headquarters—a big green canvas tent city. Some had wooden siding with screen windows. I guess you could call it a battalion headquarters.

Six or eight of us weren't terribly wounded. The rest went on to Japan or back to the States. I ended up spending about a month recuperating. Twice a day my wound was scrubbed, with stitches still in it.

They took the wire stitches out and the wound opened up real wide. They were going to send me out to the hospital ship for a possible skin graft because it was so wide. But they just left it and the corpsman scrubbed it a couple of times a day with Betadine [antiseptic] and gave me shots twice a day of penicillin with what looked like a horse syringe. It had gotten infected pretty quickly. My wound, which was about two inches wide by four inches long, took two or three months to close up completely because it kept getting reinfected. A lot of skin was gone. It finally healed as one huge scab which later sloughed off, leaving a big scar right on my belt line.

Before it was even healed up, I got orders back to my platoon. I was terrified. I just wanted to go home. I was hurt, scared, and lonely around all these strange people. Remember, I wasn't in a nice, clean, shiny white hospital with pretty nurses in white uniforms. I was in a dirt-floor tent where I climbed up on a stretcher and another corpsman scrubbed me up.

I was eventually sent out to the forward area — Vandergrift Combat Base — and rejoined my unit about a month after I was wounded — maybe the 23rd of August [1968]. When I got there, I regrouped with my unit and got harassed in the chow tent by some Marines. They used dark humor and gave me a hard time about getting wounded. They didn't say, "Welcome back and sorry you were hurt." It was more like making fun of me on some sort of sarcastic level. The teasing began when I walked in. An M60 machine gunner named Couton got up and bent over holding his side and shuffled around mocking my being wounded. This embarrassed me — and I've been angry about the teasing for years.

Something else also bothered me. They had given me a Bronze Star with a "V" for valor for action on that day, and I also got harassed about that. In fact, I got harassed by the guy who was originally holding the battle dressing on that first Marine I had helped. "You got a Bronze Star," he said. "I was down there and I didn't get anything!"

So I got a medal and then got harassed for it. And I continued to feel very strange about it because I had left that guy. It still burns a hole in my soul.

Into the Dragon's Mouth

There would be many more patrols, firefights, and horrible consequences of combat before Maddox would, himself, come in from the field. After recovering from his wounds, he and his unit manned the lines farther north at Vandergrift Combat Base. The base, also known as LZ [landing zone] Stud, was the frequent target of enemy sappers, some of whom attacked the very night Maddox arrived.

Somebody was trying to get through our wire — Viet Cong I guess. I saw a lot of firing and red tracers. I pulled out my .45 but luckily I didn't see any enemy.

A few days later, as luck would have it, we were leaving on another fresh operation. I think it was around the 25th of August [1968]. We were going into a "hot" LZ. For anyone who was with the infantry and went by helicopter, those were not the words you wanted to hear. A "hot" LZ meant enemy contact. I was still dealing with dressing my wound, which was infected and still hurting.

It was a hot LZ with more horrendous firefighting. I won't go into all the details, but it actually was among the worst of my tour. We ended up fighting on a mountain for about three days. On this operation it was 1st, 2nd, and 3rd platoons — in that order — up the mountain. Memories of the previous fight had me terrified, and I didn't want to go through that again.

Nobody yelled for me to come up this time. They instead passed the wounded down the line like sacks of bloody oatmeal. We had some pretty horribly wounded people. They had encountered mines in the trees that were command detonated. An enemy soldier on the other end was waiting for a Marine to get in just right position and then he set off the mines. The mines were hung about three feet off the ground next to a tree so when they went off, they did all kinds of damage. Our guys were getting hit by these mines and it was really tearing them up. I rolled under some trees with the platoon sergeant while mortars were going off up above.

During the first day's fighting, we were getting mortared and the whole company was retreating at a full run back down the mountain. A guy behind me was hit in the temple by a piece of shrapnel. As he came running by holding his wound, which was squirting a stream of blood, he yelled that he was "going home." This was his third time being wounded. I grabbed him and swung him to the ground to put a battle dressing on his head. He was more hysterical with joy about the fact he was getting out of there than he was concerned with the head wound.

This battle took place in late August of 1968, maybe the 27th or 28th. We fought our way back up the mountain. Not long after we got to the top, a young Marine was shot through the head and his brain was coming out like toothpaste from a small hole in his forehead. He had poked his head into a bunker and an NVA had shot him point-blank. I had to call in a medevac for him. When the chopper came down over us, a rotor blade hit a tree. Before the chopper could do anything, it took off, and I heard a high-pitched singing noise. I was also screaming and cussing because I wanted them to get this kid out of there. I later realized that the chopper could have gone down hitting the tree like that.

They finally got the kid out by lowering a basket from another chopper. As they were raising him up, part of the Stokes litter broke and he swung down with a terrific jerk. He was hanging vertically instead of horizontally like he should have been. They dragged him through the trees when they took off. Nothing was clean and nice in Vietnam.

I saw my first dead NVA on this operation. The Marines killed them in the same bunker that the kid had looked into when he was shot in the head. They blew the NVA to pieces with grenades. One guy was blown in half with his intestines strewn out and rice and flies everywhere. Another's head was blown apart with his brains clumped out on the ground and an eye hanging out of the socket by the optic nerve. They were a mess. After a while in the hot sun, they began to smell horribly.

This occurred right near where we set up base camp, so I got a work party together and we buried them in shallow graves. Later, after it rained, a hand stuck up out of the ground in a grasping position. Someone stuck an AK-47 clip in the hand. I saw it as we left the hill a few days later, a grayish hand sticking up out of the ground holding an ammo clip; it was a morbid memorial.

After that operation, we manned an artillery base for a while and got to live in bunkers. In Vietnam, as long as you weren't out on a search-and-destroy mission of some kind, everything else kind of felt safe and comfortable, at least relatively speaking. While we were manning the bunkers, we had rats about half as long as your arm. We set huge rat traps with peanut butter from our C-rations. Through the night you'd hear the rat traps going "ka-thunk" and then you'd hear the rats scratching until their last breath. I mentioned the rat bite earlier. The guy held up a can opener and said, "This gets you a couple of weeks out of the field—a rat bite." I learned why the Marines would do anything to get out of the field.

I hate to say it but corpsmen would do anything, too! It was so tough. It was too much. Some Marines would shoot themselves in the foot or leg. We had a corpsman who actually injected his knee with lighter fluid and it swelled up like a balloon. I even dreamed about it. Since I had been hit once, all I needed to do was to get hit by a little piece of shrapnel and I could get out of the field. Two Purple Hearts, you're out of the field. Three, you go home. I even fantasized that after a firefight or incoming, I would actually cut a little hole in my arm and put a piece of shrapnel in there. I'm confessing these sins because I know a lot of people who were in that situation thought like I did and then went on to feel bad about it.

Once I got out of the field, I stayed with the battalion. I was assigned to Vandergrift Combat Base and became an ambulance driver in the forward area which meant going out and getting injured Marines on base. One Marine I particularly remember. He and his friend were playing Russian roulette in the bunkers at night. They jammed a clip up in a .45 and pulled the trigger while holding the pistol to their heads. Some stupid game. This kid shot himself through the eye and it came out the back of his head. I had to go down and pick him up in the ambulance. He was dead and his friend was in hysterics. Another guy had shot himself through the foot—an "accidental discharge!" I suspected he had done it on purpose to stay out of the field, but I wrote it up as an "accident."

After my stint as an ambulance driver, I became a regular BAS [battalion aid station] corpsman. It was real good duty compared to the field, and that's where I spent my remaining five months. A dry tent to sleep and work in, hot food, and not "humping" all day looking for trouble. The worst part was the occasional incoming with rockets and mortars. I think the enemy even had some artillery on us because we were one of the last outposts before the DMZ. They hit the patients' tent twice, once wounding a guy inside.

I feel it was the corpsmen—the medics—right out there with the infantry, who really looked into the dragon's mouth. They saw the nastiest part of what the war offered.

The Departure: Not a Word Spoken

For a hospital corpsman, as with other military personnel, departing Vietnam after serving a year in a combat zone was both emotional and unnerving. He experienced mixed feelings, to be sure. He survived ceaseless fear and stress, the terror of combat, and often witnessed repeated and violent death. Returning to "the world" now engendered its own brand of anxiety and foreboding. How would he be received by a nation now turned against an unpopular war, not to mention the reception by loved ones and friends? Who but brothers-in-arms could possibly comprehend or even care what he had been through? Of more immediate concern was just to make it aboard the "freedom bird" in Danang. Would a last-minute rocket attack or sniper's bullet claim him the day before departure? And what about the comrades he was leaving behind?

HN James Maddox, Golf Company, 2nd Battalion, 9th Marines

I got my orders home at the end of May [1969]. Someone brought a little slip of paper to the BAS with my name on it telling me to report to the rear — to Quang Tri — to process out. I had a box of goodies I had been packing up to bring home from Vietnam — a poncho liner and maybe another set of utilities — no real war trophies. So I just said goodbye to people around me, and didn't even bother with the box of stuff I'd packed. I had someone drive me across a little valley to Charlie Med where I knew helicopters were going out to Quang Tri. I wanted to catch a lift on one.

So I caught a medevac chopper loaded with freshly wounded, IVs hanging everywhere. I kept thinking it might get shot down before I got to Quang Tri. "Please just make it to safety so I can go home!" I went from Quang Tri to Da Nang to catch my big commercial flight home. When that plane took off, everyone started giving the big cheer. This bothered me for years. I think I began to give the big cheer but stuffed it because that guy's face appeared — the guy I had left during our first firefight. And I just froze. I just couldn't feel good, and I carried that burden for a long time.

HN William Barber, India Company, 3rd Battalion, 4th Marines

I watched the administrative traffic and looked at the names for mine. One day my name finally appeared. It seemed like that day would never come. I got my stuff and went back to Danang on a truck convoy. When I got to Danang, I stayed at the R&R center, which was both the in-and-out processing center. There I cleaned up and got a change of clothes for the trip home.

I flew out of Danang sometime in June of 1969 and arrived at Travis Air Force Base. Since my two-year active duty enlistment was up, they processed me out. That's when I saw a lot of guys make mistakes. Because the processing-out routine took so long and guys wanted to get home so badly, they were willing to do anything to reduce the process. It became common knowledge that if you signed a waiver letter saying nothing was wrong with you, you could go home quicker. Some men had all kinds of physical/mental problems, but to get home, they signed those waiver letters. We were still so young, immature, and without any guidance. Home was security — and we needed it.

HM3 Raymond Felle, Kilo Company, 3rd Battalion, 9th Marines

I got my orders and flew to Danang and caught the Braniff plane to Okinawa. I don't remember arriving in Vietnam but I do remember leaving. I kept thinking, "Please don't let them rocket this plane!" I was talking to God. I talked to God a lot over there.

They gave us rags to wipe our faces because it was really hot in the plane until it took off. When it did, everybody started clapping.

We spent a week at Camp Hansen where I picked up the sea bag I had left there months before. It was all moldy. While on a bus to catch a flight back to Travis [Air Force Base], a sergeant got on and pointed at about six of us, including me, and told us to get off. After we did, he said six people were going on emergency leave who needed to get on the flight. Then he pointed at me and said, "You! Get back on."

When I left Travis on my way over to Vietnam, I had taken some leaves from a tree and had kept them in my wallet while I was in Vietnam. I now put those leaves back under the same tree.

HM3 John Higgins, Golf Company, 2nd Battalion, 5th Marines

I went to Danang and flew out at night. It was a big jet—a Boeing 707—and just loaded with Marines and some Navy personnel. What struck me the most was that you could hear a pin drop on that airplane. Not a word, nothing. Everyone was just sitting on that plane as if they were sitting in a church. We had a mixture of emotions. "God, I made it out alive! What about the guys we left?" A whole lot of memories were going through everybody's head and nobody was talking. I thought everyone was going to shout and cheer when we got airborne, but it didn't happen. It was just dead silence.

I sat there looking out the left-hand window into the night. For some reason, I had the sensation that we were circling. I couldn't figure it out. I saw a light out the window that didn't seem to move. It probably took me 10 or 15 minutes before it dawned on me that I was looking at a light on the end of the wing. About 20 minutes into the flight, I started to hear people quietly talking but it never got noisy in the cabin.

HM3 Dennis Noah, Hotel Company, 2nd Battalion, 5th Marines

It was the damnedest thing. They put me in a helicopter and flew me to Danang where they gave me a new set of utilities. Then I walked up the steps to a giant airplane with its engines running. At the top of the steps I turned around. Then I looked in front of me. It was like an entryway you've seen in science fiction movies where someone goes through a time portal. Half the person is still here and the other half is 10,000 light-years away. It was surreal. I'm hot, sweaty, dirty, getting shot at, and all of a sudden I walk through a time portal into an air-conditioned airplane where the crew couldn't do enough for me. All my buddies are out in the field someplace getting shot at and killed—and I'm going aboard an air-conditioned airplane to go home.

They fed us and gave us as much as we wanted. The pilots came back and thanked us. One day I'm being shot at and the next day I've got all these people trying to get me drunk. It was the damnedest feeling I've ever had in my life—or probably will ever have.

HM2 Roger Pittman,
Golf, Hotel, and Fox Companies, 2nd Battalion, 4th Marines

I couldn't believe it. I had seen a Marine killed the night before he was going to leave Vietnam. He was hit by lightning just a few feet from me. I knew that the chance of leaving Vietnam, even the last day, was not guaranteed. When I got on that two-engine plane at Quang Tri and we flew down to Danang, I knew they could still get me in Danang. I'd had seen rockets come in there. I joined up with some corpsmen I knew who were also leaving, and we had an unbelievable wipe-out party. I slept over at the Seabees because they had the best food. And the night before we were to leave Vietnam, the NVA sent us off in good style. They threw about 10 rockets into the R&R center, which was where we were going that morning when the sun came up to catch our plane out. I figured I wasn't safe until I was about 20 miles off the coast in the Pan Am 707.

HM3 Roger Ware,
Fox and Hotel Companies, 2nd Battalion, 5th Marines

The day I left Vietnam, my old company — Hotel — was out on a patrol and got in a firefight. A helo came in to fly me to Danang and I didn't want to go. I felt guilty that I was a survivor and that my job was taking care of Hotel Company. I still had friends there and felt I could make a difference. I tried every way I could to stay with my unit but it didn't work out. I lost a lot of friends in Hotel Company. Leaving was very emotional because I knew I wouldn't see a lot of those guys again. They were in combat and I wasn't. It's tough when you leave like that because you were in combat with those people and bonded with them.

7

MEDAL OF HONOR

On any given day in Vietnam, military personnel exhibited many acts of bravery and self-sacrifice. For inexplicable reasons, a young warrior dashed across fire-swept terrain to silence an enemy machine gun that was killing his buddies. A young sergeant, finding his superior wounded and dying, assumed command of the rifle company and rallied his men to lead a successful counterattack against enemy positions. A grievously wounded second lieutenant directed the landing of two transport helicopters for the evacuation of the dead and wounded, then assisted in the "mopping up" and final seizure of the battalion's objective. Without regard for his own safety, a Navy hospital corpsman ran across an active battlefield to aid a downed Marine, throwing himself upon his patient to protect him from further injury.

These heroic deeds in the face of death were common in Vietnam. Hospital corpsmen, as in other wars, always seemed to be in the thick of battle — and they paid the price. During the course of the nearly 10-year-long conflict, 681 hospital corpsmen were killed in action, the highest number lost since World War II. Thirty received the Navy Cross, 127 the Silver Star, and 290 the Bronze Star. Four hospital corpsmen were awarded the Medal of Honor, two posthumously.

The Medal of Honor has never been awarded casually. As crucial and meritorious as the act itself, the lengthy awards process to get the MOH has many obstacles: The timely testimony of eyewitnesses plus the willingness of a superior officer to do the paperwork and track the nomination through a complicated system. In addition, the granting of that rare and most coveted of medals is never a foregone conclusion until the award is presented by the president to the lucky survivor or, posthumously, to the family of an absent hero. As is often the case, the citation accompanying the award is often brief and scant in detail. The real story is usually far more dramatic.

"I Didn't Want to Commit Suicide"

HM3 Donald Ballard was assigned to Company M, 3rd Battalion, 4th Marines of the 3rd Marine Division. He had been in Vietnam about five months, having spent all that time patrolling with "Mike" Company in such places as Khe Sanh, Dong Ha, Cam Lo, and "the Rockpile," which was adjacent to the DMZ. Ballard had also seen his share of jungle warfare and treated many casualties. "I don't think that day meant much more to me than any other day. Looking back, it was similar to other actions, but on that day I was involved in some other exploits. We were constantly in firefights and lately were taking more casualties because of where we were and what terrain we were trying to hold."

May 16th, 1968, was the day I earned the medal. The situation had settled down and we decided to move off our hill. I had selected a staging area and had five or six patients lying there. I had asked some of the Marines to help me get some ponchos so we could take them down off the hill to where we could medevac them out. The helicopters couldn't land on the side of the mountain, and that's why we had to take them down to a flat, grassy area.

Because we were the only targets moving on the side of the mountain, we brought attention to ourselves. We were loading the patients onto the ponchos and getting ready to drag them down the hill when a North Vietnamese soldier threw in a hand grenade.

What are you going to do with it? You don't have too many choices. It was inappropriate but acceptable to throw a dead body on the grenade to absorb the blast. But I didn't have any volunteers and nobody wanted to play dead. Another option was to get rid of it. The third choice was to try to hide myself or run from it — and that was not going to work.

My patients — who were lying near me — couldn't do any of the above. They were wounded. I had been treating them and they were out of the war and ready to go home. Therefore, I was the only one who could do something to deal with this new crisis.

It was more of a reaction than a conscious decision. I didn't want to commit suicide. I had a wife and two kids. I had a life and I loved myself as much as I did the Marines. But again, I didn't see a whole lot of options at the time. I had to do something because the patients couldn't. I thought I could absorb the blast and save their lives. I believed that grenade was going to kill us all if I didn't do something.

I had seen the grenade come in and roll down the hill toward us. It looked like a C-ration can with a handle in it. It wasn't smoking — it just lay there. I had a flak jacket on that was supposedly bulletproof. I figured that would probably help a little bit. I wore that jacket all the time except when I was in the shower. I even slept in it. I guess I was thinking that my body would take most of the blast and save the others.

I lunged forward and pulled the grenade underneath my chest and waited. It seemed like an eternity. When you've got time to think about what you're doing, you relax. And then a second instinct kicked in and that was to throw it away. I was lying beside one of my patients, and as I rolled up off the grenade, I turned over onto him and in one motion I slung it down the hill as I rolled. I wanted to get it as far away as I could. Of course, my second worry after I threw it was, "Damn! I hope I didn't throw it on my own guys!"

The citation says that when the grenade failed to go off, I quickly continued my efforts taking care of the Marines. It doesn't say anything about me getting rid of it. It's not the kind of object you leave lying around. And I can tell you for a fact that a grenade went off in the area where I threw it. I can't tell you whether or not that was the same one but the Marines who were with me said it was.

I was glad that everybody survived it and doubly glad that I threw it in a place where there weren't any Marines. I didn't even think that anybody saw what really happened. It didn't appear to me worthy of a general flying in and saying, "You're a hero!" When I was actually being awarded the medal, they didn't tell me why I was getting it. I was thinking I had done other acts that no one else knew about.

Some Marines with me deserved the Medal of Honor more than I did. But I was the lucky one in several ways. I thank God every day.

Medal of Honor recipient HM3 Donald Ballard (BUMED Archives).

"My Days Were Over"

HM3 Robert Ingram was with the 3rd Platoon, "Charley" Company,[1] 1st Battalion, 7th Marines. He had already been in Vietnam for eight months with more than enough patrolling and jungle combat under his belt. As bad as it all seemed, nothing could prepare him for what occurred on 28 March 1966. In an operation called "Indiana," Charley Company was to be part of a blocking force intended to trap and destroy a reinforced North Vietnamese battalion.

Even though Charley Company was at half-strength, its Marines were considered seasoned and experienced. Moreover, they had already been operating in that area of Quang Ngai Province where the operation would take place and they knew the territory. It was hilly terrain with cultivated rice paddies dotting valleys between the hills. Intelligence indicated enemy presence in one of those valleys.

We flew by chopper into what they called a "safe zone" at one end of the valley. Of course, the NVA were keeping an eye on the choppers and seeing where they were landing.

As we came in, we headed toward the blocking area where we were supposed to cross the rice paddy area and set up our fields of fire. We never quite made it to that site.

We came to one hill and were about a third of the way around it when someone noticed two uniformed Vietnamese at the top. They appeared to be lookouts. As soon as they saw us, they jumped up and ran across the top of the hill. Cpl. [Richard] Mayes and I automatically took off around the left side of the hill. When we met them on the hill's back slope going down to the rice paddy, we opened up on them — just the two of us.

We were out front and as soon as we opened up, all hell broke loose. The village on the other side of the rice paddy, which was about 70 yards from where we were, absolutely lit up. You'd have thought it was the Fourth of July. There was an insurmountable number of automatic weapons opening up on us. I distinctly remember Mayes looking over at me, then turning his head and charging the rice paddy. The remaining parts of 3rd Platoon were probably 30 feet behind us as they came around the side of the hill. Then they, too, commenced to charge the rice paddy.

I think that the very moment Rick Mayes opened up, he knew he didn't stand a chance. He was about 10 feet away from me. In this case, the odds were overwhelmingly in the enemy's favor. As far as the after-action report is concerned, we estimated more than 100 North Vietnamese were in that line in the village. So it was just Rick and me out front and another 12 or 14 of our guys spread out. The two of us worked together a lot in combat. Rick would say, "Doc!" and I'd just follow.

In this situation, the enemy had set up an ambush and we had upset that ambush. Rick made it 30 or 40 feet in his charge and went down immediately. It was a miracle that nothing hit me in the first barrage. The fire power was so intense that trees were falling.

I took off after Rick and slid down behind him to see what I could do. He was pretty much out in the open. I knew it was bad but you do what you've gotta do. It was obvious he had numerous gunshot wounds. I turned his head over trying to check his pupils. And that's when they got me in the left hand — and [killed] him. He was finished. My hand was on his head when they got both of us, and [the bullet] blew his head apart.

At that point, we were about 60 yards from the line of fire with the rest of 3rd Platoon coming up behind us. And that was only 15 or 20 guys max. The rest of the company was assaulting the top of the hill. The 2nd Platoon was spreading off to the left flank. The other platoon was charging around the right side of the hill. We had nowhere to go and we had no cover.

I noticed machine gun fire coming from a cane patch to the left of the rice paddy so I tried to use the maximum amount of firepower to get in that cane patch. Of course, the other guys were coming behind me and they were just going down left and right. Some of them made it out into the rice paddy while I was firing. As I tried to back up, three of them were halfway across the paddy. One went down with multiple gunshot wounds and the other had a 3.5 [inch] rocket blown out of his hand. A projectile went through the rocket. The rocket went off but it didn't blow up. He and the other two guys were pinned down out there in the middle of the rice paddy for 45 minutes to an hour with all this fire going both ways across them.

I emptied Rick Mayes's ammunition and all but one magazine of mine into the cane patch trying to take out the machine gun until I finally got it quieted down. I started firing at the hedge line across the rice paddy. Then I got down to one magazine. You always kept one magazine in reserve. I slapped it in and took off running toward the rear. When I got about 40 feet back — about the position I started in — I saw SSgt. John Bansavage, our platoon commander, lying over there. When I turned to go after him, I got hit in the knee and that took me down. I was still out in the open with enemy rounds hitting all around me.

Nevertheless, I made it over to him as soon as I recovered my position from the knee injury. When I got in behind Bansavage, I saw that he had numerous wounds, certainly more than three. And his pupils were fixed and dilated. I threw his weapon into the bushes, grabbed his magazines, and took off back over to the right.

I had been hit in the knee but when the enemy is shooting at you, you'll amaze yourself and just go. You don't have time to pay attention to your wound when rounds are hitting all around you.

I got to a tree line perpendicular to the field of fire and tried to get a breath and some protection. I saw another guy lying back there and went to check him out. To this day, I can't remember who he was. As I leaned over him, for some reason, I looked back. An NVA was standing about 15 feet from me. I was squatted down with one knee on the ground when I turned. He shot me through the face with an AK[-47]. It moved me a good six or seven feet. I remember the bullet coming in the right side of my face and going out the other.

It's like stopping time, and all this is a very distinct memory. I remember thinking, "I'm still alive!" Of course, I couldn't hear. My vision in the left eye was little or none, and I realized I was lying on the ground with my head down. My M14 was still in my right hand. Then I recall that this guy had just shot me and he still had to be nearby. So I rolled over on my back and, sure enough, he was standing there looking down at me. I have no idea how much time went by, probably just seconds, but I rolled over and shot him. And then I lay back down for a moment trying to get my bearings as to what was going on.

It became very obvious to me as a corpsman that my days were over. The blood, the swelling, and the lack of hearing and vision were all pretty obvious. I felt like my head was literally falling apart. I didn't have any substantial holding power. I knew I was dying. I had no problem with death. I just asked the Lord to give me enough strength to finish my job — and He did so.

Then the NVA started shooting at me again. I rolled over and pulled the guy — [the one] I had been attending when I was shot — to safety. But I realized he was finished. I still can't remember who he was and that bothers me. As I began moving off to the right flank, I heard the cry for "corpsman!" coming from the edge of the rice paddy. I couldn't see who it was so I followed the little tree line, which didn't offer much protection. It seemed that a hundred people were still shooting at me.

When I reached him, he was lying out in the open and not moving. He had a through-and-through thigh wound in the left upper thigh with no bone involvement and obviously no big vessel involvement. I tried to drag him — and I wasn't very strong at this point. I made it the six or eight feet to the tree line but they were still shooting at both of us.

I stuck my rifle barrel out to him and screamed, "Grab it! Grab it!" When he did, I pulled him into the tree line.

I made my Marines carry their own bandages. I was out at that point. So I grabbed the packet he was carrying, removed two bandages, and wrapped one on the entrance wound and one on the exit. I tried to keep the bandages as tight as I could without creating a tourniquet. Then I pulled him a little further into the tree line where he had some protection. At least the enemy couldn't see him that well. And I left him there.

I then took off back to the hedge line and tried to follow it over to the right side of the area where I found numerous other dead men and a corpsman — still alive — lying in a washout off the top of the hill. It was probably four or five feet wide at some points and probably two feet deeper than the other terrain. The corpsman was lying in the middle of this wash about halfway down and in the open. With the NVA pumping rounds [at us], I went up the hill to get him.

His helmet was off and he had a grazing head wound. The bullet had not entered the skull, but instead the round had grazed the left temporal area and penetrated the skin. The bone was showing but it didn't appear that he had any obvious fractures. I couldn't find any other wounds on him. He had a pulse, was breathing, but was just knocked out.

I pushed him over to the side of the bushes by a washed out gully, then stuck his rifle off to the side and grabbed his ammunition since he didn't need it. I didn't even wrap his wound because it was not bleeding. I could not do a whole lot for him at this point.

By this time, the fight had been going on about an hour. I went back down the hill toward the rice paddy to see if some guys were down there who might be salvageable. One of the men who was in the CP [command post] group suddenly showed up and began dragging the wounded back up to the command post. I think it was Sgt. Mack Feerick. He also retrieved the man with the thigh wound I had treated earlier, and later helped move the guys from the rice paddy. We also got the corpsman out of there.

It was approaching dusk by this point, and Mack and someone else were dragging the men out. Some were dead and some were alive.

I know that I had expended 20 rounds. I had 30 rounds when I went down there. When I changed magazines, I crawled back off the little slope. It was dark and they couldn't see me. On the right side of the hill, the terraces were too high to climb so I went back around to the left side where I had originally come down. The first terrace was probably a couple of feet tall and I got over it pretty easily. When I got up to the second terrace, it was about five feet tall, and I just couldn't get over it. I kept trying to crawl up but just didn't have it.

All of a sudden, a hand reached down, grabbed me, and pulled me up over the terrace. I started walking back toward the top of the hill when I encountered my commanding officer. He later said he had no idea who I was. With the blood and the mucus, I looked like one of those guys with a beard that goes all the way down to the knees. What he saw was just slime hanging off the front of me and I was covered with blood.

We got back to the command post. I know only from what they told me that at 11 o'clock that night we had only 200 rounds of ball ammunition left and 2 grenades within the company.

The [Medal of Honor] citation says that I was responsible for saving lives that day. I'm not convinced of that. I probably saved more lives by killing the enemy than I did by being a corpsman — and that bothers me.

Robert Ingram suffered four wounds that day, the most serious being the one to his face. The bullet missed the eye but hit the base of his skull, fracturing it and both eye orbits. "It probably took about four or five weeks to start getting my vision back. I had loss of hearing; I had no smell. I had no vision and then the vision started coming back." Although both eye orbits were fractured, his eyes were miraculously unscathed. It was the surrounding trauma that caused his vision problems. "By the time I got out of the hospital, I was back to about 20-30 vision and within a couple of months it was back to 20-10, 20-15. Too bad it didn't stay that way. I got old."

8

NAVAL SUPPORT ACTIVITY HOSPITAL DANANG

In 1965, the Navy created Naval Support Activity (NSA)Danang to support the Navy and Marines operating in the northern provinces of South Vietnam (I Corps). Providing emergency and definitive medical care for Navy and Marine Corps personnel became the mission of the Naval Support Activity Station Hospital (NSAH), which soon grew to be the largest land-based medical facility in Vietnam. The advanced emergency hospital center was designed to provide specialties not usually represented in the medical battalion hospitals, such as neurosurgery, dermatology, urology, plastic surgery, ophthalmology, and ENT (ear, nose, and throat) treatment.

Construction of the hospital center began in July 1965, but three months later the Viet Cong attacked the site with satchel charges and mortars, destroying much of the compound. Despite this devastating setback, the hospital opened for business in mid–January 1966 with 120 beds. During 1966, 6,680 patients were admitted. Two years later, during the peak of American involvement in the war, the bed capacity increased to 700 with 24,273 admissions. The facility also included a dental department, preventive medicine unit, blood bank, frozen blood bank, and a detachment of the Naval Medical Research Unit-2 (NAMRU-2), then headquartered in Taipei, Taiwan.

The Naval Support Activity Station Hospital Danang admitted three categories of patients, based on the number of recovery days. Those patients whose hospitalization was expected to be 30 days or less were retained and, when fully recovered, returned to their units. The more seriously injured were treated but then evacuated to naval hospitals in the Philippines, Japan, or Guam if their hospitalization was expected to be 120 days or less. If hospitalization was estimated to be more than 120 days, the patients were evacuated to medical facilities in the United States. NSAH Danang provided care until patients were able to withstand air travel. Air Force Casualty Units provided the airlift to Clark Air Force Base Hospital,[1] the Naval Hospital at Subic Bay in the Philippines, and also to naval hospitals in Japan, Guam, and the States.

The emergency facility occupied the sandy strip on the east side of the Han River opposite from Danang, between the Han River and the South China Sea. The land was slightly hilly — no vegetation — just white beach sand. Just to the south were five famous outcrops known as the Marble Mountains, the highest peak rising 345 feet above the plains.

The hospital included several groupings of Quonset huts connected by cement walkways. Some of the walkways — ones connecting the patient areas — had a wooden roof to protect patients who were being transported by gurney. The casualty receiving area (triage), consisting of one Quonset hut and an open area with a cement floor and tin roof, was adjacent to a small landing strip. The Pre-op building and X-ray hut were side by side, just up from the receiving area. Adjacent to Pre-op and X-ray were the lower OR Quonset huts that contained two operating rooms, the Central Supply half hut, and the upper OR hut that also contained two operating rooms. The two OR Quonset huts and Central Supply were in the shape of an "H." Former hospital corpsman James

An aerial view of NSA Hospital Danang during its construction in 1966 (BUMED Archives).

Chaffee, who served at NSAH Danang from October 1967 until June 1969, sets the scene of the medical compound.

It was part of a cluster of bases just north of the Marble Mountains where the Danang perimeter ended. The hospital was across the Main Supply Road from MAG-16, a Marine Corps helicopter base on the beach. The hospital was on the west side of the road, the river behind it. On the south perimeter was a Seabee camp, and south of that camp, at the foot of the northernmost inland Marble Mountain named Nui Tho Son, was a dump. The 5th Special Forces HQ was across the road from the dump, on the beach at the foot of the big Marble Mountain, Nui Thuy Son. It is now generally referred to as "The Marble Mountain" in tourist guides. North of that was a POW compound, and then came MAG-16. Farther north, the road to the China Beach USO exited the main road. On the hospital's north perimeter was a pagoda attached to the hamlet on the east perimeter, between the hospital and the river.[2]

Anguishing Decisions

Capt. Harry Dinsmore, an experienced veteran with more than 20 years in the Navy, was NSAH's Chief of Surgery from July 1966 until August 1967. Dinsmore recalls the hospital's early days.

The staff at Danang varied between 25 and 30 people. The administrative staff consisted of 15 or 16 people plus Medical Service Corps officers and such. I can't recall how many corpsmen we had. The hospital continued to expand during the 13 months I was there. They were still in the building phase at that time, and we continued to add additional specialties as we increased the staff. Dental surgeons and plastic surgeons arrived, as did a neurosurgeon. We had a lot of head injuries in Vietnam from land mines so our neurosurgeon was kept really busy.

It went in spurts along with the battle activity. If we had an offensive like Tet or another big operation going on anywhere in I Corps, which was where we and the Marines were, a lot of casualties came in. And as it turns out, I was the main triage officer for the I Corps area for at least part of that year.

We had three major hospitals in the area: Naval Support Activity Hospital where I served, the hospital ship in the harbor at Danang, and Charlie Med in West Danang.

NSAH had a big helipad and a large reception area where the medical casualties arrived by chopper. A lot of the helicopter casualties came to us. "A lot" meant more than a dozen injured. We could handle a dozen or up to 20 with no particular problem because we had enough staff and three or four operating rooms. But when we got 60, 80, or 120, and the chopper pilots would tell us more were on the way, triage was necessary. I had to decide who went to surgery first — a very unpleasant duty because triage officers had to decide who was to be allowed to die, that is, they were not savable. When we had a large number of casualties, I would go to the administrative shack which had a radio and get in touch with Charlie Med and the hospital ship, which I believe was the *Repose.*

Our hospital in Danang was really good, especially after we got the capability of a neurosurgeon. We already had orthopedists and general surgeons. We added a urologist and then plastic surgeons were assigned.

We only received sporadic casualties if no major battles were going on. We had post-operative patients to take care of, and we made rounds every day. Once the seriously injured were stable, they were air-evaced to Clark Air Force Base Hospital in the Philippines or back to the States so we didn't have many long-term casualties. We kept those who looked like they would recover long enough to get back to active duty within two or three weeks. But other than that, we had mostly short-term patients who were air-evaced out to make room for more serious ones.

When casualties were light, we got pretty bored. After all, we were living in a bunch of Quonset huts on a sand dune with nothing to do. During those slow times, we operated on cleft lips and palates, very common congenital anomalies in the Vietnamese population. Many children had these conditions and we did corrective operations on them. The word got around and children would be brought to us. When we had light days of surgery, we'd schedule four or five harelips to do in a morning. All the surgeons did this kind of operation at one time or another, and we did hundreds of them that year. Most of the severe cleft palates were supervised by the plastic surgeon and the oral surgeon.

In addition, we treated many ARVN [Army of the Republic of Vietnam] soldiers. In addition to our long Quonset huts for our own surgical casualties, the hospital was divided into Quonsets for different tasks. The internal medicine Quonsets were in a different location from the surgical units. They treated malaria, dysentery, etc. A separate hut held 25 to 30 beds for Vietnamese soldiers. Because Danang had an ARVN hospital in the city, these South Vietnamese soldiers would be transferred to that hospital as soon as we stabilized them. We also had a Quonset hut for POWs. We actually operated on many "Charlies" [Viet Cong] who were brought in with other casualties. Interpreters and Marine guards were always in that building.

I did so many surgeries that it is hard to recall specific ones. I tried to save some tremendous liver injuries, that is, those people who would have died within a half hour. And some of them died because you can't put a completely shattered liver back together. Because we had excess amounts of blood, we could work on them for a couple of hours and try to salvage them — try to repair torn hepatic veins where blood was just pouring out. We had many of those kind of casualties and multiple amputees from land mines. Some had both legs gone, an arm gone, or maybe both arms gone. Some had been blinded — all terrible injuries.

Nurse Lt. Cmdr. Marjorie Warren evaluates a patient in triage at NSA Hospital (BUMED Archives).

But we had to try to do something for them. If we had many casualties, we just made some of the more serious injured comfortable and administered morphine. We couldn't let them take up operating room space when we had many others who could be salvaged. It was a lousy decision to make.

I remember one Marine colonel who showed up wanting to look in on some patients from his unit who had been injured by mortar fire. After he had been there a few hours walking around, he complained of a headache which kept getting worse and worse. Although he appeared uninjured, we took an x-ray of his head, which showed a metal fragment in his brain. He had no obvious external wound; he didn't even know he'd been hit. We found a wound inside his hairline where it wasn't obvious. One of the tough aspects of wartime surgery—and in civilian surgery, too—is finding foreign bodies. The body is three dimensions and an x-ray is two dimensions. To try and get that third dimension, you take lateral and front views to pinpoint exactly where a foreign body is. The x-ray showed the fragment in the posterior part of his brain; the neurosurgeon removed the fragment.

*   *   *

HM3 James Chaffee joined the Navy in 1966, went to boot camp and hospital corps school in San Diego, and then was assigned to the naval hospital in Yokosuka, Japan. After spending nine months working the wards at Yokosuka, Chaffee returned to the States and, with other young men just assigned to NSAH Danang, went to the Navy's counter-insurgency school at Coronado, California.

"They taught us about counter-insurgency techniques, winning the hearts and minds of the people — civic action programs. Then we went to Camp Pendleton for a week and marched around a lot and had weapons training. We fired the old .30 machine guns from World War II. They taught us to strip them down and put them back together."

While stationed at Yokosuka, Chaffee heard from a corpsman who had already served at NSAH Danang. "He told us how everyone at NSAH Danang carried guns and how dangerous it was. Of course, when we got there, we found that it was all nonsense. They didn't even issue weapons. And that was good. I would hate to think of all those guys running around carrying weapons."

Fully Prepared for the "Vicissitudes of Combat"

HM3 Chaffee continues with a description of NSAH Danang where patients viewed the medical treatment and attention as "paradise." But many of those Marines suffered appalling wounds and the deadly diseases endemic to a tropical locale — lung worm, cerebral malaria, dysentery, leptospirosis, scrub typhus, and hepatitis. And at NSAH Danang, triaging took on new dimensions in efficiency.

When I arrived, the facility was a major field hospital with air-conditioned wards and operating rooms. NSAH Danang had a large staff of specialists in areas ranging from tropical medicine and thoracic surgery to neurosurgery.

I was temporarily assigned to Receiving 2 — part sick bay and part outpatient clinic. Receiving 1 was next door just off the chopper pad. This was the triage where I would spend the bulk of my tour. But first I was permanently assigned to the same sort of medical ward as my previous assignment at Naval Hospital Yokosuka, Japan.

The Vietnam War would explode with the 1968 Tet Offensive, coinciding with my 21st birthday, just around the corner from my arrival. The year would be the most devastating of the war in terms of American casualties.

The hospital grew after I got there, but it was already quite a sizable place. We had concrete walkways covered with metal. Big conduit pipes drained away the water. As you went in the front gate, there was a chopper pad right near it. And right off that chopper pad was Receiving 1. Next door was Receiving 2. Off to the left, right behind Receiving 2 at the end of this little walkway, was the orthopedic ward. The entrance went right through that overflow triage just beside it. We also had an outdoor triage. The indoor triage was in a Quonset hut. Right beside it to the left was an outdoor triage with a lot of sawhorses and supplies. Both were always kept ready to go with IVs hanging. In addition, we had an overflow triage on the other side of the walkway through the entrance where we could put another 50 or 60 casualties if necessary.

Just down the walk from Receiving 2 — to your left — was an orthopedic ward. It was the one that got hit by a rocket in 1969. The urology clinic had just been built off that ward, but it had been blown up in a rocket attack that wounded a number of people.

Just to the right, and next to Receiving 1 was the armory where the weapons were kept. If casualties arrived with weapons, we'd take them away and deposit them in the armory. If someone came in with a C-4 explosive, that was also deposited in the armory.

Just down from the armory was the motor pool with ambulances. The ambulance drivers were Seabees. They would usually wait for an ambulance run at the motor pool and turn in their .45s at the armory after they got off duty. I only wore a weapon if I went outside the Danang perimeter south of the Marble Mountains. We were not allowed to do that but if I did, I'd usually borrow somebody's .45.

As you went up from the triage, you passed some clinics near the wire right at the top. Several wards, clinics, and a chapel were at the top of a hill. The medical wards were the farthest away from Triage. You would go out Triage, up the hill, and X-ray was on the left. Across from X-ray on the right was Pre-op. That's where we put patients who had been stabilized and ready to go to surgery. We'd shave them and get their x-rays. The ORs were just adjacent.

The DOA [dead on arrival] shack was right off the overflow Triage. It was just a big closet with probably enough room for maybe five or six people.

When I got to NSAH, the wards were staffed with a handful of nurses who went about their typical supervisory roles in starched white uniforms. I am not certain when they arrived, but I believe it was about the time I did because corpsmen were working the wards who had preceded the nurses. My recollection is that they were all at least lieutenant in rank. Most were lieutenant commanders, and they were led by a Cmdr. [Mary] Cannon who later made captain. Their role was largely symbolic. An uneasy truce existed between the nurses and the doctors, with the corpsmen often caught between. The areas of the hospital where corpsmen had most freedom in treating patients— Receiving 1 and 2 — were not staffed by nurses. In fact, they almost never made an appearance in either place. One nurse in the OR, however, may have been an anesthetist. She was always in scrub greens when we saw her, usually in Pre-op just above Triage across from X-ray.

Staffing was short for the large, open bay wards. A single corpsman on night duty often had to handle a ward with 60 or more patients. I remember making the temperature rounds at 0200 with a ward full of malaria patients, giving them the standard drill when their fevers were excessive: Sit under a cold shower and drink a recycled IV bottle full of cold water after swallowing five aspirin. Sometimes short on bedside manner, the wards provided a real bed, hot chow, showers and flushing toilets, and excellent medical care. To the grunt Marines— the majority of our patients— they were paradise. Transferring from the wards was nearly impossible; it took an insubordinate encounter with a nurse to get me out.

The medical ward was intensely busy, overflowing with malaria patients, most with *P. Falciparum*, which can lead to cerebral malaria and death. And we had deaths from cerebral malaria. We occasionally used quinine for a really bad case of falciparum, otherwise we dispensed the standard chloroquine and primaquine.

The lab was over-extended and samples sometimes sat unexamined for days. The standard treatment was to get a malaria slide as soon as possible. A lab tech showed me how to stain a slide with a drop of blood and examine it for parasites. The doctor had a microscope in his office and let me use it, encouraging me to take blood when a patient began the cycle of chills and fever. The nurse did not think I should be doing this duty since it was the responsibility of the lab. This led to a shouting match one day when I was examining a slide instead of mopping the floor.

We also saw Ascaris— lung worm. If one drank feces-contaminated water, the larvae grew in the stomach and migrated through the bloodstream to the lungs. The individual then coughed up and swallowed the larvae. When they reached the stomach, they turned into worms which looked like big earthworms.

We occasionally saw encephalitis or meningitis, but it was mostly malaria and hepatitis on our wards.

After the incident with the nurse, I was, in essence, fired. I was pretty certain that a captain's mast would be next, but I believe the doctor interceded, and I was transferred to Receiving 1 and that was a blessing.

The whole area of Receiving 1 was intimidating. Large signs in the covered outdoor triage beside the main walkway shouted in red —*Off Limits and Use of Cameras Prohibited.* This was the first overflow Triage. The main Receiving 1 Quonset hut was beside it.

Off Limits greeted you in red at the door to the main Receiving 1 Quonset. Inside, the place was all business. On either side of the hut near the rounded ceiling, pipes extended the length of the room suspending bottles of Ringer's lactate, which were ready for use. Pairs of sawhorses lined both sides below the pipes, pulled out to support stretchers bearing casualties as they arrived. Jelcos [catheter for administering intravenous fluids] and other equipment filled bins along the walls, and a cardiac board doubled as a pinochle table. Along the front wall, near the door, hung Unit 1 bags [combat medical bags], flak jackets, and helmets. The wall was lined with suction machines for chest tubes. The floor was concrete, stained brownish red, with a drain in the center. The room was incredibly cold, and a sickly green light from bare overhead fluorescent tubes bathed the grayish interior.

A complement of corpsmen and stretcher bearers was assigned to Receiving 1. The bearers, mainly Seabees or seamen from the fleet, kept the triage area clean and moved the patients from the chopper to Triage to X-ray and Pre-op. Sometimes they performed medical procedures we taught them in case we were overloaded.

Receiving 1 corpsmen were at the top of the pecking order — a special bunch. But you had to prove yourself, and they questioned new personnel, especially those who had served on a medical ward. It was mostly learning by doing, and the corpsmen who had served on surgery wards had a shorter learning curve.

Only one physician oversaw Receiving 1, a junior surgeon on 24-hour duty, who called the duty senior physician if surgery was required. Receiving 1 had no nurses, no anesthetists, and the doctor was not on the premises until needed. When casualties arrived, the corpsmen assessed the situation and began IVs using 14-gauge Jelcos, usually one in each arm and one in the neck. Corpsmen did venous cut-downs, inserted chest tubes, inserted tracheal tubes, and performed other emergency surgery. They were also on call to handle emergency ambulance runs and occasional chopper runs.

NSAH Danang had three triage areas. The main one was the Quonset hut. The first open unit outside was set up much as the Quonset hut — sawhorses below pipes suspending bottles of Ringer's lactate ready for use. As with the main Quonset hut, vials of emergency fluids, mainly for those in cardiac arrest, were also at hand, but I believe the sterile pack with a chest knife was kept inside.

Across the walkway, the third area was full of sawhorses and pipes, but IVs were not kept ready. This was for overflow mass casualties, and when it was needed, personnel from other areas, like the laundry or pharmacy, would be brought in to set up IVs and help haul stretchers. During the Tet Offensive,[3] the three areas were full most of the time, and stretchers were lined upon the walkway waiting for X-ray or to get into Pre-op, which was also full.

The drill with wounded was well worked out. Corpsmen and stretcher bearers ran to meet the chopper, with the bearers carrying empty stretchers in case the wounded were just stacked up on the floor of the chopper. This was often the case, particularly with the CH-46 [Sea Knight helicopter used by the Navy to deliver cargo and personnel], or if the wounded were on tanks or amtracs. Sometimes a CH-46 would be so loaded with wounded you wondered why those on the bottom didn't suffocate. I remember getting over 100 patients within an hour!

I was senior corpsman in Triage one night and went out with a flashlight and began triaging on the helicopter. I looked at the ones I thought were going to survive, took those, and sent the rest off to the hospital ship. I think the medical personnel on *Repose* or *Sanctuary* said they could handle them. The chopper was full of blood; it was just a mess.

The wounded were brought in and their stretchers placed on the sawhorses. Clothes and boots were cut off, blood pressure and pulse taken and written on bare chests in black marker. Three IVs with Ringer's were started and blood taken for cross-matching at the blood bank, but sometimes this was difficult when the pressure was so low that blood wouldn't flow. I remember seeing corpsmen do femoral sticks [inserting a needle into the femoral artery] to find blood and start an IV, only later to have to restart it when pressure would build up enough to force the blood back into the bottle. We had hit the artery and not the vein. Sometimes what flowed from wounds was Ringer's lactate. Seeing chests with 0/0 and 0 in black marker was not uncommon.

I don't recall names but I remember some cases. One casualty arrived and was dying. He had 0 blood pressure. You got used to looking at someone's eyes and could tell if he was going to die. It looked as though a light was going out behind their eyes. That signified cardiac arrest.

Even though this man had no blood pressure, I managed to get in three IVs, but he died. I could see in his eyes that he was in arrest. I didn't need to check anything else. We monitored cardiac arrest with a cardiac monitor. This guy was flat. We put a cardiac board under him and brought him back. He lived! I went to visit him on the ward after his surgery. He was so unusual. When someone went into cardiac arrest being that injured, they didn't survive. He had been shot six times with an AK-47. No organs had been hit but he had almost bled out. When he went home, he took a film canister with the bullets the doctors had taken out of him.

We had an awful lot of mine injuries. It was pretty common. Every morning we'd talk about our amputees. If you worked nights, you would be waiting for the next crew to come to relieve you. We would say, "Are we gonna get out of here before the amputee comes in?" Every day we got an amputee — every morning. One career Marine staff sergeant had lost both legs, an arm, and a hand. He was so dazed that he was trying to run off the stretcher. His face was burned and he had shrapnel wounds everywhere. A corpsman was trying to hold him down while he was screaming, "God, get me out of the compound!" He lived.

Another man came in who had a hole right between his eyes. The bullet had gone through his head and came out the other side. When he arrived, he couldn't talk and couldn't write. Everything was jumbled. We couldn't find out the name of his unit. When he left the next day, he was fine. The bullet had gone between the two hemispheres of his brain!

Circling above the room in my mind's eye, I can see the concrete floor covered with clotting blood like great mounds of liver — naked young men littering the room on blood-stained green stretchers while desperate corpsmen shouted at them to make a fist! to start an IV in the forearm, or "Bear down like you have to take a shit" was another command to try to force up the vein in the neck.

During mortar and rocket attacks we stayed with the wounded and hoped for the best. The chopper pad took enough hits just outside the triage area that the Seabees finally put up a pair of blockades of stacked railroad ties in front of the main Quonset hut and the outdoor triage to stop shrapnel. Fortunately, none of the triages ever took a direct hit but wards and an OR did.

After I left Vietnam, I buried my personal experience, studying mathematics then working in industry. A number of years had passed before I really learned about where I had been and its mission. After three decades ignoring my past, I decided I needed to go back. I searched the Web and wrote organizations, but didn't get any information. It seemed the place had been forgotten. Then one day I got a hit. I found the abstract of a paper written by some Navy physicians about a study done at the hospital, and I wrote for a copy of the paper.

Between January and June 1968, a study followed wounded patients from initial resuscitation through final disposition. Part of this study took place during my own triage service. The study was shelved for decades. Published in the March 1988 *Military Medicine*, the paper is entitled "Naval Support Activity Hospital, Danang, Combat Casualty Study." The authors were Capt. B.G. McCaughey, MC, USN, J. Garrick, M.D., L.C. Carey, M.D., and J.B. Kelley, BA. It had remained in the archives at the Naval Medical Research Institute for 20 years though Dr. Garrick had analyzed the data initially and described the results in a lecture in 1969.

The paper backs up my memory of the personnel staffing the triage-surgical theater. There were three anesthesiologists and only two nurse anesthetists. Those two nurses did not work the triage. In fact, on the rare occasion when we had a particularly difficult intubation to be performed — as on one occasion when a child blew open his mouth chewing a blasting cap — an anesthesiologist handled it, but usually the corpsmen did.

The statistics from the study make for interesting comparison. According to *The Vietnam*

War Almanac, by Harry G. Summers, a former Army infantry colonel, the mortality rate for wounded Army personnel was nearly .036, while for Marines it was about .028. The NSAH study indicates that the mortality rate at the hospital was about .021, a significant improvement. Even if the number considered DOA at NSAH is included, the figures are about .027. Of course, many factors affect these figures, only one of which is emergency unit effectiveness. But the fact that the Marine Corps bore the brunt of the fighting in I Corps, where the enemy was better equipped and trained than in other sectors, which seems to indicate that Navy corpsmen and physicians who served as medical personnel for the Marine Corps offered better service for their wounded.

A few comments in the study make these numbers even more impressive: "The types of casualties sent to NSAH were not representative of all those occurring in Vietnam, because the NSAH was staffed by a larger variety of specialists and thus more capable of handling difficult medical problems." I talked to Marines who served in the area from Chu Lai to Hue, including all the hill country around Danang and such hot spots as An Hoa. Many of them remarked on the NSA Hospital, particularly those who were wounded. I recall a retired gunnery sergeant, who had spent time with the MPs and had provided security for the hospital, saying it was the best emergency hospital in the world at the time. He was probably right. Staffed with experienced and senior medical personnel, the hospital mission was to handle the most difficult cases.

As with most of the hospitals in Vietnam, the bulk of the casualties came directly out of the field without first passing through aid stations. The helicopter made this possible, saving an incredible number of lives by shortening the time between being wounded and receiving care. This was also noted in the study: "Combat casualties were generally taken to NSAH via helicopter and without primary definitive care." This can explain how the number of Marines KIA in Vietnam was so much smaller than for the Marines in World War II — even though the number of wounded was comparable. In World War II, transit time was generally 6 to12 hours, while in Vietnam it was more like 2 to 4 hours.

The study mentions that the mean transit time was about five hours, suggesting that something else was affecting this average. The authors wonder whether it might be the result of transfer of casualties from other units. But my experience is closer to that of Dr. Garrick, who recalls the difficulty of getting choppers into hot areas, particularly at night. The Marine Corps was using CH-46s, much larger and slower than the Army's Hueys, which were more effective at getting into tight spots. I remember getting huge loads of casualties on CH-46s— wounded who had clearly been lying in the field for some time. The were covered with mud and leeches, and often dragged out of inaccessible areas on ponchos, and sometimes they had been carried on stretchers fashioned from bamboo poles and ponchos. These men were outside the norm of the transit time of two to four hours because of the vicissitudes of combat.

This article showed me clearly what I had known intuitively all those years: NSAH was a special field hospital, staffed with specialists and stocked with all the medical supplies required to be a modern emergency hospital. The spirit of the place was dedicated and proud. We would have been hard-pressed to provide better service to our wounded.

(From "NSA Station Hospital Da Nang: A Personal History" by James Chaffee, *Navy Medicine*, Jan.-Feb. 2002, Vol. 93. No. 1, pp. 9–15, and interview with James Chaffee.)

Building Up "Defenses"

Even before joining the Navy in 1966, Marie Joan Brouillette had served five years in the Air Force Nurse Corps specializing in operating room nursing. Her first Navy assignment was at Naval Hospital Portsmouth, Virginia. Then Vietnam beckoned. She had been there but a few months when she learned that nurses were needed in Vietnam.

I thought Vietnam would be an exciting assignment and I volunteered. I subsequently found out that 2,000 nurses volunteered and 18 were chosen.

Prior to deployment, all 18 nurses were ordered to Washington for a few days of orientation. All I remember from those days were discussions concerning the Vietnamese culture. We were briefed on what would be available on the base to satisfy our needs and wants and how to prepare for possible POW status. We did not discuss any of the nursing or medical aspects we might face. We would be divided into three groups consisting of four nurses in the first, six in the second, and eight in the third group because of the fear of losing 18 nurses should the plane go down.[4]

Our chief nurse had arrived with three other nurses a couple of days ahead of my group's arrival in-country. Ten of us would search the place for cleaning materials and proceed to get the compound cleaned up. That took a couple of days. Then we went to take charge of patient care. I was the nurse who had extensive operating room experience so I was assigned to the ORs along with [Lt. Cmdr.] Ruth Morlock, who had some OR training. The third group was assigned to the surgical, medical, and POW wards.

After arriving at the hospital compound, we were shown the command bunker that was our destination for cover when the sirens warned of incoming fire. We placed a pair of shorts or slacks and a sweat shirt on the foot of our bed so that we could quickly change from PJs to other clothes and then run across the beach to the bunker situated about 20 yards from the quarters. We were not issued flak jackets or helmets. We were not supposed to be in harm's way.

We felt very vulnerable running to the bunker without our protection. After the third trip to the bunker, we asked if we could stay in our quarters under our beds against the cement wall. The CO agreed and that became our routine. We all spent many hours sleeping under our beds.

On the third day in Vietnam, the sirens went off around midnight. We dressed and ran to the bunker. After the all-clear, we returned to our rooms and soon after that the chief nurse told me the chief surgeon had called and asked if the OR nurses could come to the triage area to provide assistance. He sent a jeep to pick us up and transport us to the receiving area.

It was pitch-black except for the lights of the open receiving area, which was full of casualties lying on stretchers. The wounded had been placed on sawhorses, and their IVs hung from a horizontal metal pipe suspended from the ceiling. We probably had 70 patients in this receiving area. Ruth and I proceeded to the pre-op area and ORs to determine the situation. We decided to split up. She took the upper OR hut and I took the lower one so I could keep in communication with the triage officer.

It was close to midnight when we completed the treatment of the last casualty. I believe we did 112 cases. Ruth and I walked slowly to our quarters bone-tired and in complete silence. In our own way, we were both processing the experience of the past 24 hours.

The normal routine was like this: When the choppers landed, the stretcher bearers ran out, deplaned the patients, and placed their stretchers on two sawhorses. Each bay had a team assigned and immediately began to remove ammunition, boots and clothes, and then begin an IV line on each side of the patient's neck. A patient admission chart was initiated and blood was sent to the lab for readings. After the triage officer assessed a patient's needs, he was placed on a gurney and taken to X-ray. The cement made it very easy to push the gurneys. That saved labor and time because only one person was required to transfer a patient.

After X-ray, the patient went on to the pre-op area for further treatment and preparation for surgery. If required, medical personnel inserted a chest tube and a Foley catheter and started

Opposite, top: **Lt. Cmdr. Joan Brouillette and Lt. Larry Bergman, Navy nurses, wheel a patient into one of NSA Hospital's operating rooms (BUMED Archives).** *Bottom:* **Nurse anesthetist Lt. Larry Bergman (left), monitors a surgical patient (BUMED Archives).**

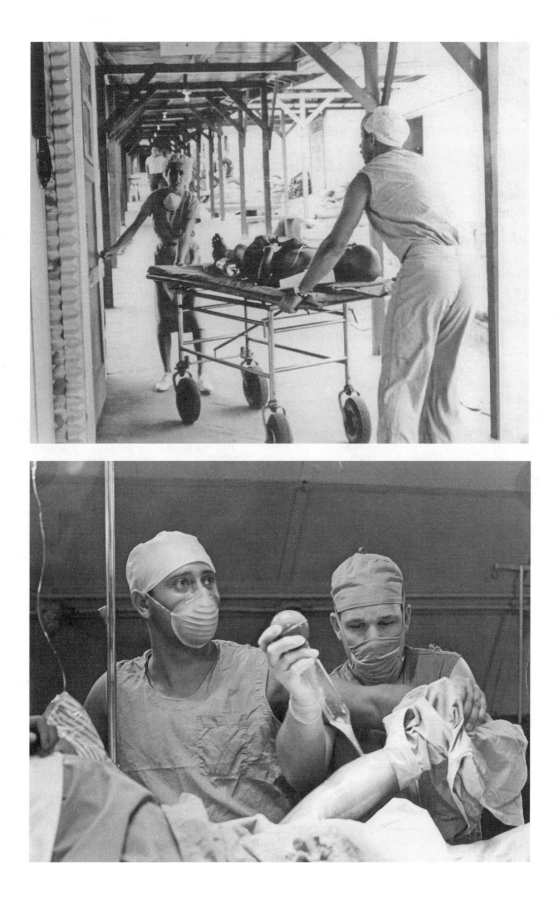

the patient on blood. While these other procedures were being accomplished, we cleaned up the patient as best as possible prior to his transfer to an OR.

It was not unusual for this type of patient to be on an operating room table within 15 minutes after being removed from the chopper. In that time, he had received a total evaluation from the triage surgeon, had blood work done, had received a blood transfusion, had gotten complete x-rays, and the appropriate surgical team or teams had been notified. The OR and anesthesia teams were ready to begin their work. When a patient had injuries to his head, chest, or abdomen and/or needed a limb or two taken care of, all three specialty teams would work simultaneously.

Sometime in the spring of 1968, we were able to rig a table very similar to one used by a pathologist in a morgue today. We rigged a shower-type hose over the table and were able to clean up many patients quickly and safely, shaving some minutes from the time needed in Preop and OR. A lot depended on how critical the patient was, the time we had, and the ability of the patient to tolerate some of the procedures we needed to do. As a result, a patient sometimes went into the operating room not all that clean, but time was vital. The choppers got the wounded to us very quickly, and they were in an operating room very quickly. That's one reason we were able to save so many of these guys.

The other reason was the staff's experience. If I remember correctly, the chief of surgery at Danang was a senior surgeon I worked with in the operating rooms at Naval Hospital Portsmouth, Virginia. Every general surgeon, orthopedic surgeon, neurosurgeon, and ENT surgeon were all experienced in their given fields. I don't remember if they were all Navy-trained or had some civilian experience.

A team of researchers arrived sometime during my year to study our processes and procedures for treating casualties. They even pitched in and helped where they could when we were receiving heavy loads of wounded. I don't think some of the injuries we saw in Vietnam would be seen outside a war zone. A lot of today's trauma treatment in our country's emergency rooms had its birth in NSAH Danang.

When Tet hit, Ruth Morlock — the other trained OR nurse — was on R&R. So that left Marge [Lt. Cmdr. Marjorie Warren] and me to cover Pre-op, four ORs, and Central Supply. I was on the day shift and sound asleep in my quarters when the sirens went off. Machine gun fire and rockets began falling close to us. We all had a gurney pad, blankets, and pillow under our beds so when the sirens went off, we dove under our beds for protection. I was under my bed up against the three-foot-high cement wall that the Quonset hut sat on. The fighting continued for hours and increased in intensity. Planes were flying very low over the quarters. I thought my life was coming to an end. I think I damaged the concrete with my hands, I was so scared.

We had no communication as to what was going on. We had no way of telling what was friendly fire or enemy fire. It was very noisy, especially when the planes were over our quarters. It seemed like this went on for four or five hours.

At dawn, the all-clear sounded and we were all anxious to get to our work areas. The air outside the nurses' quarters was heavy with the clouds and odor of gunpowder. A few dead VC were lying near the fence line approximately 15 yards from us. We later found that they were attempting to overrun our compound to reach the Marine air base.

I found some patients being processed to go into surgery. We had a steady inflow of casualties, but during the first day it was manageable. However, that situation changed later in the day and continued to be very heavy for a number of days and nights. When Marge came back for her night shift, I asked her to concentrate on the Central Supply portion of our job as the wards and the receiving area and ORs were running low on sterile supplies. We both managed a couple of hours of sleep every now and then until the flow of casualties slowed.

At the time of Tet, we had four ORs that had been in service. We also had two "MASH

Units." They were small metal box-shaped units that were totally unsatisfactory and had never been used. It was impossible to perform the type of surgeries needed at NSAH Danang. We pressed them into service controlling the type of surgery the patient needed. However, even if the patient required simple abdominal surgery, the anesthesiologist and his equipment could not fit into the unit, and he was set up outside the door. We attempted to funnel patients with wounds that could be handled with a spinal or blocks [anesthesia] into those two ORs.

Tet demonstrated that we needed to increase our capacity to handle casualties. The Seabees told me they could get steam from the base's laundry area to the Central Supply hut. The supply officer ordered a sterilizer sent over from the States. These two additions allowed us to greatly increase our ability to sterilize needed supplies. We had two sterilizers but with every three runs, one had to be off line for an hour and a half so its water tank could produce steam. So a third sterilizer and direct steam greatly improved the time and amount for processing needed supplies — no disposable linen packs existed in the 1960s.

The Seabees came to me and asked if I could use a Butler building.[5] After receiving the dimensions of the building, I provided them with a list of what would be needed to turn it into functioning housing for operating rooms. They told me they could get most of the supplies and offered substitutions which were satisfactory. I gave them drawings for four separate operating rooms with a central area for sterile supplies and a scrub sink. The scrub sink was the most difficult piece of equipment to get, but the Seabees found a long metal trough somewhere in the countryside. With a little welding, we had a scrub sink for the surgical teams.

The addition of four ORs to the six we had nearly doubled our capabilities. The MASH units were seldom used for reasons I have stated. We now had eight fully functioning operating rooms and two MASH units for relatively minor surgeries.

The Tet offensive was the first time we received so many casualties over an extended period of time, and many more days and nights stressed our capabilities as the fighting apparently increased. I have never seen such teamwork before or since my tour in Vietnam. We had no territorial limits. Everyone assigned to NSAH Danang was an equal part of the team with the same goal. Our team members did what they could — when they could — whether or not they had any medical training.

For example, the cooks kept track of the needs of the personnel in Receiving, X-ray, Pre-op, and OR. During very busy times they came to Pre-op, which was centrally located, with a meal wagon designed to transport hot food. They served staff members appropriate meals given the time of day as they were able to break for 5 or 10 minutes between patients. They provided milk shakes so we could feed the surgical teams at the operating table.

On Sundays, the chaplains came to the patient areas with their sandwich boards letting us know the time of services in the chapel. Sunday was also the day we got steak from the barbecue and vanilla ice cream. It was also the day to take the weekly malaria medication contained in bottles at the table. All this provided some stability and civility to life. The laundry personnel worked day and night to keep clean linen coming to CSR [Central Supply Room] so we could keep up with the need for sterile supplies and OR packs. It was this total dedication to the goal of saving as many lives and limbs as humanly possible by all staff members that made the goal achievable.

We weren't on the clock as long as patient care needs were there. A team went 24, 36, or 48 hours if needed. We used common sense and allowed staff — who could go no longer — some time to rest. Somehow we managed. No one ever complained.

If I remember correctly, we processed more than 8,000 patients in the ORs and completed over 12,000 procedures on these same patients. For example, one patient might have needed a limb amputated, his belly opened to have bowel surgery, and a craniotomy for a head injury. These three procedures would be done by a general surgeon assisted by an OR tech, an orthopedic surgeon, and a neurosurgeon — all working at the same time. This method — simultaneous treatment — had two advantages. First, the patient was under anesthesia for much less time which helped in his recovery. Secondly, the patient tied up the OR for about one hour versus the usual four hours if the three teams had worked sequentially.

During the time I was in Vietnam, I remember one patient above all the others. It's strange. When I was at Portsmouth, two nurses had been in Saigon back in the early 1960s — Tweedie Searcy and Bobbi Hovis. Before we left for Vietnam, Tweedie and Bobbi gave me and Ruth a going-away party. One of them said, "There's going to be a time when one patient is going to get through your defenses."

Afterward, I thought of that a lot but was doing pretty well — even through Tet. Perhaps it was a few months after Tet when that changed. I was at lunch with the triage officer when we heard the chopper come in. His beeper suddenly went off indicating he was needed immediately, so we both went to the triage area. This much wounded patient was the worst I had ever seen. His brains were coming out of his head. He had one leg blown off at the hip. The other was blown off mid-thigh. His belly was wide open. One arm was off at the shoulder joint and the other was off at the elbow. His eyeballs were lying on his cheek. His jaw was missing. And he kept saying, "I'm not dead! Please help me!"

He was one of the ones we prepared very quickly to get him to the operating room. Even up until the time he was put under anesthesia, he kept saying, "Please save me! Please save me!"

We got him off the operating table but he didn't last very long afterwards. We were unable to save him. That patient got to both the triage surgeon and myself. We both went back to our quarters and that was it. I just couldn't take anything for the next 18 hours. We had to build up our defenses again before we could go back.

So that's the patient I remember the most. It's amazing, first of all, that someone prior to him didn't get through my defenses. To this day, it's still very emotional for me.

When I think back on Vietnam, that was the most rewarding year of my life, professionally. I think I made a difference with a lot of patients — and being able to speed up the process so we could save more. With my training, everything all came together and that's what kept me going. "I've gotta get everything working right and we've gotta save these people." I didn't get emotionally involved with any of the patients. Each was a casualty we had to save. And that was it. I wasn't thinking of the person, his family, or anything else. You can't do that and remain sane.

Frozen Blood on Trial

At NSAH Danang and other medical facilities in Vietnam, treatment of large numbers of critically wounded patients required huge volumes of fresh blood. Providing them with ample supplies of that precious commodity soon became a major issue.

During the conflict, half the whole blood supply shipped to the war zone had a shelf life of 21 days. This supply quickly became outdated and had to be discarded. It was therefore necessary for fresh blood to be flown in regularly to satisfy demand, but a more reliable source had to be found. The Navy Medical Department looked to frozen blood as the answer.

Freezing red blood cells effectively stopped the clock, and the 21-day shelf life no longer applied. Once a person donated a unit of whole blood, technicians placed the unit in a centrifuge in which the blood was spun into its components — platelets, plasma, and red cell concentrate. The red cells were then treated with glycerol, a cryopreservative. If frozen without being glycerolized, ice would damage the cell walls and render the red cells useless.

Once glycerolized, the red cell concentrate was stored and frozen in containers in mechanical freezers at -80 degrees centigrade. When needed, technicians thawed the container of red cells for about 25 minutes in a water bath and then washed the red cells to remove the glycerol. Afterward, the unit was spun at high velocity to recover the red cells, which were now ready for transfusing. The once frozen blood was virtually indistinguishable from its freshly drawn counterpart and was equally effective.

The science of freezing and storing blood was not yet a decade old when the United States committed forces to Vietnam. In 1956, the Protein Foundation of Cambridge, Massachusetts, had begun a frozen blood research project at Naval Hospital Chelsea, which soon became the Navy's center for frozen blood studies.

In 1965, the Naval Blood Research Laboratory (NBRL) was born at Chelsea, and scientists soon refined the techniques for preserving and storing blood. One year later, the NBRL shipped its first unit of frozen blood to Vietnam. The new hospital at Danang— with its more than adequate supply of surgical patients— offered a perfect venue to test the frozen blood bank concept.

Lt. Robert Valeri was fully trained in internal medicine and hematology before he joined the Navy in 1962, and was assigned to what was originally called the Blood Research Lab at Chelsea. His job was to help develop a method to freeze red cells.

When I joined the Navy in 1962, the entire attitude of the military, which was really driven by the Army, was that if you went into combat, the simplest way to provide blood was to obtain it from the troops— the so-called "walking blood bank." The Navy, however, was unique. It had ships and deployments where it would be difficult to maintain a walking blood bank.

The medical community also had a tremendous amount of interest in developing blood substitutes. The major blood substitute introduced during World War II was human albumin — serum albumin. This was all brought about by technology designed and developed by Edwin J. Cohn, a professor at Harvard University. He developed the Cohn Fractionator, which enabled the separation of albumin from plasma.

About the time they were isolating these plasma proteins from blood, a veterinarian, Audrey Smith, described a study in which she froze fowl spermatozoa using glycerol. When Cohn heard about it in 1954, he decided to freeze red cells that were normally being discarded when albumin was isolated from whole blood. But first he decided to use his Cohn Fractionator to add glycerol to the red cells before freezing them.

When I arrived at Chelsea, we were using the Cohn Fractionator to take whole blood and separate it into its components, add glycerol to the red cells, and then freeze, thaw, and wash them. This technology was a research effort then and wasn't related to anything anyone would consider practical. But the principle was there.

At that time, the original Cohn Fractionator was a research tool that was being used extensively by Capt. Lewis Haynes, a Navy surgeon who was very interested in documenting the safety of glycerolized red cells. It soon became apparent that the Navy had to modify the Cohn Fractionator concept and to upgrade it into a system that would be simple and usable.

That's about the time a scientist named Jack Latham entered the picture. He used his ingenuity to design a stainless steel bowl and then a polycarbonate bowl, which could be put into a centrifuge. We in the military were very interested in this development because the Cohn Fractionator was a monster and very impractical. It was like the Statue of Liberty. Latham's technology revolutionized blood banking because his bowl could not only be used to add and remove glycerol but also to isolate plasma, red blood cells, and platelets. The original Cohn Fractionator required that the machine be dismantled, washed, reassembled, autoclaved, and then reused. Unlike the Cohn reusable system, Latham's was a disposable system.

It was our increasing involvement in Vietnam that spurred this work. As I mentioned, when I entered the service, the Army had convinced itself that "walking donors" would be able to provide the necessary blood. With the development of the Cohn system and the freezing of red cells, the Navy felt that other frozen blood products could be used in isolated areas. So this marked the major division in research funded by the Department of Defense.

The Army pursued liquid preservation of blood products while the Navy became very interested in frozen blood products. The Army researchers did not want to get involved in a complex technology. Freezing was more complex because the blood required an additive — glycerol — and a method had to be devised to do this. Freezers were also required to freeze the red cells. And then scientists had to figure out how to remove the additive from the cells once they had been thawed.

The Army pursued the simpler approach. To a donated unit of blood, researchers added a substance which would allow it to be stored beyond 21 days. When I first entered the service, the length of storage for red cells was 21 days. Then, as the Army pursued its research with additive methods to stabilize cells, the collected blood could now be stored at 4 degrees centigrade for 42 days.

The Navy, on the other hand, was very interested in freezing red cells at -80 degrees centigrade. Originally we could store the red cells for three years. Now we can store them for at least 10 years.

When I first arrived at Chelsea, the lab was relatively small because early on we probably had 8 or 10 enlisted personnel and Medical Corps officers working on site at any one time. As we became more involved in Vietnam, we trained a lot of people, including the staff in Vietnam. We also trained all military personnel involved in our frozen blood feasibility project. So we were not only collecting and freezing red cells, we were also transporting them to Vietnam. All the data were returned to our lab, and we published a number of papers concerning the experience using frozen deglycerolized red cells in a combat zone.

Dr. Gerald Moss, a surgeon at Massachusetts General Hospital, joined the Navy to get involved with this project. He was responsible for the frozen blood program at Danang and studied the patients who received the frozen red cells.

Back during the Vietnam era, the whole technology of frozen blood was complicated. The original Cohn Fractionator could never be field-tested. What we field-tested was a system of washing the cells using a principle called "agglomeration" [collecting in a mass]. If you take red cells and put them into sugar solutions, the cells will agglomerate. A surgeon, Charles Huggins, who was working at Mass General, introduced the principle of agglomeration to remove glycerol. To do that required 6.7 liters of wash solution. The red cells were frozen in huge bags, which reduced the number of units you could put in the freezer. And then you needed a tremendous amount of wash solution — at least 6.7 liters. What's more, the usable life of the deglycerolized cells was only 24 hours. This was the system that was field-tested by Moss in our lab in Danang.

"Filling Up the Tank"

Ohio native Gerald Moss completed his surgical residency at Massachusetts General Hospital and spent nearly a year in Manchester, England, involved in experimentation with liver transplantation. The subject of his research was the cryopreservation of that critical organ using glycerol. Even though Moss admits those experiments were a "catastrophic failure," the work set the stage for the rest of his professional life.

When he received orders for active duty in May 1965, Moss learned he would be assigned to the carrier USS Saratoga, *not an ideal venue for honing his surgical or experimental research skills. A providential phone call from his mentor and frozen blood pioneer, Dr. Charles Huggins, changed the direction of his medical career.*

"Are you interested in some sort of more intense surgical experience with some research?" Huggins asked.

I said, "Of course!"

He said, "Let me make a few phone calls." He called me back within the hour and said, "I've got a job for you. It's exactly what you want."

I responded, "Great! Where is it?"

"Vietnam," he said.

That began a very fascinating part of my life. I finished my residency and hooked up with Bob Valeri, who was across town at Chelsea Naval Hospital. Then I took a crash course on red cell physiology and cryopreservation.

The Navy was interested in simplifying blood transfusions for the Marines by limiting the number of blood groups — mostly O negative, and using freezing as a way to stabilize the blood supply. With glycerol, you could store red cells literally forever at -80 degrees [centigrade]. At that time, Massachusetts General [Hospital] and Chelsea [Naval Hospital] were freezing large numbers of O negative red cells.

Shortly after my crash course, I went to the Field Medical Service School at Camp Pendleton. It was essentially to prepare physicians for the realities of combat — throwing grenades, firing .45s, crawling under wire with live fire going over your head. I'd never held a gun in my hand, but it turned out to be pretty useful as events played out. I was to be a general surgeon and officer in charge of the frozen blood program for Marines in Vietnam.

Before I left Boston, I had spent time with Bob Valeri and Charlie Huggins thinking about what the clinical trials would look like — as we understood "clinical trials" back in those days. We spent time on the science side of it talking about how the study would be done.

After the training at Camp Pendleton, I went to Vietnam. In the meantime, however, the Viet Cong had blown up the new hospital at NSA Danang. It was in shambles so I was diverted to Saigon. Although I don't agree with Oliver Stone, his portrayal of the troops getting off the plane [1986 movie "Platoon"] is very accurate. The door of the plane opened and we walked out from civilian life into a war zone. I felt a blast of heat and saw a chaotic environment with lots going on — people running around, everybody in uniform. Because it was August, it was hotter than anything I had ever experienced.

We had an orientation with Gen. [William] Westmoreland shortly after we landed. He looked like a Hollywood character — a tall and very handsome guy with salt and pepper hair, and he had a presence about him. He spoke to us with tremendous confidence about the mission of the war, and I was very dazzled by him.

I was then assigned to the station hospital in Saigon as a surgeon, and I lived in an apartment house about a block or two away. My roommate was a Navy psychiatrist named Richard Gettman. We had two Chinese maids who cooked for us and cleaned house. It was a very pleasant existence inside the apartment, but when you walked out on the street, every alley was filled with people living in little makeshift containers. Beautiful kids were running around the street washing themselves in little basins beside the street and holding their hands out for whatever they could get.

I was to remain in Saigon until the frozen blood vans for the lab and the freezers arrived, and did so for three months with several other general surgeons running a general clinic. I did some surgery but it was infrequent. Most of that surgery was related to war wounds — shrapnel or land mines. We put a lot of blood vessels back together again but I didn't really do enough surgery to keep on top of my form.

In December, I received orders to go north because the vans had arrived. I flew up the coast to Danang and then began to put together the blood banking equipment. When I arrived, I found a huge complex had been created for a 1,000-bed hospital. I think they called it a station hospital for organizational reasons to keep it out of the Marine supply line, which wasn't very good. It had all sorts of high-tech equipment which I had back in Boston. I thought it was quite a logistic tour de force.

The complex was still in the process of being constructed by the Seabees and by Raymond, Morrison, Knudson. RMK was the big contractor for the military at that time, but they contracted out a lot of the work to Vietnamese locals, half of whom were probably VC.

Because we had no patients yet, the Marines would not give us a perimeter. This meant we were on our own just to the west of what the Marines called "Battalion Road," and were required to man bunkers at night — 22 corpsmen and our new CO, Capt. Bruce Canaga. To the east of Battalion Road were beaches, a Marine air group, and a Marine tank group.

We were in the bunkers every night for eight weeks until all the Quonset huts were completed. Every night as the sun went down, all of us hunkered down in the bunkers connected by voice-activated phones. The most beautiful sound in the world was the sound of a Marine tank that would cross the road and sit at the west end of the hospital and aim down into the Danang Valley where the Han River ran. Flares went off every night, and we saw firefights as the VC came down the river and tried to engage the Marine air group and the Marine tank group. Even though I knew how to fire a gun, I knew I couldn't survive a concerted attack. We were all armed with carbines — but we were not proficient. So we had helmets, flak jackets, and "locked and loaded carbines." We had every expectation that we were going to get killed. It was eight weeks of sheer, sheer terror.

This was December 1965 and it was the monsoon season — cold, rainy, and uncomfortable. Eventually, the hospital was completed. I was working with two corpsmen specially trained to work in the blood bank area along with an MSC, Lt. Jim Bates.

The blood then arrived from Boston packed in dry ice. Out came these units of frozen red cells, which we transferred to the freezers. We had a big generator and a van.

Two sandbagged vans had "Frozen Blood Bank" painted on the sides. They were like the temporary offices you see beside construction sites. One van contained a freezer maintained at -80 degrees centigrade; the other van housed a lab to make blood measurements and do calculations. We didn't have computers at that time. We recorded our data with pencil and paper.

Our freezer capacity was in the hundreds, that is, units-wise. I was responsible for the blood bank, as well as the frozen blood program. I was also responsible for transfusion medicine. Here is a description of the procedure. The Red Cross and other agencies collected the blood so its source was both military and civilian. The blood was then further refined to ensure that it was negative for a couple of common antigens.[6] These were cells that were truly universally compatible and wouldn't produce any clinically significant antibodies. It was the ideal universal donor blood. These cells were then immersed in glycerol, frozen, packed in dry ice, and shipped to us in Vietnam.

The freezers worked off electricity from a gasoline generator. These were standard -80 degree stock freezers used for science. We had a large supply of O Kell-Duffy negative red cells, and we packed them in these freezers.

The idea was to take the frozen blood, thaw it, wash it, and then use it on patients in the hospital to see how it worked. This, in essence, was a clinical trial with a waiver of consent. It couldn't have been done any other way because of the magnitude of injuries. The idea was to study patients who had been given these formerly frozen red cells.

We used machines that were developed specifically to wash the cells through the process of agglomeration. The cells were placed in very long bags with glucose and were hung up on a machine. The cells all agglomerated — settled to the bottom of the bag. The bag was then manipulated in such a way that we ended up with only the red cells at the bottom. The wash solution was then removed from the top, and we were left with about 200cc's of red cells. We used the wash solution to remove glycerol from the cells. Even though a tremendous volume of wash solution was required to produce glycerol-free cells, obtaining it never posed a logistics problem while I was there, and it never inhibited our ability to do the study.

We were part of the surgery department, and that's one of the aspects that made the arrangement work so smoothly. We never had an instant of friction or any sort of turf problems among the four or five general surgeons and anesthesiologists. Everybody was interested in the project.

I'll tell you why there was so much enthusiasm. The blood we regularly got through the system came through Saigon and then up to Danang, and averaged about 18 days since it had been drawn. That left us only a few days before it was outdated. I never saw the data published, but my memory is that the vast amount of the regular blood we received for the Marines ended up being outdated and had to be discarded. Well over half of what we got was not useable. Because the battles were episodic and unpredictable, we would outdate large numbers of units. At times we had a lot of blood but didn't have compatible units. That's why this project seemed so exciting to us. The idea was to determine whether or not the mechanics would work. It took about 20 minutes to a half hour to actually thaw the frozen red cells in a water bath, agglomerate them, and get them ready for transfusion. And despite the fact that the cells were universally compatible, we were still doing cross-matches as well.

Once the study began, we learned very quickly that the Marines who had tremendous injuries required huge amounts of fluid and blood. The typical patient used a number of units of frozen red cells and a number of units of liquid preserved blood. So most of those patients ended up with combinations. The study was confounded by the fact that military medicine was so good that if a patient didn't have a head injury, the odds were overwhelming that he was going to survive. That made the study a little more complicated.

In fact, I don't know whether or not this story has really been told as dramatically as it should. If you compare the quality of medicine between Korea and Vietnam, it was a quantum leap. I think it has to do with the fact that all medical officers in Vietnam were trained to the teeth before they came. Every time an endotracheal tube was inserted, it was done so by a trained anesthesiologist.[7] Every time a head was operated on, it was done by a trained neurosurgeon. Whenever a belly was opened, it was done so by a trained general surgeon. Every artery was operated on by someone who knew how to operate on arteries. Every bone was taken care of by a trained orthopedic surgeon. I'm sure that had never happened before in history. And frequently all these doctors were operating on one patient simultaneously. There may have been a chest injury, a head injury, a belly injury, and a leg injury. The whole team operated in unison. It was quite inspiring.

The period we observed between injury and arrival at the hospital was about 20 minutes. We had a whole Henry Ford assembly line right where the chopper landed. One corpsman manned a hose, and as the patient was lifted off the chopper, the corpsman hosed him down because most of them were injured in the rice paddies. They were covered with buffalo dung and mud. Then their clothes were removed. We then inserted big-bore IVs and gave them a lot of saline and bicarbonate. We got them rapidly resuscitated before they even got any blood. Then they were triaged.[8]

We learned that resuscitation was based on using salt water rather than dextran or uncross-matched O blood. We used the notion of "filling up the tank," so to speak, with salt water and then replacing red cell deficits with red cells. This was normal saline or Ringer's lactate. Then we carefully cross-matched red cells. These were washed, preserved red cells or the frozen cells. If we were giving O to an A, we had fewer complications than we did had we been using whole blood transfusions.

We completely transformed some patients' blood from A to O. Then you can imagine someone trying to figure out what that patient's type was once he arrived in Subic, especially when his dog tag said something different. They had mixtures they couldn't cross-match. I flew back to Subic a few times to see how these patients were doing. I spent time with the blood bankers at Subic and it was a real problem trying to identify a patient's blood type at that instant.

This wasn't a permanent blood type change, though. Once the patients began producing their own red cells, then they had mixtures of transfused cells and their own cells. The transfused cells had a half life of a month or something. Eventually the patients would return to their regular blood group. On the other hand, they may have required another operation and a transfusion in the meantime and that blood would have to be cross-matched.

The study progressed and very quickly the surgeon and anesthesiologist preferred using the frozen red cells when they were available because they were a known quantity. We knew they were pristine cells— no plasma, no white cells, no antibodies. And the blood grouping was unquestionably correct. This study was carried out between December 1965 and July 1966 when I left.

The study culminated in a paper Bob [Valeri], Chuck [Brodine], and I wrote in 1968, which was the lead article in the *New England Journal of Medicine*.[9] It took us time to figure out how to format the data. A series of Marines received large amounts of the frozen red cells. What we looked for were adverse effects or events. The fundamental question was, did the red cells hemolyze during transfusion? Was there evidence of hemolysis [excessive breakdown of red cells]? So we measured plasma, hemoglobins, urine hemoglobins, plasma haptoglobins [proteins that bind free iron in the blood]. We did everyone's creatinines [proteins produced by muscle and released into the blood], blood gases— pretty much the whole gamut. We carried out first-class, stateside, esoteric research right at the hospital, and we did all this in a war zone.

What had the study proven? One might have a thousand units sitting in a freezer so how come it wasn't used? That was the other part of the story. We had a finite period required to thaw and wash the cells and prepare them. It required a reliable source of energy to run the agglomeration machines. Was there sufficient advantage to going through this process of thawing, washing, agglomerating, and collecting the frozen red cells, as opposed to simply opening the door of a cooler and hanging up a unit of blood? The argument had to do with the reliable supply on the one hand — the frozen cells— versus the ease of using liquid preserved cells. But our job then was simply to show whether or not it was feasible, safe, and effective to use this system in a war zone. And the answer was yes.

The biggest impediment seemed to have been the whole agglomeration process. The ideal answer would be to have come up with a cryopreservative which didn't need to be washed out. But that never happened.

I stayed in the Navy an extra few years because not only was I interested in frozen red cells but something else happened while I was there. We found that a number of patients had developed pulmonary failure. These were patients who had been seriously injured and had been given huge volumes of resuscitation fluids. They developed pulmonary failure and died from what looked like pulmonary edema. The question was whether or not this was due to too much saline and not enough colloid,[10] which has an oncotic property that inhibits fluid from seeping into the lung tissue.[11] This work consumed a good part of my professional life after that. I became more focused on lung injury and less on frozen blood after I left Vietnam.

*   *   *

Vietnam was rife with disease — tuberculosis, plague, Japanese B encephalitis, leptospirosis, and helminthiasis. Among the debilitating diarrheal diseases were dysentery and cholera. Insect-borne diseases such as dengue, scrub typhus, and malaria (P. falciparum, P. vivax, P. ovale, P. malariae), added to the casualty lists. Keeping soldiers, sailors, and Marines fit for duty in this insidious environment was one of many important missions of the Naval Medical Research Unit-2 (NAMRU-2), headquartered in Taipei, Taiwan.

When U.S. forces landed in South Vietnam in 1965, NAMRU-2 already had a proud reputation fighting tropical disease. First established at the Rockefeller Institute in New York City in 1942, the unit moved to Guam where its researchers helped win the war in the Pacific.

With the end of World War II, NAMRU-2 was disestablished. Ten years later, the Navy reestab-

lished the unit as a research base in Taipei. In 1957 NAMRU-2 was converted into a self-contained, modern medical research institute with laboratories, infectious disease wards, administrative offices, and storage and repair facilities, making it one of the most advanced research centers in Southeast Asia.

NAMRU-2 already had a reputation for its work with combating cholera. Prior to Dr. Robert Phillips's development of an effective treatment of the disease using a salt-based liquid to rehydrate victims, cholera killed 40 percent of its victims. Due to NAMRU-2's work in this field, the mortality rate was reduced to 2 percent. In 1964, Navy medical personnel treated more than 2,000 cholera victims during an outbreak in Saigon with only three deaths.

As the Vietnam War heated up, the need for a sophisticated laboratory became evident. NAMRU-2, which had the expertise, opened a detachment at NSAH Danang in February 1967 to identify illnesses and seek possible cures for diseases that might affect troops in Vietnam, particularly those operating in the I Corps area in the northern portion of South Vietnam. The mission was to conduct research studies of shock, heat stress, tropical infections, insect-borne illnesses, and parasitic diseases.[12]

With the cooperation of the Naval Medical Research Institute (NMRI) in Bethesda, Maryland, the detachment's scientists also studied the treatment of hemorrhagic and traumatic shock in severely injured battle casualties. This work was performed by the Surgical Research Unit, which maintained one portion of the Intensive Care Unit at the Naval Support Activity Station Hospital (NSAH). In this area, physicians and corpsmen of the surgical unit cared for and studied patients with particular medical problems of research interest.

The detachment also conducted special projects such as the prevention of infection in combat-related injuries, the use of freeze-dried skin in treatment of war wounds, and a study of so-called "malaria or Danang lung," a medical complication arising in a certain strain of the disease.

Most non-combat casualties were caused by fevers of undetermined origin. Some were due to strains of malaria and scrub typhus, but many were caused by bacterial or viral diseases not easily identifiable by conventional tests.

Dysentery in Vietnam was not necessarily incapacitating, but was responsible for thousands of lost man-hours. The NAMRU-2 detachment provided improved diagnostic aid to assist doctors at the NSAH to treat their patients.

Septic contamination of war wounds was a particularly important study, given the number of patients being treated for wound infections at the hospital. This study concentrated on a species of bacteria that were infecting wounds inflicted by land mines, grenades, and booby traps.

Culturing the Wounds of War

Myron Tong was already an experienced researcher when he joined the Navy. With a Ph.D. from Berkeley and an M.D. from the University of California San Francisco, Tong was just the man whom Capt. Raymond Watten, NAMRU-2's commanding officer, was looking for to head the Danang detachment.

I was just finishing my first year of medical residency at Los Angeles County General Hospital when Dr. Watten selected me to be drafted into the U.S. Navy. He was looking for doctors with laboratory and clinical experience. I found many of the tropical diseases in Vietnam really interesting and unique. In addition to our research unit, the surgical unit in Danang was set up for measurements of blood volume, pulmonary function tests, etc.

I had just finished my first year of residency in July 1968 and went to Oak Knoll Hospital for orientation. I got multiple vaccinations and seven days later I was in Taipei getting ready to go to the Danang detachment in Vietnam. I didn't know a lot about the military when I arrived.

My main job was to study war wounds. I also did some work on the medical wards because that's what I wanted to do. This is when I was introduced to tropical diseases and began to study them, as well as setting up the bacteriology laboratory.

Malaria was the biggest problem but other diseases were so prevalent and so unknown to us. We only had textbooks to go on. I'm talking about leptospirosis, Japanese B encephalitis, malaria, and scrub typhus, which I had never seen before. Falciparum was the most malignant of all the malaria species. The circulatory complications were mostly in patients with falciparum malaria. We did a number of papers about the topic at the time.

A special building had been constructed for us to work in on the edge of the hospital grounds before we arrived. It had to be a laboratory building because of what we were doing using bacterial cultures and animals.[13] Laboratory supplies and whatever else we needed would be shipped from our parent unit in Taipei, and whatever we had—cultures and specimens— would be sent back to Taipei. We had a regular airlift to Taipei from Danang airport, which at the time was the busiest airport in the world; planes were landing every 20 seconds.[14]

We had 10 to 13 corpsmen, including laboratory techs and a chief, who helped me quite a bit. And I needed his help having come from the civilian world only two weeks before.

It was really a shock for me. Tet had just finished and the facility was still very active. The number of patients the medical and surgical staff saw on a daily basis at the hospital was enormous. The medical and support staff in the triage area worked really hard every day on a 24-hour basis.

Much of our research was done at the hospital. We went to the triage area and the operating rooms to get cultures from war-related wounds. Dr. Watten had the bacteriology laboratory very organized in Taipei. They would send us the culture plates and we would do the culturing and initial incubation for a particular war wound study at our research building in Danang. But we actually did studies on surgical patients, as well as tropical diseases in medical patients.

The doctors all lived together in hooches. Everybody got up at 6:30 and ate breakfast by 7. Because I was in charge of the detachment, I had to make sure the lab and staff were okay. I tried to integrate the unit into the workings and daily routines of the naval hospital.

I also set up medical meetings right in the hospital grounds. We would have conferences with doctors from the hospital, as well as those doctors working in the field, to discuss medical topics that were current and pertinent to the diseases we encountered in Vietnam.

For the surgical studies, we all went to the hospital. We began in Triage where the wounded soldiers were flown in by helicopter, then into the surgical unit to get the wound cultures. After Triage, the patients were taken straight to Surgery for debridement and other surgically related procedures. Most of the cultures we obtained were from open war-related wounds. They were then sent to Taipei and we got the results a few weeks later.

We found a lot of gram negative bacteria in the wounds, which were indigenous to Vietnam. Since the bacteria were from the soil where the men were actually wounded, we went out to the field around Danang and cultured the soil to see what bacteria were present.

From our findings, we published a paper in JAMA [Journal of the American Medical Association] entitled, "Septic Complications of War Wounds." That article really described our research unit. We must have put out 10 papers from that unit on all the diseases we studied. I have to acknowledge the fantastic cooperation we had from the physicians who served at the U.S. Naval Hospital in Danang. They deserve most of the credit for our success.

Because I was Asian, I actually made rounds on the Vietnamese prisoners while I was there—even though that wasn't my job. We had a well-guarded ward with Viet Cong and North Vietnamese soldiers who were sick with malaria and other diseases. Even though I couldn't speak Vietnamese, these prisoners were very friendly to me. This wasn't part of our research job, but it just was something that we wanted to do. They had the same diseases our soldiers had, and they also got the same treatment. Because I could speak Chinese, I also made rounds in a special compound for Chinese Communist soldiers. The compound was not on the hospital grounds but in another part of Danang. These officers also got very good treatment.

I was in Vietnam until June 1969, when I went to Taipei for the remainder of my tour of duty. Another doctor took my place in Danang. I spent my entire service career overseas. In Taipei, one of the Chinese doctors took me to the Veterans General Hospital, which is their veterans' hospital in Taiwan. I saw cases of primary liver cancer and that's what started me thinking about what caused these liver cancers. We were the first to report that the cause of the liver cancer was the hepatitis B virus. I then went into liver disease — hepatology — because of interest in those cases.

In looking back, Dr. Watten did an excellent job in organizing the research staff. It was hard to get non-military physicians to integrate with the military physicians because everyone came from a different mindset. However, we were in Vietnam to do a job, and all of us were quite committed because of the patients we had to take care of. We were all dedicated to doing a job for our country. If you talk to any of the U.S. medical personnel who were in Vietnam, they will have the same attitude. It was such a special time in our lives. It helped shape the way some of us think because of all the trauma, disease, and death we encountered.

9

SHIPS OF MERCY

The Navy has a long tradition of hospital ships dating back to the Civil War.[1] By the end of World War II, 15 of these vessels were on line in the Pacific. The newest Haven-class hospital ships were built by Sun Shipbuilding and Dry Dock Company in Chester, Pennsylvania. Converted from C-4 freighter hulls while still in the yard, Haven, Consolation, Tranquillity, Benevolence, Sanctuary, *and* Repose *arrived in the Pacific Theater just as the war was ending.*

During the Korean War, Haven, Consolation, *and* Repose *were brought out of mothballs, reactivated, and modernized in every respect into complete, state-of-the-art floating hospitals. With operating rooms, clinics, laboratories, treatment rooms, and wards, all staffed by specialists, these vessels were comparable or superior to most of the modern hospitals ashore. Each ship was equipped to provide definitive surgical and medical care.*

The three Haven sisters were almost identical. Each 520-foot-long hull had a beam of 72 feet and displaced 11,400 tons. With their single screw 9,000-shaft horsepower, geared turbine drives, the ships had a top speed of 18 knots. Each vessel had eight decks, three below the water line. All machinery spaces were located aft, leaving the entire forward portion of the vessels available for hospital spaces. This arrangement allowed the hospital to be one unit, not built around the uptake spaces and machinery trunks, as in conventional ships. All treatment rooms and wards could be accessed by wide, continuous corridors.

The surgical suite, clinics, and treatment rooms were in the center of the ship where movement from pitch and roll was minimized. The surgical suite accommodated two major operating rooms, a fracture operating room, an anesthesia room, surgical supply room, clinical laboratory, and dispensary. The dental clinic had its own fully equipped laboratory and x-ray and darkroom facilities. The radiology department contained a record and appointment office, examination room, and x-ray machines. Other hospital facilities included a dermatology clinic, a physiotherapy department, and additional laboratories.

All but Haven *had been mothballed for a second time by the mid–1950s. With the end of the first Indochina war in 1954, the namesake of the class was again pressed into service, this time to evacuate the French survivors of Dien Bien Phu. But then,* Haven, *too, returned to mothballs. When the United States committed troops to Vietnam in 1965, these very essential mercy ships were no longer part of the fleet.*

As the American presence in Vietnam grew, so did the number of casualties. The Navy needed alternative means to augment the medical companies and the soon-to-be established hospital at Naval Support Activity Danang. These means took the form of hospital ships. The geography of Vietnam's long coastline, with the combat zone adjacent to the sea, was very suitable for hospital ships. Helicopters were therefore the ideal aircraft for medical evacuation to those vessels. With control of the seas and air superiority, hospital ships could freely cruise the coast without fear of enemy attack.

First Repose *and then* Sanctuary *came out of mothballs and spent time in the yard being readied for their new missions.* Repose *had been with the Reserve Fleet in Suisun Bay, California, for*

USS *Sanctuary* cruises near Maui (BUMED Archives).

more than 10 years when she was towed to the San Francisco Naval Shipyard at Hunter's Point for an extensive overhaul in June 1965. Her helicopter landing deck, which was added in 1952, was strengthened to support the newer, larger helicopters. It wasn't until 1969 that the helo deck was expanded to handle the largest helicopters then operational in Vietnam.

Modernization also meant reconfiguring portions of the ship for maximum efficiency in handling incoming patients. The focal point for admissions was located in Triage, which in turn was located in the most accessible area of patient care nearest the helo deck. These two strategic areas— entrance to the triage area and the helo deck — were connected by an inclining ramp which enabled rapid access to and from these two locations. Triage was equipped for rapid evaluation and resuscitation of acutely ill and wounded patients.

Besides adding the latest in medical equipment, the upgrade also included a portable heart-lung machine, an echoencephalograph, and a frozen blood bank. What had remained unchanged on both vessels were the sun decks, a chapel, and lounges where recuperating patients could spend their convalescent time. Both ships were fully air conditioned.

The two remaining Haven sisters, Repose *and* Sanctuary, *had similar or identical layouts and accommodations. The three decks above the water line contained the wards, all provided with portholes. Each ward had access to the weather decks, allowing freedom of movement for the patients. All wards, with the exception of the Intensive Care Unit, had bunk-style, two-tiered beds, with three-tiered beds on the so-called "Self-Care" units. Although both ships had the expanded capability of 750 beds, experience taught that 560 patients could be managed comfortably.*

Repose *and* Sanctuary, *each with a displacement of 15,000 tons, could provide relatively smooth sailing for patients and a stable platform for her surgeons to operate. With fuel tanks topped off, each ship, traveling at its top speed of 17 knots, had a cruising radius of 12,000 miles.*

Both vessels also sported a new paint scheme — white hull with three red crosses spaced forward, amidships, and aft. Noticeably absent was the fore and aft green hull stripe from the World War II and Korean War years. The ships also had four red crosses painted on their single funnels. The white hulls and red crosses were not cosmetic changes but necessary adherence to the Geneva Conventions, which regulated the status of hospital ships as non-combatants. These international agreements, of which the United States was a signatory, also meant that both Repose and Sanctuary would operate totally illuminated at all times and carry no armament, even when sailing in hostile waters.

When she was recommissioned on 16 October 1965, Repose was a fully equipped, modern floating hospital. She departed for Vietnamese waters in January 1966 with a stopover in Subic Bay to replenish and undergo repairs. Arriving off Chu Lai on 16 February, she began taking on patients. Her beat was I Corps, and until she left Vietnam for good in March 1970, the ship supported military operations and took patients from such places as Danang, Dong Ha, Khe Sanh, Chu Lai, Phu Bai, and Quang Tri. During her three-year deployment, Repose's medical personnel treated more than 9,000 battle casualties and admitted approximately 24,000 patients for inpatient care.

Unlike her sister, Repose, which was updated for the Korean War, Sanctuary had been idle since the end of World War II so she required far more work. Mothballed with the National Defense Reserve Fleet, she was towed to Louisiana and modernized at the Avondale Shipyards. Yard workers added a helo deck, and as with Repose, she received widened ramps to permit rapid movement from the helo deck below. Four operating rooms, a dialysis machine, an ultrasound diagnostic machine, a hyperbaric chamber useful for treating gangrene and tetanus, three x-ray units, and a blood bank were included in the renovations. Modern autoclaves for sterilization were also installed. The vessel's 20 wards were updated with the latest equipment. On 15 November 1966, Sanctuary was recommissioned at New Orleans.

Four months later, after further fitting out at Hunter's Point, Sanctuary, too, headed for Vietnam, arriving in Subic Bay in April. On 10 April 1967, she took aboard her first casualties. By the end of the month, the ship had admitted a total of 717 patients with 319 combat casualties, 72 noncombat injuries, and 326 with disease. The staff also treated 682 outpatients. Only two of her patients died.

By April 1968, after a year in Vietnamese waters, Sanctuary had admitted 5,354 patients and treated another 9,187 on an outpatient basis. Helicopters had made more than 2,500 landings on her deck. The choppers brought patients from the battlefield, transferred them to and from other medical facilities, or carried passengers to and from the ship.

Occasionally granted brief rest and recreation out of the area, Sanctuary was the only Navy hospital ship left in Vietnam after 16 March 1970. On 23 April 1971, she departed Danang for the last time and headed home.

It was the intent from the very beginning that Sanctuary and Repose were not to be employed as "ambulance ships," as was the case during World War II. The main function of those vessels was to stabilize and then transport casualties to more advanced care at base and mobile hospitals in the Pacific. Although ferrying patients back to Naval Hospital Yokosuka in Japan became routine for both Repose and Sanctuary during the Vietnam War, surgery and the definitive treatment of disease returned thousands of Marines, soldiers, and sailors to their units at the front.

Injuries Most Gruesome

Born and raised in Portland, Maine, and the son of a Navy man, Arthur McFee wasn't new to the maritime environment when he joined the Navy in 1965. A graduate of Harvard Medical School, he did his surgical training at the University of Minnesota Medical School.

Even though USS Repose *had recently been refurbished and recommissioned, the ship was anything but state of the art, having been built in 1944. Despite the condition of* Repose, *McFee became a "plank owner," that is, he served from the very beginning on the newly recommissioned ship. When, in 1965, the young physician went aboard for the first time in San Francisco, he immediately realized that the vessel would need much "fine tuning" before being ready for patients.*

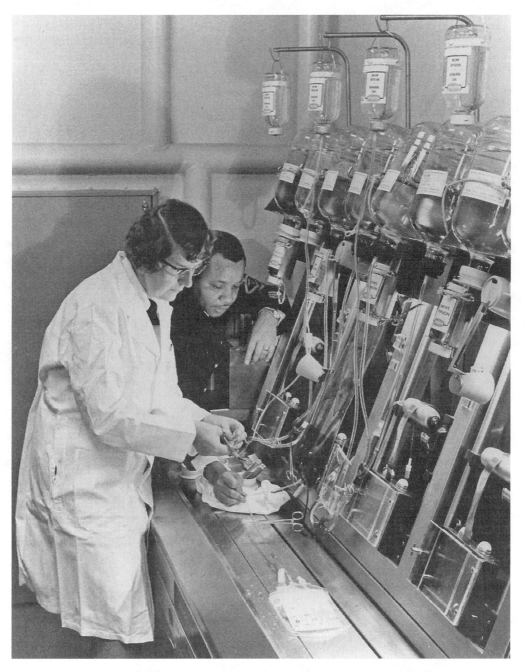

A Medical Service Corps officer and hospital corpsman use a cytoglomerator to reconstitute frozen blood aboard USS *Repose*. Both hospital ships stationed in Vietnamese waters maintained frozen blood banks (BUMED Archives).

I had been on ships before and knew what they looked like. But what I recall being impressed by was a ward of 48 beds—24 lower bunks and 24 upper bunks. Capt. [Theodore H.] Wilson, the Chief of Surgery, said, "This is going to be your ward and we're going to make it into an ICU." I thought, "My God, how are we going to give intensive care in an upper bunk?" I remember that impression rather clearly, but we figured out that problem fairly quickly once we got under way.

The *Repose* was not brand new. Even though it was newly recommissioned, it was a World War II C-4 cargo hull with a 400-foot-long crack on one side sustained during a typhoon. It had afterward been very definitely bolstered by a lot of iron plating.

I also found out that each of these Navy ships had an "IOL," an initial outfitting list. Whenever they were recommissioned, the ship was outfitted with everything the ship had when it was first commissioned according to that list. Sonny [Oran] Chenault, the urologist, brought that fact to my attention. On our way to Hawaii, he unpacked the urological clinic equipment and said, "Arthur, the only places I've ever seen this kind of equipment have been in museums. I don't know how to use the damn things!"

But the real problem was the intrinsic working of the ship itself. Its engines were never reliable. Until we went to Yokosuka in July 1966 for a month and rebuilt them, they intermittently failed.[2] It had taken us about five days to get to Hawaii. We were scheduled for two days in Honolulu but ended up staying two weeks. It was a wonderful time for all the rest of us on the medical staff because we had no patients.

Then we set out across the Pacific. At flank speed—which was about 14 knots—it took us about eight weeks to get from Honolulu to Subic Bay in the Philippines. During that voyage I experienced the specter of engine failure.

When I had first gotten on the ship, I was promoted from lieutenant to a lieutenant commander, and a lieutenant commander with a fair degree of seniority. This rank entitled me to a private cabin. It was on the starboard side of the ship's bow, which had a very characteristic "thump! thump! wham!" as the ship was under way and the bow wave washed against it. In the middle of the night, while crossing the Pacific, I was awakened many, many times by a soft "flap, flap, flap." One time I turned on the light and discovered we had no electricity. I looked out in the hallway and the emergency lights were on. I knew the ship was dead in the water in the middle of the Pacific while they were repairing those engines.

After stopping in Subic, we finally arrived off Vietnam about the 11th or 12th of March 1966. We made the voyage between Vietnam and Subic probably three or four times in March, April, May, and June, taking patients back to the Air Force hospital at Clark Air Force Base. Finally, we just had to go to a shipyard in Yokosuka, Japan, because it was the only shipyard in the Far East that could accommodate a ship our size. Once the engines were rebuilt or replaced, we went back out to sea and didn't return to Japan until we changed command in November.

I ran the intensive care unit, which was a logistical organizational problem at first. The first part of the problem was easily solved with Cmdr. Angelica Vitello, the head nurse. She ran a group of 24 nurses and 145 corpsmen assigned to the *Repose*. I had a group of 6 nurses and 19 or 20 corpsmen in the ICU. Her idea for running a nursing service was to have corpsmen in two-week rotations in every part of the ship. At that time ICUs were new and they needed experienced personnel. So she and I agreed that she would designate the 19 or 20 corpsmen she wanted in the ICU and guarantee them for one year if I would undertake to train them.

Before long, we had a stable group of nurses and corpsmen in the ICU. We subjected them to quite intensive training in practical matters such as how to set up chest suction pumps and other such procedures. Our chest suction pumps were not electrically operated but functioned with gravity. We discovered that the ship had been supplied with only three suction pumps for chest injuries. When I was on call the very first night we were in Vietnam, we took 55 casualties onboard, 11 of them with chest wounds. So we had to make do with a lot of innovative gear and rigging. Nevertheless, we did pretty well.

The ICU was pretty bad. First, the beds were abominable. All we had were cots attached to stanchions. They had no springs or mattresses but instead metal webbing for their springs and about a four-inch mattress pallet on top of that. So we had nothing that looked anything like a hospital bed except the two traction beds. The bunks were far too low on the stanchions for us to give care easily, but we made do. Beyond that, I could have had pretty much whatever I wanted if I made it known that I wanted it. For example, I had one young fellow fairly early on who was in septic shock. In the 1960s, septic shock was treated with heavy doses of steroids. The morning after his particular attack and recovery, the medical supply officer came to me and said, "Arthur, I want you to know that you've used up the ship's entire supply of hydrocortisone on one patient in one day."

Not being influenced by this kind of argument, I told him, "That is the reason you're on this ship. Now go ashore and find me some more." And he did.

As far as monitoring equipment, we had nothing compared to what is available today. We had some monitoring equipment, but it was large and bulky and wasn't what you'd see now— one on every bed in the ICU. We rolled around the equipment to whatever patient needed it because we didn't have any room to place the monitoring equipment. If we had a patient on a ventilator, we had to find a stanchion and then a clamp to hold it in place. Our ICU monitoring equipment consisted of the corpsmen who took blood pressures, vital signs, and observed. The heart and soul of the ICU care were the corpsmen and nurses. The nurses directed the corpsmen but the corpsmen did the work.

One major chore was to get rid of the 24 top bunks in the ICU. Because they were only affixed to stanchions by clamps, we easily undid the clamps, put the bunks in the hold, and nobody was the wiser. Then I had to get rid of about five or six lower bunks, which were permanently fixed to stanchions, to make room for two fracture beds with traction devices.

Once we accomplished all the preliminaries, we had a working unit of about 18 beds. The capacity of the ship was 750 patients. Not all the patients were surgical so we had an effective ratio of beds to the number of surgical beds available on the ship.

Our patient population was fairly peripatetic. The very seriously injured or the very serious triaged wounded came directly to the ICU from the operating room and occasionally from Triage. After we had effected initial treatment, we transferred them out to the regular surgical wards or back to the United States. I think the average stay in our ICU was four and a half to five days.

I would characterize my year on the *Repose* as three days of sheer terror interspersed with two weeks of absolute boredom. It all depended on who on the ground got eager and ran into a Viet Cong ambush. And then that situation could translate into 20 to 30 people in all stages of injury.

We had initially set up four triage areas and found that three of them were not useable. The only one we used was the helicopter pad on the stern. A helicopter could deliver four litter patients at a time or nine walking patients. We set up a little station right beside that helicopter pad where the four litter patients could be examined immediately. It took us five or six minutes to see all four patients and decide where to send them before the next helicopter came in.

We had a backup triage area which was our recovery room with 10 beds. We could dispatch the injured to that backup area, and they were immediately prepared for surgery. The rest of the patients were dispatched to the various wards or to ICU. It worked very well simply because we had a limited inflow of patients. We learned to handle that inflow very quickly and get them dispatched throughout the ship where we had room for them.

Beside managing the ICU, which was my primary duty, I was one of the general surgeons.

A CH-46 helicopter approaches the hospital ship USS *Sanctuary* with a cargo of sick and wounded (BUMED Archives).

We also had a few thoracic and cardiovascular surgeons, an ophthalmological surgeon, and an oral and maxillofacial surgeon, Bill Terry. Of the 24 medical officers aboard, I think 9 or 10 of them were in surgical specialties.

I remember a few specific patients. Actually, the most heartrending injuries were caused by land mines. The nastiest and most frustrating were the injuries caused by punji sticks. I recall one young man who had stepped on a land mine and lost both legs at the hip joints. His abdomen and chest had been penetrated. Both eyes were lost and he had penetrating wounds of the head. He lasted 18 or 20 hours. I was surprised he lived to get to us. His injuries were so gruesome that we could do little or nothing.

Another patient had been sent from a primary aid station on the beach. A note on his chart contained a reference to the literature: "This patient has been resuscitated according to the latest regulations established by Dr. Tom Shires of Dallas, TX." The note also cited a specific issue of the *Journal of the American Medical Association* from 1966, which promoted the administration of saline "at a rate of 10cc's of saline per kilogram body weight per hour."

The patient was a 70kg man and had received 700cc's of IV fluid for each of the 18 hours he had been in transit until he got to us. This was over-hydration of a major kind. The physicians had not taken into account the fact that such resuscitation is something that was done until the patient was resuscitated. Then the object was to establish a maintenance level. Fortunately for this patient — he was 18 years old and had wonderful kidneys — he got rid of a great deal of that fluid in the next 24 hours. But he was just one mass of water when he arrived.

I remember the severity of some of the injuries, but we had some very heartening successes. I also recall that we were the reference hospital for correcting mistakes. We were annoyed that we had to correct a lot of mistakes. One patient had a gunshot wound through his right hip into his abdomen. The doctors on the beach had felt it necessary to explore his abdomen. When they did an exploratory laparotomy, they found a significant gunshot wound of the cecum [the first part of the large intestine] and the right side of the colon. They removed the entire right side of his colon and made an anastomosis [a surgical connection or splice]. After four or five days, they sent him to us for care.

When he arrived at the triage area — and I happened to be triaging that day — his temperature was 104. I immediately sent him to ICU. When I went to see him, his temperature was 106. I noticed that he was lying on his cot in a rather funny position with his right leg sort of cocked up. When I asked him to straighten it out, he said he couldn't. It turns out that the operating surgeon had drained his abdomen with a Penrose drain[3] where he had taken out the colon, and decided the most convenient place to put it was right through the wound where the bullet had entered the body. We took an x-ray of his pelvis and noted that the bullet had passed through his right hip, clipped the femoral head off, and turned it around 180 degrees in the hip socket. The surgeon on the beach had drained a contaminated wound in his abdomen into his hip joint, which now contained about 60cc's of pus. When we got rid of the pus that night, his temperature became manageable.

A tremendous spirit existed onboard for getting the job done. Everybody on that ship felt special in being asked to commission a new hospital on an old ship and doing it from the ground up. We were a band of individuals who got to be very, very close because you couldn't go anywhere. No one was more than a hundred feet away from where he worked. We all lived within 10 feet of one another, and had a fairly profound respect for each other.

Every day at 5, we had a clinical pathological conference to discuss patients. They were unifying meetings. Nobody felt he had to come and nobody thought he had to be present every day, but a good deal of background work was accomplished at those meetings on a daily basis.

I have reflected a lot on that year aboard *Repose* and on items like chance. We replaced and rebuilt the power supply in July 1966. In November 1966, after a change of command at Subic, the incoming captain of the ship, a USNR line captain, left Subic at 4 P.M. to head into the only typhoon we had seen for months in that area. Had we not had the engine refit in July, I sincerely believe the ship would not have weathered that storm. It was a terrifying time for us all.

Teamwork at Its Finest

Dentist Bill Terry was a well-trained oral surgeon when he reported aboard USS Repose *in 1965. A graduate of the University of Tennessee Dental School, Terry received an appointment as an ensign in the Navy's Ensign Hospital Probationary Program. As soon as he completed dental school, he began a rotating internship at Naval Hospital Oakland and entered the Navy as a regular naval dental officer in 1954. Ample opportunities arose to hone his surgical skills at Oakland.*

"The trauma load was very, very heavy with fractured mandibles, maxillae, etc. At that time, we still had a few patients from World War II who were undergoing reconstruction so we were also involved with some of them."

After his Oakland assignment, Terry saw duty at the Naval Air Station at Sangley Point, the Philippines, the Naval Air Technical Training Center in Memphis, Tennessee, and additional duties at Naval Hospital Memphis. He was then assigned to the precommissioning unit for the first nuclear aircraft carrier, USS Enterprise *(CVAN-65). Terry spent three years aboard the ship before returning to Naval Hospital Oakland to complete his training in oral and maxillofacial surgery.*

As USS Repose *was being refitted at Hunter's Point Naval Shipyard in San Francisco in the fall of 1965, Terry received orders to report to the hospital ship. His experience in setting up the original dental department aboard* Enterprise *prior to its commissioning made him the obvious choice to get the old hospital ship's dental department up and running.*

Repose wasn't anything like the hospital ships of today, but it was a big white ship with converted spaces—wards, surgical suites, etc. We had all the facilities you would find in a hospital today. In addition, we had something very new. We had a frozen blood bank onboard. I think it was the first time a frozen blood bank had been put aboard a ship, and it turned out to be a great lifesaver for many of our patients. The crew consisted of 54 officers, 29 nurses, and 543 enlisted personnel, and the ship had 922 beds.

I made a list of all the surgical instruments that I would require. We set up the dental department with all the equipment for a complete range of dental services from restoring teeth to complex surgery. Because of the need for the hospital ships, we had no trouble getting almost anything we wanted, including the air-powered turbine units for dentistry, which were still fairly new at that time. We had all the surgical instruments available. The ship also had a prosthetics laboratory, where our prosthodontist, Capt. Bill Marking, could support whatever we needed for any type of dentistry. He could also fabricate temporary prostheses for injured patients who had lost part of their maxilla. Our facilities were for all types of state-of-the-art dentistry and surgery, and that included the latest anesthesia machines. No expense was spared as far as outfitting the ship.

When I received my orders to the ship, I had a lot of misgivings because, frankly, no one was available who had had experience with the tremendous trauma during World War II and Korea. They were all retired or gone. We hadn't had a war like those two wars in some time. So we experienced a lot of anticipation in just how the situation would develop.

We left San Francisco in January 1966 and stopped in Hawaii for a few days. We then arrived in Vietnam on the 16th of February. The ship was just offshore. We operated just offshore from Danang all the way north to the DMZ. We primarily supported the Marines in I Corps, but, of course, other units were operating in that region, including the Seabees, some Army units, and some South Korean and Australian troops.

As luck would have it, our first patient received aboard was a young Marine with a blast injury to his face and neck. As with 90 to 95 percent of all our patients, he arrived by helicopter. A mine had exploded taking out one of his eyes and completely filling his face with fragments. We got him within less than an hour after he had been injured, and he became my very first patient.

I was very concerned about his ability to breathe, especially with a blast injury to the neck. Because swelling had already occurred, I decided to go ahead and do a tracheostomy to make certain he could breathe properly. We then put him to sleep and I spent several hours just scrubbing and picking metal out of this young man's face and taking care of his lacerations. Because of his eye injury, the ophthalmologist also evaluated him, after which he had to remove his left eye. Fortunately, the patient had no fractures and, with the exception of the loss of his eye, he turned out just fine.

I recall another patient very well, a Marine by the name of Talley. His unit had been overrun by the North Vietnamese. When they slipped into his camp, Talley was in his tent asleep. He told me the flap of his tent was opened and a man stood over him with an automatic weapon and shot him twice through the face. The bullets took out both eyes and destroyed much of his face. He was seen almost immediately by a Navy corpsman, who treated his injuries and opened up his airway.

When the man arrived aboard the ship, his whole midface was just a bag of bones and he had lost both eyes. He was a very challenging case, and the surgery probably took several hours. I had to put him in a head frame and rig up traction devices to support his face while he healed. Again, except for loss of sight, he left the ship and healed well.

We had a unique team aboard *Repose* with almost every medical specialty represented. Capt. Theodore Wilson, the senior surgeon aboard, was the triage officer. He saw every patient who came into Triage. With his vast experience, he was able to make a rapid determination of their injuries. Then he would contact all of us who would be involved in treating that patient. Lt. Cmdr. Bill Stewart, a reserve officer, was our neurosurgeon and he was excellent. We also had an orthopedic surgeon and three general surgeons. Our ophthalmologist, Lt. Frank Hoffer, was also a reserve officer. In addition, we had two anesthesiologists plus a nurse anesthetist. She was one of our 29 nurses assigned to the ship. Other physicians included an internist, a psychiatrist, a urologist, a pathologist, and a radiologist. So we had all the specialties represented, but, initially, a plastic surgeon and an ENT were not assigned.

Our face, head, and neck team consisted of myself, the neurosurgeon, and the ophthalmologist. This team worked on every patient with a head, face, or neck injury. If a patient had multiple injuries, the whole team worked on him at the same time. Almost every patient who had been injured by missiles had abdominal, orthopedic, and facial injuries. Some even had brain injuries. So management became more or less routine. Once patients were evaluated, diagnosed, and put to sleep, all their injuries were attended to as long as they remained stable under anesthesia. When they came out of anesthesia, they had been treated to the best extent possible. You didn't hear, "We'll take care of the abdominal injury now, and then tomorrow we'll work on the other orthopedic or facial injuries." This was the ideal situation on a hospital ship because we lived on it and were available 24 hours a day. We just worked as long as necessary. Even when we were inundated with casualties, we'd operate as long as necessary. I remember one period when the whole ship was involved for about 72 hours. We took short naps between surgical procedures.

Our very excellent ICU was headed by Lt. Cmdr. Arthur McFee, and he was just outstanding. When we finished operating on a patient—and we might have a lineup of four or five patients—we didn't have to worry because Dr. McFee and his crew in ICU took over until we could find time to see the patient again.

We kept patients aboard until they were completely stable. Our rule of thumb was that if they could go 24 to 48 hours without any treatment, we could evacuate them, usually to Danang. They would be held in Danang in a holding area until they could be flown out. The problem was that sometimes the planes were late and the patients might remain in Danang for 24 hours or longer.

We put most of my patients in maxillo-mandibular fixation—the jaws immobilized and

A pilot's-eye view of USS *Repose*'s flight deck (BUMED Archives).

the teeth wired together. Naturally, they needed help in feeding. We were so concerned about this that when the ship headed back to Subic Bay, Bill Stewart, the neurosurgeon, and I decided to go to Danang with a group of our patients who were being evacuated. We wanted to see exactly what type of care they could expect to receive. We got to Danang by helicopter with our patients, and went to a tent holding area right near the airstrip. It was hot—about 110 degrees—and almost unbearable. As luck would have it, a hurricane hit. The flight that was due to take them to Clark Field for further evacuation back to Hawaii and the U.S. was canceled. So we were at Danang for almost two days. Finally, they had to take our patients to Okinawa for evacuation back to the States. That's when we developed our rule of thumb that patients should be stable enough that they could go 24 to 48 hours with just minimal care.

I left *Repose* in February 1967, and was the last of the original medical-dental staff to leave because they had held me longer. We had to have an onboard replacement and I couldn't leave until he arrived. I was finally released from the ship when we got back to Subic.

I've continued to be involved with the medical-dental profession since then. I've stated repeatedly that our patients got the best care that could be had—even now. When I go to the emergency room now, I see people sitting in that room for hours. No one was managed like that on the hospital ship. They were seen immediately and taken care of. I think we had the best system. When someone came in with an injury or with an acute illness, he was seen immediately by a group of people who had become experts in their areas. When you go to an emergency room today, the interns see you first, then one of the residents, and then the chief resident. Then, finally, an attending physician on call might see you. We didn't have that intermediate chain of command. Our patients were seen immediately by people who were very experienced, and that accounts for the good results we had.

Of our patients who arrived aboard alive, we had less than a 1 percent death rate. And that's almost unheard of. I think those are the best statistics for war casualties that had been achieved up to then.

During that time, we had 4,927 patients, and roughly 2,000 of those were severely injured combat casualties. We performed more than 2,000 surgical procedures; 1,600 were classified as "major." We administered 3,067 pints of blood during emergency lifesaving procedures.

We could keep a patient aboard if we thought he was going to be okay. I believe Gen. Lew Walt was the Marine commander at that time. As a typical Marine he said, "If these Marines are gonna be all right and ready to go back to duty in 30 days, you keep them aboard that ship because we want them back in Vietnam." More than two-thirds of all patients we received were returned to duty. That's probably a record.

We also provided 6,200 outpatient and consultation visits to the other armed forces plus the Vietnamese population. A large number of Vietnamese were brought to the ship during times when we were not extremely busy, and we would care for them. I saw patients with cleft palates, cleft lips, and tumors, some of which were completely inoperable because they were so horrendous. Yes, we took care of many Vietnamese civilians, too.

Lt. (j.g.) Kathleen Glover holds a Vietnamese child aboard USS *Repose*. During lulls in combat operations, medical personnel on hospital ships turned their attention to sick and injured Vietnamese civilians (BUMED Archives).

The Odor of Mud

Mary Lee Sulkowski joined the Nurse Corps at Niagara University as part of the Navy's Nurse Corps candidate program. She went on active duty in 1963. Her first assignment was to Naval Hospital Jacksonville. A year later Vietnam "was becoming an issue," she recalls, and shortly thereafter, when she learned the Navy was about to recommission a hospital ship, she volunteered for duty and was assigned to USS Repose.

I received orders and reported at Hunter's Point in November of 1965. We had about 15 in our group. The Chief Nurse was Angie Vitello, a very seasoned nurse. I don't know whether or not she had ever served aboard a hospital ship, but she certainly had a lot of experience in the Navy Nurse Corps. Most of us didn't know what to expect because we hadn't served in a war zone before aboard a ship. We strategized and talked about how we would adapt what we had learned stateside to the conditions we were going to encounter off the coast of Vietnam.

We sailed under the Golden Gate Bridge on January 2nd, 1966, then made a stop in Hawaii on the way over. After a layover in the Philippines, we finally arrived on station in February. We took a few patients and then had to go into Subic Bay for about three weeks because the ship had engine problems. It was a slow start but once we got back on station, we began taking a lot of patients.

I couldn't believe that I had gotten the assignment because so few nurses got duty aboard hospital ships. I felt that that's why I joined the Navy. I had read stories about Army and Navy nurses when I was a little girl, and part of the adventure was serving in a war zone. It seemed, at the time, very exciting and quite an adventure.

But you saw another side to serving in a war zone. It really didn't hit you till later. It was something you could never really prepare for.

I think part of it was being young myself and taking care of young men who were even younger than I was. The average age of the soldier, sailor, or Marine who served in Vietnam was 17, 18, 19. It was a shock, all of a sudden, to be confronted with serious life-threatening injuries and illnesses and being in a position of being responsible for giving the best care.

I've heard it said that the Vietnam War was actually two wars. The first part was before 1968. That year and the following year — 1969 — the war became a much different issue as the disillusionment and the reality of Vietnam set in. In 1965 and 1966, we were still very idealistic as to why we were there.

One of my strongest impressions of that duty was how concerned the young patients were about each other. We'd get a rush of patients — 30 patients on a unit at a time. They would tell me: "Take care of him, he's in worse shape than I am." Or I would hear: "Do you know what happened to my buddy? Did he make it aboard?" These questions have stayed with me the longest.

I don't have a good memory for details, but I do remember impressions and feelings. At times it was almost boring when we had a lull and we weren't taking on new patients. It would become very routine, and people were hopefully getting better. And then when an operation suddenly began ashore, the situation would change completely in a moment and we began receiving casualties. It could go from a lull to being incredibly busy.

Because the casualties arrived on the unit in their fatigues and boots just as they were medevaced from the field, they gave off a peculiar odor. It was the mud. God only knew when those fatigues had last been washed.

We had to go through the uniforms pretty quickly to make sure they didn't have any weapons, particularly grenades in the pockets. Then we'd line the boots up outside the ward in the hallways. It was a real sign of how many casualties our ward had taken that day because suddenly 30 muddy combat boots were lined up reeking of Vietnam mud.

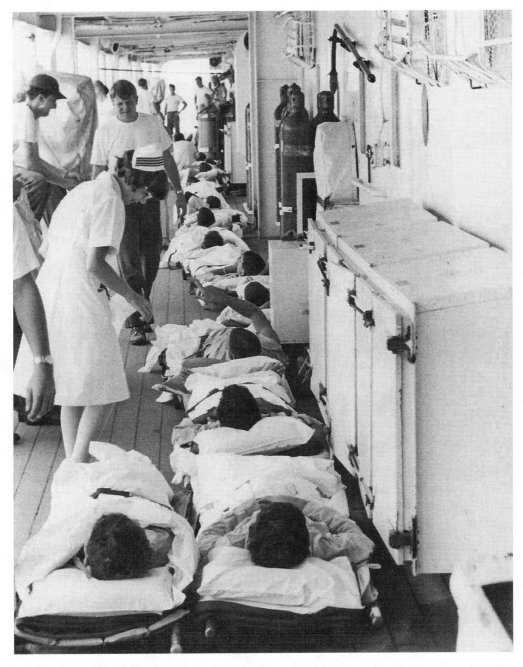

Recently arrived casualties on the deck of USS *Sanctuary* receive the attention of a Navy nurse (BUMED Archives).

I worked for most of the time on C-3, a large surgical unit that could accommodate 60 or 70 patients in triple tiers of bunks. The most serious were placed on the lower bunk. It was a sign that a patient was getting better if he went up a bunk. By the time he could hop up to the third bunk, he was doing pretty well.

We might be scheduled for an eight-hour shift but if the casualties were coming in, we'd just keep working. I recall some 12-hour shifts. People would come back after a couple of hours of sleep and start working again as the need existed. I think personal politics, which can sometimes interfere in a working situation, were probably negated in this situation because I so much appreciated people who were generous enough to give of themselves and keep working.

When the patients first came aboard the *Repose*, it was a relief for them to get out of the war zone and to be in a clean white hospital. Not only was the outside of the ship white, but we had white bed linens, nurses in white starched uniforms, air conditioning, ice cream — all the perks of getting aboard a hospital ship, let alone the medical care. Their faces said it all.

When I left the ship after 11 months, it was a very emotional time. I was one of the first nurses to leave. I got orders for recruiting duty in October 1966 and flew off the ship to Chu Lai. I then flew to Danang with some of the men who had been my patients aboard the *Repose* and were now going back to duty in Vietnam. If you could be rehabbed within 30 days, you went back to your unit. So I was leaving and they were going back into combat. And I had been in Vietnam long enough to know what they were going back to. One of the saddest memories I have is seeing their faces. They knew what they were headed for, and they also knew that they might not make it back again.

"Take Care of My Buddy First"

Frances Shea attended nursing school at St. Joseph College in West Hartford, Connecticut. Following graduation, she worked at New York Hospital, and then joined the Navy when the Korean War broke out in 1950. Honing her skills at Naval Hospital Portsmouth, Virginia, her first assignment, she soon considered herself an OR nurse.

Shea left the Navy in 1954, but stayed in the Naval Reserve while doing post-graduate work in operating technique and management. With a master's degree now under her belt, she went back on active duty in 1960, and was assigned to Naval Hospital St. Albans, New York, where she remained for two years. From St. Albans, Shea was sent on recruiting duty, her territory being Virginia, Kentucky, and portions of Indiana and North Carolina. In April 1968, she headed to Vietnam.

You didn't have a choice. We used to have a recruiters' meeting every year wherever the American Nurse Association's convention was being held. At that time the head of recruiting was Betty Murray. Those of us who had a date to rotate out of recruiting were all lined up outside a little room at the hotel that she was using as an office.

Betty Murray had a really funny voice, and you could hear what she was saying to everybody else in that room. The nurse ahead of me said she really would like to attend graduate school in Boston since she was currently recruiting in Boston. And Murray responded, "Danang will be fine."

So when it was my turn, she asked, "Miss Shea, where would you like to go?"

I said, "I'd like to go to Vietnam."

And she said, "Would you like the hospital ship? The *Repose* will be fine." She didn't say "*Repose*" or "*Sanctuary*" or "*Danang*" — I had no choice. "You're going to the *Repose*." And because I was an OR nurse, that's what I had — the operating room. So everyone who was on recruiting duty then was immediately sent to Vietnam.

I remember arriving in Danang. It was warm and filthy. The airport was just loaded with people lying all over the place. Some were GIs who were going back to the States. Others were waiting to be picked up for wherever they were going or whatever outfit they were going to. Someone told me I had to go to one of the desks and check in. I said, "I'm going to the *Repose*."

"Oh, you're lucky, she's in port."

I thought, "Oh, that's nice. I'll just get a ride down there and go onboard." But it wasn't that way at all.

I was sitting next to someone who said, "What you have to do is go out and hail a cab — hail a taxi."

I was thinking, "What kind of war is this? They have taxis?"

A truck pulled up and the driver said I owed him for a ride. I said, "I'm waiting for a taxi." And he replied, "I'm it."

I got into the truck and noticed a weapon on the seat where I was sitting. I thought, "This isn't very safe." Then he took me down to the pier. That's where the ship was supposed to be but it was out some distance. In fact, it was a 45-minute ride by launch.

It was the most beautiful ship — all white with that big red cross. It was fantastic! In those days, we wore our uniform with the bucket cap and high heels. I asked, "How am I going to climb up there?"

And someone replied, "Well, you've got to climb up that ladder."

I said, "I can't do that. They'll have to put a cargo net over or something."

He said, "Yes you can!"

The ship was at anchor but rolling, and I thought, "Oh my God; I'm gonna die before I get up there."

The first week they had me working on a ward. The OR supervisor had not left and we had no time for orientation. So the supervisor put me on a ward with the malaria patients. We had a lot of malaria and jungle rot [military jargon for jungle foot infection]. We probably had more medical cases than wounded casualties. I worked on that ward for maybe two weeks. Then I went down to the OR.

I thought it was the best experience that I could ever have because I never saw so many people work together so much. And I don't mean just the nurses and the doctors. My attitude about doctors changed because we were more of a team. They were dependent on you just as you depended on them. It wasn't that they saw you on the ward, walked off, and didn't see you again. They had to see you for breakfast, lunch, and dinner. So if you were going to have any disagreements, you had better get them settled because you were going to be with them all the time.

My day began when I went down the back ladder to the galley and picked up a cup of coffee and a roll and went downstairs to the OR. First of all, we had several categories for patients. We had the casualties, obviously. We had elective surgeries, such as hernia repairs or procedures like that.

We had the children — Vietnamese children — that either were wounded or needed reconstructive surgery, such as a cleft palate or harelip. Then there was the enemy — the Viet Cong. If someone tells you that patients weren't categorized according to who they were, they are not telling you the truth. We tried to take our American casualties first. But if it was a child, the child had to go first.

When I was running the OR, the Viet Cong came last and the Americans came first. I felt Americans shouldn't have to wait. If we didn't have any casualties, we did reconstructive surgery. So the ORs were always going — they were always active.

We also categorized patients when they came in. Now this sounds hard, but usually we tried to do our chest or abdominal cases first. And then, depending on the situation, we did our heads — our "crannies" — last because they had the least chance of survival. But what did we do with a patient who was a crannie and had an abdominal wound and an amputation all at the same time? We worked three teams. The fact that he was a crannie did not hold him back. We got him into the OR right away.

We did a lot of surgery and rarely closed the incision, but left it packed open because every case was contaminated. We didn't have any non-contaminated case because of the dirt and the weapons that were used. Sometimes the Viet Cong would pack their mortars with feces.

It was a busy, busy time and we did a lot of surgery. I think the *Repose* did over 5,000 surgeries the entire time she was out there. I know that we did 2,000 while I was aboard because for every thousandth case, the patient got a cake. On that occasion, the orthopedic surgeon came running down and said, "Hey, I've got your two thousandth case! He's a clean through-and-through in the chest."

The patient was a 19-year-old black kid. We gave him his cake and talked to him. He said, "Nobody ever had a cake for me before in my life."

I thought, "You poor kid. You had to get shot to have a cake." You remember things like that.

A gunnery sergeant arrived on the ship in March or early April [1968] from Khe Sanh, wounded through the chest. His name was Charles Perkins. He had a clean through-and-through but his color wasn't good and we had him sitting up. As he was getting ready to go into the OR he said, "How does it look, nurse?"

I said, "Hey, Gunny, it looks like a clean through-and-through and you ought to be okay."

Well, I was wrong. It was a clean through-and-through in the pancreas, through the gall bladder, through the liver. It missed the vena cava by a centimeter. The surgeons had to remove his spleen. He came back to the operating room 11 times before he died. He bled out. Everybody on the ship knew him and everybody remembers him. It was just terrible.

The skipper of the hospital aboard the *Repose* at that time was Capt. [Herbert] Markowitz, who was an orthopedic surgeon. He had been a Japanese POW during World War II. He was truly driven. Nobody got turned away. We would be working until 3 or 4 in the morning after 18 or 19 hours and he'd then come down to the OR and say, "Can I call in the choppers?" You might as well say yes because he was going to do it anyway.

One time we received a 19- or 20-year-old Marine. Everything from the hips down was gone—bladder gone, everything. But he was alive. Since his spinal cord was severed, he didn't feel anything and didn't know it. He was brought in but the surgeons didn't know what they were going to do. Nobody wanted to do that case because they knew he was going to die. Markowitz said, "I'm doing him. Nobody else is doing him."

I always respected him for that. Markowitz took the worst case, knowing that he had no chance of saving him. Yet he worked to try and save him. With what skin flaps were left, they literally diapered the patient, but he died a half hour after we got him off the table. As hopeless as the case was, he wanted that young man to at least have an opportunity to live. I respected him for that and for everything else he did, too. For him, patients came first. Capt. Markowitz met every single helicopter that came in.

The heartbreaking part was not just that these patients were so young, but they were so brave. What they said would break your heart: "Nurse, take care of my buddy first." Here he was bleeding to death and he was telling you to take care of the guy in the next rack. It was just heartbreaking. This tremendous concern for other people is what was so hard to take. It would have been easier to take it if they were mad at the Viet Cong and mad at all that had happened to them.

My corpsmen were 18 or 19 years old themselves. One, who was 21, was the old man. These young men might have had four hours of sleep, and I had to get them up for a case. And when I did, I said I was sorry I had to get them up. And they would say, "It's okay, it's okay. They didn't ask to get hit."

How did we deal with all this? How did we handle the stress? We buried it, but it came out later on. It was just like it was another day and you didn't pay any attention to it. You didn't cry. You didn't do anything. You just buried it.

A wounded Marine is offloaded on the deck of USS *Repose* (BUMED Archives).

A Tough Fight to Stay Alive

Miki Iwata was born in California but spent her toddler years living in a Japanese-American relocation camp in Poston, Arizona. When World War II ended in 1945, she and her family moved to southern New Jersey. "We went to a town called Seabrook. Seabrook Farms was a large frozen food packing company that was hiring people for their frozen food plants. About 10,000 Japanese went to Seabrook to find jobs and that's where we moved and where I was raised."

Iwata decided on nursing as a career in high school. "We all wanted to go to college or some kind of school, so nursing was the only possibility because of the scholarships."

After attending nursing school at Presbyterian Hospital in Philadelphia, she joined the Navy and was assigned to Naval Hospital Portsmouth, Virginia. But what she really wanted was an assignment aboard a hospital ship. "You can't go on a hospital ship unless you have some stateside duty," her detailer informed her. After a year at Portsmouth, she learned that nurses were being sought to staff one of the two vessels that would serve in Vietnam.

Six of us from Philadelphia who were at Portsmouth volunteered. One went to the USS *Repose*. I went to the USS *Sanctuary*. The four others served their two years and got out. We wanted to help our country, but we also thought it was unusual duty and would be a good experience. We flew from Travis Air Force Base in California and met the *Sanctuary* in Danang.

I reported with another nurse, Valerie Vitulli Newman. We were put in the SOQ [sick officers' quarters] because the nurses' quarters didn't have enough room. We had relieved somebody and they hadn't yet left. We didn't have hot water in the SOQ so we were taking ice-cold showers. The plumbing wasn't quite up to snuff either. When you flushed the toilet, it wouldn't flush. But we knew we were in a war zone and it wasn't going to be perfect.

At supper, when we told the rest of the nurses about our cold showers, one asked, "Why are you doing that? We've got hot water on the ship." It just so happened that the pipes in that particular room didn't have hot water.

Initially, I was on the medical ward and took care of malaria patients—large numbers of malaria patients. When they medevaced people to the ship, they didn't medevac one or two. They medevaced 50 or 100 either in boats or by helo. When we admitted patients, we had to have the capacity to admit them or discharge them quickly.

The beds were not cold for very long. They were warm beds because patients had just occupied them. In other words, if you had just come in and were very sick, you'd get the bottom rack. Then if you got better or somebody came who was sicker than you, you went to the next level. The racks were four high. If you were up on the fourth level, that was pretty high, and you had to be pretty well to get up to that level. If you were too good, you were off the ship.

The malaria patients ran very high fevers, and our job was to give them their malaria medication. When we gave that medication to a large number of people, we had to be organized and the patients had to be identified properly.

After six months on the malaria ward, I worked the next six months in the intensive care unit and that was quite an experience. We got patients with multiple injuries—head injuries, orthopedic surgical problems—all in one. We had cranial injuries, broken arms, gunshot wounds, and belly wounds. They might have big holes in their backs or their buttocks or both. These wounds had to be packed, cleaned, and dressed. It was labor-intensive and took a lot of people to care for one patient.

I recall several of my patients. In fact, I have difficulty going to the Vietnam Wall because I see their names and remember what a tough fight they had in order to stay alive. We never knew what happened to the patients who left the ship. When I went to Washington for the dedication of the Vietnam Women's Memorial in November 1993, a lot of those patients came and thanked us. That was very special.

"Into the Unknown"

Juel Loughney came from a Navy family. Her father served in World War I, and her youngest brother would join the Navy in 1966, the same year she did. Becoming a nurse was part of her earliest memories. "A nurse lived right across from us. I think she was in the Navy reserve because every once in a while I'd see her in her Navy uniform and I'd say, 'Someday that's going to be me.'"

She attended nursing school right out of high school, worked at Pittston Hospital near her home in Pennsylvania for the next 10 years, and then received a bachelor of science degree before joining the Navy. Following officer indoctrination at Newport, Rhode Island, she was assigned to Naval Hospital Annapolis, Maryland. In 1968, the young nurse received orders to USS Sanctuary *and soon was on her way to Vietnam.*

It was at Norton [Air Force Base] that I met three other Navy nurses who were also going to the *Sanctuary*. I had never met them before, but we became fast friends because we were the only females aboard a plane with about 250 soldiers, Marines, and sailors.

We flew to Hawaii, then to Okinawa, and then directly to Danang. From the time we left Okinawa, you could hear a pin drop on that plane. I don't think anyone said a word. Once we hit Danang, we were told to stay in our seats until we were given further instructions. As we looked out the window, we saw hundreds of our service people lined up in an enclosed area waiting to go home. It almost looked like they were cattle. When we got off the plane, we heard a big cheer from those kids. It was very intimidating, though. Here we were going into the unknown.

When we arrived at NSA [Naval Support Activity], they bedded us down in a Quonset hut. Sometime in the middle of the night, the VC began to shell the helicopter base right across from the Navy hospital. The rockets or shells went over the hospital, but every once in a while one would fall short and hit the hospital compound. It was my first experience hearing missiles going overhead. One of the nurses came in to assure us that all we had to do was get under our beds. The staff had placed flak jackets and helmets under the beds and we had to put them on.

So there I was about 2 or 3 in the morning thinking, "What in the world is a little girl like you from Pittston, Pennsylvania, doing here under this bed in the middle of a war?" It was an awakening.

The shelling went on for quite a while. The next morning, the *Sanctuary* arrived in Danang Harbor so we were finally able to be taken out to the ship. And that's when our year began.

I was just speechless when I saw that white ship with big red crosses on it. All of us were junior people—ensigns, a few jaygees, with the majority of us lieutenants. I was a lieutenant. Our chief nurse, Pat Hurst, was a commander, and her specialty was anesthesia. Her skills came in handy when they needed extra "gas-passers," as we called them. Sometimes casualties arrived in groups, and we'd run out of the anesthesia docs so she was very vital as part of the nursing staff.

I worked in "Medicine," which was on the C deck, for six months. The next six months I spent in the Intensive Care Unit. And that was it. I didn't go to any of the other wards other than for relief here or there.

It probably was the most stimulating and satisfying year of my whole life in nursing because so many of the kids we cared for were wounded and sick. Many we could not save. But if we were not there, many would not have made it home. It was a great feeling knowing that every single day we did something for somebody and made him feel better.

A typical day began when I got up and went to breakfast. The officers' dining room was separate from the enlisted mess. We were all assigned a seat for lunch. At dinner, we were seated according to rank. But for breakfast you could sit anywhere. Our food was not bad—not bad at all.

Then we went to our stations and worked however long it would take to care for our patients. Some days it was 10 hours; other days it was even longer. Many times we were too busy to get up to lunch. Often we were lucky if we could get up for supper. Many of us were working 12-hour shifts all the time, and the people working nights did not want to get up in the middle of the afternoon to dress and go to the dining room for a meal. So we asked for a big supply of peanut butter, jelly, and bread, which we kept in a small refrigerator in the nurses' quarters. Many times that was our only meal.

In September 1968, we had a change of command, as far as our CO of the hospital was concerned. Capt. [Willard] Arentzen came as the commanding officer of the hospital. I had known him as Chief of Medicine at Annapolis. When I received orders to go to Vietnam, he got his orders shortly after I did. He said, "I want you to write to me and tell me how it's going." So when he got there, he made a lot of changes. We had been working 16 hours a day. It was supposed to be 12, but most of the time it was 16. Once Capt. Arentzen arrived, he interviewed each one of us and asked what he could do to make the situation better. I think many of us said, "Take us off these 12- to 16-hour shifts." If we were needed, we were there anyway. After that, we never were assigned 12-hour shifts. We probably worked just as hard, but I thought he was very good—very human—and I was thankful when he arrived.

We saw some competition between the two hospital ships—the *Repose* and the *Sanctuary,* and also with NSA Danang. One day Capt. Arentzen called me into his stateroom. He said, "Juel,

I don't like the idea that there's animosity or competition going on among the two ships and NSA. I'm going to send you to NSA for a couple of weeks. I know they don't want you over there, but if you have to bend over backwards to please them, that's what you're going to do."

Well, I shipped over to Danang for about two or three weeks in exchange for an NSA nurse coming to the ship to replace me. That was a great eye-opener once I got to NSA. It was almost a treat for me to come off a ship where you were on top of everybody. At NSA, I had my own room in one of the Quonset huts. It was almost like being on an R&R as far as the location. Right across from the nurses' quarters was the officers' club. If I weren't on duty, I could go there. Every once in a while, I could have someone drive me to what was called "Freedom Hill." It was just one huge exchange, and it was a luxury to go there and look around. We were also able to get to China Beach. Anyway, it was a different experience for me being there for those three weeks.

We worked very hard. Our patient load was just as heavy at NSAH as it was on the hospital ship, but the living conditions made it so much easier. But then I was happy to go "home" again. By that time, it felt like the ship was home after I had been on it for so long.

When I got back, Capt. Arentzen asked me to write what I thought about the experience at NSAH. I told him that even though we had the danger of rocket attacks, I felt it was just a little easier on the nerves when you had your own space instead of being cooped up all the time on a small ship.

Besides our own patients, we also treated a lot of Vietnamese children who would go out, get guns, and kill Marines and soldiers. And then when they were injured, they were brought to us. Some were only 10 or 12 years old, and they arrived with massive wounds. Many we saved. Many we lost.

I even recall a Viet Cong patient we were caring for in an isolation room on the medical ward because he had TB plus major wounds. This man's most valued possession was a *Playboy* magazine. He would look at it and any time a nurse or corpsman came into his room, he'd hide it under his leg. He had a Marine guard because you didn't know what the Marine patients would do if they learned we had VC right down the hall. He finally died. Even though he was beyond help, we took good care of him.

Of course, we had many, many patients a few I remember very well — especially one. Rusty [Donald E. Sizemore] was a young Marine under my charge in the Intensive Care Unit. Rusty had multiple wounds, one of which was a gunshot wound through his pancreas. When he came aboard he weighed about 180 pounds. He remained in ICU for several months because we could never get him stabilized. Every time we got him to a point where we thought we could medevac him, he'd start bleeding again. I spent hours with him and felt so sorry for him. It was always, "Lt. Loughney, is it time for my pain medication yet?" I just wanted to cry with him each time he asked me that question. He always wanted to talk about going home to Florida and going fishing.

A general came frequently to give Purple Hearts, and he went to Rusty's bed. Rusty stiffened up in his bed like he was going to salute.

I became very close to him, and every time I went to the Vietnam Wall, I always had to touch his name on the Wall.

Another Marine was Charlie Rose. He was a triple amputee with only his left arm remaining. When he received his Purple Heart, he wanted to sit up in bed. The general said, "Let me help you sit up, son."

And the young man responded, "No, sir, this is all I have left and I have to learn how to use it." Talk about tears. It was a most emotional experience for those of us who witnessed it.

One afternoon, when I was in charge of the afternoon shift, I met Billy Graham, who was probably six-three. He was standing right next to our CO, Capt. Arentzen, who was all of five-six. Capt. Arentzen said, "Lt. Loughney, this is Dr. Billy Graham. If it's possible, he would like to visit your patients in ICU and pray over them."

So I led them into the ward and we went from patient to patient. He said a prayer and talked to each of those young people. It was startling to look into the eyes of that holy man. I thought I was in the presence of greatness. We had 15 beds in ICU and they were always filled. We stopped at all 15 patients' beds.

Another patient, a Lt. Clark, was a Navy pilot who had multiple injuries and had just become a father shortly after he was wounded. One of the nurses must have found a picture of his baby son in his wallet. We fastened it to one of the pipes so that he could see it, but he never regained consciousness. When Billy Graham got to him, he put his hand on the young man's head and said, "I wish the likes of President Nixon could take a look at this young man. What are we doing to our kids?"

Another patient was a southern kid named Buford. He was a quad, and couldn't move anything. The only thing he could do to get our attention was to put his lips together to make sounds. But Buford died suddenly of cardiac arrest. The images of these young Marines will be with me forever.

10

HOLOCAUST ON
YANKEE STATION

Fire has always been a ship's worst enemy, no less so in a modern navy than during the age of sail. When vessels were built of wood, almost everything aboard was combustible. A misused candle or an overturned lantern often began a chain of unfortunate events that claimed the lives of many a vessel and its crew. With no place to go, sailors had little choice but to fight the flames or perish.

Steel fighting ships added a unique list of volatile and explosive ingredients: diesel fuel, lubricants, solvents, shells, missiles, and other ordnance. Aircraft carriers provided additional hazards—JP-5 fuel to feed its hungry aircraft plus bombs and rockets to be slung beneath their wings.

When the air war against North Vietnam commenced following the Tonkin Gulf incident in the summer of 1964, U.S. carriers began operating in an area of the South China Sea soon to be called "Yankee Station." Some of the most frenetic and dangerous places to work were on the decks of such warships as Constellation *(CVA-64),* Franklin D. Roosevelt *(CVA-42),* Bon Homme Richard *CVA-31),* Oriskany *(CVA-34), and* Forrestal *(CVA-59). Young men in the prime of their lives fueled and armed aircraft, then jockeyed them into position for launch from one of the vessel's catapults. And when the missions were over, the planes and crewmen—who had survived North Vietnamese anti-aircraft missiles and gunfire—returned to the mother ship, trapped by arresting cables stretched across the deck and brought to a sudden stop.*

This routine ground on day after day and year after year, the activity waxing and waning with the war's tempo. The general calmness of the seas in the near tropical environment belied the fact that sudden tragedy could strike at any moment.

On 26 October 1966, as crewmen of USS Oriskany *were loading magnesium parachute flares into the forward flare locker in Hangar Bay 1, one deck beneath the flight deck, a flare accidentally ignited. A panicked sailor threw the burning flare into the locker, setting off other flares stacked within. The resulting blaze, fueled by burning magnesium, soon reached temperatures of 5,000 degrees and higher. The flames raced through five decks, claiming the lives of 44 men, many from the inhalation of toxic smoke. Through an unfortunate set of circumstances, many of these victims were combat pilots who had just returned from raids over North Vietnam and were resting in their quarters.*

Nine months later, a far more serious catastrophe befell USS Forrestal, *just days after she had arrived on Yankee Station and began flight operations. Shortly before 11 A.M. on 29 July 1967, crewmen were readying aircraft for the second launch of the day. Without warning, a Zuni rocket, which was mounted on an F-4 Phantom parked aft on the flight deck's starboard side, fired accidentally. The errant missile streaked across the deck taking off the arm and shoulder of a sailor before being deflected into the 400-gallon belly fuel tank of an A-4D Skyhawk parked on the port side. The Skyhawk's fuel tank ruptured, spewing JP-5 fuel onto the deck. In an instant, the highly refined kerosene ignited, spreading flames over the flight deck and trapping many of the pilots in their planes.*

The intense heat of the fire, now a blazing inferno spread by the wind, engulfed the flight deck aft, causing bombs to explode and rockets to ignite. The sailor's worst nightmare had come to pass with a vengeance.

As explosions rocked the ship, huge holes were torn in her deck, allowing burning fuel to pour through and turn the berthing spaces immediately below into death traps. Fifty crewmen succumbed almost instantly. Other men fighting the flames topside were blown overboard by the explosions.

The following accounts of the conflagration on Forrestal *and its devastating aftermath are told from four perspectives: a crewman wounded by the explosions, a physician suddenly inundated by critically injured patients, a medical administrator, and a flight surgeon-pilot aboard an adjacent carrier.*

"We Have Lost 134 of Our Brothers"

AO3 Paul Friedman was an airman specializing in aviation ordnance when he reported aboard Forrestal. *It was his first assignment. "I was just awed by how big it was. It was a proud ship with a proud crew."*

I was sleeping on the second deck, the deck right below the hangar bay. That's where most of the ship's activity was and where the mess decks were. At that time, my berthing compartment was back by the fantail in the middle of the ship.

I didn't hear the bombs going off. I didn't hear "General Quarters!" I didn't hear the first alarm, which was "Fire! Fire!" Fires happen on the carrier all the time. That's the way it was. And they were usually small fires that were quickly put out. But now we heard "Fire! Fire!" Immediately after that the GQ went off. Seconds later the first bomb exploded, but I didn't hear that and a lot of guys didn't hear it either. I was awakened by the second or third bomb blast and noticed that I had a wound. I think one of the bomb fragments came all the way down to where I was sleeping. The bulkhead next to me was cracked and I saw flames. If I had been sleeping at the other end of the bed, the shrapnel would have hit me in the head. So, in a way, it was the million-dollar wound.

One of the guys was standing next to my rack checking to see if I was all right. I noticed a red hole in the sole of my foot, right by the instep. I couldn't walk on it so I had to hop. We both decided it was time to get the hell out of there. I hobbled to the port passageway where everybody else was headed. We were all trying to make our way forward — away from where the bombs were going off. I made it over to the port side and then another big explosion rocked the ship and went right down the stairway. I saw them carrying a shipmate with a head wound. By now everyone was in the passageway heading forward. And all this time I was hopping, trying to make my way forward. I must have been slowing everybody down because one of the guys grabbed me under my arm like a twig and supported me. I still had one foot on the ground but somehow he got me to sick bay.

I saw people burned and others lying around waiting for treatment. I thought I shouldn't be in sick bay because what I witnessed I never want to see again — people with burns all over their bodies. A guy sitting next to me named Howard had a compound fracture.

All I wanted was a battle dressing and a tetanus shot. That's how much I thought about my wound. I wasn't really in any pain and it wasn't bleeding. I just wanted to cover it up. I was worried about what my mom always used to tell me. "Be careful. You'll get blood poisoning."

The chief corpsman came over and asked if I wanted morphine. I said, "No, give it to Howard." He was the one with the compound fracture.

They also brought in a chief or a warrant officer who didn't look like he had a scratch on him. Nevertheless, the corpsman told the guys who brought him in, "We can't do anything for him." He was already dead.

For my wound, they gave me one of those big battle dressings. Then time went by as I listened to the bombs going off, praying that they'd be able to stop them. They were exploding for the first 5 or 10 minutes. I heard nine detonations.

Eventually, I was taken through the smoky sick bay up an elevator to one of the choppers. I later wrote a letter to my mom about the fire.

Friedman's letter to his mother reads as follows:

"We were taken to the carrier *Oriskany*, which was half a mile away. When we landed, I was the first one off. They put me on a stretcher and carried me across the flight deck. Crewmembers and press were taking pictures but later they were ordered to stop photographing the wounded.

"I was placed on a bomb elevator which took me and my shipmates down to sick bay. They placed me in a rack next to a shipmate who had burns to his arms and his face. He was on the flight deck when the accident occurred and had jumped off the flight deck to escape the fire and burns he was experiencing. I remember him saying that during that eighty-foot descent into the ocean, he had seen his whole life go by and hoped he wouldn't hit any debris in the water below. Luckily, he was picked up by one of our destroyer escorts. Either the *Rupertus*, the *Tucker*, or the *MacKenzie* came alongside to fight the fire and pull survivors out of the water.

"When I arrived around 3 P.M. the doctors had many bad burn cases to treat, so they didn't get around to me until 5 P.M. When they did, the doctors decided not to stitch my wound but leave it with an open dressing. They cut off some skin around the wound. The doctor gave me a shot of Demerol before treating me.

"Around 8 P.M. we found out that we would be flown off again, this time to the hospital ship *Repose*. So at 3 A.M. July 30th, I was helicoptered off to the *Repose*, where they x-rayed me and said I had shrapnel in my wound and that they would take care of me. I didn't know when I'd be getting off the ship. The *Forrestal* is in bad shape and might be heading for Subic Bay [Philippines] or the States. The damage and loss of life is catastrophic. We have lost 134 of our brothers."

Friedman and many of his injured shipmates received additional treatment aboard Repose. *His wound was cleaned further and penicillin administered twice a day to ward off infection. He was then evacuated back to the States for further convalescence at Naval Hospital St. Albans New York, which was located near his home.*

"Fire on the Flight Deck!"

Dr. Gary Kirchner was new to the Navy and had little knowledge of the sea. When he was assigned to the Atlantic Fleet's aircraft carrier USS Forrestal, *he relished the idea of cruising the placid Mediterranean, the 6th Fleet's standard domain. But that illusion was quickly dashed.*

"One evening, while eating in the ward room, the subject came up and I said, 'When are we going to the Mediterranean?' It's one of those comments you make at dinner. And suddenly everything got very quiet. I knew I had just said something that probably was not quite right. One man sitting close to me said, 'Look, Doc, we're not going to the Mediterranean.'

'Oh! Where are we going?' I asked.

'WESTPAC.' [Western Pacific]

'What is WESTPAC?'

'Have you ever heard of Vietnam?'"

Even before Forrestal *departed for the war zone for its first ever combat deployment, the ship's skipper, Capt. John Beling, briefed the young surgeon on his new role — getting the ship's medical department ready for sea and ensuring that its personnel passed the pre-deployment course.* "We were not in the honors program but we did, in fact, pass. When we sailed, I remember standing on one of the sponsons[1] with a flight surgeon and him saying to me, 'Well, it's Tuesday. Here goes a whole yearful of Tuesdays.'"

It was 25 July 1967 when the 79,000-ton Forrestal *and its complement of more than 5,000 officers and enlisted men arrived on Yankee Station in the Tonkin Gulf and prepared to launch air strikes against North Vietnam. Dr. Kirchner and his staff continued to carry out routine duties in sick bay located amidship on the carrier's second deck.*

Sick bay consisted of offices, pharmacy, various examining rooms, laboratory, and an emergency room-like facility that was really where sick call was held. Two very large open wards probably capable of about 50 people in each ward plus a small isolation ward off the one side. The single operating room was marginally equipped. Although we had an anesthesia machine looking like it came out of the Second World War, there was no one to give anesthesia. So it was a contradiction in terms. I'm not going to get into that because I chose not to do so while I was there. I didn't think it was my business to reform the Navy and especially to reform the worthiness of the operating room facilities aboard. It's one of those items on a list: anesthesia machine — check, operating room — check, but it by-passed important parts of the whole process.

H Division had about 65 staff members — an administrative officer, two chiefs, a bunch of first classes, some second classes, and some strikers[2] — all with different levels of knowledge and expertise — I would say just run-of-the-mill. The senior medical officer was a meek general practitioner who spent most of his time working out of our sight. I and two flight surgeons pretty much ran the deal.

I became as heavily involved as I could be in activities on the ship other than doing my job. I'm a very early riser so I would be up around 5. After messing around with some paperwork, one of the dental officers, the flight surgeons, and I would all go have breakfast. After we returned, we'd hold sick call.

Sick call would vary considerably. If it were during a port period, it was pretty heavy, maybe 30 or 40 guys. If it was routine at sea, it was not all that many. You had the usual minor types of injuries and the usual requests for light duty chits [excuses]. It wasn't complicated. If we had some minor surgery to do, I would do it at that time, right after sick call. But I limited the activity to that which was absolutely local anesthesia and nothing beyond that. I wasn't going to take out somebody's gall bladder at sea. The surgery was minor. The biggest request was, could I remove the girlfriend's name from a tattoo?

We were on station only four days and that fourth day was startling. It was the routine I just described that pretty much saved me because I was not up on deck. I was down in the sick bay, not watching air operations. That conflicted with sick call, and I was down where I belonged.

I was treating a sailor with a busted hand. He had been brought over from one of the destroyers. I was infiltrating the fracture site with Xylocaine in preparation to reducing the fracture when I heard the 1MC [public address system] announcement "Fire on the Flight Deck!" The announcements just kept escalating, starting with "Fire on the Flight Deck!" to "General Quarters!" as 1,000-pound bombs began going off on the flight deck.

I could really feel those explosions. The lights blinked, all the trash in the overhead came down, and the ship rocked. It was a thunderous noise. The flight deck was behind sick bay and we were below the hangar deck level and forward of that part of the flight deck that was being blown apart. But it's not like we were a half-mile away. We were very, very close, as close as I ever want to be to a 1,000-pound bomb.

We began seeing the results of what was happening almost immediately. The senior medical officer came to me in the middle of all this noise and said, "Well, Gary, you understand all this; I don't. If you need any help, I'll be in my cabin." I figured, what the hell. It's better that somebody admits he doesn't know how to handle a catastrophic situation rather than trying to fake it. And by him standing down and standing away, nobody questioned what I was doing.

We were immediately confronted with a whole raft of people. It was a classic mass casualty deal — and I had no training in that field. I understood — in a limited way — about triage.

USS *Forrestal* burns following the tragic accident on her flight deck, 29 July 1967 (BUMED Archives).

But it was not all that hard. I made rapid assessments of individuals and put them in one of three categories of triage. Those who had no chance of survival I placed in a special area in the sick bay. Corpsmen attended to those with minor injuries. And for those who needed skilled medical or surgical care, I put in the third category. I knew very well I had no chance in hell that I could handle this group of people definitively. My bias was to quickly stabilize them and quickly get them off the ship to a facility that could handle them.

The help came in airlifting them off the ship to a facility that could care for them. A friend of mine came over from the *Bon Homme Richard* and said, "Hey Gary, what can I do for you? It sure looks like a helluva mess here!"

I said, "Yes. It's time to get off this ship. Get back to your ship and let me send you patients. And if you've got a spare chopper that can transport, send it over." At that time, I had no good estimate of how many people I had. I just seemed to have a helluva lot. Subsequently, I decided that with all categories lumped together, I probably had 300 people who suffered injuries of varying degrees of severity.

Even though all hell was breaking loose topside, the flight deck forward of the island was available to take helicopters. The Jolly Green Giants [HH-3E rescue helicopters] from Danang came out to the ship. I took a casualty I wanted evacuated and put him with four litter-bearers and one corpsman. Hopefully this patient had an IV in place and some morphine had been administered. The assignment was to take the man up the ladder onto the hangar deck, over to the aircraft elevator, and up to the flight deck. They loaded him onto the chopper, and off they went to wherever the chopper decided to go, whether it was to the hospital ship, Danang, or to one of the other carriers operating in the area.

We had a complete range of injuries, but it's hard to know which were the most prevalent — burns, shrapnel wounds, and some traumatic orthopedic injuries like loss of limbs. Getting them stabilized was not a problem. We had enough IV setups and more than enough morphine. In fact, I didn't pay much attention to doses. Each syrette contained a quarter grain of morphine. I had no hesitation giving it until the desired effect was achieved. It had been my

Forrestal's crewmembers struggle to save their carrier (BUMED Archives).

game plan that if we were going to leave any patients behind, we would keep them really snowed with morphine.

Because of the fire and exploding ordnance, we had many burn victims but most of them were already dead — they were incinerated. They were trapped and incinerated. It wasn't like they suffered 30 percent body burns—first-, second-, and third-degree burns. These were people who were dead of massive burns. That's what killed the majority of the people.

And all the time, ordnance was going off almost sequentially. I don't know how many minutes the bombs and rockets were going off. It's one of those situations where your judgment of time is poor. We also knew about all the firefighting because people were running up and down the passageways. Some were rolling barrels of fog foam. We were very aware that something big was going on. You would have had to be dumb and blind not to have figured that out.

At one point word was passed around to prepare to abandon ship because the temperatures in the aft magazine were rising. If they rose to a critical level, the whole damn magazine might blow up. In retrospect, it's all ridiculous because had the temperature rose to that level, and, in fact, exceeded that level, and the magazine did blow, nothing would have been left of anybody — and nothing would have been left of that ship. There would have been a gigantic hole in the ocean. We carried incredible amounts of munitions, including, I was led to believe, nuclear weapons.

In the middle of all the activity, a corpsman came by wearing a life jacket. I didn't think that was a good idea. I said, "Put your life jacket where you can find it but don't put it on. If a sailor who has a significant injury sees you in a life vest, he's gonna figure it out." So I told everyone not to wear their life vests. I never even found mine and never went to look for it. I had other problems on my mind. I thought, "We're in tropical waters. If we abandon ship, the water's warm." This is crazy thinking, but you do crazy thinking under circumstances like that.

Maybe it was 10 hours after it all began when I came up on deck to look about. I saw guys pouring seawater down giant holes in the flight deck with steam and smoke rising out of them. I saw sailors pushing stuff over the side. I have conflicting memories. Did I really see it or did I see it in movies? Or in photographs? Or did somebody tell me about it? I can't say yes or no. I have two photos I took myself. One shows four shirtless sailors with fire hoses draped across their shoulders, looking like hell, pouring water down one of these bomb holes. No, I can't tell you what I saw or heard.

When we pulled into the wharf at Subic Bay, we still had fires burning. We didn't know whether or not they would let us come alongside the wharf because of these fires. When I finally got off onto the wharf and looked at the ship, there was no question in my mind. You didn't have to be an engineer; you could just look at it. The forward two-thirds of the ship didn't look bad, but the aft one-third was destroyed.

I had absolutely nothing left to do. I never even tried to make any kind of records whatsoever. I could not make under those circumstances. I had patched a couple of people up in the operating room, but I wasn't dictating notes.

Once we were tied up, we started to have routine sick call. Most of the people who had any serious injury, I sent off the ship to the shore medical facility. Why would I want to fiddle around with them on board a severely damaged ship? Then, much to my chagrin, they elected to sail the ship back to the East Coast — 35 days at sea. And I rode it back.

It was awful. First of all, we were sitting ducks. I can't imagine anybody would have tried to take a hit at us. We wouldn't have been able to do anything about it if they had. But worse, if anybody got really sick, I couldn't get them off the ship. I had no anesthesia. A ruptured spleen is not something you want to do under a spinal anesthetic administered by a flight surgeon. Only a fool would have been too dumb to be scared. It worried the living hell out of me for 35 days. A large portion of that travel was out of range and sight. I was so damn glad to get back home, it wasn't even funny.

Oriskany *to the Rescue*

Leonard Julius was a high school dropout when he joined the Navy in 1958. After serving as a hospital corpsman for several years, the ambitious and talented 24-year-old sailor earned a commission in the Medical Service Corps, becoming the Navy's youngest "mustang"[3] at the time.

In 1967, Lt.(j.g.) Julius reported aboard USS Oriskany, *which had just been ordered to Vietnam for an eight-month cruise. His assignment was in the carrier's medical department.*

Launching and recovering aircraft for hours at a time in the Tonkin Gulf's tropical heat was exhausting for flight deck personnel and meant long hours for the rest of the crew. But as long as the flight deck was operating, the sick bay was fully manned, with one or two corpsmen stationed topside to provide first aid should their services be required.

The carrier environment was inherently dangerous and accidents frequently occurred. Fuel- and munitions-laden aircraft hurtling off the deck offered their own hazards. It was not unusual for an unwary crewman to be sucked into an aircraft engine or blown over the side by jet exhaust. On rare occasions, a cable snagged by a landing aircraft's tailhook might snap — and woe to the unlucky sailor who got in the way. Traumatic amputation of a limb or even death could result.

But then the conflagration on Oriskany *the previous year, which had taken 44 lives, had been firmly embedded in every crewman's mind. "Those were living, breathing memories to the guys who were still there," Julius recalls. "It was 'the fire' this and 'the fire' that. It had made a pretty big impact on the corpsmen and others in sick bay."*

What had occurred aboard Oriskany *back in October of 1966 was about to be eclipsed by a disaster few could have predicted. This time 134 men would die in the worst shipboard fire since World War II.*

We had just seen a few cases of diarrhea and thought some curdled milk had been the cause. After I and the sanitation tech had inspected two or three coffee messes, and I had laid down the law, we were back on a deck above the hangar deck. Suddenly I saw everyone heading toward the elevator. When we got out on deck, about four or five miles in the distance, we saw the *Forrestal* with a great big black mushroom cloud hanging over it. It was obvious that something had gone horribly wrong. I said to the sanitation tech, "I think we're gonna be busy today."

We went to sick bay and tried to get things organized. Normally, when we brought in a badly injured patient, the surgeon would take x-rays to help his diagnosis. At the time, the surgeon, Lt. Comdr. Will Williams, had a patient with a badly fractured femur. I looked in and said, "You've got to stop."

"Don't get in my way. I'm busy here," he said. He was trying to decide how he would operate on the sailor.

I then pulled him by the belt saying, "Will, you've got to take a look at what's going on out here."

When he saw the patients lined up, he exclaimed, "Oh, my God! I had better get into the OR." We didn't have another doctor at the time because the senior medical officer had gone with two flight surgeons and half the corpsmen over to the *Forrestal* to help out without telling our commanding officer. Of the four doctors on the ship, three were now gone. We would have to make do with dentists, corpsmen, and dental techs.

Shortly thereafter, the skipper of the *Oriskany* called down to sick bay wanting to talk with the senior medical officer. I didn't want to be the one to tell him the doctors were gone. I got on the phone and said, "I can guarantee you that all the medical officers are working their butts off right now. And it's difficult even for me to come to the phone because we're busy."

He then said, "Is there anything I can do for you?"

"Yes, sir. You can make sure the load of patients gets spread evenly between us and the other aircraft carrier. That will help."

And in a typical line officer mode, he replied, "What's the matter? You can't handle it?"

I said, "Captain, we can handle anything, but we do it differently when we have this many patients. You asked me what you can do for us and this is what you can do for us."

By this time I realized he knew the medical officer was gone but didn't let on. "Julius," he said, "you're a very loyal officer. I wish all my officers were like you." Then he hung up.

During the course of that day, helicopters brought us 70 or 80 patients with the worst injuries I had ever seen in my life. It just seemed to go on forever. Probably within less than an hour from the time I saw the explosion, sick bay began filling up.

And these were horribly injured men. I'm talking about a femur broken so badly that the leg was bent over double. I'm talking about a guy who was burned over 90 percent of his body with second- and third-degree burns. I'll never forget him. He was so badly burned you couldn't tell whether he was a black man or a white man. He was disfigured beyond recognition. He didn't have a lot of pain because most of his nerves were destroyed. One of the corpsmen said, "Mr. Julius, you told me you worked in a urology ward. This patient is really bad off but his only complaint is that he can't urinate."

I used to work in a urology ward when I was a corpsman, and never completely lost my touch for patient care. I had as much urological nursing skill as anybody else. So I got a catheter and passed it, which was not easy, and he was able to void. He was very grateful and said, "Thank you very much. You really helped me a lot." Then he added, "I know I'm gonna die." And, of course, he was right.

"Well, nobody ever knows when he's going to die," I said. "I may go before you."

"Oh, no. You don't have to worry. I'll be all right. I haven't done anything I'm ashamed of."

I left the man and went someplace quiet and just cried. Later he did die but not on the ship. That was one of the most significant encounters of my life. He was not a man who was afraid to die. I doubt I will ever be able to forget him.

I particularly remember two other patients—two kids who had been blown off the *Forrestal*, picked up by a destroyer, then by a helicopter, and finally brought over to my ship covered with oil. You couldn't tell whether they were hurt or not. Once we cleaned them up, we found they were hardly hurt at all. Both said, "We've got to go back to our ship."

I told them, "It's over. You're done. You've had enough for today." But after I left them, they sneaked out and went back to their ship. And they were teenagers!

We were set up like a trauma hospital. A lot of the treatment occurred outside the OR. We gave people morphine, palliative treatments, and worked to stop bleeding. But by then many of the people arriving already had their bleeding attended to and we were just trying to keep them comfortable until they could be taken to the OR. Most of what was happening was in the OR because it wasn't all that long before the other doctors came back and went into the OR with the surgeon.

The rest of the day is almost a blur. When our doctors returned from the *Forrestal*, they still had work to do, but after a while I noticed one doctor could be freed up a little. I suggested, "Let's put together a little record for each one of these patients so when they get wherever they're going, people will know what's already been done. It will improve their chances of survival."

When people left the *Oriskany* to go to the hospital ship, either the *Sanctuary* or the *Repose*, every single one of them had a record. I thought that was amazing.

Moving them off the ship, however, was somewhat difficult. Normally, we manhandled patients from sick bay up a ladder to the hangar deck, over to the deck edge elevator, then up to the flight deck where they were put aboard helicopters. This time it was different with all these patients who were so bad off with IVs running. So I called the weapons officer whom I knew quite well. I told him I wanted to use the bomb elevator which was just aft of the sick bay. He said, "You know you can't use that for transporting people."

"This is an unusual circumstance," I replied. "It's an emergency. How about forgetting the rules for a while."

He said, "Okay. But I want you to understand that the door at the top of the elevator doesn't open automatically. It's possible to squash someone against that door if we screw it up."

"Well then, don't screw it up," I said. "I'll go on the first lift."

We were communicating with the bridge at the time, telling them we wanted to move these people off the ship. When they finally told us it was time to go, I went up on the elevator with a corpsman and the first patient who was on a Stokes stretcher.

It was a black night and I couldn't see whether or not the top of the elevator was open. It was very unnerving. But we managed to get up on the flight deck when, all of a sudden, someone said, "Hold on! They're evacuating the *Forrestal*." We would have to wait while they evacuated 132 dead bodies from the *Forrestal* to the hospital ship!

I bet I stood on that flight deck for an hour with a man who was in pain, and other patients were strung out ready to move. It was infuriating. To the best of my knowledge, not too many critically injured people were left on the *Forrestal*. We already had them on the *Oriskany* because our docs had gone over there and sent them to us. Anyone who was badly injured came to our ship. Nevertheless, they evacuated all the bodies first.

It was sometime late at night after I had gone back to my stateroom and was taking a shower when the fire alarm went off. "Fire! Fire!" And my fire station was the scene of the fire. I said to myself, "I don't know if I can do this." I dried off and threw on my flight suit, which was somewhat fire-retardant. When I got there, I saw the XO [executive officer] and the fire marshal. It was just a tiny electrical fire but it really scared everyone. On my way, I had noticed that all the five-gallon cans of fire foam were gone. They had gone over to the *Forrestal*. We had nothing. If we had had a big fire then, we'd have sunk.

In Dire Need of Assistance

LCDR Allan Adeeb, Oriskany's *senior medical officer, was a "dual designator," one of a handful of men who wore both the medical officer's oak leaf insignia and the gold wings of a naval aviator. When he wasn't attending patients in sick bay, Dr. Adeeb flew A-4 tanker missions. "If somebody took a hit in the wings and was losing fuel, I'd go out and find them. They'd plug in [connect to the tanker's refueling hose] and I'd take them back to the ship." The morning of 29 July, the pilots on* Oriskany *were scheduled to fly an "Alpha strike," a major coordinated attack against an important North Vietnamese target.*

I was down in sick bay and don't recall if I was scheduled to fly that day or not. Someone said, "Hey, the *Forrestal*'s on fire!"

We all ran up topside and looked over. The *Forrestal* was nearby with smoke billowing out of it. We didn't know what had happened but the word was that something had blown up. A couple of us docs and a few corpsmen then flew over to the *Forrestal* on helicopters.

The ship was already listing and burning. Fire hoses were lying all over the place, and everybody was running around trying to put out the fire. I and my guys went right down to sick bay. Dr. [Cmdr. Louis] Herrmann was in sick bay plus a bunch of corpsmen. Everybody acted independently trying to find people who were injured and wounded. Where were they? Some were just lying there. Some were bleeding. Dr. Herrmann, God bless him, was overwhelmed because all of a sudden so many people were coming into sick bay. It was a very confusing period. Sick bay had hoses everywhere, and the place was full of smoke. He had a patient in the OR he was trying to sew up. I said to him, "Louie, I'd evacuate these people. They can't stay here. You can't operate here. We've got to get these people over to the *Oriskany*."

So somehow we instigated the evacuation. We started picking up the badly injured ones, putting them on the helicopter, and taking them over to the *Oriskany*. Even so, a tremendous number of men died en route.

Will Williams, the surgeon aboard the *Oriskany*, was the only doc left aboard, and he sent an urgent message to us. "I need help. I can't handle all these people. You've got to send some of the guys back." I flew back as did [Lt.] Blair Edwards and [Lt.] Dick Fahrenbruch. We had probably stayed on board the *Forrestal* for about two hours, but before we left, we had evacuated just about everybody we could evacuate. We figured Dr. Herrmann's docs and corpsmen could do the rest.

We knew we couldn't keep transferring the injured from one place to another. Somewhere along the line they needed to be treated. So when they were all on the *Oriskany*, we got two docs from the *Intrepid* to come over and lend us a hand. Even before all this happened, we had a sick bay full of patients on the *Oriskany*, some with aches and pains. "I've got a cold." "I've got the flu." "I can't work today." When everything began happening, we said to them, "We've got some serious business." And all these guys just got up and left. All of a sudden they became well— well enough to help.

Before long, the *Oriskany* was overloaded. Guys were on cots and on the floor. Will was operating as hard as he could, and all of us were pitching in trying to patch up the wounds. The injuries were just unbelievable! Unbelievable! I had never seen such horrific injuries.

One of the hospital ships [*Repose*] arrived, and we began transferring those who were still alive. Because a bomb elevator came right through the middle of sick bay, we were able to put these patients on the bomb elevator and take them up to the flight deck. Then they were flown to the hospital ship.

We worked around the clock until 5 the next morning. By then all the patients had been transferred to the hospital ship. We were all completely exhausted, absolutely beat. I don't think we flew even the next day.

11

HUE

In the modern annals of warfare certain place names are etched in Marine Corps history: Guadalcanal, Tarawa, Iwo Jima, Inchon, Seoul, and Hue City, to name a few. The struggle to recapture Hue from the North Vietnamese Army and its Viet Cong allies lasted 26 days. The fight took place during the Tet Offensive in February 1968, and was considered the most harrowing battle of the Vietnam War. Even today, the actual cost in human life is not really known, but it is estimated that the fighting took at least 10,000 lives; 147 were U.S. Marines and 17 were Navy corpsmen. The systematic destruction of Vietnam's ancient capital and most beautiful city presented images both traumatic and disturbing. These scenes were unsettling not only for those who fought for Hue but also for the American people who witnessed the bloodletting on the evening news.

Hue was truly an anomaly of the Vietnam War. Until the Tet Offensive, the conflict had not been about urban warfare. The war had been fought in rice paddies, jungles, hilltops, and the elephant grass of the Central Highlands. Suddenly — and without warning — Marines and soldiers were fighting a well-armed and highly motivated enemy who chose to contest every inch of ground — street by street and house to house.

The battle for Hue was brutal, numbing, and seemingly without end. Years later, veterans still recall the terror — unseen snipers at every window, the horrifying closeness of the battlefield, and the cold, damp, overcast skies. They can still hear the cacophony of explosions and the cries of wounded comrades lying in the street just out of reach. They can still see a buddy shot dead — barely an arm's length away.

This form of confined combat also meant being able to scrutinize the face of one's enemy. "City fighting," recalls Hotel Company 2nd Battalion, 5th Marines commander George "Ron" Christmas, "is the dirtiest of all fighting. It's a very intense and personal fight. Your enemy is within 35 meters or less. You see him; he sees you. One or the other wins." Christmas still sees the man who nearly killed him. "I looked over my shoulder and about 100 meters away was a North Vietnamese soldier with an RPG [rocket-propelled grenade]. As he let it go, I said, 'You've gotta be kidding me. I'm not a tank. You're not supposed to shoot that grenade at me.'"

Second Lt. Bill Rogers, assigned to Golf Company of that same battalion, remembers a careless moment that nearly cost him his life. "I had been standing sideways, looking out the window across the street and saw the guy who shot me. The NVA were only a hundred feet away. My M16 had jammed and I stepped back to see what had happened. That's when I got hit on the right side and the left thigh — two bullets from an AK-47."

Hue had a very high incidence of casualties. The weapons that killed and maimed were small arms, rocket-propelled grenades, mortars, artillery, and recoilless rifles. Many more wounds resulted from the so-called "debris effect," that is, injuries inflicted not by bullets or shrapnel but by secondary missiles. These insidious projectile fragments of concrete or steel were sent flying by impacting ordnance.

The 2nd Battalion, 5th Marines, one of two Marine battalions engaged, took some 600 casualties out of a total of 850 Marines deployed. Lt. Gen. Ernest Cheatham, then a lieutenant colonel and commanding officer of the 2nd Battalion, points out that many of his Marines were wounded at least once or twice. "A number of times — and I mean up in the dozens — Marines would receive wounds and never go back to the aid station. Or they would go back and then turn right around and come back to us. This was on their own initiative. The standard procedure was: you got wounded, you got tagged, and you got medevaced. Well, these guys would get tagged and then just turn around and come right back up to the unit." The men who followed the Marines step for step and did that tagging were hospital corpsmen.

An infantry battalion normally rated two battalion surgeons and about 50 corpsmen. But when troops of the 2nd Battalion, 5th Marines entered Hue, the battalion was under-strength both in troops and medical personnel. Nevertheless, the medical staff members did their work in the MACV (Military Assistance Command, Vietnam) headquarters or in battalion aid stations, which had been set up in abandoned buildings recaptured from the enemy. Hospital corpsmen, who were not assigned as platoon and company corpsmen, staffed these crude aid stations. Most corpsmen, however, accompanied the troops fighting to retake the city.

The most senior of these corpsmen was HMC Lou Legarie. The 43-year-old chief hospital corpsman had served most of his career with the Marines and had seen action at Chosin Reservoir during the Korean War. He was a take-charge veteran whose vast organizational experience proved invaluable once the Marines of 2nd Battalion, 5th Marines began retaking ground in the newer part of the city.

Legarie's first task was to set up an aid station near Hue University. "It was an advanced battalion aid station," Legarie recalls, "on the first deck of an apartment house." Eight to 10 corpsmen staffed this aid station, but Legarie was often the first one to assess the incoming casualties. "We'd take off all their clothes and make sure they didn't have any wounds we didn't know about." After triaging the patients and stabilizing those who would most likely survive, the medical personnel transferred them by truck to the landing zone (LZ). This particular LZ was in a nearby soccer field close to the Perfume (Song Huong) River. Although the weather had turned rainy with a very low ceiling, helicopters were the only real way of evacuating casualties from Hue to the 1st Medical Battalion hospital at Phu Bai or to one of the hospital ships offshore.

Chief Legarie's other job was assigning corpsmen to units that needed replacements. "We were short because many of the corpsmen had been killed or wounded. And it was not easy to get replacements right away because everyone was having their problems," Legarie remembers. Assigning a young man to a unit, which had just lost its corpsman killed in action, was a sobering and solemn responsibility. "I had corpsmen there at Hue City who had earned three Purple Hearts and were supposed to leave the country, but I had to use them. I'm not sure whether or not I felt guilty about continuing to use these corpsmen. Our job was to support the Marines, the wounded, and the sick, and that's what we did."

Return with Your Shield — or On It

HM3 Richard Thacker's 3rd Platoon, Golf Company, 2nd Battalion, 5th Marines was at Phu Bai when it received word that the occupants of the MACV compound in Hue were fighting for their lives and needed help immediately.

We had no contact at all with the enemy. It was a smooth ride all the way up Route 1 from Phu Bai to Hue. We were about a quarter of a mile from the MACV compound when the enemy started shooting at us. We had to get off the trucks and take cover along the streets. We then fought our way down to the MACV compound where all the Army personnel and American civilians had blockaded themselves. It was like a little Fort Apache. The North Vietnamese were in buildings, in the trees, in spider holes. They were everywhere.

Marines ease a wounded comrade down a fire escape at Hue University (BUMED Archives).

The battalion worked its way across the street to a building at the women's university, and we set up our battalion aid station in there for a couple of days. Then we had to start fighting our way from that position down that side of the river going west. The next structure across the street was the treasury building. We had to take that building, then the hospital, then the yacht club, and then the governor's mansion before we worked further on out.

I was with the forward battalion aid station. We had one surgeon with us—Dr. [Joseph] Buchignani from Memphis, Tennessee. We called him "Dr. Buck." He was assigned from 1st Med Battalion to go with us. We had a small contingent of five or six corpsmen, and we carried our medical gear in big beach bags. Everywhere we stopped we set up a battalion aid station, and the casualties were brought to us. We were the advanced mobile battalion aid station. We set up in blown-out buildings, in rooms—whatever place was secure. As the Marines moved, our forward battalion aid station moved.

Lt. Col. [Ernest] Cheatham was our battalion commander. He told Dr. Buck that we would get anything we needed. And he lived up to that because we never ran out of anything. We were supplied all the time and our needs were met.

I saw a lot of shrapnel wounds, but because snipers were really active, the majority were typically gunshot wounds of the head and upper chest.

Even though most of the civilians had packed up and left, we treated a French priest who had been shot in the stomach and had been hiding in a closet. A North Vietnamese surgeon apparently operated on him and left him there. He had been in that closet three or four days before we found him. He was in pretty bad shape but he survived.

We had some very poignant situations, too. One young Marine was brought by his comrades into our battalion aid station. He had been shot in the chest and was having trouble breathing. We were all concentrating on treating him and dealing with our own individual fear when suddenly the kid sat up on the stretcher and yelled out really loud for his mom. Then he died.

HN Dennis Howe patches up a wounded Marine as his comrades hunker down during the battle for Hue (BUMED Archives).

Another young Marine was brought in wounded really bad. He died from internal bleeding that we just couldn't stop. Believe it or not, he had played football against me in high school.

Because snipers had zeroed in on the streets, we had lots of casualties. You had to run, one at a time, trying to get across the street. It was a heck of a job trying to find cover and get those casualties because we were under such heavy fire. We were doing everything we could to retrieve them without getting ourselves shot. We'd crawl into cars, throw ropes out to them — anything we could do to protect ourselves, too.

I saw heroes everywhere. When Marines fight, they're a brotherhood. They fight as a unit, as a team. They would even go out at night to retrieve their dead. Nobody would be left in the streets. Our motto was, "You come back with your shield, or you come back on it."

Battle Logistics Made Easy

Lt. Col. Ernest Cheatham saw the medical situation from his unique position as commanding officer of 2nd Battalion, 5th Marines.

I really didn't have to think that much about medical support because we had two doctors with us, and when we went up into Hue, we got another doctor and a load of corpsmen. Later, Regiment sent us more medical support. It might sound a bit funny but the doctors we had were young guys with no real military experience — even though they certainly had acquired this experience when it was all over. Chief Lou Legarie was the one who pulled it all together and showed them where to set up and what to do. I relied pretty heavily on him.

The medical personnel were absolutely overloaded with casualties. But one of the nice parts— if you can say there was a nice part about it — was that our logistics in Hue City were reasonably easy. We fought the first 14 days and received most of our casualties during those first 14 days. We went only seven or eight blocks in that time. What we didn't have we could get reasonably quickly by just running back four or five blocks or sending a jeep or mechanical mule [flatbed utility truck] back to bring up supplies.

It was the same with medevacs. The standard procedure was that you got wounded, you got tagged, and you got medevaced. The logistical line that was required when a man was wounded and evacuated in Hue was simple. A very seriously wounded man could be evacuated back to a clearing station at the 1st Marine Regiment and sometimes be on a helicopter in 30 minutes.

It was the same situation with resupply. When we had to get food, water, or ammunition, the Navy brought it up the Perfume River. At a landing just east of Route 1, the Navy could come up in LCUs [Landing Craft Utility] and bring ammunition, food, medical supplies— anything we needed. And even when we couldn't use the roads because they had been cut or blown away, we were still able to be resupplied either by helicopter or by those LCUs. So the logistical aspects of medicine, of ammunition, of food, and of fuel were reasonably easy because of the short distances we traveled. I never got the impression from anyone on my staff, from Chief Legarie, or from any one of the doctors that they were ever low on any medical supplies.

"A Very High Casualty-Producing Environment"

Marine captain Ron Christmas was commanding officer of Hotel Company, 2nd Battalion, 5th Marines when the Tet Offensive and the Battle of Hue began. His unit had been ordered to guard two bridges and keep Route 1 open south of Phu Bai. As the fighting in Hue intensified, Hotel Company was ordered north. By 5 February 1968, Christmas's company and the rest of 2nd Bat-

talion, minus one company, had entered Hue and began to retake the city. The young officer led from the front, witnessed the human cost, and became a casualty himself.

In my company, every one of our Marines was wounded at least once or twice. The wounds weren't necessarily bullets or shrapnel but debris. A large shell hit the concrete next to you and concrete fragments became missiles. Or you tore up legs, arms, and knees in the rubble. It was a very high casualty-producing environment. In my battalion, many Marines were wounded.

I was wounded on the 13th day, hit by an RPG and then some mortars after that. I remember it so very well. We had seized the southern portion of the city by then and had pushed out into the western area. In fact, by chance we had overrun an NVA base camp. I had just called my platoon commanders to direct the fight when I looked over my shoulder and about 100 meters away was a North Vietnamese soldier with an RPG. As he let it go, I said, "You've gotta be kidding me. I'm not a tank. You're not supposed to shoot that grenade at me." It hit behind me and the shrapnel went through my left leg.

My corpsmen were beside me immediately. They wrapped the leg real good, and when I tried to get them to move me to an area where I could direct the fight, they put me down next to a building. Unfortunately, when the mortars came in, they came in straight, and my gunny [gunnery sergeant] and my radio operator dove on top of me. They didn't get hit at all but my arm was hanging out underneath and I got a few more hits.

How I was evacuated is a story. We had created our own little ambulance service. I suppose today I'd probably get in trouble for this. Our company had liberated six vehicles. Three were little hatchbacks—little jeeps—that the mail used to be delivered in. We used them as ammunition vehicles, stacking them full of small arms ammo. When we'd run low on ammo, they'd drive up as close as they could to the front line and we'd carry the ammo in.

The other three vehicles were pickup trucks with mattresses we had liberated; they became our ambulances. They pulled up one of these ambulances as close as they could, threw me on the back, and whisked me to our battalion med, which was right in the city. Battalion med patched me up a little bit and then sent me to Regimental med, which was at the stadium about 10 blocks away. It had an evacuation capability.

I was then evacuated to Danang on a CH-53 helicopter. My partner on the rack of stretchers was a wounded and captured North Vietnamese soldier.

The Bridge

John Higgins was a hospital corpsman assigned to Golf Company, 2nd Battalion, 5th Marines. The Nebraska native had arrived in Vietnam just before Christmas 1967 and had already seen action before Tet began. When the communists launched their offensive, Higgins was with a squad guarding a bridge south of Phu Bai. "I remember this little kid we called 'Johnny,' who was maybe 10 years old. If you wanted a Coke, he'd get it for you. If you wanted anything, you told Johnny and he'd get it for you. One day he said to me, 'You go away.'"

"I said, 'Yeah, I'm going away.'"

"He said, 'No. No. You go to Hue.'"

"Evidently, he must have known something was up. I really didn't think anything of it. I had no clue where Hue was. I don't think any of us knew."

On the night of January 30th [1968], I remember talking about Tet [the Vietnamese New Year]. It was going to be like Christmas and every other holiday wrapped into one. About midnight some fire erupted on the Phu Bai perimeter, but it was mostly people shooting in the air. "Oh, they're celebrating Tet." We got rocketed that night.

The next day, the 31st, we were told we were going to go help the Army. Those soldiers had run into some heavy fire. We would go up, take an objective, and be back by night so we shouldn't even take our packs, just our fighting gear.

Finally they fed us a lunch of mashed potatoes with creamed turkey over the top. Then they put the 3rd Platoon — which I was with at this point — on trucks and we headed out of Phu Bai towards Hue City. Up till this time everything we heard was just scuttlebutt; we had no real information. We were told that a village had been hit real hard, and we were going to go up and take care of the village. As we headed north by truck up Highway 1, you could see a big column of black smoke rising up in the air ahead of us. We figured it was a bunch of burning hooches. As we got closer to Hue, the column of smoke got thicker and thicker. Then we started to run into more buildings.

When we got to the canal,[1] which wasn't very wide — maybe 10 or 15 feet across. The trucks then stopped with one truck across the bridge [An Cuu Bridge], one on the bridge, and one short of the canal. In front of us was a market place. On the left side were two- and three-story buildings with an ARVN tank stuck in one with bodies hanging out of it. On the right side were awnings overhead — probably part of the market — and some regular buildings.

Then a burst of automatic fire opened up on us, and everybody bailed out of the trucks and looked for cover. We returned fire, got up, and then started walking down the left side of Highway 1 toward the tank that had crashed into the building. The tank had bullet holes in it where armor-piercing rounds had gone through it. We were all laughing and joking and doing the theme song from "Combat" [World War II television series that ran from 1962 to 1967]. None of us fully understood what we were in for.

We proceeded through the open area and took some fire off to our left. After we got through that area, we entered the MACV compound. I think it was a three-story building on the main road — Highway 1. It had the usual bunker at its main gate. Inside the gate was an open compound. It looked to us like these guys had it pretty nice. I don't remember seeing any wounded in this compound at the time, but it was obvious where rockets had exploded and blown stuff out of the brick. We also saw holes in the ground so we knew they'd been under attack.

It may have been about this time that we married up with some more of Golf Company. We got orders to cross the bridge over the Perfume River and go into the Citadel.[2] We could see the Citadel, which was a big, impressive red brick structure with a moat. It looked medieval. The Citadel wall itself was huge. A tall flagpole flew a Viet Cong flag. Later I saw a Skyraider — a prop-driven bomber — drop a 250-pound bomb on the outside wall of the Citadel and it didn't even knock a hole in the wall. The bomb just blew apart a bunch of bricks. We were supposed to go there and then head to an ARVN compound. But first we had to take the [Nguyen Hoang] bridge and that was really nasty.

That bridge was bad news all the way. It had an arch to it — a crown in the middle — so when you first got on it, you couldn't see the other end. Almost immediately, we started taking casualties — big time. The NVA were manning a machine gun on the other side. It was probably a position the ARVNs had set up to guard the bridge, but the NVA had taken it over. The bridge had steel beams that went up from the roadbed and it also had overhead beams. We had so many casualties that I couldn't treat them on the bridge. We were just grabbing the wounded and dragging them to the south end of the bridge where trucks took them back to the MACV compound.

The Army had a quad .50 machine gun [heavy barrel air-cooled machine guns] on the back of a Deuce and a Half truck [Marine workhorse truck], or a "6 by," as the Marines called them. I was plastered up against a steel beam and could hear the rounds hitting that beam — Tink! Tink! Tink! Tink! It was a good that I was a skinny little dude. I probably weighed only 125 pounds so I was able to hide behind the girder. I saw M79 grenade rounds bouncing on the concrete right in front of me. They weren't exploding, just hitting and bouncing. All this time that quad .50 was shooting ahead trying to get that NVA bunker. The Army truck was almost directly in front of me so I could see the soldier shooting when all of a sudden I saw his forehead explode. He was shot right in the forehead! As soon as he was hit, the driver of the truck backed it up all the way across the bridge.

Shortly after that I looked at where the bunker was just in time to see [Cpl. Lester] Tully charge that machine gun nest, jump on top of it, and throw a couple of grenades down inside, killing the NVA who were there. He got a Silver Star for that. Once that happened, we were free to get off the bridge.

It was late afternoon by this time, maybe 4 or 5. The north end of the bridge ended in a "T." Some of the guys left the bridge, then made a left [onto Tran Hung Dao Street]. I stopped just past the bridge where I found a Marine with a sucking chest wound [wound in which air passes in and out of the chest with each breath taken]. While I was treating him, a hellacious street fight was going on around me, as I've been told, but I don't remember it.

This man was my very first sucking chest wound. The wound was on the left-hand side and I was thinking, "This is just like they showed me in corps school." He had this little round hole, and every time he tried to breathe in, you could hear a sucking sound. Then it would bubble, bubble, bubble but not much blood came out. I rolled him over and felt along his back for an exit wound but didn't see any. I took out one of my C-ration cigarette packs, removed the cellophane, put some Bacitracin ointment on it, and stuck it right over the hole. I put a small battle dressing on top of that, wrapped it around him, and tied it as tight as I could. I then rolled him over on his good side while a couple of Marines ripped a door off a house. We loaded him on the door, put him in the back of a 6 by, and took him back across the bridge.

About that time, the guys who had started to go left down the street were coming back towards me with wounded. And that's when I learned they had been ambushed on the road and that "Doc" [HN Donald] Kirkham had been killed.

We were pretty close to the Citadel, maybe a block or so. We knew there was no way we could hold the bridge that night. Not many of us were left at that point! I took care of gunshots to the abdomen. I saw some leg wounds that weren't really serious and some shrapnel wounds that didn't amount to much. But these guys weren't going to let me do much with them. They'd say, "Get away from me. I'm okay, Doc. Go treat my buddy over there."

The most serious one I actually had time to treat was the guy with the sucking chest wound. A lot of the men I helped drag off the bridge had abdominal wounds or other wounds that were very severe but I didn't have any place to treat them without getting killed myself. We'd simply grab them by the back of their flak jackets and drag them back across the bridge. Then [HN] Terry Sutton, [HM2 James] Yount,[3] and I would run forward for more. We finally withdrew across the bridge to the south side.

On the Wrong End of a Firing Squad

Following the repulse at the Nguyen Hoang Bridge, John Higgins and his unit joined the action to regain control of the city south of the Perfume River. The fighting was no less fierce. For a corpsman not familiar with urban warfare, the learning curve was short and business was brisk and frequent.

This was just the second day and we didn't have a clue as to what urban fighting was about. It was all new to us. Jungle and paddies were all we had seen up until that point. On the third day we were sent down a road to retrieve some Air Force personnel who were supposedly trapped in a building.

We came to a church with a parking lot in the front. On the left side of the road were one-story houses. On our right was a concrete-plaster wall probably seven or eight feet high. We were walking next to that wall when the NVA ambushed us from across the street. It was like being on the wrong end of a firing squad with us pinned up against that wall. The church was directly across the street from the wall, and they were firing from that church.

On the right side of the street along the curb were some trees, then the sidewalk, and then the wall. A black Marine named Howard, who was in front of me, went down. From a recess in the wall, I began yelling, "Howard! Howard! Where are you hit?" I tried to drag him back and find where he was hit. But he turned shocky and then he was dead. To this day I don't know where he was hit.

I was sitting in that little recess with rounds popping around me. Another Marine was down to my left behind a tree. I watched him get hit three times. The first time I saw him jerk and then roll a bit going forward. Then he jerked again and I saw him kind of flip. I yelled at him to cross the street because by this time some of the Marines had gotten into a house right next to the church, and I was yelling at him to get into that house.

I ran to the house. It had two or three rounded steps that led to a door on the building's corner. I tried to kick the door in but it wasn't going to budge. When you see people kicking in a door in the movies, it's just not real. I had adrenalin going through me big time — but I couldn't get that door knocked down. I can still see pieces of concrete flying up all around me.

I then ran around the house to another door. By that time some Marines had entered the building, and the guy I had seen shot three times was in there. He had been hit in the left wrist; it was a through-and-through and didn't get the bone. He was also hit on the back left side of the shoulder which took out a hunk of skin and fatty tissue. As he moved his shoulder, you could see the action of the muscle. The third round hit the left-hand chest side of his flak jacket, which then struck a small can of cleaning solvent. It deflected the bullet just enough so that it went just underneath the skin. I could see the bullet in there. He was one lucky guy.

I wanted to start an IV on him, but when I reached down for my serum albumin, all three cans were drained. Rounds had blown holes through all of them, maybe when we were pinned against that wall. I filled out a casualty tag and we evacuated him.

It turns out that the house belonged to a Vietnamese doctor. I noted that all the labels on his medicines were in French. While we were looking around, the doctor came crawling out of a bunker, which was built in a room of the house, shouting, "Don't shoot! Don't shoot!" I'm surprised he wasn't shot. At that point we were so new to the city we really hadn't thought about searching room to room yet. And, of course, by then we had almost been massacred against a wall.

He spoke English and told us he was a doctor. He also had his wife and family with him. I wanted to take him back to the MACV compound because he was a doctor, and I figured that with all the casualties we had, a doctor would sure be helpful. But they wouldn't let us bring him back. We had to leave him there. He was probably taken out and executed.

On the fourth or fifth day three trucks were sent back to Phu Bai. They put a squad of Marines on them for protection and I went along. These 6 bys had sand bags in the back for protection because if one of the trucks went down, we'd slow down enough to grab the people off the truck and keep on going. Nothing was going to stop us.

We headed south out of the MACV compound back down Highway 1 towards Phu Bai. I lay on the bed of the truck with the Marines shooting out of it. They were throwing their magazines to me, and I was reloading them and giving them back until we shot our way out. Some of the guys later told me that the lead truck encountered an NVA soldier in the middle of the road who was firing at the truck. They ran him over. I remember this horrendous firing out the backs of the trucks and me loading magazines for the Marines. The whole time they were yelling at me, "More, more, Doc!"

Just outside the Phu Bai base, we stopped and got out. I saw holes all over the trucks. When we entered the base, I went to the battalion aid station and told them what was going on. I resupplied and got a new pair of pants because the ones I had on had the knees ripped out of them. I spent the night there. The next day we got in a convoy and headed back to Hue.

Since every available man was needed, HM3 John Higgins rejoined the fight. When he returned to the MACV compound he found yet more casualties to treat and the battle as savage as when he had left it.

One guy had a leg wound. He had caught some shrapnel in his right leg just above the knee. It had laid him open pretty good and I could see the femur. The dressing the corpsman had applied up at the front was pretty blood-soaked so I removed it and replaced it with an Ace wrap. I stuffed the Ace wrap in that big opening and then wrapped the wound with a pressure dressing again to stop the bleeding—and the bleeding stopped. By this time an Army doctor took care of most of the casualties. We then married up again with 3rd Platoon and spent several days clearing houses.

There was opposition in every house. My casualties at this point—if they were alive— were mostly shrapnel from [shoulder-fired] B-40 rockets [RPGs] that had been shooting at us. Some wounds were caused by pieces of concrete. Rounds would hit concrete and splatter. As a result, I got guys who had wounds in their faces. They didn't bleed very much and were fairly close to the surface so they coagulated pretty quickly. One man had some dirt or concrete granules in his eyes. I tried to flush those granules out with the remaining can of serum albumin I had, but that didn't work very well. So I just put a small battle dressing on it and sent him back to the MACV compound. He came back about an hour later.

I also treated gunshot wounds of the arms, legs, and abdomen by applying pressure dressings. During the first few days, when we were going house to house, a lot of NVA were down in the sewers and street drains. They were shooting at us from these low points so I saw a lot of low leg wounds—shots through the femur. I treated them with pressure dressings and morphine. Leg wounds were really painful. Some men were shot through the ankle. I saw a through-and-through of the ankle, and I'm sure the guy probably ended up losing his foot. It was a nasty wound that went right above the ankle bone. The foot was just hanging there loose. I could tell the bone wasn't really attached to anything. I had some blow-up air splints [inflatable splints used for fractured or broken bones] with me and tried to put one on but I couldn't blow it up. I don't know whether or not it was the heat that had sealed it together but I couldn't inflate it to save my life. So I used Ace wrap again. I loved Ace wrap and carried as many of them as I could get. I made a figure eight-type of dressing over the ankle and then evacuated him.

International [Harvester] Scouts [vehicles designed to be competitive with the jeep] which the guys were able to hot-wire, were all over the city. Then we'd throw our casualties in the backs and the drivers would haul ass back to the MACV compound, usually taking a lot of sniper rounds along the way. We used those civilian cars the first week we were in Hue to evacuate the wounded, and they returned with ammunition for us.

Not long after that we were sweeping along the edge of a canal back towards Highway 1 and going through an alleyway. It was heavily brushed and overgrown. As the point man came out beside a house, a machine gun opened on him and he went down. I started out to get him, and just before I got to the corner of the house, one of the Marines grabbed me by the back of my flak jacket and yanked me back. "You're not going out there, Doc!"

The platoon leader for the 3rd Platoon, Bill Rogers, who had pitched baseball for the University of Mississippi, began pitching grenades over the top of a one-story house to get that machine gun. All this time we were pinned behind the house. We tried to flank the machine gunners but they could shoot down the little alleyways on both sides of the house. I could see that Marine lying out there, and he wasn't moving. He wasn't moving an inch.

One of the grenades finally got the machine gun position, and a Marine ran out and started dragging the wounded man back. He had been shot through both legs, breaking the femurs in each. The man was in absolute, amazing pain. He had tears in his eyes but never made a whimper. I guess he had figured that if he made a move, they'd shoot him again. He must have lay out there for what seemed to me like an eternity. It may actually have been 5 minutes, perhaps 10 minutes tops.

I gave him two shots of morphine because I was afraid he was going to go into shock. He wasn't bleeding very badly so I used pressure dressings. I had told the Marines to get me some wood and they came back with what appeared to be slats off a bed. They broke them up and I used them to splint his upper legs. We then rolled him onto a poncho, and a couple of Marines took him out to the road to load him onto one of those Scouts to took him away.

We took some buildings and then part of the hospital compound. I remember seeing all these freshly used bloody bandages lying all over the place. Evidently the NVA were also using that hospital for their wounded. As we were going through one of the wards, a rocket came through a window. It made our ears ring. Some of the guys got powder burns and a little shrapnel, but nothing real serious— just small puncture wounds from shrapnel. I wiped them off and applied a small pressure dressing. If the wound was on an extremity, I sometimes took a roll of gauze, wrapped it around a couple of times and tied it. Then I wrapped some adhesive tape around it.

Taking the buildings was a platoon operation. Three squads were supposed to be in each platoon. But we were down to two. We had between 10 and 14 in each squad at a time. We'd fire on a building, and an M79 guy would try to launch something inside a window. At one point someone got a few 3.5-inch rocket launchers for us. We'd shoot those through the door but half of them turned out to be duds. They'd hit the door and just fall down without exploding. Then someone would pitch a grenade in and rush through going from room to room. If someone went down, I'd be right there with him.

Once or twice, I had a guy shot right through the wall. One Marine got a burst of fire through a wall and I ended up treating another sucking chest wound that way. By this time I was pretty numb about the casualties. It getting very routine. You did it without thinking about what you were doing. A lot of the casualties just ran together.

I always treated the sucking chest wounds the same way. The battle dressings came in a clear plastic bag and I could use that to stick over the hole. I had used cellophane from a cigarette pack on that first sucking chest wound I treated on the north side of the bridge. But by this time it was a matter of using expedient dressing — whatever you could do to stem the bleeding and keep the guy going. A piece of plastic across the wound worked well.

I remember another incident. A Marine was running into a house when ordnance exploded right beside him. When I jumped on him, I couldn't find any bleeding but he couldn't breathe. All I found were some little specks on the side of his face and his arms but nothing on his upper torso. I rolled him over but still couldn't find any wound. He was saying, "I can't breathe. I can't breathe." Then he was starting to get a little blue around the lips. I touched the side of his chest and felt a grinding sensation. The force of the explosion probably fractured his ribs and he couldn't get a breath.

I took an 18-gauge needle and stuck it into his chest and — Phst!— air escaped, and his breathing became better. There must have been air trapped in his lungs and he couldn't get it out. It may not have been by the book but you did what you could.

As the 3rd Platoon continued to clear buildings, the platoon commander, who had demonstrated his pitching prowess by taking out the NVA machine gun a few days earlier, was seriously wounded. 2nd lieutenant Bill Rogers tells what happened when meeting up with an AK-47.

I can still remember getting shot — as if it was yesterday. It's not like in the movies where a wounded John Wayne remains standing. It just knocked me against the wall and down on my back. I had been standing sideways looking out the window across the street — and I saw the guy who shot me. The NVA were only a hundred feet away. My M16 had jammed and I stepped back to see what had happened. That's when I got hit on the right side and the left thigh — two bullets from an AK-47. And I don't mean just a little scratch. One bullet went in my side right about my belt line, and the other went completely through my thigh. How it missed my femoral artery, I'll never know. That bullet could have killed me very quickly.

I had two corpsmen with me at the time. John Higgins was the company corpsman, but he was with my platoon that morning because no other unit was nearby for him to attend to; all the wounded had already been evacuated. I also had one of my platoon corpsmen, Terry Sutton. My other two platoon corpsmen had already been killed. To this day, I can't remember their names. Doc Higgins was right there and saved my life. Later he told me they didn't think I was gonna make it.

My intestines had come out the hole in my side. They were just lying there, and I was holding onto them. Doc was down on the floor working on my leg. I said, "Doc, my thigh's okay. It's my stomach that's killin' me."

"No, Lieutenant. You've been shot in the thigh, too." I had so much pain in my stomach that I didn't realize I had also been shot in the thigh. So there I was with nothing but blood from my knees to my chest and my guts were just hanging out my side.

I said, "Doc, are my girlfriends gonna be disappointed?"

He said, "No, Lieutenant, you're okay. It missed that." The bullet came right across the top of my right thigh, grazed my right leg, and dug into my left thigh. It had passed so close to my penis, I think I had a powder burn. That's how close it was.

Higgins and Sutton wrapped me up, gave me two shots of morphine, then called a jeep to get me. We were probably about a mile from the MACV compound. By then we had moved to the back of the building to get away from the firefight. They put me on a stretcher and picked me up to put me over a barbed wire fence. I weighed 185 pounds but probably more with my flak jacket. As the two corpsmen were putting me over the fence, they dropped me. The stretcher turned sideways and I reached over and grabbed the top of the barbed wire to keep from falling off the stretcher. The barbed wire just tore my arm all up. They laughed; I laughed. Considering how bad I was shot up, my arm was the least of my worries.

Higgins and Sutton got me in the back of the jeep and took me to the MACV compound. Years later, a sergeant came up to me and said, "Lt. Rogers, you don't remember me, do you? I was in the MACV compound when they brought you in, and we thought you were carrying a newborn baby in your arms. But you weren't. You were holding your intestines."

That was the situation I was in at that time. They didn't do any more work on me, but instead took me down to the river where helicopters were coming in. The radioman on the ground was talking to one of the incoming choppers and the pilot was replying. He said, "I've got room only for one more person." The guy on the ground was walking down the line and looked at about 17 of us. He stopped at me and said, "This guy goes first." I knew then I was in bad shape.

"I Just Couldn't Leave My Marines"

The hell that was Hue went on for days with no respite for the Marines and the few corpsmen who were still alive and in one piece. Numbed by fatigue and the carnage he witnessed almost minute by minute, "Doc" Higgins continued to do what he had been trained to do — stop the bleeding, treat for shock, and evacuate his patients.

After we evacuated Bill Rogers, we headed north back toward the MACV compound. They wanted us to sweep back up Highway 1 and clear out any snipers because vehicles coming into Hue were still catching sniper fire on that part of the road. We encountered a house with a cupola on top and went up to the top to get a good view. As we were coming down, a B-40 rocket hit where we just had been. One of my Marines caught a pretty big piece of shrapnel in the back of his neck. It was actually sticking out and appeared to be embedded in the spinal cord of his backbone. I was afraid to pull it out so I took two dressings and put one on each side of it to keep it from oozing any more blood. I was careful not to put any direct pressure on top of it. What else could I do? I couldn't tie it tight [around his neck]; I'd choke the guy.

A day or so later, I took care of a Marine who had taken a round on the right side of the neck. It had gotten his jugular, which was just spewing blood. What do you do? I took an Ace wrap and jammed it in there. Then I took another Ace wrap and rolled it around his neck to hold it in place and I evacuated him. The man lived! Two months later, he returned to the company, and I was very surprised he was alive. He responded to my amazed look by saying, "They told me if you hadn't done it the way you did, I'd be dead."

On 21 February, after 22 days of continuous combat, HM3 John Higgins was finally overtaken by the odds. Elements of Golf Company had already fought their way to the western edge of Hue. The Marines then encountered a railroad bridge crossing the Perfume River and a bunker protecting it at the southern end. As he had done countless times before, Higgins ran forward to treat a Marine who had been hit.

As I went inside the bunker to work on the Marine, there was an explosion. All I remember was feeling pressure and hearing a distant roar. Then I don't recall anything for a while. I was told later that a recoilless rifle round hit but it could have been an RPG.

I next remember being a half a block down from the bunker. I was sitting behind a building and holding a towel to my head. At some point I had liberated a pink beach towel — and I still have it today. Because it was wet, rainy, and cold, I had wrapped the towel around my neck and underneath my flak jacket to help keep me warm. I was holding it up against the side of my head and a Marine was standing close by talking to me. I could see his mouth moving but couldn't hear what he was saying.

I'm told now that a pretty big fight was going on but I don't remember it. By this time, the battalion aid station was located in an apartment complex we had secured. Besides myself, there were three other walking wounded. We began walking back to the battalion aid station — the three wounded guys in front of me. For some reason, I stopped and turned around just as the lead man stepped on a land mine. As I started to run out to him, a bunch of ARVNs up on a nearby wall began yelling that mines were out there. By the time they led me through the mine field, the lead man was already gone. The mine had blown shrapnel up through his abdomen and he probably died from internal bleeding.

When I got to the battalion aid station, they numbed up my arm and pulled the shrapnel from my shoulder. My canteen was resting on my right side just about kidney level. The canteen had a hole about an inch and a half in diameter in it. Inside was a big chunk of shrapnel. If I hadn't had the canteen on, that shrapnel would gotten me right in the kidney.

Since [James] Yount had been badly wounded, I was now senior corpsman. I went to the Golf Company headquarters, reported in, and then went to a room and lay on my side for the next two days. My eardrum had been damaged, and I couldn't hear anything in my right ear. I have no memory whatsoever of those two days. I had a concussion or maybe I was completely exhausted and just burned out. Every day we lost somebody else and I was reaching the end of my rope. A few days before, I had sat with my .45, looked at my foot and thought, "If I just put one bullet through my foot, I'll be outta here." I didn't do it, thank God. I don't know what stopped me. I thought it would either hurt too much or maybe I just couldn't leave my Marines.

The young corpsman didn't leave his Marines. The battle to secure the city and its environs went on for several more days. Higgins would still be in the thick of it, dodging bullets and giving aid and comfort to his comrades. "People come up to me today and say, "You corpsmen are heroes." Maybe it's modesty, but I was just doing my job."

Too Many Purple Hearts

Fox Company, 2nd Battalion, 5th Marines, in Hue from 1 February until 9 March, lost two of its corpsmen. The company's commanding officer, Capt. Michael Downs, remembers both the losses and accomplishments.

One of the corpsmen we lost was HM3 James E. Gosselin. He was killed on the 1st of February. I didn't witness Doc Gosselin's death but I wasn't far away, and so I know where it was—right in the streets. Interestingly, Gosselin was an older guy and had been in the Special Forces. He was a medic with the Army before he came into the Navy.

The second corpsman was an HM3 by the name of Charles L. Morrison. He died on the 6th of February. I wasn't far from him when he was killed. His 2nd Platoon headquarters was effectively wiped out. The platoon guide, the radio operator, and Morrison were all killed. So four out of that platoon headquarters group died by small arms fire that day. It's also a very meaningful day to me because my radio operator was also killed that day—less than an arm's reach from me.

These corpsmen lived with our corporals, our lance corporals, and our sergeants. You don't have to be around Marines and corpsmen very long to know what a tight link that is. We Marines feel that that's what we signed up for. But corpsmen signed up to go in the Navy and yet they were with us. And, of course, where there's fire, there are casualties. And corpsmen are almost always where the casualties are. If you took a group of people who had their asses hanging out, I would say it was usually radio operators and corpsmen. The enemy is not stupid. When the enemy sees an antenna, they think command and control. When the enemy sees the corpsmen, they know the corpsmen are rushing to help somebody who has been wounded.

During that period from 1 February to 9 March, our company had 21 Marines killed and 172 additional Purple Hearts. Of those 172 casualties, some had been wounded more than once. That's why I said Purple Hearts. And, in fact, some of the Purple Hearts could be one of the 21 killed if they had gotten a Purple Heart before they were killed.

Of the awards that the company received beyond the Purple Heart, we had 31 personal decorations—from the Navy Cross down through a Navy Achievement: 1 Navy Cross, 10 Silver Stars, and 17 Bronze Stars. Of the corpsmen, two received the Bronze Star. In addition to those U.S. decorations, the company received 36 Vietnamese Crosses of Gallantry. HM2 Robert J. Stout, who was the company corpsman, received the Vietnamese Cross of Gallantry.

The Citadel

The savage battle to secure Hue continued through the first two weeks of February as Marines and Army troops fought to dislodge the enemy. As ferocious as the fighting was to secure the new city south of the Perfume River, the battle to retake the old district north of the river was another story. The Citadel was a walled fortress about three miles square. It was patterned after Peking's

Forbidden City and surrounded by a moat. With its brick and masonry walls 20 to 30 feet high and 50 to 90 feet thick, the bastion now had a gold-starred blue and red Viet Cong flag flying defiantly from a prominent flagstaff. Inside the Citadel's walls were blocks of row houses, shops, a collection of pagodas, parks, residences, gardens, and beautifully carved stone buildings. The Imperial Palace was a fortress within a fortress. All structures provided an abundance of hiding places for NVA and Viet Cong soldiers. The Citadel was proving to be a very tough nut to crack, and casualties were heavy on both sides.

Two weeks after the costly repulse of Golf Company, 1st Battalion, 5th Marines at the Nguyen Hoang Bridge, that regiment's Delta Company joined the battle to take the Citadel. By then NVA sappers had blown the infamous bridge, and South Vietnamese Navy junks and U.S. Navy LCUs had to ferry troops across the river. Hostile ground fire prevented the use of helicopters. Capt. Myron Harrington, commanding officer of Delta Company, recalls the events.

Once we got inside the Citadel area itself, we joined up with the battalion CP [command post], settled the troops down in a bivouac area, and I reported to the commander for my instructions for the next day. We were to participate in the attack as the battalion was moving north to south inside the Citadel. Specifically, the tasking was to take the Dong Ba Gate, which was a piece of high ground with a tower overlooking the battalion zone of action. The fact that the North Vietnamese held that gate and were able to bring suppression fire down on the battalion precluded our advance. The tower and the wall were up on the Citadel wall, which was a built-up area some 30 feet above the street. It provided the enemy with an elevated position to fire down on us. So it was a necessary objective we had to take in order to keep moving forward.

On that particular day — the 15th [February 1968], — Delta Company alone lost six killed in action and had 33 or so who were wounded and evacuated. Some were wounded but not evacuated. I don't know the exact number but it was a significant number of casualties. I had only a hundred Marines to make the attack so I lost almost 40 percent that one day.

In some cases the Marines had received multiple light wounds and would not be evacuated for a couple of days because we just didn't have the people in the line. On the 15th of February, one of my lieutenants was wounded in the attack on the tower. I required him to stay around until he came up to me one day and said, "I can't move my leg anymore." So, at that point, I evacuated him. It was a desperate time and it was necessary to leave some Marines on the line who had injuries that were not debilitating. Though they would have been painful and uncomfortable, those Marines showed great fortitude in sticking in there and staying with their friends as long as they could.

On the 20th of February, we lost a gentleman named [HN Michael J.] Reinhold, a highly respected corpsman who went to great means to make sure that he was able to take care of the Marines. Somehow he had come across an Army-style rucksack [knapsack], which was much roomier than the Marine Corps packs that we had that time. He had filled it absolutely to the brim with medical supplies to ensure that he would be able to perform his duties on the battlefield.

As for the corpsmen who were with us, they were the unsung heroes of that battle by taking care of the wounded and the dead. It's amazing the extent these young men would go to guarantee the medical welfare of the Marines.

"Code Among Brothers"

Hospital corpsman Alan Kent was a newcomer to Vietnam and had little time to orient himself to combat. The day after arriving in Danang, he was assigned to Delta Company, 1st Battal-

ion, 5th Marines. Delta Company was supposed to be in Phu Bai, the staging area for units going into combat at Hue. "I still had my leather boots and starched utilities on," Kent recalls. "Not knowing anything, with no direction, and being in a combat environment with rockets going off, it wasn't a very secure welcome to Vietnam." He could not have known that in a few days he would be involved in some of the most brutal fighting of the war—the battle to retake Hue's Citadel.

When the choppers could fly, they'd bring in the wounded. You knew they were the wounded because they dropped them off on one side. If they were KIAs, they'd move the bodies off on the other side into a different pile. From the pile of equipment that was being recycled I got to pick my gear. This equipment had all come off the dead or severely wounded. My flak jacket was full of holes. I got a Unit 1 that was all torn up, but I was able to outfit it as best I could.

I got a .45 and ammo for it, my M16, and bandoliers of ammo. I got outfitted with the basic equipment for light infantry combat plus bottles of IV fluids I found in a connex box [transportable container]. I rolled the bottles up in whatever I could find to protect them from breaking because we didn't have plastic bags or bottles in those days. I just jammed them in my pack. Everything was glass, including the plasma expanders.

The choppers—when they could fly—came into a small LZ where the hospital company was located but the monsoons were keeping the flights down. In fact, we waited for two days at the edge of that LZ for a chopper to take us up to Hue City. Hell, every time one came in, we watched all these bodies being thrown off and the wounded coming in. Then we'd walk through an inflatable building with a long line of sawhorses and stretchers down both sides and see all these guys in agony. The Marines had arms and legs missing—massive trauma. I thought, "Oh, my God! What the hell's going on? This is hell and I'm never gonna make it outta here." I didn't have any idea what incoming rounds sounded like or any idea of how I would react in combat.

We finally got on choppers and headed up to Hue City, landing in the old ARVN compound, which had originally been a French military compound on the north side of the river. The 1st and 2nd platoons of Delta Company had already gone up the river in sampans and LCUs.

A forward battalion aid station had been set up in a semi-bombed-out building in the ARVN compound. When I got off the chopper, which had landed on the edge of a wall, tracers were coming up. We ran and got under some cover.

So there I was. It was dark and wounded guys were waiting to get out. I started to make them as comfortable as possible. They were all over the place. They were lying in corners, bleeding and in pain. Everybody was trying to make them as comfortable as possible, but the equipment was minimal at best. The conditions were ridiculous.

A doctor [Lt. James P.] Brock, a really nice guy, worked to save the wounded while I was reduced to the extreme basics. Chief Folio came in with our group and a couple of other guys. All we could do was stop the bleeding, give them morphine, a cigarette, some water, and start IVs. I used some of the IVs I had in my pack because a few of the men were shocking out on me. But, by and large, this was basic, compassionate care. There wasn't a lot of level one trauma treatment taking place!

The next morning I was taken over to where they thought Delta Company was supposed to be. A Marine named Ray Howard, a black kid, was driving one of those little flat bed utility vehicles called "mules." He should have gotten the Navy Cross a hundred times. Anyway, he said, "Get your head down, Doc. We're going." So I hung onto the rails and lay flat. Every time we came around a hot corner, he'd say, "Keep your head down; there are 'gooks' right around here." And then they'd start firing at us as we zipped up and down the streets. Sometimes he'd make a wrong turn, find some enemy crossing the road, and turn around.

Ray finally got to a place where he thought Delta Company was, and said, "Jump into this ditch right here and you'll be fine." Then he spun around and took off.

So there I was lying in a ditch on the edge of the street; I didn't move. I thought, "I'm just gonna wait for this war to be over and then I'll move." I was armed to the teeth. I came from northern Michigan and shot deer and spent a lot of time in the woods so I figured I could survive one way or another. I just hoped my luck would hold out.

Five minutes later I heard somebody. This was a long street which followed the northeast [Citadel] wall. Across the street was a little courtyard with a couple of pillars, and a house which was pretty much bombed out. From across the street, I heard a couple of grunts say, "Hey, Doc. When we tell ya, come running across the street over here."

Pretty soon they opened up with their M16s down toward the end of the street and I started running across. The NVA had a .51 caliber machine gun at the end of the street, and they were blasting anybody who came across that road. I got across without incident even though they were shooting at me.

I ended up joining the group and meeting everybody. We were up against the northeast wall of the Citadel, which surrounded the Imperial Palace. At that time, we had a little bit of a lull, and — being a real novice — I hooked up with a guy who saved my life more than one time, Tommy "Spanky" Mitchell. He was a forward air controller, a real bristly Marine from Tennessee, who had already been wounded a couple of times.

He took me under his wing and began teaching me the ropes quickly. He taught me what incoming AK-47 rounds sounded like. It didn't take long because any time you moved — if you weren't careful — the NVA were behind you using you for target practice. They would get into the sewers and crawl underneath, popping up in manholes. They had spider holes[4] all over so you had to be constantly vigilant as to what was going on.

The enemy would come right at you and not give a damn. It was very difficult to stop them. You'd pump a bunch of rounds into them and they'd end up falling down. We found out later that they all knew they were going to die anyway and were high on heroin and opium. That's why the NVA were so bold and brazen and euphoric, like in a "Scarface" movie.

We didn't have any C-rations and had hardly any water. Wells were all around the area but they were contaminated. We loaded the water up with halazone [disinfectant for drinking water] but the high levels of halazone caused diarrhea on its own. The dead bodies were bloating and decomposing so it was a very disease-oriented place. We didn't think we'd live long enough to worry about having typhus or whatever. We tried burning the enemy dead with flame throwers to keep the disease and stench down. I slept next to a rotting corpse, which I covered with a piece of tin roofing for several days.

The climate, too, was against us. It was the monsoon season. You could touch the ceiling with your hands so we had very few days that choppers could fly. And we had no air cover because of that. Due to some policy, we couldn't dump ordnance into the Imperial Palace or the Citadel because the South Vietnamese didn't want us [Americans] destroying it. And that's where all the North Vietnamese regulars were holed up with their artillery and snipers. It was off limits. We couldn't get to the heart of the Citadel. It was ridiculous trying to fight a war like this.

When we'd try to make pushes down the streets, we might get a half a block and come up against B-40 rockets, machine guns, and snipers who were all over the place. My first recollection of dead GIs was a tank that had been debilitated. The commander's head was blown in half and his brains were spilled all over the place. I still can see that skull snapped like an eggshell.

I had mentioned those two pillars in the courtyard. Lo and behold, I saw some wounded GIs across that road where that machine gun had been targeted. The NVA also had that courtyard zeroed in with their mortars. I would run out and grab guys who were getting hit and falling behind the houses or shot in the street. Then I'd drag them back and get them in that little courtyard area where I'd patch them up, stop their bleeding, and apply a tourniquet. I was doing this back and forth, back and forth. Each time I'd go out there, the NVA would shoot at me and mortars would come in.

I finally got the last guy in, put him down on the ground, and took care of him. He was okay but for a little bleeder in his arm that was pumping out, which I fixed. Then I went back to see if any others were down. I was standing by a 2 × 2 × 2-square-foot pillar when a mortar round came in and hit the top of that pillar. Some of the blast went into the courtyard and threw me across the road. Luckily, the majority of the impact went behind me. I didn't even know I was hit until later. I was in shock and just ignored what was going on. I basically ended up in the same ditch I had jumped into when I got off that mule. Everything was so surreal. When I looked back into the courtyard, all the guys I had just brought in were flopping on the ground like a bunch of fish in the bottom of a boat. So I had to take care of them once again.

I was reduced to the basic essentials—using rags or clothing or whatever else we could find. And I was all by myself. Another corpsman was wounded during this time. He was hit for a second time. Only a big hole remained where his eye had been. I managed to get him patched up, but we had to wait to evacuate the casualties until we called in naval gunfire for cover fire. And naval gunfire was coming right at us from the sea. It was not like they were shooting from behind us or over our heads or laterally. The gunfire was coming right at us. We'd call in the gunfire support to try to keep "Charley's" head down. The shells would go off about 50 meters in front of the wall with pieces of shrapnel coming off—the size of a car hood. It was amazing that anything could survive. We dumped a lot of ordnance on the city and it really didn't seem like it was doing a hell of a lot in terms of impacting the enemy's ability to fight.

Men were wounded continually — hour after hour. Some had femoral wounds with femoral bleeding and just a tremendous amount of trauma to the lower extremities or the abdomen. If I was lucky enough and could find the [source of the] bleeder, I could clamp it off. Most of the time just putting direct pressure on it didn't do it. You had to get to the source and tie off the bleeders. He's gonna lose his leg but at least you might save his life. And here I was trying to be something I wasn't. How many field-trained corpsmen have dissected out and tied off major bleeders or done a trach [tracheotomy] under direct fire? You're thinking, "I don't know if I'm doing it right but I'm just doing what I know I should do." You tried to make the game up as you went along. Even though I had all the basic stuff, I knew I wasn't a surgeon. That was the frustrating part about it. I could have used a little more training, but I guess baptism under fire is one way to solidify what you can do. It's called field experience!

By this time we were down to leading platoons with pfc's [private first class]. We had no officers. The only officer around was [Capt Myron] Harrington. All the others had either been killed or wounded. We ended up making another push, led by a guy named Dennis S. Michael, a pfc. We also had David Greenway of *Time*, Al Webb from UPI, and Charlie Mohr from *The New York Times*.[5]

Michael was leading a platoon. He'd be everywhere leading guys and never get hit. You can't believe how many times he should have been killed. So a Lt. Williams arrived. He was a lead magnet. Anywhere he went, he'd get hit. He had been in the rear because of his history. But he decided to come and help out. He, Michael, and a couple of us ran up the edge of the wall trying to get into a better position along that northeast wall. The North Vietnamese were all dug in waiting and just blew the shit out of us.

Michael got hit in the face and Williams got knocked down. He had three bullets pumped into him and was bleeding — but breathing. He had been hit in the side of his neck but he was lucky. The bullets missed his jugular. He had a little bit of a spurt from a branch of his carotid, but I was able to control it with some direct pressure. He also had some holes in his leg but none were life-threatening. I started an IV of lactated Ringer's solution and applied direct pressure to his neck and leg wounds. Maybe three months after the Battle of Hue, I ended up in the rear area at Phu Bai and there was Williams sitting behind a desk. He eventually was wounded again and was finally sent home.

Michael was the worst. When I turned him over, I saw that he had bad trauma to the jaw and face — and he wasn't breathing. By that time I had been reduced to a Ka-bar fighting knife and a little tube you used for mouth-to-mouth resuscitation. I grabbed the Ka-bar and did a cricothyreotomy[6] and slipped the tube in him. But I couldn't get it in right away because he had a lot of cartilage and a clot in there. So I took my mouth, put it on the wound, and sucked all the fragments out. Then I slipped the trach in him and got him going again. Al Webb, Dave Greenway, and Charlie Mohr were there, and they found a green shutter they used for a stretcher. They were able to get him back to that courtyard area where they were trying to stage people to protect them from the direct fire.

Michael died in that battalion aid station waiting for evacuation. He made it all the way back to the battalion aid station, but because of the lack of a way to evacuate him to a higher level of care, he expired.

From the time I got to Hue until the time I left, I was covered in blood from the top of my head to the tip of my boots. Whether it was mine or somebody else's blood, I don't know. It got to the point that it didn't make any difference after a while whether or not it was my blood. In fact, when that mortar hit the pillar earlier, I was hit but it wasn't until everything died down and I was hunkered down behind a wall that I noticed something warm running down my legs. I had been wounded in my thighs and knee with shrapnel. I had fairly decent lacerations, but no bone was showing and there was no neurological deficit at that time. So I said, "I'm staying with these guys and nothing's going to make me leave unless I get killed."

It was all about bonding. It had nothing to do with the flag or Mom's apple pie or Chevrolet. It had to do with your comrades— the guys in the unit. And that was the key to it all. You just thought that they're gonna try to keep you alive and you're gonna keep each other alive as best as you can. And that was more or less the code among brothers. And believe me, our main objective wasn't to try to foster a democratic government in some country that wanted nothing to do with us.

12

KHE SANH

Khe Sanh, as with Hue, is another name associated with Vietnam that evokes a visceral response from the Marines who fought at that isolated outpost. From January through April 1968, an estimated 20,000 to 40,000 North Vietnamese troops besieged the combat base 15 miles south of the DMZ. Khe Sanh, in the northwest corner of South Vietnam, was a mere six miles from Laos. Defending the post were 5,000 men of the 3rd Marine Division.

The compact one-half by one-mile outpost was neither strategically nor militarily analogous to the French experience at Dien Bien Phu in 1954. But the parallels between the two sieges seemed almost ghostly at the time. President Lyndon Johnson contemplated political and strategic disaster should the base be lost. "I don't want any damn Dinbinphoo," he told his advisors. Despite the fact that the 77-day siege diverted attention from the real enemy objectives of the Tet Offensive, Khe Sanh would be defended at all costs — and those costs would be heavy.

Even though an estimated 10,000 communist troops were killed by American artillery and the unrelenting rain of ordnance dropped in B-52 raids, nearly 500 Marines also died either defending the base itself or in combat securing the surrounding lush hills. As elsewhere in Vietnam, caring for the Marine casualties was the job of Navy medical personnel — physicians, dentists, and corpsmen — attached to the 26th Marine Regiment.

Prior to the beginning of the siege, two battalions of the 26th Regiment's three battalions were stationed in or around Khe Sanh. On 22 January, the day following the attack, four battalions were in place: the 1st, 2nd, and 3rd Battalion, 26th Marines, and 1st Battalion, 9th Marines. Three battalion aid stations serviced the 26th Regiment, each staffed by one general medical officer. Charlie Med, the base's largest medical facility, had three or four doctors — a surgeon, an anesthesiologist, and two general medical officers. A regimental surgeon was also assigned to the 26th Marines. When business was brisk after a major shelling, Charlie Med's staff gladly accepted that regimental surgeon's assistance.

Charlie Med was adjacent to the midpoint of the 3,900-foot-long hard-surface runway. Before the siege began, four 15 by 30-foot tents had served medical needs, one for sick call, one for supplies, and two as living quarters for corpsmen. After the initial bombardment, which began on 21 January 1968, destroyed much of the above-ground facilities, troops reinforced tent side walls with double rows of sandbags. Two tents were then designated for Triage. The first casualties from communist shelling were treated on the floors of these tents with sandbags offering the only protection.

As the frequency and ferocity of the enemy bombardment increased, Navy Seabees constructed new bunkers dug into the plateau's red clay soil, shoring the clay with timbers reinforced by sandbags. One bunker had a portable operating table, generator/battery-powered lights, and a field autoclave unit.

The season seemed to dictate the type and seriousness of the wounds. During the high plateau's relatively cool winter months of January and February, Marines were more apt to wear their flak jackets and keep them closed. As a result, incidences of serious chest and head wounds were relatively low. In warm weather, the troops were less concerned about wearing hot, cumbersome flak jackets and helmets, resulting in a higher incidence of upper body injuries. Of the 2,500 casualties treated during the siege, 95 percent were multiple fragment wounds, mostly to the abdomen and extremities; 300 of 2,500 men triaged had minor fragment wounds and, after treatment, were returned to duty. The regimen was to clean, debride, and dress the wounds and administer tetanus shots.

According to James Finnegan, one of Charlie Med's surgeons, the triage procedure was well developed and well rehearsed. Corpsmen first stripped each casualty of combat gear and clothing and then took vital signs. Blood was drawn for typing, followed by a complete examination to determine the location and gravity of the casualty's wounds. Besides the most obvious injuries, medical personnel carefully inspected the scalp, posterior part of the neck, back, axillae, and the anal, perineal, and scrotal areas. This procedure was made even more critical because x-ray equipment was not available at Khe Sanh. During the initial triage, any casualty who arrived by litter had an intravenous line inserted immediately.

Medical personnel performed emergency surgery for the most seriously wounded. The immediate goal was to stabilize and then evacuate them to more advanced facilities back at Dong Ha or aboard one of the hospital ships. The weather didn't always cooperate, making medevac sometimes impossible. The high ground looming over the base was often shrouded in fog and mist during the monsoons, masking enemy troops and limiting flying conditions. It was atop some of these hills that the most brutal fighting took place.

77 Days of Hell on Hill 881S

William Gerrard joined the Navy in 1965 wanting to be a hospital corpsman. His first assignment was to the Brooklyn Navy Yard clinic, which was unusual because he had not yet attended the hospital corps school at Great Lakes, Illinois. Following his stint at Brooklyn, he attended a 14-week course at the hospital corps school and was then assigned to Naval Hospital Portsmouth, Virginia, where he spent the next seven months.

Field Medical Service School at Camp Lejeune, North Carolina, was Gerrard's next stop before being transferred to the 5th Marine Division at Camp Pendleton for more training. Not surprisingly, Camp Pendleton was merely a way station on the road to Vietnam. The Nebraska native arrived in Danang in October 1967 and was assigned to Company M, 3rd Battalion, 26th Marines.

I was already an E-4 [Hospital Corpsman Third Class] and had taken the exam for E-5 [Second Class]. One event led to another and I was assigned to Weapons Platoon of Mike Company as a spare corpsman in case someone got hurt.

A few weeks later my senior corpsman came down with amoebic dysentery, and I ended up as senior corpsman of the company. Then my senior corpsman came back for a couple of months until his time in the bush was done.

On Christmas Eve night, the leading chief of the battalion aid station told me I was senior corpsman of the company for good. I actually thought that was a cool Christmas present at the time. All of sudden, I was medically responsible for 200 guys. About three weeks later, we went up on Hill 881S[1] [south of the Khe Sanh base] for a 24-hour operation. It lasted for 77 days!

Once or twice we got down to one meal a day while we were there. You don't put on a lot of weight eating C-rations. The best we ever had was two meals a day eating C-rations. Every ounce of what we needed — from water to food to whatever — came in by chopper. But we weren't really prepared to stay there 77 days. We had gone to Hill 881S on a one-day operation and had taken a few extra packs of cigarettes and a change of socks. And that was basically it. The prevailing command was: "You guys are here and you're staying. You have the bottom of the hill and India Company has the top of the hill."

We were there to slow up and stop the NVA if they tried to come through us. On certain parts of the hill, you could see over to [Hills] 861N and 881N and also the runway at Khe Sanh. The mission was to keep the enemy from occupying the hills which prevent them from shooting down at the base.

Our job was to cover the perimeter while India Company [3rd Battalion, 26th Marines] went over to 881N. Capt. [William] Dabney, who was "Chesty" [Lt. Gen. Lewis] Puller's son-in-law, was taking his troops over to 881N, and that was the first major contact we had for the beginning of the Tet Offensive. These troops ran into a battalion of NVA coming to attack us that very same night. So instead of evacuating us back to the base, we ended up spending the next two and a half months right there on Hill 881S.

The enemy occupied 881 North, about a click [kilometer] or two away from us. They could fire mortars and we could fire mortars back—if we could see anything, which was difficult because they had their artillery on the reverse side of the hill. They knew where we were but we couldn't see them.

The first night I was in my bunker all by myself. Grenades were flying, mortar rounds were landing, and illumination rounds were going off. I wasn't real comfortable sitting in my bunker alone not knowing what was going on. So I finally worked up my courage to go out to the trench line. As luck would have it, no one got hurt that night. We lost kids during resupply and at other times—but not that night.

Most of our contact with the enemy was sitting on Hill 881S taking mortar rounds, rockets, and some artillery. As a corpsman, I saw a lot of casualties. They were mostly shrapnel wounds, which I treated with pressure dressings. Every two or three days there was a medevac. It seems that every time we turned around, we were medevacing kids out. Most of the time they went straight to Dong Ha or Quang Tri, not routinely to the main base at Khe Sanh.

Hill 881 was pretty bare; nothing was up there. If you see pictures of World War I with guys living in the trenches—that's how we lived. We dug holes back in the sides of the trenches—two-man crawl spaces in which to sleep. I had a bunker in a 1,000-pound bomb crater. That's where we initially brought the wounded. It was below ground and considered one of the safest spots. After I treated the casualties, we'd load them on stretchers and haul them out to the "saddle."

That little saddle, located between our perimeter and India Company's perimeter, was covered by both sides, but it was where the trash dump was located. The saddle was one of the safer places for medevac birds to come in because the enemy didn't have a good view of it. For some reason, they couldn't get their mortars on the saddle quick enough to hit. It seemed like every two or three days we were in the saddle with maybe three or four shrapnel wound cases to medevac. Sometimes we'd sit there for two or three hours with these guys.

The NVA had observers spotting the hills. If more than two or three guys were out on top of the hill during daylight hours, they'd drop a round on them. I lost my Weapons Platoon corpsman that way, a kid named Jerry King [HN Doyle G.]. We heard the first round leave the tube. Then we heard the second round leave before the first round even hit. In between rounds someone yelled, "Corpsman up!" Jerry already had his gear on and jumped out the door to go to the Marine who was down. He ended up getting hit by the second mortar round. That action was probably one of the bravest deeds I ever saw. He knew it was coming and he went anyhow. At times I had gone out in answer to "Corpsman up!" When you heard that call, you grabbed your Unit 1 [medical supply bag] and scrambled. But this time I didn't get out there quick enough and Jerry got hit. I dealt with a lot of injured men on that hill. Of all the guys who were there, only 11 came off who were not wounded.

The scariest moment occurred when the NVA dropped some artillery on us from Co Roc,[2] an artillery base on a hill off toward Laos. The company gunny and the Weapons Platoon gunny said, "Hey Doc, can we borrow your foxhole to have lunch in? The rounds seem to be following us around."

I said, "Sure." They got into my foxhole, which was in the bottom of that 1,000-pound bomb crater, and I went into one of the next hooches to talk to some guys from Weapons Platoon. About three minutes later an artillery round made a direct hit on my foxhole and they were both KIA. Needless to say, it's a memory that has stayed with me.

We never saw the B-52s that bombed the enemy but we heard them. They were so high up. But then all of a sudden, you could hear the bombs hitting and the ground shook. Sometimes they were dropping them within a thousand yards of us.

When that artillery came in [from Co Roc] and hit the gunny, I got a concussion. They turned that in and it counted as a wound for me. All of a sudden a new corpsman came in and said, "I'm your replacement."

I came off the hill by chopper and went back down to the main base at Khe Sanh. There was nothing left standing. All activities were done from a bunker — a hole in the ground — and everybody lived underground. I wondered, "What are a bunch of Marines doing here? Sitting here and holding a piece of real estate is an Army job."

When we arrived in Khe Sanh, we all walked down the company street in combat formation — five yards in between down both sides of the road. When we got to the company area, I walked into the aid station and someone said, "Who the hell are you?" They looked at us strangely because we had been living on less than a canteen of water the whole time we were up there. We didn't shave and I came off the hill with 70 days' growth of beard. I had lost about 20 pounds.

"A Friendly Parachute"

Since arriving in Vietnam, Raymond Felle, hospital corpsman of Kilo Company, 3rd Battalion, 9th Marines, had seen continuous action up near the DMZ — combat at the Rock Pile, at Camp Carroll artillery base, at Ca Lu, and savage fighting on Valentine's Ridge. Felle's unit had most recently been patrolling west along the Laotian border trying to locate and destroy an NVA force reported to be operating in that vicinity. Locating the Ho Chi Minh Trail and pinpointing a reported enemy hospital rumored to be in the area were also part of the battalion's mission.

It was the beginning of summer 1968 and the 3rd Battalion had accomplished most of what it had set out to do. The unit then assembled at a landing zone carved out of the jungle and waited for transportation to Khe Sanh.

On the 19th of June, helicopters came in to pick us up — CH-46 Sea Knights. Seventeen from my platoon and I got on one of them. I recall looking out one of the windows and seeing the airstrip at Khe Sanh. You could see a burned-out plane, either a C-130 or a C-123 lying out in the middle of the runway.

I had already been out in the field for six months and was supposed to be rotating out but they couldn't get a replacement for me. So here I was heading into Khe Sanh. The helicopter was to land at a place called LZ Turkey in the southwest corner of the base. As we prepared to land, someone drove one of those small vehicles called a "mule" [small flat-bed vehicle] right under where we were going to land so the pilot aborted the landing. As he circled around to make another try, one of the parachutes used to drop supplies during the siege rose up off the ground and was sucked up by the rotor blades. When the two blades came together they exploded.

We were about 25 feet in the air and the helicopter dropped to the ground like a rock. The crash broke the back of the helicopter and the rear gate jammed shut. As jet fuel poured out everywhere, we tried to get out the back of the chopper. Everyone was screaming. I didn't know the choppers had side doors because I had always entered and left at the back. Just for a minute, I thought, "This is it. It's gonna catch on fire or blow up — and I'm dead. The inside of this chopper is the last thing I'm ever gonna see." Then someone screamed to us from a side door where the gunners normally were and we ran from the helicopter.

It did not catch fire. Over the years, I've tried to figure out why it didn't. I triaged all my men and found that they just had fuel burns. I went to the front of the helicopter. The person on the left, who I later found out was the co-pilot, was dead. His name was Lt. [Michael D.] Helmstetler. The transmission had crushed him. His helmet and everything else were down almost to the level of his pelvis. The pilot, Capt. [Lufkin] Sharp, was on the right side. Parts of the blade had come through the Plexiglas and cut his arm and leg off.

One of the other birds flying nearby saw what had happened and landed. The crew pulled the pilot out and took him aboard that other helicopter, which then took off for D-Med in Dong Ha. But Sharp died en route. When I looked in the cockpit, all I saw was a boot with part of his leg in it and part of his arm. Later they gave both Helmstetler and Sharp Purple Hearts as if they were killed by enemy action. But it was really friendly action if you consider it was a "friendly" parachute that caused the crash.

"Brave Deeds by Young Men"

Lt. Edward Feldman had been in the Navy since August 1967 and was eager to do his part in Vietnam. A month later he received orders to Camp Pendleton's Field Medical Service School. After completing the course, Feldman reported to the Marine Corps Recruit Depot in San Diego for duty. When he arrived, his new commanding officer informed him that he was a "rooster."

"So here I was among all this new terminology and all the acronyms I couldn't keep straight. I asked him what a 'rooster' was."

"He answered, 'You're just here to roost for a while because you're going to WESTPAC.'"

"I wasn't quite sure what WESTPAC was so I asked, 'Is that Vietnam?'"

"And he said, 'Yes. That's likely Vietnam.'"

Feldman arrived in Danang and was assigned to the 3rd Medical Battalion at Phu Bai. Shortly afterward, he received temporary duty orders to the 1st Battalion, 26th Marines at Khe Sanh where he was to help man that battalion's aid station.

It was January 3rd, 1968, when I got to Khe Sanh. After the hill fights in the late spring of 1967, Khe Sanh was considered a nice R&R place — a little plateau in the mountains. The base was dirty red clay. Each unit had bunkers all above ground. They were just dirty sandbagged bunkers with some living spaces. The battalion aid station was housed in large brown tents; I had two of these tents one in front of the other. One was for storage, the other for conducting sick call and seeing casualties. The BAS had a bench or two and a nice red and yellow lettered sign reading: 1/26 BAS [1st Battalion, 26th Marines Battalion Aid Station].

We had medications, stethoscopes, an ophthalmoscope, dressings, and minor surgical sets. I don't remember the sterilization equipment but I'm sure it was there. We even had electricity with light bulbs and visible wire going to what must have been a generator. To the immediate north and northwest were mountains [hills]; to the south and southeast the land was relatively flat from my line of sight.

The corpsmen were great. The day I arrived they prepared a place for me to sleep but because they had only three blankets, each guy offered me his blanket, which was a poncho liner. I wouldn't take their blankets so I remember freezing my ass off that night. Because Khe Sanh was much higher than Phu Bai, we experienced a tremendous weather differential temperature-wise. It was hot during the day even though it was January, but it got pretty cool at night.

On Sunday morning, 21 January 1968, the base was hit. There had been some activity in the preceding days on Hills 861 and 881, and we had taken one KIA and three severe WIAs [wounded in action].

That morning began at 0500 with a fierce mortar and rocket attack. By the time the siege began, I had moved into a two-person bunker but I was alone. It was a good bunker but it stood up above ground. I was very frightened. And I can underline the word "very." We were sleeping in our clothes, sleeping in our boots, and sleeping with weapons. I had unlaced my boots a bit and now was trying to tie them. My hands were shaking. I was in no position to help anyone in this bunker all by myself.

Suddenly, a huge round landed just outside my bunker. It sounded like a freight train coming in. If that shell had exploded in the passageway that led to the outside, I would have fallen into a hole the size of a Volkswagen. It had taken out our "shower" — a 55-gallon drum with a shower attached to it. The EOD [Explosive Ordnance Disposal] people later told me that it must have been an artillery round.

Fortunately, I had increased our defensive posture. I had two automatic weapon positions at either end of the triage bunker, our so-called "holding bunker." I had obtained from Lt. Col. Wilkinson [commanding officer of 1st Battalion, 26th Marines] some additional Marine personnel to operate these weapon positions.

I waited a little while and then headed for the battalion aid station but it was on fire, having taken a direct hit. The BAS was essentially gone. Instead, I went to an above-ground bunker, which was our holding bunker, and moved out the guys who had resided there in a two- or three-day hold situation; I then sent them elsewhere. They weren't wounded but just had rashes and other minor ailments.

We salvaged as much as we could from the battalion aid station tents and put all that gear into one corner. One person then started sorting out undamaged supplies and equipment so we could utilize the holding bunker efficiently.

[Lt. Feldman reading from his journal:] "A restless night but surprisingly no attacks. Slept on ward which was defended by several automatic rifles, a grease gun, [.45 caliber submachine gun], and a shotgun. Received incoming mortar rounds. These were not as bad as rockets. Continued taking casualties. Today is clear and extensive repair and resupply is going on. Removed something questionable — a live 82 round from patient's abdomen. Thoughts of mail become less important during times such as this. Many brave deeds by young men."

I heard incoming throughout the course of that day, and a lot of shells that were cooking off in the ammo dump. Resupply was going on by helicopter and fixed wing for a short time thereafter, but I don't have a firm memory of that. I know that we lost some aircraft — a C-130 and a C-123 — on the runway during the approaches. The scarring of the airstrip became more pronounced with more and more incoming. The runway soon became useless as a means of fixed wing resupply and/or evacuation.

To characterize the incoming as "sporadic" would suggest only an occasional round but that was anything but the case. On some days we'd have heavy incoming and some days it would be considerably lighter. We had one recorded day of 1,309 rounds of incoming and that was in a relatively small place. That's a huge amount of incoming! I've heard figures that are substantially greater than that. I would say that we had incoming every day, some days more than others.

My mission — the care of the wounded at the battalion aid station level — was really not taking care of serious casualties unless I was close to them. I directed the serious casualties to Charlie Med, located in the central portion of the base. It was staffed with doctors more skilled than myself. In fact, instructions went out to all personnel that serious casualties who needed really complex care and/or evacuation were to be directed to Charlie Med. Unless a serious casualty was close to 1/26 BAS which I was attached to, I didn't see a large number of company casualties. I saw the less complex cases.

I found that I needed to stay at Khe Sanh, and the way to do that was to get reassigned to Charlie Med. I told Lt. Col. Wilkinson, the battalion commander, that I needed to stay and

Lt. Edward Feldman monitors a patient's IV in the Khe Sanh bunker that housed Charlie Med (courtesy Edward Feldman).

asked him to help me get reassigned to Charlie Med. I also told Comdr. Brown, the medical battalion commander, of my desire to join his staff. I soon got my wish.

In terms of training, I was the most junior person, but the doctors I worked with instructed me. In very short order we developed a sense of triage and we all worked well together. Over the next few weeks when we had the need for definitive procedures, such as inserting a chest tube, doing a tracheostomy, taking care of very serious extremity wounds, and preparing abdominal and head wound patients for evacuation, I would not do it alone. I had neither the training nor the experience to do it. We all did that together. These guys trained, taught, and mentored me. It didn't take long to learn these procedures because the principles were clear.

The surgery we did was stabilization. We maintained what I call a "surgical capability to perform a definitive procedure," and we actually planned to do one if the circumstance was right. If that should happen, our objective would be to perform a definitive abdominal procedure — if the patient could not be evacuated or if delay would jeopardize the casualty's survival.

We soon had our test case with a wounded South Vietnamese soldier. The weather had closed in on us and we couldn't get him out. So Don Magilligan [surgeon] did the operation, Jim Finnegan [surgeon] supervised it, I assisted, and Joe Wolfe [general medical officer] gave the anesthesia. We definitively operated on this casualty in the triage bunker. We opened him up from stem to stern and did whatever had to be done. We did it because it had to be done, but we also did it to convince ourselves that we could actually perform this type of surgery if need be.

We had no x-ray so we never looked for fragments. As I said, the only open operation that we had done relative to an abdominal exploration was the one on that South Vietnamese soldier. If someone got hit in the chest, we'd put in a chest tube but never did the definitive surgery. If a casualty had a hemopneumothorax [blood in the pleural cavity], it was treated by opening the chest and placing a Heimlich chest tube and valve. If the injured had a neck wound or facial wounds, or anything that might compromise the airway, we performed a tracheostomy. Depending upon the level of consciousness, we then evacuated the casualty with an endotracheal tube in place with an ambu bag.[3]

We had a few amputations in cases where extremities were all but traumatically amputated. And we saw all manner of extremity wounds. We treated them with compression dressings and inflatable splints to stabilize the fracture.

We placed large-bore IV tubing directly into the lesser saphenous vein [in the leg]. We all became very good at that. I shouldn't say it that way. I became very good at that. The medical staff physicians were already adept!

It wasn't clear what was going to happen to the base. Rumor spread that it would be taken over by the Army and destroyed building by building. I thought that as long as Charlie Med was a functioning unit that at least two of us should remain, and Joe Wolfe and I decided to stay till the very end.

I don't know the official date the siege ended but it lasted 77 days. During the third week in April [1968], the Army's presence was more and more visible in an operation called "Operation Pegasus." It seemed that every E-2 [Private] had his own chopper. The sky was so filled with choppers, it looked like a swarm of mosquitoes or a bee's nest. I left on April 23rd. We had hot meals that night.

I saw a good deal of antagonism. We had been living in dirt, filthy utilities, no underwear, no showers. And these Army guys come up with great equipment — and lots of it — and an attitude like "we bailed you guys out." That didn't go down well with Marines and rightfully so — and certainly not after what we had endured.

"Get Me to Charlie Med!"

Combat engineer 1st Lt. William K. Gay, USMC, was assigned to the 1st Platoon, A Company of the 3rd Engineer Battalion. Gay's engineer force was attached to the 26th Regiment at Khe Sanh in late 1967. By March 1968, the strain of constant shelling and witnessing violent death every day had taken a heavy toll on Gay and his men.

I arrived in Khe Sanh in October 1967. By that time Route 9, the only land access to Khe Sanh, had already been taken over by the North Vietnamese, and the bridges had all been blown. We were resupplied only by air. Enemy contact increased in November, December, and January preceding the official siege.

An increasing number of incidents led up to the siege, which began on 21 January [1968]. A few days earlier, a recon patrol had taken a large number of casualties and several people were killed.

My platoon, part of the engineer force, lived in bunkers. People made fun of us because those bunkers were dirty with the ever-present smell of mildew and stale air. But at least we were underground. When the rounds came in that morning, many units were still living above ground. All they had around their tents were sandbagged walls or 55-gallon drums filled with dirt. Those units suffered a significant number of casualties. All we did in our bunkers was get scared as the explosions went off.

On the morning of 8 March, I told my platoon sergeant, "Ski [SSGT Ron "Ski" Sniekowski], I can't go out today." I usually took out a squad and he took one out to do some work. We always left one squad back, ostensibly to improve their defenses — to put more sandbags on the bunker. But the real reason was that these were 19-year-old kids, and it would give them a chance to be under cover for a day and decompress psychologically. So that day I said, "Ski, I can't go out. My nerves are shot." I had stopped eating by that time. In fact, I had not eaten for days other than the chocolate we got in sundry packs.

Ski responded, "Mr. Gay, you've been out every single day. Take a day off."

So I rested on top of a bunker in the sun when a beautiful woman showed up — Jurate Kazickas. She was freelancing for U.S. newspapers, and was attempting to do interviews with soldiers from New York.[4] We were all infatuated with her when she began to talk to us because she was tall, polished, very sophisticated, and very beautiful, even though she was filthy like the rest of us.

As we talked, one round came in some good distance away, causing us to begin moving to safety. The North Vietnamese forward observer that day was very good because the next rounds were right on us. I had just jumped into my bunker when I realized Kazickas was not in there with us. I went back out to get her, pushed her in, and then dove in behind her just as a round went off.

Kazickas got a lot of small dings but I got the big blast, including a very large piece that just about ripped my right buttock off. Another piece went through my right foot and shattered the joint. A piece went into my elbow and came out my shoulder, and lots of pieces ended up in both my legs and my arm. My flak jacket was almost ripped off my body, and my helmet was also badly beaten up. I knew I had been hit because I could feel the heat. I remember saying, "I'm hit! Dammit! I'm hit bad!"

I put my hand between my legs to determine if my penis and genitals had been blown off and came up with a handful of blood. To this day, where a big piece of shrapnel entered, I still have a scar about three inches long located an inch below my testicles.

My platoon corpsman was already giving me whatever painkiller he had. Shortly afterward, they threw me onto a mule — a platform with four wheels that looked like a rough-terrain vehicle of today — and took me to Charlie Med. Dr. [Donald] Magilligan was working on me when my platoon sergeant showed up. My one good hand still grasped the compass I had used to place the mines. I refused to let go of it because it was the compass we used in the minefields and we needed it. Another compass might not have the same set of errors in it. I finally gave the compass to my platoon sergeant, Ski, and the doctors continued working on me.

Once I had been stabilized, I was carried on a stretcher to where the helicopters came in. The guys who worked at the chopper landing were all volunteers — all corpsmen and other Marines — and they had a tough and miserable job. They were the men who carried the stretchers. Although the medevac choppers would feint in one direction and go to another site, it didn't take the North Vietnamese very long to adjust their artillery or rockets and drop them in.

Ironically, the day I was wounded, I was supposed to be in Bangkok on R&R, but I turned it down because I felt it was too dangerous getting in and out of Khe Sanh. The helicopters, the C-123s, and the C-130s were being shot down right and left so I wasn't real excited about getting off the ground.

I was on the last stretcher that was put on the first bird; it took off immediately. As the chopper rose, I looked down at the moonscape that was now Khe Sanh. It had once been a lush green coffee plantation. I then heard a voice say, "I made it!" I realized the voice was mine. I had made it out of Khe Sanh alive.

I and many others would not have made it out alive without the medical personnel at Charlie Med. At Khe Sanh, Charlie Med was a complete subculture with amazing people. When the siege began, those doctors were operating behind sandbag walls that weren't even full height. Prior to the Seabees building a bunker for them, the doctors were operating in different places so they all wouldn't be killed at one time. The number of people they treated and then medevaced out was just unbelievable. Charlie Med was a constant conveyor belt of injured and mangled people. Those medical folks worked day and night.

Charlie Med took care of our men. When the one corpsman assigned to my platoon wasn't helping us, he was running over to someone nearby who was wounded, patching him up, and getting him to Charlie Med.

I can't tell you how important Charlie Med was to the morale of all of us at Khe Sanh. As combat engineers, we always had to expose ourselves to enemy fire when we moved about the combat base. We found some extra courage to do so because we believed that if wounded, we would survive if our platoon mates could only get us to Charlie Med.

I can say this: Many, many more people would have died at Khe Sanh had it not been for the doctors in Charlie Med and the corpsmen and Marines who volunteered to put us on choppers. Throughout Khe Sanh we had all heard the account of the young Marine with the mortar round in his stomach — and the doctor [Lt. Edward Feldman] at Charlie Med who had saved him. That story led to the cry, "Get me to Charlie Med! They'll save me!"

"Young and Bulletproof"

As a youngster, James Thomas could see himself as an artist hanging out on Paris's Left Bank. But with a family tradition of medicine, he focused his attention on medical school. After graduating from Morehead State College in his native Kentucky, Thomas attended the University of Kentucky School of Medicine. Upon completing his internship, he decided to delay his residency and go to Vietnam. The personal intervention of an influential former Navy physician helped secure Thomas a commission as a Navy medical officer.

After the obligatory orientation at Field Medical Service School, Thomas headed for Vietnam and was assigned as battalion surgeon to the 1st Battalion, 4th Marines. It was July 1967. "When I got out to my Marine battalion, I had no idea what I was supposed to do. So I put together my own processes and my own approaches. I found out what the guy had done before me and that's what I did."

Thomas's battalion operated north of Hue and as far north as Quang Tri and Conthien. On one battalion-size operation, his unit was hit very badly. "We took a lot of casualties that night. The canopy was a hundred feet, and we couldn't bring any helicopters in mainly because we were taking a lot of fire and were concerned about getting overrun. I had a bomb crater full of dead and dying."

From the field, Lt. Thomas reported to Alpha Med at Phu Bai. But because he had experience handling casualties, he supervised the hospital's triage and performed some surgery. That knowledge soon earned him a ticket to Khe Sanh where his skills were sorely needed. He was assigned to Charlie Med as soon as he arrived.

As far as a base goes, it was a pretty raggedy place. I was not at all impressed with it as a stronghold. I had been in places where people had built some very sophisticated bunker systems — nice and neat. This place looked like it had been thrown together. Don't get me wrong. People had bunkers but the bunker system didn't impress me the way the usual Marine bunker systems did. I thought that if they hit us, we would be in trouble. You could look out and see mountains all around. From a strategic standpoint, it didn't look too cool.

When I arrived at Charlie Med, I had a jungle hut. The hooch had one small bunker, but when I had to take care of patients, I had to go upstairs to the hut. And I didn't attend to them standing up. Most commonly, I took care of them lying down.

I had decided to sleep in the bunker the night of 20-21 January, and at 5 o'clock in the morning we took our first round. I think by noon we had taken a thousand rounds. I have a photograph showing me taking care of a casualty around that time.

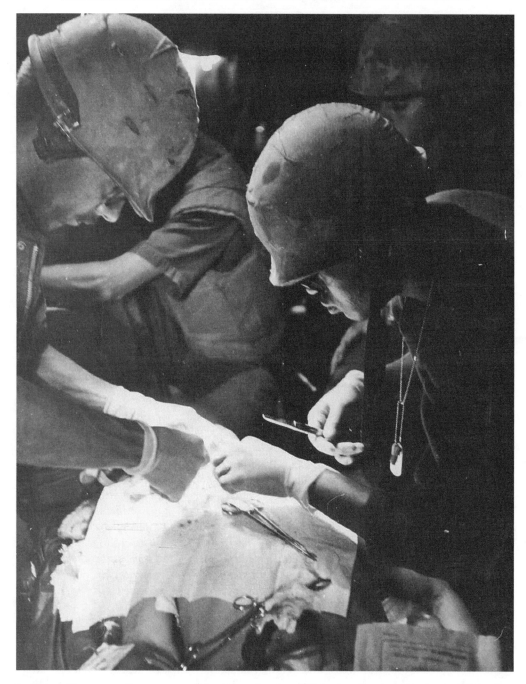

Lt. James Thomas performs emergency surgery in a bunker during the siege of Khe Sanh (BUMED Archives).

A kid came in with a bad injury to his jaw. It was pretty obvious that he had an obstructed airway. We were in that jungle hut or hooch at the time he was on a stretcher and I was on my knees. I did what I had learned to do as an intern, that is, do a tracheostomy. A corpsman helped me. I don't know whether or not the casualty survived; I just don't remember but the operation went very well. I don't actually recall the picture being taken or who took it, but I saw it in *Stars and Stripes* while I was in Nam. Photographers were around all the time, and many of them were just Marine Corps photographers.

I never got an opportunity to burrow in deeper like Jim [Finnegan] and Ed [Feldman]. The whole time I was there, I was upstairs. The hooch was sandbagged to a certain level. In case anything hit adjacent to it, the sandbags at least would prevent shrapnel from harming people. The hooches had canvas on the sides and slabs of wood. We had lots of debris from artillery — shrapnel from rounds, rockets. That debris was all over the place and zinging around us while we worked. You never knew whether or not you were going to get hit. On a number of occasions, guys would bring their wounded buddies in and then walk out and get blown away.

Was any of this frightening? It's difficult to say that because when you were doing what you had to do, you didn't pay much attention. You were young and bulletproof and had to take care of these people. Nevertheless, at times the shelling was so heavy that we treated casualties on our knees or lying down.

Circumstances eventually improved but not while I was there. I was above ground the whole time. In fact, a surgeon was brought in because there was a fear that I didn't have the skills to handle the situation. He lasted about 48 hours before going back because of the severity of the shelling. It's difficult to remember now how frequently those rounds came in, but I can assure you they came in frequently. We felt like we were going to be overrun every day, every night, every minute. The shelling was intense, but it reached a level that we soon adjusted to. We were constantly hearing rumors that someone had gone out today and didn't come back.

The perimeter was being checked continually. One time a Marine Corps pilot was dropping napalm when his plane was hit, and he came down inside the perimeter. They brought him to me at Charlie Med pretty shaken up but not seriously hurt. We shared some medicinal brandy in the bunker.

What limited the ability of anyone to provide care was a safe facility. Eventually a bunker was built underground. You also needed support personnel who would allow you to intervene to save people's lives.

To do this, you had to be able to provide blood. You also had to be able to operate in a safe circumstance. Then you had to be able to get people out as quickly as possible — those whose injuries you couldn't treat and those whom you had operated on who needed further support. This meant you had to have a way of moving patients fairly quickly.

This is how we got people in and out of Khe Sanh. The C-130 would land and taxi down the runway, never stopping. We'd run out with stretchers and load them in the back, and then the plane would take off. If we had really heavy incoming, the C-130s wouldn't come in. A number of them had been hit and pushed off to the side.

I was at Khe Sanh about three weeks, but it seemed like a very, very long time. When I left, I got out on one of those C-130s. I ran, jumped in the back of one, and hoped I wouldn't get hit.

Why were we at Khe Sanh in the first place? I think those discussions were held not only before going there, but while there, after leaving there, and even after leaving Vietnam. We were very much aware of the possible parallel between Dien Bien Phu and Khe Sanh. Everyone was aware of that siege. And I think it influenced our behavior as well in terms of making people steel their will to a great extent. But I think what happened is that the people around you became so important that you felt it was a waste of energy to talk about why you were there. It was better to use your energy to take care of these folks, and you didn't want to do anything that would prevent you from focusing on your job. You developed relationships with these guys and they became very important people.

Dentist Under Siege

Lt. Robert Birtcil arrived in Vietnam in December 1967 as a replacement for another dentist who had recently been killed in action. That dentist had been a member of 3rd Dental Company while attached to First Amphibian Tractor Battalion located at Cua Viet Combat Base.[5] In 1967, 3rd Dental Company was headquartered at and co-located with 3rd Marine Division Headquarters in Phu Bai near the ancient Vietnamese capital of Hue. The Headquarters Clinic at Phu Bai was staffed by four to six dentists, as were the clinics at Delta Medical Company at Dong Ha Combat Base and the clinic at the Sub Unit 2 compound at Dong Ha Combat Base. Once "seasoned," a dental officer might be assigned to a smaller clinic within the Dong Ha Combat Base or with the 11th Engineers. He might also be sent to one of the more remote combat bases in I Corps adjacent to the DMZ—Cua Viet, Cam Lo, Camp Carroll, or Khe Sanh.

Most of these bases reserved space for a small dental clinic staffed by one dentist. These clinics were generally equipped with one or two field dental chairs, field dental lights, sterilizer, air syringe, evacuator, and a field dental unit consisting of a compressor to power air-driven high- and low-speed handpieces. One of these suction machines sometimes doubled for abdominal lavage[6] on casualties. Field dental x-ray units were scarce.

A major problem for both medical and dental personnel was finding enough electrical power to run all the equipment. As Birtcil soon learned, 3rd Dental Company was entitled to just a single diesel generator. Since the company had at least six clinics in disparate locations, that generator was usually assigned to one of the larger clinics. Even with the Marines providing power at other clinics, demand for electrical power often outstripped the ability of the Marine Corps to provide it. Lt. Birtcil recalls, "I remember being 'down' for patient care many times for broken generators, generators that needed maintenance, and generators that—despite being sandbagged—were put out of operation by shrapnel."

In the first week of February 1968, word came that the 3rd Dental Company's dentist, who had been with the 26th Marines at Khe Sanh, was being reassigned and needed a replacement. The siege had already begun on 21 January with the initial attack by the NVA. That morning enemy fire had set off the combat base's ammunition dump with spectacular results. Ammunition "cooked off," throwing artillery rounds and other ordnance into the air and onto the combat base's flimsy structures. Needless to say, with Khe Sanh's precarious situation, volunteers needed to fill the dental vacancy were not forthcoming.

Even more hazardous was getting into or out of the base by air because air travel was the only mode of transportation. Route 9, the east-west road south of the DMZ between Dong Ha and Khe Sanh, had been closed prior to the start of the Tet Offensive. One airplane was hit while unloading supplies on the ramp at Khe Sanh. The cargo plane caught fire and went up in flames. At least one CH-53 helicopter had also been hit and destroyed. C-123s and C-130s were no longer stopping on the runway or ramp at Khe Sanh. Air crews began kicking off supplies while rolling down the airstrip. Soon they would not even land at Khe Sanh, but would employ low-altitude parachute ejection system (LAPES) delivery of supplies. Eventually the Air Force would use a high-altitude ejection system to drop supplies—with mixed results for the safety of Marines below. CH-46 and CH-53 helos would land just long enough to offload personnel and supplies, take on casualties, and immediately get airborne again—all the time risking hits by NVA gunners. With no takers to relieve the Khe Sanh dentist, Lt. Birtcil, who was then serving at the larger four- to six-dental officer clinic located at Sub Unit 2, raised his hand and volunteered for the assignment. Nothing he had previously experienced could have prepared him for duty at Khe Sanh.

I recall staying at the air terminal all day on 9 February, but no transportation to Khe Sanh was available. The weather was bad—foggy, cloudy, and overcast with some rain.

The next day I was able to get a ride on a CH-53 with some other personnel and supplies going to Khe Sanh. The overcast around Dong Ha had lifted, but once we flew into the mountain area surrounding Khe Sanh, we were in the overcast traveling through a thick fog. I was sitting in a "sling seat" at the front of the aircraft on the right side, just behind the door gunner manning a "Ma Duce" [.50 caliber machine gun]. I had a pretty good view out the door gunner's window and was watching our progress through the fog. The airspeed of the CH-53 was slow at this point as though the pilot was looking for something. All of a sudden the fog parted to the right side of the helo, and the door gunner and I were looking at a mountainside — and that mountainside was very close. Evidently the helo crew saw this mountainside at the same time I did for the CH-53 heeled over to the left and we were back in the fog. We were flying a radio beacon located at Khe Sanh Base, and something went wrong either with the beacon or the electronics in the CH-53 because I heard the crew chief shout at me.

A short time later we broke out of the fog and landed at Khe Sanh. As the rear door ramp lowered, a Marine was running toward the helo, and the crew chief was already directing people off the aircraft while other crew were throwing off supplies. The Marine who met us upon exiting the helo directed us on a run to a sandbagged area/slit trench at the edge of the ramp. We took advantage of that trench for several minutes even after the CH-53 lifted off. I don't remember any ordnance hitting the ramp or runway upon my arrival, but I probably wouldn't have known because of all the ambient noise from the helicopter.

It turned out we were in the sandbagged area just outside Charlie Med, which was located on the south side of the runway. Casualties slated for evacuation were lying there. I believe later that day a C-130 was hit. It crashed and burned on the runway.

When directed by the Marine, I grabbed my gear and proceeded in the direction of the first structure that turned out to be Charlie Med. A corpsman showed me the way to the Combat Operations Center [COC] so I could meet and report to Col. David Lownds, who was the regimental commander. In the eight weeks I had been "in country," I had cultivated a pretty good-sized handlebar moustache. Col. Lownds was standing in the middle of the room. After I introduced myself, he looked at me and said, "You're the new dentist. Okay, Doc, I've got only one thing I want you to do. Cut that moustache off!"

Of course, he was standing there with his own handlebar moustache. I said, "Yes, sir!"

Then he looked at me with a twinkle in his eye and said, "I'll bet you're wondering why I'm ordering you to do that, aren't you?"

"Yes, sir."

"Because you're the only son-of-a-bitch here with one bigger than I've got." It turned out he was just kidding me. I kept the moustache.

After reporting to Lownds on the 10th, I proceeded to the Regimental Aid bunker to check in and see who I would

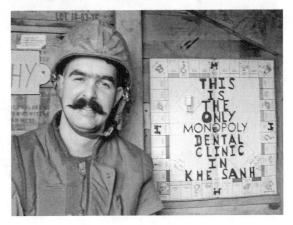

Lt. Robert Birtcil at Khe Sanh (courtesy Robert Birtcil).

be working with. Lt. [Casimir] Casey Firlit was the regimental surgeon, a graduate from medical school in the Chicago area who hoped to return to a surgical residency once his military obligation was discharged. Casey was a very competent physician who proctored me in various aspects of casualty care — wound debridement, abdominal lavage, venous cutdowns, etc. When we started receiving casualties, both of us could get real busy attempting to stabilize wounded Marines for evacuation.

Six or seven corpsmen were assigned to Regimental Aid. All of them were stand-up young men who exited the bunker after artillery attacks to help wounded Marines to the facility and then assisted with treatment. We also had a senior chief hospital corpsman assigned for Administration.

We had two dental technicians at Khe Sanh — petty officers Janowski and Donahue. Janowski was a very robustly built man while Donahue was thin and bespectacled. Both these men had established reputations as being fearless. They traveled all over the base securing C-rations for Medical, driving a water truck for resupply of Medical's potable water, and in general, scrounging up all sorts of items needed in the medical bunker. They both were also very active in assisting casualties to the bunker for treatment. As a result of the destruction of the ammo dump on January 21st and the need to resupply ammunition to the base, Marines were limited to two C-ration meals per day during the siege. Since Regimental Aid kept some Marines with minor wounds overnight or for several days before returning them to duty, we were always looking for enough C-rations and water to supply the needs of the personnel in the bunker.

Years after this episode, I read an article where the author maintained that of all the military personnel who served during the Vietnam conflict, the military personnel at Khe Sanh during the siege of 1968 became the most competent or proficient at judging when to get on the ground or get under cover during artillery, mortar, and rocket attacks. NVA forces about Khe Sanh and in the Co Roc area across the border in Laos had a wide variety of ordnance at their disposal to drop on the runway and base. This included 82mm and 120mm mortars, 122mm rockets, and 130mm and 152mm artillery rounds. I soon learned that when I heard the "pop" of a round leaving a tube, I had to get down or get into a bunker quick if I was within the azimuth of the round's travel. It might hit short by some distance, hit right where I was, or hit over and beyond where I was — but I had to get down! I always attempted to stay clear of any ambient noise, such as generators or any other equipment with an engine running, that would shroud that warning "pop." Marines and sailors at Khe Sanh, who operated mules, jeeps, and trucks, were much more susceptible to being wounded or killed because of the ambient noise of the machinery they were operating. About the only warning they would get was to watch Marines about the area diving under cover — and that was often too late. My respect for Janowski, Donahue, and all the other operators of equipment at Khe Sanh continues to this day.

Within a few days, I got myself oriented within and about the Regimental Aid Station. We had few, if any, dental patients to see except for emergencies, such as a toothache or oral-facial swelling. It was simply too dangerous for Marines to come to the aid station for anything routine. The policy on casualties at Khe Sanh was to treat and keep as many as possible. If a Marine's wounds did not absolutely require medical evacuation, he was kept at Medical, sometimes for several days, and then returned to duty.

This was a good policy for two reasons. One, it was more dangerous to attempt to leave the base than it was to remain there. Some wounded Marines, slated for evacuation, were subsequently killed during the evacuation process at the airfield. Two, the rifle and artillery battalions at the base, already below full strength for manning, could hardly expect to get replacements. But some replacements and return-to-duty wounded Marines did arrive at the base during the siege. Over the course of my time at Khe Sanh, I probably did as much medical treatment — maybe more — than dental treatment.

The weather at Khe Sanh during the first three weeks I was there remained mostly overcast with some days extremely foggy; it was still the monsoon season. Sometimes the fog would lift midmorning, but many days the fog just hung in. If ever there was an opportunity for General [Vo Nguyen] Giap[7] to direct an all-out ground assault against the base, it was during this time. Little, if any, close tactical air support could be brought to bear against an attacking NVA force in such inclement weather.

All this time NVA ordnance continued to rain down on the base. Some days it was just a few rounds. On other days it was a hailstorm of mortar, rocket, and artillery with a high of nearly 1,300 rounds one day near the last week of February. What made the mortar, rocket, and artillery attacks more intense was the fact that the actual base at Khe Sanh was not that large. It was maybe 600 yards long — east to west, and 300 yards wide — north to south.

My existence at Regimental Aid settled into going to some of the morning briefings at COC. The senior chief had been attending most of these when I arrived. We then began to share the duty, and finally I took it over. We had hours and hours of boredom punctuated by arrival of casualties that needed our complete attention. I spent a lot of time reading out-of-date periodicals, sleeping, and making the most of the two-C-rations-per-day food allowance.

On the 25th of February, I was wounded by artillery shrapnel. Early that morning B/1/26 put a patrol out to the south of the base. As the fight began to quiet down, I proceeded down to the lines to assist with casualties coming in and to get numbers of WIA/KIA to take back to COC. This patrol was decimated by the NVA in trenches outside the wire; most of the patrol were either killed or wounded. I was dogtrotting up the road from the lines toward COC when the first 45-round artillery barrage hit in front of me. I never heard the "pop" of the first round coming out of the tube because there was too much ambient noise in the area. The only warning I received was the roar of the round as it neared the ground, and that sound caused me to hit the ground. I remember being suspended in midair — and then nothing.

A corpsman in a nearby bunker came out and picked me up when the artillery ceased and assisted me to the bunker. He looked me over and determined I was not badly injured. All I had were a few puncture holes in my left shoulder and arm and in my shins. Unfortunately, a Marine who was ahead of me on the road took the full brunt of the first artillery round. I remember being in a daze, but I looked out the door of the bunker which the corpsman had assisted me to and watched others place that Marine's body on a mule.

What the corpsman found once I returned to Regimental Aid were three good-sized pieces of shrapnel buried in the back of my flak jacket, any one of which would have done serious damage. Casey Firlit dressed my minor wounds and I went to my rack. For several days I slept off the effects of the concussion in the form of headaches and a loss of hearing. I had been incredibly lucky. My heretofore sense of immortality quickly disappeared, and I learned to be much more careful after this experience.

Early one morning — the first week of March — I was sleeping in my rack, which was toward the back of the bunker, when a loud explosion quite near my area of the bunker shook me awake. Later that morning I went out of the bunker and determined that a rocket had landed within a foot of the bunker wall just outside my sleeping area. I talked it over with Casey Firlit, and we both thought we needed more protection on the roof of the bunker against mortar, rocket, or artillery. Subsequently, and early in the following few mornings while it was still overcast and foggy, I went out with a working party made up of our corpsmen and DT3 [Dental Technician 3rd Class] Robert Burdette. We all worked on retrieving 105mm shell casings from the large pile the battery of the 13th Marines had built up across the road. Over several days, we layered the roof of the bunker with 105 shell casings on top of which we added another layer of sandbags. Who knows if this would have protected any of us inside the bunker from ordnance that might hit the roof, but I thought it would help. We didn't get this additional roof protection on too soon for within a few days, early in the morning, we heard three successive loud concussive explosions just outside the bunker. I exited to take a look and found three good-sized craters bracketing the bunker — close, but no hits on the roof. One of the Marines from the battery across the road took a look with me. It was his conjecture that the NVA had bracketed the bunker with delayed-fuse artillery rounds. This was a little unusual for most of the artillery that hit the base was point-detonated fused and exploded upon hitting the ground or a surface. These craters from delayed-fuse rounds were alarming because if any of them had hit the roof, no amount of sandbag layering would have protected the occupants from serious injury or death.

At the end of March, Company B/1/26 attacked an NVA position south of the base. We received several of the wounded Marines from this action at Regimental Aid. One Marine I remember in particular had a left to right side facial wound, and the stretcher bearers brought him to us on his back. Upon initially examining him, I thought he was dead as he wasn't breathing. But he had a pulse. I pulled up on some of the eviscerated facial tissues blocking his airway and the Marine took a gulp of air. I quickly turned him over on his stomach so his facial structures lay on the stretcher. He was then able to breathe freely. I got a line in him, loosely bandaged his facial tissues, and ordered the stretcher bearers to get him to Charlie Med for evacuation.

Within the last day or so of March, the siege was over. The NVA artillery, which had caused us so much torment from Co Roc, had been attacked by Navy jets. The Navy's Bullpup missiles had silenced the NVA's artillery. These elements of the Air Cavalry Division had arrived at the base, supposedly rescuing the Marines, though the Marines didn't think they needed rescue.

By April 17th or 18th, Regimental Aid and Dental were packed up and ready to exit the base. Petty Officer Burdette and I loaded the dental equipment on one truck of a convoy leaving for Dong Ha in the morning. We traveled down Route 9 and arrived in Dong Ha at Delta Med that afternoon about the time evening chow was served. I remember getting off the truck and going to the mess for my first non–C-rations meal in 68 days. The food was wonderful, but about halfway through dinner, everyone at my table had left. I was puzzled but then one of the other dental officers at Delta Med walked over and whispered in my ear, "Bob, you really need a shower." I guess I smelled so bad that everyone at the table had lost their appetite. I had gone to Khe Sanh with two issues of utilities, one of which I wore for the first 30 days, and the second of which I had worn and was still wearing at the time of my arrival at Delta Med.

Within a day or so, I climbed on the scale and discovered I had lost 22 pounds at Khe Sanh. This is mute testimony as to what kind of nutrition a two-C-rations-a-day diet contains.

"Absolute Madness!"

When he arrived at Khe Sanh, 3rd Medical Battalion surgeon Lt. James Finnegan had already paid his dues as a surgeon at Delta Med in Dong Ha. He had been "operating on casualties and ducking the incoming" for four months. When Delta Med's commanding officer, Cmdr. Bob Brown, asked him to head the surgical team at Khe Sanh's Charlie Med, Finnegan agreed. As he jumped off the Huey gunship at the combat base, two men jumped on so quickly that he hardly saw their faces. One was the surgeon he was relieving and the other was Charlie Med's anesthesiologist. "So I was there and they were gone."

There I was the new CO of Charlie Med. Eddie [Feldman] had been with one of the hill companies—1/26 [1st Battalion, 26th Marines]. Don Magilligan was out there with one of the other Marine companies. They pulled them in to work with me. So I had Ed, Don, and [Lt.] Joe Wolfe plus 26 corpsmen.

When I got up there, Charlie Med was a little compound right on the side of the runway because—for evacuation purposes—we had to be right on an airstrip. Everything was all canvas tents with sandbags. The tents had holes in them and were flopping all over the place. It was madness!

Not too long after I arrived, incoming artillery ratcheted up to 2,000 rounds a day. Eventually the incoming got so bad that all fixed wing aircraft were banned from Khe Sanh. Then it got to the point where even getting a helicopter in and out was very dangerous. They would land and then take off in a flash! They didn't sit on that strip but for a few seconds because the minute they landed, it was unbelievable. And, of course, Charlie Med always got the secondary effect of that added incoming because the helicopters parked right in front of us.

Within a very short time, we had nothing above ground that hadn't been blown away. The corpsmen and I had little bunkers that were dug down maybe three feet in the ground with sandbags and wood on top of them. At the triage area, we just had sandbags and wood. The incoming seemed unrelenting. It was probably less at night. I don't know whether anyone has ever documented incoming rounds. I've always had this impression that the North Vietnamese did not like to fight at night. Maybe nobody does. But no matter where I was—even at Delta Med—it was less at night. If we went to our underground bunker at night, we could sometimes be in there with not too much happening.

But daytime was different. Even taking the catwalk—the wooden planks that led up from the bunkers—was a risk. We had spotted a sniper across the way, and you could never just get up and take the catwalk. You'd jump on and off of it because no one wanted to get picked off by that sniper. But as soon as we had casualties, we'd all charge from the bunkers up to the triage, which was in front right near the airstrip.

One of the hardest tasks was first off-loading the casualties. The minute the chopper would drop in, the incoming would pick up. We called the choppers "mortar magnets." You'd run out, get the casualties off the chopper as fast as you could, and they would just lift off and go as fast as they could. Then you had to bring the litter about 20 yards from the landing pad into Triage.

It was the same procedure if you were evacuating casualties. Once we got everybody stabilized and the situation was quiet, we'd call for choppers to get them over to Dong Ha or wherever else they were going. And, of course, as soon as the chopper came in, the incoming would start. We had to set up a wall of sandbags from the door of the triage bunker to the helicopter pad so we could run low behind the sandbags and try to get to the chopper without getting hit.

Every morning I was supposed to go down to a regimental briefing. A lot of mornings we had to run from truck to truck or pole to pole because of the incoming, even as you tried to walk down the path. The briefing was an out-of-body experience for me as I sat there and listened to these guys. Col. [David] Lownds was the CO of the 26th Marines at Khe Sanh. The rest of the officers were also there. Every morning they went through the intelligence reports. One officer would say, "Outside Z2 R1 Perimeter we heard these clanking noises which we think were tank treads."

Tank treads! I'm thinking, "Jesus, they've got tanks!"

Other reports would focus on the incoming, on a patrol that went here or there, or on enemy sightings. Then every once in a while Lownds would refer to the "impending invasion of Khe Sanh"—what forces the NVA had and how they were going to come in.

I pointed out that we needed some kind of protection at Charlie Med because we were getting shelled as we were caring for the casualties. I didn't see that I was getting anywhere with that argument. Finally, I had a discussion with the executive officer. "Some of these kids are getting re-wounded. It's not a good thing. It's bad enough they get wounded the first time."

And to this day, I still don't know who said what to whom, but sometime after that discussion a group of Seabees came over with a backhoe. They dug a good-sized hole in the ground, maybe 12 by 20 by 10 feet deep, which they buttressed with 12 by 12s. They then put metal Marston matting [pierced steel planks] on the top with layers of sandbags on top of that. They also built a little ramp going down into it.

Now we finally had a place where we could take the casualties! It was a pain in the ass to have to take them down the steps into the bunker, but at least we were in there with some notion of being able to stand up and take care of them without worrying about getting hit.

Lownds now felt that the NVA's attempt to overrun Khe Sanh was imminent. I remember seeing a picture of the base very clearly. The picture had curved arrows showing five routes onto the base: the primary route where the NVA were most likely to come in over here or over here, and the third route up the draw through Charlie Med. Well, that last arrow got my attention. The perimeter was a hundred yards and you could see the NVA running around out there right across the strip. You could see them through binoculars. And right behind us was a half track [vehicle with wheels in the front and caterpillar treads on the rear] with a .50 caliber machine gun on it and a couple of Marines. That was it.

I waited until the briefing was over because I never felt I had enough military moxie to even ask a question. These were all Marine combat professionals. So I got the executive officer afterwards and said, "Listen, I don't exactly know what I'm supposed to do here. I've got four docs who wear .45s and are in danger of shooting themselves in the foot at any given moment. I have 26 corpsmen who don't carry weapons because they're working on casualties, and a little half track out there. You're drawing an arrow saying that there's at least a reasonable possibility when they overrun this place—which you're absolutely certain they're gonna do at any moment now—that they might come right up the draw through Charlie Med. I'm not John Wayne. I cannot be taking care of a casualty and shooting the enemy while I'm doing it. This is not the movies. Seriously, can you put some Marines out there?"

He answered, "Don't worry, Doc. If they come up through there, the reaction force will come right away."

I asked, "Well, how long is it gonna take for them to get there if we're triaging casualties?"

He replied, "Doc, it probably will take them a little while for them to be activated and be ordered over there."

I then persisted. "When I go back, what do you want me to tell my guys? What am I supposed to do?"

He countered, "I understand that when the casualties come in, you strip them and take their weapons." He then questioned, "Don't you take all the weapons from the casualties?"

I said, "Of course."

"My suggestion," he added, "is to go back and make sure that your docs and corpsmen all have sidearms, M16s, and grenades and that you also dig fighting holes."

That's what he told me. As I walked back to Charlie Med, I thought, "Now, there's just no way that I can say to all these guys, 'Okay. We're all gonna strap on our .45s and carry an M16, put some grenades in your lapels like John Wayne, dig your foxhole, and we'll keep taking care of the casualties. If they come up the draw, we'll become a Marine platoon.'"

In all triage setups, the wooden "ammo box" sits behind the tent wall. We'd set the casualties' M16s against the wall. If they had bandoliers or grenades, we'd throw them in the box. When I think about it now, if you handed me a grenade, I'd run screaming out in the hall.

The whole situation seemed like madness, absolute madness! So I decided that I was not going to say that to the guys. We all knew the Marines were very concerned that the enemy was going to overrun the base. We felt that at any given time the NVA could try to take the base. Everyone was aware of that fact as the siege went on. That's what it was all about.

With the incoming so bad, they started air-dropping supplies. It was one of those tragic comedy situations because we would watch the planes come over—mostly C-130s—with the rear hydraulic doors down so they could drop the load off the back. We would watch the stuff coming down. Let's say that a significant percentage of it didn't land in Khe Sanh. As a result, parachutes were spread all over hell's half-acre. Sometimes we had to send out a combat patrol to rescue the supplies.

Right outside of Charlie Med was a huge collection of used parachutes, open and sprawled all over the place. Everybody knew the plan was for "Charlie" [NVA] to come over the wire and get us. The Marines were actually begging for it. In all fairness, at least the senior veteran Marines wanted them to come. This is what Marines are born for. In that context, rather than say to the men, "Get your M16 and dig a fighting hole," I said, "Guys, I've got a plan. We have lots of casualties to take care of and we can't be worried too much. We've got the Marines down there.

If we see the enemy break through and come up that draw, what I suggest is that everybody get under the parachutes. The enemy will never know we're there. They will roll right on by, and then we can go back and get our guns." At least I got a laugh from the guys. That was my famous parachute speech to the troops.

I recall many patients we worked on but none more than Jonathan Spicer. In fact, the Jonathan Spicer story has been written up in many places. It's one of the many stories that came out of Khe Sanh.

Jonathan was the son of a preacher from Miami. I think he was drafted into the Marine Corps.[8] According to the story, he immediately informed his superiors that he was a conscientious objector. He would do anything they wanted but he wasn't going to fire a gun. Somehow he was passed through basic and ended up in Vietnam. Once he got there, he was assigned to a Marine hill unit. He kept saying to his superiors, "I'll do whatever you want me to do but I will not fire a gun."

His CO was so disgusted with Spicer that he was going to discipline him in some way. But someone else said, "Let me take him and maybe he can do something else." And so they brought Spicer to me at Charlie Med.

Spicer wasn't a corpsman. He was a grunt Marine. The kid was not a coward. He just didn't want to be a shooter. So he became our main litter-bearer. He would run back and forth to the choppers under fire. This kid was fearless. We loved him. I still remember the day we were standing down in the bunker — Don Magilligan, Eddie [Feldman], and I. Suddenly somebody yelled, "Spicer's down!" He was moving litters and took shrapnel right through the center of his chest.

Physicians of the the 3rd Medical Battalion — "Charlie Med" — gather during a lull in the shelling at Khe Sanh. (Left to right) Lt. Joseph Wolfe, Lt. James Finnegan, Lt. Edward Feldman, and Lt. Donald Magilligan (courtesy Edward Feldman).

They brought him quickly into Triage, right onto the first litter. He was gone. No pulse. No blood pressure. Don Magilligan was standing beside me and said, "I think it's pericardial tamponade." This means the blood in the heart sac is compressing the heart. If a fragment penetrates the heart, first it has to go through the heart sac — the pericardium — then into the heart. If the heart sac hole is small enough, the blood will spurt out of the heart and build up in the sac and compress the heart.

I said, "Don, I think you're right." So we opened his chest, massaged his heart, put a single stitch in the hole in his heart, and his vital signs came back. Everything seemed dandy. He had been intubated with an endotracheal tube and we got him stabilized.

We then called Delta Med and told them that Spicer had an open chest wound, a sutured hole in his heart, and that we had to get him out of Khe Sanh and back to Delta Med big time. We couldn't keep anybody at Khe Sanh. Once we stabilized them, we had to get them the hell out because we didn't have the facility to do anything else.

Spicer was medevaced and for a long time nobody could find out what happened to him. I heard all kinds of stories, including one that he had died. We finally got information that he was medevaced first to Danang and then to Japan. He died in Japan "of infection." It's hard to know exactly what that means. But because of his heroism, he got the Navy Cross.

At that time a tremendous amount of newsprint covered the Jonathan Spicer story. We were very excited because we thought we had saved our boy. Years later I saw his name on the Wall.

13

PRISONER OF WAR

The day began much the same way for the men who flew the Navy's carrier-based aircraft on Yankee Station. Following an early morning briefing in the carrier's ready room about the day's mission, the pilot suited up and headed for his plane, which was already fueled and armed. Catapulted from the flight deck, he headed for his designated target — a rail yard, port facility, bridge, or power plant in North Vietnam. As he flew the aircraft, he simultaneously scanned the ground for anti-aircraft fire or the far more frightening SAM (surface-to-air missile). Even if the pilot caught a fleeting glance of the missile, it was usually too late to evade what looked like a smoking telephone pole. What each man knew was that the routine was never routine. Jet turbines, fuel lines, canopies, and control surfaces were incompatible with flak, bullets, and exploding SAMs.

Pulling out from a low altitude bombing run, the pilot's day suddenly takes a turn for the worse. He hears a thump and in an instant he notes the absence of his starboard wing. Without the option of clawing for altitude or nursing the fatally stricken A-4 Skyhawk out over open water, he "punches out." The cannon shell-activated ejection seat slams him up and out into the slip-stream with a force exceeding 30 times the force of gravity, crushing vertebrae and violently tearing the helmet from his head. His parachute has already deployed — and not a moment too soon as the ground and an angry mob await his arrival.

During the Vietnam War, 771 American military personnel became prisoners of war, most of them aviators. In 1973, 658 were returned to U.S. military control; 113 died in captivity. Although these numbers were a fraction of the 130,201 American POWs captured during World II and the 7,140 held in Korea, the prisoners of the Viet Cong and North Vietnamese suffered a singularly cruel experience. Many were injured by hostile fire prior to leaving their aircraft. The harsh ejection, often at low altitude, broke bones, dislocated joints, compressed or fractured vertebrae, and caused blunt force injuries. Once on the ground, enraged Vietnamese civilians dispensed mob justice before military personnel arrived on the scene and took control.

Then the POWs had to confront many years of captivity. For those military personnel seized in the south, many endured a living hell in Viet Cong camps deep in the jungles of South Vietnam, Laos, or Cambodia. The aviators shot down over North Vietnam were incarcerated in Hanoi's infamous Hoa Lo Prison, christened the "Hanoi Hilton" by its inhabitants, or in other lockups — Son Tay, Dan Hoi, Cu Loc, "Dogpatch," the "Zoo," and "Alcatraz," among others.

Isolation, disease, and inadequate food and medical attention were the norm. Ejection injuries went untreated as were those afflictions incurred during what can only be described as premeditated torture. What the Spanish Inquisition had once practiced in the 1500s paled in comparison to what the North Vietnamese devised in the 1960s. Recalcitrant POWs suffered the so-called "rope trick," ankle stocks, wrist cuffs, and ratchet cuffs designed to cut off circulation by degree. They also endured electric shock, sleep deprivation, solitary confinement, and beatings — brutal treatment that exacerbated existing injuries or provoked new ones.

The prisoners eventually learned that despite their best efforts to resist, every man had his breaking point. Said one former prisoner, "The only people who don't talk are Steve McQueen or John

Wayne in movies." And once that threshold had been crossed, more than a few POWs experienced self-recrimination, guilt, and despondency for having betrayed the military Code of Conduct and selling out their country. As Stuart Rochester and Frederick Kiley have pointed out in their study of American POWs during the Vietnam War,[1] the most realistic goal was to hold out against the torture as long as possible, give the enemy as little as possible, and use whatever respite that followed the torture to recover strength for the next bout. The POWs who finally were freed in 1973 already knew they would have many issues to work through — both physical and psychological.

The Rope Trick

Jack Fellowes graduated from the United States Naval Academy in 1956 and earned his wings a year later. In 1966, he was assigned to a squadron aboard the carrier USS Constellation *[CVA-64]. With 55 missions under his belt, his luck finally ran out in August of that year when enemy ground fire hit his A-6 Intruder, and he became a "guest" of the North Vietnamese. For the next seven years as a POW, he endured humiliation, torture, isolation, meager rations, and an almost complete lack of medical attention.*

Our mission that day was up in the Vinh area, a city in the panhandle of North Vietnam. We were supposed to bomb some barges in the river, but they were camouflaged and we never could find them. Although my target was in the river leading to Vinh, it was very heavily defended. Apparently, the NVA shot our right wing off—from what my wingman said. The A-6 went into a flat, inverted spin and we both ejected.

You train but you don't think you're going to be the one who has to eject. On this particular day, I was the one. Everything went according to what I expected. I had to eject inverted and I was off the seat. It was a Martin-Baker seat that used a cannon shell, and it was almost guaranteed to give you some back problems. It was a good wallop — 32 Gs — in that one microsecond. It hit me in the butt, and I was off the seat inverted. When I got home, I learned that I had suffered a compression fracture of two vertebrae in my back.

I came down right in the middle of a village. Needless to say, evasion and escape were not options. I tried to send out a radio signal, but it was too late so I just broke the radio. It was lunchtime, too, so everybody was in that village. They captured me immediately. I tried to light up a cigar but the villagers took it away from me. And that was about it.

The Vietnamese were very hostile. I didn't see a friendly face in the crowd. Someone in the village was rallying them to be excited. They took me to a part of the village that was rather concealed and kept me there for a while. And then when the airplanes went away, they marched me most of the afternoon to another village where I spent the night. I had no shoes or socks, just bare feet. I think they thought that if I kept them, I would try to escape. My back hurt but I had no idea what caused the pain. In fact, the Vietnamese solution to the problem — or to everybody's problem — was to let you sleep on a hard bed board. So I was either sleeping on a cement slab or a hard wooden board.

I was in that second village about four nights. Then the Vs [North Vietnamese] picked us up and marched us to another village. I say "us" because by this time, they had also captured my bomber-navigator who had landed in a rice paddy.

The Vs began to grill us separately. I was supposed to answer all the questions the interrogator couldn't answer. He wanted to know what our war plans were. Of course, I had no idea. The government doesn't ask me, a lieutenant commander, how we're going to go about this mission or that mission. But he seemed to think that lieutenant commanders had some weight. So he would ask me how many missions I had. When he didn't get the right answer he and his guards beat me up a little bit.

My hands were tied behind my back. The jailers untied me when I ate, but tied me up again when I went to bed. Some kid would usually be standing outside the door. I guess the guards were really concerned about us being great escape artists.

The jailers gave me a little water. Actually, it was tea, very weak tea. Somebody brought me some vegetables which looked like grass, which it was, and then a little bowl of rice. So for the first 10 days, I didn't really eat except for a cup of rice a day and a little vegetable, which was like the roots of grass. Nobody was really very interested in feeding us at all. I think they probably just wanted to get us to Hanoi. Maybe they thought that our presence in the village would get them bombed.

The North Vietnamese took us to Hanoi by pickup truck, which had a cloth across the back so that it could be closed shut. Every so often during the day, the Vs would stop the truck, open the cloth, and talk the villagers into throwing rocks at us. So they'd throw some rocks and then the curtain would be closed.

We got to Hanoi very early in the morning on September 9th. I remember looking out the back of the pickup and seeing how dark it was. Their light bulbs were about 20 watts. It was very dark and gloomy in Hanoi. We finally arrived at the Hoa Lo Prison ["Hanoi Hilton"], they let us out. I don't remember seeing too many people. They put me in a little courtyard where some people were preparing rice. Then the interrogation began.

The next morning when it was still dark, the North Vietnamese started the heavy interrogation. I didn't give the right answers so they put me in the "rope trick" by tying my arms behind my back and putting my legs in leg irons so I couldn't move them. I had police cuffs on my wrists and rope tied around the upper part of my arms between the elbows and shoulder blades. My arms were tied tightly together behind my back so I was really in a knot. Then the tormentors bent my head down to a bar and secured that. Every so often they raised me up and let me hang there. I was in that position for roughly 14 hours. It was dark when they started this—and it was dark when I came out.

My arms were injured and I couldn't use them. The guards put me in with an Air Force lieutenant named Ron Bliss. When he ejected, his helmet and his seat separated from him and his helmet then came back and hit him in the head, which made a hole in his head. The guards put him in with me to take care of me because I couldn't move my arms. After having been subjected to this rope trick, I had also suffered some cuts and bruises on my elbows and arms. So when I lay in bed these cuts would all drain. And here is Bliss trying to take care of me with this big hole in his head.

The Vs packed his head with sulphur. And with me, they tried to do whatever they could do with my arms. They put sulphur on my cuts, but my hands got really swollen. They tried to get the swelling down by using a pair of pliers to squeeze where it was swollen. I had a couple of cuts at the knuckles. My middle finger on the left hand got really swollen. They squeezed it with pliers to try to drain it. I went through that for a month or so, and finally my hands got down to what was a somewhat normal position. I couldn't move my arms from the shoulders so Bliss had to dress and feed me. He was doing everything possible to keep me alive. He was and is a great guy and real friend.

The Vietnamese were very uncomfortable with my condition because no one had actually lost the movement of his arms—although they had done the rope trick on many others. They actually took me to a little way station that had a doctor. I don't know what they expected him to do. He stuck a needle in the top of each of my hands and then started pulling out the substance, which was a clear liquid — infection liquid — but no blood. That scared them a little bit. But after a while, Bliss would exercise my arms. And, after a long time I got the feeling back in them, which was very painful. Having no feeling is bad enough but then when the feeling came back, boy!

It seemed like the Vietnamese were really worried about my condition because from then on people would tell me that when they went into the rope trick, the Vs would write the time they put the ropes on. Then they'd come back after half an hour and look at the time. If it were over half an hour, they'd relax the ropes and let the circulation come back before they put them on again. So apparently it bothered them. The interrogators didn't want me to come out of that prison with no use of my arms. That would have shown the world that they had tortured us— something they denied and continue to deny.

The second day I was with Bliss they drove us out to the "Zoo" and put us in a cell. We called it the "Zoo" because it was the only zoo in the world where the people looked out at the animals. It was just outside Hanoi. I remained at the Zoo for the next three years. I remember the guy who ordered the torture came into camp one day and said in effect: "If you don't give us the answer, remember, we took your arms. Now we'll take your legs." Then he left and I never saw him again.

Ron Bliss and I stayed together until my arms got better. As soon as the Vs felt I could do certain tasks on my own they moved him out. We had been together for 13 months before they separated us. And then I was solo for the next 15 months in the "Carriage House." It was really a garage with a big door and a bed in one corner. It was a pretty big room. It was very comfortable. I had a rat as a friend. He used to come in through a rat hole and sit there. I'd sit there and look at him. It got to where I was talking to the rat, but he never answered me.

Keeping your sanity in those conditions was important. First of all, you had to have a sense of humor. Then the POWs got the tap code going and were able to talk to each other. Here's the way it worked. You've got a 26-letter alphabet. We took a letter out—the letter K. Now you have 25. You break that 25 down to five groups of five. So, A, B, C, D, E become group ONE. F, G, H, I, J become group TWO, etc. Now K is out. So K just becomes a tap, pause, two taps, pause, tap. The rest of the letters are in groups. Group ONE is A, B, C, D, E. If I want to tap an E, I would tap the group—ONE. So I'd tap one, pause for a second and then tap the positional letter in the group, which is five. So it would be one tap, one pause, then five. Tap, pause, tap tap tap tap tap.

We did that right till the bitter end and some guys were still doing it in the hospital at Clark. They had nothing else to do.

An Air Force guy named Smitty [Carlyle] Harris brought the code into the prison. Smitty knew the code because he learned it in survival school. The instructors there told him it might be valuable just in case. Smitty said that he'd learn it but never thought he would need it. Well, he ended up as one of us and got the code passed around.

A guy would come by outside your room singing "Hello Dolly," or actually the "Hello Dolly" music, but instead of singing the actual words, he'd sing you the tap code. You had to listen to him about three times before you realized what he was doing. But that was the start of it and it worked pretty well. We got a couple of good messages by guys singing strange words to familiar songs.

Then we also used a 26-letter code which was one tap for A, and 26 for Z. You'd put your cup to the wall next to your bed and listen. Then we'd do the cup so we could talk to the wall. But the tap code was the most reliable because we could do it anytime. When people came back from torture, we would tap on the wall and try to get that person back in shape mentally. It was a very valuable code. In 1960, you could get this code from the top off a Wheaties box. I think it was the Captain Midnight Club. They would send you a club card, a decoding ring, and a code. And this was the code. Just think, a 50 cent code saved about 600 lives.

If you'd been to an interrogation, you would tell your buddies what information the Vs asked you about and what they wanted. Once you got past that, you'd tap anything that might be enjoyable to hear. We'd even tap dirty jokes. We asked people to give their histories. Where are you from and all that kind of stuff. Once you got the tap code down, you'd just tap anything to keep each other going.

When I was in the first cell with Bliss, we had a shower. Bliss had to turn it on — but no hot water. From then on all we had was well water. Ron would lift up a bucket of water from the well and pour it on me. This was done in the courtyard. We had no water in the room.

The Vs gave us shorts and an undershirt made of very coarse cotton and also what we called "long johns"— pajamas. They were long pants with a cloth belt and a shirt. And they gave us a sweater with a hood. When my arms hurt so bad, I wouldn't take a cold shower and I wouldn't let Bliss even wash me down. So after so many months of wearing the sweater, the hood rotted off. Then the sweater arm rotted off. I was almost crying when this happened. So I went to the Vs and told them that I needed a hooded sweater. They told me they didn't have any more sweaters. So I ended up with a sweater with one arm and the hood gone. I had a pair of socks and that was it.

The jailers gave us a blanket and later — when the war ground to an end — they were giving us three blankets. But for the first year I had only one blanket made of coarse cotton. The Vietnamese don't have wool. You'd wear everything to bed because all the windows were bricked up in the cells and there was no circulation. It was like a freezer in the winter and a steam bath in the summer. And then there were tons of mosquitoes. And when you put a mosquito net up at night, you couldn't see what you were doing because we didn't have any lights. You couldn't catch them because you couldn't see them.

For sanitary facilities, we used a bucket. You put the bucket outside and a prisoner would empty it. You never saw him do it. Then the guard would open the cell door and you'd take the bucket back.

I had a toothbrush but it broke right after I got it. So I ended up brushing with just a nub of what was left. The Vs gave us some toothpaste which was terrible, but it was still toothpaste. We didn't have any food that was considered good enough to decay teeth. We didn't have a lot of fats. We didn't have a lot of sugars. We had cabbage soup, pumpkin soup, grass soup, bread. In fact, the bread was pretty good when it was hot. And that was it. Two meals a day. You got kind of hungry. With the food as poor as it was, it wasn't the kind of food that would clog your arteries. It was really barren food.

In 1968, they allowed wives to send packages. If they wanted to, the Vs would give them to you. I got two packages the whole time. My wife sent about seven. One of them had bullion cubes. My wife said that she never sent bullion cubes so I don't know where the hell that package came from. One guy's wife sent him a bottle of Pepto Bismol.

The Vietnamese, by the way, provided very little of anything. They did have some medical care but it wasn't very good. A guy named Myers had developed a very serious infection on his upper leg. The Vs had cut it open, put maggots or leeches in the wound, and then bound it up. One day they came into the room, took a pair of scissors, and cut this blister that had formed. They opened it up, took out the maggots, and then wrapped it up again. I saw Myers about eight months later and you couldn't even tell he had a scar.

They told one guy, who kept getting blisters in his private parts, that he had syphilis. He said, "I can't have syphilis because the only person I've had relations with is my wife." So one guy got on the wall [tap code] and asked, "Do you ever take sulphur?"

And he responded, "I don't know."

The other guy said, "The next time they give you a pill for anything, just don't swallow it." So after a year of being told he had syphilis, he put this pill on his tongue and just licked it and he broke out in blisters. His syphilis-like symptoms were a reaction to sulphur.

The dental work consisted of a foot pedal drill. I wouldn't go in there. I did everything I could to help my teeth. The Vs would say, "Prepare to suffer." And then they'd pedal through your tooth.

If you had a toothache that was bothering you, your only choice was getting it out. You'd say, "My tooth hurts." And they would take it out. They only had the foot pedal to power the drill. Jack Bomar went in one day to get a tooth removed because it was driving him crazy. The Vietnamese took the tooth out. Once back in his cell, he moved his tongue to where the tooth was missing. Suddenly he realized that they had taken the wrong tooth out. So, in a fit, he kicked the wall and broke his toe. But he laughed about it later.

I had a tooth that was bad and drove me nuts. I took the aspirin they'd bring me and salivate on it. Then I'd stick it on the gum above the tooth and it would numb the area. When I got to Clark a year and a half later, I immediately asked, "Can I get a tooth removed?" This mean-looking guy came in and said, "I'll take it out." And I thought, "He's a tough looking hombre." But in a few moments the tooth was gone. I didn't even feel it.

Some of us would refuse to have a Vietnamese operate on us. Fred Cherry was an Air Force colonel. They had tortured him by bending his wrist and arm behind his back with such force that they broke a rib. The rib popped into the lung so they had to operate and take the rib out of his lung. Fred came back and he was fine. So they could operate if they had to.

A couple of POWs caught dysentery and the Vs gave them a drug called "cintoflin," a Chinese drug. They were given one shot and the dysentery cleared up. We had guys who got sick now and then but their roommates took care of them — even if it just meant covering them up with blankets.

I spent 15 months in the Zoo. I got to room with Jim Bell, then with Bud Day. Boy, they were tough guys. So I was really in the middle of a good crowd for the next three years and those guys got me through this ordeal.

One day they finally moved us out of the Zoo and put us in with 40 other prisoners back in Hoa Lo—the "Hanoi" Hilton. A number of the prison rooms each held 40. One room had 20 in it. Now we had someone to talk to all the time. It was really interesting exchanging thoughts and ideas. For those in the same room, we had courses in Civil War taught by Art Burer, who was from the South and maintains that the South won the war. And nobody questioned him because he was the instructor. And John McCain told Damon Runyon stories.[2] We just had normal living except that we were locked up.

Up until 1972, all the guys who came in said they didn't know what was going on the outside. Then we got a group who came in that year and they told us a lot more of what was happening. Of course, the Vietnamese talked about the Paris peace negotiations but it was gloomy because they spent a year and a half trying to figure out the size of the table.

When you're trying to survive, you tend to get right to the basic premise that I'm going to survive. So the people around you were all on the same team. Surviving with our honor became very important. We were all on the same frequency so we were all focusing on the same thoughts—surviving and helping each other out. And when you have about 600 people helping each other out, you're doing pretty well. We never gave up hope.

My family didn't learn that I was alive until November of 1971, four years and 10 months after I had been captured. In fact, I was the 61st prisoner captured.

One day the Vietnamese announced to us that we would be released in four increments. We knew the first group was going. I was supposed to be in the second group. On March 3rd, they brought in a razor blade and we shaved. Up till then, we shaved only twice a week, so this was the third time that week. We surmised that something was up. We went out the next day, March 4th.

It was raining the day I was released. When we and the Vs left the cell, they didn't close the door. Usually when we left the cell, they closed the door and locked it. So it was off to the buses and out to the airplane.

The North Vietnamese had a table with a couple of officers reading the names. As soon as we were aboard the C-141, the crew shut the door and we took off. Everyone was very quiet until the pilot said, "Feet wet." That's when we were over the water. Then the plane broke out with cheering Americans. We were free.

I spent three days at Clark [AFB] getting cleaned up. Then we flew on to Andrews [AFB] in Maryland and then to Norfolk where I saw my wife and kids. It was a great reunion after seven years. My kids were grown. It was very, very touching. And I'll leave it at that.

I went to Portsmouth Naval Hospital, where the medical staff found out that we were in pretty good shape, a lot better than expected. They took very good care of us. It was the best in the world. My teeth had problems. I needed crowns. The dental care was superb. And since then I've been taken care of very well. Navy medicine has been excellent. After I got back, I'd go down to Pensacola every year for Dr. Mitchell's program [Repatriated POW Program].

The Navy paid my way down and put me up in the BOQ [Bachelor Officers Quarters], and they paid my way back. The Navy took care of my entire treatment. Bob Mitchell's group would give me a physical. They checked me out to make sure I was all right. After about four days, they would send me home. If I needed consultations, they'd send me to Bethesda [Naval Hospital]. It worked great for me for about 15 years. Then I had a heart attack and bypass surgery. Since then I've been taken care of so well at Bethesda that I don't need to go to Pensacola.

The Hanoi Skydiving Club

Born in New Jersey and raised as an "Army brat," Paul Galanti attended the Naval Academy before undergoing flight training and earning his wings as a Navy pilot. Eventually, he began flying missions from USS Hancock (CVA-19), a vintage World War II–era carrier. Galanti's aircraft was the A-4 Skyhawk, a single-engine attack jet. "We didn't lose many of them because it was very survivable. You could lose hydraulics and still fly it disconnected unless it was like mine that had bent ailerons. When I disconnected from the hydraulics, it became uncontrollable."

Although he reported this defect to his skipper, the repair was never made. "When I disconnected at slow speed, the jet had an excessive rate of roll. I could trim it out as long as I had electricity. But that was still unsatisfactory. I downed it for that reason but my skipper said, 'Bring that son of a bitch out here to the ship; we need it.'

"I said, 'Skipper, the ailerons are bent.'

"He answered, 'That's all right; it flies okay with hydraulics.'

"There was a big note on the yellow sheets saying, 'Do not disconnect this aircraft. Bent ailerons.' Of course, I couldn't know that a few days later I would have to try to disconnect it."

On 17 June 1966, while flying the same ailing A-4, Galanti was shot down over North Vietnam. His troubles had just begun.

The weather was bad for the first mission and we couldn't get in. We went up and down the coast and finally came back and jettisoned our bombs into the water. We got back to the ship and were briefed for the second mission. We briefed a second target but knew we probably weren't going to get in there either. Then our skipper, who had just come back from a flight, said, "Hey, we've got some boxcars at Qui Vinh, which is right on the coast. Go and hit those."

So we did and that's where I got shot down. You don't see Qui Vinh on any of the new maps. It's northeast of Vinh right on the coast where North Vietnam pinches in and is the narrowest part of the country.

I was on a dive-bombing run and got hit with automatic weapons. I didn't know until after the war what had happened. I knew something hit the airplane and knocked out all the electricity. Then the engine shattered. The plane rolled over hard and headed for the ground. I punched out and became a member of the "Hanoi Skydiving Club."

I was hanging for a second or two in my parachute and then I looked down and saw tracers around me. I think they were shooting at other airplanes in the flight. Then I got hit in the neck. I felt a sting and didn't know what it was. It wasn't until I had come down in some bushes and saw the blood all over that I realized I had been hit. I had a survival radio and requested a strafing run but the flight leader said he didn't want to do it because he wasn't sure exactly where I was. So I told them to send the helicopter back because all the North Vietnamese had guns and they would surely have shot it down. "See you after the war," I said, thinking it would be over in about six more months.

The people on the ground were pretty rough. I got bashed on the head. Then they took my pistol, all my flight gear, stripped me down to my underwear, tied me to a tree, and lined up to shoot me. They had army shirts on but wore farmer trousers. I think they were militia, and carried old bolt-action rifles. These were not happy campers because a few moments before I had been bombing a bunch of railroad cars just up the road. A North Vietnamese army guy came over and made them stop.

The bullet that had hit me just tore the skin off. I didn't have anything to clean it with. All I had was my old dirty underwear and I was barefoot. Right after I was captured and tied to the tree, they cut me down. Then a guy with a red cross on his arm — who I assumed was a medic — came over and poured some iodine on my wound. A huge scab formed and it attracted all kinds of maggots. It was just a mess but it eventually healed.

I spent 12 days traveling mostly by foot north to Hanoi. We moved almost always at night through village after village. I was joined in a few days by a couple of Air Force guys who had been shot down two days before I was. They wouldn't let us talk to each other the whole time we were going north but I did get their names [Maj. Alan P.] Lurie and [1st Lt. Darrell E.] Pyle, an Air Force F-4 crew.

We got to Hanoi on the 29th of June which was the first day our planes bombed Hanoi. That was a very exciting arrival. The Vietnamese went crazy because we hadn't bombed the city before. I spent three days in a cell with no food or water, and I think they forgot about me when the air raid happened.

After three days I started yelling because I was dying of thirst. Then they came in and that's when my interrogation started. I was being held in "Heartbreak Hotel," a part of Hoa Lo Prison where the North Vietnamese kept prisoners during their initial interrogation.

I didn't know anything. I had written the schedule for my squadron and didn't know what the missions were for the next day until the last plane had landed. That was deliberate. The intelligence guys knew about it, but the pilots never found out about it until the last plane landed. The interrogators wanted to know the name of the ship, the squadron, the names of other people in the squadron. Obviously we resisted. They didn't like defiance so they tortured us.

They kept trying to get us to write statements to read on their radio condemning the war. I got tortured twice at this stage of the game. When I was first captured, the guy who was doing the torturing didn't speak English so that didn't work very well. They cut off the circulation above my elbows and pulled the elbows together in back until they touched. They tied another rope tightly around my ankles. Then they pulled the rope back around my neck so that I was bent like a pretzel until my feet touched the top of my head backwards. I was left in that position until my thinking was "corrected."

This happened to me four times. The first time I didn't feel my hands for six months afterward. That first time they had an English speaker. I took it as long as I could, probably an hour, before my arms were black so I told them I'd talk. When they took the ropes off the pain was worse as the blood went down to where the ropes had cut off the circulation.

Then they asked me four questions — name, rank, serial number, and date of birth. The question I wouldn't answer was, "Are you married?" I said, "I can't answer that." When I did that the second time, they put the ropes back on and this time they didn't take them off until I answered more questions. I mean I was a hurtin' puppy.

This torture went on for about three days, off and on. They kept me awake. The guard banged me on the head with a rifle butt and his fist. An English-speaking sergeant behind a desk obviously got a big kick out of beating people up.

Then they took me out and gave me a set of brown coveralls that had the word "Tu-31." It turns out that "tu" means prisoner. All I could think of was that these guys had been a French possession at one time and the French word for "kill" is "tuer," so I figured they gave me this clothing so I would be shot. Sure enough, that night they put me in a jeep with another POW, Lt. Col. [Robinson] Robbie Risner, and handcuffed us together. I thought they'd take us out and shoot us. That was the "Hanoi March." So my introduction to camp was getting marched through Hanoi with 500,000 Vietnamese yelling and screaming and throwing objects at us and kicking us. It was not a fun time. That's the way I got to see downtown Hanoi on July 6th, 1966.

The guards took me back to the same cell afterwards. I had a cell mate for one night, Len Eastman, who had been on the *Hancock* with me. Len had come to the *Hancock* to replace another guy who was a POW, and Len got shot down after I did. The reason so many POWs were grouped together at that time was that they had brought all these guys in from outlying camps for the march. They were interrogating them that night and forcing statements out of them saying that we were receiving lenient humane treatment. I thought that was the ultimate irony.

The North Vietnamese had only eight cells and one was a shower. We washed the dishes and showered there — but didn't take a shower too often. That camp was mainly a torture camp used for interrogation.

The only people who don't talk are Steve McQueen or John Wayne in movies. We finally figured that out and started telling lies. You'd just keep lying and lying. If they'd ask you your name, you'd give them the wrong name. It finally would stop when they realized they were just getting garbage. But they did the torture and beatings about once a quarter after that — just to keep their interrogators trained.

After the initial interrogation, they moved me to another camp called the "Zoo." They brought me back in September to meet with a French woman reporter from *L'Humanité*, the French communist daily. When she showed up, I acted like I didn't speak very good French. But the word got out that I was alive. That's how my wife found out. The North Vietnamese let us write home sporadically. She got about 20 letters from me over the course of the seven years.

For food, we had pumpkin soup and rice. Pumpkin soup was made from the meat of a pumpkin thrown in some water with some pig fat to make it greasy. And then we sometimes got rice or occasionally some bread. They baked the bread in the camp. The ration was bread about twice the size of a dinner roll and a little bowl of soup. We would get that twice a day. That went on for six months, and then it changed to a green soup with what looked like collard greens boiled in water. We got that green soup for six months. We lost a lot of weight even though we ate every bit of food we could get.

We could smell their food cooking and it smelled just like an Oriental restaurant. Occasionally, on holidays, they'd spice the food up a bit or we'd get an orange or one beer for two guys.

A doctor ran around the camp; he sometimes became a dentist. He showed up periodically but I saw him only twice through the whole seven years. When I ejected from that airplane, I was going almost 600 miles an hour. I had a low-altitude, zero-delay lanyard hooked up to the parachute so as soon as I came out, the parachute popped. I went from 600 miles an hour down to a walking speed — too fast a transition for the body to handle. It separated almost every joint in my body. The gunshot wound was almost irrelevant. The worst part was the dog-gone joints. And then I had to walk on them. The Vietnamese just snapped them back in. The first six months were terrible. We were not treated for any of these injuries. Whatever healed, healed and whatever didn't, didn't.

As far as my teeth were concerned, I was supposed to have a dental appointment the day

I went on my mission. My teeth never bothered me. Of course, I never had any sugar and I could rinse out the rice with water. They gave us a toothbrush. My problems never got any worse. They did have a dentist. A guard would get on a little bicycle to power the drill. And, of course, they had no anesthesia. Fortunately, I never had to experience that but some of the guys who did have to experience dental treatment said it was worse than the torture. The dentist would get in there and kill the nerve and basically just kill the tooth. The process of going through all that dental work was horrible.

I was in and out of solitary for a total of two years. The longest stretch was about nine months, which came shortly after I met with the French woman reporter. Then they brought a guy in from my ship who had been shot down five weeks before I was. The two of us were in that cell for five or six months. When they'd get new shoot-downs, we'd clean their clothes. The guards wouldn't let us talk to these new POWs but we taught them the tap code anyway.

You'd live for the moment you could talk to another American. We tapped on the wall. I was in total isolation only a couple of times, never more than a week. I had contact with Americans the rest of the time I was in POW camp.

I went back through every class I'd ever taken, reflew every flight I had ever flown in the Navy, every trip in a car. All these memories are back there somewhere and all the cobwebs go away. Pretty soon I was watching my own life like it was a movie.

On the 29th of June when that bombing raid happened, we weren't sure what was going on, but Robbie Risner, who had been there for a while and was a senior Air Force POW, had been brought back for an interrogation. He was in the room when the guards went crazy with the bombing and they left. Robbie then started talking to us. He told us how to do the tap code. So we had it easy. Later on, when I had to teach it to other guys, it was harder because you had to show them to tap using one tap for A and 26 taps for Z. Later on after [Seaman Douglas] Doug Hegdahl came home in the summer of 1969, I think the Navy started teaching the code in survival school. It didn't matter what we heard and communicated, just the fact that we heard something was a big morale boost.

I moved all over the place but not frequently. Several camps were inside the big Hoa Lo complex. The various camps were in a series of wings called "Little Vegas." Each of the wings was named after one of the hotels in Las Vegas. I was out at the Zoo for a short while. Then I was at Son Tay, the camp the Green Berets raided and found empty.[3]

Toward the end of the war when the bombing started in earnest and Hanoi was getting hit pretty hard, the North Vietnamese moved about half of us up to a camp near the Chinese border. They did this so that if a bomb hit, we wouldn't all be wiped out. We were the only leverage they had on Uncle Sam. We called that camp "Dog Patch." The camp had no electricity even though a car battery ran the PA system to make sure we got our daily dose of propaganda. That wasn't a bad time for us. They must have realized the war was almost over.

The torture pretty much stopped after Ho Chi Minh died in September of 1969 [2 September]. Our camp had a few torturing incidents after his death; it usually involved somebody embarrassing or hitting a guard. The North Vietnamese stopped using POWs for propaganda after Ho's death. We were tortured strictly for punishment.

We could usually tell what was going on by switching the propaganda. The North Vietnamese said the Tet Offensive [beginning in late January 1968] was just a raving success. And according to the media back in the U.S., the offensive was a success. But the guys who were involved in this fighting said repelling the offensive was one of the most glorious victories in the history of our armed forces. It got reported totally backwards in the States. So we just reversed whatever their propaganda said. Whatever they said, we knew the opposite was going on. They'd say, Dr. Benjamin Spock is talking against the war and was thrown in jail. "See, you take baby doctors and throw them in jail."

I was up on the Chinese border when the Christmas bombing took place. The bombing stopped up north in March of 1968 when the peace talks started. So we didn't hear anything from March of 1968 until the Son Tay raid. We had been in Son Tay but they moved us out. We were five miles east when we heard SAMs and airplanes going over. We weren't sure what was going on but figured that it had to be good. Then we heard nothing until 1971 when the bombing started. For a while the North Vietnamese even cut off the propaganda radio so we didn't have any news. We didn't have any new shoot-downs because nobody was flying up north. We went for about two years with no news.

When the bombing started up again, we began thinking we might finally get out. We were so far north that we didn't hear the B-52 raids. But as soon as the Air Force started putting B-52s over North Vietnam, we knew we would be going home momentarily. We didn't know about the mining of the harbors, but all the incidents that brought the war to a close had been planned in 1965 but they weren't executed until 1972. Once they got the full brunt of bombing, the war stopped — and almost instantly. Sixty days after the bombing pause, I was home.

We knew something was up because the Vietnamese began screaming about the B-52s. All of a sudden, some trucks came into our camp up near the Chinese border, and we got into the trucks during daytime. We were handcuffed — but not blindfolded — and drove all the way back to Hanoi in the daytime, which was really unusual.

Once we got to Hanoi they threw us in a bunch of rooms at Hoa Lo. These were the same rooms we had been in before the Son Tay raid. We were lined up in those rooms by shoot-down date. It went from the earliest ones right on up. I was in the second bunch and all the guys in my room were about the same vintage of shoot-down. One of the camp interrogators then read us the Paris Agreement [January 1973]. One of the stipulations was that they had to read the Paris Agreement to us within 24 hours. It basically said that three groups were to be home within three months. We figured that meant sick and wounded first, and then shoot-down order next.

I was number 87 out of the group and got on the third airplane. The slew of people who had just been shot down in the B-52s during the Christmas bombings were also there.

The North Vietnamese took us to Gia Lam Airport in buses. We lined up and our names were called. We then went up and saluted the American colonel. A medic grabbed us because he thought we were going to go berserk. We were then escorted to the C-141 airplane. We boarded, they sealed it up, and away we went.

Everyone was quiet. We decided beforehand that it would be totally dignified; nobody was going to show wild elation. When you look at photos, we're all serious. We did that because we didn't want them to use it for propaganda showing what a group of happy campers we were. When the crew sealed the aircraft, someone said, "These bastards are going to shoot us down." It got pretty quiet until the pilot called, "Feet wet." Then we started yelling, screaming, and hugging. We knew they couldn't shoot us down because we were over the ocean. And then all the guys lined up to smell the flight nurses' perfume.

When we landed at Clark AFB [the Philippines], the authorities were concerned about the press bothering us so each of us had an escort officer assigned. As soon as our plane landed, my escort went over to the terminal and got me on the manifest for the first plane out. Then we went to the hospital and my escort ran me through up to the front of every single line saying, "He's got to be in this line. He's on the first airplane back." Everybody just backed up.

I didn't need a lot of medical care at that point. I was just scrawny. The dental team cleaned my teeth and the doctors checked to see if everything was working okay. They kept some of the guys at Clark for a while. Everybody wanted to get home. And I got on that first plane back to the States.

From Clark we went to Hickham [AFB in Hawaii]. We refueled and went on to Travis [AFB in California]. At Travis everybody was split up; then we came into Norfolk on a C-9. Jeremiah Denton, Jim Mulligan, and I went right to Portsmouth Naval Hospital. They tried to keep the press away from us. They weren't sure what our reaction was going to be.

Every morning for five or six days two intelligence debriefers went over details about our imprisonment. They didn't want to accidentally leave anybody behind so they asked us about everything that happened. Our memories were pretty clear then. I told them about everybody I had run into, the rundowns of every camp I was in, and the dates we switched camps. They tried to line that up with people they knew who were missing to make sure they had everyone accounted for.

I still suffer from the injuries I got as a result of punching out of the aircraft and from the torture. But remember, I was on flight status so the doctors never found out about a lot of those injuries. The Navy was pretty good about it. Navy personnel set up a program in Pensacola at the Naval Aerospace Medical Institute [NAMI], which had come out of the Thousand Aviators program begun in 1941. A Navy team of specialists had been tracking these guys for years. Dr. [Robert] Mitchell was at Pensacola doing the Thousand Aviators study in 1969, and the Navy realized that this tracking would be great information to have when the POWs came back. The program would have a control group to study and these former POWs to research to see if they had any long-term effects. So Dr. Mitchell started tracking us when we got home. It became a serious problem only when specialists found that some of the guys shouldn't be flying. Doc Mitchell would ensure that these former POWs would stay on flight status. But a gentlemen's agreement existed among the doctors that these former pilots wouldn't get orders to go flying. That way they wouldn't lose their flight pay.

At the beginning, the doctors found little ailments like worms and various parasites. My vision had gone down to the point where I should have been wearing glasses. The medical staff wasn't sure whether or not that was normal aging or vitamin deficiency. I had some blind spots then — which I still have. I had a lot of neurological problems which they couldn't duplicate — like shooting pains in my arms and legs. I never said anything about pains in my back and neck because I thought that was just aging. I was an old guy; I was 34.

Just before I retired [at age 42], I said that I wanted to go through every clinic and have everything on paper. I had never complained about any orthopedic injuries because I didn't have any broken bones.

I was sitting out in the waiting room and a doctor [Joseph Ricciardi] came out and yelled for a corpsman to get all the residents. So they all came in and I heard them talking about these 75-year-old bones in a 42-year-old body. "Wait a second," I thought. "I'm 42. I wonder if that could be me?" And sure enough, I had this horrible, crippling arthritis in my shoulders, back, and neck from the ejection and having had my shoulders separated so many times.

Dr. Ricciardi was responsible for the fact that post-traumatic osteoarthritis is now presumptive from the VA's standpoint. If you were a POW and got that, you don't have to prove service-connection. It's presumed to be service-connected. He really did a good service for all POWs.

I've gotten so used to my old injuries, I can't tell whether or not I suffer from them. But I was diagnosed with MS [multiple sclerosis] a couple of years ago. Some of the symptoms I had back then, such as the shooting pains, might have been from the MS; I don't know. The doctors could never duplicate the little ailments I've had over the years. I don't even think about the arthritis anymore.

Operation Homecoming

The following narrative is from an article originally published in the September 1973 U.S. Navy Medicine (Volume 62, September 1973, pp. 6–11), written by two flight surgeons (Michael D. Stenberg and R. Paul Caudill, Jr.), who escorted the recently freed Vietnam captives back to the States.

In February 1973, "Operation Homecoming" began. Six flight surgeons, residents at the Naval Aerospace Medical Institute in Pensacola, Florida, joined three Army, seven Air Force

The first group of prisoners of war awaits release at Hanoi's Gia Lam Airport, February 1973 (Naval Historical Center).

flight surgeons, and two Air Force School of Aerospace Medicine staff members at Clark Air Force Base in the Philippines. Their job was to escort the newly freed POWs from Hanoi and provide in-flight medical care. The group was subdivided into nine teams of two members each.

The evacuation aircraft were C-141 Starlifters reconfigured for their special cargo. Each plane had 42 airline seats, 15 feet of troop seats along each bulkhead, 20 litters, and a "comfort pallet," which consisted of two lavatories and a galley in a single unit.

All the Hanoi missions were similarly conducted. Each C-141 carried a flight crew, public affairs officer and photographers, a military escort, three medical technicians, three or four flight nurses, one or two Medical Service Corps officers, and two flight surgeons.

The returnees tolerated the high noise and extremely low humidity flight environment well. Medical personnel encouraged them to keep well hydrated and to use the available wax-impregnated cotton ear plugs.

The POWs came aboard the C-141s quickly as they were released, which made triage difficult. The medical crew could only accomplish rapid visual inspection and hasty questioning during the brief time before takeoff. The returnees who appeared to be weak or sick, or who were presumed to have acute medical conditions, were placed on litters. Immediately after the last returnee had boarded, the crew secured the doors and the engines started. On some flights, the cheering began almost immediately. On others, it was only after the pilot announced, "Feet wet," which indicated they had cleared North Vietnamese airspace and were over the ocean, that the former POWs burst into cheers. They jumped from their seats, joyously greeting each other and the crew. No amount of planning or foresight could have adequately prepared the flight and medical personnel for the moving and vivid experiences of greeting these men, taking their first steps out of the hands of their captors.

Once outbound from Hanoi, the flight surgeons resumed their rapid triage and evaluation, notifying the Air Force hospital at Clark of special needs or problems. During the three-hour flight, staff interviewed each returnee, taking notes that would be accompanying each patient to the hospital.

Following the initial intensive hospital evaluation at Clark, the returnees were scheduled for long flights back to the U.S. Teams of two flight surgeons again reviewed all medical records and made preflight visits with the patients whom they would accompany aboard the C-141. The specially configured aircraft and its medical crew provided a direct extension of inpatient hospital care.

It became apparent that although most of the returnees were in good general physical condition, many had not slept adequately in the hospital; some began to manifest signs of sleep deprivation during the flight. Quiet counseling and gentle, but firm direction nudged them into litters for as many as six hours of uninterrupted sleep. Many of the men wanted to discuss personal problems, and they sought medical opinions and information, particularly in connection with their future in aviation careers. The flight surgeons tried to answer these questions and provide short-term psychotherapy.

Doctor of the Repatriated

Capt. Robert Mitchell's reputation as the dean of Navy flight surgeons goes back many years. In a Navy career that spanned more than four decades in uniform, he became most famous for his work with the "Thousand Aviators" project. Begun in 1940 by Dr. Ashton Graybiel, the "Pensacola Study of Naval Aviators," as it was originally called, investigated the value of physiological and psychological testing in predicting success in the Navy's flight training program. After World War II, researchers saw the potential of this information they had collected — a considerable data base of medical statistics on this homogenous group of aviators. Re-evaluation of their health status over time had yielded a trove of information about the natural aging process, cardiovascular health, and morbidity and mortality rates. With this successful and well-established protocol in place, Dr. Graybiel the mentor and Dr. Mitchell the student found new subjects for their well-honed research techniques — the newly repatriated Vietnam prisoners of war.

Prior to Vietnam, no long-term study had ever been conducted on repatriated prisoners of war with respect to the cause and forecast of disease or psychological problems. Following World War II, repatriation examinations were performed on about 60 percent of Pacific Theater repatriates and 20 percent of those liberated from the European Theater. Following the Korean War, 85 percent of repatriates had examinations. However, these were one-time examinations with no follow-up. Unlike their neglected predecessors, the repatriated Vietnam prisoners of war would find themselves treated as precious cargo.

The Repatriated Prisoner of War Program is a takeoff on the Thousand Aviators study, and, in fact, we're still seeing Thousand Aviators piggybacked on the POW program. It's a rare week that I don't have at least one or maybe two of the Thousand Aviators come in. Of course, they're now averaging about 86 years of age.

Dr. Graybiel and I had been following the Thousand Aviators over the years. I started working with him in 1955 when I came to Pensacola, and we were seeing them at five-year intervals. When word came that the North Vietnamese were going to repatriate the prisoners of war, our idea was: Why not just follow these people the same as we had been following the Thousand Aviators? And that's exactly what happened.

A group of us got together at San Diego in 1972 and planned the repatriation program, basing it strictly on what we had been doing with the Thousand Aviators. We were going to look at them both physically and psychologically. The programs were set up in such a way that half the study was to be physical and the other half psychological. We had our own staff at Pensacola, the group that had been working with the Thousand Aviators. When we started in with the repatriates, we were well set up to do it.

The repatriated prisoners of war were brought from Hanoi to Clark, and were then farmed out to Navy, Army, and Air Force hospitals throughout the United States. Many of them went to the West Coast; many came to the East Coast. We also had other POWs who were not aviators; Marines and a few Army people in the group who were primarily picked up in South Vietnam and taken north.

Believe it or not, we had only one Navy enlisted man in the group but we also had a number of enlisted Marines. The Navy enlisted man was Doug Hegdahl. Hegdahl had been stationed aboard the *Canberra* [CAG-2]. One night in the South China Sea, he went up on deck just as the big guns were being fired, and the concussion knocked him overboard. He swam around for a few hours and some Vietnamese fishermen picked him up and took him ashore. He still works at the SERE [Survival, Evasion, Resistance, Escape] School in San Diego. When the POWs were released in 1973, I was here in Pensacola and we started seeing them in January of 1974.

We had all three services represented — Navy, Army, and Air Force. We were interested in what had happened to these people as a result of their captivity. In other words, did they have physical disabilities? Did they have psychological disabilities? Just how were they doing?

Our psychiatric people were doing a big part of the interviewing. I was doing all the physical exams. In fact, I personally examined every man who came in annually up until 1991. I didn't miss a man.

Overall, they were doing surprisingly well. We expected that they would have many physical and psychological problems, but most came back in good condition. The malnourishment wasn't as much as one might have expected because during the last year the North Vietnamese had started to feed them better. The POWs weren't as bad off as they had been in previous years. However, we saw a lot of evidence of no medical treatment or simply bad medical treatment.

For example, the prisoners who had fractures had not been properly treated. During the time they were in captivity, they also developed things like beriberi [vitamin deficiency disease] and skin diseases, which were not treated properly. We saw evidence of these conditions when they came back. Some of them had horrendous orthopedic problems that had not been properly cared for. One man's arm is foreshortened such that the hand is about halfway up the arm because the bones were broken. He had been badly injured when he ejected. After the Viets picked him up, they thought he was dead so they tossed him into a grave. When they started to pour the dirt in on him he awoke and sat up and was then pulled from the hole. He had severe injuries.

Another man came back with a leg fracture that had not been treated properly. One leg was about four inches shorter than the other. He was eventually operated on and his good leg was shortened to match the bad leg. In fact, 103 of the men had significant orthopedic problems.

Dentally, the men weren't really that red hot. They needed dental work but not as much as I had predicted.

We found their psychological health surprisingly good. We expected they would come back with all sorts of problems, but they did better than we anticipated. This study raised several interesting points. We have seen more in the way of psychological problems in the enlisted group than in the officer group. We attribute that discrepancy to the fact that the officers were better trained. Most of them were college graduates and were better able to cope with the situation. I think that's why most of the aviators came back in pretty good condition. That's not to say we didn't see problems but certainly fewer than I initially expected.

When we did the planning in 1972, the Army and the Air Force had their own programs. Unfortunately, the Army study petered out altogether after a year because the fellow who was running it decided that it was interfering with his practice. He recommended to their Surgeon General that the program be discontinued. The Air Force ostensibly had a study, but if you talk to the Air Force people, you'll find that their research program didn't amount to much. I was seeing 16 of the Air Force people here. These fellows were coming in at their own expense from various areas and I'd run them through the program.

When we first started our study on the POWs, we were bringing the former prisoners in for a period of five days because we were doing some very special work on them. In the latter years, that time in some cases dropped to one to three days, depending on what was being done. We certainly tried to give them the best possible care.

"Every Sort of Vile Damage"

Four years after the end of the Vietnam War, Capt. Joseph Ricciardi, an orthopedic surgeon, arrived in Pensacola, Florida, "the cradle of naval aviation." It was then he began seeing Dr. Robert Mitchell's referrals, former POWs who were at that time part of the Repatriated Prisoner of War Program. Most were aviators who had suffered high-speed ejection injuries following shoot-downs over North Vietnam. These injuries were left untreated by their captors and/or aggravated by harsh and often disfiguring torture during their captivity. Dr. Ricciardi's annual evaluation of these POWs and getting to know them personally became the most fulfilling part of his medical career.

I got to Pensacola in 1978. Within a month of getting there, I was asked by one of the clinic nurses to see a patient who didn't have an appointment. I asked her why I should do that. I wasn't on call but the on-call guy wouldn't see him, and the head of the department was too busy. She said, "These are our POW patients. We don't know when they're going to be coming in, and many of them need orthopedic consultations." I thought, nobody is too busy to see one of the POWs. So that's how I started seeing all the patients Capt. Bob Mitchell was referring.

I trained in a county hospital and saw every sort of vile damage that one human could inflict on another. But it took all my New York–New Jersey smarts and toughness to sit down and not cry when these patients would matter-of-factly describe how their bones were broken and dislocated on ejection. They told me how they were repeatedly tortured by having their arms pulled out of sockets to get information, and how they were routinely beaten and mistreated.

I was in Pensacola from 1978 to 1987, and I saw POWs every year who needed orthopedic evaluations. Working with these men and trying to absorb some of the horror that they went through was one of the most tremendous experiences I've ever had.

Dr. Mitchell would send me a typical military consultation request. "Please see this 42-year-old aviator, RPOW [returned prisoner of war] with a history of ejection injuries to the shoulders and other injuries to the arms and legs." So I would sit down with the patient and try to make a list of all the body parts that hurt. And then we would examine every injured part and take x-rays on a yearly basis. Many of the POWs had had ejection injuries to their knees, their upper extremities, or both. They were routinely not treated or maltreated by their captors. A number of the men had dislocated shoulders.

One of the favorite tortures the North Vietnamese used was to bring the POWs in for a questioning session and then repeatedly redislocate their shoulders. A number of men had had their hands tied behind their backs. Their elbows were also tied together behind their backs, if you can imagine that. Ropes were passed around their wrists and thrown over a beam in the ceiling. The men were then pulled up with their hands behind their backs until their shoulders would tear, dislocate, or break.

This resulted in a significant number of very traumatic injuries. What we learn with every war is that untreated orthopedic injuries lead to early arthritis. So these were men who had to deal with pain and with injuries that were left untreated anywhere from one to seven years. Many of them came back with less than normal function in their arms, legs, and spines.

I tracked the POWs who I saw along with a very well put-together control group that Capt. Mitchell had assembled. I was able to show a comparison in my statistics with the POW group having a much higher rate of osteoarthritis and nerve injuries than the control group. When you have had your arms and wrists tied behind your back or are manacled by your legs for months, your nerves will be subjected to pressure and will stop functioning. You can then have foot drop[4] or wrist drop.[5] You can also get carpel tunnel syndrome and ulnar nerve injuries.

Fortunately, I was in a position in about 1988 or 1989 to testify at the VA Special Committee on POWs in Washington. As a result of Dr. Mitchell's work and some of the reports I made, the VA has considered degenerative arthritis in a POW as presumptively coming from active duty and from the POW injury. They don't have to prove a service connection — the service connection is presumed. This connection also holds true for nerve injuries. I was just a person in the right place at the right time able to document these POW–related injuries.

I took x-rays year after year on these POWs and noted that their joints wore out faster than the control groups' joints. I saw only a few nerve injuries in the control group. For a long period of time, the POW group was so malnourished that their heart disease rate was much lower than the control group. And it wasn't until they'd been back about 10 years and had been eating well and getting into a more indulgent lifestyle that their heart disease rate started to catch up to the rest of the population.

The malnutrition they experienced had another down side. When you don't have fat, you don't get four vitamins — A, D, E, and K. So most of these men have some visual acuity problems worse than the control group. They certainly had poor nerve nutrition, which is why I think the rope tortures left them with so many permanent nerve injuries. The nerves had no way to completely recover physiologically. So the starvation diet had some positive aspects, but it also had negative aspects in terms of their vision and their nerve function.

A number of these ex-prisoners had had surgery between 1973 when they were repatriated and 1978 when I first saw them. But I did a number of operations on these men, primarily for the nerve problems — taking the pressure off nerves, carpel tunnel releases, ulnar nerve transpositions, and more recently, two shoulder rotator cuff repairs. Some of them had already had their knees worked on. I saw a range of injuries in one POW I never could have imagined could be sustained by one individual. I sat down with this man for the better part of two hours and catalogued all his injuries. I picked up one he didn't even know about because when I x-rayed his hip, the x-ray techs got far enough down at the thigh for me to see a healed thigh fracture. He had been beaten up very badly and then placed in leg irons on the concrete deck for months. His femur was fractured and he was unaware of it because the rest of his body was so horribly beaten up. The femur healed and he never knew about it.

This man also made a documentary for the Navy about what he'd done. He was filmed swimming in a pool at a naval facility. The documentary showed that he couldn't run anymore, but he was still doing his physical fitness training. But while he swam, he wasn't moving his left shoulder. I saw him in the morning then saw the film at lunch time. I examined his left shoulder in the afternoon and found an undiagnosed fracture in that shoulder. That man had at least nine separate orthopedic diagnoses. I saw any number of people with six, seven, and eight diagnoses — specific parts of their bodies that were fractured, dislocated, damaged, or otherwise injured. It was just incredible! I will probably never see that kind of abuse again in my practice.

I believe it really helped those men to be part of a POW community. I think one person all by himself in isolation for six or seven years would have a hard time keeping his sanity and not giving up if he were by himself. But these men fed each other. They cleaned each other. They tolerated each other's dysentery. When a fellow would break under torture, they'd all point out to him that everybody breaks under torture. I think an understanding of the Code of Conduct was greatly improved. What the POWs had to do for themselves was come to an understanding that a man would hold out until he was afraid of losing his life, a limb, or his sanity. And after that, you just had to make the torture stop. They're all tough guys. They all had their limit but they all stuck together as a community, with about a half-dozen traitorous exceptions. They were just an outstanding example of what good human conduct can be in adverse situations. And I'm proud to be in the same military with these sailors, soldiers, airmen, and Marines. It is just wonderful to know these people and know about them.

After I had been seeing Bob Mitchell's patients for about a year, he said, "I want you to come to lunch with me and two other guys in the program." I sat opposite him during lunch. To my right and to my left were two Medal of Honor winners. And there I am, a very junior lieutenant commander sitting between a vice admiral, a Navy captain, and an Air Force colonel. I didn't close my mouth once during the whole lunch because I was in such awe of these Medal of Honor recipients. I just sat there with my head turning like I was watching a tennis match. When you sit down at a table with heroes, you learn not to talk.

14

MENDING

Weapons of modern warfare took a heavy toll in Vietnam. Anti-aircraft guns and surface-to-air missiles claimed a brutal number of pilots and aircrew flying missions over North Vietnam. South of the DMZ, North Vietnamese and Viet Cong troops, equipped and resupplied by China and the Soviet Union, were rarely short of high-velocity automatic weapons, rocket-propelled grenades, mines, mortars, and artillery.

Viet Cong guerrillas augmented their arsenal with "low-tech" but equally deadly weapons. Skilled at converting undetonated American ordnance into what are now referred to as "improvised explosive devices," these masters of the booby trap exacted untold casualties. Other deaths and injuries resulted from grenades triggered when unsuspecting troops tripped invisible wires stretched across jungle paths.

And explosives were not always required. So-called "punji sticks"— sharpened bamboo stakes sometimes smeared with human excrement— lurked in hidden pits, poised to skewer and then infect the unwary. Even nails protruding from camouflaged boards could inflict serious damage. The enemy understood too well the old military maxim: A wounded soldier is preferable to a dead one because his evacuation and subsequent care remove several other combatants from the action.

The results from this mayhem were certainly similar to what had been seen in previous wars — punctured vital organs, disembowelment, limbs blasted and splintered beyond recognition, disfiguring burns, and fatal or debilitating head wounds. Corpsmen on the scene stepped into the breach as they had always done. They arrested hemorrhage with battle dressings and tourniquets, administered morphine, splinted fractures, and, when possible, started intravenous serum albumin or other life-preserving fluids. Insuring the patient's evacuation up the chain to more capable medical care was the next priority.

Battalion hospitals, Naval Support Activity Hospital Danang, or hospital ships took up the slack. Once patients were evaluated, skilled surgeons repaired what limbs they could or reluctantly resorted to amputation when necessary. Less seriously injured patients who recovered quickly from their wounds returned to action. Those requiring additional treatment or a long convalescence continued their journey aboard aircraft equipped for medical evacuation to Clark Air Force Base in the Philippines, Yokosuka Naval Hospital in Japan, and then to other naval hospitals back in the States. For many a soldier, sailor, or Marine, the road back to a "normal" life was long and arduous.

Flight Surgeon to the Rescue

Lt.(j.g.) Dennis Earl was deployed aboard the aircraft carrier USS Oriskany (CVA-34) on Yankee Station. His unit was Air Wing 16 of VA-163 Squadron. Earl had already flown 62 combat missions without major incident, but his 63rd mission over North Vietnam turned out to be his last. It was 20 October 1967.

We launched off as a flight of four. [Lt. Cmdr.] Jim Busey and I were flak-suppressors for two other A-4s that were carrying Walleye air-to-surface missiles. The objective was to take out a bridge and we were to knock back the flak—if there was any. One of the A-4s vaporized the bridge with the first Walleye.

Then we split up and went two for two into different areas. Jim Busey and I were flying backup to check out some water-borne logistics craft in the Yellow River area. These were barges camouflaged on the banks of a river. We were headed back to take those out with our weapons, and were doing some road reconnaissance en route. I was flying behind Jim, and I was weaving down a road at 3,000 feet, a little above and behind him, crossing from his left to right. I was finishing up the cross from his left to right about a mile behind him. That's the usual formation for road reconnaissance. You stay out of phase with each other and usually leave a mile separation. If the lead can then spot a target in time, such as trucks at a road intersection, and describe them, the pilot following could then pop into a roll-in position and roll in on the targets. In the middle of doing this maneuver, I got hit by triple A [anti-aircraft] fire being shot at Jim.

The projectile, which was a 12.7mm shell about the size of a .50 caliber, came in the lower forward nose section just above the nose wheel well. It penetrated a couple of bulkheads and split in two on the left rudder pedal. Half of it got my left foot and the other half got the tibia of my right leg. It had just enough energy to do the job because the boat tail bullet was lying on top of the boot that had split. The other half was projecting out the other side of my G-suit [pressure suit] after it had gone through my tibia.

As soon as I was hit, I jinked to make sure nothing else was coming up, then I checked out the airplane. I first checked the engine instruments to make certain I didn't have a compounding problem. I knew I was in some kind of trouble but wasn't sure what it was. At first I thought it might have been a surface-to-air missile because we didn't have any indications of anything happening. But I knew right away I was in quite a desperate situation and bleeding a lot. A nose wheel and unsafe gear lights were flashing, as well as a couple of other annunciator lights. Smoke filled the cockpit, and I wasn't sure if I was going to be able to fly the plane out of there.

We were just south of what they called the "Hourglass [Hong] River" close to a karst ridge. It was geographically close to Phu Ly, which was a major center for North Vietnamese transportation. North Vietnam is narrow. Down in that area it was probably no more than 40 miles wide. We were only about a third of the way in from the coast, maybe less than that. Fortunately, in a jet like the A-4, the rudder pedals aren't really needed in normal coordinated flight so I could use the stick for control. In most jets with swept-back wings, you don't need the rudder unless you're trying to exaggerate a turn rate.

I notified Jim Busey and told him I had taken a hit and had two broken legs. That got his attention. He told me to turn toward the coast. Your first inclination is to get away from land so you wouldn't get picked up and incarcerated. So I turned to the east and pickled off the weapons I had left. This means getting rid of ordnance. You can pickle them either deliberately over a target or just get rid of them to lighten the plane. On that mission I had six Mark 82s—"daisy cutters," which together weighed about 3,000 pounds.[1]

It was about a 25-minute flight back. This was when Doc [Lt. Cmdr. Allan] Adeeb came into the picture. He was listening to the calls on the radio and suggested that I inflate my G-suit to put compression on the injury to reduce the bleeding.

The lower bladder of my G-suit was punctured, but if I held my hand on the G-suit actuator, I could actually inflate it without pulling Gs by pushing down on a plunger. That would cause a restriction in the upper bladders which weren't damaged. And this restriction reduced the blood loss. But, at that point, the blood was starting to clot up anyway. I also was in a lot of pain, especially in my left foot.

As for the right leg, the bullet had just enough energy to do its job, which was to take a chunk out of the tibia about a half-inch wide. I was able to fly with my right hand and lift the weight off my right leg with my left hand. I did that for the 25 minutes it took to get back to the ship.

I never felt like I was going to pass out but the ship's crew thought I might so they rigged the barricade for my recovery. It was probably the best landing I ever made. I had told them I didn't need that barricade but they rigged it just in case, and I wasn't going to argue with them. The ship was still in a turn as I made my approach. I didn't do the normal 350-knot break turn and come back around and land. I just did a long left-base entry, and when the ship steadied, I made it straight in.

As soon as I felt the tug on the wire, I pulled it to idle and the airplane nosed into the barricade. Then I shut the engine down. They brought out a forklift with a pallet and mattresses on it, which they pulled alongside the cockpit. A couple of corpsmen helped me stand up on my left foot. Then they eased me into a litter after which they strapped me down and lowered the forklift.

I then knew I was in a weapons elevator going below right to sick bay. With a shot of morphine, I was starting to feel better.

In sick bay I first met the doctors who were going to work on me — Dr. Gallitano and Dr. Adeeb. Shortly after I hit the flight deck, Dr. Adeeb landed and the two of them went to work. They cut off my G-suit and my boots and started a drip. I woke up in a cot in sick bay with a cast up to my hip on the right leg and a half-cast up to my knee on the left leg and foot.

The round had gone through the ball joint of my big toe so I don't have that joint anymore. The adjacent toe was fractured but the doctors didn't have to anything beyond splinting it. The docs put two K-wires[2] through the tip of my big toe down through the ball joint, and into the bone extending back from the big toe. They lined up all the bones and stabilized them. They then removed some skin from my left thigh and did a skin graft over the missing skin. That procedure amazed the doctors when I got to Pensacola. This skillful grafting had not resulted in the kind of infection they had previously seen in patients coming back from Vietnam.

About six weeks after I got back to Pensacola, the doctors removed those K-wires. I was still in a half-cast on my left foot but I could walk around on it. They put a walking cast on it and I used crutches for my right leg. I had a cast that went past my right hip all the way down the leg, so it was held in that position until it knitted across the gap. I no longer had any wires or screws.

I was married in February without the cast but was still on crutches. My brother carried my wife across the threshold for me.

* * *

Lt. Cmdr. Allan Adeeb, senior medical officer on Oriskany, *was a "dual designator," one of a handful of men who wore both the medical officer's oak leaf insignia and the gold wings of a naval aviator. When he wasn't attending patients in sick bay, Dr. Adeeb flew A-4 tanker missions. "If somebody took a hit in the wings and was losing fuel, I'd go out and find them. They'd plug in [connect to the tanker's refueling hose] and I'd take them back to the ship." Adeeb was in the air that day flying such a mission.*

Jim Busey was nearby and I heard this conversation about Denny Earl bleeding and that he didn't know if he was going to make it back. So I called Jim and said, "Tell him to inflate his pressure suit. That will act like a tourniquet." Busey then radioed Earl and told him to inflate his G-suit, which he did, and then he made it back to the ship.

I landed when they were already getting him ready for surgery. Al Gallitano was the general surgeon. I came down right from the flight deck, took off my flight suit, put on my scrub suit, went in and helped operate on this guy without missing a beat. Al was such a great doc. In those days, they taught the surgeons a lot of orthopedics. We had Denny off the ship and back to the States in about 36 hours.

Lt. Alphonse Gallitano had been aboard Oriskany *for only a few days when the badly injured pilot was brought into the carrier's operating room.*

Earl had taken a large caliber round through his right lower leg, which shattered it. He nearly lost the leg; it was almost shot off. He had also lost a fair amount of blood. We controlled the bleeding, gave him blood, and repaired the broken tibia. I hadn't seen wounds caused by high-caliber bullets before.

We stripped off all his clothing, debrided the dead and badly injured tissue, and irrigated the wound. We then aligned the broken fragments of bone and put Earl in traction. While he was in traction, I put him in a cast. It wasn't an extensive operation. I think it took only an hour or two. Dr. Adeeb assisted me.

Overcoming the Odds

Following his serious wounding during the Battle of Hue, Capt. Ron Christmas was to be evacuated to NSA Danang. But since so many casualties were pouring into Danang at that time, he ended up at the Air Force medical facility on one side of the Danang Air Base. As he recalls, he was "lost" in the system for nearly two months.

My poor wife knew that I was wounded but didn't know where I was. I ended up in the Air Force system. I'm not sure if I got malaria or something else. But I got a huge infection and temperature.

I remember waking up on a ward with no other patients around. Suddenly I see a figure in white. And I thought, "Is this something in the beyond or what?" It turned out to be an Air Force nurse. All the casualties had been moved on, but because I had this infection from the wounds, the medical staff kept me there.

Then they evacuated me down to Cam Ranh Bay, which was still in the Air Force system, where my wounds were debrided more extensively. I had taken shrapnel from the RPG [rocket-propelled grenade] in the back of my left knee. The doctors later determined that the shrapnel took both the nerves—the motor and the sensory nerve—and created an aneurysm on the major artery. We didn't know about this aneurysm at the time. The wound was filled with debris with a huge infection resulting. The other shrapnel wounds from the mortars were to my arms but they were not major.

About six weeks passed before they evacuated me to the Yokosuka Naval Hospital. That was the first time I was able to call my wife. While I was there, the wound still would not heal so they decided to go in. Fortunately, the surgical team included a vascular surgeon. After putting a tourniquet on my leg, the surgeon went in behind the knee. The artery burst and they tied it off. They then separated the veins as much as possible and — because they were able to keep the leg stationary for about 48 to 72 hours—the veins picked up the flow. While I didn't have a pulse, at least I had blood flow to the foot. They had talked about taking the leg before but I said, "No!" Now they thought about it again but I ended up keeping it.

Eventually, I was evacuated to the Philadelphia Naval Hospital and then went through a series of three or four surgeries. The first was to repair the artery. The doctors took a vein from my right leg, clipped the clot out of the major artery in my left leg, and dropped in the vein. That vein has worked from that time on.

Then they went after the nerves. They were able to pull together the sensory nerve with all its million circuits. But the motor nerve was just too badly gone and scarred so they couldn't do anything.

Through the years, I've regained sensation all the way down through my ankle. I was able to stay in the Marine Corps, "hide" for a while, and get well enough to run and push. I've got a very fused ankle that's a bit off on a cant and atrophied below the knee, but it has never stopped me.

Another point to remember. Philadelphia Naval Hospital was the amputee center at the time. If you ever felt sorry for yourself, you climbed in your wheelchair and went down to the wards. After visiting that ward, you didn't feel sorry for yourself anymore.

"I Canceled My Policy!"

Bill Henry became an officer through the Officer Candidate School and was commissioned into the Marine Corps Reserve in 1966. Following a bout with collapsed lungs and subsequent lung surgery at the National Naval Medical Center in Bethesda, Maryland, he didn't arrive in Vietnam until November 1967. He soon found himself in command of 2nd Platoon, Hotel Company, 2nd Battalion, 3rd Marines. For three months the battalion patrolled an area south of Danang and south of Marble Mountain, encountering sniper fire, booby traps, and other enemy-harassing activity.

At the end of the Tet Offensive of 1968, Henry and his Marines began patrolling farther north near Phu Bai and the DMZ. Henry's battalion participated in Scotland II, an operation to the west of Khe Sanh. They were given the grim task of recovering 40 bodies who had been casualties of an ill fated patrol — Charlie Company, 1st Battalion, 9th Marines. The remains — thought to be on the side of a hill and in enemy territory — had already been on the ground for six days.

The recovery operation was well planned with two or three battalions involved. After the hills were secured, Henry's unit was ordered to follow and recover the remains. A helicopter would then fly the body bags out.

But the plan went terribly awry. With the assigned unit unable to secure the hill, Henry's platoon, which expected to complete its mission very quickly, was forced to spend the night without equipment — even to dig foxholes to secure themselves. Enemy artillery rained down on the platoon causing many casualties. Lt. Henry was one of them.

I initially did not experience very much pain considering that a fragment went through the center of my right foot, another through my right back, and I had burns up my left arm. Most people suspected it was a 105mm artillery round. I didn't have any remnants of shrapnel left in me; everything that hit me went through me.

The corpsman couldn't get my shoes off, but he packed the wounds to try to slow the bleeding and wrapped my chest as well. Then I was hauled in a poncho back up the hill. A gunship, which was flying in support of our mission, dropped down and picked me up. They threw me on the floor and a gunner put his foot in my back to hold me in. We then flew about two miles back to Khe Sanh.

When we got there, the helicopter landed right outside the door of the aid station and men ran out with an empty litter and pulled me onto it. From the time the helicopter hit the ground, no more than 15 seconds went by before they were out, had me on the litter, and had me back down into a shaft leading into the aid station [Charlie Med].

By virtue of having been at Bethesda, I was well experienced with the Navy medical system and understood how corpsmen, doctors, and nurses worked so well together. When I was taken deep into this aid station at Charlie Med, a very senior corpsman looked at me and saw I was an officer. He said, "Well, Lieutenant, it looks like you're going to have an occasion to use your Blue Cross/Blue Shield."

I looked up at him and said, "You know, Doc, when I got my Navy doctors, I canceled my policy!" And that just broke everybody up.

The medical staff took great pains to clear away the boots and clothes and were able to attack the wound in an effort to stop most of the bleeding, which was very serious. They had a tremendous amount of work to do. The shrapnel that hit my foot went through my boot. I'm sure they did a fair amount of debriding because just to get the boot off my foot would have required a great deal of cutting and hacking. Then they tried to remove the leather pieces from my foot. It was a real mess.

I was probably at Khe Sanh for a few hours before they took me out on another helicopter to Dong Ha. I recall a huge concrete slab out at a triage unit with water hoses and brushes.

I did not receive any shots for pain until I immediately went into debriding surgery at 1 o'clock in the morning. Mind you, I had been hit in the field about 2 o'clock in the afternoon.

The doctor singled me out to go in for surgery and said that I was bound to have internal damage. I said, "Doc, you picked the wrong one. I'm okay. I've had the upper lobe of my left lung taken out. I know what it feels like to have something wrong inside, and there's nothing wrong in there.

He said, "It can't be. "The shrapnel round hit the big muscle that goes down your back."

He took me into X-ray, and it turned out that I did not have any internal damage. The shrapnel had entered my chest underneath my arm and went straight across my rib cage from right to left from under the arm around to the back. It then exited just before the backbone. It was like a fillet knife had scraped the rib cage off. It was that close. The doctor said that if that shrapnel had been an eighth of an inch closer, it would have sent those bones into my chest cavity and I wouldn't have had a chance. It actually didn't go inside the ribs at all. It just went through the meat and took all the muscle out — tore that muscle out.

After the x-ray, they put me aboard a C-130 with a lot of other casualties and headed to Phu Bai. From there, they sent me to Danang to be evacuated from the country. I went to the 249th Army General Hospital in Tokyo because the big Navy hospital in Japan — Yokosuka — was full.

Then I went through another debriding surgery. I had "wound care" three times a day. The corpsmen or nurses pulled out the gauze from the wounds, poured in peroxide, and used tweezers or forceps to remove all the dead skin or tissue from the foot. Then they would repack it.

It was quite a scary procedure because I had recalled that one of our corpsmen had been seriously wounded just south of Danang in mid–March, and he contracted gangrene and died. It just had me horrified that I was not getting correct wound care. I was insistent upon having my wounds checked to make sure they stayed clean. And it was a very painful routine to pull that gauze from those wounds and have peroxide poured in every day.

I went home on an Air Force C-141 that had stacks and stacks of litters against each side and down the middle. I wound up at Millington [Naval Hospital Memphis], Tennessee, which was the closest hospital to my home in Mississippi. I was assigned to the SOQ [Sick Officers Quarters]. And as was the practice, every time you changed hospitals a doctor had to be present when the wounds were opened, and he had to prescribe the new round of medications. Nurses and corpsmen didn't have the authority to see the first one. When I got assigned and was sent to the ward, I kept screaming to get my wounds checked because it had been a full day of travel, and I had not had my wounds opened and looked at.

It was on a weekend when I got into the hospital, and very few doctors were around. An internist was on duty, but he didn't know much about orthopedic care. I know that for a fact because where it used to take 15 minutes to bubble those gauzes out of my foot, he reached down with one hand and pulled that gauze out. This old hospital I was in had the pipe running down the roof of the building. I thought I could reach that pipe when he grabbed those pieces of gauze and pulled them out. It was pretty brutal.

I went through some fairly extensive surgeries. Having previously had some surgery at Bethesda, I knew the status of the hospitals. Bethesda was one of the best in the world. I was sad that I didn't get assigned to go back there. But, as it turned out, a young orthopedist from Wisconsin named Dr. George Lucas was at Millington. My foot was so destroyed that you could put your hand or finger in the top of my foot and touch the bottom layer of skin all the way across my foot. He brought the bones back and overlapped them some way. I'm not exactly sure what he did. Nevertheless, he reconstructed my foot — which is unbelievable. The foot is intact but I have a big hole right in the middle of it, and the center of the arch to the front is turned outward. To this day it still works although I experience some pain and swelling from time to time. He was just a phenomenally talented man.

*   *   *

Lt. Cmdr. George Lucas was an orthopedic surgeon on the staff of Naval Hospital Memphis, Tennessee, located in Millington. He graduated from medical school in 1961 and was drafted into the Navy. When he arrived in Millington, Lucas had had only one year of practice under his belt, but he was immediately named chief of orthopedics. The physician he was replacing had just left for Vietnam.

I acquired a lot of experience in orthopedics during the two years I spent in Memphis. But I also developed an interest in hand surgery at that time, and that's basically what I've done ever since. Part of that interest was fostered by the wounded from Vietnam who showed up at Millington. I began specializing in hand wounds and peripheral nerve injuries when I was in the service.

At Millington, we received airevac patients practically every day — and in every stage of injury. The most common injuries were compound leg fractures resulting mostly from mines. But we saw a lot of upper extremity injuries such as gunshot wounds that would knock out the medial or radial nerve.

If the injuries looked like they were going to take many months to heal, those people would be boarded out and sent to a Veterans Hospital. But I did a fair bit of reconstructive upper extremity procedures that could be resolved in a few months, such as stabilization of hand fractures.

I was the only orthopedist who was fully trained, although I usually had three other people with me. These were guys who were just out of medical school and might have had a year of internship. So the three or four of us ran the service. The hospital at that point was manned mostly by reservists since the regulars had gone to Vietnam.

As I recall, Bill Henry had a severe foot injury and actually lost a part of his foot, which was going to be a problem in terms of walking and running. That outlook was devastating to him. We did some skin grafts and stabilized his fractures but he lost part of his foot. I think he had three or four procedures and achieved some mobility as a result of our work.

I remember one interesting sidelight about this patient. I came from Wisconsin. I had trained in Wisconsin and was practicing in that state when I got drafted. Three or four newly minted nurses who had just finished nursing school were at Millington at the time. The Navy had sponsored their education so they owed the Navy a few years. They showed up at Millington and because they were from Wisconsin, I got to know them rather well. Henry ended up falling in love with one of these girls and married her. They were married while he was still in our custody and I went to their wedding. It was a Catholic wedding and they had to kneel at the altar. When they finally stood up and marched out of the church, he was limping. I said, "Gee, Bill, you're going to ruin my reputation by limping in front of all these people."

Taking Flak Through a Flak Jacket

William Weise volunteered for duty in Vietnam while still stationed in Korea in 1967. A week before arriving in Vietnam in October 1967, he was promoted to lieutenant colonel and assigned to the 3rd Marine Division. Less than two weeks later, he took command of BLT (Battalion Landing Team) 2nd Battalion, 4th Marines. "At the time I was about 50 miles below the DMZ visiting a battalion that was on an operation when I got orders in the middle of the night to get up there and take command." Weise retained that command until 2 May 1968 when he was critically wounded during the Battle of Dai Do.

Dai Do, named for a village complex, was located south of the DMZ near the Cua Viet River. The battle began on 27 April when Weise's 2nd Battalion surprised a much larger force of North Vietnamese regulars heading south from the DMZ. The NVA's move was threatening Dong Ha, the headquarters of the 3rd Marine Division. For the next three days, 2nd Battalion engaged the enemy in a series of fierce firefights. Because NVA soldiers had dug themselves into camouflaged one-person holes called "spider holes" plus trenches and even abandoned buildings, the Marines were forced to dislodge them at great cost.

In the late afternoon of 2 May, after days of brutal and often hand-to-hand fighting, Lt. Col. Weise was seriously wounded. After taking shelter in a trench with several of his men, his sergeant major was killed and both his radio operators wounded. Moments later, as Weise continued firing his M16 at the enemy, an AK-47 round ripped through his flak jacket. The round punctured his lower left side and lodged between his fourth and fifth vertebrae, dangerously close to his spinal cord. With both legs temporarily paralyzed and bleeding from several other shrapnel wounds, he was in no condition to continue the fight.

Capt. J. R. Vargas, commander of Golf Company, managed to drag his superior about 50 meters out of the line of fire as the enemy began to overrun the position. Others then assisted Weise back to Dai Do where corpsmen administered basic first aid. They then placed him and other wounded aboard amphibian tractors for transportation to the nearby Cua Viet River. Gentle hands then transferred the wounded aboard "skimmers"— outboard motor-powered craft — for a nine-kilometer trip downriver to a secure helicopter landing zone out of enemy range.

"This is where the wounded got their first real medical treatment other than what the corpsmen could do," Weise recalls. At this point physicians and corpsmen performed triage and stabilized the casualties. "They stopped the bleeding, splinted obvious fractures, and, when necessary, pushed the intestines back in." In Weise's case, the medical personnel administered an IV of serum albumin, a scene captured by a civilian photographer.[3]

All my corpsmen were just terrific. They saved a lot of lives. We had 297 medevacs and 81 KIAs in that three-day battle, including corpsmen. But we considered our corpsmen Marines anyhow. In fact, some of the best Marines I had were Navy corpsmen.

All casualties were initially taken out to the *Iwo Jima* until their facilities were filled, and then they moved them to the hospital ship or to Able Med at Dong Ha. The reason for transferring them to the *Iwo Jima* was because she was the flagship of the Special Landing Force and that's where my battalion rear was located — my headquarters. I stayed in that sick bay until we arrived in the Philippines.

When I first arrived in sick bay, the staff took an x-ray, found where the bullet was lodged, removed it, and stuffed the path it had made with gauze to keep it open and draining and prevent infection. When they removed the gauze in a few weeks, it healed up pretty nicely. As soon as that bullet came out, I had feeling in my legs again and was up and walking within a couple of weeks. I wasn't supposed to— but I did. A year later, I was as good as I ever was.

Stabilized for his wounds, Lt. Col. William Weise awaits evacuation at a triage station near Dai Do. Navy physician Lt. Runas Powers (second from right) aids other casualties (courtesy William Weise).

Written in Blood

Second Lt. Michael Holladay arrived in Vietnam in November 1967. Shortly thereafter, he found himself commanding officer of 1st Platoon, Company K, 3rd Battalion, 9th Marines. His beat was the territory just south of the DMZ near the 700-foot-high Rockpile and the infamous Route 9, the road to Khe Sanh. The routine was varied and enemy contact was frequent and violent.

It was a good platoon. We had taken few casualties—a few men wounded in some fistfights along the way—but no one had been killed. Because the situation had heated up so rapidly during Tet of 1968, the decision was made to kick off "Operation Pegasus" to relieve the Marines at Khe Sanh. We were at Ca Lu, the closest place where they could mount the operation. Ca Lu was going to become an operational base for Pegasus. The 1st Air Cavalry would come with their abundance of helicopters and make the push to Khe Sanh.

On the afternoon of 26 March, our company—Kilo—was ordered to head back to the Rockpile, which was not far away. But en route we were diverted to join up with Echo Company, 2nd Battalion, 9th Marines and search for the infamous NVA hospital.

We moved out on the afternoon of the 26th, hooked up with that unit, and set up for the night. The next morning we kicked off. The plan was to spread out through open country, try to push through any opposition we encountered, and look for this mysterious hospital.

Late on the afternoon of the 27th, we set up before dark. Normally, while the rest of the company was setting in, we sent out patrols to check out the area. I took out a "fan patrol." You went out from one point on the clock and came in at another point on the clock. At about 1630, I took a patrol out to the west and returned about 1800 as darkness was setting in. We hadn't found anything. We then began setting up our area of the perimeter when we got word that our company commander wanted us at about 1845 up at his position, which was off in the center of the large two-company perimeter.

I made my way there and began discussing what we had done that day and to plan for the next. About 1900—in the middle of the discussion—we heard the first mortar tubes popping. It wasn't the normal one or two but a large number of them. When you heard a mortar, you supposedly had about 12 seconds at most to make a decision before they began hitting.

The platoon commanders started moving to their areas of the perimeter, and I began running back to my area. A mortar round hit to my left rear about two feet away. Fortunately for me, the round broke up in small chunks. We had learned that if the mortar rounds broke up in large chunks, you were dead. We didn't wear lower body armor, just flak jackets. I still had my helmet and flak jacket on. It was customary in the evening, right after "Stand to,"[4] to take off my helmet and flak jacket and go to a soft cover [cloth cap] because it was just quieter. You could move around and hear sounds better. We had some moonlight that night but it was still so damned dark.

The mortar round instantly struck me down. I later learned from Doc [Ray] Felle and others that it knocked me out for a while. Most of the fragments hit on the left side, shredded the flak jacket and broke my left arm. My left arm and hand also picked up some shrapnel. Pieces entered just below the flak jacket on the left side and busted up my left hip. The force caused me to hit the ground in such a way that the impact ended up breaking off the lower part of my right hip and also filled my right leg with some shrapnel. And I took a couple of pieces just above the flak jacket on the left side and in the neck. A fragment had just barely grazed the major vessels in my neck, and I was losing blood fairly dramatically.

When I sat up, I was swallowing so much blood I really thought I was going to drown. I couldn't keep the blood from running down into my throat so I tried to lean over. Doc Felle peeled off what was left of my flak jacket, which was pretty well shredded on the left side and back. As he kept trying to push me down, I kept trying to sit up.

Then came the second mortar barrage. At that point, Cpl. [Will] Williams took off his flak jacket and put it over my head, shoulders, and upper body. He then pushed me down on the ground and Doc Felle lay on top of me. Will had his helmet on and he crouched around and held on to both of us so he was the more exposed at the time.

Doc Felle tried to determine where all the wounds were and obviously came to the conclusion that my neck was the most serious because of all the blood I was losing. Cpl. Williams tore off his skivvy shirt and they wrapped it around my neck. Then they began dragging me over to the nearest hole, which was the mortar pit.

By that time, I thought I was gonna drown. When I tried to stand up, I just couldn't. My right leg felt like it was on fire. In the process of dragging me to the mortar pit, the second half of the second barrage came in — maybe two or three extra rounds.

Meanwhile, Doc Felle hit me with morphine and wrote what he had done on my chest — everything by the book. He actually wrote it in my own blood. Even before the chopper came, he gave me more. The shrapnel felt like it was burning holes in me. In fact, I've still got about a pound left in me; some of it has made its way to the surface over the years.

Cpl. Williams managed to reach the company commander who was able to get a helicopter inbound. It was an old H-34 and the pilot was amazing. You talk about a hero. He turned on his lights so he could see where to set down. It was heavily mountainous terrain near the Rockpile, and we were in a rolling plateau area with an abundance of rock structures.

About that time the next barrage began but Cpl. Williams stood up and waved him in. I can still see him silhouetted between me and the lights of the helicopter as it came across the perimeter. Doc Felle was still lying on top of me and trying to deal with the blood loss.

Even though the ground was rocky and mortar rounds were still coming in, Cpl. Williams got the helicopter to where it was at least hovering. Four Marines then got me on a poncho and dragged me over to where they could get up underneath the helicopter. They tried three times. On the third attempt they hoisted me high enough for the bird to get down enough so they could shove me in the door.

I hadn't died yet and didn't think I would. I was maintaining my optimism. I was now less concerned about my neck because I no longer felt I was drowning. At that point my legs became my main concern. I couldn't stand up; there was just too much pain.

When we landed at Delta Med that night, Operation Pegasus had just kicked off and the 1st Air Cav was taking enormous casualties. The NVA were eatin' the 1st Air Cav alive. As a result, Delta Med was receiving all kinds of casualties.

They rolled us casualties on big gurneys into Delta Med and stripped us completely except for dogtags. I was just colder than hell and could not warm up. They immediately began jamming plasma into me while a corpsman covered me with blankets. He said, "It won't make any difference how much we put on top because we're putting cold plasma inside."

As I lay there, a mortally wounded gunnery sergeant lay beside me on another gurney. A chaplain came over, looked down at me, and said, "Lieutenant, just relax. Take it easy. You're not going to die!"

And that settled the issue right there. Talk about credibility. He had it! The calming effect was just amazing. He then went to the gunnery sergeant and said, "Gunny, you're gonna die. It's time and if you haven't already done so, it's time we had a talk."

The gunny had been gut-shot and was hurt bad. Within the next 30 minutes, he tried to make peace with everything that came to his mind, but he just didn't make it through his laundry list.

Meanwhile, they were attending to me. I knew — or thought I knew — where all the hits were but nobody had yet told me what was actually wrong with me — and I didn't ask.

I was then put on a stretcher, placed on the back of a jeep, taken to a C-130, and immediately flown down to Danang. When they rolled me into the medical facility, a doctor asked me where they had taken blood.

I found that amazing. Everywhere I stopped, they had taken blood. So now they took some more and then I was x-rayed. Shortly thereafter, in a stretcher, I was again deposited on another jeep and strapped in. Someone instructed me to hold two bottles, one with plasma and the other containing glucose.

When we got to the airstrip, a sergeant came over and said, "I'm a master sergeant in the Air Force, lieutenant, and I'm gonna take care of you. We really appreciate what all you guys are doin' up there."

I don't remember landing on the hospital ship, but I vividly recall being in some kind of prep room and having a corpsman shave my entire damn body with the proverbial dull razor. I felt like he pulled half my hair out. I was hit right about 1900, and now I was being prepped for surgery aboard the USS *Sanctuary* a little after 0100—just five hours later.

I awoke from the surgery on the bottom rack in what was called the SOQ [Sick Officers Quarters]. My mouth was completely wired shut. A feeding tube went down through my nose to my stomach. My left arm was in a rig which kept it at 90 degrees. The right arm from the shoulder down to the elbow was along my side, and the elbow was at 90 degrees going straight up. My left-hand fingers were free. I had a cast-like apparatus from my waist down to my kneecaps.

One night, while I was still on the ship, I recall grabbing hold of the springs on the rack above me because I thought I was drowning. I kept shoving Kleenex in my mouth. And the pain was such that I was kept constant medication—morphine. I developed a blood clot in my right leg that required them to break open the cast, dig in there, and get that damn clot out.

After my stay on the *Sanctuary*, which I think was around nine days, I was taken to Danang to the overnight Air Force facility and prepped for movement to Guam. The trip from Danang to Guam was the worst part of my whole experience. Everything I experienced through nine months of hospital time seemed insignificant compared to that trip. The plane was a C-141. We were stacked in litters with me on the top. It was hotter than Hades up there. Because I was on my back in this cast arrangement, I couldn't take a leak so the nurse or corpsman was always having to help me. I was absolutely miserable.

The flight took 10 hours. I couldn't roll up on my side, and my left arm was sticking up and jabbing into the skin of the plane. Nevertheless, the Air Force nurses and doctors on that plane were just superb. They couldn't have been more kindhearted.

We got to Guam in the late evening and I was rolled into the transient ward of the naval hospital. A doctor made the initial check and disposition on me. He said that over the next few days he would remove the cast on my arm and redo it. He was also going to remove the wire from my mouth and take the tubes out. I could then start eating soft foods and that generally life would improve to some degree. I told him that what I really wanted was a sandwich. He said I wouldn't be able to eat it. I wasn't begging him but close to it. He finally relented and said I could try it. Well, I tried and it didn't work at all. I then realized that he knew what he was talking about!

At that time I didn't know that all the nerves in the left side of my face had been severed. I have been numb to this day from the point of my chin back to the top of my ear. That left side of my face—up to the high cheek bone just under the eye and the left side of my tongue— has been without any sensation for years.

Because of all the nerve damage, it was damn near impossible to swallow anything. It took me most of the time I was in Guam, which was from mid–April until the end of June 1968, to get to where I could chew a little bit. But I had to drink great amounts of liquid to wash everything down. I still do all my chewing on the right side. I can't control anything with the left side. But I've learned to live with it.

At that point, I wasn't ambulatory. My hip was still pretty well locked down. I then learned the extent of my injuries because the medical team began to look more closely and inform me what was going on. I had taken a piece of shrapnel in the arm, which had broken a bone, but it had healed all right. My lower body seemed to have been the problem. I had taken shrapnel in the left hip, which really chewed it up. The right hip was broken at the ischium and remains so to this day. The lower part of the circle was broken off and it's down an x number of centimeters below. The whole time I was in the Marine Corps, the doctors told me that at some point in my life it was going to become a foreign body. Because of the time required for recuperation, the doctors eventually made the decision that I was going back to the States.

The next day I was moved to the amputee ward on the bottom floor. The wards were set up like most hospitals with courtyards in between them. This ward was not air conditioned but instead had big fans. We wore blue cotton trousers but no shirts. Outside the ward we had to wear our striped seersucker bathrobes but we never wore shirts.

The doctors finally took the contraption off my pelvic area that was keeping me immobilized. I was then able to take a shower and it was amazing. To this day I can still remember that sensation. It was the first shower I had since I left Okinawa back in November 1967. In Vietnam, we just grabbed water out of a stream or got some out of a water can. We lived out of our canteens and helmets.

It was about this time that I first saw myself. I looked in the mirror and was amazed at how much weight I had lost. In those days I was running about 170. I was now down to about 130.

Then began an "observation period." It became a lesson about life and the realities of war that to this day plague me. I have dreams and, on occasion, nightmares. If I'm watching the evening news and see some discussion about a particular hospital, I have instant memories of seeing a lot of youngsters in incredible contraptions, and I know what they will be carrying with them the rest of their lives.

I have such vivid memories. Directly across from me was a kid — a corporal — who was a triple amputee. Every day the staff sedated him to get him to relax at night. He was in the "monkey bed," which was a four-poster with rails hooked together at the top. He had his left arm intact but was missing the right arm above the elbow and both legs above the knee. Every morning the nurses came to wake us and get the day started. They awakened him and the chow would be brought in. They sat him up in the rack and he'd eat. Then after he pushed the cart away, he would make a lunge and grab hold of the rail at the top with his left arm. Then all day long he would bounce and grab, bounce and grab, going all around that bed. You could hear the bed springs as he did this all day. All day. Then after chow at night, he'd be sedated all over again. This routine must have gone on for two or three weeks. After a while you just didn't hear the bedsprings; you just knew he was in motion.

Down by the nurse's station on the left side was the "round bed." It was a round contraption that had a bed suspended in the center of it. When I first got on the ward, I saw a young lance corporal who had been there just a day or two. He had been hit by white phosphorus — Willy Peter — and been severely burned. They had him in this round bed and every so often — maybe every 30 minutes — they turned the bed and put gauze material on his other side. The time on that side would be up, and then they'd keep the process going.

Every time they turned him, you'd hear blood-curdling screams. After a while that sound didn't cause you to stop what you were doing. You just got used to it. The mind is amazing. And, of course, we were living inside of this very small world. Without the spell being broken, you became very used to what was inside of it. I don't think the kid in the round bed made it for quite a month. He got gangrene. The doctors started by amputating some toes. They moved all the way up to his groin on one side and just above the knee on the other. Then he died.

As my body was healing, the atmosphere in the hospital just seemed to become increasingly intense as more and more injured were always arriving. The average civilian has no idea concerning the level of expertise and the amount of energy that are expended to keep a serviceman alive when he's come out of the combat environment. The injuries I saw coming into that hospital seemed to get worse and worse.

The hospital finally established an SOQ because so many officers were arriving; I was then moved. By the time I left Guam, I knew several of the lieutenants who were coming from other units. Some of them had been in my Basic School at Quantico. One had been in my officer candidate class. The SOQ had lots of junior officers. The life expectancy of a Marine second lieutenant was about 20 minutes in those days. Enough wounded lieutenants were in the SOQ to set up an infantry battalion.

We had a potpourri of injuries on that ward. One of the lieutenants was from 2nd Battalion, 9th Marines, and I had come from 3rd Battalion, 9th Marines. He had had both legs amputated. He was older than the rest of us, was married, and had a couple of daughters. He was very despondent. I remember going to his Silver Star award ceremony. That occasion was one of the few times I'd ever seen him smile. He tried several times to commit suicide. He just desperately did not want to go back to the States. I never knew what happened to him.

Most everybody—but four or five of us and that burn victim—were amputees or had major orthopedic injuries. We were asked to help the nurses with the kids who were having difficulty cleaning their wounds. So I helped organize a little group and we'd move around in our wheelchairs helping out. That was one of the highlights of the day. You got real used to the sights, smells, and sounds. If you were ambulatory and able to go outside in a wheelchair or a lawn chair, you'd go into the center courtyard about an hour or two after lunch. If you could sit up and had an arm to use, you could pass a tennis ball around. We'd form a huge circle and throw the tennis ball back and forth. If the ball got away, the nurses would retrieve it.

I was still attached to pain medicine. One day the doctor said, "I'm gonna get you off of any kind of pain medicine because you shouldn't be needing it anymore. You're healing well enough. You're gonna have aches but you might as well get used to it because you're gonna have them forever. It will settle into its own routine so let's get on with it."

It was very obvious to me that I really wanted this stuff. I couldn't go to sleep at night because I thought I was in pain.

One day a nurse appeared on the SOQ ward named Margaret Wilkinson. Her married name is Crowe. She was called Maggie. She was a tall, blonde lieutenant. When she came on the ward, it changed the whole tone. She was stern but not hard. She wasn't a tough, grizzled nurse. She was just, "Hey, guys, here's the way it's gonna be so let's have some fun while we're here."

She was always smiling and laughing, and had an amazing amount of warmth. I credit her with singularly getting me off those medications.

In the course of a week, by sitting for a couple of hours in the evening by the rack, and talking and bringing me a cold washcloth and a pail of cold water to swab off with, Maggie got me off the doggone stuff. She was the single support source that made the difference. Nobody else took that kind of interest. I was just part of a growing populace of wounded Marines and sailors. Maggie became very influential in my recovery.

The time I spent in Guam was profoundly influential on my future as a Marine officer. It didn't diminish my aggressiveness. A lot of officers might be fearless and assume that everybody else is. What the hospital experience did for me was to make me understand what I was all about. And that was from the time I hit Delta Med in Dong Ha all the way to the time I was released from the Naval Hospital at Beaufort, South Carolina. I'm talking about the whole experience — what it took to just get me back from where I was. People look at me and say, "We can't even tell you were injured."

The doctor who worked on my neck was good. I've got a six- or seven-inch scar from behind my ear that runs all the way around to the front of my neck on the left-hand side. That surgeon put the incision right in the crease. Unless I point it out, the average person doesn't look twice at it. I've always wanted to track him down and thank him for what he did.

But the real point is that the whole experience changed me. I think about what it takes to support that aspect of warfare and all that's required. And then there's the amazing skill of the medical people who put folks like me back together.

"Getting Them Back on Their Feet — Even If They Didn't Have a Foot"

In the early 1960s, Margaret Wilkinson Crowe was inspired by Ben Casey, Dr. Kildare, *and* The Nurses, *which were the popular TV medical programs of that era. After attending Riverside School of Nursing near her home in Newport News, Virginia, she joined the Navy. Naval Hospital St. Albans, New York, was her first assignment.*

It was 1966 and many of her patients on the orthopedics ward were recently arrived Vietnam casualties. In the spring of 1967, Lt. Wilkinson headed for her next assignment — Naval Hospital Guam.

I worked in orthopedics and then the "air evacuation ward." It was a central location where all the casualties came in. It was like a disaster triage team. Every patient who came in was seen by a physician. They were then fed, bathed, and had their dressings changed. Orders were written and the patients were stabilized for the night. Then they went to their respective units. We received anywhere from 20 or 30 patients and sometimes as many as 150 at a time. Usually they arrived three or four times a week.

It seems incredible that you could get a hundred patients and they'd all be seen, bathed, fed, medicated, and orders started on every one of them before they were bedded down for the night. It was almost an impossible task — but it wasn't.

People were on call every time an airevac came in so we had a team of physicians, a team of nurses, and a team of corpsmen, and the staff. Once everything was done — once all the orders were written — then that team could leave and the staff stayed to get the patients through the night.

We attended patients with some pretty horrific injuries such as traumatic amputations. I hadn't had any training for treating these kinds of injuries. In fact, people have asked me about working with traumatic amputations. At the time it seemed normal. I had already seen orthopedic injuries at St. Albans but the ones at Guam were fresher. The patients had dirt in the wounds. From the time of injury to their arriving at the hospital might be less than 24 or 48 hours. They were stabilized in Vietnam and then they either came to us or went to Japan. Usually they had been seen some place else prior to our seeing them. Depending upon how stable they were, they may have come directly to us within a day or two of the injury.

We cleaned them up and changed their dressings. We were assessing, assessing, and assessing to see where they should be placed. We'd get patients who had to go straight to surgery. Something might have happened in flight. They might have gotten very unstable during evacuation, or they would get to us and start bleeding. It was really a trial by fire for us but it seemed normal then. It wouldn't seem normal now.

The hospital was laid out with open units — open bay — with beds in rows and 40 or 50 patients on a unit. The dependent units were rooms but it was open bay for the soldiers. We had some private rooms for critically ill or infectious patients who should not have been in the mainstream. But it was mostly open bay so you could see a lot of what was going on by looking down the areas to do a quick assessment.

I worked on the officers' unit. If they didn't have an airevac, then you worked on other units. Mine was mostly orthopedics. That's where I met Col. [2nd Lt. Michael] Holladay. He did very well with his injuries. His were potentially very life-altering injuries but because of his fortitude and determination, he had minimal, if any, residual effects. He also he had a full career in the Marine Corps, which is even more amazing. He went to the other extreme. He was going to do whatever it took.

I saw the same kind of determination among some of my other patients. That certainly was a different time. We were all young. I don't think we realized some of the ramifications. For me it seemed like these casualties were all just taken in stride. Nothing seemed abnormal.

We could deal with anything. "This is the hand you've been dealt so how are we going to get you through it? How are we going to get you on your feet?"

And that was the main goal — getting them back on their feet — even if they didn't have a foot. Anything was possible. At that time I was initially blessed with having physicians who were really good. They were top of their line and doing state-of-the-art techniques. Some of the procedures that were done really enabled some very seriously injured patients to get a new lease on life.

We would see horrific injuries. Someone had stepped on a land mine. These physicians would say, "Okay, that happened. Now what? This is what we need to do."

Number one, we were dealing with a young, healthy population. So many new procedures were possible. I felt like I was on the cutting edge. That whole period was really incredible.

When I got out of the military in 1970, I didn't go back to work in a hospital until January of 1971. I saw that nothing was done the way it was done in the military. Now we have so much to work with and we don't seem to be doing quite as much. Military nursing was much better. I still look back on those days—they were the best. We really accomplished a lot with very little. Back then every day was different. As a young nurse, it was learning, learning, learning. And when I left I felt I could do anything as a nurse.

Corpsman Down

HM3 Bob Ingraham served with Lima Company, 3rd Battalion, 1st Marines in Quang Ngai Province, South Vietnam. On 5 March 1966, the second day of Operation Utah, his platoon engaged elements of the 21st Regiment of the People's Vietnam Army, commonly known as the NVA — North Vietnam Army. Operation Utah was the first major engagement between the Marines and regular North Vietnamese troops. Ingraham, having been in Vietnam for only 37 days, was seriously wounded in the ensuing battle for a hillock named "Hill 50."

To the Marines of 3rd Platoon of Lima Company, 3/1, the sunny, warm morning of 5 March 1966 hardly seemed dangerous. Just ahead of us Marine Phantom jets were dropping napalm into what appeared to be an empty field. But throughout much of the night, the entire area had been subjected to heavy bombing and an artillery barrage which no one could have survived. In short, we did not seem to be faced with a direct threat to the platoon.

Our anxiety increased when we started receiving fire from a nearby hill — "Hill 50," whose name I would learn many years later. The Marines returned fire. But then word was passed to cease fire — South Vietnamese troops had fired on us by mistake. We relaxed and moved up the hill. No one on our side knew that Hill 50 was a maze of tunnels and spider traps. We didn't know that we were walking, oblivious, into a trap set by heavily armed North Vietnamese soldiers. And then the trap was sprung.

The assault on 3rd Platoon by light and heavy weapons was sudden and furious. Enfilading fire made it nearly impossible to find safety. One of the first casualties was our platoon leader, Lt. Eugene Cleaver. He only remembers raising his hand to order us forward when a blow from a large caliber bullet struck him in his chest near his right shoulder.

A bullet penetrated a rifleman's helmet and pulverized the top of his head. He was breathing but as good as dead when I reached him. A sergeant sustained a pumping chest wound. While I was bandaging him, he twisted away from me twice shouting, "Grenade!" Enemy soldiers we couldn't even see tossed grenades over the high, dense brush that surrounded us. Shrapnel pierced the buttocks of a Marine hugging the ground next to me.

After doing what little I could for Lt. Cleaver and the sergeant, I learned of a wounded Marine farther up the hill. I soon found him. He had been eviscerated. Amazingly, he was still conscious and calm. I didn't know how I could possibly have helped him. A Marine farther down the hill yelled, "I'm gonna throw a grenade over you guys! I'm gonna get that sniper!" Naturally I didn't want to be killed by a Marine grenade. I was starting to dive for the ground when a rifle discharged to my right and very close to me. In what seemed like the same instant, a bullet slammed me to the ground. It was like being hit by a giant's sledgehammer.

The bullet hit me on the right side of my right thigh about six inches above the knee. It shattered the femur and blasted out through my inner thigh. I realized instantly that I had been badly wounded. My right foot was turned backwards. Another corpsman, HN Larry W. Skonetski was nearby when I was shot. "Ski!" I shouted. "The bastard shot me!"

I had enough strength to lower my fatigue pants to examine the wound. The bullet had left a blue-rimmed hole on my outer thigh, about the diameter of a 7.62mm M14 or AK-47 round. I remember that one North Vietnamese soldier who was killed that morning had been using an M14. The entry wound was hardly bleeding. On my inner thigh, a trickle of blood oozed from a patch of mangled flesh that looked like fresh hamburger. My femoral artery was apparently intact. I could wiggle my toes: I had no major nerve damage.

In case I started bleeding heavily, I removed my belt and put it around my thigh to use as a tourniquet, but the effort exhausted me and I couldn't tighten it. Fortunately, as it turned out, a tourniquet was unnecessary.

I tried to inject myself with a morphine syrette, which was standard equipment in our Unit 1 medical bags. Morphine syrettes consist of a single dose of morphine in a foil tube, similar to a small toothpaste tube with an attached hypodermic needle. To use a syrette, the seal first has to be punctured with a thin pin which is stored in the hypodermic needle. Because my attempt to puncture the seal failed, the tube burst in my hand when I tried to inject myself. It was the only syrette I had.

The battle raged on. Nearby, a well-concealed rifleman continued to shoot. I assumed he was the one who had shot me. I could hear him operate the bolt of his rifle. If he was using an M14, it might have jammed so that he had to load each cartridge manually.

It seemed that every time an enemy rifleman fired, a Marine screamed. I began to fear a "human wave" attack. I unholstered my .45 pistol and held it on my chest, determined to kill the first Vietnamese I saw. I was overcome with hatred for all Vietnamese. Fortunately my hatred lasted no longer than the battle itself.

I was almost completely incapacitated not by pain as such but by extreme discomfort. My skin became ultra-sensitive. Even the small bits of debris, which were raining from the sky after nearby explosions, hurt like hell! No word adequately describes one of my sensations—my entire body began to "vibrate." I wasn't shaking. Instead, every cell in my body seemed to be buzzing with an electric charge. Then I began getting agonizing cramps in the muscles of not only my wounded leg but my good leg as well. The sun, now high overhead, began to roast my exposed skin. I had been unable to pull my fatigue pants back up after lowering them to see my wound. Sweat soaked my uniform. Oddly, I don't remember being thirsty.

Eventually, a Marine crawled up the hill to help us, but he was shot through the shoulder. The eviscerated Marine kept asking if he was going to die. I tried to reassure him, but I don't know to this day whether or not he lived. Another Marine moved up the hill to help us and was also shot. Finally, Skonetski reached us and managed to put a battle dressing on me. I don't know what, if anything, he did for the eviscerated Marine.

The rate of gunfire and explosions had slowed by then. Eventually, Skonetski and three other Marines half-carried, half-dragged me down the hill on my poncho. And that hurt! I screamed every time my butt hit a bump. I don't think I'd been given any morphine. With every bump, I could feel the shattered ends of my femur grating. I worried that the jagged bones would cause more bleeding.

At the base of Hill 50, helicopters were starting to evacuate wounded Marines. I talked

HM3 Bob Ingraham awaits evacuation. A fellow corpsman has given him first aid as noted by battle dressings and a casualty tag (courtesy Bob Ingraham).

with the Marines. One was crying. His best friend had just been killed before his eyes. I asked Ski to take a picture of me and I took one of him. Ski's photo shows me holding my helmet tight to my head. I was afraid because bullets were still flying. The out-of-focus, back-lit picture of Ski shows a broad, encouraging smile that helped to put me at ease. He wasn't faking it. He was confident that I'd be OK. I wish I could thank him for what he did for me that day.

Later, at a field hospital, corpsmen bandaged my wound more thoroughly, immobilized my leg in a splint, and packed me off to the hospital ship USS *Repose* [AH-16].

I recall seeing the *Repose* from the helicopter before landing, but I don't have any memory of the arrival itself. I remember lying on a gurney in a dark passageway for what seemed like hours. Corpsmen eventually wheeled me into the operating room. My femur was badly fractured. An x-ray shows shattered pieces of bone and fragments of the bullet lodged in my muscles. The exit wound on my inner thigh told just part of the story. The muscle for several inches around the exit wound — and all the way down to the femur — had been turned to pulp by the bullet and had to be excised. Skin and some muscle around the entrance wound had to be trimmed away as well. I received two units of whole blood during the surgery.

When I left the OR, I had some new hardware — a threaded steel rod that went completely through my right shin about six inches below my knee. The rod stuck out an inch and a half on each side. It would later anchor the traction weights which would stretch my thigh muscles and hold my femur at its original length while it healed.

When the surgeon was finished, nurses and corpsmen packed the wounds with cotton and bandages. Then they encased me in plaster from my right foot all the way up to my armpits and down to my left shin. I was like a parcel ready for shipping.

I don't recall much about my short time on the *Repose*. I probably was getting morphine or Demerol regularly; I don't remember being in pain and I slept a great deal. I was also receiving prophylactic antibiotics at this time. Gunshot wounds are dirty by definition; infection was a certainty.

Hanging on chains from a frame over my bed was a bar that I could use to pull myself up. Its main purpose was to make it easier for me to use a bedpan. However, it also allowed me to see the ocean through a nearby porthole. The *Repose* steamed constantly in big circles, or so it seemed. A former *Repose* crewman later told me that the ship sailed back and forth between Chu Lai and Da Nang.

I wrote a letter to my parents a day or two after the surgery. In handwriting even worse than my normal bad scrawl, I explained how I was shot, the extent of my wounds, and that my recovery would be long. I did not mention that I might lose my leg. I'm not sure that I even knew just how serious my wound was.

After perhaps three days on the *Repose*, I was flown to Danang. The next morning a C-130 Hercules evacuated me to Clark Air Force Base Hospital in the Philippines where I would stay overnight. I was able to talk to my parents from the hospital via a telephone-ham radio link. That was how they learned that I had been wounded — before they received my letter.

The next morning I joined scores of other wounded men on a huge C-141 Starlifter. I recall little about that flight, but remember being in a huge, dark, noisy cavern filled with stretchers. Nurses and medics ran back and forth constantly. I had little pain but my bladder had become badly infected, apparently from poor sterile technique when I was catheterized on the *Repose*.

I assumed that most of the wounded on the Starlifter were Marines from Operation Utah, but not until years later would I learn just how bad the casualties were. Historical records are not in full agreement, but it is clear that at least 94 Marines were killed and some 278 were wounded. According to the 3rd Battalion's "Combat Operation After Action Report," dated 11 March 1966, 42 Marines were killed and at least 100 were wounded. Ten Lima Company Marines had been killed and 20 wounded, including myself.

The Starlifter landed in Hawaii where an officer came onboard to hand out Purple Hearts. I then remember being at the hospital at Travis Air Force Base near San Francisco. The next day I reached my destination, the Naval Hospital at Balboa Park in San Diego. I have fleeting memories of my arrival. I must have been sedated for the entire trip, and exhausted as well. I do recall, all too clearly, when corpsmen removed my cast and the dressing from my wound. The blood-soaked cotton had dried and was firmly stuck in place. When the corpsmen pulled it away, it felt like they were tugging flesh right off my leg. It was worse than being shot. I was put into traction where I would remain for the next 111 days.

About a week after I arrived at Balboa, my parents and girlfriend, Susan Overturf, flew from New Mexico to visit me. Susan and I started corresponding when the 3rd Battalion was still training in Okinawa. During her visit to San Diego, I asked her to marry me and she accepted.

My infections slowly yielded to antibiotics, and skin grafts helped to prevent the formation of excessive scar tissue — but scarcely improved the appearance of my leg!

Early in the summer I got out of traction. Corpsmen attached a carpenter's hand drill to the threaded pin in my shin and backed it out. I wish I had been given some Demerol for that procedure! Then they wrapped me in another large cast from my right foot up to my armpits. At last I could hobble about on crutches. I got my first liberty and had my first date with Susan!

In August, I got a new, smaller cast which immobilized my right leg only. I also had my first leave home to New Mexico. Then it was back to San Diego for a few more months. Finally, late in 1966, I was fitted for a brace and told that I would have to wear it for the rest of my life. Never again would I be able to bear my full weight on my right leg, which could break easily and might not heal a second time. Instead, when I stood or walked, I would literally be "sitting" on the brace, bearing my weight on the right ischial tuberosity, my "sit bone." The brace gave me a lot of freedom and the ability to bathe at the cost of some discomfort and inconven-

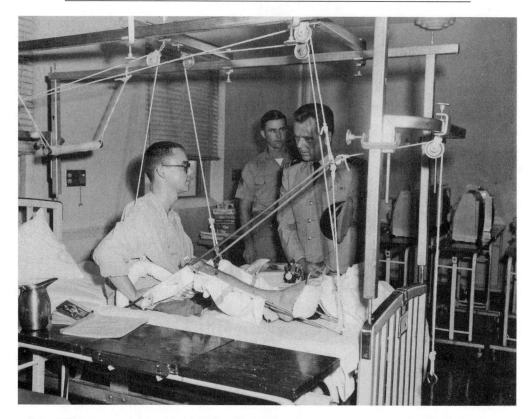

Bob Ingraham recovers from his wounds at Naval Hospital San Diego. His visitor is actor and Navy Reserve officer Lt. Cmdr. Jackie Cooper (courtesy Bob Ingraham).

ience. It was hinged at the knee so that I could sit down with reasonable ease, but I could walk only with a stiff-legged limp. A modified government-issue shoe was attached to it. Very stylish.

In December, I limped up and down endless passageways at Balboa, getting signatures from various Navy doctors and administrators who had to approve my discharge. I said goodbye to Balboa Naval Hospital and flew to Kansas City, Missouri, to be admitted to the Veterans Administration hospital. Susan was already in her first year of teaching in Kansas City, Kansas, and I planned to enroll for the spring semester in pre-journalism classes at the Kansas City campus of the University of Missouri.

I got some good news at the VA hospital. An orthopedic surgeon told me to throw my brace away. The Navy, it seemed, had been overly cautious with its warnings. Susan and I married on 27 December 1966. Soon after our honeymoon, I began going without the brace in our apartment, and in a few more days ventured outside without it. At first I had a deep limp. The atrophied muscles in my right leg could scarcely support my weight. In a short period of time, however, I was walking almost normally.

It's hard to believe, looking back on my experiences on Hill 50, that I have been able to live an active life of hiking, backpacking, running, and cross-country skiing. The more difficult trial I faced — although I did not know it at the time — was the struggle to put Vietnam behind me. Counseling did not exist at that time, and I was unaware that combat veterans do not necessarily enjoy the luxury of packaging the past and hiding it away in a dusty attic. My greatest challenge loomed ahead — coping with the psychological trauma of combat.

15

FULL CIRCLE

Even before Saigon fell on the last day of April 1975 ending the Vietnam War, the final stage of America's exit — Operation Frequent Wind — had already begun. This so-called "aerial Dunkirk" was the large-scale helicopter evacuation from Saigon of American staff and selected South Vietnamese personnel and their families who had been trapped by the North Vietnamese offensive. Marine helicopters flew out to sea to land their passengers aboard carriers and amphibious assault ships lying offshore. But waves of Vietnamese military helicopters packed with refugees followed in their wake seeking any vessel that might offer a landing deck.

Frequent Wind — involving 44 ships, 6,000 Marines, and 120 Air Force tanker aircraft — had without warning turned into an immense rescue mission of Vietnamese fleeing their homeland. Chaos followed as South Vietnamese pilots set their aircraft down on already crowded flight decks, creating indelible images of the war's finale. Empty of fuel, some choppers were forced to land in the sea. Looking like dying birds, they beat their rotors to fragments. As men, women, and children swarmed from aircraft, Navy crewmen stripped the helos of any useable equipment. The helicopters were then shoved over the side to make room for more incoming aircraft with cargoes of refugees.

Thousands of seaborne refugees then appeared in every conveyance that would float — ships, landing craft, fishing boats, and barges. Refugees in this second wave were even more desperate. Many had been at sea for several days and suffered from hunger, dehydration, seasickness, and eye infections. Legions of displaced Vietnamese had suddenly and unexpectedly become wards of the U.S. Navy. Ironically, many of them had begun their odyssey in 1954 when they fled North Vietnam for South Vietnam aboard U.S. Navy transports. Who then could have imagined that the Navy would again be called upon to help fleeing Vietnamese refugees make the transition to a new life. The story of Navy medicine in Vietnam had tragically come full circle.

"From Every Direction"

HM2 Randy Hudson joined the Navy in 1971. After hospital corps school in San Diego, he drew an assignment at Naval Hospital Portsmouth, Virginia, then went for preventive medicine training in Oakland, California. He soon received orders to the carrier USS Hancock *(CVA-19). "It wasn't my choice. It just happened that way."*

Being a corpsman, I was assigned to sick bay. My specialty training at Oakland was in preventive medicine. I was given a tiny office in sick bay aboard *Hancock*. After that I didn't have much to do with anybody else because preventive medicine was such a unique specialty.

I arrived aboard in September 1973. *Hancock* was the Navy's oldest carrier, and we knew this was going to be the last WESTPAC [Western Pacific] cruise. The ship was in drydock at the time with a lot of dirt and a great deal of painting going on. It was a really loud, messy place to be. In fact, we didn't have our first shakedown cruise until 18 months later.

When we got under way in the spring of 1975, we thought we'd go to Hawaii and then the Philippines. About halfway to Hawaii, the skipper got on the 1MC [loudspeaker] and filled us in on the situation. He said we were changing course. We had no Internet back then so we believed everything the skipper said. He was the source. He told us we were going to be involved in a bigger operation and that our role would probably remain as support. We'd let the air wing off in Hawaii and take helicopters aboard.

After we left Hawaii and headed for the Philippines, we thought we'd probably just float around and not get very involved with any of the activity because of our carrier's age. But while in the Philippines, circumstances apparently began getting hotter. In fact, the skipper told us the situation was quite precarious as we headed back out toward Vietnam.

Nevertheless, we still didn't think we were going to take aboard any evacuees because Operation Frequent Wind initially emphasized air evacuations from the airport in Saigon. But after the enemy bombed Tan Son Nhut airport, we began conducting helicopter evacuations. The situation escalated from that point and Vietnamese began descending on the embassy. They were even plucking people off the embassy roof.

When we heard that evacuees would soon be arriving aboard *Hancock*, our senior medical officer reminded us that they would be coming from a plague-endemic area. As a safety precaution, those of the crew who had not had the plague immunization received shots. This was one of the worst shots I've ever had. We were then instructed to dust the incoming evacuees with Lindane[1] using old-fashioned hand pump sprayers.

My first encounter with these refugees occurred when they came off the helicopters. We had been given some rudimentary Vietnamese lessons prior to that time period. I don't know whether we were speaking gibberish or actually speaking the language, but we said, "Yamaki," which means "Cover your eyes, and then turn around so we can spray you down." In retrospect, I wonder if any of that spraying was effective or even necessary. It was a dignity issue to me. I looked at that period of evacuation several years later and said, "What a welcome to America!"

Some of the evacuees were elderly. Others were families with children. Some refugees were our age. There were more children than I expected to see. Adults with young children wanted to get out more than anybody else to protect their kids.

We called them "refugees" but they weren't in wretched condition. They were from Saigon, a big city, and were mostly middle class. None of them were in rags, and they seemed to be in pretty good condition.

I suspect many were very frightened having just left their country — their homes — and having to get on a helicopter. I don't know if anyone had an outright panic attack but there was definitely an air of excitement and urgency. Crewmembers on the *Hancock* shouted, "Come on! Get out of the helicopter! Get on down here!" Everything happened so fast!

I saw a lot of helicopters land. In fact, it's amazing that we had only one casualty and that was a Marine helicopter. To this day, I'm still very surprised we didn't have any mid-air collisions because they were coming from every direction. It was complete chaos. Those helicopters were coming so frequently, the sky was dark from jet exhaust. Most were Hueys but there were also a few Chinooks flown by Marine crews. They carried large numbers of refugees.

I understood many of the helicopters were ready to run out of fuel so it was getting to be a desperate situation. So many choppers were trying to land that our crew began pushing them over the side to make room for more.

Once all the evacuees were onboard, we began steaming toward the Philippines. By this time the whole hangar bay was crowded with people. Some of the crew had the opportunity to visit with them. Most didn't speak very good English but I was able to get some Vietnamese money — a 1,000-dong note and some coins — for souvenirs.

Everybody was all spread out sleeping on the hangar deck. Some had their own blankets. Everyone brought a bag containing their most prized possessions.

To accommodate their personal needs, wooden troughs had been set up rather quickly on the port and starboard sides. Seawater moved along the troughs and then emptied near the fantail. I asked, "What in the world is that thing for?" Answer: the toilet facility. The skipper didn't want all those refugees wandering around the *Hancock* trying to find a toilet.

But the refugees didn't use the troughs for that purpose. They began washing their clothes in them. I don't know whether or not they were also using them for toilets. They may have been washing their clothes up forward and then toileting aft.

Feeding all those refugees took a long time as they walked through the enlisted mess deck. I don't know whether they ate down there or brought their food up to the hangar bay, but it took hours to get through the chow line.

When we got to Subic, the refugees were off-loaded. Many went to Guam. Many years after I got out of the Navy, I was director of a gastroenterology lab at Texas Tech University in Lubbock. One of our gastroenterology fellows was Asian. When I asked him where he was from, he said he was originally from Vietnam.

"When Saigon fell in 1975," he told me, "we were transported by helicopter to an aircraft carrier, the USS *Hancock*."

I never got to talk to that fellow again, but it was an interesting coincidence and a great story.

Vietnam's "Dunkirk"

Paul Jacobs was commanding officer of USS Kirk (DE-1087) during South Vietnam's final days. The Maine Maritime Academy graduate had assumed command of the ship the previous summer of 1974. The nearly four-year-old vessel was designated a destroyer escort specializing in anti-submarine warfare, but at 438 feet length, Kirk was much larger than her World War II forebears. When South Vietnam's fight for survival reached its denouement in early spring 1975, Kirk was ordered under way at "max speed," for the western Pacific. Capt. Jacobs describes what happened.

We were ordered under way at max speed to rendezvous with the USS *Hancock* [CVA-19] in Hawaii. When we got there, they were already loading supplies and helicopters onto the *Hancock*. She had a locked deck, which meant that nothing could fly off and nothing could move.

The *Hancock* was an old ship. The only flyable asset between us and the *Hancock* was my LAMPS [Light Airborne Multipurpose System] helicopter. The captain of the *Hancock* and I communicated each day. He got his planes moved around so when we got to the San Bernardino Straits, he could launch his jets and send them into Cubi Point for storage. At that time, the *Midway* came down from Yokosuka. So I was plane-guarding two aircraft carriers in the middle of the San Bernardino Straits going 30 knots with junks all over the place. And half the time they were moving helicopters from the *Midway* to the *Hancock* at night.

First we went to Cambodia for Operation Eagle Pull,[2] and when that episode was over we went to stand off Vietnam. After being on station a few days and since we were not sure when Saigon was going to fall, *Kirk* and *Hancock* were ordered to Singapore for a port call. We had just arrived, tied up, and were ready to shut down the boilers when suddenly we received orders for an "Emergency Underway" to return to Saigon. After getting all our crew back aboard within four hours, we proceeded down the Singapore River at night.

We exited the river and headed north. With all the shipping out there, it was like being on the freeway. I radioed a nearby tanker and asked whether or not any Maine Maritime graduates were aboard. The radioman replied that the chief engineer was a graduate of Maine Maritime Academy. When he got on the radio, he said he remembered my dad. I then asked a big favor. "I don't want to keep dodging these junks while we head north. Can I pull in behind you and have you crank up your speed? I can make about 27 knots and I need to get up off Saigon because it's about to fall."

He answered, "Be my guest. Haul in behind. We will increase speed to get through the ships so we can catch up with the *Hancock*."

When we arrived close to South Vietnam on the 28th of April, we found many Navy ships already out there to support the evacuation. Thousands of small boats made my radar scope look pure white. It began to look like Dunkirk as these people were fleeing from Saigon. We took the Vietnamese people from small boats and helicopters. We were getting so many refugees that they began to outnumber the crew. When we had taken aboard as many as we could, we offloaded them to an MSC [Military Sealift Command] ship and returned to our position.

Each of these small boats were loaded with 30 to 50 people. You could smell them even before they came alongside. The refugees were filthy and probably hadn't had a bath in a week. And they had no food. We'd move the people to one side and then hose down the empty side to get rid of human waste. Then we had the people move to the clean side and our crew would hose down the dirty side.

We had to remove all the live ordnance from the boats that were coming out to us. They had firearms, ammo—you name it. We put all that ordnance at the rear of the ship. Before long, the small arms were piled four feet high.

We then received a message to get rid of all the animals the people had brought along. They wanted me to take pets from the kids and throw the animals over the side. So the XO said, "What do you wanna do, Captain?"

I replied, "You answer the message. Tell the powers that be that the action is done, and then don't do a goddam thing!" Had I followed that order, I would have had a riot on my hands.

We had converted the first class lounge into a makeshift maternity ward. When I went back there with my Vietnamese interpreter to see the setup, everyone was talking at once. It was chaos. Finally, I took a piece of pipe and hit the bulkhead. Whang! Suddenly, a dead silence. I said to the interpreter, "You tell those women to get busy and have one of these babies onboard. That will be their ticket to the U.S."

They all began to smile. I was trying to help their morale and also make it easier for the enlisted guys to supervise them. I then took one of my aviation seamen from the flight deck, Seaman [Donald] Cox, and told him to get another buddy and take care of one of the Vietnamese women [Lan Nguyen Tran]. He said, "What do I do?"

"First, you need to give her a bath," I replied, "and then you walk her around. You can't let her sit down. Then you feed her some saltine crackers to help with the seasickness. Take some of your shirts and make her a maternity gown. You and your buddy will be responsible for her until we get into Subic Bay."

In the intervening years, we found her. She now lives in Long Beach. Her daughter went to Long Beach State and graduated with honors. She came with a daughter and son to the USS *Kirk* reunion in 2005, and Seaman Cox was her escort at that reunion. In just a few hours all of us—officers and men—had transformed the *Kirk* from a man-of-war to a humanitarian ship. This was the situation that confronted my sailors.

This movement of refugees lasted for three days. We started sinking the boats they abandoned because they were a menace to navigation. We then began steaming east toward Subic Bay.

Not long afterward, I received a call from the 7th Fleet Admiral [Rear Admiral Donald Whitmire], about sending me a military advisor named Richard Armitage. I was to take orders from him and act in the highest traditions of the United States Navy.

Over 30 ships—the remnants of the South Vietnamese Navy—along with the Vietnamese CNO [Chief of Naval Operations] and other key personnel were at Con Son Island, about 140 miles from Saigon. The admiral went on: "Mr. Armitage knows these folks and speaks the language. Your job is to escort these ships east to Subic Bay."

I was to get these ships under way, feed the people aboard, and provide them with medical care. Initially the order was *Kirk*'s job alone but soon USS *Cook* [DE-1083] would assist us.

At the time, I thought Armitage worked for the CIA. I learned he was a graduate of the Naval Academy. So I took him aboard and headed west back toward Vietnam. He, the executive officer [XO], and I then began planning how we would accomplish our mission.

I said, "When we get there, you pick out the key Vietnamese personnel and bring them back to the ship. Then we'll stand off. You'll have all day, the rest of that night, and all the next day to plan how you're going to do this."

I told Armitage and my XO, Lt. Cmdr. Richard McKenna, that we would go into the island right after dark and that I'd drop him, McKenna, and 8 or 10 of my senior enlisted men so they could make an assessment. What would I need to get these ships started? Would the *Kirk* have to take any of these ships under tow?" Could the Vietnamese personnel get them under way or would I have to do that?

When we arrived, we saw Swift boats, landing craft — everything that was left of the Vietnamese Navy. The Vietnamese CNO and his staff came aboard and we planned the operation. I went back the next night and offloaded them and about 50 of my enlisted men — electricians, enginemen, etc. — to help get the engines on these boats started. Once they got them all up and running, we headed east the next morning making about 5 knots.

The Vietnamese vessels of all types were loaded with refugees, many of them families of

Refugees find safety on USS ***Blue Ridge*** (Naval Historical Center).

these officials. I have no doubt that they all would have been slaughtered had they stayed behind. At the very least, the communists would have put them in "re-education" camps.

I found two Vietnamese women who could speak English. They were married to U.S. officers or enlisted men. I put one on the bridge as my communicator to talk to the Vietnamese ships. Each of the ships had a U.S. officer or petty officer aboard and I could communicate with each of them. I told them what course I was taking. At night the Vietnamese vessels were right in close; during the day, they'd spread out. Thank God, it was flat, dead calm. If it hadn't been, we would have lost a lot of these small ships.

When we had medical incidents at night, I had to prioritize these emergencies. I had my chief corpsman, Chief Steve Burwinkel, go from one ship to another in the captain's gig or whaleboat checking on the refugees. The Vietnamese woman on the bridge coordinated this operation. She would tell me what case was serious and which boat needed our corpsman. From the bridge, I kept track of all the emergency medical cases on a tally sheet so I could direct Chief Burwinkel to go to specific refugee ships. My officers or enlisted men who were on those vessels would radio the medical emergencies to us.

"What ship are you on and where are you located?" I would ask. "Give me a bearing to *Kirk*." I had the names of all the Vietnamese ships on a sheet and generally where they were located. And this process went on 24 hours a day. We were also feeding these refugees and getting them water. In fact, water was the big issue. We distilled water, put the water in five-gallon cans, and sent these cans to them.

What Chief Burwinkel accomplished was unbelievable! I only knew about the emergencies he handled. I didn't know about all the other tasks he performed.

After we expended all our medical supplies, the Air Force dropped us 55-gallon drums filled with medical supplies. We then sent our boat out, wrestled those drums aboard, and brought them back to *Kirk*.

Those Vietnamese just cannot express their appreciation enough for what the officers and men of *Kirk* did for them. They are so gracious and are dying to pay their respects to the United States Navy. The Navy could, if it wanted to, have the reunion of all reunions in San Diego aboard the *Midway* for the sailors and refugees of Operation Frequent Wind.

A Girl Named "Kirk"

USS Kirk's *independent duty corpsman, HMC Stephen Burwinkel, represented the vessel's small two-man medical department. Independent duty meant that as a highly trained and experienced petty officer, he worked without supervision of a physician. His patient load was soon to increase.*

It was 28 and 29 April when all hell broke lose and Saigon fell. Operation Frequent Wind really started for us on the 29th when we began taking on refugees. Our LAMPS helicopter was fortunately broken at the time because it was in the hangar and not on the flight deck when the first Vietnamese helo landed. Soon another one landed on our flight deck and that filled up the deck.

I was truly amazed when the second pilot landed. I thought, "He can't put this thing down here." But sure enough he did. Then the helicopters started coming out like butterflies or hornets circling around us and other ships.

We had to push those first two Hueys over the side to make room for other incoming choppers. Another one landed on our fantail so that filled up the flight deck again. To get that Huey on the fantail out of the way, our LAMPS pilot flew it off the ship then re-landed it on the flight deck. So now we had two more Hueys up there.

A vacated South Vietnamese Huey is pushed over the side of USS *Blue Ridge* to make room for more incoming choppers (Naval Historical Center).

At that point, a CH-46 [Sea Knight helicopter] came along and the pilot acted like he was going to land. When he saw that our flight deck was fouled [obstructed by aircraft] and couldn't land there, he came around toward our fantail. But it was obvious that he couldn't land there either. Our first class storekeeper [Jeffery Swan] spoke some rudimentary Vietnamese. He got on the radio and in very broken Vietnamese told the pilot not to land. The pilot then hovered about 10 feet over the fantail and people began jumping out the back.

Some incurred minor injuries such as broken ankles, but most refugees were uninjured. In fact, quite a few unsung heroes among our crew began catching these refugees. One mother threw her little 4-year-old boy out and a sailor caught him just like he was catching a baseball out of the sky.

After the helo was empty of passengers, the pilot flew some distance from the ship, rolled the helo on its side, and landed it in the water. When it hit, rotor blades went everywhere. When all the debris stopped flying around, he climbed out the window, jumped into the water, and popped to the surface. By that time our motor whaleboat was in the water to pick him up.

Soon we were maxed out with about 150 refugees aboard. Good old Capt. Jacobs, being the hard charger he was, went around looking for more. In fact, he came to sick bay all excited and said, "Doc, I think we found a lady who's pregnant!"

I said, "Skipper, we don't need any pregnant women on this ship." As it turned out, we ended up with five pregnant ladies.

"Please, Doc," he said, "tell me that one of these ladies will have a baby aboard ship."

That possibility didn't really cause me any anxiety because a previous tour in Morocco included duty in the delivery room. The process of a woman giving birth wasn't fearful to me. My third class [petty officer], in fact, asked me, "Chief, what are we gonna do if one these ladies has a baby?"

"I assume we'll witness the miracle of birth," I replied.

As it turned out, one of the women went into labor but then stopped. None of them delivered aboard ship. In a space we called the "Ballroom," we had set up a mini maternity ward and that's where we kept these five pregnant women under observation.

The refugees were in pretty good shape despite the fact that I had some concerns I had voiced to the skipper. I thought about tuberculosis, dysentery — all the diseases endemic in Vietnam. But these refugees were the upper crust of Vietnamese society. They were wives and family members of Vietnamese officers and were wealthy enough to get out first. In fact, many came aboard with shoe boxes full of gold, which we confiscated to prevent a situation in which theft might occur. We gave the people a receipt. Our supply officer collected a lot of gold.

We rigged up some canvas awnings on the O-1 level and refugees were soon living up there. We also granted them some head privileges. But the 150 refugees we had taken aboard taxed our food and water situation.

Kirk was then ordered to move down to Con Son Island near Vung Tau. When we got there on the 1st of May, we found what was left of the Vietnamese fleet. And this is when all the fun and games started for me. Between rendezvousing at Con Son Island until we got to the Philippines, I spent all my time going from ship to ship to see what I could do for these refugees. I was basically holding sick call.

A first class bosun's mate and one of the other chiefs went with me. They went aboard to make sure that these people weren't armed. I can't tell you the number of .38 caliber pistols, shotguns, and rifles that we threw into the South China Sea. As we found these weapons, we tossed them over the side.

The refugees seemed to be very relieved that the initial danger was over. They were out of Vietnam. They were away from all the hell and disorder in Saigon. They were very apprehensive, of course, because they didn't know where they were going. In many cases, families had been split up. Mom was there with the kids. Who knew where dad was or vice versa? But generally, they were a calm, cool, collected group of people considering what they had just been through.

I discovered two Vietnamese armed forces physicians on one of these refugee ships. Both spoke pretty good English. I thought my luck had changed. I said, "When I go back to the ship and get some more supplies, I'll bring you stethoscopes and whatever else you need."

One answered, "No, the war is finis. And we are finis." They would not offer any assistance.

I said, "At least I'll bring you back some medical supplies."

The other answered, "No, we're not doing anything. We're refugees like everybody else."

I was pissed, to put it very plainly. "Wasn't this typical," I thought. "No wonder these guys lost the war."

Sometimes I'd go back to the *Kirk* during the day to replenish my supplies, such as Ace bandages and battle dressings. Usually I'd do these medical checks until dark, then come back aboard to get something to eat and change my clothes. Then I'd start out again the next morning. A few times because of certain circumstances, I spent significant time aboard some ships — sometimes all night. I didn't want to take the chance of trying to find the *Kirk* in the dark.

These refugees had a lot of minor medical problems. I saw many cases of conjunctivitis caused by the unsanitary conditions and being worsened by exposure to the sun. Conjunctivitis — pink eye — is highly contagious. In fact, if I caught it, I was afraid that would be the end of it. Your eyes get swollen and you can't see.

I quickly ran out of ophthalmic ointment. I desperately needed something to treat diarrhea, large amounts of antibiotic ophthalmic ointment, and diapers. A C-130 arrived and dropped barrels of supplies. I think I had more Kaopectate and Lomotil than I had ever seen in my life.

One of the problems that contributed to this horrendous scenario was the unsanitary situation. The ships discharged wastewater directly from the heads into the sea, especially the older ships. The Vietnamese on the aft end of the ships would get water out of the sea to wash their faces and bodies so they were using water contaminated with fecal material. I tried to explain to more than one commanding officer not to let the people do this but instead to insist that they go up forward and get their water. In most cases, however, this was impractical because the freeboard [distance between the water and the main deck] up forward was too high and they couldn't lift a heavy bucket successfully. They could do it at the aft end where there was less freeboard.

After the third day, I began seeing upper respiratory problems and some trauma. One situation was very unusual. I came across a man on one boat who had been gut-shot. I could see his intestine and that's why I thought he couldn't survive but would probably die of peritonitis. I noticed that he had already been treated by someone. He had a dressing and what looked like sulfa powder. A Vietnamese officer wanted me to take him back to the *Kirk* but I didn't know what I would do with him back on the ship.

But he ended up back aboard the *Kirk*, and I waited for him to die. I opened up the table in what we called the "after battle dressing station" and inserted an IV. I then got a young third class [petty officer] and showed him how to take blood pressure and change the IV. Then I said, "This guy is yours until we reach the Philippines or he dies. Don't give him anything to drink except to wet his lips."

But the old coot didn't die. When we got to the Philippines, he was taken to surgery at [Naval Hospital] Subic Bay. Afterward, he did just fine — sitting up and smiling. He was a tough old man.

We came across a large civilian freighter — the *Tan Nam Viet* — which was loaded to the

Crowded with refugees, ***Tan Nam Viet*** wallows dead in the water awaiting USS ***Kirk***'s assistance (courtesy USS *Kirk* Archives).

gills with refugees. The XO, a few other people, and I went aboard that ship. That's when my adventure started. I recall what Dick McKenna, the XO, said: "Doc, you need to stay aboard and see what you can do for these people. And I'll be right back in about four hours to get you." Two days later they came back and got me.

Of course, I didn't have a lot with me. I had my Unit 1 and some penicillin. We identified a woman who spoke some English, and I used her as my interpreter. She brought me a baby I thought was already dead. The baby was listless and unresponsive. I listened to its lungs and determined it was still alive but was in very bad shape, probably pneumonia.

I had no way to figure out the baby's weight and what the penicillin dosage should be. But I administered a great big dose of penicillin. And I'll be darned if it didn't work. The next day this baby was not only alive and well; it was pretty pissed off! It was hungry and crying.

I recall another incident. An LSM [Landing Ship Medium] we had given the Vietnamese showed up in very bad shape loaded with refugees. I went aboard and could see that the ship, which was taking water through the bow doors, was sinking; the doors wouldn't close properly. A young Vietnamese lieutenant was acting as the CO. I asked him if he spoke English and he said yes.

"Do you know your ship is sinking?"

He answered, "Yes, I know that."

At that point we went alongside another Vietnamese Navy ship and that's when the refugees on the well deck and the deck above it realized the ship was sinking — and they panicked. As we were close by the other ship, the crew put two wooden gangways across to that vessel. Then one of the men panicked and pushed a woman in front of him and she fell into the water. I don't know what happened to her after that. A Vietnamese officer walked right behind this man, put a gun to his head, and executed him right on the spot. Suddenly it was just like a church. Everybody quieted down and went over to the other ship without further incident.

One refugee had a severe leg injury, a compound fracture of the femur. I applied a Thomas half-ring splint to immobilize his fracture but could see that he had to have open orthopedic surgery, which meant getting him to a ship with a doctor. That ship was the *Flint* [AE-32], which had a physician and an operating room.

Remember that we had taken two Hueys aboard the *Kirk*. The front end of one and the back end of the other had been damaged. Our LAMPS detachment took the good front end and the good back end and married the two to make one good Huey.[3] Then we loaded this refugee with the leg injury in a Stokes stretcher and got him on the now functioning Huey. One of our LAMPS pilots did the flying.

In taking off, we snagged one of our radio antennas and tore a hole in the bottom of the Huey. We had to land so they could patch the hole with duct tape; then it took off again. Of course, I was sitting back on the deck of the helo because all the seats had been taken out. The pilot said, "Hey Doc, if something happens and we go in the water, you need to push yourself out the door, pull those things on your Mae West, and you'll pop to the surface."

I remember responding to the pilot through the mike, "What about this guy who's in the Stokes litter?"

One of the pilots answered: "He's bought the farm [been killed]." When we landed on the flight deck of the *Flint*, they took the guy off and we left. I assume the man made it. At least I hope he did.

Caring for the pregnant women was one of the jobs that cut into my time. After I did my rounds during the day, I'd come back, they'd tie the Swift boat up, and we'd tow it along as if it were an extra lifeboat or dinghy. My third class corpsman, Mark Falkenberg, and I would compare notes and catch up. It might be 11 at night or midnight before I got a few hours of sleep.

In the morning, we'd get the engine started on the Swift boat, which often was not immediate. It was long overdue for an overhaul. Then I'd go up and down the lines of boats doing my rounds.

Luckily the weather held during our crossing to the Philippines—no bad storms. That was good because some of those boats would never have made it had we gotten into some heavy seas.

We had only one real tragedy. A young mother with five or six children had been brought aboard the *Kirk*. One of them, a boy about a year old, had pneumonia. He responded to treatment and was doing real well. For all practical purposes, he was cured. But while I was out on my rounds, the first class bosun's mate said, "Doc, we just got a radio message and we've got to get back to the *Kirk* right now." When we returned to the ship, I found that the mother had been feeding the baby a bottle. He coughed and aspirated the formula from the bottle. Due to his compromised lungs, he died.

Somehow, we found the father on one of the other ships, and brought him to the *Kirk*. Then we had a formal burial at sea of this little baby. That really shook me up.

By this time we reached Subic Bay and unloaded our passengers, our ship was in total disarray. Our daily cleaning routine had come to a screeching halt. I was stripped of all my supplies.

When we arrived in Guam, we had a reunion with some of the people from the *Tan Nam Viet*. In fact, the first of the pregnant ladies [Lan Nguyen Tran] gave birth on Guam. If it was a boy, she promised to name her child "Kirk." But it was a girl so her middle name is "Kirk."

Hueys Over the Side!

Before Lt. Cmdr. Hugh Doyle became Kirk's *Chief Engineer, he had already seen duty aboard two other Navy vessels. After volunteering for duty in Vietnam, he was then rewarded with an assignment to Destroyer School in Newport, Rhode Island, for engineering training. "Since nobody wanted to be a chief engineer," Doyle recalls, he received orders to* Kirk, *a nearly brand-new warship.*

I'm not sure how we actually learned of Operation Frequent Wind. We originally were directed to take part in Operation Eagle Pull, the evacuation of Cambodia [12 April 1975]. Eagle Pull was uneventful because it was very quick. We got in, took a few hundred people out, and the mission was over. This mission was nothing like what would happen in Vietnam.

We were in a normal deployment, the second for *Kirk* with nothing unusual about it. She was a new ship, having been built in 1972. I made the 1973–1974 deployment as chief engineer so I was one of the old hands when I went on her second cruise. I don't recall thinking much about Vietnam because most activity there had died down — at least for us but certainly not for the Vietnamese. How we were actually selected to take part in Frequent Wind, I just don't know. But as it turned out, it was good for us.

When we came out of the Cambodian operation, we went right to Singapore for a port call. I recall both boilers had been taken down for maintenance, which put us out of operation. But suddenly we were put on a 24-hour notice to get under way. My memory of this from the standpoint of the chief engineer is: "Hey, you've got to put those boilers back together in 12 hours!" And then an hour later a new order arrived: "You've got to have them back together in 8 hours!"

Soon it became very obvious that something big was going on. I had two boilers disassembled with bits and pieces scattered all over the fire room. We went into high gear. As we were heading out from Singapore to go to Vietnam, we were still putting one of the boilers back together, having gotten under way on the other boiler.

The original Frequent Wind plan was very lock-step. It was get in there, send in our big helicopters, pick up as many people as we could take out of Saigon, and bring them out to the large ships. Our job was to sit there and act as an anti-aircraft asset. We were concerned that North Vietnamese jets, which were thought to be operating out of captured Tan Son Nhut and Bien Hoa airbases, would harass the evacuation fleet. So *Kirk* was to provide protection for the fleet. We had no inkling there would be any Vietnamese Air Force helicopters involved. No one aboard *Kirk* even anticipated a mass evacuation.

Our first indication the helicopters were coming was to observe the blips on the radar and then to actually see them. All of a sudden we saw 1, 2, 8, 12, 15, and 25. Then there were swarms of helos heading our way. It was totally unexpected.

It was a natural decision for the Vietnamese pilots. A pilot had a Huey fully loaded with fuel. His family was standing next to him, and out over the horizon he knew there were U.S. ships. It didn't take a genius to see the big picture and say, "Kids! Get in the airplane. We're going!" And they did that in great numbers. We had no advance warning. The refugees just started coming.

Because we were a small ship, relatively speaking, the first helicopters flew right over the top of us. The pilots knew the bigger ships were out on the horizon. From their altitude, they could probably see them —*Blue Ridge, Hancock, Midway* — and all the rest of the ships that the big helicopters could land on. These CH-53s and CH-46s were shuttling the embassy personnel.

Then, unexpectedly, small Hueys began showing up. It seemed that everyone got the same idea at the same time. The Vietnamese knew the evacuation was going on. They could see Marine Corps and Air Force helicopters heading for the embassy. So they all took off and followed them back out to sea. There were certainly a lot of large-deck, multi-spot flight decks out on the horizon for them to land on.

However, a number of the Vietnamese Air Force Hueys were very low on fuel. Many of the Vietnamese Air Force pilots had never flown over blue water. They normally flew over rivers and paddies but had never been out to sea. It was a strange environment to them. Some were concerned they would run out of fuel. We thought it would be a professional challenge to take one helicopter aboard the *Kirk*.

That idea seems like a joke today but at the time we were very naive. I was up in CIC [Combat Information Center]. The captain was very interested in taking one aboard, but we were getting frustrated because helicopters kept flying right over the top of us in great numbers. You could look around and maybe one 90-degree quadrant of the sky would have 15 or 20 helicopters at various altitudes and distances— and all heading out to sea. The captain [Paul Jacobs] kept saying, "Can't they see our flight deck? Can't they tell that there's something right here? Why don't they land on us?"

We had a first class storekeeper named Jeffery Swan who had had a couple of tours in Vietnam; he could speak rudimentary Vietnamese. He was called up to CIC where he began broadcasting, "Ship 1087. Land here!" He was attempting to get the Huey pilots to recognize who we were. This went on hour after hour. Our air controllers were broadcasting on the guard circuit —121.5 — the frequency everybody guarded.

After so many hours one of the Huey's turned inbound to us and landed, a cause for great joy on our part. We thought, "Finally we took part in this!" That first helo was the personal helicopter of the deputy chairman of the Vietnamese Joint Chiefs of Staff and his entourage.

When it landed, we planned to chock it down, save it as a trophy, and bring it back in so everyone would be proud of us. Then we looked up and there were three more, all on short final [about to land]. I shouted, "Oh my God, what have we done?"

Capt. Jacobs made a very quick decision. He ordered, "Okay, get the refugees out of it and throw it over the side." But we didn't throw it over. We pushed it up on the port side of the hangar. But when the second one landed, it clipped the rotor of the first one. Capt. Jacobs said,

"We can't have this; we're going to have a huge accident." So we repositioned that first one on the port side of the hangar further forward and pushed its tail over the side to get it out of the way. Then we pushed the second one over the side, and started taking the rest of the helos. They would land, discharge passengers, and then crewmembers would push the empty helos over the side.

Every time we took refugees off a helicopter, we should have logged their names and the helicopter's serial number. But we didn't. Too many were landing and too much was going on. With few exceptions, we didn't even know who the refugees were or how many were on each helicopter. We have a picture in our cruise book of one helicopter flying up one side of the ship. It was jammed with more than a dozen people — all women and children. And these Hueys were designed to carry six men. We ended up taking 157 refugees on the first 14 helicopters that landed on *Kirk*.

By the end of the operation, we received a total of 16 Hueys and 1 CH-47 Chinook. This big Chinook carried 10 refugees, but it was much too large to land on our flight deck. While I was inside with the team, the decision was made for the pilot to hover over our fantail, drop his tailgate, and disgorge all his passengers onto our fantail.

Without my knowledge, the helicopter hovered over us for about 10 minutes while all the refugees jumped out. Then the pilot flew the aircraft away from the ship and hovered it with his wheels in the water for about 10 minutes while he took his flight suit off. I'm a pilot and I still can't understand how he did this. He sat there by himself without a co-pilot and flew a big twin-engine, twin-rotor Chinook with wheels in the water. And while he was sitting there with what seemed like "three" arms flying the helicopter, he somehow got out of his flight suit and dropped it out the window.

He finally rolled the helicopter to the right. As the rotors smashed into the water, he jumped out the pilot's window to the left. The doors were open on either side of the ship so we could hear the crash and see bits and pieces of the rotors flying over the ship and splashing all around us. The pilot avoided the wreckage and swam away. Not only was he an incredible pilot but he somehow kept his wits about him while he performed that unbelievable maneuver. It was just amazing!

Some of the crew became "John Waynes" at that point. You couldn't stop our guys. Five or six sailors ran out on the fantail and jumped over the side, swimming like crazy to that helo and dragging life jackets with them. They didn't realize that the helicopter was now empty. All the refugees were standing behind us on the fantail. Now we had to be concerned about getting our own sailors out of the water. Half of them hadn't even put their life jackets on before they jumped in. Our motor whaleboat drove over and picked up the lone Vietnamese pilot, who was calmly paddling his way through the water. Most of the trouble was getting the *Kirk* sailors into the same boat.

Because these refugees were in the know, they knew their country was falling to the communists. For many years some of them had been converting a lot of their personal wealth into gold and diamonds. Our disbursing officer, Craig Compiano, had to take an incredible number of small gold bars — tiny ones — probably no bigger than a Wrigley Spearmint gum stick. Individually, they were very small but collectively that was a lot of money. This was the reason the pilot of the Chinook went through all the trouble of taking his flight suit off. He had gold in the suit which weighted him down. When he hovered over the ocean and took his flight suit off, he also was throwing away his life savings. Even though he had saved what turned out to be 10 lives and done an extraordinary feat of flying, he just couldn't be consoled. All he had in the world were the skivvies on his back.

The first phase rescuing the helicopter refugees lasted a few days. On Tuesday, the 29th of April, we took aboard four helicopters. On Wednesday we took another three helos. We took one more on Thursday, a transfer helicopter from one of the LSTs.

The refugees who landed aboard the *Kirk* were transferred over to one of the other ships on the second day. An LCM [Landing Craft Medium] from the *Mobile* (LKA-115) came alongside and the 157 refugees went aboard. Soon they went to one of the MSC [Military Sealift Command] ships in the holding area. Then we stood by the rest of Wednesday afternoon watching many boats come out. The number was just incredible!

A lot happened on April 30th. We were told to go to Con Son Island but our mission was really to pick up Richard Armitage from the *Blue Ridge*, the task force's flagship, and deliver him to the Vietnamese Navy rendezvous anchorage. We were told to rendezvous with the *Blue Ridge* and do a small boat transfer. Armitage came aboard in civilian clothes armed with a pistol on his side. He sequestered himself with the captain in the captain's cabin for a few hours. Armitage said, in effect, "I'm going to give you orders and you follow me." At the time, the captain didn't like hearing that from this young guy so he got on the secure voice to the admiral and the admiral said, "Yup, take your orders from Armitage." So we did.

We steamed down to Con Son Island overnight, arriving there early on Thursday morning. And that's where we met up with a milling throng of ships. Ships and boats were all over the place. Some were anchored; some were just drifting. We saw everything from a PBR — a small patrol boat — all the way up to a former U.S. Coast Guard cutter and destroyer escorts. We probably saw 50 vessels. And they were covered with refugees. Many at Con Son Island had been there for some time. During the previous month, several cities had been evacuated — Danang, Nha Trang, and a number of others down the coast as the North Vietnamese moved south toward Saigon. Many of these refugees had been picked up by chartered American merchant ships — *Pioneer Contender*, *Pioneer Challenger*, and a number of other chartered merchant ships. These ships were sent for the sole purpose of picking up refugees from port cities up and down the coast, telling the refugees to "just get aboard; we're going south."

The situation was ripe for trouble — violence and mob rule. Some of this chaos and anarchy got out to the press weeks before the Saigon evacuation. Marines were put aboard these ships to quell the uprisings. Those people were eventually offloaded at Con Son Island. I have no idea about their living conditions ashore. When it was time to head for Subic, 25,000 to 35,000 refugees boarded 32 Vietnamese Navy ships.

We started out shepherding the boats but then began bringing some of these refugees aboard *Kirk*. We were on our own that Friday running about like a sheep dog around the outsides of this long formation. Four or five ships accompanied us: USS *Cook* [DE-1083], USS *Tuscaloosa* [LST-1187], USS *Deliver* [ARS-23] — a submarine rescue ship, USS *Lipan* [TATF-85] — an ocean-going tug, and USS *Abnaki* [ATF-96].

Chief Burwinkel and Hospitalman Falkenberg represented us — they were our entire medical department. The USS *Cook* also had two corpsmen. Our ships were identically manned as far as numbers of medical personnel. *Tuscaloosa* probably had more medical personnel than we had. One of the collateral duties of an amphibious ship like the *Tuscaloosa* is to provide medical services to the troops aboard. So you might have had a chief petty officer, a first class petty officer, and maybe two corpsmen. *Lipan*, *Abnaki*, and *Deliver* probably each had one corpsman.

For a time a doctor from USS *Mobile* and some of *Mobile*'s corpsmen came aboard and were on loan to us for a few days. So the full medical contingent for the formation was an on-loan doctor for about 25 percent of the time, our own chief, the chief from the *Cook*, a junior corpsman from *Kirk*, a striker[4] corpsman from the *Cook*, probably four total corpsmen from the *Tuscaloosa*, a couple of corpsmen from *Mobile*, and one independent duty corpsman each from *Lipan*, *Deliver*, and *Abnaki*. Each of the ships made rounds — house calls. Chief Burwinkel would go aboard a Vietnamese LST with 3,000 people, and in an hour he would be aboard another LST with 3,000 more refugees.

Tan Nam Viet was a Vietnamese freighter we helped Friday and Saturday. Chief Burwinkel stayed aboard from Friday night until Saturday morning and saw some 600 patients! The numbers were overwhelming.

I recall a small former Navy LSM (HQ-402) coming over the horizon and heading toward us. The lookout called out, "Here comes a small boat!" Well it wasn't a small boat. It was probably about 200 feet long. We thought it was steering a sinuous course as it appeared to be weaving its way. It was very down by the bow. A flashing light aboard signaled that it needed help and was sinking. They were taking that sinuous course because they were forced to steer by hand. The steering motors that drove the big steering units weren't working, and they had jury-rigged the rudder to try to get it amidships without success. The rudder, however, kept flopping back and forth. But the ship had another problem: It had twin screws and only one engine was functioning.

We boarded the ship with several of our people, including HMC Burwinkel. It was very clear that they knew they were sinking, but they just couldn't pump the water out.

A few thousand people must have been aboard. We got word to Armitage, who was now aboard the Vietnamese headquarters ship — their flagship — and told him we had a ship loaded with refugees many miles back and that it was sinking. We told him we needed one of the Vietnamese ships to come back to us and evacuate them.

One of the Coast Guard cutters, with only the crew aboard, returned to where we were, came alongside the HQ-402, and began transferring the refugees. It wasn't an orderly evacuation. They had placed wooden planks from one ship to another and people were scrambling aboard like ants. That's when the little girl was pushed over the side. Shortly after the rescue ship pulled away, the HQ-402 sank.

We had the kind of illnesses that come from mass crowding without sanitation, including diarrhea and dysentery. A few days out of Subic, diarrhea was rampant throughout the fleet because the refugees had been living in such close quarters for a week. We were completely out of Kaopectate. Somehow we got word back to Subic that what we really needed was Kaopectate. The only way to obtain it in quantities and fast enough to make it worthwhile was to fly it out. The Air Force provided a C-130 and dropped a 55-gallon drum. Once we took the watertight top off, we saw that it was full of Kaopectate bottles. And we needed every bottle for the estimated 32,000 people.

As we got closer to Subic Bay, the situation became tense. One of our electronics technicians and one of our officers were aboard a Vietnamese LST. They noticed that some of the Vietnamese had shortwave radios and were listening to the BBC. One of the reports stated that [Ferdinand] Marcos had said that since the Philippines had now recognized North Vietnam or the People's Republic of Vietnam, the Philippine government would have no choice but to send the 32,000 refugees back to their home country of Vietnam.

A lot of consternation erupted about that! But someone must have laid some heavy words on Marcos because he eventually relented. Nevertheless, all that uncertainty required us to delay entry into Subic while all this diplomatic finagling was going on.

We faced many questions: What would the refugees think? What would happen among the 32,000 people if we made an abrupt right full rudder and headed back toward the west? How would we get the word out? How would we keep them calm and let them know that we weren't really going back to Vietnam, especially since they had heard rumors about returning to their country?

We made a huge full circle of the entire 32-ship formation, which took the better part of the day to complete. And because that turn was so gradual, nobody aboard the ships was the wiser. They didn't realize that we were turning. I don't know who thought of this huge full circle but it was a great maneuver. It was probably Capt. Jacobs's idea.

I'm always concerned that we don't slight the other ships involved in this operation. They weren't just cardboard. They were there for a reason — and they performed very professionally.

Recording History in the Making

From 2 to 6 May 1975, Hugh Doyle recorded three cassette tapes in his stateroom, which he sent home to his wife, Judy. They were candid, extemporaneous observations of rapidly moving events. Untarnished by the passage of time, these excerpts offer a "you are there" quality to the human drama that marked the end of the Vietnam War.

Taped Excerpt 1: [Another helicopter] came in and landed like the first, right on the flight deck. They shut the engine down, they all jumped out. And we had about, oh, maybe 12 more people in that plane. They were a Vietnamese Air Force Lieutenant, his wife and his children, and some of his buddies—as many people as they could jam on the helicopter.

About 10 of us pushed that plane over the side, and I almost went over with it! Luckily, someone grabbed me by the belt and held me on the deck. But we pushed it over the side, and about five minutes later another one came in and landed. We got all those people out, disarmed them—they were heavily armed, everybody had a gun—and we pushed that aircraft over the side. That was the second one to splash. Then the fourth helo came in and also landed. We pushed it over the side like the other two. By that time, we'd thrown three helicopters in the water and had one on deck. I know you probably don't believe any of this, but it's all true!

We took all those people up onto the 02 level, just behind our stack and made lean-to's and laid mats and all kinds of blankets and things out on the deck for their babies. There were all kinds of infants and children and women, and the women were crying. Oh, it was a scene I'll never forget.

Taped Excerpt 2: There were stories—horrible stories—that I heard from the refugees. As he was loading his helicopter, one man had his family killed in front of his eyes. They were standing there, waiting to get on the helicopter, when they were machine-gunned. He was the pilot and was sitting in the helicopter looking at them. They were all lying dead. The town—Can Tho, I think—was being overrun at the time, so he turned and ordered anyone there aboard. They just swarmed aboard the helicopter. He took off and landed aboard our ship with a couple of bullet holes in him but without his family. It was really sad. There have been all kinds of stories of mass slaughters. It's a horrible thing to even think about but it is apparently happening.

Taped Excerpt 3: As fast as they landed, we emptied these planes and pushed them over the side. They would land, and about three minutes later I would stand on the bridge wing and look back over the side, and there would be a helicopter falling over the side and crashing into the water. One of the last ones we took that night was an Air America airplane [helicopter]. It's supposedly owned by the Central Intelligence Agency but they'd never admit it. It was absolutely beautiful. That was the last plane we took that night so we didn't throw it away.

Taped Excerpt 4: The first wave of refugees all came by helicopter. The second wave came by fishing boats, and they covered the horizon. Somebody in the wardroom that morning told me, "You ought to see all the fishing boats!" I thought I was going to see 10 or 12 fishing boats. I went out on deck and saw 10 or 12 hundred fishing boats! I'm not kidding you! I looked over toward the beach, which was about 12 miles away, and there were so many fishing boats, I could hardly see the water. They were all swarming out, all flying Vietnamese flags, going as fast as these little old junk-type boats could go. One ship looked like someone had taken a candy bar, laid it on the sidewalk, and let the ants get at it.

The ships were taking them as fast as they could, but there was a bit of panic. This was because the fishermen and peasants in the boats were a lot less "sophisticated" than the military people and urban families who had come out on the helos the previous day. The helo people were relatively calm. The Vietnamese fishermen and peasants, on the other hand, were just in a frenzy.

"The Lucky Few"

Joseph Pham was born in Hanoi just as the Japanese invaded Indochina in World War II. At age 6 his family fled to their ancestral village far from Hanoi to escape fighting between the Vietnamese communists and the French, who had returned to reclaim their colony. He recalls hiding in rice paddies "to avoid the bullets and the cross-fire."

In 1952, his family returned to Hanoi. Two years later they left for Saigon as part of the mass migration following the Geneva Accords of 1954 that partitioned Vietnam. When they arrived in the South Vietnamese capital, Pham's father and mother opened a retail shop in Saigon where they sold religious icons. While attending the University of Saigon, he witnessed the coup against Ngo Dinh Diem in early November 1963 and the chaos that followed.

Pham was fluent in English by then, having been taught the language at a young age by a British teacher. As the United States became more involved in his country, Pham, as with many others, sought economic opportunities with the Americans. He worked for the U.S. government as a medical interpreter.

In 1967, Pham was drafted into the South Vietnamese Army. After attending the ARVN Officer Candidate School at Thu Duc Military Academy, he reported for duty on the first day of the Tet Offensive in 1968. As a new second lieutenant, he led a company securing an outpost in one of the most active military zones, only a few miles away from a communist underground sanctuary. Because of his language background, he was assigned to work with American advisors and later transferred to work with them at a training center for ARVN Regional and Popular Forces.

Pham was soon transferred to the ARVN Language School where he taught basic conversational English to Vietnamese service personnel. Twice Pham went to the United States to receive more language training at the Defense Language Institute at Lackland Air Force Base in Texas.

When he returned to Saigon in the summer of 1974, U.S. combat forces had already left following implementation of the Paris Peace agreement. Despite that treaty, the North Vietnamese continued to press their advantage. By early spring 1975, the situation in the northern part of South Vietnam deteriorated as coastal cities fell one by one, sending streams of refugees south. When ARVN forces abandoned the Central Highlands, South Vietnam's fate was sealed.

I remember vividly what had been happening to our country those last few days of that fateful month of "Black April." My unit was on the outskirts of Saigon across from the military general hospital. At that time my wife was pregnant, but I had to stay with my unit almost every day because we were on high alert.

On the 28th of April, the Viet Cong attacked Tan Son Nhut Air Base with rockets and mortars. The sky was illuminated with a firestorm that could be seen miles away. Yet on this night a handful of us officers and other fellow soldiers were placed on highest alert to defend our unit compound of the Vietnam Armed Forces Language School, just a stone's throw away from the air base and the US/DAO [Defense Attachment Office]. Even though the violence kept unfolding before our eyes, we had to defend our compound as best we could. People were fearful of the collapse of Saigon at any time because so much chaos was going on in the city. I felt the collapse would come sooner rather than later — and I was in the middle of it.

On the following day, 29 April 1975, I received a call from my pregnant wife early in the morning reporting that she had a contraction. I got excited yet panicked at the news. What was I going to do under the circumstances? What hospital would be open at that time? With that excuse I got permission to leave the compound and see what I could do to help my wife in labor.

The streets were congested with refugees and all kinds of vehicles, mostly scooters overloaded with people trying to get out of the city. Some Vietnamese military units were coming in from other parts of the country and discarding their uniforms so they would appear to be civilians. Many had only a handgun to defend themselves. We all felt helpless and hopeless. We would rather flee than let ourselves be captured and persecuted by the communists.

I was determined to take my near-term pregnant wife and our 4-year-old son to find ways to flee the country. We packed up a few possessions on our tiny scooter and tried to get out of Saigon.

We had heard rumors that the U.S. would pick up some of the people — those who had worked with them — at certain rendezvous places. We went from one rendezvous site to another with a slim hope of being rescued by one of the many helicopters evacuating others to safety. In some places people had gathered and it was very chaotic. But because of my young child and my wife's condition, I felt helpless. If I had been by myself, maybe I could have waited for a helicopter. But I had a family. Our hope was fading rapidly as the night and terror fell upon the city. We were struggling to find our way home late that night to regain our strength for another escape attempt the following day.

When day broke on April 30, 1975, my family of three climbed on our tiny Honda scooter and headed toward the docks. That was our only chance and our last hope. We snaked our way through traffic with people jamming the streets. Scooters running out of gas were abandoned and all kinds of clothes and military uniforms were strewn on the sidewalks. Several helicopters — overloaded with people — were seen crashing into a residential area causing houses to burn to the ground.

As soon as we made it to the docks, the bad news blared on radios nearby: the South Vietnamese government announced its surrender to the communists. With no time to think, we dashed into Vietnam's Naval Shipyard where we saw a medium landing ship with many people aboard. Later it was estimated that it held about 5,000 people. It was the *Lam Giang* (HQ-402), a landing craft that had been given to the Vietnamese Navy. We were among the last few people who boarded the ship before the gangway was withdrawn. We quickly learned that it had no crew and was disabled. It didn't even have a mechanic. Nevertheless, someone somehow managed to repair the engine. What we didn't know at that time was that the ship was leaking very badly.

Eventually, we raised the white flag and moved out of the shipyard and Saigon Harbor about 3 o'clock in the afternoon. The Viet Cong were celebrating their victory at the time so they probably didn't care about a ship moving slowly down the river. No one shot at us.

As the ship reached the rallying point at Con Son Island on May 1 and because of her disabled condition, all the refugees aboard were transferred to other ships. The severely damaged HQ-402 finally sank. From the time we came aboard the landing craft until we were transferred to the larger ship we had not eaten anything for two days, except for a few drops of precious water.

The entire Vietnam Navy fleet was at Con Son Island — about 32 ships altogether. A day later a relief team from the USS *Kirk* came aboard our refugee ship bringing water, medical supplies, and some food. The relief team asked if any people were aboard who were sick and ladies who might be pregnant. There were five pregnant women, two who were at or near full-term. I was among a few people who could speak English so I raised my hand and said that my wife was pregnant.

By order of the *Kirk*'s captain, Paul Jacobs, these women and their families were transferred and resettled aboard *Kirk* under the expert care of Chief Hospital Corpsman Stephen Burwinkel. They were given accommodation in the senior petty officer compartment, which turned out to be a very nice makeshift maternity ward considering the circumstances.

It was a wonderful experience. After my wife and the other pregnant women were settled in the ship's makeshift maternity ward, I volunteered to join the relief team to help bring food and other supplies to different refugee ships in the fleet.

From May 4th to May 6th, I went out with Chief Burwinkel on his rounds and we brought along food and water. The food was mostly fruits like apples, oranges, and some candies. There weren't many supplies aboard the *Kirk* but we brought what we could. Chief Burwinkel provided the medical care and I acted as the interpreter.

During that time I think I had some sense that we were going to Subic Bay because that was the closest port to Vietnam. When we arrived in the Philippines, we all left the *Kirk* and the pregnant women were transferred to the naval hospital on the base. I accompanied them for their examinations. After that, we returned to the docks, boarded a merchant ship, and headed for Guam.

After we arrived in Guam, my wife and two other women gave birth to their babies at the Naval Regional Medical Center. All three brand-new babies were girls! The fourth pregnant woman gave birth to her daughter aboard one of the merchant ships on their way to Hawaii.

We had mixed feelings. We were glad to reach the freedom we were seeking but were also sad, knowing that from that time on we would no longer be able to return to our country and the people we left behind. So we had to accept our situation.

They took us to "Tent city" at Orote Point — on Guam's western coast — that had been erected to receive refugees. About that time, my son came down with the measles and had a very high fever. The next day they transferred my family to the BEQ [Bachelor Enlisted Quarters]. My son was treated at the hospital tent clinic.

On the 18th of May, when my wife began having labor pains, she was taken to the Naval Regional Medical Center. I was not allowed to go with her because my son was still recovering from the measles. She was very scared and did not speak any English at the time. She gave birth to our daughter that same day. Four days later, another woman had a baby. Then a third lady had a child. One of these women named her daughter after the *Kirk*.

After the birth of our daughter, we went to Camp Asan on Guam's western shore until the 23rd of June. When the camp was closed due to tropical storms, we were moved to Hickam Air Force Base in Hawaii. From there we were flown to a refugee camp at Camp Pendleton, California, aboard a big C-141.

The camp had big tents, more refugees, but it was very organized. It was a processing center where refugees were finally allowed to leave and join their sponsor families. My sponsor lived in Texas. Because my daughter had trouble eating the regular formula, she had a diarrhea problem. Our request to leave the camp was therefore approved sooner than it was for others. We spent only four days in Camp Pendleton before being flown to our sponsor's home near Fort Worth, Texas.

I count myself among the lucky few. So that's why I try to get any opportunity to return the favor to my community because of my deep sense of gratitude to the people who saved us. This is especially true of the *Kirk* people and all those who saved our lives and brought us to freedom.

I haven't had an opportunity to go back to back to Vietnam since the war. I am the oldest son in the family. According to Vietnamese tradition, the oldest son has to take care of the parents when they are old. While my mother was still alive, I was unable to leave the country. I'm waiting for the opportunity to take my children to Vietnam — my birthplace. My son, who is 34, has been there twice.

"Angel from the Sky"

Lan Nguyen Tran was 17 in April 1975. Her parents and grandparents were transplanted northerners, having left Hanoi during the mass exodus of refugees aboard U.S. Navy ships in 1954. She was born and raised in Saigon. In 1974, Lan married a man 12 years her senior. Her husband, a member of the South Vietnamese Air Force, was stationed at Tan Son Nhut Air Base. As South Vietnam crumbled into chaos and the fall of Saigon appeared imminent, Lan prepared to give birth to her first child.

My grandparents knew about communists and knew we could not live with them. So with a group of people they bought a boat, which was nearby on the river in Saigon just waiting for the right time. A boat tied up near our boat left a few days earlier, but the government brought it and the people on it back. So that wasn't a good time to leave the country.

On the 28th of April, my husband called from the air force base at Tan Son Nhut. He told my grandparents and the rest of the family to go to the boat and leave.

I did not go with them but instead went to Tan Son Nhut with my mother and my other uncle, a doctor. My aunt worked for an American company so that's why she got a permit to leave in an airplane. But it was too late for me because by the time I got there the communists put rockets in the airport. My mom told me that we had better get out and that she would take me to the hospital because I would have the baby at any time.

But when I got back home, everybody had already gone so I feel so lonely. I didn't have a chance to go to the hospital. When one of the drivers came back to my grandparents' house, I ask him, "Is that boat still there?"

He said, "Yes!"

I said, "Would you please take us to the boat?"

He said he would but first he had to take another wife, pregnant like me, home because she didn't want to leave. She said it was too much hassle to leave when she was pregnant. I told the driver, "No, no. I want to go with you. After you drop that woman, then you take us to the boat."

He said okay, he would do it. But it was very difficult to get from my grandparents' house to the boat because it was about 9 P.M. on the 29th of April. It was raining and storming and people were running. It was very hard to get through the traffic.

Finally we got to the river but the boat wasn't there. Far away, I see the other side of the river and the boat and recognize that boat. I asked the driver, "Is that the boat on the other side of the river?"

After he looks, he says, "Yes."

And I said, "How we can get over there? There's no way we can swim. It's too far away."

Then some people wearing military clothing and guns asked my driver, "Hey, you want to rent a little boat so you can get to that big boat?"

The driver said, "Yes." Then he ask how much.

And they say, "You don't have to pay much. Anything will be okay."

But by the time they are saying that, they take the bag from our driver which had all our valuables. He had taken it from me earlier saying, "You are pregnant. Don't keep it. Let me keep it for you. Bad people will take it from you." My mother's money and jewelry were in there so I give to him.

Suddenly the bad people take the bag from his hand and run. He then follow them to take it back so they shoot at him. I say, "Hey, stop! Stop! They will shoot you so don't run after them!"

They didn't hurt him, just make him scared. As it turned out, there was no small boat at all. They were just trying to take advantage of us.

But suddenly I saw the boat from the other side of the river come over to where we were. It was very strange. But I was very glad. I say, "Hey, the boat is here!"

But I still could not get in the boat because of the rocks on the riverbank, which were very slippery. My mom called and then the people on the boat hear my mom. They ask, "Who is that?"

My mom say our names and then three of my husband's cousins come down to help me climb on the boat. My mother was with me. Then they could not go under the bridge because the water is so high. But finally that night, the water is lower and we are able to go under the bridge and go down the river.

But before that, we heard a lot of gunfire. The [South Vietnamese] soldiers were shooting at whoever wanted to leave the country. Actually they didn't shoot at us but were just shooting in the sky. The gunfire was very loud to scare us, but finally the boat was able to get down to the ocean.

I'm now on the boat with my mom and my in-laws. My husband was not there. He is still at the airport—Tan Son Nhut—because he want to stay until the last minute. He had to stay. He said, "It's no good for a soldier to leave."

There is a Vietnamese doctor in the boat. I am feeling pain and they thought I will have a baby. And with all I had been through they thought I can have the baby at any time. It is already nine months. So they thought I would have baby on that boat. But luckily I don't have the baby, just the labor pains.

Later on, we feel our boat shaking a lot. When I look up from the bottom of the boat I see this very big ship. It was so big I was not able to see the whole ship at once. They don't come up next to our boat but instead they use the canoe [motor whaleboat] to come over to us with the translator and give us some food and water. Then they told us they would return.

A Vietnamese Navy ship named *Ly Thuong Kiet* [HQ-16] later came over and we went aboard it for safety. It's lucky that the ship was empty.

They provided us with food because we had nothing. We stayed on that ship for about two days. Then the translator and others from the *Kirk* came over to help us. One day Mr. Pham, the translator, came over and said that the people on the *Kirk* wanted to take people who were sick or those women who were over seven months pregnant.

I say no because they wanted me to go alone and I wanted to stay with my mother. So they took both of us. It was very dangerous the way they took me. First they had to put me in a basket and lower me by hand down to the ocean. It was a very dark night and was very scary. I thought, "Oh, my God! Maybe I will drop into the ocean." Several sailors down there in the canoe take me from there.

Then they took me to the *Kirk*. They put me in a basket and lifted me with some machine. It was very dark and all I could see were the orange vests the sailors were wearing. When I got there I was so tired and I again had a labor pain. They take me to the doctor [HMC Stephen Burwinkel]. But he said, "Not yet."

After that they put me into a big room with about five other pregnant women. They felt I was the one who would have the first child. Other people had had their second pregnancy but for me it was the first.

The captain knocked on the door and came over to say "Hi" to us. He said, "Hurry, we want one child born and we want the child named for the ship. The ship will then be a sponsor of the baby. So hurry! Hurry!" He was smiling and everyone remembers that.

But no one have a baby on the ship. Capt. Jacobs give one of the crewmembers, Mr. [Donald] Cox, a special assignment to take care of the pregnant women and their families. Every day he would come over and take us to the breakfast room where the sailors eat. We get in line like the other sailors. The food so good! But all I eat is a little bit of corn. I don't feel like eating anything.

Donald Cox was young, too. He told me he is 19. Every day he took me up on the deck so I can have some fresh air. I saw other helicopter parked there on the deck. One day he have a Polaroid camera. He took my picture and I took his picture in front of the helicopter.

But we get along well even though at that time I don't speak English. I just understand a little bit but I don't speak. In high school we learned a little but didn't have a chance to practice anything. But somehow I understand him perfectly and he understand my language.

I stayed on the ship for 12 days. It took so long but at that time we did not know why. Now I do. Capt. Jacobs told me at the reunion why it take so long. Halfway to the Philippines, he got the order to go back to Vietnam to help with other refugees. He thought if he turn the ship around during the day, maybe we will know and be scared. So he wait for night when we are asleep, and he slowly turn back to Vietnam. And that's why it take 12 days in the ocean.

Before I get off the ship at Subic Bay, Donald Cox give me a picture of him and my picture. Then he put something on the back of his picture. He say something like: "I'm sorry to see you go." He told me he have a girlfriend in California. He told me if I cannot locate my husband and I need help, here is his girlfriend's address.

When I get to Subic Bay, they first put me in the naval hospital right away. When I get in there, I was the only one. I felt scared and lonely so I told the sailors that I wanted to go out with the other Vietnamese people. So they let me go. I just stay in Subic Bay for one night.

The next day they put us on a big commercial ship and took us to Guam. From that time I don't feel hungry and do not eat. I remember they give everybody one box of food with cigarettes, fruit cocktail — a military ration. I give it away to other people. I just get one can of fruit cocktail, that's all.

When we arrived in Guam, they took me to the U.S. Navy Hospital there. And that night I have a baby, a little girl. I remembered that Capt. Jacobs had said he wanted to put the name of the ship for the baby. But because I have a baby girl I cannot put first name Kirk for the baby girl. So her middle name is Kirk. My husband's last name is Tran and my maiden name is Nguyen. And then her middle name is Kirk, and her first name is Giang Tien, which means "angel from the sky." So my child's name is Tran-Nguyen Kirk Giang-Tien.[5]

BABY KIRK 4 MONTHS IN BALTIMORE - MARYLAND 09-75

Tran-Nguyen Kirk Giang-Tien ("Baby Kirk") and mother Lan Tran (courtesy USS *Kirk* Archives).

I stay for three days in the hospital in a twin bed with my baby in a big room with other patients. On the third day I saw Capt. Jacobs come in with other sailors to visit the Vietnamese refugee patients. He saw me and asked my baby's name. And I told him. After that I don't see him until the reunion.

When the baby was 10 days old, we flew on an airplane to Camp Pendleton near San Diego. I then went to the Red Cross and they try to reunite people missing in three camps. One was in Arkansas, one in Pennsylvania, one in Florida. They find my husband in Fort Chaffee in Arkansas. He went to the Red Cross, too.

He told me he left Vietnam on the morning of April 30. He said he was in the last group to leave. They went by helicopter. He said it wasn't working and they had to fix it. Finally, they were able to fly to Thailand. I don't remember where he went from there. It was three months since I had seen him. He didn't know that I had made it out of Vietnam. A friend later told me that while he was at Fort Chaffee, every day he went to the Red Cross to see if my name was there. He could not find it and was losing hope. Every day he cry. The other pilots had been able to take their wives. He had stayed longer because he followed military orders and so now he felt guilt because he was unable to take care of me.

We were at Camp Pendleton for six months before we got a sponsor [church] in Baltimore, Maryland. In September 1975, I, my baby, my husband, his parents, and his sister and brother moved there and lived in Baltimore for nine months. Nine months after we arrived in Baltimore, we moved to California.

In May 2005, Lan Tran, her 30-year-old daughter, Tien "Baby Kirk," and son James were reunited with the captain and crew of USS Kirk at an emotional reunion in Orlando. Her husband died in 2001.

"Lan's Sailor"

Donald Cox joined the Navy in 1972 and was trained in anti-submarine warfare systems as a helicopter air crewman. An assignment as part of HSL-33 Air Detachment 4 aboard USS Kirk three years later marked his second western Pacific cruise. Like his fellow crewmen, Cox soon discovered that his humanitarian skills would trump the skills he had acquired as a warrior.

We were flying daily routine radar picket and utility missions. We took off before dawn and flew up and down the coast between the battle group and the beach looking for hostile sea craft. After two hours, we were relieved on station by another aircraft. Later, most days, we picked up some mail or supplies from the aircraft carrier and delivered them to the ships in the battle group. The government of South Vietnam was falling, and the action up north near the DMZ was heating up. I didn't pay much attention as information about what was happening was limited to the radio broadcasts. My focus was on flying and maintaining the aircraft.

The action in Vietnam began in earnest when we were down in Singapore. We were enjoying some shore leave for a couple of days in mid–April. The day before we got the call to go to Nam, the skipper decided to make a run south to the equator. He wanted to do this so that we "polliwogs" could become "shellbacks."[6] Just a few hours above of the equator, we got orders to return and proceeded north to Vietnam. That was the call we were waiting for. Operation Frequent Wind had begun.

When we turned around and headed back, we stayed busy checking our equipment to make sure everything was in perfect condition for what we would face. Everyone was ready to do whatever the mission called for.

At that point we knew we weren't there to do what the Navy had been doing for the past many years—causing death and destruction. It was clearly a mission to help save lives. This realization is what changed our attitude toward what we were doing. As with any humanitarian service, nothing motivates a person more than the feeling you get when you are helping others. A person changes his attitude about people in need and about his fellow sailors. I feel this experience is what helped draw us together as a crew. We were surrounded by all those high tech weapons and trained on how to use them. But when the moment came, we would much rather save lives than take them.

The operation was rather slow to start. A helicopter would fly out from the beach. General Quarters would sound and then the helo would sometimes land on our ship or fly over to one of the other ships. Mike Washington and I were the "designated rescue swimmers." We stayed in our wetsuits with our swim gear at hand in case one of these helicopters crashed while landing. We were prepared to get into the water and help rescue any survivors on a moment's notice.

One helo, a CH-47, was too big to land on the deck so the pilot hovered over the deck and the passengers jumped into the waiting arms of the *Kirk* crew. The pilot, following instructions from our pilots, then ditched the aircraft 50 yards off the starboard side of the ship. I will never forget how at that moment Mike and I were on the main deck in our wetsuits with orders to enter the water to save the pilot. Before we could jump into the water, seven or eight sailors jumped from the flight deck above us into the ocean with intentions of saving that pilot. This act clearly shows the selflessness and courage of the men of the USS *Kirk*. The captain's gig motored over and picked up the pilot and all our men who were in the water.

Since our helicopter wasn't functional and the helicopters that had landed were secure, the air detachment didn't have anything for us to do so we augmented the security team looking after the refugees. We couldn't let them run unescorted around the ship so when any of the women were feeling too claustrophobic or just needed to get away from the group for a few minutes, I escorted them up to the flight deck.

Lan [Tran] and her mother requested through the interpreter to spend more time above decks. The skipper instructed me to see to their [Lan and her mother's] needs. I was instructed to help where I could and to take care of these people and make them as comfortable as possible. If there was a medical problem, I was to get hold of Chief Burwinkel.

Neither Lan nor her mother could speak any English but, being nine months pregnant, Lan wanted to spend a lot of time on deck. She would often ask to go upstairs so I'd take her and her mother up above decks and sit with her and we talked. She talked in Vietnamese and I spoke in English. Neither one of us really knew what the other person was saying. More than anything, I think she just needed to get some sunlight and have someone to talk to. I could see in her face the fear, loneliness, and loss from leaving her homeland. I developed a strong affection for her.

She claims she was 17. I think she may have been a little younger. She was about the same age as my little sister. Her husband was quite a bit older and was a Vietnamese army pilot. She thought I was a pilot. That brought us closer.

Very easily she could have been younger than she claimed. I was only 20 at the time. Interestingly, during the 10 days we were transiting, we spent a lot of our waking hours together. When I was below decks, she would come over and ask to have me take her above deck or take her to eat. Her mom always came with us as an escort.

On the way to Subic Bay my job was just taking care of the ladies. We also had to perform burials at sea. One young boy Chief Burwinkel had treated for pneumonia aspirated some food and died. The funeral itself was simple. I was asked to play Taps on my trumpet at the proper time when they consigned the baby's body to the ocean. You see, Mike Washington and I both played the trumpet. We had brought our instruments onboard for the cruise to enjoy and entertain anyone who would listen.

The funeral was a very dignified event. I remember afterwards asking Joseph [Pham] as we returned below decks, "Is there anything we can do?" He looked at me and said, "No. You've done too much already." It was all very touching and left an indelible mark in the life of this 20-year-old sailor.

Lan monopolized my time. When I showed up at the compartment where they were housed, she came over and stayed close to me. That was okay with me. I was helping these refugees who had just lost everything. I had purpose and felt we were making a positive difference in their lives.

Up until the time we disembarked them, we felt something bad might happen. The ships we escorted were constantly breaking down so we were sailing slowly. More than anything else I was pleased that the refugees were now going to be safe and taken care of.

Toward the end of the trip, we were up on deck and I wanted to remember her. I was sensitive that she was another man's wife. I took the first photograph of her alone. She looked very young and very pregnant. Then I took a second photo of her together with her mother. I asked her to take a photo of me in my most manly pose in front of one of the Hueys. I wrote my name and squadron information on the back of the photograph and she wrote her name on the back of her photograph. I kept the two of her and she kept the one of me. Over the years, I've kept the photos of her in one of my keepsake boxes but haven't been able to find that box. These pictures were our only link.

After the ship pulled into Guam, I went to the hospital because I wanted to see Lan and the baby. There she was with the new baby who was only days old. I spent a few minutes with her. I was not concerned as I saw everything was okay. We knew they were all going to be transported to the U.S., but Lan was very worried. And this was one subject Joseph [Pham] had mentioned to me when he was interpreting back on the ship. She didn't know what to do to find her husband. So before she left the ship, I got some information regarding who she should contact in the Red Cross to locate her husband. I think her husband was in Arkansas when she finally got to Camp Pendleton. I had given her instructions regarding how to go about submitting her name and his name to the Red Cross to identify the two as being married. This started the process for the Red Cross to reunite them.

I made contact with the crew association around 2003. I had swapped sea stories with Bon [James Bongaard] about my Vietnamese friend and her child [Tien Kirk] named after the ship. Some time in 2005, I got a call from Bon. He said, "Don, I think you might be the one we're looking for."

"What are you talking about?" I asked. He then explained how they had located Lan. It seems that she had originally identified somebody else in the cruise book as being "her sailor." At the time she couldn't find her picture of me as it had been packed away. In the course of her conversations with the skipper and Bon, Bon realized that our stories matched.

He asked me a couple of questions and we communicated a few times via email. We came to the conclusion that I was Lan's sailor. I shared the information with my wife, Jackie. She was very supportive of me making contact with Lan. Bon gave me Lan's phone number and I called her. During that hour conversation, we shared some reminiscences and discovered that we were indeed the two people who had been looking for each other for the last 30 years. Soon after we spoke, we exchanged family photos and vital information.

I finally got to meet Lan at the *Kirk* Orlando reunion in 2005. I had just arrived and was in the hotel lobby with my wife waiting to check in. The skipper, XO, Bon, Lan, and her two kids — Tien and James — had all come out of the elevator and stopped in the lobby to discuss dinner plans. I had my back to the elevator and didn't see them. Jackie poked me and said, "There's Lan! There she is!"

Lan was just as beautiful as the last time I saw her — a little older, but just as beautiful. Tien, the *Kirk* daughter and namesake was there as well as her brother, James. When I walked over to Lan's group, she recognized me in an instant as our eyes met. I wish I had a picture of our meeting but no one thought about a camera. We hugged a lot and there were a lot of joyful tears among all present. It was a very emotional meeting.

Our families spent a lot of time together during that weekend. Both Tien and James are very attentive to their mother's needs and take very good care of her and their grandmother, Can. The only downside for me is that Lan's husband wasn't there. He died in 2001. I regret not having been able to meet and get to know him.

"All They Have Is Each Other"

Odette Willis joined the Navy Nurse Corps at age 19. "I remember calling my dad and saying, 'I'm joining the Navy. If you don't sign for me, I'm going to join the Navy anyway when I'm 21 so you might as well sign.'"

While at her first duty station, Naval Hospital Philadelphia, Lt.(j.g.) Willis was given 30 days' notice that she might be assigned temporary additional duty, location unknown. Shortly thereafter, she flew to Guam to help staff the Naval Hospital. South Vietnamese refugees were on their way.

We arrived in Guam about 3 o'clock in the morning and were taken to the hospital. At 4 o'clock the hospital supervisor said, "Okay, here's the situation. You are going to be working with Vietnamese people who are being brought in and need medical care. We have three shifts.

The day shift is 10 hours. The evening shift is 10 hours. The night shift is 8 hours." My specialty was medical-surgical so I ended up working on the acute care med surg unit.

The hospital had three units at the time. The communicable disease unit housed patients who had anything contagious, such as TB, dengue fever, malaria, typhoid, and typhus. We also had a basic medical-surgical ward and a pediatric unit. For the three months I was there, we had a total of 598 patients between the three units.

Ours was not the only medical facility on Guam. The hospital at Anderson Air Force Base took some of the load. Camp Asan was also opened, as well as clinics at what became known as "Tent City" at Orote Point.

Most of the refugees who arrived in Guam were those who had come aboard ships. Some had crowded onto tankers. When they opened the hatch of one of the tankers, I saw a sea of people. It looked just like someone had opened a can of worms with body after body tangled together. Some of these vessels had been at sea for 30 days before they got to Guam. The refugees were pulled from the ship's hold and taken to Tent City.

All patients who were dehydrated or ill and required hospitalization came through us. Among the first few people evacuated from South Vietnam were the wealthy. They had brought suitcases filled with money — not clothes, not food — but money. But most of our patients were peasants with very little or no education. Many were elderly. We saw everyone from newborns to people over 100. Based on interpreter reports, several of our patients were near or over 100 years old!

During my first night at the hospital, I put in IVs, inserted Foley catheters, put down nasogastric tubes. In fact, I learned more nursing skills the first night I was there than I had in the two years I was at Philadelphia. These people were in frightful condition. They were so dehydrated, we were hanging one IV an hour on some of them.

Many people arrived who had been separated from their families. Every person brought to a camp had his or her name listed in English, Vietnamese, Cambodian, Laotian, or Korean because all those nationalities were represented. Lists were printed every day and posted. People stood in front of those lists for hours reading the names to see if anybody was related to them. And if they were, officials set up a camp-to-camp transfer.

I witnessed many reunions. In my journal I wrote about two old women in their late 60s. "They were walking slowly arm in arm up and down the ward. They help each other in and out of bed and tend to each other's needs. Their families, lost in the shuffle of the evacuation and lost in the shuffle of the refugee camps, are gone. And now all they have is each other."

Most of them were scared to death because they couldn't understand us and weren't sure where they were. All of a sudden they had been uprooted. Now they were in an environment with electric lights, flush toilets, flowing water, and machines they'd never seen before, especially if they had lived in the jungle. Once they got used to us or as they talked to each other over time, they began to understand what was going on and what we were going to do for them. And they appreciated it.

They were scared for another reason. Our hospital was on a hill overlooking Camp Asan and Agaña, which was the capital city and also where the main airport was. Every time a plane landed or took off, it came over the hospital and those people would scatter. They often ended up underneath the beds huddling and scared to death because this was a sound they knew. When a plane came over, it meant a bomb was about to drop on them.

We fed them rice and basic foods for the longest time. If we fed them anything they weren't used to, they ended up with nausea, vomiting, and diarrhea.

A few young teenagers were already in the hospital when I first arrived. One was about 16 years old. She had worms that had actually grown in her lungs, and had been given de-worming medication. Whenever she began coughing, you had to grab a pair of gloves and run to help her. A worm was coming up and it was necessary to help pull it out before she choked to death.

A 14-year-old boy had reached Guam aboard one of the U.S. ships that had plucked some of the refugees from a small boat. While still at sea and just before they arrived, the boy had a seizure. They brought him to the hospital and he was placed on a respirator and completely monitored. We took care of him for about two weeks but he didn't make it.

Before the child died, his father, a wealthy businessman from Saigon, had shaved his long, straight, shiny hair off as a sacrificial offering for the life of his son. His wife and daughter had thrown themselves onto the floor of the hospital in hysterical tears. The patients outside the room sat quietly, stone-faced. Some were crying.

On the opposite page of my journal was a letter written by the father in English. I'll read the letter.

> Dear friends and employees of the U.S. Naval Hospital Guam. Allow me to introduce myself: Mr. Huong Van Chi. My wife Li Tai Pu and my daughter from Saigon.
>
> My son Huong Van Minh just passed away last night at the Naval Hospital in Guam after an illness of more than one week. I want to take this occasion to express my deepest appreciation to the employees of the hospital, especially the doctors and nurses and corpsmen for their constant day and night care and their concern for my son. It has been beyond my imagination to see this, especially on the part of the doctors and other medical personnel. I just want to reveal my deepest thanks for your help at a time when we are at our lowest point as refugees fleeing from the communists who took our country regardless of our wishes. Respectfully,
>
> Huong Van Chi and family

Another image stands out in my mind. As we began winding down, those OB patients who had delivered their babies were brought to our unit for care after delivery. I tried to teach a mother–newborn baby class through an interpreter. No one had ever tried to teach them how to take care of their kids. It was something that came natural to them. I had tried to teach them how to bathe their babies, how to feed them, and procedures like that. They laughed and laughed.

One patient had delivered her seventh boy and another her sixth girl. They were all name-tagged as was our custom. Just as we were discharging one of the families, we realized that the mother did not have the right baby. We couldn't figure it out so we took the baby back to the nursery. We finally determined that they had the wrong baby. The mother who had given birth to the boy had the girl. The mother with all the girls had the boy. We swapped babies and made sure everything was correct.

When we were again about to discharge the mother, the mother with the girls again had the boy. An interpreter told us what was going on. Both mothers had all the same sex children. They didn't want the same sex so they simply swapped them. In their country that would have been perfectly okay. The one who had the boys didn't need any more boys to take care of the parents when they grew old. But the one with the girls needed a boy to have a man in the family when the parents got old.

Because the babies were technically born in the United States, we could not allow them to just swap babies so we kept them an extra day and went through a complete adoption process so they could take each other's babies home.

Many years later, I try to share my experiences because it was one of the most rewarding experiences of my life. Not only did I learn far more nursing than I ever imagined, but helping people who wouldn't be helped otherwise was a superb experience. It was hard work and long hours in wretched conditions but it was worth it.

Confronting War's Darker Side

Lt. (j.g.) Linda Daehn was new to the Navy. As a staff nurse she worked the surgical ward at Naval Hospital Camp Pendleton. Preparing to transfer to the hospital's surgical ICU, her supervi-

sor suddenly told her those plans were on hold. "She asked me to set up a ward from scratch for refugees who were going to be arriving any day. I was the division officer for the ward in charge of the unit." It was spring 1975.

We had moved our surgical ward from the old building to the second floor of the new hospital [Camp Pendleton]. Because some empty wards were available at the time, we went to work straightening up one of them. We made beds and tried to acquire some basic supplies. Within a few days, patients began arriving. It began with under 10 patients, but very quickly we were filled to the gills. To staff the new ward, some personnel were pulled from the rest of the hospital and others were assigned temporary additional duty. Very quickly this space had been turned into an infectious disease ward.

As I recall, the patients were very poor. Many had tuberculosis. Their chest x-rays were almost white from disease. Of course, the sputum had TB in it so we had to teach them about Kleenexes and not to spit on the floor. Many of the patients were pretty gaunt and weren't well nourished. Then a measles outbreak occurred out at the camp which was in the middle of the base. Although clinic-sick call services were available, we also hospitalized a few of those patients.

To treat the TB, we administered isoniazid pills and gave injections of streptomycin daily. We lined these folks up at 6 in the morning and had them inhale medication that would make them cough. Then we collected sputum samples. When those samples came back negative, we could release them from the hospital and, hopefully, they would continue to take their medications.

Some of the patients improved, but all we could do with those who had terrible cases of TB was to try keeping them from spreading it to others. When someone has had most of his lungs taken over by that disease, it's pretty hard to see a lot of improvement.

There was a vast age difference between the youngest and oldest patients. One patient was about 102 years old. Another was a little 12-day-old baby with the measles.

One patient we treated early on was a fellow in his late 20s with some kind of kidney disease. Because he spoke English, he became our main interpreter. Although other interpreters were in the building, often it was just easier to ask him to help. He was a big boon for us.

Another patient sticks in my mind. I don't recall why he was brought to the ward, but he was very depressed. At that time some of the precautions we now have in our hospital wards were not in place. One of the treatment room was unlocked. It contained a cart with a variety of supplies which included a bottle of acetone with a skull and crossbones label. Somehow the patient got his hands on it and tried to commit suicide by drinking it. We then transferred him down to our psych ward but he managed to hang himself using some of the curtains. His wife, who spoke no English, was devastated by her husband's suicide.

One lady of about 80 had somehow become separated from her family in the evacuation and we ended up placing her in a nursing home in Oregon. Many families were split up. A lot of tragic stories unfolded among those individuals.

People who had experienced many hardships in their lives—and endured—figured they could get through this ordeal, too. Family members who were housed in the camp visited the patients. They arrived by the bus-load. We never knew how many people we would have to feed for lunch but we always managed to feed everybody. The visitors also used our showers, which was a luxury for them.

I was so naive at that time. I had gone to college in the era of protests against the war in Vietnam and knew what was going on over there. I never felt guilt, but I was very sad for some of these Vietnamese patients who knew they were never, ever going to go home. They had left everything they had and now they were in a strange country. I was very glad to help them because they were so needy. But I also wondered about the transition they would have to make and how that would go for them.

Epilogue:
The Journey Back

The Vietnam War took a heavy toll in lives and treasure. Tallying that cost was straightforward. More difficult to measure was the lasting impact on the war's survivors. During the 30 plus years since the fall of Saigon, some veterans still find Vietnam part of their everyday lives — "a ghost that never leaves," as one former hospital corpsman put it. Moreover, the current conflicts in Iraq and Afghanistan have triggered painful psychological responses in those who thought Vietnam had long been laid to rest. Sleeplessness and anxiety affect some; survivor's guilt and profound sadness haunt others.

In Vietnam, the role of warrior and healer often became indistinguishable. Men trained to preserve life were compelled to take up arms and kill an enemy who specifically targeted them — because they were corpsmen. Circumstances demanded this bloodshed, even though their creed dictated non-combatant status. More than a few veterans still struggle with that reality.

Those who worked in hospitals or aboard the two hospital ships witnessed war's everyday results — death, mangled young bodies, and intangible psychological trauma. Triage officers, forced to "play God," decided who would live or die. Despite heroic efforts, surgeons would lose a 20-year-old Marine on the table as 15 more of his hideously wounded comrades awaited their turn. But there was no time for grieving. That would come later. Nurses, often the same age as their patients, fought to maintain their composure. "Losing it," while tenderly caring for these young men, was not an option. The tears were put on hold.

Having conducted more than 100 interviews with Navy medical personnel and their patients, I learned what Vietnam still means for them. I ended each interview by asking the same question: "Do you still think about Vietnam?" Their answers provide an eloquent and poignant conclusion.

Darby Reynolds [Nurse]

When I got home there was no reception. There was nothing negative. Just nothing. It was like coming back from a trip and that was it. It took awhile to adjust. Certain sounds would trigger responses, such as when a car backfired. It could be perfectly quiet then I would hear a noise, and I would be off the chair and ready to dive somewhere quick. I don't think anyone came back from Vietnam without having some difficult times. It is a very trying time for me around Christmas because of everything that had happened. I would just as soon avoid these memories if I could.

I saw so much death so soon — young people. If you see a car accident or you know an older person is dying who has lived a long life, you can accept that. But when I saw all those young men coming in and dying, it took its toll on me.

317

James Maddox [Hospital corpsman]

It was a quiet homecoming. I arrived home late at night, alone, only to learn the bad news that my mother was sick and in the hospital with cancer, which she eventually died from. They didn't want me to worry about her while I was in Nam so they never told me when I was over there. It was a real shock to find out that night.

I recall talking to my father that night in the kitchen about how I left that wounded Marine. It really bothered me and still does. He told me, "Son, we make a lot of promises to God at the time. If we get out of a mess, we promise to do this or that. But we don't fulfill those promises as we get safe and grow older."

Even though my dad and I ended up not getting along for years after Vietnam, what he told me that night has stuck with me. Other memories from Vietnam have also remained with me. I still recall a young Chicano kid. When I was back from the field at the battalion aid station, one of my jobs as a corpsman was to decide which wounded were healed and capable enough to go back to their unit in the field. This kid was really begging me not to send him back but I had to.

A little later I learned a unit had been hit out in the A Shau Valley. I accompanied the chaplain to Charlie Med and saw the dead in body bags. One of them was the Chicano kid. Just a few days earlier he was alive pleading with me not to send him back to the field.

So I came home with some guilt — and the guilt seemed to harden into place later. I was so ecstatic about being home that I put those memories out of my mind for a time but the psychological problems came later. I had recurring nightmares. I would be extremely anxious both in the dreams and when I awoke. I had those dreams for years.

Certain sights and sounds would set me off. Blinking plane lights at night were upsetting. The sound of a car door closing in the distance is similar to a mortar hitting. I developed some phobias, and I was left with a general insecurity about being safe.

I've gone to counseling through the VA and saw a counselor once a month. When I lived in California in 1987, I even went to a meeting called the "Young Vets Program." I went through a lot of that so-called "tough love" therapy, which was "in" at that time. I've had my problems with anxiousness and depression. On the whole, I'm doing pretty good now — and real good at times. But I still have my ups and downs.

Mary Lee Sulkowski [Nurse]

My tears come as a surprise even though a lot of the memories are gone. So much is blurred, and I tend to remember just some of the happier moments. But those of us who worked in the medical profession have a legacy of sadness that stays with us and it becomes part of us. I think that's where the tears come from. War is just very sad and it profoundly affects people. What stays with me are the patients I've treated as a psych nurse since being with the VA. I've worked with the post-traumatic stress disorder that many of those men still have 35 years after Vietnam.

George Harris [Medical Service Corps officer]

When I think about Vietnam, I try to remember the good parts. I had some good times, too. But what has stayed with me all these years are the sights and sounds associated with the wounded, the dying, the dead, and then the smells associated with all the injuries and death. I can remember the smell of blood, or the smell of someone's body being opened because you opened it or because it was opened as a result of a wound. I can remember the smell of a body that was blown up. I can still smell burned flesh. It has been 38 years since I was in Vietnam, and those odors have never gone away. I've been to the Wall twice since it was put up, once because I got dragged there. I just can't go. It's too personal. I can see those guys. Even though I didn't know them, I can see them. I know who they are.

James Ryskamp [Physician]

I dream about Vietnam maybe once a month. In the dream, I'm back in-country. I wake up in the morning and say to my wife, "I was in Vietnam." And it's not like today. It's like it was back then. It's funny how those memories come back.

James Finnegan [Physician]

I don't have nightmares in the sense that I lie awake at night thinking horrible thoughts about something that happened in Vietnam. I do have recollections which recur frequently that I'll never stop thinking about. But I'm mentally healthy enough and secure enough in who I am to recognize them for what they are — memories that I'll just never get rid of. Hardly a week goes by when I don't have some reminder of what I did.

Long ago every surgery textbook started with a chapter on military history. The opening chapter of one of them had a quote at the top: "The only victor in war is the surgeon." Based on my experience in the last 35 years of medicine, this statement is absolutely and unequivocally true. I came back from Vietnam with a new professional credential. I now carry the label "Vietnam Combat Surgeon" for the rest of my professional life. To this day, I can walk into a room and someone will say, "Jim was a surgeon in Vietnam."

Richard Thacker [Hospital corpsman]

I spent 22 years in the Navy. Toward the end of my career, I started having some memory situations about the war and some issues I had to deal with — post traumatic stress conditions. I never met a man who went to Vietnam and saw combat who hasn't dealt with issues after that. They didn't know anything about post-traumatic stress at the time. Now they know everything in the world about it and are able to deal with it. And I'm glad. In a way, it's sad I didn't get that initial de-programming and treatment which would have helped me. I don't blame the military; they did their best. But they learned from us. Now the young men and women who experience combat are a lot better off when they come home. If de-programming isn't done, the stress stays inside and one day it will find different ways of coming out. And it can happen 20 or 30 years later like it did with me.

The stress comes out in bad dreams and hyper awareness of my surroundings. Different smells would set off memories. Diesel fumes were the biggest triggers of all. The pop, pop, pop of a Huey flying overhead would bring back memories. But I worked my way out of all that. I think we all had to deal with it in our own way.

Michael Downs [Marine Corps officer]

I don't think much about Vietnam anymore unless young Marines of today want to talk about it or places like Fallujah [Iraq] are in the news. That battle is compared to the Hue City fight. I've talked to guys who were over in Fallujah, and what needs to be understood is that no two experiences are ever alike. The two cities are different and the enemy is different. But it's interesting to compare and contrast.

I'm very fortunate in the sense that I've never lost a wink of sleep because of any of my experiences in Vietnam. The constitution the Lord provided me is such that I don't labor over what could have been. I always did the best I could and couldn't have done any better. So there's no value in second-guessing and I don't do it.

Alan Kent [Hospital corpsman]

The adjustment to coming home was a bitch. Here you are in Vietnam where everything was trying to kill you—from the populace to the animals to the environment. Then, all of a sudden, you come out of that and are put into a completely different environment where you're supposed to react in a more socially acceptable way. It's very difficult to separate yourself so immediately. How can you sleep in a bed? How can you sleep without your weapon next to you? The readjustment was tremendous.

When I came back home to Hancock, Michigan, I couldn't sleep in my regular bed. We had a basement and I slept there for a time. My mother said, "Forget about all the stuff that happened. You're home now. Finish college. Do this. Do that." This was the way the world expected people to react and it's not so easy when you've been in ongoing trauma for 11 months—a constant physical and emotional bombardment. I remember walking down a hometown street with a friend of mine and someone behind me clapped his hands. Well, it sounded just like an AK-47 and I was down on the street. I was so bloody embarrassed it was unbelievable!

Immediately after I got back, I thought about Vietnam all the time. It was constantly in my dreams because my biggest fear was going back and getting killed. I really don't think about it too much anymore. Let me put it this way. I had a lot of issues, including survivor guilt. I tried to apply coping mechanisms I used when I was in combat. Well, it doesn't work in a socially refined environment. I eventually had to say, "I really have to straighten out these issues." And with the help of some very smart psychologists—friends of mine—we were able to put a group together and resolve these issues.

I had never been married and never thought I deserved to have children. I had a real problem with responsibility after the war due to all the burdens I had to shoulder when I was in Vietnam.

Resolving all this didn't happen until 1985. Once I did it then I was okay with myself and accepted myself as being okay. I'm not a coward for living and being alive and having survived. I realized I deserved to be loved and I deserved to have a family. I got married to the most wonderful lady in 1989 and we've got two kids, a son, 14, and a daughter, 12. That's the unfortunate part about it because they are the focus of our lives and right now I'm looking into my longevity, which is in question because of respiratory cancer. I've been through this before. It's all a plus. I most likely should have been blown away 38 years ago.

William Gerrard [Hospital corpsman]

Vietnam is a ghost that never leaves. It was part of my life for 365 days and some of what happened was mind-boggling. I'm still adjusting to it. That's the one place where the military truly screwed up. The biggest mistake the military made was getting us home to our families. How do you tell your family about someone who was killed next to you? You could talk about what happened with someone you had shared the experience with. But you couldn't tell your brother, your sister, your mom, or your dad about those incidents.

So all of it got buried, never got ventilated, and a lot of it is still there. Right after I opened my business, I found a website about Khe Sanh. I visit that website almost daily and read the notes I post there myself.

Marie Joan Brouillette [Nurse]

For a long time after I got back from Vietnam, I remember being very sensitive to loud noises like the backfire of a car. I'd have a tendency to dive under my desk. To this day, I'm still a little jittery when I hear an unexpected noise.

When I remember Vietnam, I think of all the lost lives. It's sad. I don't think Vietnam ever left me. Shortly after I retired, someone from a TV station called and wanted to discuss Vietnam. I recall that I was very short with her. I said, "I just can't turn that on and off so easily." I just didn't want to deal with it. It was still pretty raw for me and never far away.

Gerald Moss [Physician]

I think about Vietnam all the time. I have a little talk I put together for students entitled "Vietnam Recalled." I take them through the context and the time — the Berry Plan and the pivotal phone call I got from Charlie Huggins asking me if I was interested in an adventure. And that's exactly what it was. The result was that it affected the rest of my professional life. I'm still interested now — almost 40 years later — in precisely what I was interested in during my time in Vietnam — taking care of Marines. You never know where life is going to take you.

Juel Loughney [Nurse]

When we got home from Vietnam, we got a big greeting from our families but that was about it. I was home only a couple of days when my sister-in-law and I went out shopping in our little town of Pittston, Pennsylvania. I looked around and everyone was having such a wonderful time. I wanted to scream at them: "Why are you enjoying yourselves when we have kids dying right now in Vietnam?" It is hard to get used to the fact that people didn't know what was happening on the other side of the world. But I guess I feel the same way today.

Frances Shea Buckley [Nurse]

After I got back, recalling these events made me so angry. I knew that if I didn't see somebody, I'd lose my temper, and I couldn't afford to do that. I went to a civilian therapist. In therapy, she said, "You are not angry; you're furious." When I told her what had made me so angry, she said I also had some problems with Vietnam which I needed to talk about. And so I did. I also learned that what was important then was no longer important now.

My anxiety level also changed. I wouldn't get as stressed out about certain situations as I might have prior to going to Vietnam. While in Vietnam you had to get into an acceptance mode. The ability to work together with people was very important. You had to get along with everyone because you were living on the same ship for 365 days — a reality that made a difference. It did change my life.

After Vietnam I went to Boston where I taught nurses OR procedure. I soon had to get out of it, not because of the nurses but because of the doctors. These guys hadn't been in a combat situation. Nevertheless, they would be very demanding. They would say, "We've got an emergency." They had never experienced what had been an emergency to us in Vietnam. What might have seemed an emergency to them, we wouldn't have taken out of a dressing room. Our "emergency" would have been taken to a little aid station, had his wound debrided, and that would have been it.

I had a Vietnam problem. I denied it but I think I had a problem. None of us ever talked about it. About a dozen of us who had been in Vietnam together had never said that anything bothered us. That was not good but that's the way it was. We do now. If I couldn't say I had a hard time, how could I expect young kids to say it? Recently I spoke to a group coming back from Camp Pendleton. I did an exercise with them. Based on that, the nurse in charge told me they were making arrangements to ensure that those who wanted to could talk to a therapist. You just can't bury those experiences. It comes out some place.

Michael Holladay [Marine Corps officer and patient]

When I was on active duty, I actually thought about the combat I'd experienced. And when it was necessary to use that experience as lessons learned, I tried to keep it in that context. Since I have retired, I have had more time to think and reflect. And since the U.S. went into Iraq, I think a lot about it. I've probably had more sleepless nights, more nights lying awake trying to go to sleep, or just waking up in the middle of the night. Or out of the blue, a memory will come back. I find it occurring more and more.

It's not the memories of combat that give me the most trouble. It's the time I spent in the hospital. I will never forget the sights and sounds from the moment I was medevaced until I was released. Some of those memories are at the top of the scale in humor and loving kindness. Many others are at the bottom.

Doc Felle, my corpsman from Vietnam, and I communicate regularly. Three or four of my contemporaries who have retired are now discovering they have the PTSD syndrome. I think anyone in the world who has ever been in combat has something on that laundry list.

William Barber [Hospital corpsman]

When I returned from Vietnam I couldn't sleep very deeply. I had a short temper and a chip on my shoulder. I wouldn't let anyone come up behind me, and I resented those who hadn't gone to Vietnam. I later learned it didn't matter how I felt or what I said so I just withdrew into myself.

John Higgins [Hospital corpsman]

I knew all along that I had Vietnam problems. I'd drink every night until I passed out. I did that for a lot of years until about 1997. Then I realized it was killing me. I also found myself sitting on my bed with a shotgun one day and knew that this was not gonna work. That's when I went to the VA.

The VA doctors put me on an antidepressant right away. I quit drinking. The antidepressant helped me sleep at night so I didn't need the alcohol anymore. I went on a monthly basis to visit with a social worker. The psychiatrist who saw me originally transferred to another VA Hospital out in Arizona. Then the VA eliminated some staff at the hospital and I went for a time without a psychiatrist. I eventually got a new psychiatrist and a new case worker. I go on a monthly basis to see the case worker, and I see the psychiatrist every three or four months.

I can't help it. Vietnam is a daily thought in my head. My flashback can consist of a smell and what that scent came from. The smell is burned flesh, blood, or the rotten tobacco the Vietnamese smoked in those villages. I can smell it right now. It's amazing. If I'm cutting some meat and I get some blood on my hands, that sight and odor can trigger the flashback. I can remember days on end when I looked at my hands, and I would have dried blood around the rims of my fingernails and on the back of my hands. It was dried blood from the Marines I'd worked on. And I didn't have any way to wash my hands. After a while I didn't care anymore. It just became a way of life.

Vietnam influences my life every day. I have a short fuse. The trigger could be something minor and I'll blow up. But if you leave me alone, 10 or 15 minutes later, I'll calm down. My wife has learned over the years what not to do. You don't get into an argument with me. If I scream and holler, get out of the room. Ignore me and go away. There's a sad legacy of what it has done to my children. I have three daughters and I can see my own behavior in all three, particularly in my middle daughter. I'm the most dominant personality in the house and they grew up around that kind of personality. I feel bad about it but I can't go back and change it. All I can do is understand what they're going through.

I don't go to movies because I don't like sitting in a room full of people. I'm fairly isolated. I don't go out and socialize with people. I stick around my house for the most part. I also spend time working in my yard and I do crafts. I pretty much live in my basement. I sleep down there; I have my TV down there. My wife, Beverly, says that's my bunker.

It's good therapy for me just to get it out. It helps to talk about it. It's never going to cure anything. No one is ever going to wave a magic wand over me and make Vietnam go away.

Bob Ingraham [Hospital corpsman and patient]

My wife and I became Canadian citizens in 2003. We would have done so sooner, but my ultra-patriotic mother-in-law, a member of the DAR [Daughters of the American Revolution], might have had a stroke! We decided to become Canadians after both of Susan's parents had died. My father was already dead, and while my mother did not applaud our action, she understood.

Not a day goes by that I don't think about my experiences in Vietnam, but I don't often dwell on them. I've had some psychological difficulty. I'm hyper-alert and cannot easily relax. It's as if I'm always on watch. I don't readily trust people and I don't trust governments or politicians at all. I'm afraid I have a fairly black outlook on life. I've never been officially diagnosed with PTSD, but I exhibit most of the symptoms. However, for a long time—18 years in fact—I lived a fiction that said I hadn't been affected in the least by what I saw and did in Vietnam. I held that notion because I was "in-country" for only 37 days, not counting my time on the *Repose* and at the hospital in Danang. I could not possibly have been traumatized psychologically.

In the mid–1980s, I began suffering serious insomnia and depression. My doctor suggested that I attend a "Come Alive" seminar at The Haven, a personal development center on Gabriola Island, British Columbia. To this day I don't know how it came about, but during a late-night talk with a counselor, I had a classic flashback of an incident that left me grief-stricken. It was a shattering experience. That night I learned that it was not only my body that had been traumatized by Vietnam. In subsequent months I had two more flashbacks that stunned me with their power. I had not realized it before, but part of me—a part deep within my subconscious—had never left Vietnam at all.

It took several years of counseling before I was able to cope with the worst of the demons. That finally came about because of a counselor who was adept at a new therapy at that time, EMDR [Eye Movement Desensitization and Reorganization]. Because of EMDR, certain memories of especially traumatic events no longer have the power to move me to tears. I have clear memories of the events themselves, but for the most part it's as if I am watching them as a detached observer and not as a participant.

Many people assume that I would want to forget everything about my experiences in Vietnam, but that's not the case. A complete person is a collection of all the incidents that have occurred in his life, both the good and the bad. I can no more forget Vietnam than I can forget how to breathe or blink.

Margaret Crowe [Nurse]

I think about that time but not in a bad way. Several years ago, at one of our nursing meetings, I was asked to come as a Navy representative. An Army nurse and an Air Force nurse also attended. Their experiences were very different. When it was my turn, my take on the war was unlike theirs. I really enjoyed that time because it was a special time. I don't think I was a hero. It was a time that I just did what I was supposed to be doing.

There was not much room for discussion during my era. You just did it. You didn't say, "I don't believe I like that option" or "I don't want to do that." You did what you were supposed to do. We knew what the procedure was and we did it.

No one was saying, "You girls are great. You're doing a wonderful job." That was never a part of it. So, as I said, I don't think of myself as a hero.

I often wonder what happened to our patients. When the memorial to the Vietnam nurses in Washington was dedicated several years ago [11 November 1993], some of us nurses went. I had no notion how that occasion would be. In fact, a group of us who had been at the Naval Hospital in Guam were going to meet and just have a good time. I was really awestruck by what was going on. Many patients were at that memorial looking for their nurse, and some nurses were looking for their patients. I was surprised at the impact we all had on these men. I hadn't realized that we mattered as much as we did.

William Gondring [Physician]

I knew I had to go back to Vietnam. I wanted to set up a program through the Vietnam Veterans of America. We would go back to Rach Gia and provide some kind of support to our colleagues who were less fortunate. I made a presentation to our Vietnam Veterans of America chapter in St. Joseph [Missouri]. I then made a presentation to the state chapter to enlist its support. Some people started crying, some began yelling, some said that all the Vietnamese ever did was to send our boys back in boxes. I knew the situation wasn't going well when my Vietnamese physician colleague, who was also at this meeting, began crying. I just couldn't believe that some people hadn't found closure with the past and gone on with the next part of their lives.

I was selected to be one of the international fellows of AOFAS, the American Orthopedic Foot and Ankle Society. We set up a hospital at the Orthopedic Rehabilitation Institute in Vinh and took care of cases, both children and adults. These patient cases were not necessarily related to the war. Vinh is significant because this was the port where the PT boats that attacked the *Maddox* came from in early August 1964. The city was completely destroyed by American naval air during the war.

We also took care of Agent Orange cases. We knew it was Agent Orange because one of that chemical's ingredients, dioxin, causes chromosomal aberrations. Normally, we never see patients with no arms, no elbows, no shoulder joints.

I also treated polio and post-polio cases, congenital feet, and even a pit viper case. At Vinh I met an NVK [North Vietnamese] surgeon who had fought in the war. We operated together as colleagues at the institute and went out and drank together. Occasionally we would go to dinner with the entire hospital — nurses, anesthesiologists, anesthetists, scrub techs, surgeons, and the hospital administrator. The interchange and fellowship were wonderful.

This experience was an awakening for me. I was just a colleague and a comrade. We had similar experiences, only on opposite sides. Here's what my Vietnamese friend said: "That is the past. This is the future." That says it all.

William Mahaffey [Physician]

Our generation returning home in late 1966 didn't face quite the traumatic reception that the guys faced three and four years later. We got the "It's nice to have you back" comment. We didn't see any of the hostility. The anti-war feelings were not high when we returned.

After I left the Navy, I used my GI Bill to take some classes, one of which required a field trip involving history. So I chose to take a field trip and study the history of religion in Vietnam. I went back with a group of about six or eight people. The tour was headed by an activist priest who at one time had chained himself to the gates of the embassy in Saigon, as they called Ho Chi Minh City then. He was quite an anti-war activist but was a great guide. We had a fine tour.

It was good to get back to Vietnam. I didn't know what the word "closure" meant prior to that trip. At that time — 1992 or 1993 — Westerners were still very rare on the streets of Saigon. People came up to us and said, "Where you from?" The people still loved us even though the government up north was still at odds with our government.

The best I can say is that the trip represented closure, and I hadn't accomplished closure yet with Vietnam. I still have resentment that so many of our young people were killed in Vietnam. I cannot put those memories aside. But by going back, I realized that life goes on and that I could not live with those old memories forever. I just had to say, "Well, I've come back now. Vietnam is still here." It was time for me to return to living my life without feeling hostile toward the Vietnamese about what happened.

Raymond Felle [Hospital corpsman]

I wanted to return to Vietnam but on my own terms. I wanted to go back on top of Valentine's Ridge and then go where Will Williams was killed on April 30th, 1968. Those two places were very important to me.

I waited until relations with Vietnam got better and then went in June of 2003. It was a good feeling knowing that I was going to be able to accomplish what I wanted to. But I also wondered, "Can I handle this? Can I do this on my own?"

When we landed, I saw military people — both men and women — wearing North Vietnamese uniforms and with the characteristic stars on their helmets. But now they were smiling at me. It seemed surreal.

I rented a guide, a car, and a driver for the week. We found Valentine's Ridge and I hiked up to the very top where the battle was, took pictures, said prayers for the 10 Marines and the corpsman who were killed, and hiked back down. I was hoping to find old spent shells or some sign that we had been there but I found nothing. I cut a couple of trees at the top of the ridge and brought them home for walking sticks. I gave one to Col. Holladay and kept one.

We then went to Khe Sanh and I walked around taking pictures. I saw some barbed wire sticking out of the ground; I cut pieces of the wire to bring home. I also brought a bag of dirt from Khe Sanh, which a customs officer took away from me when I got back to the States. I told the customs person, "I know that bag of dirt doesn't mean a whole lot to you, but I was in Vietnam. I fought on this soil, and it means a lot to me and the people who were in my battalion."

"I'll autoclave it and mail it back to you," he said.

"Yeah, sure," I responded.

Two days later it arrived by FEDEX.

It's not really a closure. My experience in Vietnam will never close. But I was able to do what I wanted during the week I was there. I wanted to go to where Will was killed — and I did. I hiked out into the rice paddies, which are still there, and filmed the whole landscape. I said a prayer for him and brought back some dirt. And that's what was meaningful for me. It was my ability to go back on my terms. If any peace can be made, that's how I made it.

Robert Ingram [Hospital corpsman]

Twenty-five enlisted guys got back together in 2000. One of them said, "Let's go back to Nam." I wasn't too crazy about the idea. But they insisted that I go with them. Once again, you've got a team. Not much left of it, but you've got a team. I kept asking myself, "What in the hell are you doing? Why do you want to go back there?" Of course, my wife, my boss, and everybody else who knew me asked the same question: "Why do you want to do this?"

I told them I wasn't sure. "The guys want to go back and they want me to go with them. They've gotta have their corpsman, right?"

So, against my wife's wishes, 13 of us took off for Nam. We went back to most of the places where we had battles. We also left some money in the village where the big battle had taken place. It was a significant amount of money because we wanted to build a memorial for all who died there back on 28 March 1966 — the Marines, the villagers, and the North Vietnamese.

Psychologically, this is an important point. The NVA were just like we were. They were sent out there to do a job. They didn't have any personal contempt or hate for us. We didn't have any personal contempt or hate for them. It's an unforgettable experience to kill somebody, particularly when you realize that they're just doing their job like you are. But you don't have a choice.

So our memorial was very meaningful to us. We left $3,000 in cash. We had an agreement with the village chief, and we actually drew up a contract right there. The work was to be done by the village people. One of the NVA police who had accompanied us first said that he knew someone who could come in and build it. But we said no. That was not what we wanted. And since it was our money, we were calling the shots. We wanted the villagers to be able to build the memorial for several reasons. It was their village. A few people were there during the battle. They totally understood why we were building it because we discussed it with them. They were very passionate about what we were doing. And we wanted the people in the village to benefit from that work — in cash.

They have very little money — about $150 a year max income per family. So $3,000 is a lot of money. They bought and dragged the materials down from the mountains. Before they were through, they ran out of money and then put their own money into it. And they donated their labor.

Thirteen of us went back again the following year. This time we were able to get closer to the village than we had the previous year when we had hiked about eight or more miles to get there. We got within five miles of the village the second time. When we got halfway there, the villagers started coming out and then followed us. They saw these Marines coming down the trail and they just dropped everything. Everybody came out of the rice paddies.

It was kind of eerie. By the time we got to the village, we must have had 200 to 300 people around us. The little schoolhouse — also built with the money — was probably about 30 by 14 feet. They had made wooden desks and painted the plastered walls all different colors that you see in the Orient. They were very proud of that schoolhouse and so pleased that we had come back to see it. We had told them the year before that we were going to come back the following year on this same day — and we did. We then had a little service celebrating what they had done.

The memorial, about 50 feet behind the school, was in three sections. The center represented the village, and the villagers had carved in a huge stone in that center the names of the people they knew who had died that day. They had written something in English on the stone indicating that we were their liberators. The NVA didn't like that very much. On the other side, the villagers had made an inscription in Vietnamese which said something about men who fight in war not for personal gain but because they're fighting for their country. That addition made the NVA feel a little better.

It was a nice piece and we were very proud that it was there, not for our purposes but for everybody in the village. Those kids are going to hear that there was a war, that the Marines were not bad people, that the North Vietnamese were not bad people, and that the villagers just happened to be there. They needed to know it was important to pay respect to all who died there that day — on all sides.

I was very pleased to see they had actually built the memorial and that they had put themselves into it. I was also impressed when I learned they had completed it even after they had run out of money. And I was thrilled someone hadn't stolen the money and run off with it. I didn't expect to see the villagers with that much pride over the past, even though most of them were not there in 1966 and didn't know anything about the battle. It's like a history book for them.

The village chief at that time had a daughter who was going to college in Saigon. She was back in the village in 2001 when we came. She was going to be the teacher at the school. One of our interpreters came from that village as a child. He was only 22 years old. He wasn't there in 1966. In the bus on the way back he said, "You have no idea what you have done for this village. The possibility of these children ever having any education at all or having a desire to be educated is nil. You have created a situation where this may be one of the most educated villages in all of the Central Highlands area."

We've sent pencils and pens. One of the guys is married to a Vietnamese girl and she purchased books and sent them there for the school. We've gotten a lot of financial support from our group. Out of those 13 guys and a few others who wished to donate, we're talking $18,000 to $20,000 worth of materials that went to the village which was used for both the memorial and the school. They all felt good about it — and I felt good about it.

Roger Pittman [Hospital corpsman]

I went back to Vietnam in 1997 with a few of the Marines I knew from that era. Why had I gone? I didn't know the reason at the time, but it came to me gradually while I was there. During the trip, we sat around and talked. It started off with sea stories but eventually we talked about the inner thoughts we were having and what they meant.

We had been there a week or two, but as we went through the villages we'd fought in, we felt uneasy. Each of us wanted to have a weapon in our hand to get ready for the shit to go down. But it didn't. The peace was there.

We remembered an area — Mai Xa Chanh through Lam Xuan. Lam Xuan was hell. Above Lam Xuan about half a click [kilometer] was an abandoned little village called Nhi Ha. If you went to Nhi Ha in 1968, you were going to die. That was guaranteed.

It was now 1997. They bussed us in as far as we could go, then we hiked a short way into Nhi Ha. The village was still small but it had a little elementary school. Some kids were dismissed while we Americans were there. They came out of the schoolhouse onto a grassy little slope where we were eating our box lunches. Greg, one of the guys in our group, had a bottle of bubble soap. He stood upwind from these kids who ranged in age from about 5 through 12. They stood on that grassy slope while Greg blew bubbles across their faces. As they reached up and tried to grab the bubbles, they screamed with delight. Watching this, I realized the war was over.

APPENDIX 1: THE CAST

ALLAN ADEEB left active duty in 1969, joined the Navy Reserve, and continued to fly A-4s until he retired from the Reserve in 1976. He practices anesthesiology in Jacksonville, Florida.

JULIUS AMBERSON retired from the Navy in 1970 after a career that began as an enlisted radioman in World War I. He was a mining engineer after that war, and was active in prospecting, drilling oil wells, and designing power plants. He also practiced medicine for 15 years. During World War II, Amberson rejoined the Navy Reserve as a commander in the Medical Corps and served with epidemiology units in the Middle East, Africa, India, and the Mediterranean. After the war, he led a military medical expedition from Cairo to Capetown. He died in 1988.

DONALD BALLARD left the Navy in 1970 and joined the Army's Officer Candidate School program. He retired as a colonel in 2000, and now operates a cemetery and funeral business in Kansas City, Kansas. He is also a real estate developer and a residential and commercial landlord. He resides in Kansas City, Missouri, and remains active in the Medal of Honor Society.

WILLIAM BARBER stayed in the Navy Reserve until 1981, attended college, and earned a degree in management and a graduate degree in finance. He received a commission in the Medical Service Corps in 1981 and retired in 2005. He makes his home in Bastrop, Texas.

ROBERT BIRTCIL was released from active duty in 1970 but remained in the Navy Reserve, advancing to the rank of rear admiral and Deputy Chief of the Navy Dental Corps before retiring in 2000. For his Vietnam service, he was awarded the Bronze Star with Combat V, the Purple Heart, and the Vietnamese Cross of Gallantry with silver star. He owns and operates a hay and cattle ranch near Spokane, Washington.

STANLEY BLOUSTINE remained in the Navy Reserve after the war while practicing in a multi-specialty clinic in Illinois. After completing a residency in plastic surgery, he worked in that field, opened a private practice, and joined the Army Reserve. After an assignment at Fort Campbell, Kentucky, Col. Bloustine transferred to Madigan Army Medical Center at Fort Lewis, Washington. He served with the 14th Combat Support Hospital at Bagram Air Base, Afghanistan, then returned to Madigan. He retired in 2008 and lives in University Place, Washington.

MARIE JOAN BROUILLETTE, after her year in Vietnam, had several hospital assignments including Naval Hospitals Chelsea, Massachusetts, and Millington, Tennessee. After a 25-year Navy career, she retired in 1984 as Director of Nursing Services at Naval Hospital Camp Pendleton, California. Capt. Brouillette resides in Escondido, California.

FRANCES SHEA BUCKLEY, following her assignment aboard USS *Repose* (AH-16), reported to Naval Hospital Chelsea, Massachusetts, as an operating room instructor for nurses. She then served as Assistant and then Director of Nursing Services at the National Naval Medical Center Bethesda, Maryland. Her next assignment was as Director of Nursing Services at Naval Hospital San Diego, California. Promoted to rear admiral in 1979, she was selected as the ninth Director and 14th head of the Navy Nurse Corps. Rear Admiral Buckley retired in 1983 and currently lives in San Diego, California.

STEPHEN BURWINKEL retired in 1989 after a 30-year Navy career, and then worked for CHAMPUS and Humana. He retired "for good" in 1997, and makes his home in Pensacola, Florida.

JAMES CHAFFEE, after leaving Vietnam, taught first aid at the Officer Candidate School in Newport, Rhode Island, before being discharged in 1970. He attended college, obtained a mathematics degree, and then worked in research and development helping to perfect the Global Positioning System. He subsequently started his own company, which concentrated on missile and navigation research and development. He currently resides in Cedar Park, Texas.

ERNEST CHEATHAM retired as a lieutenant general in 1988 after serving more than 35 years in the Marine Corps. He lives in Virginia Beach, Virginia.

GEORGE RONALD CHRISTMAS received the Navy Cross for his actions at Hue. He retired from the Marine Corps in 1996 with the rank of lieutenant general, and now works for the Marine Corps Joint Forces Command. He is President of the Marine Corps Heritage Foundation, and makes his home in Stafford, Virginia.

H. PAUL CHURCHILL is a retired auto worker and resides in Port Huron, Michigan.

WINIFRED COPELAND was a member of the last surgical team to serve in the Mekong Delta town of Rach Gia. Her team was withdrawn in September 1967. She retired from the Navy as a captain in 1979, and lives in Oceanside, California.

ANNA CORCORAN retired as a commander in 1977 after 26 years. She divides her year between Cocoa Beach, Florida, and Marshfield, Massachusetts.

DONALD COX left the Navy in 1977. He worked as an electronics technician, attended school, worked for a helicopter manufacturer, and earned degrees in electronics technology, computer science, and software engineering at National University in California. He is currently a principal systems engineer at Raytheon Missile Systems in Tucson, Arizona.

MARGARET WILKINSON CROWE left active duty in 1970 and went into civilian nursing. She retired from the Navy Reserve in 2003, taught nursing at Roane State Community College in Knoxville, Tennessee, and retired in 2007. She lives in Knoxville.

LINDA DAEHN retired as a captain in 2003 after 30 years. She makes her home in Mount Pleasant, South Carolina.

HARRY DINSMORE, for his heroic action at NSA Danang, received the Navy Cross. He retired from the Navy in 1967, and practiced medicine in Punxsutawney, Pennsylvania, until retirement in 1991. He died in 2003.

THOMAS DOOLEY resigned from the Navy in 1956. By that time, he was already known to Americans from his best-selling *Deliver Us from Evil*, which was serialized in *Reader's Digest*. With proceeds from this book and supplies donated by pharmaceutical firms, he and three former Navy colleagues went to Laos, where they set up a small hospital at Nam Tha. Dooley turned this facility over to the Laotian government in 1957. He then lectured, traveled the fund-raising circuit, and made many TV appearances promoting his humanitarian efforts in Laos. Following publication of his second book, *The Edge of Tomorrow*, he and Washington physician, Peter Comanduras, founded MEDICO (Medical International Cooperation Organization). Dooley returned to Laos where he operated another small hospital until cancer forced him to return home for treatment. He died in 1961, one day shy of his 34th birthday.

MICHAEL DOWNS retired from the Marine Corps as a brigadier general in 1992 after 31 years of service. He is currently Director of the Personal and Family Readiness Division in Manpower and Reserve Affairs at Marine Corps Base, Quantico, Virginia. He was awarded the Silver Star for his heroic action at Hue.

HUGH DOYLE, after his assignment aboard *Kirk* (DE-1087), served as executive officer of USS *Fanning* (FF-1076) and retired from the Navy in 1987 with 20 years of service. As a civilian, he was a management consultant, worked as chief estimator and project director at the Derecktor Shipyard, and retired in 1993. He now lives in Middletown, Rhode Island.

DENNIS EARL retired in 1984 and now flies for the Navy as a contract pilot training weapons systems operators. He resides in Pensacola, Florida.

STEPHEN EDMONDSON returned from Vietnam and was assigned to Naval Hospital Chelsea, Massachusetts. He practiced psychiatry for 25 years in Atlanta, worked as a civilian psychiatrist at Fort Benning in the Georgia state hospital system, and now practices part-time in the Georgia prison system. He lives in Clayton, Georgia.

EDWARD FELDMAN was awarded the Silver Star for his heroic surgery removing live ordnance from a wounded Marine during the siege of Khe Sanh. He is an obstetrician-gynecologist practicing in Thousand Oaks, California, and is an advisor to the California Veterans Board.

RAYMOND FELLE left the Navy in 1970, returned to school for a degree, and was an ultrasound technician for 25 years. In retirement, he is battalion archivist for his old outfit — the 3rd Battalion, 9th Marines "finding people and collecting history." For his action in saving 2nd Lt. Michael Holladay, he was awarded the Bronze Star with Combat V. He resides in Portland, Oregon.

JACK FELLOWES taught leadership at the U.S. Naval Academy after he returned home, followed by a tour with the Bureau of Personnel. His last assignment was with the Disability Board at the National Naval Medical Center. He retired in 1986 and works as a liquor inspector for the City of Annapolis, Maryland.

JAMES FINNEGAN, after leaving the Navy, returned to the University of Pennsylvania to complete his surgical residency training. He then became an associate professor of surgery at the Medical College of Pennsylvania, and then a full professor in 1983. He continues to practice thoracic surgery at the Cooper University Hospital in Camden, New Jersey.

ROSARIO "RUSS" FISICHELLA, following his return from Vietnam, became Force Medical Officer of the Atlantic Fleet. He was also commanding officer of Naval Hospital Portsmouth, New Hampshire, and Deputy Director of the Naval Regional Medical Center, San Diego. He retired from the Navy in 1975. Back in civilian life, Dr. Fisichella worked in the health service of San Diego State University, and then practiced medicine in Poway, California, for 20 years. He is now retired and lives in San Diego, California.

PAUL FRIEDMAN, after recovering from his wound, was discharged from the Navy for a previous injury. He is active in the USS Forrestal Association and resides in Coral Springs, Florida.

PAUL GALANTI, following his return from captivity in North Vietnam, remained on active duty and became executive officer then commander of the Richmond recruiting district. He spent his last three years in the Navy at the U.S. Naval Academy as a battalion officer training midshipmen for leadership. He retired in 1982 with 20 years service. Galanti then worked for the Virginia Pharmaceutical Association and then as director of the Virginia Medical Society. Of his days as a POW he says: "Those guys I lived with in Hanoi are closer than any brothers. Our reunions are still the happiest things I go to. If I have to miss one, it depresses me incredibly because it's the only place I go where I don't hear anybody complaining about anything." He lives in Richmond, Virginia.

ALPHONSE GALLITANO served two years in the Navy and then practiced medicine in Waltham, Massachusetts. He also served as an assistant professor of surgery at Boston University before retiring in 2005. He makes his home in Lincoln, Massachusetts.

WILLIAM GAY, after recovering from his wounds, made an inter-service transfer to the Army. He retired after 21 years service and now works for Computer Sciences Corporation in Fairfax, Virginia.

WILLIAM GERRARD left the Navy in 1969 but returned to the Navy Reserve three years later. He retired from the Reserve in 1987 and now lives in Weatherford, Texas.

WILLIAM GONDRING, following his return from Vietnam, served another two years on active duty before joining the Reserve from which he retired in 1994 after 30 years. He now practices orthopedic surgery in St. Joseph, Missouri. "I have two significant remembrances in my office in honor of Advisory Team 54. One is a rifle I brought back and another is a VC flag."

SAMUEL HALPERN was discharged from the Navy in 1965, returned to the University of Oklahoma for a residency in internal medicine, followed by a year in nuclear medicine. He then practiced radiochemistry with the Veterans Administration in Los Angeles before moving to the University of California San Diego in 1970. He retired in 2006 and lives in San Diego.

MYRON HARRINGTON was awarded the Navy Cross for his actions at Hue. He retired from the Marine Corps in 1990 with the rank of colonel after a 30-year career. He retired as headmaster of Trident Academy in Mount Pleasant, South Carolina, in 2007, and resides in Charleston, South Carolina.

GEORGE HARRIS, following his return from Vietnam, became commanding officer of the 3rd Medical Battalion headquartered in Okinawa, had duty at Headquarters Marine Corps, the Health Sciences Education and Training Command, and the Naval School of Health Sciences. He then served as Executive Assistant to the Navy Surgeon General, and was commanding officer of the Naval School of Health Sciences before retiring in 1990 with 39 years of service. Harris then took the job of Vice President of Executive Affairs at the Uniformed Services University of the Health Sciences, retiring from that post in 1998. He now works as a hospice volunteer and lives in Manassas, Virginia.

BILL HENRY was medically retired from the Marine Corps after his treatment at Naval Hospital Millington, Tennessee. He then married a nurse he met there, returned to school, earned a master's degree, and spent 28 years as an employee of Mississippi State University. He retired in 1997 and now spends his time "chasing Mississippi State sports and fishing" near his home in Starkville, Mississippi.

JOHN HIGGINS was discharged from the Navy in 1970 and returned home to Lincoln, Nebraska. He joined the Nebraska National Guard in 1972 and was assigned to an air ambulance company, retiring from the Guard in 1993. As a civilian, he worked in a Lincoln hospital for several years assisting with autopsies. He then worked for 24 years at the University of Nebraska. His continuing battle with post-traumatic stress disorder ended that career in 2003, when he retired on a medical disability. He resides in Lincoln, Nebraska.

G. GUSTAVE HODGE, following his Vietnam tour, was assigned as battalion surgeon for Fleet Marine Force Atlantic. He left the Navy in 1968, and practices orthopedic surgery in Bellingham, Washington.

MICHAEL HOLLADAY, after recovering from his wounds, made the Marine Corps his career. He served another tour in Vietnam as a company commander, and retired with the rank of colonel after 28 years of active service. He lives in DeLand, Florida.

BOBBI HOVIS retired in 1967 with just over 20 years of Navy service. She resides in Annapolis, Maryland, and is the author of *Station Hospital Saigon: A Navy Nurse in Vietnam, 1963–1964*.

RANDY HUDSON was discharged from the Navy in 1976. He then attended nursing school and became a registered nurse. He is currently Director of Education at Southwest Regional Medical Complex in Lubbock, Texas.

ROBERT INGRAHAM, following his discharge from the Navy, received a journalism degree and moved to Canada where he worked for the Canadian Wildlife Federation in Ottawa. He taught in the public school system in Prince George, British Columbia, for 17 years, and then opened and operated a photography studio for 10 years before retiring in 2001. He lives in Vancouver, British Columbia.

ROBERT INGRAM is operations manager for Jacksonville Family Practice Associates in Jacksonville, Florida. He received the Medal of Honor in 1998, 32 years after he was first nominated for the nation's highest honor.

MIKI IWATA left USS *Sanctuary* (AH-17) in 1969, then was assigned as a coronary nurse to: Naval Hospitals Annapolis, Maryland; Chelsea, Massachusetts; and Charleston, South Carolina. After additional training, she became a nurse practitioner and subsequently worked at: Naval Hospital Memphis, Tennessee; Annapolis, Maryland; Orlando, Florida; Guantanamo Bay, Cuba; and Pensacola, Florida. She then received orders to USS *Yosemite* (AD-19). "I learned to be a Navy officer, not only a Navy Nurse Corps officer. I also managed to earn my surface warfare medical officer pin. That's a proud accomplishment." She retired in 1995 after a 29-year career, and lives in Orlando, Florida.

PAUL JACOBS retired from the Navy in 1984 after commanding three ships and serving as Director of Undersea Surveillance. He is Senior Vice President and Chief Financial Officer of Federal Resources Corporation in Fairfax, Virginia.

LEONARD JULIUS continued his Navy career after his *Oriskany* (CVA-34) assignment, retiring in 1978. He enrolled in college and then completed his degree before earning a master's degree and an MBA. After several positions as an administrator of a community mental health center and also a small free clinic in Morehead City, North Carolina, and as a senior purchasing agent for the state, he now works part-time and resides in Emerald Isle, North Carolina. "I'm still a retired naval officer. And my checks still say lieutenant commander, MSC, USN."

ALAN KENT was awarded the Bronze Star with Combat V for his action at Hue. He was discharged from the Navy in January 1969. After graduating from the University of Alabama, he received a master's degree specialty in surgery and urology from the University of Nebraska, and completed a residency as a physician assistant at Montefiore Hospital in New York City. Kent worked for many years at the Veterans Administration Hospital in Iron Mountain, Michigan. He died in 2008.

G. GARY KIRCHNER left the Navy in 1968 and practiced general surgery for 38 years. He served as Coroner of Lancaster County, Pennsylvania, from 2004 to 2007.

JUEL LOUGHNEY, after her Vietnam assignment, saw duty at the Naval Hospital and Hospital Corps School in San Diego, followed by tours of duty in the Philippines and graduate school at Fresno State University. Her service included: department head and interim Director of Nursing at Naval Hospital Long Beach, California; Director of Nursing Services at Naval Hospital Great Lakes, Illinois; Nurse Corps Career Plans Officer at the Bureau of Medicine and Surgery; Director of Nursing Services both at National Naval Medical Center and aboard USNS *Comfort* (T-AH 20 during Desert Shield/Storm; and Executive Officer, Naval Hospital Newport, Rhode Island. She retired in 1995 after 29 years active service and now lives in Virginia Beach, Virginia.

GEORGE LUCAS left the Navy in 1969 after a two-year tour and returned to his orthopedic practice. He resides in Wichita, Kansas.

ARTHUR MCFEE, after leaving *Repose* (AH-16), spent a year at Naval Hospital Charleston, South Carolina. He then left the Navy for the University of Texas Health Science Center in San Antonio, which had not yet been completed. "Twice in my life, I've had this unbelievable opportunity to build something from the ground up." He spent the rest of his career in San Antonio, retiring in 2001 with the title Professor Emeritus. He divides his time between homes in San Antonio, Texas, and Santa Fe, New Mexico.

JAMES MADDOX was awarded the Bronze Star with Combat V and the Purple Heart for his Vietnam service. Following discharge from the Navy, he returned to college and earned a bachelor's degree in art and a master's degree in Communications/Instructional Technologies. He then worked as a museum technician and a graphic artist for California State Parks and Recreation before moving to Pennsylvania. He continued his artwork, volunteered in a hospital emergency department, and taught art to pregnant teens in Harrisburg. Now semi-retired, he resides in Gibsonia, Pennsylvania.

WILLIAM MAHAFFEY returned from his Vietnam tour on New Year's Eve 1966, and resumed duty at Naval Hospital Portsmouth, Virginia. He then requested orders to Camp Pendleton so he could remain with the Marines. Following that tour, Dr. Mahaffey left the Navy after four and a half years of active duty. He practiced as a civilian for a short time, but rejoined the Navy and specialized in submarine and diving medicine, before earning a master's degree in public health. He retired in 1988 and lives in Upper Sandusky, Ohio.

ROBERT MITCHELL retired in 1980 but was retained on active duty to carry on his work with the repatriated POWs, the former Iran hostages, and the "Thousand Aviator Study." He again retired in 1991 after 45 years in uniform. Despite retired status, Dr. Mitchell maintains an office at the Naval Operational Medical Institute, where he continues with his life's work.

GERALD MOSS left Vietnam in 1966 and was assigned to the Naval Medical Research Institute in Bethesda, Maryland, where he was also in charge of the surgical research lab. He left the Navy in 1969 and became Chief of Surgery at Cook County Hospital where he established a frozen blood bank. "There were logistic and expense issues and so it was not a permanent enterprise," he recalls. He subsequently became head of surgery at Michael Reese Hospital in Chicago and professor at the University of Chicago. He retired as Dean of the University of Illinois Medical School in 2004, but continues as a consultant on a study comparing hemoglobin-based oxygen carriers to packed red cells.

DENNIS NOAH left the Navy in 1969, and then attended school part-time. After receiving a commercial pilot's license, he returned to school full-time, earning his bachelor's and two master's degrees. He is currently a vice president of Manufacturers and Traders Trust Company in Baltimore, Maryland. "I'm also a part-time professor and a licensed Coast Guard ship's master. I like to keep busy."

JOSEPH PHAM, following his escape from South Vietnam, eventually settled in the Pacific Northwest with his family. A certified court interpreter, he has worked in the Washington court system in King and Snohomish counties.

ROGDER PITTMAN, following his tour in Vietnam, returned to college, earned a degree in archaeology, and attended Duke University's physician assistant program. He currently works as a physician assistant in the emergency room at Natividad Medical Center, Salinas, California.

DANIEL REDMOND left the Navy in 1957 and practiced law in Washington, D.C., until his death in 2000.

A. DARBY REYNOLDS still had a whole career ahead of her after she returned from Vietnam with a Purple Heart. A snapshot from that time shows her receiving the award in her nurse's uniform. "When they told us we would be awarded the medal, they insisted that we wear our blues. But I felt we should be in our nurse's uniforms because that's what we were there for. So, they relented and that's how we received our Purple Hearts—in nurse's uniforms and caps." She retired from the Navy in 1988, and resides in Dover, New Hampshire.

JOSEPH RICCIARDI left the Navy in 1998 and joined an orthopedic practice in Berryville, Arkansas, run by his former commanding officer, Alice Martinson, one of the first female orthopedists in the Navy.

BILL ROGERS was discharged from the Marine Corps in 1970, returned home to Earle, Arkansas, and grows rice on the farm that has been in his family for 65 years.

JAMES RYSKAMP remained in the Navy for 15 years before resigning in 1971. He then joined the Navy Reserve and retired with the rank of captain in 1995. He is now part owner of a surgery outpatient center in Fresno, California, where he practices cosmetic surgery.

DAVID SCHWIRIAN was medically discharged from the Marine Corps in 1968. He is a field engineer employed with a manufacturer of drilling accessories for quarries and mines, and makes his home in Springdale, Arkansas.

FRANCES SHEA (See Frances Shea Buckley)

DENNIS SHEPARD, after his discharge from the Navy, went back to Southeast Asia as an employee of MEDICO. He served with Dr. Tom Dooley in Laos providing medical care to a rural population that had never seen modern medicine. He subsequently attended medical school, and now practices ophthalmology in Santa Maria, California.

JAMES SOLIDAY retired from the Navy in 1992 as a commander in the Medical Service Corps, having earned the Bronze Star with Combat V and the Purple Heart with gold star. He is currently commander of VFW Post 9044 in Big Run, Pennsylvania, and resides in Punxsutawney, Pennsylvania.

MARY LEE SULKOWSKI left the Navy but stayed in the health care profession, working for the Veterans Administration as a psychology nurse. She lives in Buffalo, New York.

DAVID TAFT left the Navy shortly after his return from Vietnam, but returned to active duty in 1989 and served during the 1990–1991 Gulf War. He received the Navy Cross for the heroic surgery he performed in Vietnam. He resides in Seattle, Washington.

BILL TERRY retired from the Navy in 1974 after a 20-year career. Afterward, he held a professorship at the University of North Carolina in maxillofacial surgery and was chairman of the Graduate Division in oral and maxillofacial surgery. He retired from that position in 1995, and now does consults, conducts seminars, and writes from his home in Chapel Hill, North Carolina.

RICHARD THACKER left the Navy after his return from Vietnam but reenlisted three years later. He retired as a chief hospital corpsman in 1989 and makes his home in Covington, Georgia.

JAMES THOMAS, after returning from Vietnam, served another year in the Navy at Naval Hospital Chelsea, Massachusetts. Of his Vietnam homecoming he recalls: "I was in uniform and hadn't been out of Vietnam a week. I was at the Los Angeles Airport thinking about going back home and wondering if I really wanted to do that. In the booth next to me people were talking: 'Did you see the gown she had on last night and how horrible it was?'

"I had all I could do to keep from standing up and shouting, "What in the hell is wrong with you people? Don't you realize what's going on somewhere on the other side of the world?"

Dr. Thomas is currently Program Director, Vascular Surgery, University of Kansas Medical Center in Kansas Citfy.

MYRON TONG is Director of Hepatology and Associate Director of the Liver Cancer Center at the UCLA School of Medicine and chief of the Liver Center at the Huntington Medical Research Institutes in Pasadena, California. He also maintains a private practice in Pasadena treating liver disease.

LAN TRAN resides in Long Beach, California, and works for the Social Security Administration.

FLORENCE ALWYN TWYMAN, after returning from Vietnam, served two years at Naval Hospital Bremerton, Washington. Her last assignment, before retiring in 1968, was as chief nurse at Naval Hospital Quantico, Virginia. She lives in Walnut Creek, California.

ROBERT VALERI served 23 years on active duty before retiring. He continues as Director of the Navy Blood Research Laboratory in Boston, Massachusetts, having already spent more than 45 unbroken years in the blood research field.

ROGER WARE, following his return from Vietnam, made a career in the Navy, serving as a flight corpsman, and then aboard several vessels before again being assigned as a flight corpsman with the 4th Marine Air Wing based in Aurora, Colorado. After another assignment aboard ship, he was accepted to the Navy's commissioned chief warrant officer physician assistant program. He served as a physician assistant aboard the aircraft carrier USS *Theodore Roosevelt* (CVN-71) and was aboard when that vessel participated in the first Persian Gulf War. His next and last assignment was as an instructor at Basic School in Quantico, Virginia. He retired in 1997, as the last commissioned warrant physician assistant in the Navy. He lives in Elkins, West Virginia, where he is also Senior Vice Commandant for the Marine Corps League.

WILLIAM WEISE received the Navy Cross and two Purple Hearts for his action in the Battle of Dai Do. He retired from the Marine Corps in 1982 as a brigadier general after 31 years of service, and resides in Alexandria, Virginia. He is currently working toward the installation of a monument to the 2nd Battalion, 4th Marines at the National Museum of the Marine Corps.

ODETTE WILLIS served 13 years on active duty in the Navy Reserve, and retired in 2003 with 32 years service. She teaches nursing at George Mason University in Fairfax, Virginia.

ALMON WILSON became Chief of Surgery at U.S. Naval Hospital, Yokosuka, Japan, following his tour in Vietnam. He had many other assignments, including personal physician to the Chairman of the Joint Chiefs of Staff, Commanding Officer, Naval Hospital Great Lakes, Illinois, Medical Officer of the Marine Corps, and Manager of the Fleet Hospital Project. The fleet hospitals that saw action during the Gulf War of 1990–1991 and the Iraq War of 2003 owed their existence to R.Adm. Wilson's vision and planning. He died in 2003.

USS *SANCTUARY* (AH-17), as with her sister ships of the *Haven* class, was built during World War II as a cargo vessel. After launching, she was converted and fitted out as a hospital ship. While en route to Japanese waters to participate in the invasion of Japan, the war ended and *Sanctuary* was diverted to the task of evacuating and treating liberated prisoners of war. Later the ship returned patients from overseas bases to the United States until June 1946. In August of that year, *Sanctuary* was decommissioned and placed in the Navy Reserve Fleet. Fifteen years later, the ship was stripped and transferred to the Maritime Commission Reserve Fleet.

In 1965, the Navy reacquired *Sanctuary*. After a total overhaul and modernization, the hospital ship was recommissioned in 1966 and headed for Vietnamese waters, where she supported operations in I Corps. One year later, the ship had admitted 5,354 patients and treated another 9,187 on an outpatient basis. *Sanctuary* was again decommissioned on 15 December 1971.

Subsequently, the ship was converted for use as a dependents' hospital and as a commissary/Navy exchange retail store. Two women officers and 60 enlisted women were assigned for non-medical duties. When *Sanctuary* was recommissioned in November 1972, she became the first Navy ship with a mixed male-female crew. In September of that year, the vessel cruised to South America on a humanitarian-good will mission.

Sanctuary was decommissioned in 1975 and remained in mothballs until 1989 when she was struck from the Navy Register and transferred to the Maritime Administration for disposal. The ship was subsequently sold to Life International, which hoped to use the ship to train medical personnel in Africa. Unable to raise funds to accomplish its goal, *Sanctuary* was turned over to the Project Life Foundation of Baltimore, Maryland, in 1992. This organization's mission is to teach new skills to people overcoming substance abuse. Today, the old veteran resides at a pier in Baltimore, a short distance from Fort McHenry.

USS *REPOSE* (AH-16), after shuttling patients around the Far East during late 1953 and early 1954, was decommissioned later that year. For more than 10 years, she lay at anchor in mothballs with the National Defense Reserve Fleet at Suisun Bay, California, until the Navy reactivated her in 1965 for another war, this time in Southeast Asia. After reconditioning, *Repose* was recommissioned at Hunter's Point Naval Shipyard before heading for Vietnam waters. In February 1966, the vessel began cruising offshore near the DMZ, providing medical support for I Corps operations. By 1970, the "Angel of the Orient" had witnessed 14,000 helicopter landings, admitted over 24,000 patients, and treated more than 9,000 battle casualties. She returned home in 1970 and was decommissioned. Stricken from the Navy register in 1974, the veteran of three wars was transferred to the Maritime Administration for disposal.

APPENDIX 2: MEDAL OF HONOR CITATIONS

Ballard, Donald E.

Rank and organization: Hospital Corpsman Third Class, United States Navy, Company M, 3rd Battalion, 4th Marines, 3rd Marine Division.

DATE: 16 MAY 1968

Citation:

For conspicuous gallantry and intrepidity at the risk of his life and beyond the call of duty while serving as a Corpsman with Company M, 3rd Battalion, 4th Marines, 3rd Marine Division in connection with operations against enemy aggressor forces in the Republic of Vietnam. During the afternoon hours, Company M was moving to join the remainder of the 3rd Battalion in Quang Tri Province. After treating and evacuating two heat casualties, Petty Officer Ballard was returning to his platoon from the evacuation landing zone when the company was ambushed by a North Vietnamese Army unit employing automatic weapons and mortars, and sustained numerous casualties. Observing a wounded Marine, Petty Officer Ballard unhesitatingly moved across the fire-swept terrain to the injured man and swiftly rendered medical assistance to his comrade. Petty Officer Ballard then directed four Marines to carry the casualty to a position of relative safety. As the four men prepared to move the wounded Marine, an enemy soldier suddenly left his concealed position and, after hurling a hand grenade which landed near the casualty, commenced firing upon the small group of men. Instantly shouting a warning to the Marines, Petty Officer Ballard fearlessly threw himself upon the lethal explosive device to protect his comrades from the deadly blast. When the grenade failed to detonate, he calmly arose from his dangerous position and resolutely continued his determined efforts in treating other Marine casualties. Petty Officer Ballard's heroic actions and selfless concern for the welfare of his companions served to inspire all who observed him and prevented possible injury or death to his fellow Marines. His courage, daring initiative, and unwavering devotion to duty in the face of extreme personal danger, sustain and enhance the finest traditions of the United States Naval Service.

Caron, Wayne M. (Posthumous)

Rank and organization: Hospital Corpsman Third Class, United States Navy, Headquarters and Service Company, 3rd Battalion, 7th Marines, 1st Marine Division (Rein), FMF

DATE: 28 JULY 1968

Citation:

For conspicuous gallantry and intrepidity at the risk of his life above and beyond the call of duty while serving as Platoon Corpsman with Company K, 3d Battalion, 7th Marines, 1st Marine Division, during combat operations against enemy forces in the Republic of Vietnam. While on a sweep through an open rice field in Quang Nam Province, Petty Officer Caron's unit started receiving enemy small-arms fire. Upon seeing two Marine casualties fall, he immediately ran forward to render first aid, but found that they were dead. At this time, the platoon was taken under intense small-arms and automatic-weapons fire, sustaining additional casualties. As he moved to the aid of his wounded comrades, Petty Officer Caron was hit in the arm by enemy fire. Although knocked to the ground, he regained his feet and continued to the injured Marines. He rendered medical assistance to the first Marine he reached, who was grievously wounded, and undoubtedly was instrumental in saving the man's life. Petty Officer Caron then ran toward the second wounded Marine, but was again hit by enemy fire, this time in the leg. Nonetheless, he crawled the remaining distance and provided medical aid for this severely wounded man. Petty Officer Caron started to make his way to yet another injured comrade, when he was again struck by enemy small-arms fire. Courageously and with unbelievable determination, Petty Officer Caron continued his attempt to reach the third Marine until he himself was killed by an enemy rocket round. His inspiring valor, steadfast determination, and selfless dedication in the face of extreme danger, sustain and enhance the finest traditions of the United States Naval Service.

Ingram, Robert R.

Rank and organization: Hospital Corpsman Third Class, United States Navy, Company C, 1st Battalion, 7th Marines, 1st Marine Division.

DATE: 28 MARCH 1966

Citation:

For conspicuous gallantry and intrepidity at the risk of his life above and beyond the call of duty while serving as Corpsman with Company C, 1st Battalion, 7th Marines, against elements of a North Vietnam aggressor (NVA) battalion in Quang Ngai Province Republic of Vietnam on 28 March 1966. Petty Officer Ingram accompanied the point platoon as it aggressively engaged an outpost of an NVA battalion. The momentum of the attack rolled off a ridge line down a tree covered slope to a small paddy and a village beyond. Suddenly, the village tree line exploded with an intense hail of automatic rifle fire from approximately 100 North Vietnamese regulars. In mere moments, the platoon ranks were decimated. Oblivious to the danger, Petty Officer Ingram crawled across the bullet spattered terrain to reach a downed Marine. As he administered aid, a bullet went through the palm of his hand. Calls for "Corpsman" echoed across the ridge. Bleeding, he edged across the fire swept landscape, collecting ammunition from the dead and administering aid to the wounded. Receiving two more wounds before realizing the third wound was life-threatening, he looked for a way off the face of the ridge, but again he heard the call for corpsman and again, he resolutely answered. Though severely wounded three times, he rendered aid to those incapable until he finally reached the right flank of the platoon. While dressing the head wound of another corpsman, he sustained his fourth bullet wound. From sixteen hundred hours until just prior to sunset, Petty Officer Ingram pushed, pulled, cajoled, and doctored his Marines. Enduring the pain from his many wounds and disregarding the probability of his demise, Petty Officer Ingram's intrepid actions saved many lives that day. By his indomitable fighting spirit, daring initiative, and unfaltering dedications to duty, Petty Officer Ingram reflected great credit upon himself and upheld the highest traditions of the United States Naval Service.

Ray, David R. (Posthumous)

Rank and organization: Hospital Corpsman Second Class, United States Navy, 2d Battalion, 11th Marines, 1st Marine Division (Rein), FMF.

DATE: 19 MARCH 1969

Citation:

For conspicuous gallantry and intrepidity at the risk of his life above and beyond the call of duty while serving as a Corpsman with Battery D, 2d Battalion, 11th Marines, 1st Marine Division at Phu Loc 6, near An Hoa. During the early morning hours, an estimated battalion-sized enemy force launched a determined assault against the battery's position, and succeeded in effecting a penetration of the barbed-wire perimeter. The initial burst of enemy fire caused numerous casualties among the Marines who had immediately manned their howitzers during the rocket and mortar attack. Undaunted by the intense hostile fire, Petty Officer Ray moved from parapet to parapet, rendering emergency medical treatment to the wounded. Although seriously wounded himself while administering first aid to a Marine casualty, he refused medical aid and continued his lifesaving efforts. While he was bandaging and attempting to comfort another wounded Marine, Petty Officer Ray was forced to battle two enemy soldiers who attacked his position, personally killing one and wounding the other. Rapidly losing his strength as a result of his severe wounds, he nonetheless managed to move through the hail of enemy fire to other casualties. Once again, he was faced with the intense fire of oncoming enemy troops and, despite the grave personal danger and insurmountable odds, succeeded in treating the wounded and holding off the enemy until he ran out of ammunition, at which time he sustained fatal wounds. Petty Officer Ray's final act of heroism was to protect the patient he was treating. He threw himself upon the wounded Marine, thus saving the man's life when an enemy grenade exploded nearby. By his determined and persevering actions, courageous spirit, and selfless devotion to the welfare of his Marine comrades, Petty Officer Ray served to inspire the men of Battery D to heroic efforts in defeating the enemy. His conduct throughout was in keeping with the finest traditions of the United States Naval Service.

Appendix 3: Small Arms

North Vietnamese Army (NVA) and Viet Cong

Most small arms employed by the North Vietnamese Army and Viet Cong were of Soviet manufacture, or produced by several Warsaw Pact nations, or China. Later in the war, North Vietnam produced weapons patterned after Soviet and Chinese models.

Rifles, Carbines, and Automatic Weapons

AK-47 semi-automatic/automatic rifle 7.62mm
SKS semi-automatic carbine 7.62mm
MAT49 submachine gun (French)7.62mm
PPSh41 submachine gun "burp gun" 7.62mm
Type 56 semi-automatic/automatic assault rifle (Chinese) copy of AK-47
DP light machine gun 7.62mm
RPD general purpose machine gun 7.62mm
Type 24 heavy machine gun 7.62mm

Grenades

Offensive or concussion (stick grenades based on Soviet RGD 33)
Fragmentation (based on Soviet RGD 33)
Anti-armor
RPG-7 (Rocket propelled grenade)

United States and Army of the Republic of Vietnam (ARVN)

All small arms employed by U.S. forces were of domestic manufacture. During early American involvement, and up through 1965, U.S. advisors and ARVN troops were often armed with Korean War vintage M1 Garand rifles, and M1 and M2 carbines. The NVA and Viet Cong possessed the legendary AK-47 assault rifle, capable of semi-automatic and fully automatic fire. When combat Marines arrived in March 1965, they brought with them the M14 rifle, then the standard weapon for the U.S. military. Although the M14 was capable of both semi-automatic and fully automatic fire, excessive recoil made the weapon very difficult to keep on target during automatic fire. As a result, most M14s were only configured in semi-automatic mode.

It was not until the troops began trading in their M14s for the new M16A1 assault rifles in 1966 that Marines and soldiers finally had the firepower they needed. The M16 was capable of both semi-automatic and automatic fire.

Rifles, Carbines, and Automatic Weapons

M14 semi-automatic/automatic rifle 7.62mm
M14 (M21) semi-automatic sniper rifle 7.62mm
M40 sniper rifle 7.62mm
Winchester M70 sniper rifle .30-06
M16A1 semi-automatic/automatic rifle 5.56mm
M60 machine gun 7.62mm
Browning machine gun .30

Grenades

Mark 2 anti-personnel hand-rifle grenade
M-203 40mm grenade launcher
M-79 40mm grenade launcher

Anti-armor

M-67 90mm recoilless rifle
M-72 60mm light anti-tank weapon
M-20 3.5 inch rocket launcher (Super Bazooka)

Glossary

Amebiasis: The state of being infected with amebae, especially with *Entamoeba histolytica*. The intestinal form is amebic dysentery.

Anastomosis: Removing a damaged portion of an artery or intestine and re-attaching the vessel or organ end to end.

Anectine: Trademark for preparations of succinylcholine chloride.

Arbovirus: Any of a group of viruses, including the causative agents of yellow fever, viral encephalitides, and certain febrile infections, which are transmitted to man by mosquitoes and ticks.

Atropine: A substance derived from belladona, hyoscyamus, or strammonium, or produced synthetically. Used to relax smooth muscles, to increase heart rate, or topically to dilate the pupil of the eye.

Aureomycin: Trademark for preparations of chlortetracycline hydrochloride. Used as an antibacterial and antiprotozoan.

Autoclave: An apparatus employing steam and pressure for sterilizing.

Barosinusitis: A condition produced by a difference between the atmospheric pressure of the environment and the air pressure in the paranasal sinuses.

Barotitis: A condition of the ear produced by exposure to differing atmospheric pressures.

Benzalkonium chloride: A water-soluble mixture of ammonium chloride derivatives, occurring as an amorphous powder or in gelatinous lumps. Used as an antiseptic and disinfectant.

Benzoin: A balsamic resin with an aromatic odor and taste. Used as a topical protectant.

Betadine: Trademark for preparations of povidone-iodine.

Bird respirator: A medical respirator invented by Forrest Bird.

Bleeder: Any large blood vessel cut during a surgical procedure.

Cannula: A tube for insertion into a duct, cavity, or blood vessel.

Catgut: A sterile, absorbable suture material obtained from collagen of healthy mammals. Originally prepared from the submucous layer of sheep intestine.

Catheter: A tubular, flexible, surgical instrument for withdrawing fluids from (or introducing fluids into) a cavity of the body, especially for introduction into the bladder through the urethra for the withdrawal of urine.

Carpule: A glass tube usually containing a premeasured dose of anesthetic.

Cauterization: The destruction of tissue with a hot iron, electric current, or a caustic substance such as phenol.

Chloramphenicol: An antibiotic substance originally derived from cultures of *Streptomyces venezuelae* and later produced synthetically. Used as an antibacterial and antirickettsial.

Chloromycetin: Trademark for preparations of chloramphenicol.

Chloroquine: A water-soluble compound occurring as a white, or slightly yellow, crystalline powder with a bitter taste. Used as an antimalarial.

Chlortetracycline: See Aureomycin.

Clonazepam: A compound (benzodiazepine) used as an anticonvulsant and in the treatment of panic disorder.

Colostomy: The surgical creation of an opening between the colon and the surface of the body.

Compazine: The trademark for preparations of prochlorperazine maleate, a major orally administered tranquilizer and anti-emetic.

Contracture: A condition characterized by fixed

high resistance to passive stretch of a muscle, resulting from fibrosis of the tissues supporting the muscles or the joints.

Cricothyreotomy: An incision through the cricoid cartilages for passing a tube.

Curare: A substance derived from tropical plants of the genus *Strychnos*. Used for arresting the action of the motor nerves.

Cutdown: The creation of a small incised opening, especially over a vein (venous cutdown), to facilitate venipuncture and permit the passage of a needle or cannula for the withdrawal of blood or administration of fluids.

Cytoglomerator: A machine for washing preservative from thawed red blood cells.

Debridement: The surgical removal of foreign material and dead or contaminated tissue from or adjacent to a wound until surrounding healthy tissue is exposed.

Demerol: Trademark for meperidine (pethidine) hydrochloride. A white, odorless powder, soluble in water and alcohol. Used as a synthetic narcotic analgesic.

Dramamine: Trademark for preparations of dimenhydrinate, which is a white, odorless, crystalline powder soluble in alcohol and chloroform. Used as an anti-nauseant.

Dysentery: An infectious disease marked by inflammation and ulceration of the lower part of the intestines.Characterized by chronic diarrhea and severe dehydration.

Edema: A swelling caused by abnormally large amounts of fluid in the subcutaneous tissues.

Epidemic hemorrhagic fever: An acute infectious disease characterized by fever, peripheral vascular collapse, and acute renal failure.

Epidural anesthesia: Anesthesia produced by injection of the anesthetic agent between the vertebral spines and beneath the ligamentum flavum into the extradural space.

Episiotomy: Surgical incision of the vulvar orifice for obstetrical purposes.

Excision: Removal of a growth or organ by cutting.

Fascia: A sheet or band of connective tissue surrounding, supporting, or binding together internal organs or parts of the body.

Furacin: Trademark for preparations of nitrofurazone.

Furadanatin: Trademark for preparations of nitrofurantoin.

Gangrene: Death of large amounts of tissue due to an interruption of circulation followed by invasion of bacteria and putrefaction.

Granulation: The formation in wounds of small, rounded masses of tissue composed largely of capillaries and fibroblasts, often with inflammatory cells present.

Guillotine amputation: The rapid amputation of a limb by a circular movement of the scalpel and then cut of the saw. The entire cross-section is left open for dressing. This procedure is performed when primary closure of the stump is contraindicated because of the possibility of recurrent or developing infection.

Halazone: A white crystalline powdery acid used as a disinfectant for drinking water.

Hemangioma: A tumor consisting of dilated or newly formed blood vessels.

Hemoglobin: The oxygen-carrying pigment of red blood cells.

Hemostasis: The arrest of bleeding either by the physiological properties of vasoconstriction and coagulation or by surgical means.

Hemostat: A small surgical clamp for constricting a blood vessel. Sometimes used as a locking plier for gripping a suture needle or surgical blade.

Heparin: An anticoagulant used in the prevention and treatment of thrombosis and in the repair of vascular injuries.

Impetigo: A streptococcal infection of the skin.

Induction: The introduction of unconsciousness by use of anesthetics.

Laparoscopy: Examination of the interior of the abdomen by means of a laparoscope.

Laparotomy: A surgical incision into the abdominal cavity through any point in the abdominal wall.

Levin tube: A gastroduodenal catheter of sufficiently small caliber to permit transnasal passage.

Lidocaine: A white or yellow crystalline powder soluble in alcohol and chloroform. Used as a topical anesthetic.

Ligation: The application of any substance such as catgut, cotton, silk, or wire. Used to tie a vessel or strangulate a part.

Mercurochrome: Trademark for preparations of merbromin, a topical antibacterial.

Merthiolate: A water-soluble powder used as an antiseptic.

Metaphen: Trademark for preparations of nitromersol, a compound used topically in solution or tincture as a local anti-infective.

Morphine: An opium derivative used as a narcotic painkiller.

Nasogastric tube: A tube inserted into the nose and down the throat through which nourishment can be administered.

Nembutal: Trademark for preparations of sodium pentobarbital. A hypnotic used as a sedative, anticonvulsant, pre-anesthetic in surgery, or an adjunct to anesthesia.

Nitrofurantoin: A powder used as an antibacterial agent in infections of the urinary tract.

Nitrofurazone: A powder used as a local anti-infective.

Nitrous oxide: A colorless gas (N_2O) used as a general anesthetic or analgesic. Also called laughing gas.

Novocain: Trademark for procaine hydrochloride. Used as a local anesthetic.

Payr clamp: A crushing clamp used in resections of the stomach, intestine, and colon.

Pediculi: Lice.

Penicillin: The so-called miracle antibiotic of World War II. Noted for its antibiotic properties by Sir Alexander Fleming in 1928, penicillin was first isolated from the penicillium mold in 1940. During the next several years, U.S. pharmaceutical firms began producing penicillin in quantities that made a huge impact in the treatment of Allied casualties during World War II. In common usage during the Korean and Vietnam wars.

Perineum: The space between the anus and scrotum.

Periosteum: A specialized connective tissue covering all bones of the body, and possessing bone-forming potential.

Peritoneum: The strong colorless membrane that lines the abdominopelvic walls and surrounds the viscera.

Peritonitis: Inflammation of the peritoneum accompanied by exudations of serum, fibrin, cells, and pus.

Plasma: The liquid part of blood, as distinguished from the suspended elements, such as platelets and red blood cells. Before serum albumin and whole blood were available, plasma was commonly used as a blood volume expander for the prevention and treatment of shock.

Pneumothorax: An accumulation of air or gas in the pleural space, which may occur spontaneously or as result of trauma or pathology.

Popliteal: Pertaining to the posterior surface of the knee.

Povidone: A synthetic polymer used as a plasma volume expander.

Povidone-iodine: An amorphous powder used as a local anti-infective agent.

Primaquine: An orange-red, odorless crystalline powder (primaquine phosphate) with a bitter taste. Used to eliminate liver stages of *P.vivax* or *P.ovale* malaria.

Pyrogenic: Inducing fever.

Ringer's Solution: A clear, colorless liquid, which is dissolved in purified water. Contains sodium chloride, potassium chloride, and calcium chloride.

Roseola: Any rose-colored rash, such as seen in measles and syphilis.

Saphenous vein: Pertaining to or associated with a saphena, either of two large superficial veins of the leg.

Serum albumin: The principal protein of blood plasma. When administered intravenously, albumin draws fluid from surrounding tissues and helps increase blood volume to counteract shock.

Shock: A collapse of circulatory function caused by severe injury, blood loss, or disease.Characterized by pallor, sweating, weak pulse, and very low blood pressure.

Smallpox: Variola; an acute infectious disease caused by a poxvirus.

Sodium pentothal: A commonly used anesthetic administered intravenously to induce general anesthesia.

Spica cast: A figure-8 cast with turns that cross one another at the shoulder or hip.

Spinal anesthesia: Anesthesia produced by injection of local anesthetic into the subarachnoid space around the spinal cord.

Stilette: A wire run through a catheter or cannula to render it stiff.

Stokes stretcher: A wire mesh and wood slat litter invented by Navy physician Charles F. Stokes. Stokes served as Surgeon General of the Navy from 1910 to 1914.

Streptomycin: A bactericidal antibiotic used chiefly in the treatment of tuberculosis.

Stryker frame: A rigid structure consisting of canvas stretched on anterior and posterior frames on which the patient can be rotated around his/her longitudinal axis. Commonly used in treating patients with broken backs.

Succinylcholine chloride: A white, odorless crystalline soluble in water, alcohol, and chloroform. Used as a skeletal muscle relaxant.

Sulfa drugs: A group of antibacterial compounds first introduced in 1936 to prevent or treat infection before penicillin came into general use in the mid–1940s. The World War II sulfa quintet included sulfanilamide, sulfapyridine, sulfathiazole, sulfadiazine, and sulfaguanidine.

Syrette: A single-dose, collapsible tube with an attached sterilized hypodermic needle sealed in tinfoil.

Tamponade: Compression of the heart by pericardial fluid.

Terramycin: Trademark for preparations of oxytetracycline. Used as an antibacterial and antirickettsial.

Tetanus: An infectious, often fatal, disease caused by the toxic effect of *Clostridium tetani*. The bacteria usually enters the body through wounds. Characterized by violent muscle spasms, rigidity resulting in trismus (lockjaw), and respiratory failure.

Tetracycline: An antibiotic used as an antiamebic, antibacterial, and antirickettsial.

Tetracaine: A fine, white powder used as a local and topical anesthetic.

Thorazine: Trademark for preparations of chlorpromazine hydrochloride. A tranquilizer and antiemetic with a distinctive sedating effect.

Trachoma: A chronic and infectious disease of the conjunctiva and cornea caused by the bacteria *Chlamydia trachomatis*.

Traction: The act of drawing or exerting a pulling force used principally in the treatment of fractures.

Triage: The sorting and classification of casualties to determine priority of need and proper place of treatment.

Typhus: Any of a group of related arthropod-borne infectious diseases caused by species of *Rickettsia*.

Urticaria: A vascular reaction of the skin marked by the transient appearance of smooth, slightly elevated patches (wheals), which are redder or paler than the surrounding skin and often attended by severe itching.

Vascular graft: The reconstruction of a damaged vessel by splicing in a section of vein.

Viscus: Any large interior organ in any one of the three great cavities of the body, especially in the abdomen. Viscera is the plural form.

Yaws: A usually nonvenereal, systemic, infectious disease caused by the spirochete *Treponema pertenue*, and most commonly occurring in children of tropical regions.

Xylocaine: Trademark for preparations of lidocaine.

Zephiran: Trademark for preparations of benzalkonium.

CHAPTER NOTES

Preface

1. Shulimson, Blasiol, Smith, and Dawson. *U.S. Marines in Vietnam: The Defining Year 1968*, p. 587.

Chapter 1

1. Task Group 90.8 was a sub-unit of Naval Task Force 90.

2. DDT's adverse and long-lasting impact on the environment was unknown in 1954, but it was the most effective insecticide then available.

3. A Navy term defined as "requisitioning" a needed item without benefit of official paperwork.

4. A syndrome named for physicians Pierre Marie and Adolf von Strümpell characterized by a rheumatoid arthritic spinal condition.

Chapter 2

1. Three Americans and dozens of Vietnamese were killed.

2. A smokeless, slow-burning powder used as a propellant in munitions.

3. The Viet Cong frequently planted these sharpened sticks in shallow pits beneath roads or paths. Their purpose was to pierce the feet of unwary soldiers.

4. These were, in fact, South Vietnamese PT boats on their way back from attacking two North Vietnamese offshore islands. The covert raids, known as OPLAN 34A, were supported by the Central Intelligence Agency.

5. James B. Stockdale was shot down on a later mission and spent the rest of the war as a POW. He was the senior officer at the "Hanoi Hilton."

6. The bullet recovered was a 14.5mm slug.

Chapter 3

1. "Remarks at a Dinner Meeting of the Texas Electric Cooperatives, Inc.," 4 May 1965.

2. Irregular (militia) troops recruited from the local civilian population.

3. Catgut sterilized and impregnated with chromium trioxide to prolong its tensile strength in tissues.

4. A heavy grease used to protect ferrous metal from the elements.

5. A fiberglass, outboard motor-powered boat, usually under 20 feet in length.

6. Magnesium flares fired at night to illuminate the ground below and also used for signaling.

7. A steel plate upon which the mortar tube is mounted.

8. The surgical creation of an opening into the trachea through the neck and the insertion of a tube to facilitate breathing.

9. A green work uniform, the Army and Air Force equivalent of fatigues.

10. Connex containers are 20- and 40-foot steel shipping containers used to send goods by sea, rail, or road on the backs of semi-trucks.

11. In 1960, the Navy transferred the hospital ship USS *Consolation* (AH-15) to the People to People Health Foundation, sponsor of "Project Hope." Under her new name SS *Hope*, the vessel visited ports in Southeast Asia, Africa, the Caribbean, and South America, providing treatment and training native hospital personnel in advanced medical and public health procedures.

12. "Puff the Magic Dragon" was the name given to AC-47 aircraft equipped with Vulcan rapid firing cannons. These planes could saturate a designated area with overwhelming firepower.

Chapter 4

1. Operation Harvest Moon was launched on 8 December 1965 with U.S. Army and Army of the Republic of Vietnam (ARVN troops). The Marines were engaged the following day.

2. Mike boats were designated LCM (Landing Craft Mechanized). They were designed to land heavy equipment or trucks, trailers, and tanks on a beach.

3. Capt. Harris tells another story of how to take charge during pre-deployment. "We had a 6 by 6 [truck] with a window that didn't work. Col. Widdecke had been on me to get it fixed but we couldn't get the parts. A nameless mechanic and a lance corporal came to my office one day while we were on Okinawa and asked to borrow my jeep to go on a 'supply mission.' They started out with a battery and by the end of the day had traded all the way up to a whole 6 by 6 door, complete with operating window. They installed the door and brought the truck by my office to show it off, complete with a big white Army star on the door! I sincerely thanked them and told them to take the truck to the motor pool and get the door painted.

"Next morning, Col. Widdecke came to our motor pool to see if the window had been repaired. You could vaguely see the outline of the star and I know Widdecke saw it, but he simply smiled when we showed him that the window worked. He then walked away. Now that is teamwork and innovation of the highest order!"

4. Water tanks carried on trailers.

5. A blood vessel that hemorrhages uncontrollably.

6. The Berry Plan, created by Dr. Frank B. Berry, Assistant Secretary of Defense for Health Affairs in 1954, allowed for new physicians with a military obligation to choose among three options: entering the armed service of their choice immediately after internship and returning to their residencies after service; entering the armed services two years after medical school and completing their residencies after service; or entering the service after completion of residency training. The plan deferred thousands of physicians from the draft to complete their residencies before entering on active duty.

7. The term "combat fatigue," used extensively by World War II psychiatrists and psychologists, transitioned into what became known as "post-traumatic stress disorder" (PTSD) after the Vietnam War. In 1989, in response to congressional action, the Veterans Administration established the National Center for Post-Traumatic Stress Disorder to deal with this condition prevalent among veterans.

8. The 1987 film *Good Morning, Vietnam* depicted the story of Air Force broadcaster Adrian Cronauer.

9. The man at the front of the column.

10. Official fighting and utility knife used by Marines.

11. The M113 armored personnel carrier was an amphibious tracked vehicle armored with half-inch to 1-inch steel. It could reach speeds of 40 mph or more. It had a two-man crew and room for up to 11 soldiers.

12. Antipersonnel mines that shot out hundreds of small steel balls in a fan-shaped direction.

Chapter 5

1. The 60mm mortar round of the Vietnam era weighed about 3 pounds and was nearly 14 inches long.

2. Shortly after this incident, HM1 Daniel Henry was killed in a mortar attack.

Chapter 6

1. *Navy Medicine*, January–February 1988, pp. 13–21.

2. Wilson, Almon C. *Reminiscences of Rear Admiral Almon C. Wilson, Medical Corps, U.S. Navy, (Retired).* Interviewed by Paul Stillwell, 15 February 1989, p. 101.

3. Marine fighting and field uniform. Known as "fatigues" in the Army.

4. Despite the Geneva Accords, which stipulated that a hospital corpsman could be armed only with a defensive weapon — a pistol — to protect himself and his patient, as in other wars, this custom went by the boards. As his predecessors learned during World War II, a red cross on a helmet was akin to a bull's-eye. During the Vietnam War, both North Vietnamese regulars and the Viet Cong frequently targeted corpsmen and radiomen. By eliminating one or both of these two essential components, they degraded a unit's ability to function. As a result, many corpsmen went beyond the standard .45 automatic pistol and armed themselves with rifles, shotguns, and other weapons.

5. The Unit 1 medical bag contained a wire splint, aspirin (1 bottle), Tetracaine ophthalmic, Povidine iodine, atropine, 4 by 6 battle dressings, triangular bandages, camouflage roller gauze, cravat bandages, gauze field dressing, adhesive tape, Band-Aids, thermometer, rubber airways for children and adults, bandage scissors, tourniquet, mechanical pencil, and casualty tags. Morphine syrettes were added when going into combat.

The Unit 1 could also accommodate a surgical kit,

which contained forceps, small scissors, bullet probe, needles and suture, scalpel handle, and No. 5 scalpel blades.

Despite being an issued item, the Unit 1, with its distinctive shape, was shunned by combat-experienced corpsmen who quickly learned that wearing the bag attracted unwanted enemy attention. Instead they carried medical supplies and equipment in gas mask bags, ammunition bandoliers, and other containers.

6. In 1967, Secretary of Defense Robert McNamara ordered the construction of an electronic infiltration barrier below the DMZ. It consisted of seismic and electronic sensors designed to track vehicular and human movement along the Ho Chi Minh Trail.

7. To clear a spent shell casing from the firing chamber, the cleaning rod was inserted into the muzzle and the round pushed out from the front.

8. On 27 April 1968, the 2nd Battalion, 4th Marines encountered a very large force of North Vietnamese pushing south from the DMZ, many of whom were entrenched in Dai Do and surrounding villages. After vicious fighting, very costly to both the Marines and an Army battalion, the NVA were defeated. Dong Ha, the enemy objective, had been saved.

9. Father of Senator John S. McCain.

10. The handgrips on these early M16s were made by the California toy manufacturer and embossed with the company logo.

11. Operation Tuscaloosa sent 2nd Battalion, 5th Marines into the Song Thu Bon Valley to neutralize a Viet Cong force operating there.

12. Maddox recalls, "A year and a half after this interview, thanks to the marvel of the Internet, I was able to contact a former Marine buddy, Carl Johnson, through the 2/9 website. He was still in touch with Bob Murdock, who had made it and was, as I suspected, paralyzed. I contacted Bob and we talked a long time on the phone."

Chapter 7

1. Charlie Company's nickname was "Suicide Charley," a label earned at Guadalcanal and allegedly misspelled by a Marine who painted the name on a flag made from a discarded parachute. The unit's reputation was enhanced by the company's willingness to take on very dangerous missions in two other wars — Korea and Vietnam.

Chapter 8

1. Clark Air Force Base Hospital offered short-term medical care for patients who were on their way to other treatment facilities.

2. From "NSA Station Hospital Da Nang: A Personal History" by James Chaffee, *Navy Medicine*, January–February 2002, Vol. 93. No. 1, pp. 9–15.

3. The Tet Offensive began 30 January 1968 and continued into early June.

4. Memories of such a tragedy were still fresh. During the Korean War, a transport crashed off the Kwajalein atoll in the Pacific on 19 September 1950, taking the lives of 11 Navy nurses.

5. A prefabricated metal building made by the Butler Manufacturing Company.

6. An antigen is a substance that stimulates an immune response, especially the production of antibodies.

7. James Chaffee recalled that when he came to NSA

later on, corpsmen were routinely inserting endotracheal tubes, chest tubes, and doing venous cut downs—when necessary. "Often, we did procedures without a physician telling us to do them or even present to watch."

8. Chaffee does not remember seeing patients being hosed down when he arrived. "They may have done it earlier and then stopped. And we did a lot of triaging before we ever got an IV in them. I remember triaging on crowded '46s, deciding by flashlight who we would take and who we would send to the *Repose* based on whether they looked savable. And when we saw 30 or more guys littering the deck of one of those noisy monsters at night—not even on stretchers, that is a hell of a thing for a corpsman to decide."

9. *The New England Journal of Medicine*, Vol. 278, No. 14, April 4, 1968, pp. 747–752.

10. A material of two or more components and a mixture intermediate between a homogeneous solution and a heterogeneous mixture.

11. In blood plasma, dissolved compounds have an osmotic pressure. A small portion of the total osmotic pressure is due to the presence of large protein molecules. This is known as the colloidal osmotic pressure, or oncotic pressure. Because large plasma proteins cannot easily pass through capillary walls, their effect on the osmotic pressure of the capillary interiors will balance, to some extent, the tendency for fluid to leak out of the capillaries. In conditions where plasma proteins are reduced, for example, from extreme blood loss, the result of the much lessened oncotic pressure can be edema—excessive fluid buildup in tissues such as the lungs.

12. Capt. Raymond Watten, NAMRU-2's commanding officer, recalls traveling to Saigon in July 1966 to convince officials from MACV (U.S. Military Assistance Command, Vietnam) that the detachment was necessary.

13. Lab spaces included two large animal rooms, three microbiology labs, glassware washing and storage rooms, virology lab, and quarters for watch personnel.

14. More than 10 tons of research laboratory equipment from test tubes to refrigerators were airlifted from Taipei to Danang for the detachment.

Chapter 9

1. *Red Rover* was a captured Confederate sidewheeler that had been reconfigured as a hospital for the care of the sick and wounded.

2. The problem was a defective feeder pump.

3. A drain made by drawing a strip of gauze or surgical sponge into a tube of gutta-percha. This device provides an open channel for the exit of fluids or purulent material from a cavity, wound, or an infected area.

Chapter 10

1. A platform projected outboard from the side of a ship.

2. Sailors learning the skills of a specific Navy rating: in this case to become hospital corpsmen.

3. An officer who was previously enlisted.

Chapter 11

1. The Phu Cam Canal ran from the Perfume River and bordered the southern part of the more modern half of Hue.

2. The old walled city on the north side of the Perfume River.

3. Terry Sutton was later killed in action at Hue; James Yount was wounded.

4. A shoulder-deep, protective hole, often covered by a camouflaged lid, in which a soldier can stand and fire a weapon.

5. Greenway, Webb, and Mohr were awarded Bronze Stars, the only civilians so awarded.

6. An incision through the cricoid cartilages for passing a tube.

Chapter 12

1. The U.S. military measured the elevation of hills in meters, thus giving them their name.

2. The North Vietnamese positioned heavy artillery on Co Roc Mountain near the Laotian border. Well shielded in caves, these guns were on tracks and could be rolled out for firing. Hospital corpsman Raymond Felle recalls, "Anything we fired back from Khe Sanh would either go over the top of the mountain or slam into the front of it. The only way to get at them was to bomb them by jet."

3. A manual resuscitator, which consisted of a flexible squeeze bag attached to a face mask, used to ventilate a patient.

4. Tad Bartimus, Denby Fawcett, Jurate Kazickas, Edith Lederer, and Ann Mariano, *War Torn: The Personal Experiences of Women Reporters in the Vietnam War*, New York: Random House, 2004.

5. Lt. Robert Perry Mills, Jr., was the only Navy dentist to be killed by hostile action in Vietnam. Mills had been serving with the 3rd Dental Company attached to the 3rd Marine Division headquarters at Phu Bai.

6. The irrigation or washing out of an organ.

7. The defeat of the French during the first Indochina war insured Vo Nguyen Giap's reputation as a military strategist. His role as chief military leader of North Vietnam continued in the war against U.S. forces.

8. The Marine Corps was sometimes forced to rely on the draft when the pool of volunteers was insufficient.

Chapter 13

1. *Honor Bound: American Prisoners of War in Southeast Asia 1961–1973*, p. 165.

2. The future senator spent five and a half years as a POW.

3. This unsuccessful commando raid took place on 21 November 1970.

4. Condition in which the foot hangs in a flexed position.

5. Condition resulting from paralysis of the extensor muscles of the hand and fingers.

Chapter 14

1. A 500-pound general purpose bomb.

2. Kirschner wires (pins) are designed to hold bone fragments together.

3. Gen. Weise recalls one of the photographers taking the picture without his permission. "I had told him not to but he took it anyway. I told one my sergeants, 'Take that damn camera away and rip the film out.' The photographer was very apologetic. 'I'm sorry, sir. Please don't do that. I promise I won't show that to anyone.'" Despite

that promise, the photo was published in several newspapers, including the *Philadelphia Inquirer*. Philadelphia was Weise's hometown.

4. The act of occupying an assigned position to defend against an attack.

Chapter 15

1. An insecticide used in agriculture and for the treatment of head lice and scabies.

2. The 12 April evacuation of 159 Cambodians, 82 Americans, and 35 other nationals from Phnom Penh.

3. *Kirk*'s chief engineer, Hugh Doyle, recalls the specifics of this operation: "Kirk's aviators removed the tail pylon, drive shaft, and tail rotor from one of the helicopters we were preparing to throw over the side, and re- placed the damaged tail assembly on the helicopter we had saved up on the port side of the flight deck. This 'cannibalization' took only a few hours, and the repaired Vietnamese helicopter was then pushed back into position on the flight deck, refueled, and made ready for one more mission."

4. A sailor who has not been trained in the specialty but earns on-the-job skills that will enable him to change his rating.

5. As is customary with Vietnamese names, the surname appears first. Once the refugees became resettled and "Americanized," many reordered the name sequence.

6. In this centuries-old seafaring ritual called the "Order of Neptune," landlubbers—"polliwogs"—who have never crossed the equator, are initiated into the brotherhood of "shellbacks" by undergoing a series of ordeals.

BIBLIOGRAPHY

Published Sources

Butler, David. *The Fall of Saigon*. New York: Simon and Schuster, 1985.

Chaffee, James. "NSA Station Hospital Da Nang: A Personal History." *Navy Medicine*, January-February 2002, pp. 9–15.

Dooley, Thomas A. *Deliver Us From Evil: The Story of Viet Nam's Flight to Freedom*. New York: Farrar, Strauss and Cudahy, 1956.

_____. *Doctor Tom Dooley, My Story*. New York: Farrar, Strauss and Cudahy, 1962.

Finnegan, James O. "Triage at Khe Sanh." *Gynecology & Obstetrics*, Vol. 135, July 1972, pp. 108–110.

Fisher, James T. *Dr. America: The Lives of Thomas A. Dooley, 1927–1961*. Amherst: University of Massachusetts Press, 1997.

Fisichella, R.A. "Navy Hospital, Saigon." *Military Medicine*, Vol. 131, No. 2, February 1966, pp. 145–147.

Freeman, Gregory A. *Sailors to the End*. New York: Avon, 2002.

Halpern, Samuel E. *West Pac '64*. Boston: Branden, 1975.

Herman, Jan K. "Field Medical Service School: Training a Different Kind of Corpsman." *Navy Medicine*, January-February 1988, pp. 13–21.

The History of the Medical Department of the United States Navy, 1945–1955. NAVMED P-5057. Washington, DC: Bureau of Medicine and Surgery. 1955.

Hooper, Edwin B., Dean C. Allard, and Oscar P. Fitzgerald. *The United States Navy and the Vietnam Conflict: The Setting of the Stage to 1959*, Volume 1. Washington, DC: Naval History Division, Department of the Navy, 1976.

Hovis, Bobbi. "Coup in Saigon: A Nurse Remembers." *Navy Medicine*, November-December 1997, pp. 16–21.

_____. *Station Hospital Saigon: A Navy Nurse in Vietnam, 1963–1964*. Annapolis, MD: Naval Institute Press, 1992.

Karnow, Stanley. *Vietnam: A History*. New York: Viking, 1983.

Laurence, John. *The Cat From Hué: A Vietnam War Story*. New York: PublicAffairs, 2002.

Marolda, Edward J. *By Sea, Air, and Land: An Illustrated History of the U.S. Navy and the War in Southeast Asia*. Washington, DC: Naval Historical Center, 1992.

_____ and Oscar P. Fitzgerald. *The United States Navy and the Vietnam Conflict: From Military Assistance to Combat 1959–1965*, Volume 2. Washington, DC: Naval History Center, Department of the Navy, 1986.

Mavroudis, Constantine. "Physicians and the Navy Cross: A Treatise on Courage." *Surgery*, Vol. 110, No. 5, November 1991, pp. 896–902.

Mitchell, Robert E. "The Vietnam Prisoners of War: A Follow-Up." *Foundation*, Fall 1991, pp. 28–36.

Moss, Gerald S., C. Robert Valeri, and Charles E. Brodine. "Clinical Experience With the Use of Frozen Blood in Combat Casualties." *New England Journal of Medicine*, Vol. 278, No. 14, April 4, 1968, pp. 747–752.

Nolan, Keith W. *Battle for Hue: Tet 1968*. Novato, CA: Presidio, 1983.

_____. *The Magnificent Bastards: The Joint Army-Navy Defense of Dong Ha, 1968*. New York: Dell, 1994.

Olson, James S., and Randy Roberts. *Where the Domino Fell: America and Vietnam 1945–1990*. New York: St. Martin's, 1991.

Professional Knowledge Gained from Operational Experience in Vietnam, 1965–1966. NAVMC 2614. Washington, DC: Department of the Navy, Headquarters United States Marine Corps, 24 February 1967.

Redmond, Daniel. "Reminiscences of Passage to Freedom." *Navy Medicine*, January–February/March–April 1989, pp. 33–36.

Rochester, Stuart I., and Frederick Kiley. *Honor Bound: American Prisoners of War in Southeast Asia 1961–1973*. Annapolis, MD: Naval Institute Press, 1999.

Sanger, Quintin M. "Hemostats and Barbed Wire." *Navy Medicine*, January-February 1997, pp. 14–18.

Sharp, U.S.G., and W.C. Westmoreland. *Report on the War in Vietnam (As of 30 June 1968): Section I, Report on Air and Naval Campaigns Against North Vietnam and Pacific Command-wide Support of the*

War, June 1964-July 1968. Section II, Report on Operations in South Vietnam, January 1964-June 1968. Washington, DC: U.S. Government Printing Office, 1968.

Shulimson, Jack, Leonard A. Blasiol, Charles R. Smith, and David A. Dawson. *U.S. Marines in Vietnam: The Defining Year 1968.* Washington, DC: History and Museums Division, Headquarters Marine Corps, 1997.

Snepp, Frank. *Decent Interval.* New York: Vintage, 1977.

Stenberg, Michael D., and R. Paul Caudill, Jr. "Navy RAMs in Operation Homecoming." *U.S. Navy Medicine,* Vol. 62, September 1973, pp. 6–11.

Strange, Robert E., and Ransom J. Arthur. "Hospital Ship Psychiatry in a War Zone." *American Journal of Psychiatry,* Volume 124, Number 3, September 1967, pp. 37–42.

Terry, Bill. "Facial Injuries in Military Combat: Definitive Care." *Journal of Oral Surgery,* Vol. 27, July 1969, pp. 551–556.

Todd, Olivier. *Cruel April: The Fall of Saigon.* New York: W.W. Norton, 1990.

Tong, Myron. "Septic Complications of War Wounds." *Journal of the American Medical Association,* Vol. 219, No. 8, February 21, 1972, pp. 1044–1047.

Wilson, Almon C. *Reminiscences of Rear Admiral Almon C. Wilson, Medical Corps, U.S. Navy, (Retired).* Interviewed by Paul Stillwell, 15 February 1989, pp. 69–121, U.S. Naval Institute, Annapolis, MD, 2002.

Unpublished Sources

Amberson, Julius M. "Operation Passage to Freedom: 17 August 1954–19 May 1955," Lecture, U.S. Navy Medical School, 1 June 1955, Amberson Biography File, Bureau of Medicine and Surgery Archives, Washington, DC.

Copeland, Winifred. Letter to Veronica Bulshefski, 30 March 1967, Vietnam File, First Person Accounts Folder, Vietnam War Collection, Bureau of Medicine and Surgery Archives, Washington, DC.

Dooley, Thomas A. Letter to Melvin A. Casberg, 21 August 1954, Thomas Dooley File, Bureau of Medicine and Surgery Archives, Washington, DC.

Haven File, "Operation Repatriation," Bureau of Medicine and Surgery Archives, Washington, DC.

Report of the Bureau of Medicine and Surgery on Battle Casualty Management Meeting. Study performed at Surgical Research Unit, Naval Support Activity Hospital, Danang, Republic of South Vietnam, 1973. Unpublished report in the Bureau of Medicine and Surgery Archives.

Report of USS *Haven* (AH-12) "Operation Repatriation." *Haven* File, BUMED Archives, Washington, DC.

First-Person Accounts

All interviews conducted by the author and preserved in the Oral History Collection of the Navy Bureau of Medicine and Surgery Archives, Washington, DC.

Adeeb, Allan. Interview, Washington, DC, 25 October 2005.

Ballard, Donald. Telephone interview, 15 January 2004.

Barber, William. Telephone interview, 23 March 2005.

Birtcil, Robert. Telephone interview, 4 January 2005.

Bloustine, Stanley. Telephone interview, 26 October 2004.

Brouillette, Marie Joan. Telephone interview, 26 May 2005.

Buckley, Frances Shea. Telephone interview, 7 June 2005.

Burwinkel, Stephen. Telephone interview, 23 January 2007.

Chaffee, James. Telephone interview, 9 June 2004.

Cheatham, Ernest. Telephone interview, 20 October 2005.

Churchill, Paul. Telephone interview, 4 January 2006.

Christmas, George, Ronald. Telephone interview, 25 February 2005.

Corcoran, Anna. Telephone interview, 26 May 2004.

Cox, Donald. Telephone interview, 25 April 2007.

Crowe, Margaret. Telephone interview, 18 January 2005.

Daehn, Linda. Telephone interview, 27 May 2004.

Dinsmore, Harry. Interview, Punxsutawney, PA, 5 October 1989.

Downs, Michael. Telephone interview, 15 November 2005.

Doyle, Hugh. Telephone interview, 29 January 2007.

Earl, Dennis. Telephone interview, 14 November 2005.

Edmondson, Stephen. Telephone interview, 27 June 2005.

Feldman, Edward. Interviews, San Diego, CA, 14 and 15 February 2004.

Felle, Raymond. Telephone interviews, 23 and 24 November 2004.

Fellowes, Jack. Telephone interview, 18 December 2003.

Finnegan, James. Interview, Kansas City, MO, 9 September 2004.

Fisichella, Russell. Telephone interview, 5 February 2004.

Friedman, Paul. Telephone interview, 7 November 2005.

Galanti, Paul. Telephone interview, 1 April 2004.

Gallitano, Alphonse. Telephone interview, 14 November 2005.

Gay, William. Interview, Washington, DC, 7 January 2008.

Gerrard, William. Telephone interview, 8 November 2004.

Gondring, William. Telephone interviews, 22 and 24 September 2004.

Halpern, Samuel. Telephone interview, 27 April 2004.

Harrington, Myron. 8 December 2005.

Harris, George. Interview, Washington, DC, 14 January 2004.

Henry, Bill. Telephone interview, 19 April 2005.

Higgins, John. Telephone interview, 10 June 2005.

Hodge, G. Gustave. Interview, San Diego, CA, 14 February 2004.

Holladay, Michael. Telephone interviews, 30 November, 9 December, and 16 December 2004.

Hovis, Bobbi. Interview, Annapolis, MD, 2 December 1994.

Hudson, Randy. Telephone interview, 16 January 2007.

Ingraham, Robert. Telephone interview, 30 May 2006.

Ingram, Robert. Telephone interviews, 4 and 18 November, 16 December 2003.

Iwata, Miki. Interview, Williamsburg, VA, 12 May 2004.

Jacobs, Paul. Interview, Fairfax, VA, 29 December 2006.

Julius, Leonard. Telephone interview, 19 July 2005.

Kent, Alan. Telephone interview, 9 December 2005.

Kirchner, G. Gary. Telephone interview, 26 July 2005.

Loughney, Juel. Telephone interview, 14 March 2006.

Lucas, George. Telephone interview, 30 September 2005.

McFee, Arthur. Telephone interview, 19 July 2005.

Maddox, James. Telephone interviews, 9 and 23 June 1999.

Mahaffey, William. Telephone interview, 17 December 2003.

Mitchell, Robert. Telephone interview, 8 January 2004.

Moss, Gerald. Telephone interview, 5 November 2004.

Noah, Dennis. Telephone interview, 22 September 2005.

Pham, Joseph. Telephone interview, 11 February 2007.

Pittman, Roger. Telephone interview, 10 February 2005.

Reynolds, Darby. Telephone interview, 27 April 1998.

Ricciardi, Joseph. Telephone interview, 6 February 2004.

Rogers, Bill. Telephone interview, 26 July 2005.

Ryskamp, James. Telephone interview, 10 November 2004.

Schwirian, David. Telephone interview, 3 January 2006.

Shepard, Dennis. Telephone interview, 29 August 2003.

Soliday, James. Interview, Washington, DC, 27 August 1992.

Sulkowski, Mary Lee. Interview, Las Vegas, NV, 13 May 2003.

Taft, David. Telephone interview, 25 August 2004.

Terry, Bill. Telephone interview, 13 June 2005.

Thacker, Richard. Telephone interview, 16 May 2005.

Thomas, James. Interview, Kansas City, MO, 9 September 2004.

Tong, Myron. Telephone interview, 4 April 2006.

Tran, Lan. Telephone interview, 12 April 2007.

Twyman, Florence Alwyn. Telephone interview, 19 November 2003.

Valeri, C. Robert. Telephone interview, 5 August 2004.

Ware, Roger. Telephone interview, 15 March 2005.

Weise, William. Telephone interview, 29 December 2004.

Willis, Odette. Telephone interview, 27 May 2004.

INDEX

Numbers in **bold italics** indicate pages with illustrations.
Page numbers in *italics* indicate notes.

A Shau Valley, South Vietnam 131, 318
Abnaki, USS 302
Adeeb, Allan 209–10, 270–72, 329
Adler, Michael 16
Afghanistan 1, 317
Agent Orange 324
"Alcatraz" (prison camp), North Vietnam 251
Alwyn, Florence *see* Twyman, Florence Alwyn
Amberson, Julius 13–14, 15–19, 20, 329
Amebiasis 1, 4, 30, 341
Amebic dysentery 30, 231, 341
American Nurse Association 192
An, Nguyen Phouc 48
An Hoa, South Vietnam 112, 115, 163, 337
Arentzen, Willard 197–98, *198–99*
Armitage, Richard 292, 293, 302, 303
Arnold, Homer 81
Asherman, Aldon 88
Ashworth, Ray 79
Asquith, Richard 104

"Baby Kirk" *see* Tran-Nguyen Kirk Giang-Tien
Back, James 107
Baie d'Along, Gulf of Tonkin 10, 11, 12
Bain, Keith 42
Ballard, Donald 113, 115–16, 150–51, *151*, 329; Medal of Honor citation 151, 336
Ban Me Thuot, South Vietnam 51
Bangkok, Thailand 26, 130, 238
Bansavage, John 153
Bao Dai, Emperor 25
Barber, William 109–13, 131–34, 147, 322, 329
Barcott, Jan 26
Bates, Jim 172
Bearson, Lawrence O. 46, 51
Beeby, James 46, 49, 51, 52
Behrens, Jerry 117, 119
Beling, John 202
Bell, Jim 256

Benevolence, USS 178
Bergman, Larry **165**
Berry, Frank B. *346n*
Berry Plan 80, 88, 321, *346n*
Bin Chi, North Vietnam 18
Birtcil, Robert 242–46, **243**, 329
Bliss, Ron 253, 254, 255
Blood supply 54, 84, 168, 171; frozen blood 78, 155, 168–74, 179, 181, 186, 333; "walking blood bank" 30, 78, 169
Bloustine, Stanley 57–60, 329
Blue Ridge, USS **293**, **295**, 300, 302
Bomar, Jack 256
Bon Homme Richard, USS 200, 204
Bongaard, James 313
Brink, Francis 34
Brink Hotel, Saigon, South Vietnam 30, 34, 36, 37, 38
Britten, Sydney 19
Brock, James P. 226
Brodine, Charles E. 174
Bronze Stars 109, 120, 144–45, 150, 224, 330, 332, 333; awarded to civilians *347n*
Brouillette, Marie Joan 163–64, **165**, 166–68, 321, 329
Brown, Bob 236, 246
Buchignani, Joseph 214
Buckley, Frances Shea 321–22, 329, 334
Buddhists 27, 31, 50
Bui Van Luong *see* Luong, Bui Van
Bulshefski, Veronica 56
Burdette, Robert 245, 246
Burer, Art 256
Burns, Paul 31, 32
Burwinkel, Stephen 294–99, 302–3, 306, 309, 312, 329
Busey, Jim 270, 271

Ca Lu, South Vietnam 93, 117, 118, 119, 233, 278
Cam Lo, South Vietnam 115, 121, 123, 150, 242
Cam Ranh Bay, South Vietnam 272

Cambodia 9, 56, 61, 62, 115, 299, 314; Operation Eagle Pull 291; Viet Cong camps 251
Camp Asan, Guam 307, 314
Camp Carroll, South Vietnam 113, 116, 120, 123, 126, 233, 242
Can Tho, South Vietnam 63, 304
Canaga, Bruce 172
Cannon, Mary 160
Carey, L.C. 162
Caron, Wayne M.: Medal of Honor citation 336–37
Casberg, Melvin A. 22, 23
Catholics 9, 12, 15, 17, 31, 34, 49, 64, 275
Catinat Wharf, Saigon, South Vietnam 3
Caudill, R. Paul, Jr. 262
Cavallaro, USS 10
Central Intelligence Agency (CIA) 13, 53, 54, 57, 293
Chaffee, James 155–56, 158–63, 329, *346n–347n*
Chandler, Jim 86
Chau Doc, South Vietnam 61–64
Cheatham, Ernest 110, 211–12, 214, 215, 329
Chenault, Oran 182
Cherry, Fred 256
Chi, Huong Van 315
China, People's Republic of 269, 339
China Beach, South Vietnam 69, 156, 198
Cholera 17, 51, 57, 174, 175
Cholon, Saigon, South Vietnam 31, 34
Christmas, George "Ron" 211, 215–16, 272–73, 330
Chu Lai, South Vietnam 68, 72–76, 80, 163, 180, 192, 287
Churchill, Paul 94, 330
The Citadel, Hue, South Vietnam 217, 218, 224–29
Civil War, U.S. 1, 106, 107, 178, 256
Clark Air Force Base, Philippines 30, 71, 72, 155, 157, 182, 263, 269, 287, *346n*
Cleaver, Eugene 284

Co Roc, South Vietnam 232, 233, 244, 246, *347n*
Cohn, Edwin J. 169
Cohn Fractionator 169, 170
Colonna, Jerry 30
Compiano, Craig 301
Con Son Island, South Vietnam 292–93, 296, 302, 306
Con Thien, South Vietnam 114, 121, 136, 239
Consolation, USS 178, *345n*
Constellation, USS 200, 252
Cook, USS 293, 302
Cooper, Jackie **288**
Copeland, Winifred 56–57, 330
Corcoran, Anna 7–9, 330
Corpsmen *see* Hospital corpsmen
Cox, Donald 292, 309, 311–13, 330
Crowe, Margaret Wilkinson 282, 283–84, 324, 330
Crumpton, Frances L. 37
Cu Loc, North Vietnam 251
Cua Cam River, North Vietnam 10, 14
Cua Viet River, South Vietnam 126, 129, 130, 242, 276
Cytoglomerator **181**, 342

Dabney, William 232
Daehn, Linda 315–16, 330
Dai Do, Battle of (April-May 1968) 127–30, 276
Dai Do, South Vietnam 127–30, 276, 335, *346n*; triage station **277**
Dan Hoi, North Vietnam 251
Danang, South Vietnam: aerial view of Charlie Med **81**; arrival of U.S. combat troops 1, 68; departure of troops 147–49; evacuation 302; field hospital 60; Quonset huts 72; *see also* Naval Support Activity Hospital
Danang Air Base, Danang, South Vietnam 57, 272
Danang Harbor, Danang, South Vietnam 82, 157, 197
Danang Valley, South Vietnam 172
Davis, David 16
Davis, Ray 97
Day, Bud 256
DDT (insecticide) 9, 12, 17, 18, 20, 21, 23, *345n*
Deliver, USS 302
Dengue 1, 174, 314
Denton, Jeremiah 261
Diem, Ngo Dinh 25, 31, 32, 33, 34, 38, 305
Dien Bien Phu, North Vietnam 3, 5, 7, 9, 10, 13, 15, 178, 230, 241
Dinsmore, Harry 101–3, **103**, 107, 156–58, 330
Do San Peninsula, North Vietnam 16, 19
"Dogpatch" (prison camp), North Vietnam 251
Dong Ha, South Vietnam 113–16, 121, 123, 128, 130, 140, 180, 231–32, 234, 245–47, 276, *346n*;

medical battalion 76, 89–92, 113; medical facility 89, 91, 143–44, 231, 242, 246, 282; patrols 150; shelling of 89; triage area 89, 90, 274
Dong Ha Combat Base, Dong Ha, South Vietnam 89, 242
Dong Tam, South Vietnam: corpsman **109**
Dooley, Thomas A. 21–23, **22**, 330, 334; books and lectures 13, 330; duty aboard USS *Montague* 22–24; Haiphong assignment 13, 15, 16, 19, 22–24; role in Operation Passage to Freedom 7, 13, 22–24, 79
Downs, Michael 224, 319–20, 330
Doyle, Hugh 299–304, 330, *348n*
Duong Van Minh *see* Minh, Duong Van
Dysentery 1, 13, 17, 70, 126, 157, 159, 174, 175, 342; *see also* Amebic dysentery

Earl, Dennis 269–72, 330
Edmondson, Stephen 97–100, 330
Edwards, Blair 209
Eisenhower, Dwight D. 25
Encephalitis 160, 174, 176
Enterprise, USS 186
Estes, USS 15

Fahrenbruch, Dick 209
Falkenberg, Mark 298, 302
Feerick, Mack 154
Feldman, Edward 95–97, **236**, **249**, 331; heroic surgery 103–4, 239, 330; at Khe Sanh 95, 103–4, 234–37, 239, 246, 249, 330; Silver Star award 107, 330
Felle, Raymond 116–21, 322, 325–26, 331; action in saving Michael Holladay 120–21, 277–81, 331; battle of Valentine's Ridge 116–18, 233; Bronze Star award 120, 331; departure from Vietnam 147–48; at Khe Sanh 233–34, *347n*
Fellowes, Jack 252–57, 331
Finnegan, James 88–91, 231, 236, 241, 246–50, **249**, 319, 331
Firlit, Casey 243, 245
Fisichella, Rosario "Russ" 28–31, 331
Forrestal, USS 200–209, 331; burning **204**; crewmembers **205**
France 3, 5, 7, 13
Franklin D. Roosevelt, USS 200
French Foreign Legion 3, 5, 7, 9, 11, 16
Friedman, Paul 201–2, 331

Galanti, Paul 257–62, 331
Gallitano, Alphonse 271–72, 331
Garrick, J. 162, 163
Gay, William K. 237–39, 331
Geneva Accords 3, 9, 11, 15, 18, 25, 305, *346n*
Geneva Conventions 73, 180

Gens, Lou 26, 28
Gerrard, William 111, 231–33, 320, 331
Gettman, Richard 171
Gia Lam Airport, Hanoi, North Vietnam 261, **263**
Giap, Vo Nguyen 244, *347n*
Gipson, George 142, 143
Gleason, Edward 16
Glover, Kathleen **189**
Gondring, William 45–47, 49, 50–56, 324, 331
Goss, Larry J. 118
Gosselin, James 224
Graham, Billy 198–99
Graybiel, Ashton 264
Greenway, David 228, 229, *347n*
Grindell, James 19
Guadalcanal, Solomon Islands 211, *346n*
Guam: blood supply 84; naval hospital 7, 120, 155, 280–83, 307, 310–15, 324; refugees 291, 314, 315; during World War II 174; *see also* Camp Asan; Orote Point
Gulf of Tonkin Incident 38–44
Gulf of Tonkin Resolution (1964) 38, 44
Gulf War (1990–91) 1, 334, 335
Gutshall, Richard 61

Ha Tien, South Vietnam 53
Haiphong, North Vietnam: abandoned military barracks 19; evacuation of refugees 10–24; French naval base 18; orphanage 17; refugee camp **14**
Halpern, Samuel 38–44, 331
Han River, South Vietnam 155, 172
Hancock, USS 257, 259, 289–92, 300
Hanoi, North Vietnam: airport 261, **263**; American POWs 251, 253, 254, 256, 258–65, **263**, 331; diplomats 13; exodus of refugees (1954) 305, 307
"Hanoi Hilton" *see* Hoa Lo Prison
Harrington, Myron 225, 228, 331
Harris, Carlyle ("Smitty") 254
Harris, George 73–80, 139, 318–19, 331, *345n*
Haven, USS 3–9, **8**, 178
Hawaii 26, 182, 186, 189, 190, 196, 287, 290, 291, 307
Haynes, Lewis 169
Heath, Donald R. 15
Hegdahl, Doug 260, 265
Helminthiasis 174
Helmstetler, Michael D. 234
Henry, Bill 273–75, 332
Henry, Daniel B. 105–6, *346n*
Hepatitis 1, 20, 30, 159, 160, 177
Herman, Allan 135
Herrick, John J. 40, 43, 44
Herrmann, Louis 209
Hesli, Philip 96
Higgins, John 148, 216–24, 322–23, 332

Ho Chi Minh *see* Minh, Ho Chi
Ho Chi Minh City, Vietnam *see former name,* Saigon
Ho Chi Minh Trail 20, 130, 131, 233, *346n*
Hoa Kanh Children's Hospital, South Vietnam *52*
Hoa Lo Prison ("Hanoi Hilton"), Hanoi, North Vietnam 251, 253, 256, 258, 260, 261, *345n*
Hodge, G. Gustave 92, 332
Hoffer, Frank 187
Hoi An, South Vietnam 45, 57–60
Holladay, Michael 109, 117–21, 277–83, 322, 325, 330, 332
Hope, Bob 30–31, 37
Hope, SS 63, *345n*
Hospital corpsmen 2, 108–49; Medal of Honor recipients 109, 113, 150–54, 332, 336–38; see also *names of individual corpsmen*
Hospital ships 178–99; *see also Haven,* USS; *Repose,* USS; *Sanctuary,* USS
Hovis, Bobbi 26, 31, *32,* 36, 168, 332
Howard, Ray 226
Howe, Dennis *214*
Hudson, Randy 289–91, 332
Hue, Battle of (February 1968) 2, 211–29, *214,* 230, 272, 330, 331, 332
Hue, South Vietnam 2, 97, 163, 211–29, 272, 319, 331, *347n*
Hue University, Hue, South Vietnam *213*
Huggins, Charles 170–71, 321
Humphrey, Hubert 25
Huong Van Minh *see* Minh, Huong Van
Hurst, Pat 197
Hutton, Ray 106–7

Imperial Palace, Hue, South Vietnam 227
Inchon, South Korea 211
Indochina: Chinese families 17; evacuation of refugees 10, 18–19; first Indochina war (1954) 178, *347n*; French colonial rule 3, 25; French soldiers 4, 5, 6, 7; invasion by Japanese (World War II) 304; opium and hashish 12; *see also* Cambodia; Laos; Vietnam
Ingraham, Bob 59, 284–88, *286, 288,* 323, 332
Ingram, Robert R. 152–54, 326–27, 332; Medal of Honor citation 337
Intrepid, USS 209
Iraq 1, 317, 319, 322, 335
Islam 6, 9
Iwata, Miki 195–96, 332
Iwo Jima, USS 65, 127, 276
Iwo Jima, Japan 130, 211

Jacobs, Paul 291–95, 300–301, 303, 306, 309–10, 332

Japan: World War II 194, 195, 304, 335; *see also* Iwo Jima; Okinawa; Yokosuka
Jimerfield, Craig *109*
Johnson, Carl *347n*
Johnson, Kim 104
Johnson, Lyndon B. 25, 44, 45, 51, 230
Julien, Renee 4
Julius, Leonard 206–9, 332
Jungle rot 109, 117, 127, 193

Kaufman, Penny Chloe 25–26
Kaufman, Richard 18
Kazickas, Jurate 238, *347n*
Keelung, Taiwan 40
Kelley, J.B. 162
Kennedy, John F. 25, 34, 46
Kent, Alan 113–14, 225–29, 320, 332
Khe Sanh, Siege of (January-April 1968) 95, 98–100, 103–4, 119, 230–50, 278; emergency surgery *240*
Khe Sanh, South Vietnam 97–100, 119, 130, 132, 180, 194, 230–50, 277–78, 325, 330, *347n*; aid station 273–74; bunkers *236, 240;* "Charlie Med" physicians *249;* combat base 97; dentist 242–46, *243;* patrols 150; visited by veterans 325; website 320
Khe Sanh Valley, South Vietnam 130
Kian Giang Province, South Vietnam *see* Rach Gia
Kiley, Frederick 252
King, Jerry 232
Kirchner, G. Gary 202–6, 332
Kirk, USS 291–313, 330
Kirkham, Donald 218
Korean War: battles 211; Chosin Reservoir 212; field medicine 111; hospital ships 3, 178, 180; medical treatment 2, 80; outbreak of (1950) 25, 192; post-war repatriation examinations 264; POWs 251; small arms 339; transport crash *346n*; trauma 186

Lam Xuan, South Vietnam 327
Lan Nguyen Tran *see* Tran, Lan Nguyen
Land mines 51, 87, 101, 157, 171, 175, 184, 223, 284
Lang Dong Bao Thuong, South Vietnam 95
Laos 9, 93, 132, 230, 232, 244, 330, 334; Viet Cong camps 251
Latham, Jack 169
Leavitt, Ira *139*
Legarie, Lou 212, 215
Lewis, David 107
Lewis, John L. 48
Lipan, USS 302
Lodge, Henry Cabot 26
Loughney, Juel 196–99, 321, 333
Lownds, David 243, 247
Lualhe, Maurice 7

Lucas, George 275, 333
Luong, Bui Van 15
Luong, Nguyen Van 101–3, *103*
Lurie, Alan P. 258
Lyons, John 102–3

MacIntosh, Pierre 5
Maddox, James 110–11, 113, 140–47, 318, 324, 333, *346n*
Maddox, USS 38, 39, *39,* 40, *44*
Magilligan, Don 236, 238, 246, 249, *249,* 250
Mahaffey, William 80–88, *86,* 325, 333
Mai Loc, South Vietnam 126
Mai Xa Chanh, South Vietnam 327
Majestic Hotel, Haiphong, North Vietnam 20, 21, 26
Malaria 1, 4, 13, 17–20, 85, 123, 167, 174–76, 193, 196, 272, 314, 341, 343; cerebral malaria 159, 160; prophylaxis 30; treatment 23, 137, 157
Marble Mountains, South Vietnam 155, 156, 159, 273
Marcos, Ferdinand 303
Marking, Bill 186
Markowitz, Herbert 194
Marseille, France 7, 9
M*A*S*H (movie) 88, 91, 332
Mason, Ruth A. 37
Mayes, Richard 152, 153
McCain, John S., Jr. 134, *346n*
McCain, John S., III 256, *346n*
McCaughey, B.G. 162
McFee, Arthur 180–85, 187, 333
McKay, Bernadette 46–50, 51
McKenna, Richard 293, 298
McNamara, Robert *346n*
McNamara Line 117, 120, *346n*
Medal of Honor Society 329
Medals of Honor: awarded to hospital corpsmen 109, 113, 150, 151, 332; citations 336–38; nomination 134
Medical Civil Action Program (MEDCAP) 46, 59, *59,* 66–67, 80
Mekong Delta, Vietnam 2, 47, 51, 52, 56, 109, 330
Menard, USS 10, 23
Michael, Dennis S. 228, 229
Military Provincial Health Assistance Program (MILPHAP) 45, 57, 58, 60–65
Minh, Duong Van 34
Minh, Ho Chi 15, 20, 25, 260
Minh, Huong Van 315
Missing in action (MIA) 97, 199
Mitchell, Robert 257, 262, 264–68, 333
Mitchell, Tommy "Spanky" 227
Mobile, USS 302
Mohr, Charlie 228, 229, *347n*
Montague, USS 21, 22, 23
Morlock, Ruth 164, 166
Morrison, Charles L. 224
Moss, Gerald 170–74, 321, 333

Mulligan, Jim 262
Murdock, Bob 142–43, *346n*
Murray, Betty 192

Nam Tha, Laos 330
Napalm 53, 118, 135, 143, 241, 284
Naval Support Activity Hospital, Danang, South Vietnam 1, 2, 109, 155–77, 197–98, 269; aerial view during construction *156*; mortality rate 163; operating room *165*; patients in triage *158*
Navy Crosses 103, 106, 107, 109, 131, 134, 150, 224, 250, 330, 331, 334, 335
Navy Nurse Corps 56, 190, 313, 329, 332
Newman, Valerie Vitulli 195–96
Ngai, Vu Thi 17
Ngo Dinh Diem *see* Diem, Ngo Dinh
Nguyen Hoang Bridge, Hue, South Vietnam 216–18, 225
Nguyen Phouc An *see* An, Nguyen Phouc
Nguyen Van Luong *see* Luong, Nguyen Van
Nha Trang, South Vietnam 28, 29, 30, 31, 35, 36, 302
Nhi Ha, South Vietnam 327
Nixon, Richard M. 199
Noah, Dennis 112, 134–36, 148, 333
North Vietnam: aviators shot down 251; recognition of, by Philippines 303; weapons 339; see also *names of specific places*
Nui Tho Son (mountain), South Vietnam 156
Nui Thuy Son (mountain), South Vietnam 156

Okinawa, Japan: blood supply 84; landing exercises 10; medical battalion headquarters 28, 287, 331; supply point 69–70, 75, 78
Okinawa, USS 65
Operation Frequent Wind 289–316
Operation Homecoming 262–64
Operation Passage to Freedom 9–24, 79, 109; refugees boarding ship *11*
Operation Pegasus 119, 237, 278, 279
Operation Repatriation 3–9
Oran, Algeria 6–7, 9
Oriskany, USS 200, 206–10, 269–72, 332
Orote Point, Guam 307, 314
Osborn, Raymond *52*
Osier, Herb 41, 43
Overturf, Susan 287, 288

Paris Peace agreement (1973) 21, 261, 305
Parrish, John 89
Pasteur Institute 50, 52
Perfume (Song Huong) River,

South Vietnam 212, 215, 217, 218, 223, 224, *347n*
Perkins, Charles 194
Pham, Joseph 304–7, 309, 312, 313, 333
Phat Dien, North Vietnam 18
Philippines 84, 303; *see also* Clark Air Force Base; Subic Bay
Phillips, Robert 175
Phu Bai, Vietnam 216–20, 226, 229, 234, 239, 242, 273, 274; airfield 68, 89; arrival of U.S. combat troops 68; battalion aid station 113; dentists 242, *347n*; hospital 139, 212; medevac missions 139, *139*; medical battalions 68, 75, 89, 97–99, 212, 234; Quonset huts 72
Phu Ly, North Vietnam 270
Pittman, Roger 114, 121–31, 148–49, 327, 333
Plague 1, 80, 174, 290
Platoon (movie) 112, 114, 171
Pneumonia 4, 13, 70, 71, 85, 133, 298, 299, 312
Pojeky, Ruth 46, 49–50, 51
Ponder, Ken 79
Post-traumatic stress disorder (PTSD) 99–100, 319, 322, 323, *346n*
Powers, Runas *277*
Princeton, USS 65
Prisoners of war (POWs): American military personnel 194, 251–68, 331, 333, *345n*; French military personnel 3, 5; Viet Cong 157
Puller, Lewis 232
Punji sticks 35, 85, 119, 184, 269
Purple Hearts 86, 121, 146, 198, 212, 224, 234, 287, 335; received by Navy nurses 37, *38*, 333–34
Pyle, Darrell E. 258

Quang Nam Province, South Vietnam 45, 57, 336; *see also* Hoi An
Quang Ngai Province, South Vietnam 152, 284, 337
Quang Tri, South Vietnam 45, 95, 97, 139, 144, 147, 148, 180, 232, 239, 336
Quang Tri Province, South Vietnam 45, 95, 336
Querville, Jean 13, 18
Qui Vinh, North Vietnam 257

Rabies 1, 52, 94, 127
Rach Gia, South Vietnam 45, 47–49, 51, 56, 324, 330
Rach Gia-Phu Dinh Hospital, Rach Gia, South Vietnam *47*, 48–57
Ray, David R.: Medal of Honor citation 337–38
Raye, Martha 87
Red River, China-Vietnam 15, 16, 17, 18
Red River Delta, North Vietnam 10, 12, 16, 19
Redmond, Daniel M. 10–15, 333

Reese, William R. 118
Reinhold, Michael J. 225
Repatriated Prisoner of War Program 264–66
Repose, USS 1, 2, 80, 86, 178–99, 286–87, 323, 329, 333, 335, *347n*; capacity 1, 179; dental department 186–89; flight deck *188*, *195*; frozen blood bank 179, *181*, 186; helicopters 76–77, 161, 179, *195*, 202; living quarters 82; medical specialties 2, 187; radio communication 78, 157; statistics 180, 335; treatment of *Oriskany* crewmen 202, 208, 209–10; Vietnamese child *189*; wounded marine *195*
Reynolds, A. Darby 34–37, *38*, 317, 333–34
Ricciardi, Joseph 262, 266–68, 334
Richman, Ann 35, 36
Risner, Robinson ("Robbie") 259, 260
Rochester, Stuart 252
The "Rockpile" 115, 117, 150, 233, 277–79
Rogers, Bill 211, 220–23, 334
Rope trick 251, 253–54
Rose, Charlie 198
Ryskamp, James 319, 334

Sabin, Lorenzo S. 15, 16, 19, 23
Saigon, South Vietnam: apartment house 1, *27*, 29, 34, 35; fall of (April 30, 1975) 289, 291, 307; French soldiers 3; government 25; harbor 4, 306; terrorist activity 1, 29, 30, 34, 35, 36, 37; U.S. Embassy 109, 325; *see also* Station Hospital Saigon; Tan Son Nhut Airport
Saigon River, South Vietnam 4, 32
Sam Hai River, South Vietnam 75
San Francisco, California 89, 175, 179, 181, 186, 287
Sanctuary, USS 1, 2, 76, 92, 94, 109, 161, 178–99, 208, 280, 332, 335; capacity 1, 179; casualties on deck *191*; cruising near Maui *179*; helicopters 76–77, 161, 180, *184*; medical specialties 2; statistics 180, 335
Sanger, Quintin M. 46
Saratoga, USS 170
Schwirian, David 93–94, 334
Scrub typhus 1, 159, 174, 175, 176
Searcy, Owedia ("Tweedy") 26, 36, 168
Seoul, South Korea 211
Sharp, Lufkin 234
Shea, Frances *see* Buckley, Frances Shea
Sheen, Charlie 112
Shepard, Dennis 19–21, 334
Shires, Tom 185
Silver Stars 97, 107, 109, 120, 150, 218, 224, 282, 330
Singapore 291, 299, 311
Sizemore, Donald E. 198

Skonetski, Larry W. "Ski" 285, 286
Smallpox 1, 13, 17, 343
Smith, Audrey 169
Sniekowski, Ronald ("Ron") 104, 237–38
Soliday, James 60–65, 334
Son Tay, North Vietnam 251, 260, 261
South China Sea 10, 40, 58, 155, 200, 265, 296; *see also* Tonkin, Gulf of
South Vietnam: surrender to communists 306; Viet Cong camps 251; see also *names of specific places*
Soviet Union 269, 339
Specialists, medical: simultaneous treatment by 2, 167–68, 173, 187
Spicer, Jonathan 249–50
Spock, Benjamin 60
Station Hospital Saigon, Saigon, South Vietnam 1, 27–31, *32*, 34–35, 109, 332
Stenberg, Michael D. 262
Stewart, Bill 187, 188
Stockdale, James B. 43, *345n*
Stone, Oliver 112, 171
Stout, Robert J. 224
Subic Bay, Philippines: hospital ships 180, 182, 188, 190, 292, 293, 299, 309, 312; naval hospital 155, 173, 297, 309–10; refugee ships 303, 306; wharf 206
Sulkowski, Mary Lee 190–92, 318, 334
Summers, Harry G. 163
Sutton, Terry 218, 222, *347n*
Swan, Jeffrey 295, 300
Sweeney, William G. 46, 50, 51

Taft, David 105–7, *106*, 334
Taipei, Taiwan 155, 174, 175, 176, 177, *347n*
Taiwan *see* Keelung; Taipei
Tan Chau, South Vietnam 61–62, 65
Tan Nam Viet (Vietnamese freighter) *297*, 297–98, 299, 302
Tan Son Nhut Airport, Saigon, South Vietnam 26, 30, 33, 290, 300, 305, 307, 308
Tani Binh, North Vietnam 18
Tap codes 254, 255, 260
Tarawa Atoll, Gilbert Islands 130, 211
Terry, Bill 185, 186–89, 334
Tet (Vietnamese New Year) 56, 216
Tet Offensive (January-June 1968) 97, 113, 159, 161, 167, 211, 215, 260, 273, 305, *346n; see also*

Hue, Battle of; Khe Sanh, Siege of
Thacker, Richard 114–15, 212–15, 319, 334
Thailand 310
Thailand, Gulf of 47
Theodore Roosevelt, USS 335
Thomas, James 239–42, *240*, 334
"Thousand Aviators" project 262, 264, 265, 333
Tigers, attacks by 1, 92–94
Tinh-Bien, South Vietnam 62
Tong, Myron 175–77, 334
Tonkin, Gulf of 10, 38–44, 200, 203, 206
Tourane, Vietnam 11; *see also present name*, Danang
Tourane Bay, Vietnam 69
Trachoma 1, 13, 21, 24, 344
Tran, Lan Nguyen 292, 299, 307–13, *310*, 311, 334
Tran-Nguyen Kirk Giang-Tien ("Baby Kirk") 310, *310*, 311, 313
Triton, South Vietnam 62
Tuberculosis 1, 13, 83, 136, 174, 296, 316, 343
Tully, Lester 218
Turner Joy, USS 42–43
Tuscaloosa, USS 302
Twyman, Florence Alwyn 25–28, 334

Unit One medical bags *110;* carried by corpsmen 110, 117, 136, 226, 232, *346n;* supplies 134, 136–137, 285, *346n*
U.S. Agency for International Development (USAID) 45, 46, 56, 57, 61, 62, 64

Valentine's Ridge, South Vietnam 116–19, 233, 325
Valeri, C. Robert 169–70, 171, 174, 334
Vargas, J.R. 276
Vargas, Manuel S. 129
Viet Minh 3, 7, 9, 10, 12, 15, 18
Vietnam: ancient capital 211; coastline 178; partition along 17th Parallel 9, 21, 25, 305; *see also* North Vietnam; South Vietnam
Vietnam Veterans Memorial, Washington, D.C. 2, 88, 109, 196, 198, 250, 319
Vinh, North Vietnam 252, 257, 324
Vitello, Angelica 182, 190
Vo Nguyen Giap *see* Giap, Vo Nguyen
Vu Thi Ngai *see* Ngai, Vu Thi

The Wall *see* Vietnam Veterans Memorial
Walt, Lewis 72, 189
Ware, Roger 111–12, 136–40, 149, 335
Warren, Jerry 102
Warren, Marjorie *158*, 166
Washington, Mike 311, 312
Watten, Raymond 175, 176, 177, *347n*
Webb, Al 228, 229, *347n*
Weise, William 123–25, 128–29, 276–77, *277*, 335, *347n–348n*, 351
Westmoreland, Katherine 28, 29
Westmoreland, William 28, 31, *103*, 171
WESTPAC (Western Pacific) 39, 202, 234, 289
Wheeler, Bernard 97
Whitman, Walt 107
Whitmire, Donald 292
Widdecke, Charles E. 74, 75, *345n*
Widdel, Eric 66
Wilkinson, Margaret *see* Crowe, Margaret Wilkinson
Williams, Clifford "Will" 120, 207, 209, 278–79, 325
Willis, Odette 313–15, 335
Wilson, Almon C. 68–73, 97, 108, 335, *346n*
Wilson, R.D. 46, 47
Wilson, Theodore H. 182, 187
Winn, Walter C. 9, 10, 12, 13
Wolfe, Joseph 236, 237, 246, *249*
Wooster, Barbara A. 37
World War I 91, 196, 232, 329
World War II: aircraft carrier 65; concentration camps 44; destroyer 40; hospital corpsmen 21; hospital ships 178, 180; Japanese invasion of Indochina 304; kamikazes 40; medical research unit 40; naval hospitals 25; post-war repatriation examinations 264; POWs 194, 251; trauma 186

X-ray: mortar round lodged in chest of soldier 101, *102*

Yokosuka, Japan: naval hospital 7, 22, 25, 28, 158, 159, 180, 269, 272, 274, 335; shipyard 182
Yount, James 218, 223, *347n*

Zink, Richard 108
The "Zoo" (prison camp), North Vietnam 251, 254, 256, 259, 260